SHAKESPEARE SURVEY

ADVISORY BOARD

Aspects of *Macbeth*
Aspects of *Othello*
Aspects of *Hamlet*
Aspects of *King Lear*
Aspects of Shakespeare's 'Problem Plays'

SHAKESPEARE SURVEY

AN ANNUAL SURVEY OF

SHAKESPEARE STUDIES AND PRODUCTION

55

King Lear and its Afterlife

EDITED BY

PETER HOLLAND

CAMBRIDGE
UNIVERSITY PRESS

PUBLISHED BY THE PRESS SYNDICATE OF THE UNIVERSITY OF CAMBRIDGE
The Pitt Building, Trumpington Street, Cambridge, United Kingdom

CAMBRIDGE UNIVERSITY PRESS
The Edinburgh Building, Cambridge CB2 2RU, UK
40 West 20th Street, New York, NY 10011-4211, USA
477 Williamstown Road, Port Melbourne, VIC 3207, Australia
Ruiz de Alarcón 13, 28014 Madrid, Spain
Dock House, The Waterfront, Cape Town 8001, South Africa

http://www.cambridge.org

First published 2002

Printed in the United Kingdom at the University Press, Cambridge

Typeface Bembo 10/12 pt   *System* LATEX 2ε [TB]

A catalogue record for this book is available from the British Library

ISBN 0 521 81587 8 hardback

Shakespeare Survey was first published in 1948. Its first
eighteen volumes were edited by Allardyce Nicoll.
Kenneth Muir edited volumes 19 to 33.
Stanley Wells edited volumes 34 to 52.

EDITOR'S NOTE

Volume 56, on 'Shakespeare and Comedy' will be at press by the time this volume appears. The theme of Volume 57 will be '*Macbeth* and its Afterlife'. Submissions should be addressed to the Editor at The Shakespeare Institute, Church Street, Stratford-upon-Avon, Warwickshire C V 37 6H P, to arrive at the latest by 1 September 2003 for Volume 57. Pressures on space are heavy; priority is given to articles related to the theme of a particular volume. Please either enclose postage (overseas, in International Reply Coupons) or send a copy you do not wish to be returned. Submissions may also be made via email attachment to pholland@nd.edu. All articles submitted are read by the Editor and at least one member of the Advisory Board, whose indispensable assistance the Editor gratefully acknowledges.

Unless otherwise indicated, Shakespeare quotations and references are keyed to the modern-spelling Complete Oxford Shakespeare (1986).

Review copies should be addressed to the Editor, as above. In attempting to survey the ever-increasing bulk of Shakespeare publications our reviewers inevitably have to exercise some selection. We are pleased to receive offprints of articles which help to draw our reviewers' attention to relevant material.

Volume 41 of *Shakespeare Survey* carried the first of Niky Rathbone's listings of professional Shakespeare productions in Britain; this volume carries the last of the fifteen she has assembled. All interested in Shakespeare in performance owe her much for showing us the astonishing range of Shakespeare stage-work throughout the UK. The feature will be continued by others in subsequent volumes of *Survey* but her achievement deserves our collective thanks.

P.D.H.

CONTRIBUTORS

ISKA ALTER, *Hofstra University, New York*
JANET BOTTOMS, *Homerton College, Cambridge*
WILLIAM C. CARROLL, *Boston University*
THOMAS CARTELLI, *Muhlenberg College, Pennsylvania*
KENT CARTWRIGHT, *University of Maryland*
MICHAEL CORDNER, *University of York*
MICHAEL DOBSON, *Roehampton Institute, University of Surrey*
R. A. FOAKES, *University of California, Los Angeles*
RICHARD FOULKES, *University of Leicester*
ANDREW GURR, *University of Reading*
ROBIN HEADLAM WELLS, *Roehampton Institute, University of Surrey*
JONATHAN HOLMES, *Royal Holloway, University of London*
MARK HOULAHAN, *University of Waikato, Hamilton, New Zealand*
JOHN J. JOUGHIN, *University Of Central Lancashire, Preston*
JOHN JOWETT, *Shakespeare Institute, University of Birmingham*
RICHARD KNOWLES, *University of Wisconsin-Madison*
SONIA MASSAI, *St Mary's College, University of Surrey*
DREW MILNE, *Trinity Hall, Cambridge*
EDWARD PECHTER, *Concordia University, Montreal, and Victoria University, British Colombia*
RICHARD PROUDFOOT, *King's College, London*
ERIC RASMUSSEN, *University of Nevada*
NIKY RATHBONE, *Birmingham Shakespeare Library*
NIALL RUDD, *University of Bristol*
KIERNAN RYAN, *Royal Holloway, University of London*
WILLIAM O. SCOTT, *University of Kansas*
SIMON SHEPHERD, *Central School of Speech and Drama, London*
LESLIE THOMSON, *University of Toronto*
PETER WOMACK, *University of East Anglia*

CONTENTS

vii

CONTENTS

ILLUSTRATIONS

LIST OF ILLUSTRATIONS

KING LEAR: A RETROSPECT, 1980–2000

KIERNAN RYAN

I

Since the 1960s, when it usurped the throne securely occupied till then by *Hamlet*, *King Lear* has reigned supreme as Shakespeare's masterpiece and the keystone of the canon. The last twenty years of the twentieth century have seen the play fall prey to a whole new tribe of critics, many of them hostile and bent on Bardicide. But none of them inclines one to doubt R. A. Foakes's prediction that 'for the immediate future *King Lear* will continue to be regarded as the central achievement of Shakespeare, if only because it speaks more largely than the other tragedies to the anxieties and problems of the modern world'.[1]

As the touchstone of literary value and star witness in defence of the discipline, the tragedy is fated to be the target of every critical approach keen to stake its claim to priority. The most persuasive account of what Shelley deemed 'the most perfect specimen of the dramatic art existing in the world'[2] seizes the flagship of the entire subject. *King Lear* has consequently become an exemplary site of contention between the leading schools of contemporary criticism; and to examine the most influential rival readings of *Lear* is to bring into focus not only the key disputes dividing Shakespeare studies today, but also the current predicament of criticism itself.

In his survey of critical views of *King Lear* between 1939 and 1979, G. R. Hibbard noted that 'a crucial shift was taking place round about 1960, not only in the controversy as to whether *King Lear* is, or is not, a Christian tragedy, but also in critical assumptions and methods'.[3] Looking back on accounts of *Lear* over the last two decades, it is plain that an equally crucial shift in assumptions and methods was taking place around 1980. In the 1960s, the Christian paradigm that had governed criticism of the play for most of the century was displaced by two new critical dynasties: on the one hand, upbeat humanist views of the tragedy as vindicating the value of human suffering; on the other, downbeat conceptions of *King Lear* as Shakespeare's *Endgame*, a vision of existence as a brutal, pointless joke. But with the advent of the 1980s, as the flood tide of theory began to lap round Stratford's sole claim to fame, this divided dispensation surrendered its sway to a fresh generation of critics, for whom the meaning of *Lear* was inseparable from questions of language, gender, power and the unconscious.

Shakespeare's greatest tragedy is now densely colonized by most breeds – and some curious cross-breeds – of poststructuralist, feminist, new-historicist, cultural–materialist and psychoanalytic criticism, and within each of these approaches, to make matters more complex, different tendencies can be discerned. The diversity of the readings they have spawned, however, masks a shared commitment to criticism as an inescapably political activity. It is this feature above all that distinguishes the

[1] *Hamlet Versus Lear: Cultural Politics and Shakespeare's Art* (Cambridge, 1993), p. 224.

[2] 'A Defence of Poetry', in *Shelley's Poetry and Prose*, ed. Donald H. Reiman and Sharon B. Powers (New York, 1977), p. 489.

[3] '*King Lear*: A Retrospect, 1939–79', *Shakespeare Survey 33* (Cambridge, 1980), pp. 1–12; p. 9.

new wave of Shakespeare criticism from the Shakespeare criticism that preceded it, and that attracts the antipathy of more traditional scholars. Hitherto, critical quarrels about the vision of *King Lear* had been pursued with little thought for its bearing on the social and ideological problems of the present. But from the 1980s onward the issue was no longer whether *King Lear* counselled affirmation or despair, the way of the cross or the wisdom of oblivion. What mattered was whether the play sustained or subverted oppressive structures of power and perception in its world and our own.

II

For a number of scholars and critics, however, such interpretive issues begged the fundamental question of which text of *King Lear* one was talking about. New departures in criticism on the tragedy were accompanied by the revival of doubts about the authority of the editions on which the criticism was based. The arcane erudition of the textual scholar and the radical scepticism of the postmodern critic forged an unlikely, but mutually advantageous, alliance to scupper complacency about the identity of *King Lear*. For once, hard-core theory buffs could anchor their abstractions in evidence collated in the Rare Books Room, while editorial skills disdained as nitpicking drudgery could sell themselves as sexy, as the cutting edge of theory in practice.

In point of fact, the textual problem posed by *King Lear* was hardly news when it was dug up and dusted down by the 'new revisionists' in the late 1970s. Every serious editor of the play since Pope and Johnson has had to grapple with the fact that it exists in two substantive versions, the Quarto of 1608 and the Folio of 1623, which differ from each other in a number of significant respects. The Quarto contains about 288 lines or part-lines that are not in the Folio, including the whole of 4.3; the Folio includes some 133 lines or part-lines that are absent from the Quarto; and between the two texts there are over 850 verbal variants. Most editors, ancient and modern, aware that neither text represents a reliable transcription of the script as

performed by Shakespeare's company, and seeing no grounds for dubbing one version authentic and ditching the other, have created a single conflated text, incorporating as much of both versions as possible and using their best judgement to choose between the verbal variants. This might seem a reasonable solution to a tricky problem, especially when editors mark the points of conflation and emendation clearly and spell out the criteria for their decisions, so that readers may judge for themselves. But in 1978 Michael Warren published an article arguing that such mongrel texts violate the integrity of the Quarto and the Folio, which should be regarded as two distinct plays, marking successive stages in Shakespeare's conscious artistic revision of *King Lear*. To splice Quarto and Folio together was to pine for a single, pristine version of the play that never existed.[4]

Warren's contention unleashed a debate which peaked in the mid 1980s, but continued to reverberate throughout the following decade, and is only now showing signs of petering out. With the backing of further articles and books by Warren, Gary Taylor, Steven Urkowitz, Stanley Wells and John Kerrigan among others,[5] the bi-textual theory of *King Lear* rapidly became all the rage. It reached its apotheosis in the 1986 Oxford edition of *The Complete Works*, which published the Quarto and Folio texts side by side, and claimed confidently on the dustjacket that 'For the first time, *King Lear* is here printed both as Shakespeare originally wrote it and as he revised it, some years later, in the light

---

4 'Quarto and Folio *King Lear* and the Interpretation of Albany and Edgar', in *Shakespeare: Pattern of Great Excelling Nature*, ed. David Bevington and J. L. Halio (Newark, 1978), pp. 95–107.

5 See in particular Gary Taylor, 'The War in *King Lear*', *Shakespeare Survey 33* (1980), pp. 27–34; Steven Urkowitz, *Shakespeare's Revision of 'King Lear'* (Princeton, 1980); and Gary Taylor and Michael Warren (eds.), *The Division of the Kingdoms: Shakespeare's Two Versions of 'King Lear'* (Oxford, 1983), which contains key essays by Wells, Kerrigan, Urkowitz and the editors. Seminal contributions to the debate were also made, from quite different standpoints, by P. W. K. Stone, *The Textual History of 'King Lear'* (London, 1980), and Peter W. M. Blayney, *The Texts of 'King Lear' and their Origins. Volume 1: Nicholas Okes and the First Quarto* (Cambridge, 1982).

of performance.'[6] More parallel-text editions have followed in the wake of Wells and Taylor,[7] and the 'new revisionists' have not ceased to defend their thesis against the assaults of the unconvinced.[8] But the ranks of the latter, which include Philip Edwards, David Bevington and Frank Kermode, have swelled, and their objections to the two-*Lears* hypothesis have dealt it a series of body blows from which it looks unlikely to recover.[9]

It is not simply that there is no way of proving that Shakespeare himself made the cuts and revisions in the Folio, which could just as well have been made by someone else or by several other people at different times. The problem is that most of the cuts and revisions are not convincing on artistic or theatrical grounds anyway. In the Folio *Lear*, moreover, as Richard Knowles lethally observes:

> No speech of any length is rewritten to make it substantially different in content or style, no new scenes or episodes are added, no changes are made in the order of existing scenes or episodes or speeches, no new characters are added, no named characters are omitted (or renamed), no new speeches are made to introduce or elaborate upon themes or to provide new and different motives. The reassignment of speeches may represent no more than normal scribal or compositorial error. If F *Lear* represents a new 'concept' of the play, it is remarkably limited in its means of revision.[10]

Even R. A. Foakes, who finds the evidence for Shakespeare's revision of *King Lear* persuasive, concludes that 'the reworking of *King Lear* is not so thorough as to mean that we have to think of two plays'.[11] So for his 1997 Arden edition of the tragedy he decided, like the overwhelming majority of recent editors, that the most prudent and practical solution was to produce a conflated text. *Plus ça change.*

III

For critics intent on the deconstruction of *King Lear* – an ambition which enjoyed a lively vogue in the 1980s – the textual controversy, like the Dover Cliff scene, was a gift horse in whose mouth few were prone to look. In his 1986 article 'Textual Properties', Jonathan Goldberg was swift to infer from the proliferation of *Lears* that the text of the tragedy was innately indeterminate, because 'Every text of a Shakespeare play exists in relationship to

---

[6] Stanley Wells and Gary Taylor (eds.), *William Shakespeare: The Complete Works* (Oxford, 1986).

[7] Most notably Michael Warren (ed.), *The Complete 'King Lear', 1608–1623* (Berkeley, 1989) and René Weis (ed.), *King Lear: A Parallel Text Edition* (London and New York, 1983). *The Norton Shakespeare*, gen. ed. Stephen Greenblatt (New York and London, 1997), which is based on the Oxford edition, hedges its bets by including a conflated text alongside the Quarto and Folio versions.

[8] See, for example, Gary Taylor, 'The Rhetorics of Reaction', in *Crisis in Editing: Texts of the English Renaissance*, ed. Randall McLeod (New York, 1994), pp. 19–59; Grace Ioppolo, 'The Idea of Shakespeare and the Two *Lears*', in *Lear from Study to Stage: Essays in Criticism*, ed. James Ogden and Arthur H. Scouten (Madison and London, 1997), pp. 45–56; and Steven Urkowitz, 'Preposterous Poststructuralism: Editorial Morality and the Ethics of Evidence', in *New Ways of Looking at Old Texts II*, ed. W. Speed Hill (Binghamton, 1998), pp. 83–90.

[9] See especially Philip Edwards, review of Urkowitz, *Shakespeare's Revision*, and Stone, *Textual History*, *Modern Language Review*, 77 (1982), 694–8; Sidney Thomas, 'Shakespeare's Supposed Revision of *King Lear*', *Shakespeare Quarterly*, 35 (1984), 506–11, and 'The Integrity of *King Lear*', *Modern Language Review*, 90 (1995), 572–84; Marion Trousdale, 'A Trip through the Divided Kingdoms', *Shakespeare Quarterly*, 37 (1986), 218–23; David Bevington, 'Determining the Indeterminate: The Oxford Shakespeare', *Shakespeare Quarterly*, 38 (1987), 501–19; Frank Kermode, 'Disintegration Once More', *Proceedings of the British Academy*, 84 (1994), 93–111; Ann Meyer, 'Shakespeare's Art and the Texts of *King Lear*', *Studies in Bibliography*, 47 (1994), 128–46; Stanley Cavell, 'Skepticism as Iconoclasm: The Saturation of the Shakespearean Text', in *Shakespeare and the Twentieth Century*, ed. Jonathan Bate, Jill Levenson and Dieter Mehl (Newark and London, 1998), pp. 231–47; Robert Clare, 'Quarto and Folio: A Case for Conflation', in *Lear from Study to Stage*, ed. Ogden and Scouten, pp. 79–108; Richard Knowles, 'Two *Lears*? By Shakespeare?', ibid., pp. 57–78, and 'Merging the Kingdoms: *King Lear*', *Shakespearean International Yearbook*, 1 (1999), 266–86.

[10] Knowles, 'Two *Lears*?', pp. 63–4.

[11] Foakes, *Hamlet Versus Lear*, p. 111. Stanley Cavell sums the matter up thus: 'the sense that it is the same play under change is as strong as the sense that each change changes the play' ('Skepticism as Iconoclasm', p. 237).

scripts we will never have, to a series of revisions and collaborations that start as soon as there is a Shakespearean text.'[12] For this supposition dovetailed with his contention in 'Perspectives: Dover Cliff and the Conditions of Representation' that *King Lear* contrives in that scene to dive off the cliff after Gloucester, vanishing into a void in which no ground of cognition survives: 'In *King Lear* nothing comes of nothing, and the very language which would seem (to us) solidly to locate the world slides into an abyss, an uncreating, annihilative nothingness.'[13]

In 'Shakespeare, Derrida, and the End of Language in *King Lear*', which rode shotgun in the same volume as Goldberg's 'Perspectives', Jackson I. Cope also drew strength from the gospel according to Warren and Urkowitz. 'There are two texts. And therefore none. Or, rather, three or five', he averred, displaying the rampant indecisiveness of the full-blooded deconstructionist. Cope's *King Lear* is 'an absent pre-text', at whose heart lies 'the transcendent absurd which defines language as nothing come to unrest in never'.[14] In this it differs sharply from the *Lears* conjured up by Terry Eagleton and Malcolm Evans, who proved that not all deconstructions of the play need come so inexorably to naught. For Eagleton, the tragedy tosses all and nothing, mind and body, sense and insanity into a vortex of reversals that confounds such false dichotomies to release us from their spell. By forcing the binary oppositions on which its vision depends to cancel each other out, the play undermines the mentality that holds hierarchy in place to this day: 'only the coupling of two negatives can hope to produce a positive'.[15] Evans begins by proposing, much like Goldberg, that 'The view from the cliff-edge, inscribed in the theatrical trope of the supplement, is the absent centre of the play, a regress into the "nothing" spoken by the Fool'. But, unlike Goldberg, he goes on to suggest intriguingly that the void in *King Lear* is an inverted expression of the 'utopian plenitude' obliquely adumbrated by the play.[16]

Scepticism about the objective existence of *King Lear* as a text has not only made strange bedfellows of some critics, but also trapped them in stark contradictions. Neither Gary Taylor nor Terence Hawkes might seem to have much in common with their deconstructive brethren, but they do both subscribe to the view that, as Taylor puts it in *Reinventing Shakespeare*, the Bard 'has become a black hole', and that 'We find in Shakespeare only what we bring to him or what others have left behind.'[17] In 'Lear's Maps', Hawkes is equally adamant that 'No "play itself" is ever available to us.'[18] There is no primal *King Lear*, we are assured, only a succession of revisions and rewritings on which we place our self-mirroring constructions. Hence in *Reinventing Shakespeare* Taylor dwells not on *King Lear*, but on the Victorian novel Bradley turned it into; while in 'Lear's Maps' Hawkes targets Granville-Barker's politically loaded wartime production of the play, which he understandably finds more rewarding than Shakespeare's non-existent text. How Taylor squares his editorial commitment to Shakespeare the reviser with his critical commitment to Shakespeare the black hole is as baffling as his ability to deliver, in *Moment By Moment By Shakespeare*, an acute conventional close reading of *King Lear* which exposes the aridity of both these pursuits.[19] But it is no more baffling than Hawkes's subsequent short book on *King Lear*, whose intimations of what lies beyond language Hawkes reveals through a trenchant analysis of Shakespeare's diction, making nonsense of his insistence that 'there is no "play itself", only our different readings of it'.[20]

---

[12] *Shakespeare Quarterly*, 37 (1986), 213–17; p. 216.
[13] *Shakespeare and Deconstruction*, ed. G. Douglas Atkins and David M. Bergeron (New York, 1988), pp. 245–65; p. 254.
[14] Ibid., pp. 267–83; pp. 269, 277.
[15] *William Shakespeare* (Oxford, 1986), pp. 76–83; p. 78.
[16] *Signifying Nothing: Truth's True Contents in Shakespeare's Text* (Brighton, 1986), pp. 224–34; pp. 226, 228.
[17] *Reinventing Shakespeare: A Cultural History from the Restoration to the Present* (London, 1990), pp. 410, 411.
[18] Hawkes, *Meaning By Shakespeare* (London and New York, 1992), pp. 121–40; p. 136.
[19] 'Revolutions of Perspective: *King Lear*', in *Moment By Moment By Shakespeare* (London, 1985), pp. 162–236.
[20] *William Shakespeare: King Lear* (Plymouth, 1995), p. 41.

IV

From a province of criticism which regards *King Lear* as a play programmed to self-destruct or an essentialist delusion, it is refreshing to turn to a realm ruled by critics who are confident that the play exists and that it secretes not only a determinate significance, but also a definable political purpose, which can be teased out by restoring it to its early modern matrix. As the doyen of new historicism, Stephen Greenblatt, declares in his much-cited essay on *Lear*, 'Shakespeare and the Exorcists': 'Deconstructionist readings lead too readily and predictably to the void; in actual literary practice the perplexities into which one is led are not moments of pure, untrammeled *aporia* but localized strategies in particular historical encounters.'[21] Historically disposed critics of *King Lear*, however, diverge as much from each other as they do from the adepts of deconstruction. Indeed, the closer they move to the play's original context, the further the prospect of consensus among them recedes.

New historicists and cultural materialists may have hogged the limelight in this sector of *Lear* studies, but that has not stopped radical historicists of a less modish cast, whose roots are shamelessly pre-postmodern, from surviving right alongside them. For these critics, who might be characterized broadly as Marxist and humanist in orientation, *King Lear* is first and foremost a dramatic enactment of the transition from a feudal to a capitalist culture. Through the twin tragedies of Lear's and Gloucester's families, the play explores the human cost of embracing acquisitive individualism and kissing the medieval pieties goodbye. 'In all this is pictured', concludes Victor Kiernan, 'the tormented process of social change, the whirlpool at the conflux of two eras, and the impossibility of any smooth, easy progression from one to another.'[22]

The million-dollar question for critics of this stamp is where the play's final sympathies lie, and on this issue most of them see eye to eye. Some, like Kiernan and Franco Moretti,[23] see *Lear* as recognizing, not without misgivings, the need to move forward into the future, and as paving the way for the new order by demystifying the old. Walter Cohen even glimpses in the play utopian premonitions of the Levellers and Diggers.[24] But the majority, including David Aers, John Turner and David Margolies, tend to agree that the tragedy is equally disenchanted with the waxing and the waning world views, but unable to envisage 'any real alternative beyond the disintegrating traditional order and the utterly destructive individualism which emerges from it'.[25]

Postmodern Marxist scholars, on the other hand, are disinclined to grant *King Lear* any such capacity for dispassionate critique. In *The Poetics of Primitive Accumulation*, Richard Halpern identifies – at inordinate length – an ultimately 'retrograde movement'[26] in the play towards the comfort zone of feudalism. And in 'The Ideology of Superfluous Things: *King Lear* as Period Piece', Margreta de Grazia mounts a fearfully abstruse argument to demonstrate that *Lear* is not just an artefact of the

---

[21] *Shakespeare and the Question of Theory*, ed. Patricia Parker and Geoffrey Hartman (New York, 1985), pp. 163–87; p. 164. This sentence was excised from the version of the essay reprinted in Greenblatt's *Shakespearean Negotiations* (Oxford, 1988), pp. 94–128.

[22] '*King Lear* (1605–06)', in Kiernan, *Eight Tragedies of Shakespeare* (London and New York, 1996), pp. 104–23; p. 108.

[23] 'The Great Eclipse: Tragic Form as the Consecration of Sovereignty', in Moretti, *Signs Taken for Wonders: Essays in the Sociology of Literary Forms* (London, 1983), pp. 42–82.

[24] *Drama of a Nation: Public Theatre in Renaissance England and Spain* (Ithaca, 1985), pp. 327–56.

[25] David Aers and Gunther Kress, 'The Language of Social Order: Individual, Society and Historical Process in *King Lear*', in David Aers, Bob Hodge and Gunther Kress, *Literature, Language and Society in England 1580–1680* (Dublin and Totowa, 1981), 75–99; pp. 98–9. See also John Turner, '*King Lear*', in Graham Holderness, Nick Potter and John Turner, *Shakespeare: The Play of History* (Basingstoke and London, 1988), and David Margolies, '*King Lear*' and '*King Lear* II', in *Monsters of the Deep: Social Dissolution in Shakespeare's Tragedies* (Manchester, 1992), pp. 14–42 and 68–79.

[26] '"Historica Passio": *King Lear's* Fall into Feudalism', in *The Poetics of Primitive Accumulation: English Renaissance Culture and the Genealogy of Capital* (Ithaca and London, 1991), pp. 215–313; p. 247.

feudal era, but an aggressively 'anti-Early Modern' text, in which 'the ideology of superfluous things holds the status quo in place by locking identity into property, the subject into the object'.[27] It is ironic that Halpern and de Grazia have to muster the headiest resources of materialist theory in order to arrive at the same judgement of *King Lear* as critics of a more conventional bent, using humbler conceptual tools.[28] In this respect, they have nothing to teach their close kin, the new historicists, much of whose ingenuity has likewise been spent on exposing *Lear*'s complicity with the status quo.

In *Power on Display*, for example, Leonard Tennenhouse construes the play as a strategy of the stage calculated to mystify, and so sustain, the authority of the Jacobean state. Taking his cue from Foucault's *Discipline and Punish*, Tennenhouse contends that the original function of *King Lear* was the exemplary torture of a royal miscreant, who has violated the taboos that safeguard the mystique of sovereignty.[29] Greenblatt's approach in 'Shakespeare and the Exorcists', from which I quoted earlier, is incomparably subtler, but the bottom line is basically the same. Greenblatt detects in Harsnett's *A Declaration of Egregious Popish Impostures*, which Shakespeare drew upon for Poor Tom's ravings, the surreptitious logic of the entire tragedy. *King Lear* appropriates the obsolete charades of religion, Greenblatt suggests, to clinch the bewitchment of the audience through the rituals of drama. The play strives in part to unsettle official values, but it does so as a ploy to win the spectators' consent to their own subjection. Greenblatt takes a similar tack in 'The Cultivation of Anxiety: King Lear and his Heirs',[30] which pivots on the affinities he discerns between the play and a nineteenth-century American Baptist's account of breaking his infant son's will. Greenblatt's bleak conclusion is that *Lear*'s cultural mission was to suspend its audience in a state of trepidation that reinforced their political docility.

Not all new historicists, it should be stressed, hold that *King Lear* is the sly secret agent or the hapless dupe of domination. In *Puzzling Shakespeare*, Leah Marcus pulls the contextual focus as tight as it could be, pinpointing for analysis the performance

of the tragedy before King James on St Stephen's Night, 1606.[31] In an attempt to nail at last the play's original objective and effect, Marcus spotlights its topical allusions to James's character and policy, and considers the influence the saint's story might have had on the royal spectators. But she is forced to infer that Shakespeare's attitude to his monarch in *King Lear* is, to say the least, ambiguous, and could have been slanted towards endorsement or indictment according to the audience. Annabel Patterson, however, has no doubt where Shakespeare's true sympathies lay when he wrote the play. Her relocation of *King Lear* in its time in *Shakespeare and the Popular Voice*[32] leads her to surmise that the man who penned Lear's speech to the 'Poor naked wretches' of his realm (3.4.28–36)[33] set out to speak for the victims of power, using every trick in the book to throw the censor off the scent.

Patterson's brand of new historicism is the kind most congenial to cultural–materialist critics of *King Lear*, who share the new-historicist belief in transporting texts back to their time, but who are more open to the possibility that works like *Lear* were either subversive from the start or can be read in ways that serve progressive aims in the present. The seminal cultural–materialist reading of the tragedy is Jonathan Dollimore's '*King Lear* and Essentialist Humanism'. As its title intimates, Dollimore's account signals a break not only with previous Christian and existentialist approaches to

[27] *Subject and Object in Renaissance Culture*, ed. Margreta de Grazia, Maureen Quilligan and Peter Stallybrass (Cambridge, 1996), pp. 17–42; p. 31.

[28] See, for example, Jerald W. Spotswood, 'Maintaining Hierarchy in *The Tragedie of King Lear*', *Studies in English Literature 1500–1900*, 38 (1998), 265–80.

[29] *Power on Display: The Politics of Shakespeare's Genres* (New York and London, 1986), pp. 134–42.

[30] Greenblatt, *Learning to Curse: Essays in Early Modern Culture* (New York and London, 1990), pp. 80–98.

[31] 'Retrospective: *King Lear* on St Stephen's Night, 1606', in *Puzzling Shakespeare: Local Reading and its Discontents* (Berkeley, 1988), pp. 148–59.

[32] Oxford, 1989, pp. 106–16.

[33] Textual references are to the Arden *King Lear*, ed. R. A. Foakes (Walton-on-Thames, 1997).

the play, but also with Marxist readings that harbour an attachment to humanist sentiments. 'King Lear is, above all', Dollimore maintains, 'a play about power, property and inheritance', which rejects the notion of the noble tragic victim ultimately redeemed by death as an 'essentialist mystification'. It offers instead 'a decentring of the tragic subject', whose consciousness is revealed as the construction of the material conditions that govern his plight.[34]

Subsequent cultural–materialist responses to Lear have languished in the shadow of Dollimore's powerful essay. In 'The Information of the Absolute', Francis Barker detects arresting connections in the play between property and personality, and between tragedy and topography. But, unlike Dollimore, who sees King Lear as a Brechtian radical tragedy, Barker finds that 'Lear ends in textual and discursive compromise',[35] stranded between its radical and its reactionary impulses. The cultural–materialist preoccupation with 'power, property and inheritance' in King Lear is given a topical twist in Richard Wilson's Will Power. Wilson resurrects the old-historicist analogy between Lear's story and the real-life case of Brian Annesley in an attempt to prove that the play revolves round 'the tragic cultural implications of testamentary power',[36] which foreshadow the dispossession of the Crown itself later in the century.

V

Three things are conspicuously missing from most historicist accounts of King Lear during the period under review. One is the suspicion that Lear may not be fully explicable in terms of its time, because its imaginative vision is straining towards the future, not slumped inside the past; however radical and subversive it is held to have been in its day, the tragedy remains the past-bound expression of a vanished world, the prisoner of a retrospective critical viewpoint. The second thing is close attention to the language and form of King Lear, which in some cases, as Greenblatt's essays illustrate, merely affords a pretext to discuss another text altogether. And the third is a sustained consideration of gender

and the representation of women in King Lear, an oversight which feminist critics have not been slow to point out.

Just as Marxists, cultural materialists and new historicists have tended to polarize around the politics imputed to the text, so feminist readings have tended to divide into those who think the tragedy reveals a patriarchal Bard and those who maintain that it provides a critique of misogynistic masculinity. Within both these camps, moreover, distinctions can be drawn between critics who rest their case primarily on historical evidence, critics who call psychoanalytic theory to witness, and critics who shuffle both these methods together.

Kathleen McLuskie's arraignment of Lear as a phallocratic morality play, which stereotypes women as saintly or satanic and makes sure our empathy is invested in the tormented patriarch, has achieved, as Ann Thompson notes, 'notoriety as exemplifying some sort of dead end for feminism'.[37] But McLuskie is also a cultural materialist, and her critics too often overlook the fact that her condemnation of the play's sexual politics is the prelude to an attempt to read Lear against its historical grain to radicalize its modern impact, giving us 'the pleasure of understanding in place of the pleasure of emotional identification'.[38] Whether it marks a dead end or not, male critics have been quick to muscle in on McLuskie's act. Writing from 'a materialist, non-humanist perspective', David Simpson, for example, argues that in King Lear 'Paternalism is exposed to criticism only in

[34] Dollimore, Radical Tragedy: Religion, Ideology and Power in the Drama of Shakespeare and his Contemporaries (Brighton, 1984), pp. 189–203; pp. 197, 202.

[35] Barker, The Culture of Violence: Essays on Tragedy and History (Manchester and Chicago, 1993), pp. 3–31; p. 31.

[36] Will Power: Essays on Shakespearean Authority (Hemel Hempstead, 1993), pp. 215–30; p. 230.

[37] 'Are There Any Women in King Lear?', in The Matter of Difference: Materialist Feminist Criticism of Shakespeare, ed. Valerie Wayne (Hemel Hempstead, 1991), pp. 117–28; p. 126.

[38] 'The Patriarchal Bard: Feminist Criticism and Shakespeare: King Lear and Measure for Measure', in Political Shakespeare: New Essays in Cultural Materialism, ed. Jonathan Dollimore and Alan Sinfield (Manchester, 1985), pp. 88–108; p. 105.

order that it might be subliminally reaffirmed'.[39] A less equivocal analysis of the play's sexual posture is supplied by Peter L. Rudnytsky, the title of whose essay, ' "The darke and vicious place": The Dread of the Vagina in *King Lear*',[40] cannot be accused of beating around the bush.

Nor, for that matter, can Philippa Berry's eccentric account of the play in 'Cordelia's Bond and Britannia's Missing Middle', possibly because in *Lear* 'for many miles about / There's scarce a bush' (2.2.492), as Berry herself points out. Berry yokes a cultural–materialist approach, rich in antiquarian lore, to a deconstructive compulsion to turn the topical into the tropical at every opportunity. Her aim is to explain the role of Cordelia in '*King Lear*'s strikingly scatological refiguration of James's new British kingdom'. But the essay's obsession with cloacal issues reduces the text's politics to a misogynistic pathology rooted in the rectum: 'a morally compromised kingship is implied to have an unsettling association with a suggestively feminized anality'.[41] 'Blow winds and crack your cheeks!' (3.2.1) will never sound quite the same again.

Two feminist essays on *King Lear* outshine all the others, casting new light into the darkest reaches of the tragedy. In 'The Absent Mother in *King Lear*', Coppélia Kahn sets out 'like an archaeologist, to uncover the hidden mother in the hero's inner world'. Her psychoanalytic excavations unearth a play which, far from being a devious apologist for patriarchy, depicts instead the 'tragedy of masculinity', dramatizing the cost of 'repressing the vulnerability, dependency and capacity for feeling which are called "feminine"'. At the very point when 'a masculine identity crisis' in Jacobean society was provoking the reinforcement of patriarchal authority in reality, Shakespeare was aggravating that crisis by staging 'Lear's progress toward acceptance of the woman in himself'.[42]

A much less sanguine – indeed, a diametrically opposed – view of the misogynistic monarch is taken by Janet Adelman in 'Suffocating Mothers in *King Lear*'. At first it looks as though Adelman intends to angle in the same lake of darkness

as Rudnytsky and Berry: the blind Gloucester's 'bleeding rings' (5.3.188), we are told, transform his face into a horrific image of a menstruating vagina, and 'the very wetness of the storm comes to seem a sexual wetness, a monstrous spilling of germens'.[43] But the essay rapidly mutates into a compelling reversal of Kahn's reading. Adelman's *King Lear* is not so much a covert plug for the maternal impulse in men as a seductive masculine fantasy in which that impulse is exterminated. In a bold final twist of her argument, however, Adelman refuses to gender as exclusively male a mother-complex by which women, including Adelman herself, are just as afflicted as men.

VI

The essays by Kahn and Adelman provide a natural bridge to those critics whose overriding concern with the play is psychoanalytic, and who prefer to treat *King Lear* on the couch rather than in the context of Jacobean culture, or in response to modern political imperatives. Symptomatic readings of this sort are less interested in *Lear* as a poetic drama, with its own distinctive idiom and design, than as a diagnostic challenge or a confirmation of the theory brought to bear on it.

---

[39] 'Great Things of Us Forgot: Seeing *Lear* Better', in *Futures for English*, ed. Colin MacCabe (Manchester, 1988), pp. 15–31; p. 18.

[40] *Modern Philology*, 96 (1998–9), 291–311.

[41] Berry, *Shakespeare's Feminine Endings: Disfiguring Death in the Tragedies* (New York and London, 1999), pp. 135–66; pp. 135–6.

[42] *Rewriting the Renaissance: The Discourses of Sexual Difference in Early Modern Europe*, ed. Margaret W. Ferguson, Maureen Quilligan and Nancy J. Vickers (Chicago and London, 1986), pp. 33–49; pp. 35, 36, 47, 46. A sympathetic male view of men in *Lear* as practising their own form of mutual care and kindness, which owes nothing to, and fears nothing from, femininity, is provided by Peter Erickson's essay 'Maternal Images and Male Bonds', in his *Patriarchal Structures in Shakespeare's Drama* (Berkeley and London, 1985), pp. 103–15.

[43] Adelman, *Suffocating Mothers: Fantasies of Maternal Origin in Shakespeare's Plays, 'Hamlet' to 'The Tempest'* (New York and London, 1992), pp. 103–29; p. 111.

Thus Marjorie Garber hails Shakespeare as the 'ghost writer of modern theory'[44] and, pushing *King Lear* itself to one side, uses Freud's essay 'The Theme of the Three Caskets' to expose the repressed identification of the father of psychoanalysis with Cordelia's papa. The latter stays centre-stage in William F. Zak's full-length study *Sovereign Shame*,[45] which defines Lear's malady as his vain mental flight from the disgrace he has inflicted on himself. In Kay Stockholder's judgement, however, the king's kink is the 'sadistic pleasure' he reaps from 'punishing in others his secret lusts'. The downside of this disorder is his affliction by 'images of malodorous female genitalia' and 'a drive towards the love-death sublimation of the infantile oral merger'.[46] Fortunately Lear's quest for relief from this unsavoury syndrome is accounted a success. The aged monarch seems to be stalled at the oral stage in Val Richards's view, too. Her Lacanian take on the tragedy sees it as 'the dramatization of a primal crisis at the Mirror stage, resolved through the shifting play of the scopic drive'. Cordelia's 'Nothing, my lord' (1.1.87) is equated with 'the proffering of a milkless nipple', the trauma of which pitches her octogenarian progenitor into a 'psychotic breakdown',[47] which weans him from his infantile narcissism and forces him – admittedly a tad late in the day – to grow up at last.

Such enlistings of *Lear* as a therapeutic parable seem entirely plausible when set beside more portentous attempts to inflate it into an allegory of Lacanian theory. In their protracted, impenetrable meditation on the tragedy in *After Oedipus: Shakespeare in Psychoanalysis*, Julia Reinhard Lupton and Kenneth Reinhard allege that we are faced not only with a psychotic sovereign, but also with a psychotic play, albeit (*pace* Berry) 'a play without a fundament'. That their interpretation of *Lear* 'serves to articulate the constitutive nodes of intransigent nonmeaning', as they disarmingly confess, cannot be denied: the play, they assure us, 'unwittingly points towards the analytic path of traversing the fantasy which it nonetheless fails to achieve'. But the fleeting hope that we are being had is dashed when they write, without a trace of irony: 'If, as the

title of this half of the book indicates, "LEAR" and "REAL" are anagrams of each other, a longer, more paranoid palindrome suggests itself here: "LEAR'S IN ISRAEL".'[48] *After Oedipus* at least has the merit of making Philip Armstrong's Lacanian analysis of the play, '*King Lear*: Uncanny Spectacles',[49] seem as lucid as Freud himself, although it is quite tough going too. Tough going can be tolerable when the pay-off is some startling insight. The trouble with these two essays is that the mental graft they demand is rewarded by the restatement of familiar points, less pretentiously made by previous critics, about visual self-consciousness and the limits of representation in *King Lear*.

VII

It will be apparent by now that, of the many critics surveyed so far, not one has been deterred by Hazlitt's qualms: 'We wish that we could pass this play over, and say nothing about it. All that we can say must fall far short of the subject; or even of what we ourselves conceive of it.'[50] *King Lear* has been confidently rehoused in its historical habitat, pressed into the service of today's political agendas, and subpoenaed to verify the assumptions of deconstruction and psychoanalytic theory. By and large,

---

[44] 'Freud's Choice: "The Theme of the Three Caskets"', in Garber, *Shakespeare's Ghost Writers: Literature as Uncanny Causality* (New York and London, 1987), pp. 74–86; p. 74.

[45] *Sovereign Shame: A Study of King Lear* (Lewisburg, 1984).

[46] 'King Lear's Quest for "An Ounce of Civet"', in Stockholder, *Dream Works: Lovers and Families in Shakespeare's Plays* (Toronto and London, 1987), pp. 118–47; pp. 121, 136, 145.

[47] '"His Majesty the Baby": A Psychoanalytic Reading of *King Lear*', in *Shakespeare in the Changing Curriculum*, ed. Lesley Aers and Nigel Wheale (London and New York, 1991), pp. 162–79; pp. 166, 170, 177.

[48] 'Part Two: The *Lear* Real', in *After Oedipus: Shakespeare in Psychoanalysis* (Ithaca and London, 1993), pp.145–229; pp. 209, 191, 228, 217.

[49] Armstrong, *Shakespeare's Visual Regime: Tragedy, Psychology and the Gaze* (Basingstoke, 2000), pp. 30–56.

[50] *Characters of Shakespeare's Plays*, in *Complete Works*, ed. P. P. Howe, 21 vols. (London, 1930–4), IV, p. 257.

it must be said, our understanding of the tragedy, and why it still matters so much, is the richer for it. But the credibility of all these approaches is hobbled by the same blatant flaw: an abject neglect of *Lear*'s qualities as a work of art; a failure to engage in detail with the poetic language and dramatic form that are indivisible from its identity as a source of pleasure and an object of study. In fact, so marked is this neglect of the aesthetic dimension, that one cannot help wondering whether it is a condition of certain kinds of reading, which might collapse if put to the test of close textual analysis.

Be that as it may, it has been left to an older generation of critics to keep the flame of formal interest in *King Lear* alight over the last twenty years. To restore one's sense of the play as a unique configuration of crafted discourse, displaying its own intricate texture, structure and trajectory, it is to these critics one is obliged to turn. The critical tragedy of *King Lear* is the gulf that yawns between their priorities and those of the most influential modern approaches to the play.

It is true that valiant attempts have been made to bridge this gulf, most notably by R. A. Foakes and Harry Berger, Jr. In *Hamlet versus Lear*, Foakes seeks 'to integrate a reading that is conscious of general social and political resonances affecting our age with a defence of the Folio texts as embodying the best reading versions we have of these plays. These readings and the defence of the Folio texts in turn are enmeshed with and support a clarification of the dramatic design of the plays, that is also necessarily partial and a product of the present time'.[51] The aspiration is admirable and deftly formulated, but the reading of *Lear* Foakes delivers is oddly flat and superficial, teetering on the brink of mere synopsis. Much more impressive is Berger's endeavour to fuse the psychological analysis of character and a poststructuralist conception of textuality in two scintillating essays on *King Lear*, which owe everything to their exact scrutiny of the wording of the play.[52] As Berger himself admits, the cynical slant of his method does tend to find 'lodged in the fine tissues of rhetoric'[53] proof of the characters' darker purposes to the exclusion of anything else. Nevertheless, his idiosyncratic accounts

of *King Lear* linger in the mind, not least because they give an inkling of what could be achieved if the play's diction and design set the critical agenda.

In the meantime, the blunt truth remains that *King Lear* 'ultimately baffles commentary', as Harold Bloom observed at the end of the 1990s. 'Something that we conceive of it', wrote Bloom, harking back to Hazlitt, 'hovers outside our expressive range', because it lies 'beyond the categories of our critiques'. Bloom's own candidate for that 'something' – the play's 'horror of generation' and vilification of familial love – is suggestive, but scarcely fits the bill.[54] Nor is any reading apt to be a match for the play, if it does not square up to what Winifred Nowottny, writing in *Shakespeare Survey* over forty years ago, called 'the magnitude of the stylistic mystery in *King Lear*'. Despite the lapidary brilliance of Nowottny's analysis, the solution to the mystery is still going begging, not only because 'the terms in which to discuss this style have eluded us',[55] but also because no one has yet found a way to connect the play's style to its stance on the issues that animate it.

This is not to disparage the profound contributions to our knowledge of *King Lear* made by John Bayley and Stephen Booth at the beginning of the 1980s. On the contrary, no critics in recent years have come closer to the source of the play's 'stylistic mystery', including Frank Kermode, whose splendid book *Shakespeare's Language* is defeated by the language of *Lear*.[56] Bayley's grasp of how 'the play slips out of every area for which there is something appropriate and intelligible to be said', of how it 'undermines the kind of expression that a play

---

[51] *Hamlet versus Lear*, p. 145.
[52] '*King Lear*: The Lear Family Romance' and 'Text Against Performance: The Gloucester Family Romance', in Berger, *Making Trifles of Terrors: Redistributing Complicities in Shakespeare* (Stanford, 1997), pp. 25–49 and 50–69.
[53] 'Text Against Performance', p. 51.
[54] '*King Lear*', in Bloom, *Shakespeare: The Invention of the Human* (London, 1999), pp. 476–515; pp. 476, 484, 488, 489.
[55] 'Some Aspects of the Style of *King Lear*', *Shakespeare Survey* 13 (1960), pp. 49–57; p. 49.
[56] '*King Lear*', in *Shakespeare's Language* (London, 2000), pp. 183–200.

relies on',[57] shows a critical finesse that makes most of the criticism covered in this retrospect seem crude and schematic by comparison. Booth displays a similar reluctance to flatten *King Lear* into a diagram or construe it as a symptom of something else. In *King Lear, Macbeth, Indefinition and Tragedy*, he proposes that 'the greatness of *Lear* arises from the confrontation it makes with inconclusiveness',[58] and provides an invaluable conspectus of the strategies it deploys to defy closure, which range from reiteration and regression, through the pursuit of irrelevance, to the confusion of categories and the confounding of meaning. As a result, as with Bayley, *Lear* comes alive as a work of verbal and theatrical art in a way that is beyond the reach of historicist, feminist and psychoanalytic approaches as they are currently conceived.

At the same time, there is no denying that formal accounts like Bayley's and Booth's are the poorer for their blindness to the insights that the most gifted exponents of these approaches have achieved. As criticism of *King Lear* moves into a new millennium, the challenge is to devise ways of tackling the play that can see the imprint of an era in the turn of a phrase, a clue to the psyche in the pitch of the verse, and the text itself as a version of history, without sacrificing its poetry to its politics. Such readings might do justice at last to Joseph Wittreich's recognition, in his pathbreaking study of the play, that '*Lear* is an historical mirror in which, beholding the past, we catch prophetic glimpses, however darkly, of the present and the future.'[59] They might even blaze a trail, given the iconic status of *King Lear*, for a transformation of the practice and the politics of criticism.

---

[57] 'The King's Ship', in Bayley, *Shakespeare and Tragedy* (London, 1981), pp. 7–48; pp. 23, 27.

[58] *King Lear, Macbeth, Indefinition and Tragedy* (New Haven, 1983), pp. 5–57; p. 16.

[59] '*Image of that Horror': History, Prophecy, and Apocalypse in 'King Lear'* (San Marino, Calif., 1984), p. 11.

HOW SHAKESPEARE KNEW *KING LEIR*

RICHARD KNOWLES

Lewis Theobald thought that Shakespeare gave a tragic ending to his *King Lear* 'to vary from another, but most execrable, Dramatic Performance upon this Story: which I certainly believe to have preceded our Author's Piece'. From that work, the anonymous *True Chronicle History of King Leir* (1605), Theobald quotes some lines of 'such Poetry as one might hammer out, *Stans pede in uno*', so 'That *Shakespeare* ... may stand acquitted from the least Suspicion of Plagiarism.' From the initial doubt that the 'silly old play', as Edward Capell called it, had much or any influence on Shakespeare, we have today come to the contrary opinion of a recent critic that '*The True Chronicle Historie* was a remarkably pervasive presence in Shakespeare's career for well over a decade and exercised considerable power in shaping the formal and thematic structure of several quite different plays.' Edmond Malone doubted that Shakespeare had ever read the 1605 edition of *Leir*, preferring to think that it was published after the first appearance of Shakespeare's play so as to cash in on its stage success. Rather, Malone supposed, Shakespeare had known the old play before its publication in 1605: 'without doubt he had often seen it exhibited; nor could he have found any difficulty in procuring a manuscript copy of it ... I suspect, however, the old play had been published in 1594'. Though Henslowe records performances of a 'kinge leare' on 6 and 8 April 1594, and though a 'Chronicle historye of Leire kinge of England', presumably the same play, was entered in the Stationers' Register a month later, no evidence exists that it was published at that time, and Walter Greg thought that Shakespeare more probably had access to a manuscript copy than to any such early edition. Kenneth Muir proposed that Shakespeare might have acted in the play early in his career; perhaps he could have done so if, as Scott McMillin and Sally-Beth MacLean have recently suggested, he was a member of the Queen's Men. Most recently Stanley Wells has inclined to the latter theory as being consistent with Shakespeare's apparent early and continual awareness of the play, though conceding that 'there is no comprehensive study' of such influence.[1]

This, then, is the range of opinions, all of them still current, about Shakespeare's acquaintance with the only dramatic version of the Lear story before his own: that he somehow knew the old *Leir* play but was little influenced by it, or was somewhat influenced by it, or was very much influenced by it not only in *Lear* but in some dozen of his other

---

[1] Shakespeare, *Works*, ed. Lewis Theobald, 7 vols. (1733), vol. 5, pp. 217–18, quoting Horace, *Sat.* 1.4.10; Shakespeare, *Comedies, Histories, & Tragedies*, ed. Edward Capell, 10 vols. (1768), vol. 1, p. 55; Martin Mueller, 'From Leir to Lear', *Philological Quarterly*, 73 (1994), 121; Shakespeare, *Plays & Poems*, ed. Edmond Malone, 10 vols. (1790), vol. 1, p. 353; Philip Henslowe, *Henslowe's Diary*, ed. R. A. Foakes and R. T. Rickert (Cambridge, 1961), p. 21; 'Stationers' Records', in W. W. Greg, *Bibliography of the English Printed Drama to the Restoration (BEPD)*, 4 vols. (1939–59), vol. 1, p. 11; W. W. Greg, 'The Date of *King Lear* and Shakespeare's Use of Earlier Versions of the Story', 4, *Library*, 20 (1940), 384; *King Lear*, Arden Shakespeare, ed. Kenneth Muir (1952), p. xxxii; Scott McMillin and Sally-Beth MacLean, *The Queen's Men and their Plays* (Cambridge, 1998), pp. 160–6; *The History of King Lear*, Oxford World's Classics, ed. Stanley Wells (Oxford, 2000), p. 12, n. 1.

plays; that he read a lost early edition of the play, or remembered seeing the play acted, or himself acted in it as a Queen's Man or later as a Chamberlain's or King's Man; or that he acquired and used a manuscript of it, before its publication in 1605; or that he mainly used the printed edition after its publication in 1605, whatever previous knowledge of the play he may already have had. I wish here to take another look at the evidence, such as it is, for each of these possibilities; to argue that some of them are demonstrably less probable than others – indeed, that most of them are baseless and others are improbable in the extreme; and to construct a narrative that accounts adequately and consistently for all the known facts, including some new ones, relating to Shakespeare's possible access to, knowledge of, and use of the *True Chronicle History*.

SHAKESPEARE'S USE OF THE 1605 TEXT

George Steevens remarked only one point of resemblance between *Leir* and *Lear* – a father kneeling to his daughter – and thought it 'not improbable' that Shakespeare 'might have seen' the old play and adopted that detail from it. Since then many more points of similarity have been found; yet there has persisted a curious reluctance to attribute these likenesses to Shakespeare's actually having known the edition of *Leir* published in 1605. Some editors, from Malone to Greg and Muir, have simply wanted to date the composition of *Lear* before the second half of 1605; *Leir* would not then have been published, since it was not entered for publication until 8 May. The impulse to date *Lear* in 1604 or early 1605 arises naturally from the difficulty of fitting a large number of plays between *Measure for Measure* and *Othello* in 1603–4 and *Coriolanus* in 1607 – the possible candidates include *All's Well, Timon, Lear, Macbeth,* and *Antony and Cleopatra,* all of which may have been written by the end of 1606.[2] *Lear* has seemed easier to put back in time than some of the others; but if it is heavily dependent on the printed *Leir*, then it must have been composed in late 1605 or the following year, a time apparently already crowded with other plays.

A more general reason for the reluctance to make the printed *Leir* a source of *Lear* is the obviously great difference between the pleasant old historical romance and Shakespeare's harrowing tragedy. Since the two plays are worlds apart generically, emotionally, philosophically, stylistically and substantively – the old play lacks the Gloucester subplot, the Fool, Lear's madness, the storm scenes and the tragic ending – many critics have doubted that Shakespeare had much or any recourse to the text printed in 1605. Thus George Lyman Kittredge: 'Shakespeare owes little to the old play except the impulse to write a new one. Now and then a phrase reminds us of something in *King Lear*, but these resemblances are trifling.' Recently Stanley Wells, though he thinks a manuscript or the printed book to be the most likely source, still leaves open the possibilities that Shakespeare may have been familiar with the play only 'from seeing it performed long before, or from acting in it ... The nature of his indebtedness to this text suggests easy familiarity rather than close consultation'.[3]

On the other hand, since the appearance in 1904 of Wilfrid Perrett's magisterial book on the sources of *Lear*, many studies of the two plays have pointed out a growing number of similarities between them – more, in the judgement of such critics as Geoffrey Bullough, Dorothy Nameri, and Reginald Foakes, than can be explained by memories of seeing or acting the play years prior to its publication.[4] Before taking up the questions

---

[2] George Steevens, ed., *Twenty of the Plays of Shakespeare,* 4 vols. (1766), vol. 1, p. 16; Malone, *Plays & Poems,* vol. 1, pp. 352–3; Greg, 'The Date of *King Lear*', 383–4; Muir, *King Lear,* pp. xxii–xxiv; Greg, 'Stationers' Records', vol. 1, p. 20; J. Leeds Barroll, *Politics, Plague, and Shakespeare's Theater* (Ithaca, NY, 1991), p. 176.

[3] Shakespeare, *Works,* ed. George Lyman Kittredge (Boston, 1936), pp. 1195–6; Wells, *History of King Lear,* p. 11.

[4] Wilfrid Perrett, *The Story of King Lear from Geoffrey of Monmouth to Shakespeare,* Palaestra 35 (Berlin, 1904); Geoffrey Bullough, ed., *Narrative and Dramatic Sources of Shakespeare,* vol. 7: *Major Tragedies* (London and NY, 1973), pp. 270, 276; Dorothy E. Nameri, *Three Versions of the Story of King Lear* (Salzburg, 1976), p. 9; *King Lear,* Arden Shakespeare, ed. R. A. Foakes (Walton-on-Thames, 1997), p. 90.

of whether Shakespeare relied on memory or a manuscript or the 1605 edition of *Leir*, it may be useful to begin by simply listing the almost hundred details common to these two plays but found in virtually none of the other sources. I shall do this in narrative form, and to keep numerals to a minimum I will (usually) not give act–scene–line numbers for *Lear*, a play with which everyone is familiar, but only Bullough's through-line numbers for *Leir*. All of these similarities (along with other more tenuous ones that I have ignored) have been pointed out by previous commentators.[5] I am simply collecting them in one place so that they may be seen in the aggregate; their number and specificity will, I expect, persuade even the most sceptical that Shakespeare's knowledge of the old play was neither casual nor remote, but recent and detailed.

On the characters and themes of *Lear* the old play had limited effect. The basic characters of the story were historical givens; but it is possible that Kent owes something both to Leir's faithful servant–companion Perillus and to the waggish servant of the French king, Mumford, who boasts of bluntness (386–9); that Oswald picks up his servile willingness to connive and murder for a mistress from both the courtier Skalliger (796–816) and Gonorill's Messenger (1006 ff.); that Gloucester's faithful old servant in 4.1 is also owing to Perillus; that Albany derives his character from Gonorill's mild husband, Cornwall, who early on begins to have doubts about her treatment of Leir (see, e.g., 945–66); and that Burgundy owes his presence to a hint, unique in the sources, of a rival suitor for Cordella (115–16). One would not expect the old play, which continually exemplifies contemporary providential theology,[6] to share many philosophical ideas with the profoundly questioning *Lear*, but there are occasionally common themes of the importance of natural law and bonds (896–905, 1264–74), the justice of the heavens (1909–10), the fact that death is not the worst one can expect (1470, 2077–80), the need to cultivate the powerful (872–5), the virtue of patience (numerous lines), and so on – all fairly commonplace ideas but not found in the other sources.

The action of *Leir*, on the other hand, provides to *Lear* countless episodes and particular details of action that are not found in any of the other versions of the Lear story. Although Shakespeare collapsed *Leir*'s first eight scenes of leisurely exposition into one, dispensed with the scenes in France, and introduced a tragic ending, he followed the beginning and middle parts of the play in numerous details. Leir's queen is dead (1–4), and Leir prepares to resign his rule because he is weary of earthly cares (26–8), hoping in the process to avoid future problems of succession, maintaining peace, and protecting against foreign hate (43–55); only in *Leir* and Spenser's *Faerie Queene* does the king resign his rule. He entertains (though he does not embrace) a plan, hinted in *Mirror for Magistrates*, to reward his daughters according to their degree of love (37–42). During her sisters' professions Cordella speaks deflating asides (254, 274). She declares herself unused to flatter (302), and (later) names that fact as the cause of Lear's displeasure (654–5). To Leir she says that she cannot express her love (277–8) but that her deeds will speak for her (278), that she gives Leir the love that she owes him (279–80) – as she later says, because he begot and bred her (2307–12) – but (like Ragan, 270) will 'happely' love a future husband. Lear rejects her answer and accuses her

---

5 See esp. *King Lear*, Arden Shakespeare, ed. W. J. Craig (1901), pp. xxx–xxxv; Perrett, *Story of King Lear*, pp. 143–289 passim; *King Leir*, Shakespeare Classics, ed. Sidney Lee (London and NY, 1909), pp. xxxviii–xliii; Allardyce Nicoll, *Studies in Shakespeare* (1928), pp. 139–55; Greg, 'The Date of *King Lear*', 386–97; Muir, *King Lear*, pp. xxvi–xxxii; Robert Adger Law, '*King Leir* and *King Lear*: An Examination of the Two Plays', in *Studies in Honor of T. W. Baldwin*, ed. Don Cameron Allen (Urbana, 1958), pp. 112–24; Bullough, *Narrative*, pp. 337–402, notes passim; Nameri, *Three Versions*, passim; Donald M. Michie, ed., *King Leir* (Madison, Wis., 1979; NY, 1991), pp. 31–9; Peter Pauls, 'The *True Chronicle History of King Leir* and Shakespeare's *King Lear*. A Reconsideration', *Upstart Crow*, 5 (1984), 93–107. The following quotations and line references from Shakespeare's *King Lear* are taken from *The Riverside Shakespeare*, ed. G. Blakemore Evans (Boston, 1974).

6 See William R. Elton, King Lear *and the Gods* (San Marino, 1966), pp. 63–71; Bullough, *Narrative*, pp. 281–3; John L Murphy, *Darkness and Devils: Exorcism and* King Lear (Athens, Ohio, 1984), pp. 119–34.

of pride (285). Later the king of France, uniquely in the sources, conducts his own suit of Cordella, and she (rather than Lear) tells him she lacks sufficient dowry (681–91). Perillus seeks unsuccessfully to interpose on Cordella's behalf (562–8), angering Leir (569–73). Leir says his oath to disown her is irrevocable (505–10), and he actually divides his land (although by lot, as in *Faerie Queene*, not by giving away a coronet) (550).

Gonorill accuses Leir of 'extremes' of behavior (195); she and Ragan both accuse Leir of senile dotage (181, 758, 784, 1188; the charge occurs in *Mirror for Magistrates* also). Gonorill complains of daily taunts from Leir (776–7), and encourages her servants to disgrace him (759–60); both Gonorill and Ragan want to force a showdown with Leir (839–40, 1155–6). Though Gonorill grows cold to Leir, he tries not to notice (2262–4), but ultimately she drives him to tears (865). She restrains half his 'pension' (763) or 'portion' (807); in *Lear* the allowance is called 'exhibition' and 'sizes'. In his rage he calls a daughter (Cordella, not Gonorill) bastard (312). Perillus shows up after Leir's first daughter shows her perfidy (866–7). Leir does not recognize Perillus (868 ff.), who attempts to comfort his master with the thought that Leir has two other daughters left (909). Gonorill's husband Cornwall urges her to be not 'partiall' (841). Gonorill writes a letter of false slander (984), and her messenger carries it to Ragan (1032–4). Cornwall begins to doubt the wisdom of his wife's actions and begins to act independently of her (945 ff.). Ragan improperly mistreats a king's ambassador (1966–7). Ragan hypocritically welcomes Leir, intending to cast him out (1118–56). Leir kneels before a daughter (Cordella, not Ragan) (2300 ff.). Ragan makes an unfilial outburst, siding with Gonorill (1172 ff.). Leir questions reason's adequacy to justify behavior (896–905). Leir rebukes Gonorill for the "vaine expense" of a "new fashioned gowne" (782–5). After being rejected by his daughters, Leir wanders with Perillus (1094, 1991). Thunder is heard (1634, 1739). Leir reviews all he has done for his daughters, for which gratitude is due, asking Perillus rhetorically, 'did I euer . . . giue thee halfe my Kingdome?' (888–905). Ragan plots Leir's (and Perillus's) death

(1318; cf. 3.6.89, often overlooked, and 4.5.11–13, 37–8). Leir (like Gloucester) learns that he has counted on his false child for help (1606–30).

Cordella prays to regain her father's love (1077 ff.) and comes to England to re-establish Leir's 'right' (2561); cf. 4.4.23–9. British citizens revolt against their present rulers to help Leir (2524–8); they are a people greatly tax'd (2524–6), as in *Lear* they are those whom 'the rigor of our state/Forc'd to cry out' (5.1.22–3). In the events leading up to the final battle, Gonorill forces a reluctant Messenger to show her some letters meant for another, as Regan attempts to do with Oswald; like Oswald, he fears punishment for showing them (995–1005). Later Ragan wonders what has become of a servant who has not returned, as Regan does of Oswald (2361–5). A disguised child (Cordella) and her parent (Leir) call each other 'father' and 'daughter' before recognizing each other (2218–21), as do Gloucester and Edgar. Perillus counsels Leir (as Edmund counsels Gloucester) against despair (2078–80). Perillus calls for heavenly punishment of the murderous children (1649–52), and Cambria affirms divine justice (1909–10); Albany does both in 4.2. Leir feels shame (2048–64) before his reunion with Cordella. Ragan flatters the Messenger to win him over (1205), and he promises without qualms to murder the old king (1214–19), as Oswald vows to murder Gloucester. She only hints at the deed to be done, as Edmund later does in instructing the Captain to murder Lear and Cordelia. When confronted, Leir asks his assigned murderer to strike, as Gloucester asks Oswald to do (1659–60). Leir has a reconciliation scene with Cordella, found in no previous version. She weeps when she sees his plight (2236–7). The French king, like the gentleman or physician in *Lear* 4.7, warns Cordella not to overtax Leir with the emotion of reunion (2196–8); joy might kill him, as it later does Gloucester. Cordella prays that Leir's health may be restored by a medicinal draught (2188–90), and praises Leir's servant for his loyalty (2335–6). Cordella asks blessing and pardon of Leir (2322–6); Leir kneels to his daughter (2300 ff.). Leir offers to resign his life to atone with Cordella (1577–85), as Lear offers to take poison for the same reason. After the battle, when Ragan is shown incriminating letters – 'Knowest thou these letters?' at *Leir* 2586, 'Know'st thou this paper?' in *Lear* 5.3 – she (as Goneril) tries to snatch and tear them.

Virtually none of these details of action is in the other sources for *Lear*. Some of them might grow naturally out of the dramatic situation and so might occur by coincidence to two dramatists working independently with similar material. In other cases some transmutation has occurred, especially through a certain amount of reordering and reassigning of the details. In the aggregate, however, there seem to be too many close similarities to be explained by coincidence or by distant memories of a performance experienced as many as ten to fifteen years earlier. Indeed, the more details *Lear* seems to derive from *Leir*, the less likely it is that the rest are entirely coincidental. In the mass, they seem evidently to derive from a fairly close recent acquaintance with the old play, which, as Greg says,[7] Shakespeare seems to have read with some care.

One would not expect much linguistic influence, and one does not find much:[8] the regular verse and plain style of *Leir* aim at very different effects than does the chiaroscuro intensity and vast range and variety of *Lear*'s language. Shakespeare never follows *Leir* line by line, and we cannot expect the continual echoes of the source that we find, e.g., in Enobarbus's portrait of Cleopatra on her barge. Nonetheless, a significant number of verbal correspondences have been found. Parallel speech–acts in the two plays sometimes contain echoes of language or metaphor. Before addressing his court, Leir hints of a 'further mystery' (144), as Lear of a 'darker purpose'. Gonorill assures Leir, 'I prize my love to you' (240), and Regan, asserting love equally great, urges Lear to 'prize me at her worth'. As George Ian Duthie pointed out, Leir's 'reuerse/Our censure' (505–6) and Perillus's 'ruthlesse doome' (567) contain elements of Kent's 'Reuerse thy doome' (Q) and 'Reuoke thy doome' (Q) from the analogous altercation in *Lear*.[9] In the same argument Leir says 'Urge this no more, and if thou loue thy life, no' (569); Lear says, 'Kent, on thy life no more.' Perillus replies, 'Ah, who so blind,

as they that will not see' (577), and Kent says 'See better, Lear.' Later in the play Leir asks Ragan in disbelief, 'did I giue thee all?' (2144); Lear exclaims to Regan in disbelief, 'I gave you all.' Skalliger calls Gonorill 'shame to all thy sexe' (811), and Perillus calls her 'monster, shame unto thy sexe:/Thou fiend in likenesse of a humane creature' (2581–2); Cordelia calls both sisters 'Shame of ladies', and Albany scolds the 'devil' Goneril: 'Proper deformity shows not in the fiend so horrid as in woman . . . Bemonster not thy feature.'

Sometimes phrases from the old play seem to appear in *Lear* in quite a different context. For instance, the same collocation of monster, deformity, and fiend is made by Lear:

> Ingratitude! thou marble-hearted fiend,
> More hideous when thou show'st thee in a child
> Than the sea-monster.　　　　(1.4.259–61)

Or consider the following passage from *Leir* 505–16:

> LEIR Cease, good my Lords, and sue not to reuerse
> Our censure, which is now irreuocable . . .
> Then do not so dishonour me, my Lords,
> As to make shipwrack of our kingly word.
> I am as kind as is the Pellican,
> That kils it selfe, to saue her young ones liues:
> And yet as ielous as the princely Eagle,
> That kils her young ones, if they do but dazell
> Vpon the radiant splendor of the Sunne.

Little can be made of the allusion to the Pelican, which had appeared in *Richard II* and *Hamlet* before its occurrence in *Lear* 3.4.75. One does hear, however, Lear warning Kent, 'thou hast sought to make us break our vow,/Which we durst never yet', and even more strikingly one is reminded of Lear's oath a few minutes earlier as he exiled

---

7　'The Date of *King Lear*', p. 397.

8　See Alfred Hart, *Stolne and Surreptitious Copies: A Comparative Study of Shakespeare's Bad Quartos* (Melbourne and London, 1942), pp. 21–32, 41, 63.

9　George Ian Duthie, ed., *Shakespeare's* King Lear: *A Critical Edition* (Oxford, 1949), pp. 125–6. F1's 'reserue thy state' and 'reuoke thy guift' are further from the wording of the source play.

Cordelia, swearing 'by the sacred radiance of the sun'. Leir, however, is not here threatening exile to anyone, simply reaffirming his plans to bestow his daughters in marriage. In another such transposition, it is Leir who says 'think me but the shaddow of my selfe' (1111) but the Fool (in F at least) who answers Lear's question 'Who is it that can tell me who I am?' with the reply 'Lear's shadow' (1.4.230–1). Perillus describes Leir, enduring Gonorill's provocations, as 'the myrrour of mild patience' (755), but it is Lear later in the storm who says 'I will be the pattern of all patience.' Ragan threatens to scratch out Cordella's eyes (1906), a threat similar to Lear's at 1.4.307–8. Several characters compare Leir's daughters to vipers (811, 1653, 2345, 2558, 2584; see also *Mirror for Magistrates*); Lear and Albany compare them to serpents. Leir speaks at length of weeds growing amid sweet and healthful herbs (2050–62), Cordelia describes in detail such a mixture in Lear's crown of weeds and flowers. Leir describes his daughters as 'florishing branches of a Kingly stocke' (225), the cast-off Cordella feels herself a 'branch' of that 'stock' who is now 'Withered and sere' (1242–3), and the King of France promises to be unto her 'another stocke' whose 'continuall sap' will 'make thee flourish' (1244–7); but it is Albany who warns Goneril, 'She that herself will sliver and disbranch From her material sap, perforce must wither.' A Captain says angrily of negligent watchmen, 'A whirl-wind carry them quick to a whirl-poole' (2486), but it is Edgar who talks of 'whirlpool' and 'whirlwinds'. Shakespeare had referred to whirl-winds in several previous plays, but the word 'whirl-pool' appears only once, in *Lear*; there is every likelihood that it derives from *Leir*, for it appears in no other version of the Lear story, nor in Shakespeare's other sources for this play, Samuel Harsnett's *Declaration* and Sidney's account of the Paphlagonian King in *The Arcadia*.

Greg may be right that none of these echoes was conscious: 'The whole thing has been fused and transmuted in the alembic of his genius ... As he wrote, ideas, phrases, cadences from the old play still floated in his memory below the level of conscious thought, and ... now and again one or

another helped to fashion the words that flowed from his pen.'[10] That memory, however, seems to Greg and others to have been vivified by recent and close acquaintance with the only other known dramatic treatment of the Lear story before Shakespeare's. Evidently score upon score of details from the old play were fresh in his mind.

It has occasionally been suggested, especially by some of those inclined to date *Lear* before the 1605 quarto of *Leir*, that Shakespere's knowledge of the old play might have come from his recently seeing a performance of it.[11] That theory has not been advanced much in recent years, as more and more similarities between the two plays have been discerned; even so retentive a memory as Shakespeare's might not have called up so many particulars from mere exposure to a performance, even a recent one. The title-page of the 1605 quarto does claim that the play 'hath bene diuers and sundry times lately acted'. Most critics have too easily doubted the truth of the claim. *Leir* is a well-made play and had played successfully, and other old plays no better than it were sometimes revived. Later in this essay, however, I shall give reasons why performances of *Leir*, if they occurred in the decade before the composition of *Lear*, probably would not have taken place in London but in provincial towns, thereby reducing markedly the chance that Shakespeare ever witnessed any.

THE MEMORY OF AN ACTOR

Is it possible that so many details from the old *Leir* were stored in Shakespeare's mind because he had once committed much or all of the play to memory in order to act in it? The idea was proposed by Karl Wentersdorf in 1950 and by Hardin Craig in 1951, refined by Kenneth Muir in 1952, and repeated as recently as 2000 by Stanley

---

[10] 'The Date of *King Lear*', p. 397.

[11] E. K. Chambers, *William Shakespeare: A Study of Facts and Problems*, 2 vols. (Oxford, 1930), vol. 1, p. 470; Thomas Marc Parrott, *Shakespearean Comedy* (NY, 1949), p. 295. Parrott also thinks that 'there can be no doubt whatever' that Shakespeare read the printed book.

Wells. It has lately received new impetus from McMillin and MacLean, who think (as most scholars do) that *Leir* was a Queen's Men play and (as Alfred Pollard, Wentersdorf, G. M. Pinciss, and others have argued) that Shakespeare was once a Queen's Man.[12]

Muir observed, influentially, that during seven of the eight passages he quotes from *Leir* that have 'verbal parallels' in *Lear*, Perillus is on the stage. 'That', Muir concluded, 'may have been Shakespeare's role.' It is a shrewd guess, but one without weight, being based on only a small fraction of the parallels of action and language noted above. In fact Perillus is on stage during just about half (49 per cent) of the lines spoken in *Leir*, and even so is absent during more than thirty other parallel passages that the critics have discerned. Muir's seven parallels no more prove that Shakespeare acted in the play than that he read it.

That Shakespeare was once a Queen's Man must remain at present no more than a speculation, since we have no firm evidence of his acting career before he appears in the Lord Chamberlain's company in 1594. Pollard thought that the jealousy of Robert Greene, who wrote a number of plays for the Queen's Men, was most easily explained if Shakespeare had *acted* in those plays and thereby, rather than by plagiarism, had been beautified with Greene's feathers. But Greene could perfectly well have been jealous of a competitive upstart who (without Greene's university training) was suddenly enjoying spectacular success writing for one or more rival companies. The fact that Shakespeare wrote later versions of several plays once owned by the Queen's Men – *The Troublesome Raigne of King John, The Famous Victories of Henry V, King Leir* – has suggested to Pollard, Wentersdorf, Pinciss and others that he had familiarity with and access to those old plays because he had once acted in them. But familiarity and access were probably not a problem in any case: as E. K. Chambers remarked, 'These were all in print before he needed them.'[13]

Recent scholarship seems to be giving at least as much weight to the likelihood that the young Shakespeare acted in several companies that are known to have performed his early plays, none of them the Queen's Men. The performance record of these plays in the early 1590s suggests that he was with Lord Strange's Men until 1592 (*1H6, Tit.*), then with Pembroke's company until it broke up in 1593 (*2* and *3H6, Shr., Tit.*), then perhaps briefly with Sussex's Men until they broke up in spring 1594 (*Tit.*), and thereafter with the Lord Chamberlain's Men.[14] If he had acted with the Queen's Men, the most important company of the 1580s and early 1590s, his earliest plays would probably not all have been acted by other companies. When the Lord Chamberlain's company was formed in 1594, it acquired actors from the old Strange's–Derby's company and from Pembroke's via Sussex's,[15] but no identifiable actor from the Queen's Men, who continued in existence as a touring company for another decade. There being no clear evidence that Shakespeare ever was a Queen's Man, and some reason to think otherwise, there is accordingly no reason to think that he ever acted in *Leir*, a play not known to have been performed by any other company than the Queen's.

LEIR'S EARLY INFLUENCE ON SHAKESPEARE

The notion that the old *Leir* influenced several early plays of Shakespeare seems rapidly to be becoming

---

[12] Karl Wentersdorf, 'Shakespeares Erste Truppe', *Shakespeare Jahrbuch*, 84–6 (1950), 128; Hardin Craig, 'Motivation in Shakespeare's Choice of Materials', *Shakespeare Survey 4* (Cambridge, 1951), p. 32; Muir, *King Lear*, p. xxxii; Wells, *History of King Lear*, p. 12; McMillin and MacLean, *The Queen's Men*, pp. 160–6; Alfred W. Pollard, 'Introduction' to Peter Alexander, *Shakespeare's Henry VI and Richard III* (Cambridge, 1929), pp. 13–21; G. M. Pinciss, 'Shakespeare, Her Majesty's Players and Pembroke's Men', *Shakespeare Survey 27* (Cambridge, 1974), pp. 129–36.

[13] E. K. Chambers, *The Elizabethan Stage*, 4 vols. (Oxford, 1923), 2:202. Speculations that manuscripts of these plays passed to the Chamberlain's company are briefly discussed later in this essay.

[14] So Chambers, *The Elizabethan Stage*, vol. 2, p. 338; Andrew Gurr, *The Shakespearian Playing Companies* (Oxford, 1996), pp. 175–6, 262–3, 269–72. It is uncertain who first acted *Err., LLL,* and *TGV*, and when; the Chamberlain's Men have been proposed for all three, in 1594 and later.

[15] Gurr, *Shakespearian Playing Companies*, p. 279.

accepted wisdom. Wells cites recent assertions by Meredith Skura and Martin Mueller that *Leir* influenced *Richard III, Titus, Taming of the Shrew, Merchant of Venice, Richard II, Much Ado, As You Like It,* and *Hamlet,* as well as such post-*Lear* plays as *Coriolanus* and *Cymbeline.* Other writers have made similar claims for influence on *1* and *2 Henry VI* and *King John.* At least some of these claims are also accepted by McMillin and MacLean. Once thought to be a play too silly and feeble to have influenced Shakespeare much if at all, now *Leir* is apparently gaining stature as a source to be reckoned with as seriously as Holinshed and Plutarch, at least if one judges by the number of plays it is supposed to have shaped. Here is Martin Mueller: 'Without *The True Chronicle Historie* we would not have *King Lear* or *As You Like It,* while *Richard III, The Merchant of Venice,* and *Hamlet* would be quite different plays.'[16] In view of their number and apparent weight, such assertions are due for some critical assessment.

I should say at the outset that I find none of these claims of *Leir*'s early influence completely convincing, and most of them vacuous. They are based repeatedly on the kind of dubious analogy that Richard Levin has called 'Fluellenism'.[17] Repeatedly the arguments for *Leir*'s influence take the form, 'Play A is similar to play B in certain (very few and often very general) respects; therefore play A is a source for play B.' Reasonable questions whether the points of similarity might derive from a wholly different source C, or from a store of common generic features, or from commonplace ideas or theatrical fashions of the time, or whether essential differences outweigh accidental similarities, or even whether the direction of influence might be the reverse of what is asserted, are all too seldom addressed at all. Nor is any explanation ever offered how the old play remained so vividly in Shakespeare's thoughts year after year. Some claims are based on demonstrable error: for example, Skura apparently believes that *Leir* 1605 is a 'reprint' or 'republication' of an earlier first edition, presumably consulted by Shakespeare.[18] No such edition exists, and in all probability none ever did, as Greg has shown (see below). Claims are also exaggerated from one critic to the next: although

Geoffrey Bullough says only 'Cf. *R3,* IV.4.369–89 for a series of oaths rejected', Mueller reports that Bullough 'rightly sees' the brief swearing scene in *Leir* (1625–33) 'as the source for a similar exchange in' *Richard III* 4.4, a claim that Bullough does not make. Skura goes further, claiming actual appropriation – 'Other lines from the scene appear in *Richard III* 4.4.369–89' – though in fact there are no lines common to the two scenes.[19]

The avalanche begins slowly in 1912 with a single essay by Robert Adger Law,[20] who argues that Clarence's death scene in *Richard III* was influenced by *Leir*'s near-assassination (Scene 19, 1431 ff.). Though conceding some points of likeness to the murder scene in Marlowe's *Edward II,* especially the 'grotesquely humorous conversation of the murderers before the deed', Law carefully lists several general likenesses between the scenes of *Leir* and *Richard III:* sleeping royalty about to be stabbed, the hired murderer(s) warned not to be dissuaded by the victim, the victim waking in fear from a dream symbolizing what is about to take place, the victim swapping counter-charges with the assassin(s), who tell(s) him that the relative he trusts is the instigator, and the victim making (one) murderer relent by warning of divine wrath and earthly consequences. Law also acknowledges that 'Differences between these scenes in the number of murderers, number of victims, background, general effect, *dénouement,* and specific details have been purposely left out of account, in order to make the resemblance as clear as possible.' Law tries to collect verbal similarities as well, but except for a couple of phrases – *sit by*

[16] Wells, *History of King Lear,* pp. 11–12; Meredith A. Skura, *Shakespeare the Actor and the Purposes of Playing* (Chicago and London, 1993), pp. 285–6; McMillin and MacLean, *The Queen's Men,* pp. 162, 224; Mueller, 'From Leir to Lear', 195.

[17] Richard Levin, *New Readings vs. Old Plays* (Chicago and London, 1979), pp. 209–11.

[18] Skura, *Shakespeare the Actor,* p. 287.

[19] Bullough, *Narrative,* p. 377 n.; Mueller, 'From Leir to Lear', 204; Skura, *Shakespeare the Actor,* p. 285.

[20] Robert Adger Law, 'Richard the Third, Act I, Scene 4', *PMLA* 27 (1912), 117–41. Quotations are from pp. 119 n., 131, 135, and 136.

me/sit . . . with you, stab him as he sleeps/stab them bravely while they sleep, never wake until the great judgment day/never wake until doomsday – they are at best common words or synonyms that might grow naturally out of the similar occasions. Two others from scattered parts of the play – *The fitter for the King of heaven* (both plays) and *in heaven, where thou shalt never come/to heaven, Where . . . you never mean to come* – are somewhat more suggestive. To Law, 'The resemblances are of such a nature that one would believe them to be due to conscious imitation.' Facing squarely the difficult question of which text was prior to the other, Law relies on a doubtful argument: that whereas Shakespeare would naturally improve on an earlier play, the anonymous playwright would not have taken such a good scene in Shakespeare and botched it so badly as to produce the 'crude, feeble, and childlike' scene in *Leir*. 'The case', he admits, 'does not admit of definite proof'; and of course the less talented author of *Leir*, aiming at very different effects in writing a pious romance rather than a sensational melodrama like *Richard III*, might easily have produced a less dramatic and less effective scene from borrowed material.

Although Law's shrewd and careful argument has been absurdly misrepresented – Thomas H. McNeal, for instance, says, 'Law pointed out years ago that this episode [in *Leir*] was taken over nearly intact' in *Richard III* 1.3 – it has won the attention of such scholars as Dover Wilson, Wolfgang Clemen, and Bullough. Indeed, Hermann von Friesen had noticed in 1876 that the two scenes resembled each other, though very superficially (*zwar oberflächlich*), and Wilfrid Perrett in 1906 had concluded as Law did: 'No one, after comparison, would dream of deriving the longdrawn dulness of [*Leir*] from the brilliance of Shakespeare's dialogue. But I am inclined to think that Shakespeare had met with [*Leir*] before he wrote R. III.'[21]

A few further parallels have been discerned. Perrett had noticed before Bullough 'the series of proferred [sic] oaths rejected as invalid by the interlocutor in this same scene of [*Leir* 1625 ff.] and in R III, IV, iv, [366] ff.' In *Leir* the murderous Messenger swears by the usual triad of heaven, earth, and hell, and Richard by the more extravagant

series of his 'George, . . . Garter, and . . . crown', the world, his father's death, himself, God, and the time to come; the speech-acts are similar, the language completely different. McNeal argues that as Gonorill (Ragan, rather) bribes the Messenger to murder her father, so Richard III, 'imitating Gonorill', bribes Tyrrel to murder the little princes; 'Thus from *Leir* Shakespeare learned a special design for murder: the heartless instigator of crime, the cowardly assistant, and the helpless (often sleeping) victim. The weapon is the dagger.' The design, however, is not special at all but generic Machiavellianism whose ingredients are common in contemporary plays: see below. Meredith Skura says that Leir's kneeling before his would-be murderer to save the life of Perillus 'certainly was a primary source for the murder of Clarence, the "begging prince", in *Richard III* (there was no such scene in the chronicles)'. There is no such scene in *Richard III* either. Although Clarence once refers to himself as a 'begging prince', he does not kneel or beg; indeed, as Antony Hammond points out, he speaks to the murderer in the second-person singular as a superior to an inferior throughout the interview, and his 'entreaty' is framed in monitory and imperative terms, not supplicatory ones.[22]

Though some similarities of incident between these two roughly contemporary plays are highly suggestive, the details in *R3* may have come from elsewhere than *Leir*. C. H. Herford finds two other analogues for Ragan's somewhat clownish hired assassin: 'After the manner of Lightborn with Edward in the dungeon (*Edw. II.* v. 5.), or Gloster with

---

[21] Thomas H. McNeal, 'Shakespeare's Cruel Queens', *Huntington Library Quarterly*, 22 (1958–9), p. 43; *Richard III*, New (Cambridge) Shakespeare, ed. J. Dover Wilson (Cambridge, 1954), p. xxxii; Wolfgang Clemen, *A Commentary on Shakespeare's Richard III* (Göttingen, 1957), tr. Jean Bonheim (1968), p. 89 n.; Bullough, *Narrative*, pp. 373–7 nn.; Hermann, Freiherr von Friesen, *Shakspere-Studien*. Vol. 3: *William Shakespere's Dramen von 1601 bis zum Schlusse seiner Laufbahn* (Wien, 1876), p. 86; Perrett, *Story of King Lear*, p. 114, n. 2.

[22] Perrett, *Story of King Lear*, p. 114; McNeal, 'Shakespeare's Cruel Queens', 48–9; Skura, *Shakespeare the Actor*, p. 285; Antony Hammond, ed., *Richard III*, Arden Shakespeare (London and NY, 1981), pp. 183–4 n.

Henry in the Tower (*3 Hen. VI.* v. 6.), he holds a catlike dialogue with the two helpless old men.' Perrett also thinks he is is 'modelled closely on the "messenger" and murderer in "Edward II", except in that his attempt on Leir must fail. He is as resolute as Lightborn, and thinks as little of murdering a man ([1212–19, 1313–15]); is not likely to relent if his victims "speake fayre" ([1347–51]); and is to be murdered too when he has done the deed ([1352–3]).' Wolfgang Clemen adds,

Almost all the murderers of pre-Shakespearian drama . . . displayed comic and coarsely realistic characteristics . . . Other murderers felt pangs of conscience and remorse, either before or after the deed (*Leir*, Sc. xix; *True Tragedy*, 1295; *Woodstock*, v, i, 231; *Wounds of Civil War*, 1008; cf. also *2 Henry VI*, III, ii); other victims were at first ignorant of the identity of the real instigator of the crime (*Edward II, Leir*); other murderers called upon their victims to offer up their last prayers and prepare themselves for death (*Massacre at Paris*, 1016; *Leir*); others seemed to read their falls in the murderer's face (*Edward II*, 2429; *Massacre*, 996; *True Tragedy* 1281 f.); and other murderers recited their orders to the keeper who then let them in and gave up his keys (*Edward II; True Tragedy*, 1204) . . . [In *Woodstock*] the two murderers are clearly differentiated, the second suffering from pangs of conscience . . . [Fn.:] So are the two murderers Dent and Will in the *True Tragedy*: Dent feels remorse before the deed but is quickly talked round by Will and is then quite determined again.

In *Woodstock* the second murderer is (like Ragan in *Leir* 1346) wary of the victim's pleas: 'If thou lett'st him speak but a word, we shall not kill him' (5.1.216–17). Law himself even finds an analogue in the prose romance *Fryer Bacon* on which Greene founded his play; there Bacon fills his would-be assassin with religious dread, gets him to drop his dagger, and converts him to Christianity. One might also recall that Black Will and Shakebag in the pseudo-Shakespearian *Arden of Feversham* are also coarsely comic, are sharply differentiated, and have at least one moment (vv. 15–28) of faltering resolve.[23]

As for Clarence's dream, it is the longest of several guilty dreams in the play, designed, as Clemen says, to symbolize its 'dominant theme of guilt and

expiation'. It 'adopt[s] as its model dreams from classical drama dealing with conscience and judgment', and in its details of the soul's journey to the underworld may be owing to *Aeneid* VI, Dante's *Inferno* (III, 109), and above all the *Induction to the Complaint of Buckingham (Mirror for Magistrates)*, as well as to Kyd's *Spanish Tragedy* (1.1.20) and *1 Tamburlaine* (2026, 2037, 2245). 'Shakespeare was not the first Elizabethan dramatist to make use of dreams in his plays to predict, to warn, and to anticipate; Greek tragedy, the epics of Horace and Virgil, and the works of Seneca [*Troades*, Andromache's dream, 433 ff.] all contained useful models for later writers. *The Mirror for Magistrates*, certainly known to Shakespeare, contains a warning dream which accurately captures the dream-atmosphere (*Anthony, Lord Rivers*, 470–87).' Among other dreams in Elizabethan plays Clemen lists *Selimus* 2215 ff.; *Leir* 1479 ff.; *Woodstock* IV, ii, 6; and *Alphonsus of Aragon* 1355 ff. To the tradition of dream-visions of hell Harold Brooks adds *Odyssey* 10, Ovid's *Metamorphoses*, some twenty-five descriptions or allusions to hell in Seneca, and especially *Faerie Queene* 2.7.26, 3.4.43, and 3.8.37.[24] Given all these alternatives, it is hard to identify *Leir* as the probable source.

Another obvious difficulty, recognized by Law and Mueller, is to establish which work is prior. *Leir*'s existence is first recorded in a performance on 6 April 1594. Greg thought the play might have dated from before plague closed the theatres in 1592, but the Queen's Men could have acquired and mounted it during their absence from London in 1592–4. Perrett gives evidence that *Leir* borrowed details from Spenser's *Faerie Queene* as well as an incident from Lodge's *Rosalynde*; both of these

---

[23] Shakespeare, *Works*, Eversley Ed., ed. C. H. Herford, 10 vols. (1899), vol. 9, p. 10; Perrett, *Story of King Lear*, p. 113; Clemen, *Commentary*, pp. 88–90; *Woodstock*, ed. A. P. Rossiter (ed. 1946), pp. 156–7; Law, 'Richard the Third', 139; *Arden of Feversham*, in *Minor Elizabethan Tragedies*, ed. T. W. Craik (1974), pp. 236–7.

[24] Clemen, *Commentary*, pp. 69, 77; Harold Brooks, '*Richard III*: Antecedents of Clarence's Dream,' *Shakespeare Survey 32* (Cambridge, 1979), pp. 145–50.

works first appeared in 1590. Less persuasively, he derives the setting of Leir's and Perillus's ambush (a thicket) from Lodge's *Euphues Shadow* (1592). The date of *Richard III* is equally indeterminate; though the play is often put as late as 1594, its Arden editor Antony Hammond (and others) think it may have been written as early as 1591.[25] Though *Leir* seems the more old-fashioned play, *Richard III* may have preceded it. The few similar phrases in *Leir* and *Richard III* may suggest some unclear relationship between the two plays. Since neither work saw print until many years after 1591, any influence of one on the other would probably have been through performance. Conceivably the author of one play acted in the other, but the relatively few similarities of phrase and incident may indicate only that one author saw (and remembered a few details from) the other play.

Law also speculates whether *Leir* influenced Shakespeare's *King John*. He concedes that the scene in *John* in which Hubert spares the life of Prince Arthur after long conversation and change of heart is more probably derived from *The Troublesome Reign* than from *Leir*. He finds, however, a 'kinship' of language – three or four commercial terms in *John* 3.2 corresponding, he thinks, to Gonorill's phrase 'make great account' (1005) – in comparable scenes in which a royal person (Gonorill, John) is hinting murder to a henchman. The similarity, if any, is of the slightest, since Gonorill's phrase is not commercial to begin with: in such phrases *account* had meant 'consideration, esteem' since the fourteenth century (*OED*, sb. 11). Law's closest echoes of language are two phrases from *Leir* and *John* that have no counterpart in *Troublesome Reign*: *her colour comes and goes* (1173) / *The colour of the King doth come, and go* (4.2.76), and *The King hath dispossest himselfe of all* [his lands] (744) / *The king hath dispossest himselfe of vs* [i.e., our allegiance] (4.3.23).[26] These two verbal parallels are far from conclusive. Though Shakespeare nowhere else speaks of facial colour coming and going, he does describe it often enough as being given, possessed, changed, turned, abandoned, forsaken, stolen, etc., and *come and go* would be a natural phrasing, in the commonest of words, for the fluctuation he

describes here. He uses forms of *dispossess* only six times; that the first three are in *John* may suggest that it was for Shakespeare a new word of the moment. He need not have found it in *Leir*, however, since it is used (though not reflexively) in both of his sources: Holinshed, vol. 3 of *Chronicles*, 193/2/6, and *Troublesome Raigne*, part 1, line 1640.[27]

In a later essay McNeal attempts to show that the romantic Margaret of *1H6* is modelled on Cordella in *Leir* and becomes the 'completely vicious' woman in *2H6* by the example of Gonorill and Ragan. The meeting of Margaret and Suffolk in *1H6*, he thinks, may derive from the meeting of Cordella and the French King; in both cases a princess in distress meets a foreign prince, who falls in love at first sight, recognizing that she is of royal blood and fit for a throne; the lady thinks herself unfit because she lacks a dowry; identities are revealed and a marriage is arranged; each princess will depart for a new home across the English Channel (though in opposite directions); and the nobles discuss the appropriateness of the marriage. McNeal admits that the similar details, which are of course staples of the romance genre, are only suggestive. No weight can be placed on the coincidence that France has a 'Palmer's staff' (698) and in a different play, *2H6* 5.1.97, York tells Henry he is fit for a palmer's staff. McNeal's 'likenesses of phrase' all consist of obvious choices of common words: *queen, sceptre, crown, I am content, whatsoere thou art, labyrinth, wondrous praise, dames, perfections*. The similarities of 'thought' are also of the most ordinary kind.[28] He has no better success with verbal parallels between *Leir* and *2 Henry VI*; in twenty lines quoted he finds only *proud, all the court*, and *hop without a head*. The first

---

[25] Greg, (Rev. of Sidney Lee, ed., *King Leir*, 1909), *MLR* 6 (1910), 515; Perrett, *Story of King Lear*, pp. 99, 102–4, 113, 116; Hammond, *Richard III*, p. 61.

[26] Robert Adger Law, 'King John and King Leir', *Texas Studies in Literature and Language* 1 (1960), 473–6.

[27] See Geoffrey Bullough, *Narrative and Dramatic Sources of Shakespeare*. Vol. 4: *Later English History Plays* (1962), 4:46, 116.

[28] Thomas H. McNeal, 'Margaret of Anjou: Romantic Princess and Troubled Queen', *Shakespeare Quarterly*, 9 (1958), 1–10.

two are plainly insignificant, and the third phrase is 'a common one in Elizabethan drama', he admits, citing variants of it in *The Troublesome Reign of King John* 5.78, *Selimus* 1. 104, and *James IV* 2.2.144. *OED* (Headless, *a.* 1b) gives examples of the 'grimly jocular phr. *to hop headless* = to have the head struck off, to be beheaded' from *c.* 1330 to 1635. In one more pair of lines the only verbal links are the common word *pity* and the only partly similar images *melt as butter doth against the Sun/cold snow melts with the sun's hot beams*; both the latter two comparisons were proverbial.[29]

Having derived Margaret from Gonorill and Ragan, McNeal goes on to derive from those same two originals all of Shakespeare's 'murderous women' who rant and rail at a weak husband or a lover and accuse him of too much pity, who curse their own feminity and wish they were men. He names not only Margaret, Goneril, Regan, and Lady Macbeth, but, surprisingly, 'charming Beatrice of *Much Ado* . . . , one member of the tribe not a queen', indeed 'hardly . . . one of the wicked sisters at all'.[30] Besides tossing off one or two misanthropic sallies, Beatrice does of course instruct Benedick to 'Kill Claudio!' (4.1.289). But this is one of the great comic moments in the play; audiences always gasp with laughter at her extravagant overreaction and then enjoy watching Benedick wriggle. No harm ever comes from Beatrice's outburst of loyalty to Hero, and it is nothing like the implacable malice of Margaret or Lady Macbeth, who help commit actual murders. Moreover, Shakespeare had many another model (if he needed one) for his murderous queens, from Ovid, Seneca, and Tacitus, the Bible, Holinshed, and recent history: he knew of Medea, Jezebel and Queen Mary, and for dramatic models had Queen Videna in *Gorboduc*, Queen Elinor in *Edward I*, and Catherine de Medici in *Massacre at Paris*, to name some obvious examples.

Nonetheless, Jacquelyn Pearson hunts for further 'suggestive verbal parallels' between *Leir* and *Much Ado*. Ragan says 'Oh God, that I had bin but made a man' (2371) and Beatrice (*Ado* 4.1.306) says "Oh God, that I were a man!" But Eleanor in *2H6* 1.2.63, possibly before *Leir* was written, exclaims 'Were I a man, a duke', and

Shakespeare uses the formula 'O God, that' in *1H6* 4.3.24, *R3* 4.1.48, and (with different meaning) *R2* 3.3.133. Additionally, Pearson notes, as the Messenger will face the Devil, 'And try a bout with him for a scratcht face' (*Leir* 1314), so Beatrice's husband is doomed to 'a predestinate scratched face' (*Ado* 1.1.126–7). The threat is frequent in Shakespeare: see *Err.* 4.4.104 (actually plucking out eyes, as in *MND* 3.2.298), *2H6* 1.3.141–2, *R3* 1.2.126, *Luc.* 1472, and many later plays. Both Ragan and Beatrice speak of 'working dayes' (*Leir* 114, *Ado* 2.1.303–4) in a depreciative sense; but Shakespeare often uses the term thus (in *H5*, *AYL*, and elsewhere), as do his early contemporaries Greene and Lodge (see *OED*).[31]

Additionally, Pearson imagines, the comic Watch in *Leir* (Sc. 27, 29) gave Shakespeare the idea of a comic Watch in *Ado*; both are inclined to be sleepy, and both make comic inversions of sense. Indeed, the Second Watchman's confusion of 'vice' (2444) with 'advice' is, she suspects, the origin of Dogberry's habit of using words that say the opposite of what he means. Clownish malapropism, however, was heard in Elizabethan plays long before *Leir*. The clown John Adroynes in Whetstone's *2 Promos and Cassandra* (1578) threatens an informer 'For reforming a lye, thus against mee'. Corebus the Booby in Peele's *Old Wives Tale* (1588–94) demands for Jack a 'Christmas burial.' Piston garbles Cicero in *Soliman and Perseda* (1589–92) – 'O extempore, O flores!' (1.3.131). The clown Adam in Greene and Lodge's *A Looking Glass for London and England* (1587–91) calls 1 Ruffian an 'incarnative knave' (1.2.45) whose father was an 'honest man . . . and in great discredit', and he later attempts to seduce the Smith's wife, 'offering a borachio of kisses to your

---

[29] McNeal, 'Margaret of Anjou', 46–7; Morris Palmer Tilley, *A Dictionary of Proverbs in England in the Sixteenth and Seventeenth Centuries* (Ann Arbor, 1950), B 780; R. W. Dent, *Shakespeare's Proverbial Language: An Index* (Berkeley and Los Angeles, 1981), S 593.1.

[30] McNeal, 'Margaret of Anjou', 41, 50.

[31] Jacquelyn Pearson, *'Much Ado about Nothing* and *King Leir', Notes and Queries* 226 (1981), 128–9; McNeal, 'Margaret of Anjou', 47.

unseemly personage' (3.3.17–18).[32] The vice of us-ing wrong words in an attempt to appear learned, perhaps a consequence of inkhornism, had long since received its own name – *cacozelia* – from the rhetoricians, who provided examples from con-temporary life: a Cambridge Provost was saluted, 'You are a worshipfull Pilate, and kepes a bominable house', and a witness refuted a plaintiff as 'an un-rude fellow, and very contagious among his neigh-boures'.[33] In any case, several years before 1598 Dull had agreed that 'the pollution holds in the ex-change', Launcelot had wished Gobbo to 'frutify' in a 'suit . . . impertinent to myself', Mrs Quickly had urged Pistol to 'aggravate your choler', and Bottom had rehearsed 'most obscenely and coura-geously'. Dogberry need no more credit his mode of speech to the Second Watchman than Beatrice her existence to Gonorill.

Elsewhere Pearson argues that *Richard II* also shows the influence of *Leir*, pointing out very gen-eral similarities while ignoring essential differences. For instance, while it is true in a general way that both Leir and Richard cease to be king, Leir will-ingly abdicates, Richard is overthrown. Leir has 'undone my selfe' [i.e., resigned] (902) willingly, Richard will 'undo [i.e., undeck] myself' (4.1.203) under duress. Richard will exchange his sceptre for a Palmer's staff in humiliation, Cordella will happily accept a Palmer's marriage proposal. Leir feeds his children like the generous pelican parent, Richard taps his forebears' blood like ruthless pel-ican offspring. Cordella should try to forget her cruel family as indifferently as if they were dead, Richard's Queen should accept her loved husband's death in advance because it is inevitable. Several parallels of thought are all commonplace: pride goes before a fall, death is the worst that can hap-pen, company lightens a journey, language is some-times inadequate. But the 'most striking' similar-ity is 'not verbal but visual': in Scene 24 Lear and Cordella repeatedly kneel to each other and rise again, and in *Richard II* 5.3 York kneels to beg for Aumerle's execution and his Duchess kneels to save her son's life.[34] Again the resemblances are general and unremarkable: each scene has three men and a woman, the motive for kneeling is to seek pardon,

one person in each instance vows never to rise, at issue in each scene is the relationship of a father and child. The last detail shows how different the scenes essentially are: Leir's and his daughter Cordella's 're-lationship' is one of mutual love and forgiveness, while York is grotesquely and comically trying to secure the death of his own son. Except for one bit of ordinary stage business, kneeling, the scenes are hardly analogous.

That same stage business, nonetheless, has been invoked repeatedly to show *Leir*'s influence on other plays. Skura compares *Richard II* 5.3 with a different scene, *Leir* Sc. 19, where the old king begs the hired murderer to kill him but to spare Perillus's life. Again there is no similarity except that a chara-cter, Leir, kneels in supplication. Leir and Perillus are not engaged in a contest of kneeling as are York and his Duchess; indeed Perillus does not kneel at all. Skura elaborates further: the same scene in *Leir* 'may have contributed to the kneelings that dom-inate [sic] *Titus Andronicus*, as victim after victim is newly surprised by his captor's cruel indifference', and (contrary to Law's conclusion) 'Shakespeare would use the scene again in *King John*'.[35] She gives no reason why such a common action in drama and in life as kneeling should need one specific source in all three plays, *Richard II*, *John*, and *Titus*. Alan Dessen and Leslie Thomson report that in stage

[32] Pearson, '*Much Ado*', p. 128; Whetstone, *Promos and Cassandra*, in Mark Eccles, ed., *Measure for Measure*, New Var-iorum Shakespeare (NY, 1980), p. 352; George Peele, *The Old Wives Tale*, ed. Frank S. Hook, in *Life and Works*, ed. Charles T. Prouty, 3 vols. (New Haven and London, 1952–70), vol. 3, p. 403; *The Tragedye of Solyman and Perseda*, ed. John J. Murray (NY and London), p. 15; Thomas Lodge and Robert Greene, *A Looking Glasse for London and England*, ed. George A. Clugston (NY and London, 1980), pp. 135–6, 184.

[33] George Puttenham, *Arte of English Poesie* (1589), p. 210; Thomas Wilson, *Art of Rhetoric* (1553), fol. 87ʳ; Henry Peacham, *Garden of Eloquence* (1577), sig. G3ʳ; Sr. Miriam Joseph, *Shakespeare's Use of the Arts of Language* (NY, 1947), pp. 75–7; Muriel C. Bradbrook, *The Growth and Structure of Elizabethan Comedy* (1955), pp. 34–5.

[34] Jacquelyn Pearson, 'The Influence of *King Leir* on Shake-speare's *Richard II*', *Notes and Queries*, 227 (1982), 113–15.

[35] Skura, *Shakespeare the Actor*, p. 285. On pp. 145–6 'may have contributed' is inflated to '[was] probably borrowed'.

directions in English Renaissance plays, 'Over 300 figures are directed to *kneel/kneel down* (a small percentage of the actual onstage kneeling).'[36] Such an ubiquitous piece of stage business can hardly show dependence of one particular play on another.

Martin Mueller's attempt to show that *Leir* profoundly affected *As You Like It* requires little attention, since he does not identify a single detail in *As You Like It* that derives from *Leir* rather than from Shakespeare's obvious source, Lodge's *Rosalynde*. Rather, he argues that *AYL* was intentionally written as an 'anti-Lear', by which he means an 'anti-*Leir*':

The father's efforts [in *Leir*] to manipulate the daughter's marriage cost him his throne. The daughter's [Rosalynde's] clever manipulation of events [i.e., wooing Rosader] produces an outcome in which the daughter's choice corresponds to the father's wishes and restores him to his throne. I think Shakespeare saw this contrast [between the beginning of *Leir* and the ending of *Rosalynde*] and designed *As You Like It* from the beginning as a comic counterpoint to a Lear drama.[37]

Whatever 'contrast' Shakespeare may have noticed between *Leir* and *Rosalynde*, it was certainly not the one that Mueller offers on the basis of his misunderstanding of both works. Leir's efforts to manipulate Cordella's choice of husband do not cost him his throne; he is determined to divide his kingdom among his daughters from his very first speech in the play (lines 30–1), before the question of Cordella's husband ever arises, and in fact that question never does arise in the abdication scene and so has nothing to do with his angry rejection of her. Nor does Rosalynde's choice of Rosader restore Gerismond; that is entirely the result of a wholly separate action, a battle successfully waged by the Peers of France to defeat the usurper Torismond.

Two other plays remain to discuss, *Merchant of Venice* and *Hamlet*. Perrett points out an allusion to Jason and the Golden Fleece in both Sc. 4 (352–3) of *Leir* and in *MV* 1.1.169–72, and speculates that this coincidence may confirm some 'slight degree' of dependence of *MV* on *Leir*. McNeal points out that the allusion is repeated in *MV* 3.2.241–2.

For Mueller this is the first of several 'echoes' of *Leir*, a play without which *Merchant* would have been 'quite different'. Indeed, 'Gratiano may be said to quote the Gallian king' in *Leir*.[38] This claim is unlikely and unprovable; the story of Jason was well known to many writers. Arthur Golding's 1567 translation of Ovid's *Metamorphoses* – from which Shakespeare probably knew this story, took the spelling *Colchos* (*MV* 1.1.171), and had already borrowed language and details for *Midsummer Night's Dream* and other plays – uses the phrase 'golden fleece' several times (7.7, 70, 206, 215, 282). Thomas Cooper's *Dictionarium*, appended to his well-known *Thesaurus* (1565), describes how Medea 'intertained y[e] aduenturous Iason commyng to Colchos to wyn the golden fleese'; many writers learned their mythology from Cooper. John Russell Brown finds the same phrase in allusions to the Argonaut myth in John Lyly's *Euphues* and in Geffrey Whitney's *Emblems*, in the latter case referring to Sir Francis Drake. In any case, in 1596 Gratiano need not have been quoting from *Leir*: in Marlowe's *Jew of Malta*, an undoubted source for *MV*, the villain Ithamore, comically adoring the courtezan Bellamira, says to her (4.2.89–90), 'I'le be thy *Jason*, thou my golden Fleece.'[39]

---

[36] Alan C. Dessen and Leslie Thomson, *A Dictionary of Stage Directions in English Drama 1580–1642* (Cambridge, 1999), p. 125.

[37] Mueller, 'From Leir to Lear', 201. Mueller's further argument that the 'contamination' in Shakespeare's mind of *Leir* and *Rosalynde* produced both the hostile brothers in *Lear* (which derive immediately from Sidney's *Arcadia*) and the 'dynastic interlace' of sexual relations between the children of a ruler and his friend, i.e. between Hamlet and Ophelia and between Edmund and Goneril and Regan, depends on analogies too general and far-fetched to be taken seriously.

[38] Perrett, *Story of King Lear*, p. 111 n.; McNeal, 'Margaret of Anjou', 7; Mueller, 'From Leir to Lear', 195.

[39] Arthur Golding, tr., *The .xv. Bookes of P. Ouidius Naso, entytuled Metamorphosis* (1567), pp. 137–8, 141–2; Thomas Cooper, *Dictionarium* (1565), sig. L6; *The Merchant of Venice*, Arden Shakespeare, ed. John Russell Brown (1955), p. lv; John Lyly, *Works*, ed. R. Warwick Bond, 3 vols. (Oxford, 1902), 2:21; Geffrey Whitney, *A Choice of Emblemes* (1586), p. 203; Marlowe, *Works*, ed. Fredson Bowers, 2 vols. (Cambridge, 1973), 1:316.

Encouraged by this 'echo', however, Mueller finds others. 'The basic donné of the Portia story and its scenic structure in all probability have their roots in the opening scenes of the Leir play, in which the King seeks to control the marriage choice of his youngest daughter by imposing on his three daughters a contest in which they choose by pleading.' As before, Mueller misstates the facts: in *Leir*, the daughters are not pleading but are speaking to persuade Leir of their love. Leir had intended earlier to force Cordella to accept his choice of husband as proof of her love, but the scene never comes to that point. This court interrogation of the king's daughters, of course, is hardly analogous with the several casket scenes in *Merchant*. Except that a father wishes to influence a daughter's choice of husband – a common dramatic situation found in *Two Gentlemen, Midsummer Night's Dream, Merry Wives, Othello,Cymbeline*, and countless other Renaissance plays – no other similarities exist, though many differences do: one father is alive and the other is dead; one acts disastrously on sudden whim, the other successfully by a carefully drawn legal document; Leir has chosen a particular husband, Portia's father has not; there are three sisters and three suitors in one play, and three male suitors for one woman in the other; in one play two sisters compete with a third in order to disgrace her, in the other the suitors compete for a bride; in neither competition is there 'pleading'. Mueller further attempts to ally *Merchant* with *Leir* as 'a play about "good" and "bad" daughters', while having to concede that 'Jessica is no Goneril, and Portia is a very complex case'.[40] Portia does, of course, follow to the letter her father's arrangements for choosing among suitors, and there is no need to agree with Mueller's claim that in promising obedience to Bassanio 'she lies'. Besides, Shakespeare had already written about 'good' and 'bad' daughters, in Katherina and Bianca Minola.

Finally, *Hamlet*. Greg finds what may be 'fortuitous' parallels between *Leir* 1467 and 2453 ff. and *Ham.* 3.3.73 and 5.1.15 ff. In the first case the hired murderer says of the sleeping Leir and Perillus 'Now could I stab them bravely', somewhat as Hamlet, sword in hand, says behind the praying Claudius, 'Now might I do it pat.' In the second case, the clownish 2 Watchman proves by choplogic and the use of imaginary props that putting his nose in a pot of ale is the same as lighting a beacon fire, while in *Hamlet* 1 Clown uses an imaginary man and imaginary water to elucidate crowner's quest law on suicide. In the first case, the plots both require a hesitating killer, who naturally enough announces his intent; their speeches are not remarkably close, nor the vocabulary or phrasing unusual. In the second case, 1 Clown is doing the same kind of comic illustration that Launce had already done years before in describing his parting from his family (*TGV* 2.3.14–32). In perceiving meaningful similarities here Greg acknowledges that he may be 'just imagining things' – a reasonable suspicion.[41]

Mueller's third parallel, 'Perhaps the most striking verbal echo of *The True Chronicle Historie* in any Shakespearean play', surprisingly 'does not appear to have been noticed'. The speeches in question are Leir's opening lines to his nobles, asking their advice, now that the late Queen's obsequies have been performed, about how to marry off his daughters (*Leir* 1–9), and Claudius's speech to the court justifying his marriage so soon after the death of his brother (*Ham.* 1.2.1–14). As elsewhere, Mueller describes the similarities in general terms and with inaccuracies that make the scenes seem closer than they are: 'In both speeches the king consults with his council as his thoughts move from wake to wedding ... Hamlet stands apart ... [and] breaks his silence with an aside, exactly like Cordella.' Justifying one's own squalid incestuous marriage is very different from anticipating three proper future ones for one's daughters; but what more obviously invalidates the comparison is the phrase 'exactly like Cordella', since Cordella is not present in the scene from *Leir*. Mueller finds a corroborating 'verbal echo' of Skalliger's 'our *quondam* Queen' (33) in Claudius's 'our sometime sister, now our queen', though conceding that Shakespeare uses 'quondam

---

40 Mueller, 'From Leir to Lear', 208–9, 211.
41 W. W. Greg, 'Shakespeare and *King Leir*', *TLS*, 9 Mar. 1940, p. 124.

queen' elsewhere – i.e., *3H6* 3.3.153 – , thereby neutralizing its value as evidence of borrowing from *Leir* here. Finally, Mueller reaffirms Greg's first parallel, that of the hesitant murderers: 'Both [assassins] have a commission, both come upon their victim at prayer, both fail to act.' Unfortunately, both do not 'come upon their victim at prayer' – Leir and Perillus are asleep – and, though both ultimately 'fail to act', the Messenger in *Leir* is paralyzed by fear of divine or worldly retribution, Hamlet by the wish to take more adequate revenge. Kenneth Muir had suggested of Greg's two parallels that they might have both derived from the *Ur-Hamlet*, an idea that Mueller rejects as inconsistent with his concept of that unknown play.[42]

I conclude that the evidence for *Leir*'s influence on Shakespeare's early plays is small at best and illusory at worst, that the arguments based on it suffer from over-generality, exaggeration, inaccuracy, and error, and that other explanations for the supposed parallels or echoes – similarity of dramatic situation, generic conventions, alternative or commonplace sources, and even reversible chronology – prevent the case for *Leir*'s influence from being persuasive. It is repeatedly vitiated by the availability of countless other possible sources besides *Leir*. Moreover, no adequate explanation is ever offered of how the old play exerted a continuous influence on Shakespeare for a decade when no edition of it existed. Quite possibly Shakespeare and the author of *Leir* at some point in the early 1590s saw or even acted in the other's play(s). If Shakespeare was a member of Sussex's Men in April, when they were sharing the Rose Theatre with the Queen's Men, he could have seen the Queen's company's two recorded performances of *Leir*.[43] There is no evidence that Shakespeare himself ever acted in the play at all, let alone repeatedly; it is improbable that he owned a manuscript of a play in the repertory of a company other than his own; and it is unlikely in the extreme that he kept seeing it acted by others year after year. It is hard to imagine by what other means he would recurrently have been reminded of small, particular details of action or language that he is supposed to have adopted in play after play throughout the first half of his career. It seems to me that the kind of

occasional similarity that appears, particularly between *Leir* and *Richard III*, would most likely derive from one playwright's keeping an eye on the performances of another's new work, and then consciously or unconsciously emulating a few bits of it. But most of the evidence itself for *Leir*'s continual influence I think is chimerical. I find no reason to agree that '*The True Chronicle Historie* was a remarkably pervasive presence in Shakespeare's career for well over a decade and exercised considerable power in shaping the formal and thematic structure of several quite different plays.'[44] I find it just as easy to believe that Shakespeare never encountered *Leir* until he read it in Stafford's edition of 1605.

SHAKESPEARE'S ACCESS TO A MANUSCRIPT

Malone imagined that Shakespeare could have read *Leir* in manuscript before the play was published in 1605, and Greg provided a scenario of how a Queen's Men's play of 1594 could have been in his possession in the early seventeenth century: 'There can be little doubt that the moribund Queen's company sold a manuscript of *King Leir* to White in 1594. If this was identical with the manuscript which Stafford acquired and printed in 1605, it had presumably remained for the eleven intervening years in the hands of stationers, and Shakespeare is very unlikely to have had access to it.' White's manuscript, he speculates, was likely to have been one of the 'very bad texts' that came into printers' hands in 1594; 'in that case it was certainly not the manuscript printed by

---

[42] Mueller, 'From Leir to Lear', 205–7, 216; Muir, *King Lear*, p. xxxii.

[43] The two performances of 6 and 8 April 1594 named earlier in this essay were recorded in a column of plays performed by 'the Quenes men & my lord of Susexe to gether' (*Henslowe's Diary*, ed. Foakes and Rickert, p. 21). The heading is generally taken to mean, not that the two companies had temporarily merged their members, but rather that they were playing in the same theatre on alternate days. See Gurr, *Shakespearian Playing Companies*, p. 175.

[44] Mueller, 'From Leir to Lear', 121.

Stafford. This (i.e., Stafford's manuscript), there-fore, may have remained till 1605 in the stock of some theatrical company.' Greg imagines that first it 'remained as a pledge in Henslowe's hands', then passed to Alleyn, who was leading the joint Strange's–Admiral's company, thence 'somehow' to the Chamberlain's, where eventually Shakespeare used it and then 'was careless enough to let it get into the nimble hands of Simon Stafford'. Of this tissue of unsupported speculation perhaps only a person of Greg's great authority and assurance could say, 'This, of course, is guesswork' but 'not altogether improbable', 'not too fantastic'.[45] It is nonetheless gravely weakened by the simple fact that the manuscript printed by Stafford is appar-ently not a 'play-house manuscript', as Greg with-out the slightest attempt at proof declared it was, but is, in the opinion of others who have studied the text, an authorial clean copy or scribal tran-script lacking signs of theatrical use.[46]

Even though his answer was far-fetched and probably wrong, Greg as usual was asking the right questions: if Shakespeare used a manuscript, how did he acquire it, and what was its nature? No one has thoroughly investigated the possibilities. Let me begin by surveying the several manuscripts that could have existed, must have existed if past specu-lations about them have any foundation. They are:

1 The Queen's Men's original playbook, used in 1594 at the Rose Theatre.
2 A manuscript acquired by the printer Edward White and registered to him in 1594.
3 A playbook used by an unknown company ca. 1605.
4 A manuscript procured by the printer Simon Stafford and registered to him in 1605.
5 The manuscript printed by Stafford and pub-lished by Wright in 1605.
6 A manuscript acquired by the Chamberlain's Men in or after 1594 and used by Shakespeare before 1605.
7 A manuscript acquired privately by Shakespeare himself.

Although Peter Blayney has recently shown that the production of a scribal copy of a play was not very expensive,[47] one might justifiably ask why so many copies of *Leir* would ever have been made; a company normally needed only the first, its one legible official playbook (and the plot schema and actors' parts derived from it). We should therefore not be surprised to find that not so many copies are likely ever to have existed.

The first of these manuscripts, a playbook bear-ing the Master of the Revels' licence to perform the play, was possessed by the Queen's Men and was very likely used as the basis for rehearsals and as a guide to the book-holder during performances. *Leir* had just been very successful at the Rose Theatre, bringing receipts of 38 and 25 shillings at its performances on 6 and 8 April; it could doubt-less have been performed successfully again. That the company would have parted with the official book of this play when they left London in 1594 is unlikely in the extreme, since they would there-after have been unable to perform the play if chal-lenged by town authorities to prove that it had been licensed.[48] Whatever Henslowe meant when he reported in May 1594 that the Queen's Men re-cently 'brocke & went into the contrey to playe', they were not about to cease to exist as a company, nor were they even, in Greg's word, 'moribund'.

---

[45] Greg, 'Shakespeare and *King Leir*', 384–5. Greg did concede, 'I have no great liking for this hypothesis.' George Ian Duthie, 'Introduction' to *King Lear*, New (Cambridge) Shakespeare, ed. J. Dover Wilson (Cambridge, 1960), p. xiv, thinks it 'has nothing in it inherently unlikely', at best a lukewarm en-dorsement. I know of no other.

[46] Greg, 'Shakespeare and *King Leir*', 380; Wilfred T. Jewkes, *Act Division in Elizabethan and Jacobean Drama 1583–1616* (Hamden, Conn., 1958), p. 201; Michie, *King Leir*, p. 21. Greg does note that 'the text is thoroughly good . . . The printing, moreover, is generally correct and the punctuation unusually careful.' See also n. 53.

[47] Peter W. M. Blayney, 'The Publication of Playbooks', in *A New History of Early English Drama*, ed. John D. Cox and David S. Kastan (New York, 1997), pp. 392, 418, n. 19. The cost was between 2 and 3 shillings.

[48] *Henslowe's Diary*, ed. Foakes and Rickert, pp. 21, 7. The Mas-ter of the Revels licensed performances of the play through-out the country as a whole, and his judgement and authority in these matters were deferred to by local authorities. See Gurr, *Shakespearian Playing Companies*, p. 42.

Rather, they ceased to be centred in London, instead touring widely and successfully in provincial towns for almost a decade (as they had done for most of their previous existence). Henslowe must have known that they intended to do so, since he lent fifteen pounds to his nephew Francis Henslowe to purchase a share in the company at that time, payable upon his 'Retorne owt of the contrey'. From incomplete surviving records McMillin and MacLean identify more than a hundred provincial performances through late 1602 into early 1603 when, upon the Queen's death, the company apparently disbanded. Towards the end of that nine-year period, to be sure, the company very likely became a smaller troupe with fewer star actors, having a reduced touring capacity and presumably limited capital to acquire new plays.[49] Under such conditions they would naturally have revived and repeated successful older plays such as *Leir*, and could have done so only if they had kept a number of their licensed playbooks when they went into the country in 1594. If Stafford's 1605 title-page tells truth, and *Leir* had been 'diuers and sundry times lately acted', the Queen's Men would have been the most likely actors until 1603; no other company has been proposed or easily suggests itself.

Edward White registered the second of these manuscripts for publication on 14 May 1594. White never published the play, and ownership of it passed at his death in 1613 to his son and heir Edward the younger, who operated his father's shop until his own death in 1624. On 29 June 1624 the younger White's widow transferred ownership of a *Leire* (and other plays) to Edward Aldee (Allde), who died in 1627. On the death of Allde's widow the copyright for *Leir* was assigned to her stepson Richard Oulton on 22 Apr. 1640. White's heirs evidently assumed continuous ownership of the play.[50] His manuscript was probably not the Queen's company playbook, for reasons just offered above. Confirmation is found in the other manuscripts that the Queen's company sold off in May 1594, none of which has been identified as a playbook. On the same day when he bought *Leir*, White procured four other plays, at least one of them, Greene's *Friar Bacon and Friar Bungay*, from the Queen's Men. Like

Leir this play had just been successful in several performances at the Rose, and was later revived by another company and reprinted well into the mid-seventeenth century. The Queen's Men are not likely to have sold off their official playbook of such a popular play in 1594, and one of its recent editors believes that White's 1594 quarto was printed from a non-theatrical manuscript. On the same day in May 1594 another printer, Thomas Creede, acquired another Queen's Men's play, *The Famous Victories of Henry V*, and on 19 June, their *True Tragedy of Richard III*. Whatever difficult manuscripts lie behind Creede's subsequent editions of these plays – McMillin and MacLean hypothesize scribal accounts of company dictations, possibly to provide multiple or backup texts for use when the company had split into two touring groups – they were clearly too garbled and mislined to be the company's official, licensed books. Creede also acquired the Queen's Men's *Selimus*, which he printed in 1594 without registering it; this is based, according to Peter Berek, on an 'authorial text never intended for the stage'. In each of these cases the Queen's Men seem to have been raising needed money by selling to printers their expendable duplicates; the playbooks themselves were most probably being retained for use on tour in the coming years.[51]

---

[49] *Henslowe's Diary*, ed. Foakes and Rickert, p. 7; McMillin and MacLean, *The Queen's Men*, pp. 66–7, 175–88.

[50] Greg, 'Stationers' Records', vol. 1, pp. 20, 34, 53, and *BEPD* no. 213, 1:337–8. White never printed any of his five plays; Adam Islip printed *Friar Bacon* in 1594 and Peele's *David and Bethsabe* only after another five years, in 1599. White's other two plays besides *Leir*, namely *John of Gaunt* and *Robin Hood and Little John*, are not known ever to have been published. As Peter Blayney notes (pp. 386–9), there was a glut of plays in 1593–5, and in the best of times printers recovered costs within five years on only one in five plays. There was no great incentive to publish *Leir*.

[51] For the later life of *Friar Bacon*, see Greg, *BEPD* no. 121, vol. 1, pp. 206–7. For *Famous Victories* and *True Tragedy*, see McMillin and MacLean, *The Queen's Men*, pp. 113–20; for *Selimus*, Peter Berek, "*Locrine* Revised, *Selimus* and Early Responses to *Tamburlaine*," *Research Opportunities in Renaissance Drama*, 23 (1980), 43. According to its editor J. A. Lavin, the manuscript behind White's 1594 edition of *Friar Bacon* was not a theatrical prompt-book but an authorial text marked

The third manuscript of *Leir* would be the play-book owned and being used by an unknown company sometime before or in 1605. The claim 'divers and sundry times lately acted' on the title-page of Stafford and Wright's 1605 edition would make most sense for an old play like *Leir* if it meant also 'in divers and sundry places', that is, in various towns on provincial tours. The Queen's Men, the original owners of the play and now wholly a travelling company, would have been the most likely performers. By the turn of the century, given their probably straitened circumstances – a diminishing company, an aging patron, and limited capital – they were more likely to be recycling a few successful old plays than commissioning new ones. Such revivals of a few old plays would more easily have sustained a provincial touring company than a company based in London; a touring company could repeat the same few plays in each town it visited, a London company needed to provide new fare every few days, month after month. When eventually the Queen's company disbanded after her death in 1603, and apparently no successor company under a new patron regrouped from its remnants, the sharers probably sold off their remaining assets, including (if they could find buyers) their handful of now unuseful playbooks.

Such events could explain how Simon Stafford in 1605, so long after the play's first composition and performance, might have come to acquire the fourth conceivable manuscript in our list. Clearly he did procure a manuscript of the play, for on 8 May 1605 he claimed copyright by entering in the Stationers' Register under his name 'A booke called the Tragecall [*altered from* Tragedie] historie [*interlined*] of Kinge Leir and his Three Daughters &c[es]. As it was latelie Acted.' Though he transferred ownership on the same day to John Wright,[52] who ultimately published the play, Stafford was clearly the manuscript's original buyer. One can only speculate how he came across it, and why he bought it. He almost certainly did not buy the manuscript that Edward White had held onto for eleven years, for in that case the Stationers' Register would have recorded a transfer from White to Stafford;[53] instead, Stafford

claimed original ownership. Moreover, if White had sold the manuscript outright to Stafford in 1605, his heirs could not legitimately have continued to claim ownership of it, as they did. Stafford may conceivably have chanced upon a manuscript

---

up to a limited extent for production (New Mermaids, 1969, p. xxxiii).

John Danter acquired another Queen's Men play, Peele's *The Old Wives Tale*, on 16 April 1595; his edition of that year seems also to its editors Frank S. Hook (1970, vol. 3, pp. 351–6) and Patricia Binnie (Revels Plays, Manchester, 1980, p. 20) to be based on authorial papers, not a theatrical manuscript. In 1594 Creede registered two other plays that may have belonged to the Queen's Men, Greene's *James IV* (also on 14 May) and the pseudo-Shakespearean *Locrine* (20 July). The manuscript behind the first of these seems to both J. A. Lavin (New Mermaids, 1967, p. xii) and Norman Sanders (Revels Plays, 1970, pp. lvii–lx) to be author's foul papers, and that behind the second appears to Jane L. Gooch (ed. 1981, p. 36) to be a clear author's or reviser's manuscript or a transcript of this. Paul Werstine (privately) doubts the reliability of the conclusions of Lavin, Sanders, Binnie, and Gooch, because the distinguishing marks on the basis of which they detect authorial manuscripts may also be found in some theatrical manuscripts. Only Daniel Seltzer asserts that a theatrical manuscript lies behind any of these known or possible Queen's Men plays; he has an 'overall impression' that *Friar Bacon* (Regents, Lincoln, Neb., 1963, p. xi) is 'very likely printed from theatrical copy'. In his single paragraph on the question, however, he adduces only one stage direction, conceding that it is 'not the sort of instruction which would have been of any use to the prompter', and cites without discussion a half-dozen others which could be 'either authorial or theatrical in origin'.

Edward White acquired another play by Peele in 1594, his *David and Bethsabe*, printed by Adam Islip five years later in 1599, and sometimes suspected (albeit not by McMillin and MacLean) of being a Queen's Men play. Its corrupt state – gaps in the action, a passage cut and misplaced, three choruses missing, a ghost character – may suggest a reviser's working copy rather than a finished playbook, though none of these features by itself would rule out a theatrical manuscript. See Chambers, *The Elizabethan Stage*, vol. 3, p. 461, who calls the play a 'boil-down'; Arthur M. Sampley, 'The Text of Peele's *David and Bethsabe*', *PMLA* 46 (1931), 659–71; Jewkes, *Act Division*, pp. 127–8; *George Peele*, ed. Sally Purcell (S. Hinksey, 1972), p. 91.

52 Greg, 'Stationers' Records', vol. 1, p. 20.
53 That at least would have been the case if White had published his manuscript in 1594, as Greg, 'Lee's *King Leir*', p. 516, says, adding, 'The entry of 1605 practically proves that that of 1594 had been inoperative.'

of the play in private hands – a manuscript in addition to that owned by the Queen's Men and to that being held by Edward White – and eleven years after the play had last been performed in London, he may have decided that on its own literary merits it deserved publishing. That is possible but not very likely. More explicably, he could have bought it from a member of the theatrical company that had always owned the play, that had (as he reports) 'lately' been performing it (thereby showing its viability), but that now had no further use for it and so were finding a publisher to buy it. Such a scenario would depend less on chance discovery and a printer's whim and would avoid proliferating imagined manuscripts unnecessarily. It would also explain two peculiarities of Stafford and Wright's edition: the facts that, contrary to common practice, neither an acting company nor a theatre is named as selling points on the title-page. No theatre could be named, of course, if for almost a decade the Queen's Men had performed only at constantly changing venues on tour; and to advertise the play as having been formerly acted by a company now several years defunct would not attract readers looking for the latest thing in plays. Better just to say truthfully if vaguely that the play had been performed 'lately' (generously defined) and often, as Stafford does.

But here is another mystery: though Stafford may have got his manuscript from the Queen's company after its demise, that manuscript seems not likely to have been the copy for his and Wright's 1605 edition. Again to avoid unnecessary proliferation of manuscripts, we might assume that a touring company like the Queen's Men in their latter days did not travel with multiple copies of their plays in their wagon; they seem to have been willing to dis-emburden themselves of a considerable number of duplicate copies of them when they left London in 1594. In practice they needed only one, the official playbook with its licence to perform.[54] That would be sufficient to refresh memories in rehearsal and to regulate performances. If that was their only surviving copy in 1603, it is what Stafford would have bought from them. After years of provincial touring, that book might well be fairly battered

and illegible, having been subjected to occasional adjustments and revisions and very likely shortened to allow playing by a reduced troupe. It might not have been very attractive printer's copy. But the manuscript behind the 1605 edition is obviously a remarkably clean, orderly, and well lined and punctuated one, and the play version it contains seems designed to be cast with the full fourteen men typically needed in Queen's Men's plays in the early 1590s,[55] not with a later, reduced troupe. Moreover, the manuscript behind the 1605 edition shows no signs of preparation for theatrical use by a reviser or book-holder; that very clean copy was probably either an authorial manuscript or a scribal transcript from authorial papers.[56] Even if Stafford had acquired from the Queen's Men a clean transcript of their playbook, it would still look in many respects like a playbook; the 1605 printed text does not.

Apparently, then, according to the scenario I have been developing, Stafford may have acquired a playbook, but Wright did not publish one. The distinction of a fifth hypothetical manuscript behind the 1605 edition, different from the one procured by Stafford, may help explain several puzzling facts. One is that Stafford no sooner registered his manuscript on 8 May 1605 than he transferred it, on the same day, to John Wright, on the condition that Wright own the copy (and publish the book) and that 'Simon Stafford shall haue the printinge of this booke'.[57] Another is the surprising coincidence,

---

[54] They had already sold one duplicate copy of *Leir* to Edward White in 1594. In their later years the company had probably been reduced in numbers and so no longer needed to keep multiple copies, as perhaps they had done in the 1580s and early 1590s, when they divided into two branches. See McMillin and MacLean, *The Queen's Men*, pp. 43–6, 61–6, 211. It is impossible to prove, of course, that some such copy did not survive and was somehow conveyed to Stafford in 1605.

[55] See McMillin and MacLean, *The Queen's Men*, pp. 100–2, 107, 189–93.

[56] See n. 45. Greg's assessment in 1910 (p. 518) was that the stage directions in the printed *Leir* did not prove that its text had been recently or ever acted.

[57] See Greg, 'Stationers' Records', vol. 1, p. 20.

if that is what it is, that John Wright had formerly been the apprentice of Edward White, who had originally purchased a manuscript of 'The moste famous Chronicle historye of Leire kinge of England and his Three Daughters' from the Queen's Men in 1594. And a third is the detail that the transfer was, as the Stationers' Register records, effected with the special attention of one of the Wardens: 'by consent of M^r [William] Leake'.

Greg says of this transfer of copy from Stafford to Wright:

Indeed, simultaneous entry and transfer is always a little suspicious: it may, of course, be only a device on the part of the seller [Stafford] to secure for himself the job of printing; but it may also mean that the purchaser [Wright] insisted on the procurer of the copy [Stafford] taking the responsibility of entrance. Stafford's reputation, moreover, was notoriously bad. Wright was at the very beginning of a long career: it was his first entrance of copy. He had been apprenticed to Edward White on 24 June 1594, the month following the latter's entrance of *King Leir*, and was by him presented for his freedom, which he took up *per patrimonium* on 28 June 1602 ... It has been suggested that Wright stole the book from his master White. There is no ground whatever for suspicion ... If this had been stolen from another stationer it is unlikely that the publisher [Wright] would have risked entering it in the Register or would have put his name and address on the edition he issued. Moreover, it is clear from the entries themselves that the copy had been obtained not by Wright at all, but by Stafford. The fact that Wright had been White's apprentice is a mere coincidence.[58]

I think that Wright's involvement is more than coincidence, but I agree that he was almost certainly acting honestly. It would have been remarkable if his first act at the beginning of a respectable career were to pirate a manuscript from the master of many years who had just given him entrance to his profession, thereby immediately risking his professional standing; and equally remarkable if White had not brought action against him for such an act of ingratitude and theft. However Wright came by his ownership of *Leir*, it is clear that he thought himself its rightful owner until he died in 1646: although *Leir* is not named in the transfer from John

Wright senior to his brother Edward on 27 June 1646, on 4 April 1655 that title was transferred from Edward Wright to the bookseller William Gilbertson.[59] Apparently, as we have seen above, Edward White and his heirs considered themselves owners of the play, doubtless because White had first bought and registered a manuscript of it in 1594 and had never formally transferred his rights to publish it; and meanwhile John Wright and his heirs understandably considered themselves owners, because Wright had acquired and registered a manuscript and printed it in 1605. Later John Wright (or his heirs) would justifiably have understood that, since he had entered and published the book, all future rights to publish the play were his. The question of later ownership, if anyone was even aware of it, seems never to have become an issue.

We cannot know what happened during the manoeuvrings over ownership in 1605, but I wish to suggest an explanation that accounts for all or most of the facts. It assumes, as Sidney Lee and Donald Michie have suggested, that Wright was allowed to publish *Leir* as a result of 'a friendly negotiation between the master, White, his former apprentice, Wright, and the third party, Simon Stafford'.[60] The following I think could have happened and may have happened. Stafford honestly acquired a theatrical manuscript of *Leir* from one of the former sharers of the now-dissolved Queen's Men and, intending to publish it, registered his ownership on 8 May 1605. Immediately, however, owing to the care or good memory of one of the wardens at Stationers' Hall, he was made aware that

---

58 Greg, 'The Date of *King Lear*', 379–80. Katharine F. Pantzer, in *A Short Title Catalogue of Books Printed in England, Scotland, & Ireland ... 1475–1640*, 2nd edn, ed. W. A. Jackson, F. S. Ferguson, and Katharine F. Pantzer, 3 vols. (1986–91), vol. 3, p. 190, says that in this entry the Stationers' Register 'erroneously specifies "per patrimonium"', a phrase that means by virtue of his father's being a stationer. John Wright was the second son of the stationer Thomas Wright, though apprenticed to Edward White. As for Stafford's reputation, Wright trusted him to do a good job of printing, and he did.
59 See Greg, 'Stationers' Records', vol. 1, p. 63.
60 Michie, *King Leir*, p. 4, enlarging on Sidney Lee (ed. 1909), p. xvi.

Edward White still held copyright from 1594. Having paid good money for his manuscript, he approached White to find a way to salvage the situation. White agreed to do two good deeds at once: to allow his fellow-stationer Stafford to make good on his investment by printing the play, and to allow his recently freed apprentice Wright to publish it. This chain of events would partly explain the 'coincidence' that young John Wright ever got involved in Stafford's transactions at all. With the supervision and approval of one of the wardens, Mr William Leake, White arranged to transfer publication rights to his former apprentice Wright – an easy favour to grant, since in eleven years of ownership he had never shown any interest in publishing the old play, and it had been out of sight and mind of the London public for more than a decade. At first perhaps he transferred informally 'not necessarily the recognized ownership of the property in question . . . but only whatever right or claim he might have to it';[61] later, as I shall suggest, he may possibly have handed over his own long-unused manuscript as well. Because Stafford had already got his manuscript entered in the Stationers' Register, Wright may not have thought it worth insisting that that recent entrance be voided and a formal transfer from him to Stafford be substituted; instead he agreed to a second transfer from Stafford to his former apprentice Wright. Thus Wright could start his career by publishing *Leir*, and Stafford, stipulated in the S. R. entry as the printer, could after all make a profit on his investment in a manuscript.

The manuscript behind *Leir* (1605), as we have seen, shows no signs of theatrical provenance, but seems rather to exemplify one of several kinds of non-theatrical copy released by the Queen's Men in 1594. It looks, indeed, like just the kind of manuscript that White might have bought in 1594 and entered for publication, and that his novice apprentice Wright might have seen in White's shop a month later when he began work there. Quite possibly White, to help make Wright's first publishing venture in 1605 as successful as possible, allowed the printer Stafford to borrow temporarily his original clean, non-theatrical manuscript, perhaps for consultation by Stafford's compositors when they

were in doubt about readings in the marked-up and worn theatrical manuscript that Stafford had acquired from the actors; or White may even have handed over his long-unused manuscript outright, letting others take the risk of publishing it that he had never wanted to take.[62]

Such an account is of course almost completely speculative; it is offered here only in the hope that a narrative which may explain a number of questions about the printing of *Leir* is preferable to no narrative at all. It does at least offer an explanation for the appearance in print of the old *Leir* so long after its brief life on the London stage in 1594, and justifies the claims, often doubted, made on the title-page of its 1605 edition, of a more recent stage life. One other virtue of this account may be that it keeps to a minimum the number of manuscripts that have been supposed to be in circulation. Five are reduced to two, and those are of a very ordinary kind and provenance. An authorial or scribal fair copy owned by the company (in addition to its playbook) is sold off for ready cash in 1594 when the company leaves London. After remaining unprinted for a decade, this manuscript ultimately is made available, by the printer who first bought it, to his former apprentice, who publishes it in 1605. The second manuscript, the company's playbook

---

61 Michie takes this distinction from W. W. Greg, *Some Aspects and Problems of London Publishing between 1550 and 1650* (Oxford, 1956), p. 80.

62 A simpler possibility might be that the Queen's Men, sometime after 1603, sold Stafford not a battered playbook but a clean manuscript kept all those years in the lodgings of one of the sharers. Stafford could have got White's permission to print this copy, without needing to swap for a better one. One might then speculate that White had not printed his 1594 manuscript because it was disorderly foul papers, the company having retained a cleaner copy of the play in its original 1594 state. Such a possibility would not make much difference in the narrative I have been imagining; some kind of manuscript would still have passed from the Queen's Men to Stafford after their breakup, and its printing by Wright would have been arranged with Edward White. The single objection to it is that it requires the existence and survival of yet one more additional manuscript during the decade after 1594. And if this clean manuscript survived and got printed in 1605, why not those of other Queen's Men's plays?

of 1594, is kept and used on tour for several more years until the company disbands. Thereupon it also is sold to a printer, who then sets in motion the negotiations that will result in the old play's being published, though perhaps from a better copy than his own. If in fact the old theatrical copy was ultimately unused by Stafford, it may have been shelved or discarded, or even lent or given to White in exchange for his original.

The sixth possible manuscript is the one, in Greg's scenario, supposedly long owned by the Lord Chamberlain's company and eventually used by Shakespeare before the publication of *Leir*. There is no way, of course, to prove that such a manuscript never existed; but several reasons make its existence unlikely. First, theories about Henslowe or the Chamberlain's men acquiring such a manuscript when the Queen's Men 'broke' in 1594 are based on the misunderstanding that the company was financially 'broken', that it 'broke' up and disbanded, or at best survived in tatters. The evidence now provided by McMillin and MacLean from the Records of Early English Drama (REED) tells quite a different story: that, having lost court patronage, finding London unprofitable, and anticipating stiff competition from the newly formed 'duopoly' of the Admiral's and the Chamberlain's men, the Queen's Men returned to their original and long-standing practice of touring, which they continued actively for almost another decade. For that they needed to retain their stock of playbooks of recently successful plays. They would not have sold usable playbooks to rival companies, and no play of the Queen's Men is known to have been performed by another company during their remaining years. Nor could other companies have mounted performances from duplicate manuscripts while the Queen's Men still held and from time to time used the original playbooks bearing the Master of the Revels' licence. Another company could of course find a playwright to write new plays based on the old, and in time Shakespeare did so for several Queen's Men plays – perhaps *Richard III*, surely *King John* and *Henry V*, and ultimately *King Lear*; but for each of these a printed version had already appeared in time for Shakespeare to use it in composing his play.[63] There is no evidence that the Chamberlain's Men ever performed the old *King Leir*, or that Shakespeare attempted to write his own *Lear* until about the time when the printed edition of *Leir* appeared.

Roslyn Knutson 'feels sure' that a number of plays migrated to the newly formed Chamberlain's Men in 1594, but concedes that she 'cannot determine on present evidence which they were'; nonetheless she names *Leir* as a 'logical candidate'. If the Chamberlain's Men had in 1594 acquired *Leir*, which had brought in good receipts in two performances at the Rose in April, one might expect to see it among the list of plays performed jointly or alternately by the Admiral's and Chamberlain's companies at Newington Butts two months later, from 3 June onwards; but its name does not appear there. Andrew Gurr similarly speculates that some Queen's Men plays, including *Leir*, accompanied 'one or two' former Queen's players into the new Chamberlain's company, but he is apparently unable to name any Queen's men who made that shift. In fact none of the Queen's players, listed by McMillin and MacLean, is known to have gone to the Chamberlain's Men. If John Heminges had ever been a Queen's man, and he is only hypothesized to have been, he had ceased to be one by 6 May 1593, a year before the Queen's company played *Leir* in London, and so he could not have carried off their playbook (if it even existed yet) to the Chamberlain's company.[64] The other conceivable candidate, Shakespeare, cannot be shown ever to have been a Queen's man.

One other possibility remains: that Shakespeare himself somehow, at some time, acquired his own

---

[63] There is no agreement whether the Queen's Men's play *The True Tragedy of Richard III* (registered 19 June 1594, published 1594) appeared before the composition of Shakespeare's *Richard III* or whether it can be considered a source for that play.

[64] Roslyn Knutson, *The Repertory of Shakespeare's Company 1594–1613* (Fayetteville, Ark., 1991), pp. 9, 59; *Henslowe's Diary*, ed. Foakes and Rickert, pp. 21–2; Gurr, *Shakespearian Playing Companies*, pp. 279–80; McMillin and MacLean, *The Queen's Men*, pp. 194–7.

personal manuscript of the *Chronicle History*. One might suppose, for instance, that although he would not have had access to such a copy while the Queen's Men were touring in the provinces between 1594 and 1603, he might have acquired one at roughly the same time when Simon Stafford bought his, after the company's dissolution in 1603. If so, he would have been able to write his *Lear* well before the summer of 1605. The theory is unappealing on several grounds, however. It once again multiplies manuscripts unnecessarily; it requires the odd coincidence that both Shakespeare and Stafford sought out the same old-fashioned play from the Queen's Men sharers at about the same time; it imputes to the Queen's Men something close to double-dealing, in selling the same play to two different investors; and it lacks a clear motive for Shakespeare's interest. The players had an obvious motive to sell the play to a printer, Stafford, and he to buy it; but they would have had no obvious expectation of hawking this very old play to London's pre-eminently successful playwright of the moment, nor is it clear why Shakespeare would have sought out an old-fashioned play not seen in London for more than a decade. Even Stafford's acquisition of it may have been fortuitous; no other Queen's Men's plays seem to have been published by anyone after 1605. The simpler explanation seems preferable: that Stafford somehow found and printed the manuscript, and that Shakespeare subsequently read the newly published old play when it appeared, and then put his mind to transforming it – as he had previously done, apparently, with editions of old plays about King John and Henry V.

The following seem to me to be the most probable conclusions to draw from the foregoing discussion. Shakespeare may have seen the old *Leir* in 1594 or before, and it may have influenced his handling of a scene or two in *R3*, though there is no reason to accept either possibility as proven. He may have seen it acted after 1594, but if during the next decade it was being performed only occasionally in the provinces by the Queen's Men, his seeing it during that time is unlikely. Despite an occasional suggestive similarity, there is no convincing evidence that the old play exerted a continuing influence on one play of Shakespeare's after another for the next ten or fifteen years, nor any easy explanation of how, if unpublished, it could have done so. There is no known reason to believe that Shakespeare ever acted in the play, whether with the Queen's Men before 1594 or with the Chamberlain's Men afterwards, or that the Chamberlain's Men ever provided a manuscript of it for him to rewrite, or that he himself acquired a manuscript from stationers or another company for that purpose. It is possible, however, to construct a plausible narrative of how the playbook of the old play was held by the Queen's Men until 1603 and then sold to Simon Stafford, who arranged with Edward White and John Wright to publish the play in 1605. There is no compelling reason to think that more manuscripts than these two, the actors' playbook and the stationer's alternate copy, were in circulation before Shakespeare wrote his play. Shakespeare's *Lear* shows in nearly a hundred significant details a close familiarity with the old play as it exists in the 1605 edition. That he shows this knowledge in about 1605, the year of the old play's first publication, and that he did not insofar as we know attempt an earlier version of the Lear story, strongly imply that he read Stafford and Wright's edition when it appeared. If that edition suggested to him the writing of his own play, then *King Lear* was mainly written in the extremely busy time between summer 1605 and its first recorded performance, on 26 December 1606, at court.

CONTRACTS OF LOVE AND AFFECTION: LEAR, OLD AGE, AND KINGSHIP

WILLIAM O. SCOTT

Imagining a legal context for Lear's abdication and division of his kingdom plunges one into a morass of power and kinship struggles, and complicates what otherwise seems, perhaps too readily, a wholly foolish decision by him. Reading the play in this manner can help to bring out a degree of dilemma in Lear's initial situation, and the ironies that result from his choices. The dilemma and the ironies may indeed concern not only family relations of love but the circumstances of both royal and paternal power. Moreover, there are indications that commoners in Shakespeare's time, at least in rural areas, sometimes arranged for themselves a more modest legal version of Lear's attempt to secure his final years while shaking off the cares of age.

A starting point, then, would be Lear's announced purpose 'To shake all cares and business' either 'of our state' (Quarto) or 'from our age' (Folio).[1] It is well known that kings cannot really dispose of their kingdoms to others in this way – or should not, in the thinking of Shakespeare's time, at least by dividing the land.[2] But commoners could reduce the cares of age by giving away their property (or by setting up a use, that is, a trust) in return for maintenance in their old age, though it is unknown how many did. There are forms in the oft-reprinted source for boilerplate legal documents (among them the preamble to Shakespeare's will), the *Symboleography* of 1590 and later, by William West, of the Inner Temple. One document, entitled 'A gift of goods and chattels, with couenants to find the donor necessaries, and performe his will', gives all the donor's 'leasses, farmes, and termes of yeares, cattels, implements, housholdstuffe, beasts and cat-

tell, and all other his other goods, aswell reall as personall, moueable as vnmoueable whatsoeuer', and all his precious metal and coins, but reserves one

---

[1] 1.1.38 (Q and F). Citations are from *King Lear: A Parallel Text Edition*, ed. René Weis (London, 1993), though I have consulted also *The Parallel King Lear 1608–1623*, prepared by Michael Warren (Berkeley, 1989). In this essay I have been greatly helped by suggestions by James A. Brundage, Michael Hoeflich, and Richard Hardin – though I will not bind them to agree with all of it. Earlier versions were read at the Shakespeare Association of America conference in Miami, 14 April 2001, and at the Hall Center for the Humanities, University of Kansas.

[2] For a thirteenth-century English statement of the obligation of the Crown to maintain and defend all lands 'without diminution' that became a principle of inalienability and indivisibility, see Peter N. Riesenberg, *Inalienability of Sovereignty in Medieval Political Thought* (New York, 1956), pp. 14–15. (This book appeared too late for Ernst Kantorowicz to use in his oft-cited work.) Nonetheless, sale of Crown lands for revenue, mentioned by R. A. Foakes in the Arden edition (Walton-on-Thames, 1997), p. 17, went on unhampered by this principle. Elizabeth made extensive sales of them, especially to finance military activity in the 1590s; she appointed several commissions for land sales by letters patent under the Great Seal between 1559 and 1601–*The Estates of the English Crown, 1558–1640* (Cambridge, 1992), ed. Richard Hoyle, pp. 15–17, 29 (Hoyle), 116 (Madeleine Gray). The requirement to affix the Great Seal on such transactions, cited by Foakes, could in effect actually have enabled Elizabeth to tighten administrative control of its use for various purposes, by limiting access to it and keeping records of its employment, as in a document of February 1592 (*Calendar of State Papers, Domestic*, 1592, no. 73). Restrictions on alienation of Crown lands by James in 1604 and 1609 were apparently aimed at limiting his gifts of land (as distinct from sales) and protecting the estates from exploitation by clients (Hoyle, *The Estates*, pp. 21–2). Interestingly, in his *Trew Law of Free Monarchies* James had rejected the

messuage (that is, dwelling and adjacent property).[3] Later the document provides that 'In consideration whereof' (in return for the foregoing) the recipient of the gift covenants that he and his executors

shall and will find and prouide to the said R. [the donor] during his naturall life, conuenient and sufficient meat, drink, and apparell. And also one comely and decent Parlor or chamber for the said R. to lie in seuerally, with fire and candle necessarie, during his naturall lyfe, and one person to attend vpon him during the time aforesaid.

In this case, there is no sign that the recipient is related to the donor, but merely someone who accepts an agreement to support an aged person in retirement (with the terms specified in some detail), in return for that person's whole wealth.

The other indenture (section 425) provides that 'aswell in consideration of the naturall loue and affection which he beareth towards his children, and of the fatherly care which he hath of their preferment and aduancement, as for diuers other good causes him hereunto especially mouing', the father gives his children 'all his goods and chattels whatsoeuer'. But again there is a major proviso:

Neuerthelesse, it is fully concluded, condiscended, and agreed, by, and between all the said parties to these presents, in maner and forme following: that is to say, That it shall and may be lawfull to and for the said [father], at all and euery time and times hereafter, during his life naturall, if he remaine so long vnmaried, peaceably and quietly to haue the vse, occupation, increase, and profits, of all the said goodes and chattels, without any lawfull let, suit, trouble, expulsion, or incumbrance of them

by the children or their agents. Unlike Lear, this father has reserved entry and use of his property to himself for the time being. Agreements of these two sorts (that is, with children or with unrelated persons) were registered and apparently enforced in manorial courts from the thirteenth through the seventeenth centuries.[4] There may indeed have been good reason, in some situations, to secure such maintenance even from one's own relatives: although the Poor-Relief Act of 1601 required lineal kin to assist persons in need (with money, not housing, at least for adults), its enforcement was doubtful.[5]

West's documents mention the concept of 'consideration'. This notion of a basis for exchange, as expounded by legal historians, gave more flexibility

---

argument that his (Scottish) coronation oath constituted a contract with the people and (at least claiming to speak 'in play' in justification of a wrong) spoke of a right to give or take away the lands of the realm (which he held as feudal lord) to subjects according to his judgment of their good service, though he might temper his actions by voluntary observation of the law (King James VI and I, *Political Writings*, ed. Johann P. Sommerville (Cambridge, 1994), pp. 73–4, 81).

[3] *The First Part of Symboleography* (London: Thomas Wight and Bonham Norton, 1598), part 1, book 2, section 424. On the relationship to Shakespeare's will, see Samuel Schoenbaum, *William Shakespeare: A Documentary Life* (Oxford, 1975), p. 246. An account of West and his book is given by Eric Poole, 'West's *Symboleography*: An Elizabethan Formulary', in *Law and Social Change in British History*, ed. J. A. Guy and H. G. Beale (London, 1984), pp. 96–106. He says that West's book 'was, from the 1590s until at least the time of the Civil War, the principal collection of precedents [i.e. legal forms] in use among English practitioners' (p. 96). West is also discussed by E. A. J. Honigmann and Susan Brock, *Playhouse Wills, 1558–1642* (Manchester, 1993).

[4] Descriptions of some are given by Pat Thane, *Old Age in English History* (Oxford, 2000), pp. 75–81. Samples of early manorial court records, from which the provisions of such contracts can be inferred, are given by L. R. Poos and Lloyd Bonfield, *Select Cases in Manorial Courts 1250–1550: Property and Family Law* (London, 1998). See also Shulamith Shahar, *Growing Old in the Middle Ages*, trans. Yael Lotan (London, 1997), pp. 154–7; Margaret Spufford, *Contrasting Communities: English Villagers in the Sixteenth and Seventeenth Centuries* (2nd edn, Stroud, 2000), p. 162, and 'Peasant inheritance customs and land distribution in Cambridgeshire from the sixteenth to the eighteenth centuries', in *Family and Inheritance*, ed. Jack Goody, Joan Thirsk, and E. P. Thompson (Cambridge, 1976), pp. 173–5; and Keith Thomas, 'Age and Authority in Early Modern England', *Proceedings of the British Academy*, 62 (1976), 236–7. A blend of marriage settlements with provisions for keeping control of property in the father's hands for his lifetime is mentioned for earlier times by Richard M. Smith, 'The Manorial Court and the Elderly Tenant in Late Medieval England', in *Life, Death, and the Elderly: Historical Perspectives*, ed. Margaret Pelling and Richard M. Smith (London, 1991), p. 41. On the underrated but pervasive influence of manorial courts in everyday life, see Christopher Harrison, 'Manor Courts and the Governance of Tudor England', in *Communities and Courts in Britain 1150–1900*, ed. Christopher Brooks and Michael Lobban (London, 1997), pp. 43–59.

[5] Paul Slack, *Poverty and Policy in Tudor and Stuart England* (London, 1988), pp. 84–5.

to commercial contracts than an older payment-and-delivery-of-goods model, to adapt to an increasingly service-based economy and (by allowing for exchanging promises of future performance) to the volatility of sixteenth-century prices and supplies.[6] It could express reciprocal benefits, as in West's example of the bargain by an unrelated person to maintain the aged donor in exchange for his property; or it could take the form of a motivation for a benefit, such as the 'love and affection' (a standard legal phrase) that the father feels for his children in making his gift of property (even the limited gift in the example).[7] In the preliminaries of his book, West also identifies the common-law 'consideration' with the 'causa' of civil law, a broader concept of a reasonable basis or motivation for entering into an agreement (part 1, book 1, sect. 10). There may be something legally problematic about such trading of property for promises of future service, a mixture of property law and contract law; but West's examples suggest doing it, and, as already described, it was actually done for several centuries. In such an agreement both the timing of the exchanges of benefits and the enforcement of a complete exchange are crucial, as Lear finds to his cost. Moreover, Lear seems to blend the two meanings of 'consideration': he asks for professions of love and affection (and therefore, he assumes, loving care) from his daughters as being motivated in return for his gift. Since, if one can apply the contractual concept here, consideration relates only to the present and future but not the past, he is making a sort of contract to buy future love.

But Lear does more: in the Folio (lines 42–3) he announces that he is going 'to publish / Our daughters' several dowers' (apparently meaning dowries), and the word appears later in both texts (F lines 106, 126; Q lines 98, 118). This is clearly good enough if done before marriage of any of the daughters (as in Shakespeare's various sources), and still valid for dowry gifts of land afterward.[8] Marriage agreements made properly before the fact, as evidenced by West, could, as Lear seems to want, actually accomplish or promise the accomplishment of several purposes at once: one document, in this case by the groom's father in part to set up a dower for the

couple regardless which survives the other, establishes an agreement of the parents that the parties will marry, promises to set up a use for the benefit of the couple (i.e. the dower or jointure, distinct from a dowry), and reserves a portion of the estate for the father while he lives (in effect like the retirement security in the contracts mentioned before).[9] Part of the critics' disagreements about what Lear is

---

6 J. H. Baker, 'Origins of the "Doctrine" of Consideration, 1535–1585', in *The Legal Profession and the Common Law* (London, 1986), pp. 369–91; Baker, *An Introduction to English Legal History*, (3rd edn, London, 1990), pp. 387–8; S. J. Stoljar, *A History of Contract at Common Law* (Canberra, 1975), pp. 33–68. On the economic issues, see Ibid., pp. 33–4, 37.

7 Baker gives the meanings, on the one hand, 'in return for', and on the other, 'because of' or, more personally, 'having taken into consideration' or 'being moved by' (*Legal Profession*, p. 374). A.W. B. Simpson, in contrast, puts the emphasis on motivation – *A History of the Common Law of Contract* (Oxford, 1975), p. 321.

8 Based on a 1568 decision, Hunt v. Bate, Simpson discusses a hypothetical situation in which 'a father, instead of promising a dowry before or at the time of marriage, promises it a few days later; such a promise will be given for a past consideration, and will therefore be unenforceable' (p. 435); but he finds the consequence, in this case of a money settlement, inconsistent in comparison with the unchallenged ability to raise uses in land in that way.

9 West, part 1, book 1, sect. 87. The document in section 84 sets up a use in land as jointure after the couple have already married. Ann Jennalie Cook describes some of these elements in marriage settlements: the dowry or portion from the bride's family, the jointure (sometimes called a dower) from the groom or his family to provide for his wife in case of widowhood, and the groom's family's provision for 'a living allowance for the couple and the husband's inheritance at his father's demise' (*Making a Match: Courtship in Shakespeare and his Society* (Princeton, 1991), p. 121). To these may be added, sometimes, reservation of sufficient wealth to maintain the father for life. At least for daughters and younger sons, Bonfield says that the father 'would make an *inter vivos* gift (generally on their marriage) or a bequest in his will', and 'the father decided the amount of portion and the time it should pass to the child' ('Property Settlements on Marriage in England from the Anglo-Saxons to the Mid-Eighteenth Century', in *Marriage, Property, and Succession*, ed. Bonfield (Berlin, 1992), p. 291). With regard to creating a use to benefit the couple, Bonfield says that 'For the purposes of marriage and family settlements, it was determined [in the Court of Chancery during the fifteenth and sixteenth centuries] that marriage was sufficient consideration to raise a use, and that "natural love and affection" between parent and child was likewise

actually trying to do may come from just this mixture of objectives, as well as from the flawed nature of his efforts to accomplish them.[10] In one grand and quasi-legal gesture he wants to fulfil all his wishes; and when Cordelia's bluntness frustrates him, his improvised measures are still more faulty.

If one puts all the factors together, it seems that Lear has a family interest, as well as a dynastic one, in settling his inheritance and taking into account his daughters' marriages, with the objective that, as he says in the Folio, 'future strife / May be prevented now' (lines 43–4). Absent any positive action on his part, the principle of primogeniture, with respect to royal title though not to property inheritance, would have provided that on his death rule would go to his eldest, Goneril – surely not a desirable result.[11] Indeed, Amy Louise Erickson, writing on wills in connection with women's ownership of property, suggests that the practice of making wills presumably was exercised precisely because the testators wished to soften the effects of primogeniture on property inheritance.[12] Insofar as his own love and affection are motivations for Lear in his gifts of property as dowers (in effect anticipating a will), they might have led him, as he acknowledges, to set his rest on his most-loved youngest child, and following his instincts in this way might indeed have been his best course except that it could have left her vulnerable to the scheming of her sisters. And unfortunately Lear tries to determine on the spot the love and affection on his three daughters' part that might both motivate and compensate for his gift, in the sense of a reciprocal value 'Where [in the words of the Folio] nature doth with merit challenge' (line 52).

The timing of the gift is carefully but disastrously planned: Lear announces his coming abdication of royal power (and in effect paternal power too), and makes a promise of future power that is supposed to be given commensurate with his daughters' present assertions of love and affection. And how can these assertions be commensurate, given Lear's own inflated estimate of the worth of kingship? He considers that, as he later reminds Regan, he is giving them all – and so they tell him insincerely, as invited, that they love him all.

Thus his expression of his own love and affection through gifts of the parts of his kingdom is an

competent' (p. 302). Elsewhere Bonfield observes that the governing law on uses at the time, the Statute of Uses of 1536, 'encouraged the execution of pre-nuptial marriage settlements which contained provisions both for jointure and for the transmission of the estate between the generations' (*Marriage Settlements, 1601–1740* (Cambridge, 1983), p. 3). See also Smith, note 4 above.

[10] Charles Spinosa thinks that Lear means not to make a grant or gift but to set up a use, on the basis that Kent urges him to revoke his gift but that common-law grants were irrevocable ('"The Name and All th' Addition": *King Lear*'s Opening Scene and the Common-Law Use', *Shakespeare Studies* 23 (1995), 184 n.57). This is possible as a part of what Lear is doing, though it seems to rely too much on the Folio reading of 'gift' (line 162); in the Quarto it is 'doom' (line 153), which can easily apply to the disowning of Cordelia, the act that prompted Kent's protest in the first place. Likewise the Quarto's 'Reverse thy doom' (line 139 – in contrast to F's political 'Reserve thy state', line 147) fits quite clearly into Kent's conviction that Lear errs about Cordelia. B. J. and Mary Sokol think that Lear's 'dower' for the two married daughters seems at first to be 'an intended *inter vivos* gift of lands' (*Shakespeare's Legal Language* (London, 2000), p. 99, s.v. 'dower'). Again this seems to cover a portion of what Lear tries to do. They say rightly that 'The ambiguities of Lear's family relations, and of his giving and not quite giving away his royal state . . . , are crucial in the play.' Richard Wilson argues that Lear's intended favoring of Cordelia resembles Henry VIII's use of the strong power given to donors in the 1540 Act of Wills to favor his youngest (and Protestant) daughter (*Will Power* (Detroit, 1993), p. 223). He also (pp. 220–3) invokes the case of Brian Annesley, which concerns a contest between two of Annesley's daughters over his competency to make the will in which he had favored one of them, Cordell or Cordelia; and Wilson argues further that Annesley was in effect 'a "sojourner" in the house', traditionally entitled to board and lodging (pp. 216, 276 n.123). The documents cited by Wilson in support of the notion of the sojourner are all in fact like West's sample retirement agreements. So that seems to be the appropriate legal form to compare with Lear's situation.

[11] Royal succession differed from common-law practice, under which inheritance was divided among daughters if there were no sons. See Spinosa, pp. 160 and note 40; also B. J. and Mary Sokol, pp. 56, 151; and Sir William Holdsworth, *A History of English Law* (5th edn, London, 1942), III, 174 (coparcenary). Richard Strier compares the situation of Henry VIII before the birth of Edward as male heir (though there is the additional problem there that the eldest daughter was Catholic) (*Resistant Structures* (Berkeley, 1995), pp. 178–9); he also makes the point about

almost-simultaneous wielding and undoing of paternal and royal power to enforce the shows of filial love and affection. His expectations of reciprocity that go with his gifts resemble the social constraints of the gift economy.[13] Available in Shakespeare's time was an idealistic version in Seneca's *De Beneficiis*; and of course Shakespeare gave Timon a more cynical view.[14] Practices in James's court suggest indeed that the latter was more apt.[15] The boundary between gift and contract may be hard to determine, or at least subject to historical interpretation; writing of French practices, Natalie Zemon Davis says of a written agreement between a mother and daughter to provide the parents with food, fire, and other necessaries 'for God' in exchange for a vineyard, '*Is* this a gift? readers may be asking. Isn't it just a contractual payment? By the criteria of the sixteenth century, it was a gift, one of the variety of gift practices that flourished.'[16] The formalities of expectation about gift exchange also had a counterpart in the 'hard' economy, in the frequent informal and reciprocal extension of interest-free credit, in which a loan in one direction eventually cancelled out a past loan in the other, that is described in Craig Muldrew's study of lending and borrowing practices.[17] But of course the two contending daughters do not feel the old informal constraints or trouble themselves about present consideration for Lear's already-completed gift.

The Fool's counsel on giving and not giving, and on what one can expect from either, sometimes has a cynical purport, in a way that befits the dilemmas of Lear's position. He tutors Lear about prudence thus:

> Have more than thou showest,
> Speak less than thou knowest,
> Lend less than thou owest,
> Ride more than thou goest,
> Learn more than thou trowest,
> Set less than thou throwest ...
>
> (F 1.4.111–16; Q lines 110–15)

and more. The context of this – banishing two of the daughters, the rent of the land that comes to nothing, cleaving the egg in the middle, and (in the Quarto) a rhyme against the lord that counselled

Lear to give away his land – looks backward to Lear's mistaken gift. But the pattern of keeping something in reserve suggests, in the Fool's sardonic version, that Lear's error was not so much in his making the gift itself as in the fact that it was total, that he has nothing with which to repeat it, to buy more love and affection (or the appearance of it). Says the Fool, one must commit multiple wrongs to make a right.

The implication is stronger in a rhyme in a later scene (in the Folio only):

> Fathers that wear rags
>   Do make their children blind,
> But fathers that bear bags
>   Shall see their children kind.
> Fortune, that arrant whore,
> Ne'er turns the key to th'poor.   (2.4.41–6)

Goneril. In January 1567 Edmund Plowden wrote a defence, prudently left in manuscript, of the claim of Mary Queen of Scots as Elizabeth's successor, based on the idea that king's daughters cannot inherit divided realms as commoners' daughters can receive divided property (Marie Axton, *The Queen's Two Bodies* (London, 1977), p. 31). There is a great difference between such inheritance on death and Lear's attempt to effect a division while he still lives; but the memory of worries about such contingencies might influence an audience's reaction to Lear's effort.

[12] *Women and Property in Early Modern England* (London, 1993), p. 78.

[13] Marcel Mauss, *The Gift*, trans. Ian Cunnison (London, 1954); Marshall Sahlins, *Stone Age Economics* (Chicago, 1972); Pierre Bourdieu, *The Logic of Practice*, trans. Richard Nice (Stanford, 1990).

[14] The parallel with Seneca (and the critique in *Timon*) is discussed by John M. Wallace, '*Timon of Athens* and the Three Graces: Shakespeare's Senecan Study', *Modern Philology*, 83 (1986), 349–63.

[15] David Bevington and David L. Smith, 'James I and *Timon of Athens*', *Comparative Drama*, 33 (1999), 56–87.

[16] *The Gift in Sixteenth-Century France* (Madison, 2000), p. 33. Nonetheless the 'gift' is specified in writing, with carefully delineated obligations in return (as it would have had to be under a French edict of 1539 on *inter vivos* donations – Davis, p. 32). (On pp. 71–2 Davis discusses *Lear*.) Stoljar says (p. 58) that, in order to distinguish a bargain from a gift in the contract practices in the early-modern period in England, there had to be a prior request for a benefit, along with some indication that the intention was to make a bargain rather than a gift.

[17] *The Economy of Obligation* (Basingstoke, 1998).

In such a naughty world as Lear's, it might not be only he who could profit from, and feel the sting of, such admonishments about ragged fathers: West's samples of gift indentures suggest that the lessons could apply to parents whose former wealth and power was less than regal. Such a possibility would give more pertinence for an audience to the Fool's teachings. It would also sharpen a dilemma, one that is naturally most acute for a king like Lear but that could unsettle any father, whose wisdom might after all not really extend to knowing his own child. Lear's instincts originally told him right about his children, it seems; but his legal arrangements (made vastly more difficult by his royal status, as well as by the characters of his daughters and their husbands) necessarily departed from these. He could not protect himself from the legal risks, either, by merely asking for professions of love and good faith.

The Fool's counsel can be pressed further for its implicit questionings. Is buying love a necessary though corrupt practice? Once one starts, can one never stop? Unless one times one's purchases very carefully, will one eventually be reduced to penury and dependence anyway? Is a purchased kindness the best that one can hope for? The Fool's attachment to Cordelia indicates his awareness that she is not subject to these strictures. His counsel, then, may perhaps be taken partly in the same ironic spirit, at least now that Lear has been reduced to his current lowly state, as the Fool's advice to Kent to be obsequious toward the great: 'When a wise man gives thee better counsel, give me mine again. I would have none but knaves follow it, since a fool gives it' (F 2.4.65–7; Q lines 53–6). Indeed, what the Fool says to Kent has its oblique application to Lear too: for Lear as well, 'there's no labouring i'th'winter' (F lines 59–60; Q lines 47–8), and there might seem to be little way to survive but by attaching himself to 'the great [wheel] that goes upward' (whichever daughter that might be) and letting it draw him after. In effect Lear tries to do that, as best he can, later in the scene, when he attempts to bargain for the remnant of his knights. Lear and Kent alike are in fact dependants – and outcasts as well, though the Fool doesn't know that of Kent. On first meeting Kent, the Fool put Lear in that subordinate position too by chiding Kent 'For taking one's part that's out of favour' (F 1.4.94; Q line 92).

The Fool casts himself, and Kent by his advice, in the role of imprudent loyalist who eschews the counsel that is meant only for knaves:

> That sir which serves and seeks for gain
>   And follows but for form,
> Will pack when it begins to rain,
>   And leave thee in the storm.
> But I will tarry, the fool will stay,
>   And let the wise man fly.
> The knave turns fool that runs away,
>   The fool no knave, perdy.
>
> (F 2.4.68–75; cp.Q lines 57–64)

Until the inversions of the last two lines, this is a retreat from irony into direct statement for himself and Kent of the virtue of serving in adversity without recompense. But that directness entails in contrast, in Lear's situation, an irony of application: in his current state Lear has nobody with a claim of past or present authority over him to whom he can, or wants to, be loyal. Ironically he does indeed pack when it begins to rain, because his daughters have denied him the consideration that he thought due him, in return for his gifts to them.

In his mad ravings Lear makes an ironic inversion of the idea of compensation that rewards love and affection, one not available by process of law, in his plea for the heavens' punishment of those who fail of these loyalties. The only trial that he can conduct is an insane mockery. But the sole vengeance that he can find emotionally satisfying is much in excess of the wrong, one that strikes flat the thick rotundity of the world and spills all human germens. He has of course no contract with the gods, only a rough sense of injustice that he is more sinned against than sinning; and even a human presumption to judge of such matters was reproved by God (the human mind and power being incommensurate with God's) in the parallel case of Job. Moreover, the living model that Lear has of retribution for wrongdoing, Edgar's tale of the corrupt servingman punished by demonic possession, is a fiction.

This incommensurate condemnation Lear matches later with an equally bitter and disproportionate pronouncement of pardon: 'die for adultery. No, / The wren goes to't, and the small gilded fly / Does lecher in my sight' (F 4.5.108–10; Q 4.6.108–10). The terms of amnesty hardly sound like forgiveness. Cynthia Herrup has noted in seventeenth-century criminal jurisprudence a pattern in which the law prescribes severe punishments but sentences are freely commuted, a judicial practice that translates into criminal justice the theological concepts of human frailty, repentance, and mercy.[18] Lear's version of mercy almost parodies the pattern with a harsh sentence that is ironically paired with a severe and irrational remission. Indeed how could he do otherwise, given his cynical conclusions (in the etymological sense) that 'a dog's obeyed in office' and 'The usurer hangs the cozener' (F 4.5.151–2, 156; Q 4.6.151–2, 156)? Whatever equality prevails in the forensic and governmental systems must consist only of the lowness of the parties.

In his reunion with Cordelia, Lear assumes a proportionality of hatred (or at least lack of love) to wrongs suffered:

> If you have poison for me, I will drink it.
> I know you do not love me, for your sisters
> Have, as I do remember, done me wrong.
> You have some cause, they have not.
>
> (F 4.6.66–9; Q 4.7.69–72)

But she, true to what she has always been, dismisses that reasoning: 'No cause, no cause.' From the start, she had always rejected such attempts at parity in specific treatment. For her, the 'bond' according to which she loves her father is founded more broadly in general care and caring:

> Good my lord,
> You have begot me, bred me, loved me. I
> Return those duties back as are right fit;
> Obey you, love you, and most honour you.
>
> (F 1.1.94–7; Q lines 85–8)

These are givens (even if not always observed) of the parent–child relationship, products or signs

of the natural love and affection that the law acknowledges and assumes to persist whatever the particular kindnesses, gifts, and benefits may or may not be. Lear, conscious of loving her most of his daughters, is wounded that she expresses nothing more particular, especially after the hyperboles of her sisters. (Lear need not be fully deceived by the other two, whom he did not prefer in his feelings: Laurence Olivier registered amusement, maybe satisfaction, at Regan's jibe at Goneril that her expression of love, in the Folio's words, 'comes too short', line 71, as if he perhaps even wanted to incite that rivalry, as well as receive their flattery.) But Cordelia's settled love has the virtue, as Lear now comes to realize in their reunion, of outlasting great wrong and severe trial. It observes recompense but avoids vengeance. Indeed it actually exceeds recompense: in the crisis Cordelia really lives out her two sisters' empty professions, leaving her husband behind and jeopardizing her life (and of course losing it) in what amounts in action to loving her father all.

In his readiness to go to prison with Cordelia, Lear puts aside all but a detached interest in court news. What matters to him now is an exchange with her that will cancel the past, as well as that can be done: 'When thou dost ask me blessing, I'll kneel down / And ask of thee forgiveness' (5.3.10–11). He has hit upon what each most needs. But of course his vision is illusory.

This is a play of reciprocities, or frustrated expectations of reciprocity, but it is a play of excesses too, whether of condemnation or of pardon (either ironic or real). Lear finally attains what rest he can in the settled love and affection of the kinship bond that had seemed too little to him. But even then, given the long journey over adversities, there must be another trading of benefits: the long-denied blessing for the long-unsought forgiveness.

---

[18] 'Law and Morality in Seventeenth-Century England', *Past and Present*, 106 (Feb. 1985), 111–12; *The Common Peace* (Cambridge, 1987).

HEADGEAR AS A PARALINGUISTIC SIGNIFIER IN *KING LEAR*

ANDREW GURR

Ophelia's identification of Hamlet as mad because when he visited her in her chamber he did not wear a hat suggests strongly that in the original performances he had one on his head at least for his opening scenes. His urgings to Osric to put his own hat to its proper use in Act 5 indicate that he was wearing it again by the play's last act. Our current neglect of headgear with its multiple functions as what the specialists in body language like to call a paralinguistic signifier has lost us several potent features not only of the original staging of *Hamlet* but of *King Lear* with its panoply of regal and ducal crowns and their varying status, and Lear's own progressive shedding of all his headgear. That loss is accompanied by an even bigger one: access to what actually happened in the original performances of the two divergent versions of its conclusion. The evidence about the wearing and not-wearing of headgear in the first performances of *King Lear* repays careful study.[1] We have regrettably little evidence about what the original players of *Lear* might have worn, but the indications about headgear in the text strongly suggest that the author expected it to be used significantly. The play's choice to open the 1606 Christmas entertainments at Court argues, if nothing else, that the players took considerable care over the correctness of their royal and courtly regalia.

Two substantial features in the first stagings of *King Lear* would have affected the early audiences more than they have current critical readings, in large part because both would have been far more conspicuous in the original staging than they are

in the written text. The first visible feature was Albany's attempt at the end of the play to repeat Lear's own mistake by offering to divide his rule between the two surviving earls, a reminder of and contrast with the play's opening, marked by the ducal coronet on Albany's head. The second was the way that the headgear of the three participants in that closing moment signalled Albany's intention to continue the decline in the social ranking of Albion's rulers that Lear had initiated. Albany with his ducal coronet, addressing the two earls, should have set himself in the same posture as Lear with his crown addressing the two dukes at the opening. Kent and the new Earl of Gloucester, to whom Albany offers his coronet, wore the headgear marking their rank, velvet bonnets, as a marked contrast to the coronets that Cornwall and Albany wore when they were with crowned Lear at the opening.

The decline in headgear through the play was a feature reminding the early audiences of Albion's fall into its old disunity: small realms, governed by minor nobles, each at odds with its neighbours. King James had hailed the glorious new unity of Britain in his first speech to the English Parliament

---

[1] The chief contributors to the questions about the crowns and coronets in *King Lear* are G. P. Shand, 'Lear's Coronet: Playing the Moment', *Shakespeare Quarterly* 38 (1987), 78-82; and R. A. Foakes, 'King Lear: Monarch or Senior Citizen?', in *Elizabethan Theater: Essays in Honor of S. Schoenbaum*, ed. Brian Parker and Sheldon P. Zitner, (Newark, NJ, 1996), pp. 271–89.

in 1604: 'Do we not yet remember', he asked,

> that this Kingdome was divided into seven little King-domes, besides Wales? And is it not stronger now by their union? And hath not the union of Wales to England added a great strength thereto? Which though it was a great Principalitie, was nothing comparable in greatnesse and power to the ancient and famous Kingdome of Scotland... And now in the end and fulnesse of time united, the right and title of both in my Person, alike lineally descended of both the Crownes, whereby it is now become like a little World within it selfe.[2]

Albany's offer to re-divide the kingdom, distributed once already between the two son-in-law dukes by Lear, to an even lower-ranked pair of earls, is no testimony to his grasp of the events he has witnessed. Such a process of continued division was recognizably taking Albion back to its ancient 'little Kingdomes'. Kent's withdrawal from the share-out makes only a minor amendment to Albany's uncomprehending repetition of Lear's act of division. The way this last incident in the play was reflected in the possible games with the headgear worn for it by the original performers offers some peculiar perspectives on the different versions the variant texts offer for the actual conclusion.

On St Stephen's Night in 1606 in the great chamber at Whitehall the King's Men staged a very dangerous game.[3] Their usual ploy of showing their king and patron the modesty of their attempts to simulate the reality of kings and their courts on stage was intensified for the court performance of *King Lear* by a local allusion laid out for deliberate shock-effect in the opening words. For the two play-earls to specify rivalry between the two named play-dukes Albany and Cornwall in the presence of the two real dukes, Prince Henry, who had just been made Duke of Cornwall, and his young brother, who had been the Duke of Albany since 1601,[4] and to do so explicitly in the context of a disunited kingdom, was an audacious and extremely risky attempt to make the courtiers sit up and take note of how the old play had been rewritten in order to emphasize its application to the current debate over the union of the two kingdoms of England and Scotland. On the face of it, in the players'

thinking this story about 'the division of the kingdoms' was designed to make an explicit exhibition of the dystopia that must follow disunification. Its very first lines made it a blatant piece of propaganda supporting the policy currently being urged on the two Parliaments by the company's own royal patron, who was there at the performance.[5] That daring piece of politics raises two questions. First, how assertively was the royal status of dukedom declared at the court performance by the ducal coronets that feature in the play? Secondly, what version did the court see of the several alternative stagings with the ducal headgear that might have been offered at the end of the play?

When the play's first lines were spoken on St Stephen's Night a lot of eyes would have turned immediately to the Master of the Revels, Sir Edmund Tilney, if he was present for the performance that he had chosen for that prime day of festivity

---

[2] Speech to the Upper House of Parliament, 19 March 1604, quoted in Charles Howard McIlwain, *The Political Works of James I* (Cambridge, Mass., 1918), pp. 271–2. '*The Kings Majesties Speech in Parliament, 19 March 1603*' was made available in print from Robert Barker, the King's printer, soon after the speech was given.

[3] The King's Men performed nine plays at Court in the 1606–7 season. *King Lear* was given pride of place on the opening night of the festivities, St Stephen's Night (now Boxing Day). For a full account of performances at Court, and a summary of the evidence for the staging of the St Stephen's Night performance of *King Lear*, see John H. Astington, *English Court Theatre 1558–1642* (Cambridge, 1999), p. 240.

[4] For the general context of the Boxing Day performance, see Leah Marcus, *Local Reading and its Discontents* (Berkeley, 1988), pp. 148–59.

[5] The thought that the young princes might have become rivals for the king's crown was evidently not a problem in 1606. It might have been more troublesome later, since there is a record of James being greatly upset by a play that Prince Charles's Men staged at court on 10 January 1620. According to the Venetian Ambassador, 'the comedians of the prince, in the presence of the king his father, played a drama... in which a king with his two sons has one of them put to death, simply upon suspicion that he wished to deprive him of his crown, and the other son actually did deprive him of it afterwards. This moved the king in an extraordinary manner, both inwardly and outwardly.' Quoted in G. E. Bentley, *The Jacobean and Caroline Stage*, 7 vols. (Oxford, 1940–68), vol. 1, p. 214.

('Have you heard the argument? Is there no offence in't?' There was little likelihood of Tilney being seen as a Hamlet figure).[6] The Master, explicitly enjoined to allow no living persons to be represented on stage, and having allowed this play to be shown at the royal court, must have known he was prompting a *frisson* at the very outset of the performance. For the first two speakers to mention the Dukes of Albany and Cornwall must have seemed to be sailing very close to the wind. James's two young sons, the twelve-year-old Henry, newly created as Duke of Cornwall and his six-year-old brother Charles, the Duke of Albany, were not actually in attendance that night, but the players could not have known that in advance, and their titles were familiar to all. Moreover, Charles's title 'Albany' was recognized as referring explicitly to his Scottish origins, since it was his original Scottish dukedom. He had been made the Duke of English York on 6 January 1605, but his Scottish title remained in use. When he was given an acting company to patronize in 1608 it was registered in the provincial records at Norwich, Leicester and even at York itself as 'the lord Albones players'.

A little quick consideration must have reassured the watching courtiers. Tilney at least must have been confident that it was free of offence. Indeed, we might speculate about his prior awareness of how the play's subject could be put to 'application'[7] about the not-yet united state of England and Scotland at that moment. The very obviousness of its application must have been, on second thoughts to the listening courtiers, a guarantee that it was properly licensed. The mythical ancient British kingdom of Albion, created by Brutus of Troy, and affirmed in the play by its antique setting and the use of 'British' instead of 'English' at 3.4.172 in F and 11.169 in Q, and Scene 20.242 in Q (where the Folio text has 'English'),[8] was a vision that well suited James's political hopes. On the face of it the ancient Albion of *King Lear* provided the perfect precedent for his wish to unite his two crowns, his dual paralinguistic signifiers, and enjoy the renewal of the mythical single united kingdom.

We know that King James was present for the performance of *King Lear* at Court on 26 December 1606, the first play of the season, as he was for all nine of the King's Men's plays that winter. If the young dukes had also been present[9] the pointedness of the ducal names announced by the first speakers would have been prominent visually as well as verbally, in their coronets. We have lost today much sense of how blatantly obvious was the application of the names of the two dukes, and the way their titles were affirmed by their visual signifiers, the headgear paraded at court from 1603 onwards. Dukes and ducal coronets were a novel feature at James's court. First established in England by Richard II, all ducal titles had disappeared by the thirteenth year of Elizabeth's reign. She executed her last Duke (Norfolk) in 1571, and never renewed any of the other old ducal titles. None of Elizabeth's most eminent and senior grandees was ever more than an earl. By contrast James had made his sons dukes while they were still in Scotland, and

---

[6] James was there, but there is no evidence for either prince nor any record of anyone else who attended the performance. See W. R. Streitberger, ed. *Jacobean and Caroline Revels Accounts, 1603–1642*, Malone Society Collections xiii (Oxford, 1986), p. 20, and Astington, *English Court Theatre*, p. 240. The Duke of Lennox is not specified as going either, though he was more likely to have been a spectator than the coronetted princes.

[7] Jonson may well have had the court performance of *King Lear* in mind when he noted in his 1607 epistle to *Volpone* that 'application ... is grown a trade'. *Volpone* is closely related to *King Lear* in its images of monstrosity as well as its time of composition for the same company of players. A play viewed as propaganda for the royal policy in a play by the King's servants would expect its applications to be licensed, unlike Jonson's earlier games with *Sejanus* for the same company. Jonson might well consider such a practice as a workmanlike exploit, part of the royal servants' trade.

[8] Line references are from the Norton Shakespeare. Quotations from the Quarto or Folio texts of *King Lear* are from the facsimile edition, *The Complete King Lear 1608–1623*, prepared by Michael Warren (Berkeley, 1989). In either text of *King Lear* 'British', and 'Britain' or 'Briton' were used far less frequently than they were in *Cymbeline*.

[9] In 1605-6 James went to forty-nine Court performances, eleven-year-old Henry to nineteen (including all those staged by his own players), and five-year-old Charles, who was not yet the patron of a company of players, to two. Princess Elizabeth, ten at the end of 1606, was not made patron of a company until a year after her younger brother, and is not on record as attending plays in these years.

he gave his cousin Lennox an English dukedom in 1603. Lennox and the two princes with their ducal robes and coronets were the most conspicuous feature of the Jacobean court that emphasized its difference from the Elizabethan.[10] The relief felt nationally that the childless Elizabeth had been replaced by a monarch with two sons made them and their princely status into a substantial prop to James's English crown.

Headgear as a feature of social status was the most prominent way of signalling a man's rank. In staging *King Lear*, what modern productions and modern study even of the original staging tend to miss is how potently the headgear worn in 1606 would have supported that view. In the first scene of the original production a lot of hats were on stage putting out signals about the relative eminence of their wearers: one royal crown, three ducal coronets, two earl's velvet hats, along with a variety of other signifiers. On St. Stephen's Night 1606 the golden headgear of rulers monarchic and ducal was on show both on stage and in the audience at Whitehall. What happened to the stage versions, including the declining succession of hats worn by Lear, is well worth registering.

The Tudor sumptuary laws, which prevailed against all the violations that new fashions as well as social climbing introduced until James abolished them in 1604, were most scrupulous and detailed in specifying what the different ranks of the aristocracy were allowed to wear. Only kings and dukes could wear golden crowns on their heads, and ducal coronets were markedly smaller and less elevated than the 'archée' royal crown. Earls wore a less distinct costume, differentiated from dukes chiefly by the absence of gold, except for a single ornament on their velvet hats, although the rest of their clothing could be similar: 'Earls and above that rank and Knights of the Garter in their purple mantles' were permitted to wear 'cloth of gold, sylver tissued, silke of purple color'.[11] The golden circlet of a duke's or prince's headgear was a mark of his proximity to the throne. Elizabeth's abolition of her dukedoms may have reflected her instinctual dislike of the visible features of ducal wear as much as her fear of

rivalry and rebellion from those eminences nearest her own rank.

In the original staging of *King Lear* at the Globe one of the strongest visual marks of the play's progress and its point as royalist propaganda was the decline or declension of the headgear that its authority figures wore. At the outset King Lear entered wearing his crown, followed by his two sons-in-law wearing their ducal coronets, and a third coronet was carried onstage ready to be presented to the new duke, whichever between France or Burgundy was to be Cordelia's husband. It was borne ahead of Lear at his entry, as specified in the Quarto stage direction.[12] In contrast to such golden signifiers of authority, Kent and Gloucester, the two earls who begin the play with their discussion about the ducal succession to Lear, wore velvet hats with no more gold on them than the medals or ornaments that the Sumptuary Laws prescribed for that level of Elizabethan nobility. Albany's and Cornwall's princely coronets were visibly shrunken versions of Lear's own elevated and substantial circlet. More gold was on show on the players' heads for this scene than anywhere else in Shakespeare. Lear's gesture in dismissively handing the third coronet to the two dukes heightened the spectacle's garish colours still more.

In this early production the headgear changed through the play as authority shifted. For Lear's

---

[10] Shakespeare knew very clearly the distinction between a crown and a coronet. In *The Tempest*, Prospero makes the differentiation when at 1.2.135 he tells Miranda that part of his brother Antonio's deal with King Alonso was to make Milan a subordinate dukedom to the kingdom of Naples, and to 'subject his [Antonio's] coronet to his [Alonso's] crown'.

[11] Under the original sumptuary laws earls were permitted to wear, besides their cloth of gold and purple silks and their gentlemanly velvet, merely a golden ornament on their velvet hats. The laws are listed in diagrammatic form by Frances Elizabeth Baldwin, *Sumptuary Legislation and Personal Regulation in England*, (Baltimore, 1926), pp. 228–9.

[12] Directors and editors have taken different views about the coronet. R. A. Foakes, in his Arden 3 edition, pp. 14–16, notes the distinctiveness of James's 'archée' crown, and accepts the idea that the third coronet was intended for Cordelia's new husband.

second appearance after the opening throne-room scene, in 1.4, he must have worn a hunting hat. The flourish ('*Sennet*') of trumpets that announced his initial entry was echoed in parody for this second entry by the more ordinary brass of hunting horns, marked in the Folio text's stage direction '*Hornes within*'. This was an entry in more relaxed mode, escorted by his knights, from a day given over to King James's favourite pastime. By the time the storm scene blew up the original Lear had lost even the hunter's protection against bad weather, since at Scene 8.13 in Q the Gentleman tells Kent that 'unbonneted he runnes' (cut in F). His loss of headgear in the storm became his version of Poor Tom's nakedness, the concluding item in his loss of all material possessions. In the last section of the play all Lear secured for his head was the parodic crown of flowers with which he returned to Cordelia, and which he may have kept on until he died at the end of the play.[13] This decline in his headgear, from the golden crown of the opening, to the hunting cap that James himself always preferred for his outdoor activities, to a nominal nudity like Tom's in the storm, bareheaded while he raged against the hurricanoes, and on to the flowery parody of what Kent still insisted on seeing in his face before he went mad, was designed to mark the shifts in Lear's mind and his status as the story developed, and perhaps the matching declension of national authority and control.

By the end of that production Lear lay dead, and the sole remaining wearer of a golden circlet, Albany, offered to resign his authority to the two remaining earls, Kent and the new Gloucester. The headgear of this surviving trio provided a visual marker for the decline in power of a divided kingdom, from royal crown to ducal coronets and now to the earls' velvet bonnets. It is a nice question, which we must come to later, whether it was the duke Albany or the earl Gloucester who was chosen to make the final authoritative speech in these first productions of the play, at the Globe and then before King James. Certainly whichever speaker it was who spoke of this sad time was registering the question whether the shrinkage of authority that

runs progressively through the play (or regressively, if you see the play as propaganda for James's desire to unite his two kingdoms), was to be seen continuing through to the present time and the divided kingdoms which were James's preoccupation in 1605.

When Shakespeare rewrote the old *King Leir* for the King's Men[14] the most conspicuous change was to make the old play's sons-in-law not the 'King of Cornwall' but a duke, and to transform the 'King of Cambria', or Wales, into the Duke of Albany, or Scotland. Since Henry had been made Prince of Wales in 1606 as well as Duke of Cornwall, the change was as obvious as it was pointed. The old Queen's Men's play ignored Scotland altogether as a part of the united kingdom that King Leir ruled over, but the times and political circumstances had changed since then. In Shakespeare's revision the names suggest that the Duke of Cornwall was given Wales and the west, while Albany was given Scotland, leaving the third part, England, by far the most opulent of the three (as James's presence in London testified), to be awarded to the husband of the third daughter, Cordelia, recipient of the third coronet, and hence of course to Lear himself.

That is why the third ducal coronet was such a feature of the play's opening. The Pied Bull Quarto of 1608 supplies this stage direction for Lear's regal entry in 1.1: '*Sound a Sennet. Enter one bearing*

---

[13] Foakes, 'King Lear: Monarch or Senior Citizen?', 283, considers that he might have regained his crown by this point, through a complex process of acquisition from Edmund to Edgar to himself. No stage directions or indications in the dialogue give any support to this idea.

[14] The likelihood that several of the Queen's Men plays were allocated to the Lord Chamberlain's Men in 1594, when the new duopoly was established, notably *The Troublesome Reign of King John*, *The Famous Victories of Henry V* and the ur-*Hamlet*, all of which Shakespeare had rewritten by 1600, gives his decision to rewrite *King Leir* in 1605 an immediate reason that intensifies its 'application' to James's political interests in that year. For his adaptation he consulted a number of sources, perhaps most notably Holinshed, where he would have found a more searching history of the legend. But I have little doubt that for his contemporaries, the names Cornwall and Albany would give the play its most immediate 'application'.

a Coronet, then Lear, then the Dukes of Albany, and Cornwall, next Gonorill, Regan, Cordelia, with followers.' If the 1608 quarto text does give any indication of the version staged at Court in 1606, this third coronet was the central exhibit of the ceremony that Lear then conducted. He explains his plan to the speculating nobles with evident glee at his secrecy, telling them that he is not going to divide the kingdom into two, as they had been thinking and perhaps fearing, but into three. There will now be a third duke to enjoy the share-out, and the third and so-far unoccupied coronet is intended for him. That is why Lear has ordered France and Burgundy to be fetched into the royal presence. One of the two lords of the great lands south of England is to get Cordelia, and with her the third British dukedom and the best share of Lear's to-be-disunited kingdom. He has it all, quite literally, mapped out.

Cordelia's refusal to follow his plan, and his consequent denial of the third coronet to her husband, turns the vacant circlet of gold into a neat visual indication of the impossibility of Lear's original scheme. After Cordelia has upset it, he dismissively tenders that now-redundant emblem of partial authority to Cornwall and Albany, saying 'This Coronet part betwixt you.' (Q; '...betweene you' F). The golden circlet, an unbreakable image of the circle that to Aristotle signified perfection, dangles idly between them. Neither duke can take it up: nobody could wear half a crown. Lear's angry and dismissive gesture destroys with it, all unknowing, his own expectation that he will keep his crown when he delegates authority to the two wearers of the lesser golden emblems. The king's crown now vanishes from the stage along with Lear's authority. In the succeeding scenes both Albany and Cornwall wear their coronets, and are called dukes by loyal Gloucester, but Lear never recovers his signifier of authority. The declension of his headgear through the rest of the play registers the inadequacy of his expectation that, while giving up the labour of government to the dukes, he could retain 'The name and all the addicions to a King'.

Other hints beside the shifts in his headgear uphold the view that after the opening scene Lear is recognizably unkinged. Gloucester still insists on

calling him king, and there are other references to his former status. But Goneril in 1.3 simply calls him 'my Father', and in the next scene the disguised Kent, for all his view of the authority in Lear's face, can only call him 'Master', like the servant to any lord. Lear's own knight in this scene calls him merely 'my Lord'. Oswald draws attention to his reduced status by naming him to his face 'my Ladies Father'. This scene lays more emphasis on his loss of status than later scenes, when he is again addressed by his royal title, and it also calls in question Albany's new power as Lear's successor. The confrontation between downgraded parent and contemptuous daughter intensifies when Albany joins the scene with his visible new authority as coronet-wearer, to find Lear raging at Goneril's decision to strip him of his trappings. Lear turns on him, demanding, with resonant emphasis on this manifestation of female control, 'Is it *your* will?' Albany's evident lack of knowledge about what is going on shows his poor command of what the disguised Kent said he still saw in Lear's face. 'My Lord, I am guiltlesse, as I am ignorant', he protests (F adds the half-redemptive qualifier 'Of what hath moved you.') It is Goneril who is in control. She overrides Albany's attempts to find out what is going on. A ducal yet uncomprehending authority figure adds a touch of incongruous colour to a scene swelling with black fury. His lack of comprehension – in utter contrast to the gross likemindedness of the other husband and wife, Regan and Cornwall, in a later scene – stands as a first example of the losses that Lear's forsaking of his crown are leading to. The two texts of the play present distinctly different Albanys, the earlier of whom it is thought might have been played by Shakespeare himself.[15] It is the stage

---

[15] I have some difficulty with the methodology of Donald Foster's *Shaxicon*, which identifies the sequence of Shakespeare's parts by the distinctive recurrence of their vocabulary in later plays, and particularly in Foster's identification of Albany as one of his parts in 1605. Albany's role in the play as the only authority figure who survives to the end is so central to its conclusion that any revisions, such as those claimed for the Folio text, must have been given special attention. The Shaxicon evidence here comes close to being whirled in a circular argument.

presentation of Albany, the senior survivor, and the level of his comprehension of the events by the end of the play, that is the last and largest of the issues considered here.

The other coronetted figure, Cornwall, on his reappearance in 2.2. makes a strong contrast to Albany. This is a powerful scene. For the first time since Scene 1 the word 'King' recurs, and each time it is applied to Lear, not Albany or Cornwall. Old Gloucester refers to Lear as 'King' and Cornwall as 'the Duke', possibly in a direct indication that Cornwall continues to wear his coronet, and certainly a reminder of the lowering of the new ruler's rank. Cornwall is the figure of power now. He enters accompanied by his host Gloucester to find Kent fighting with Oswald and Edmund, and promptly imposes his power by putting Kent in the stocks. This second authority figure is as ignorant as Albany of what is going on, but his reaction is manifestly an unjust one. The contrasting injustices of Albany's submission to his wife's control and Cornwall's brutish (British) and summary punishment of Kent give graphic testimony to the changes in authority. Moreover, the prior show of Albany's lack of control or comprehension offers little reassurance about any return to unity once Cornwall is killed. If the invasion by the might-have-been third duke, France, were not enough evidence of division, we have seen that Albany has a lot to learn if he is to replace Lear as an authority figure. What he tries to do in the final scene with his by now singular authority colours all the different possible versions of the play's ending profoundly, both as components in the propaganda game, and in the larger philosophical and theological implications. In both texts of the final scene he makes two attempts to exert the control that his coronet should give him, with Cornwall dead, France defeated and all three daughters beyond remarriage, and twice the ex-king Lear checks him. The whole scene is redolent with the King's Men's point about the chaos that comes from the forsaking of single authority. Its ostensible function as pro-royalist propaganda is qualified chiefly by Albany's behaviour as the sole heir to rule. That behaviour appears to shift drastically in its presentation between the two texts.

The difference between the two versions of *King Lear*, the first version as reflected in the Quarto of 1608 and the distinct version in the Folio of 1623 (from a revision made in 1611?), where the final speech moves from Duke Albany to Earl Edgar, if it was a calculated change (a necessary consideration: there is no sign of any preparation for the transfer in the section leading up to it), presents us with too many alternative ways of reading the staging of the conclusion for comfort. Like any frayed rope, there are so many loose strands that no single strong re-connection can be possible.

In both texts Albany employs the royal 'we' to issue the first of his attempts to be authoritative. Q in its entry direction and speech headings calls him 'Duke'. The coronet on his head asserts his right to take control (I quote from the F version; Q is identical, although set as prose):

> You Lords and Noble Friends, know our intent,
> What comfort to this great decay may come,
> Shall be appli'd. For us we will resigne,
> During the life of this old Majesty
> To him our absolute power. (5.3.271–5)

The status quo will be restored. Before he beats that redemptive retreat, though, he singles out the old earl of Kent and the new earl of Gloucester, Edgar, for particular reward, restoring their lost titles and territories to them. Then he goes on to a general proclamation, extending his restoration of justice to the entire kingdom.

> All Friends shall
> Taste the wages of their vertue, and all Foes
> The cup of their deservings. (5.3.277–9)

But Lear breaks in on that hopeful proclamation of restored order with his bleak assertion that no such earthly reimposition of justice is possible. He sums everything up in those wonderfully allusive and denying words 'And my poore Foole is hang'd' (5.3.280). Every word in that simple countervention is telling. 'And' is the effect of injustice that discounts Albany's hope; 'my' reasserts Lear's own responsibility for the disaster; 'poor' echoes France's valuation that Lear so signally failed to understand earlier, that Cordelia is 'most rich being poor', the spiritual overriding the material; 'fool' links paternal love and simplicity with Lear's other sheltered speaker of truth; and she is hanged, the fate of the criminal and, since crucifixion was a Roman form of hanging, of Christ. This gratuitous alteration of the ending to the old play, where Cordella lives on, united to 'the Gallian king' (a kindlier conclusion affirmed in Tate's sentimental union of Cordelia with Edgar), is set here against Albany's attempt at making a return to the normality of the status quo out of which Lear broke at the beginning of the play. In the face of that appalling fact, his well-meaning rewards and punishments have no value. Hanging is a judicial punishment, a curious choice of means for Edmund's murder. Applying the connotations of such a distinct form of killing to Cordelia's death makes a fool of any coronet-wearer, however well-meaning. Albany's innocent and well-intentioned desire to restore the old order shows no growth of stature either in his authority or in his understanding.

Shakespeare uses Albany to underline the enormity of Cordelia's murder. His helplessness is a mark of how inadequate earthly attempts at justice must be (and, in the process, perhaps, how unimportant the play was as royalist propaganda). The point carries through to the very end of the play, because there, in the second of his attempts to control events, Albany does it again. As the sole surviving authority figure, with Lear dead at his feet, he offers to repeat quite exactly Lear's own original mistake that started the trail of destruction. He tries to divide the kingdom a second time. In a woefully diminished version of Lear the king's giving his authority to two dukes, Albany the duke now offers it to two earls. It is a distinctly unimpressive demonstration of his grasp of what has been going on. In spite of all the visible evidence in the bodies on stage of what happened when control was handed down from a king to two dukes, he is prepared to allow it to descend further from himself as the one surviving duke to a pair of earls. Dualism runs throughout the play as the enemy of unity. The singular Cordelia is said by the anonymous Gentleman to redeem mankind from the general curse of 'twaine', and although Albany calls the two earls his friends, 'you twaine', their duality as much as their lack of golden headgear signals a further decline from the unified regal control that the play started with. That is the negation of Albany's timid attempt to renew Lear's initial error. The offer does him no credit, and gives little hope of future unification, as any rough survey of England's history through the time of James's 'seven little Kingdomes' would have affirmed to Jacobean listeners.

There is a particularly tantalizing question about Albany's last gesture for which no evidence survives, either from the 1606 version of the play as it is represented in the Quarto text or from the alternative Folio text. It would be logical for Albany to accompany his offer of authority with its emblem, that paralinguistic signal on his head. If he was imitating Lear's own initial announcement, he would keep his coronet on his own head, as Lear kept his crown. But it is possible that the act of making a wholesale renunciation required him to do more, and to offer the surrender of his signifying headgear too. If he was making a serious proposal of renunciation, as he surely was, a gesture offering his coronet to the two earls would be a kindlier, infinitely shrunken version of Lear's angry gesture with the third coronet to Cornwall and Albany in the opening scene. The two earls were being offered half a coronet each. Then Kent's immediate rejection of the offer would have left the signifier dangling, as it leaves us. We are stranded in utterly conjectural territory, wondering whether, if Albany's offer of the golden circlet was a literal one, Kent's refusal would have left it in Albany's hands, so that it went back onto his head, or whether it then found its singular way into Edgar's hands, and stayed there. This is where we have to curse Shakespeare's chronic economy in writing his stage directions. This question, who might have held or worn the remaining coronet, raises in its most acute form one of the trickiest aspects of the two-texts problem. The presence of Albany's coronet as a feature of the play's closure leaves us with not just two possible and alternative resolutions to the play but four.

If at the Court performance in 1606 Edgar was left with the coronet in his hands or on his head, such a posture would look very different from the later version, since the earlier text gives the last speech to Albany, while the Folio allocates it to Edgar. The last four ponderous lines sound quite different if delivered by a coronet-wearing Albany. They are different again if given by Albany while Edgar holds the coronet, and even more different if delivered by Edgar without the golden headgear. The fourth option, Edgar speaking while holding the coronet, is the only choice possible for those who need to see some expression of hope for the future expressed by a single and fully comprehending speaker in the last speech (I quote F again; Q gives the plural 'have' in the third line):

> The waight of this sad time we must obey,
> Speake what we feele, not what we ought to say:
> The oldest hath borne most, we that are yong,
> Shall never see so much, nor live so long.
>
> (5.3.298–301)

The second line, about putting what we feel ahead of what we ought to say, sounds in Albany's mouth like a self-reproof, an expression of regret that he had tried to issue rewards and punishments in the face of what Lear held up to him. It works against his attempt to re-divide the newly united kingdom, and could be read as a sign that he now has a better understanding. In Edgar's mouth, on the other hand, it sounds more like a reproof to the fumbling and uncomprehending Albany, and a fatalistic acceptance of the foolishness of this great stage. If Albany speaks it while holding or wearing the coronet, the lines become a reluctant acceptance of his responsibility, now with the clearer knowledge that his offer of the coronet had ignored, although nothing has occurred in between to open his eyes. If he speaks them while Edgar holds the emblem of authority, it would mark his recognition of what the play has at last taught him. Edgar is the sole heir, and the kingdom will not be re-divided. If as in the Folio text Edgar says the last words, and does so while holding the coronet, they indicate both his recognition and the general shrinkage marked by the headgear that takes authority from kings down to earls. If he speaks them while Albany still retains the coronet, he is expressing the resignation of the

lesser beings who survive, and his words direct attention away from the survivors to dead Lear and the on-stage corpses of his three daughters. The four choices each mark a distinct point in the huge gamut, from religious hope to pessimistic nihilism, that so many critics have distinguished in the play's conclusion.

There is one possible, and easy if not comforting, solution to this multi-choice dilemma, which in these variable forms surely entertains more alternatives than the original players would have bothered to canvass. This solution requires us to see the change in the last speech-heading between the Quarto and Folio texts as accidental, and allows us to set up Edgar as the single heir to a united Britain, and the speaker of the final words. A version of the play starting with Lear as king, passing authority to the two sons-in-law as dukes, and finally making Albany as the surviving duke offer it to the two earls has a striking consistency. The symmetry of the declension in rank argues that the golden token of authority should end up in Edgar's hands. The steps down from king to dukes and duke to earl collapse if Albany retains the coronet and speaks the last words, as he does in the Quarto text. So the Folio version must rule. This explanation has the convenience of reducing the final difference between Q and F to a compositorial slip in Q. The case for the F text's being, at least in this one instance, a distinct revision, however discreet, of the play's now-embarrassing 'application' to the defunct politics of 1605-6 lapses. And having a single version of the play simplifies life beautifully. The Folio version might be upheld as the nearest thing we have to a non-variable authorial input, identical in 1605, at court in 1606, and consistent thereafter.

But however convenient that may be, it is still outweighed by the predominant likelihood that *King Lear* was designed in 1605 to be judged as a token of support for James's desire to unify his kingdoms. The fact that the play texts survive in multiple forms, the record of a flow rather than a fixity, is a mark of how quickly the local readings could be displaced. Even the two surviving versions of the text understate the multitude of ways the early stagings might have presented the play. Those four or more ways of playing the closure might well reflect distinct versions of the early performances. Which, if any, was the author's own original preference and which of them might show any changes he or his fellow-players might have introduced in later years we have no way of knowing. Certainly as performed at court in December 1606 the play was meant to appear, at least on the surface, as a blatant piece of propaganda upholding the desire of the players' patron to make his two crowns into one, and the strengths of a united kingdom under a single head. Tilney's approval of the text as performed with the names cited in the very first line is ample testimony for that. The versions of the conclusion that most intensify the dystopia of the final act might be seen as concomitants of that work of propaganda, readings of the play whose urgency disappeared when the two Parliaments denied James his hope. The choice, for instance, of having Cordelia murdered so gratuitously, the most emphatic of all the changes that Shakespeare made from the Queen's Men's *King Leir*, its familiar (recently published)[16] precedent, might, if we were determinedly reductive, simply be seen as the most graphic of the many examples that the play provides of the horrors that come from de-unifying the state. Seeing the two earls in their hats being offered the surviving coronet as a parody of the initial gift of authority to Albany and Cornwall would have renewed that grim vision. As propaganda the play has to indicate that there is no hope that could possibly emerge from its dystopian image of a dualistic future.

Such a local reading brings little content to the modern reader, since the original circumstances were so transient. Moreover this reconstruction of the staging has inevitably in crucial areas to be inferential. The hard evidence of headgear-wearing is no more than hinted at in the dialogue and stage directions. The fixity of one's idea about the rest depends on how far one expects the Jacobean Court to have been thorough in following its own sumptuary expectations over the clothing that went with social rank. Readings of the moment when Albany tries to reproduce Lear's original error in dividing his kingdom are made no easier by the multitude of possible stagings of the responses to that idea, and the degrees of generosity which they leave for our opinions of Albany and Edgar as re-unifying rulers. Still less do they give much guidance to the reading or readings which the play's original author might have given to the weighty philosophical and religious connotations that derive from Cordelia's murder and its impact on the play's conclusion.

The pits of idle speculation go very deep here. They do give a distinct deep resonance to the differences between studying Shakespeare on the page and on stage. On the page we can hold all these possible conclusions at the same time, and make our personal choices, leaving, if we can bear to (though critics rarely manage to do that) the ending as problematic, contingent, or even simply unclear. On stage the choices are made for us, and they might well have been altered more than once between 1605 and 1611, or whenever the last speech was reattributed to Edgar, if not by a compositor happy to be coming to the end of his stint of type-setting.

---

[16] *King Leir* was first entered in the Stationers' Register in May 1594, re-entered to the eventual printers in May 1605 and published in the summer of that year.

WHAT BECOMES OF THE BROKEN-HEARTED: *KING LEAR* AND THE DISSOCIATION OF SENSIBILITY

DREW MILNE

In *A Dictionary of English Folklore*, Jacqueline Simpson and Steve Roud cite William of Newburgh's account of the case of an active corpse which surfaced in Alnwick (Northumberland) in 1196. This corpse emerged nightly from its grave to roam the streets, corrupting the air with 'pestiferous breath' and bringing plague. Two men dug up the corpse and found it closer to the earth's surface than expected. They hit the corpse with a spade and from the wound gushed 'such a stream of blood that it might have been taken for a leech (*sanguisuga*) filled with the blood of many people'. So they tore the heart out, dragged the body away, and burnt it, thus, according to folklore, putting an end to the plague.[1] Simpson and Roud cite this story as evidence of a specifically English folklore of vampires. There is some distance to be travelled from the twelfth century imagination of the heart to the twenty-first century imagination of television dramas like *Casualty* and *Buffy the Vampire-slayer*, but such poetics of the heart suggest powerful social illusions at work in representations linking the body and its disturbed spirits to corpses, death and the soul. Television hospital dramas such as BBC's *Casualty* provide a contemporary rhetoric of symptoms and cardiac treatments through apparently realist representations of medical treatments, even if such representations are largely a stage for emotional dramatizations of the heart. The US television series *Buffy the Vampire-slayer*, by contrast, dramatizes some of the allegorical potential in mythologies of the bloodless soul. The programme's darkly comic telling of the triumph of good over evil nevertheless presumes an ironic distance from anything approaching a scientific investigation into the heart. The gulf between rational biology and myth is played with rather than experienced as a crisis, suggesting a dissociation of sensibility between the resources of dramatic realism and those of mythic or allegorical representations of evil and poetic justice.

A report from the court of Queen Elizabeth suggests that things were not so easily dissociated in the world of Shakespeare. In 1599 one of Queen Elizabeth's maids of honour called Margaret Radcliffe died, apparently heart-broken and grief-stricken, after the death of four of her brothers within a matter of months, two slain in Ireland, and two from fever. Her premature death aroused curiosity and a letter by Philip Gawdy provides the following account of how her death was received:

Ther is newes besydes of the tragycall death of Mrs. Ratcliffe, the mayde of honor who euer synce the death of S.[r] Alexander her brother hathe pined in suche straunge manner, as voluntarily she hathe gone about to starue her selfe and by the two dayes together hathe receyued no sustinaunce, whiche meeting withe extreme greife hathe made an ende of her mayden modest dayes at Richmond vppon Saterdaye last, her Ma.[tie] being present, who commaunded her body to be opened and founde it all

---

[1] See the entry 'vampires' in Jacqueline Simpson and Steve Roud, *A Dictionary of English Folklore* (Oxford, 2000), p. 374. The source of this story is William of Newburgh's *Historia Rerum Anglicarum* (*c.* 1200), book v, chapter 24, translated by Joseph Stevenson, *The Church Historians of England*, volume IV (London, 1861). The text is available on-line at: <http://www.fordham.edu/halsall/basis/williamofnewburgh-five.html#24>

well and sounde, sauing certeyne stringes striped all ouer her harte. All the maydes euer synce haue gone in blacke. I saw it my selfe at court.[2]

Margaret Radcliffe's death prompted a brief, acrostic elegy from Ben Jonson.[3] Resonances of this remarkable dissection could also be traced through other poems from the period, such as John Donne's poem 'The Dampe', which begins:

> When I am dead, and Doctors know not why,
> And my friends curiositie
> Will have me cut up to survay each part,
> When they shall finde your Picture in my heart . . . [4]

As if to test the late Petrarchan poetic conceit of a broken heart, it seems that Queen Elizabeth ordered a dissection of Margaret Radcliffe's body to see if some natural form or cause could be found to explain her seemingly unnatural death from a broken heart. As Michael Neill comments: 'If someone suspected suicide, they were disappointed, for the body bore no trace of poison; instead they found what must have seemed like incontrovertible evidence of a broken heart, physical proof of an emotional crisis whose status normally hovered between metaphor and medical fact.'[5] Even now, within modern scientific objectifications of the body, it is open to question how far a clear distinction can be drawn between medical 'facts' and emotional conditions.[6] For the court of Elizabeth there was a significant gulf between the anatomy of physical heart-strings and the anatomy of the soul. Dark hopes are invested in the ability of the emergent theatre of dissection and medical experiment to provide better answers than the theatre or poetry of love.[7]

An echo of Margaret Radcliffe's anatomical fate can be heard in *King Lear* when Lear declares: 'Then let them Anatomize *Regan*: See what breeds about her heart? Is there any cause in Nature that makes these hard-hearts?' (*King Lear* 3.6.34–6)[8] But the status of Lear's own heart is perhaps even more interesting. The hardness of Lear's heart seems to complement the blindness of Gloucester, as if to illustrate Jesus' quotation from Isaiah in the gospel of St John: 'he hath blinded their eyes and hardened

their herte that they shulde not se with their eyes and lest they shulde vuderstande with their herte.'[9] But what might a post-mortem reveal if the anatomists were allowed to get their hands

---

[2] Quoted from E. K. Chambers, 'The Court', *Shakespeare's England*, eds. various (Oxford, 1917), 2 vols, vol. 1, pp. 79–111 (p. 87). See I. H. Jeayes, ed., *Letters of Philip Gawdy* (London, 1906), p. 103. For discussion see Michael Neill, ' "What Strange Riddle's This?" Deciphering *'Tis Pity She's a Whore'*, in Michael Neill, ed., *John Ford: Critical Re-visions* (Cambridge, 1989), pp. 153–79; and Michael Neill, 'New Light on "The Truth" in *The Broken Heart*", *Notes and Queries*, n.s. 22 (1975), 249–50.

[3] See 'On Margaret Radcliffe', *Ben Jonson: Poems*, ed. Ian Donaldson (London, 1975), p. 24.

[4] John Donne, 'The Dampe', *Poetical Works*, ed. Herbert J. C. Grierson (Oxford, 1929), p. 57.

[5] Neill, ' "What Strange Riddle's This?" ', 156. See also Michael Neill, *Issues of Death: Mortality and Identity in English Renaissance Tragedy* (Oxford, 1997).

[6] For a challenging discussion of the separation between medicine and spiritual healing see Gillian Rose, *Love's Work* (London, 1995).

[7] For a broader discussion of anatomy and dissection see Jonathan Sawday, *The Body Emblazoned: Dissection and the Human Body in Renaissance Culture* (London and New York, 1995). See also Francis Barker, *The Tremulous Private Body* (London, 1984).

[8] A reading from *The Norton Facsimile of the First Folio of Shakespeare*, ed. Charles Hinman (New York and London, 1996), 2nd edition, p. 807, 2033–5. The first Quarto text reads: 'Then let them anotomize *Regan*, see what breeds about her / Hart is there any cause in nature that makes this hardnes'. *King Lear* Q1 (1608), *Shakespeare's Plays in Quarto: A Facsimile Edition*, eds. Michael J. B. Allen and Kenneth Muir (Berkeley, 1981), p. 687. Subsequent references to Shakespeare's plays are readings taken from these facsimile editions, although line references are supplied, for convenience, from the Stanley Wells and Gary Taylor Oxford edition, referring, for *King Lear*, to their edited text of the Folio edition.

[9] St John 12:40 quoted from Cranmer's 1539 translation, *The English Hexapla: Exhibiting the Six Important English Translations of the New Testament Scriptures* (London, 1841). Jesus appears to be quoting the lines from *Isaiah* VI, 10, which the authorized version translates as 'Make the heart of this people fat, and make their ears heavy, and shut their eyes; lest they see with their eyes, and hear with their ears, and understand with their heart.' *The New English Bible* translates these lines as 'This people's wits are dulled, / their ears are deafened and their eyes blinded, / so that they cannot see with their eyes / nor listen with their ears / nor understand with their wits.' The shift to wits points to the difficulty of translating hearts.

on Lear's heart? There is something inappropriate about imagining such a response to Lear's death, as if a literal-minded resistance to the play were incapable of recognizing the body's physical conditions as embodiments of more spiritual sufferings. And yet, as I hope to suggest, the play's dramatization of tragical death reveals how an Elizabethan or Jacobean audience might associate tragic poetics with medical diagnosis in ways that create difficulties for modern performers and audiences. Related to such associations there are a range of surprisingly awkward and unanswered questions about the status of the actor's bodies at the end of *King Lear*. These questions open out into historical questions about the conventions of stage death, the biological and medical understandings of death and the tragic dramatization of the causes of death. Recent critical debates have focused on the textual problems of *King Lear*.[10] These debates are important for an understanding of the textual variants in different versions of the end of *King Lear*. This essay, however, suggests ways in which implicit directions for performance and the implied staging of the actor's body need to be analysed, not least if we are to make sense of *King Lear* for modern performance. The already unstable play-text needs to be read with an eye for the implied physical actions of the actor's body, and for the modes of gestural implicature which establish tensions between the actor's body and the body of the role being performed. The difficulty of sustaining a dramatic relation between the actor and the emotional state of the roles being played makes *King Lear* a particularly acute illustration of Diderot's paradox.

How, then, does Lear die? How does the play dramatize the causes of his death? In the Folio text there are a number of suggestive stage directions. The Quarto's direction 'The bodies of Gonerill and Regan are brought in' becomes, in the Folio text, 'Gonerill and Regans bodies brought out' (5.3.206). Both Quarto and Folio texts have the direction, 'Enter Lear with Cordelia in his armes' (5.3.231). As John Jones observes, editors have tended to interpolate the word 'dead' after Cordelia's name in one of the more famous stage directions in world drama, but Shakespeare's early

audiences did not know she was dead any more than Lear himself is sure.[11] The tendency of editors to overplay their hand in attempting to explicate the text undermines the purposeful ambiguity of Cordelia's entrance. While the status of stage directions is difficult to assess, both these directions are unusual and unusually important for the staging of the scene. It seems at least plausible that they are an essential part of the way Shakespeare conceived and wrote the end of the play, or that they provide some record of how the play was staged. Either way, there are practical difficulties amid the disintegration of anything approaching funereal pomp in the scene's unravelling. The actors playing Goneril and Regan also have the unenviable task of being dragged on while pretending to be dead. It is hard enough to avoid appearing ridiculous when called upon to die on stage, but there is a peculiar challenge in being brought on stage and then made to play dead. Audiences are often amused by signs of life in actors playing dead. To illustrate the problem, the stage manager's reports for Nicholas Hytner's RSC production note that at the Barbican performance on 6 May 1991: 'Miss Kohler had a recurring cough. Penny Jones played the dead Goneril to save her the discomfort of stifling her coughs.'[12]

It is usually hard enough to get dead bodies off the stage and no practical dramatist would bring dead bodies back onto the stage unless an important point were being made. It is even harder, however, to carry an actor on to the stage in your arms. The image of the three sisters back on stage, united again in death for the first time since the beginning

---

[10] The debates rumble on from P. W. K. Stone, *The Textual History of King Lear* (London, 1980); Peter W. M. Blayney, *The Texts of 'King Lear' and their Origins*, i. *Nicholas Okes and the First Quarto* (Cambridge, 1982); and, Gary Taylor and Michael Warren, eds., *The Division of the Kingdoms: Shakespeare's Two Versions of 'King Lear'* (Oxford, 1983). For a succinct account, see John Jones, *Shakespeare at Work* (Oxford, 1995).

[11] Jones, *Shakespeare at Work*, p. 234. Compare the commentary in *King Lear*, ed. R. A. Foakes (Walton-on-Thames, 1997), p. 385.

[12] I am grateful to Pascale Aebischer's research for unearthing this illustration of corpses and corpsing.

of the play, makes plain the consequences of Lear's initial rejection of Cordelia. It is possible, for example, to block the staging of the three sisters to echo their positions in the opening scene. But this tragic tableau is fraught with difficulties. The actor playing Lear needs, for example, to be strong enough to bring on the body of Cordelia if his entrance is not to appear clumsy. Similar difficulties are evident in the stage business and 'heavy sight' (4.16.42) of Antony's dying body being hoisted aloft in Act 4 of *Antony and Cleopatra*.[13] Various solutions can be found for coping with the weight of Cordelia's body, but performance history suggests that much of the effect of this scene depends on Lear's display of physical strength in his final hour. Even on a relatively small stage, however, it is a considerable physical feat to carry a body across the stage in a manner which does not leave the actor purple in the face and out of breath for his ensuing lines. Modern editors, such as Stanley Wells and Gary Taylor, have helped the actor playing Lear by inserting a stage direction to indicate that Lear puts Cordelia's body down between saying 'She's dead as earth' and 'Lend me a Looking-glasse' (5.3.236), as if to indicate the moment when Lear needs his hands free. But even the fittest of actors might worry about the physical demands of the gestures involved. The line 'O your are men of stones' (5.3.232) takes on a rather different sense if the effect is to illustrate the way in which those on stage do not come to Lear's assistance to relieve him of the weight he is carrying.

Scholars have tended to assume that this part was written for Richard Burbage and, if so, Burbage would have been about forty-two when *King Lear* was performed before James I on the 26 December 1606. Perhaps Shakespeare wrote this direction knowing that Burbage would be strong enough to carry on the body of the boy playing Cordelia. The effect seems not to have been repeated until Edmund Kean: 'When Edmund Kean, with a great deal of courage, decided to be the first to restore the death scene to the Tate version he moved awkwardly, short as he was, carrying his Cordelia, and some among the audience were amused.'[14] As Marvin Rosenberg reveals, some curious practical

solutions have been found: 'Gielgud's portage was easier with a concealed sling which made it seem that he carried her on one arm. This was one of Granville-Barker's favorite inventions to give Lear the appearance of massive strength...'[15] The significance of this strength was given a suitably resonant dramatic weight by Paul Scofield, eliciting Rosenberg's somewhat romanticized description: 'Scofield yielded a sense of the inward suffering that carried through from IV, vi; outwardly on his hard frame the blows that sagged him slightly seemed more psychic than physical, the bludgeoning of despair....'[16] The gap between the psychic and physical emerges as an important performance parameter for the possibilities of gestural implicature afforded by this playtext. If the moment were written for a strong Burbage, capable of carrying a boy actor with ease, then the moment only becomes difficult for subsequent actors if they lack Burbage's strength. Assuming that these practical staging dynamics are integral to the scene, however, why might Shakespeare stress physicality at such an important moment?

On internal evidence the fictional Lear is in his eighties, or 'four-score and upward' (4.6.54). The actor needs accordingly to establish an awkward relation between his own strength and the considerable strength of the aged Lear. The staging of this moment defines the casting for the play of a strong but ancient Lear against a featherweight Cordelia. Indeed, any actor hoping to play the part has to reckon how old they can be to suggest an appropriately ancient frame before they are themselves too ancient to play the part. The actor has

---

[13] Recent attempts to recreate original staging conditions have yet to resolve how this scene might have worked. At the performance I attended of Mark Rylance's production at the new London Globe in 1998 the audience applauded the physical achievement involved in raising Antony into the gallery, such that the line 'Heere's sport indeede: / How heauy weighes my lord?' (4.16.33) became an occasion for comedy.

[14] Marvin Rosenberg, *The Masks of King Lear* (Newark, 1972), p. 311.

[15] Rosenberg, *The Masks of King Lear*, p. 311.

[16] Ibid., p. 311.

to relinquish the crown of theatrical possibility before theatrical mortality catches up with them. Paul Scofield, perhaps the most remarkable of modern Lears, played the role in Peter Brook's production while, like Burbage, in his forties. This points to the importance of Lear's physical strength despite his years. Perhaps Shakespeare's concern is to show that the Lear of Act 5 is still physically strong, despite his advanced age, and despite all that he has gone through, including the weakness of his ruined body and mind in Act 4. This is emphasized by Lear's revelation, confirmed by a gentleman, that he has killed the slave that was hanging Cordelia. As Lily B. Campbell has suggested, Lear remains enslaved to his passions and wrath.[17] To the end Lear is wracked by the violence of his passions, passions that finally overcome him, even if it is a wonder that he endures so much. His physical actions suggest that after all he has been through, Lear has still failed to become patient. Indications that he still has a powerful body to support his powerful passions dramatize the heroic stature of Lear's renewed strength, adding pathos to his emotional state in his final moments. The audience might also be made aware that Lear need not have resigned his kingdom for want of physical strength. In this sense, the play makes it clear that Lear does not die because his flesh is weak while his mind is still strong. Rather the reverse, Lear's flesh is shown to be heroically strong, while his mind or heart is broken.

If the strength needed to carry Cordelia makes getting out of breath a difficulty for the actor playing Lear, this scene is also difficult for the actor playing Cordelia. The business of the looking glass and the feather, however fictionally or imaginatively staged, threatens to reveal that the actor playing Cordelia is alive. As with the part of Lear, the playtext involves a difficult identification between the actor playing Cordelia and Cordelia's fictional body. The scene might descend into farce if Lear pursues his inquiry so vigorously that it becomes evident that Cordelia is indeed still breathing. The stage business turns this risk into a dramatic effect, by dramatizing the uncertainty as to whether Cordelia is dead. It is possible that she may come back to life, as many an audience have wished, if

only for one last moment of poignant speech and brief resurrection before subsiding. Desdemona, for example, rises from her seeming death for a few last words in which, even in death, she confirms her true innocence as a wife, attempting to absolve Othello by saying that nobody but herself has committed murder. A comparable pathos of innocence, guilt and forgiveness might be drawn out if Cordelia were resurrected to utter a few last words. Stranger things happen in Elizabethan and Jacobean plays. The staging of Mercutio's death in *Romeo and Juliet* emphasizes the shocking reality of death amid what at first seems a mere scratch. The deaths of Romeo and Juliet also emphasize the ambiguity of stage corpses and their ability to come alive. In the final act of Webster's *The White Devil* Flamineo 'riseth' to reveal that the pistols with which he has been shot 'held no bullets' (5.6.148–9). Even when he is finally killed by sword wounds he manages 'to recover like a spent taper' (5.6.262) for his final speech. Elsewhere Bottom's performance of the death of Pyramus suggests the potential comedy of over-acted stage deaths. The dramatic effects possible when an actor on stage might appear to be playing dead are also evident in *2 Henry IV*, when Prince Henry, not usually rash or unobservant, prematurely tries on the crown, having observed that: 'by his Gates of breath, / There lyes a dowlney feather which stirres not: / Did hee suspire, that light and weightlesse dowlne / Perforce must moue' (4.3.162–5). In both this moment and in *King Lear*, the motionless feather is staged as a theatrical illusion that highlights the difference between the living actor and the acted corpse. Given that Shakespeare has altered his sources to kill off Cordelia it is possible that some among his audience imagined that Cordelia would indeed live. The audience is made to share Lear's uncertainty and his desire that Cordelia might live. This uncertainty has the added advantage of stopping the prospect of physical farce from over-determining the scene's

---

[17] Lily B. Campbell, *Shakespeare's Tragic Heroes: Slaves of Passion* (Cambridge, 1930), especially chapter 14, '*King Lear*: A Tragedy of Wrath in Old Age', pp. 175–207.

pathos by making the artificiality of the theatrical illusion into a dramatic ambiguity. A similar effect and uncertain diagnosis is dramatized in the mutual death scene of Romeo and Juliet: any sign that the actors playing Romeo or Juliet are merely pretending to be dead simply adds to the pathos of their potential to wake up in time or to come alive.

If we apply the drama of uncertain death to Lear himself, however, a rather different picture emerges. In the Folio version Lear's last words are 'Do you see this? Looke on her? Looke her lips, / Look there, looke there' (5.3.286–7). While attention is perhaps focused on Cordelia's lips or on Lear's hands, Lear dies. The stage direction '*He dis.*' (sic), perhaps indicates a relatively sudden death, with his dying drawn out over his vocal repetitions. This effect is perhaps paralleled by the repeated death groans of 'O, o, o, o' in the Quarto text, groans comparable to those of the dying Hamlet in the Folio text. In the Quarto text of *King Lear*, however, Lear's final line is 'Breake hart, I prethe breake', and this suggests a different way of performing Lear's last moment. Having been trained earlier in the scene to see how death on stage can be ambiguous, the responses of Edgar and Kent suggest a rapid shift from the possibility that he has merely fainted towards the wish that he would be better dead than that there might still be life or breath in him. Against Edgar's remarks 'He faints, my Lord, my Lord.' and 'Looke vp my Lord', Kent pleads for Lear's heart to let him die: saying first 'Breake heart, I prythee breake' (5.3.288) and then 'Vex not his ghost, O let him passe, he hates him, / that would vpon the wracke of this tough world / Stretch him out longer.' To which Edgar replies 'He is gon indeed' (5.3.287–91). These lines overcome the possibility that the audience might imagine that Lear has merely fainted. Moreover, Kent's line 'Breake heart, I prythee break' echoes an earlier interchange in which Lear asks Kent 'Wilt breake my heart?' to which Kent replies: 'I had rather breake mine owne' (3.4.4–5). But to what or whom is Kent's plea 'Breake heart, I prythee break' directed? Is it implied that Kent is calling on Lear's flesh to release Lear's soul? Or is Kent calling on Lear to give up his ghost, to let himself go into

death? It might even be argued that he calls on his own heart to break, wishing for a journey into death. The situation is further complicated by returning to the Quarto text, which ascribes 'Break hart, I prethe break' to Lear himself, as if Lear were calling on his own heart to break, somehow willing his own disintegration and dissociation of sensibilities.

There is much that is ambiguous, moreover, in the lines which lead up to the moment of Lear's death.[18] Lear's line 'Pray you vndo this Button' (5.3.285) for example, can be performed to suggest a variety of states of mind immediately prior to Lear's death. Many actors have performed this scene with Lear in dishevelled costumes, with no top button to undo. Accordingly, the line has been performed as if Lear is out of his mind and gestures to an imaginary button which somehow holds his spirit within his body. Performed thus it is as if he were asking for his ghost to be allowed to pass out of his body or as if he were afflicted by another attack of the 'mother' or 'hysterica passio' (2.2.231–2). The line has also been performed to refer to a button on Cordelia's clothing, such that Lear is trying to allow Cordelia to breathe and sees that her clothing is constricting her breathing. This interpretation is somewhat implausible if we remember that Cordelia has been hanged. It is usual to bare the neck when hanging someone rather than allowing their dress to interfere with the processes of execution, and the scene is often staged with signs of rope burn around Cordelia's neck. If Lear is calling for his own button to be undone, this suggests that Lear needs to be dressed with some kind of buttoned up shirt, rather than being dressed as a dishevelled prisoner of war. In a number of recent productions

---

18 Ingenious commentaries are offered by a number of editors of the play. Discussion of the button can be found in Marvin Rosenberg, *The Masks of King Lear* and in Philip C. McGuire, 'Open Silences and the Ending(s) of *King Lear*', *Speechless Dialect: Shakespeare's Open Silence* (Berkeley, 1985), pp. 97–121. See also Nicholas Brooke, 'The Ending of *King Lear*', *Shakespeare 1564–1964*, ed. Edward A. Bloom (Providence, Rhode Island, 1964), pp. 71–87; and John Shaw, '*King Lear*: The Final Lines', *Essays in Criticism*, 16 (July 1966), 261–7.

the implication of the need to unbutton Lear's shirt has been staged as if Lear were experiencing something rising in his gorge or as if suffering the onset of a cardiac arrest that necessitates the need to loosen tight clothing. The New Variorum Edition noted the following interpretation:

where any other mind would have confined itself to the single passion of parental despair, Shakespeare contrives to indicate by a gesture the very train of internal physical changes which are causing death. The blood gathering about the heart can no longer be propelled by its enfeebled impulse. Lear, too weak to relieve the impediments of his dress, which he imagines cause the sense of suffocation, asks a bystander to 'undo this button'.[19]

This line implies a physical drama, then, perhaps even an implicit stage direction for the costume appropriate for his entrance with Cordelia in his arms. The thematics of fresh and soiled garments confront the social, physical and metaphorical constrictions of clothes.[20]

Whatever costume decisions are made, the microdrama of this button, whether it is Lear's or Cordelia's, suggests that either Lear or Cordelia might need room for air to breathe. More poetically, it might be that Lear's vital spirit, ghost or blood is trying to release itself. There are pitfalls for a modern audience familiar with the appropriate first aid treatment for someone who faints or someone undergoing a heart attack. The scene surely descends into dark farce if a modern audience begins to imagine that Lear's death is the result of botched first aid in the hands of Edgar and Kent. It is also implausible that Lear dies from the physical exertion of carrying the body of Cordelia on stage, as if paying the price of lifting a heavy weight. The drama of Lear's body in these final moments seems designed to show that Lear does not slip away quietly. His howls and the cry of 'Never never never' (5.3.284) suggest that he dies with considerable strength remaining and with defiance. Indeed, like many a tragic hero, Lear reasserts his tragic status as he loses life by highlighting his heroic strength in death. Put differently, Lear loses tragic status if his death is staged as though he were simply exhausted or as if dying of natural causes. There is

nevertheless a temptation for the modern actor to borrow from the performance rhetoric popularized by hospital dramas to perform Lear's death by clutching his sides as if experiencing cardiac arrest. Most performers and audiences have nevertheless preferred, without too much questioning, to believe that Lear, after a heroic renewal of strength and painful recognition of the consequences of his failed love for Cordelia, dies of a broken heart. Indeed, the choreographed series of signals dramatizing Lear's final moments seem designed to confirm this view, not least Kent's line 'Break heart, I prythee breake.' But it is here that the historical specificity of Lear's tragic body emerges. Expressions associated with dying from a broken heart indicate a historical gulf between the performance diagnostics of modern medicine and the poetics of grief-stricken and heart-rending love. If death from a broken heart is not to be confused anachronistically with a heart attack, how can the actor playing Lear perform death to suggest that Lear dies from a broken heart? If a heart attack constitutes a sudden but natural cause of death, what gestures are appropriate to indicate a tragic death from unnatural causes?

Marvin Rosenberg offers a sketch of different ways of performing the play's conclusion through the power of visual imagery at the point where words fail:

Gielgud, dying grandly in joy at his perception of apotheosis in Cordelia; Forrest, frankly hallucinating her reviving, staring vacantly into space; Carnovsky, shocked to death at the horror of Cordelia's stillness . . . Scofield's silent death: sitting bolt upright, his eyes looking into the mystery of things . . . Booth suggested a man afraid,

---

[19] Ed. Horace Howard Furness, *A New Various Edition of Shakespeare: King Lear* (New York, 1963) (reprint of the original 1880 edition). Furness quotes *The Quarterly Review* (April, 1833), p. 197.

[20] See, for example, Thelma Nelson Greenfield, 'The Clothing Motif in *King Lear*', *Shakespeare Quarterly*, 5 (1954), 281–6; Dean Frye, 'The Context of Lear's Unbuttoning', *English Literary History*, 32 (1965), 17–31; and Maurice Charney, ' "We put fresh garments on him": nakedness and clothes in *King Lear*', in *Some Facets of* King Lear, eds. Rosalie L. Colie and F. T. Flahiff (London, 1974), pp. 77–88.

exhausted by suffering, confronting Cordelia at the end with a dreadful terror, as if in fear not only of what was, but what was to come; he died in the grand style of Forrest, standing suddenly erect, in a final spasm as a king... The physical agony could be spectacular – Mikhoels told how an actor named Zacchoni drew applause when, at the last moment, his beard jerked suddenly, stiffly up, simulating an actual physical death; but the quieter passing could emphasize Lear's release from suffering, the escape from life, as with Macready, who simply sank back...[21]

The most delicate questions of performance involve the extent to which Lear 'wills' his death. If death from a broken heart means that Lear's body is physically strong but that his heart is not strong enough to bear his unnaturally severe burdens of grief, then it is possible to suggest that what is meant by heart is not the physical heart but a metaphorical heart, where heart stands poetically for Lear's heart and soul. If Lear's ghost or spirit leaves the body when he dies, then the breaking of the heart suggests the severing of the relation between physical flesh and the spirit or soul. If death from a broken heart suggests a situation in which Lear's heart, like the rest of his body, is strong and that Lear is, so to speak, big-hearted, then the key question is the relation between Lear's mind and his heart. If Lear's flesh is strong while his mind is weak, then perhaps Lear's mind gives up the ghost. In this sense, it would be Lear's mind rather than his heart which cannot face the weight of grief involved in recognizing that Cordelia has died because of Lear's actions. Unable to face reality, his mind gives up and the resulting strain is too great for the heart to bear. But this comes close to suggesting that Lear dies in a state akin to madness because he cannot face the full consequences of his actions and the workings of fate.

The conventional and somehow more 'tragic' interpretation involves thinking instead that Lear finally gives up the ghost when he realizes that Cordelia is dead, coming to some recognition of the mentally unbearable situation he is in part responsible for. As Lear puts it earlier, 'she liues: if it be so, / It is a chance which do's redeeme all sorrowes / That euer I haue felt' (5.3.240–2). By the

same logic, if she does not live, all the sorrows that Lear has ever felt are faced with the added burden of this fatal chance which has killed Cordelia. There is a delicate balance between suggesting that Lear wills his own death, and that his mind or heart decides that enough is enough; or, alternatively, that it is the combination of mental and physical suffering involved in recognizing his tragic situation which kills him. It is evident, however, that Lear is in some sense strong, but that the situation is too tragic for someone as strong as Lear to endure, and that this defines the extremity undergone by his tragic body.

These different possibilities are difficult to perform. The tragedy is diminished if Lear dies from natural causes, rather than from the unbearable weight of the unnatural causes his body and mind have endured. This poetic and psychologically plausible form is sufficiently determinate for audiences not to have been too bothered by the awkward question of how, poetically *and* medically speaking, it is possible to die from a broken heart. The staging of bodies highlighted by the stage directions indicates how Shakespeare's playtext has succeeded in giving readers and audiences sufficient confidence that Lear does not die of a heart attack due to physical weakness or old age; that he does not commit psychological suicide; and that he doesn't die mad. None of which makes it easy for actors to suggest the metaphor of a broken heart within bodies that are alive and kicking. What are the appropriate gestures? From the perspective of modern medicine, it is possible to question the poetics of death by insisting on some clarification of the play's physiology of the heart. What if the metaphor of the broken heart is understood more literally, as if there were some continuity between broken hearts and heart attacks through which to understand the poetic expression 'broken heart'? Did Shakespeare, for example, believe that it was possible in reality for people to die of a broken heart, or is death from a broken heart a colloquial idiom here given tragic form in ways which

[21] Rosenberg, *The Masks of King Lear*, pp. 319–21.

inadvertently prefigure what has become known as a heart attack? Are heart attacks brought on by natural causes or by the more unnatural extremes of emotional tragedies?

Perhaps the most important internal evidence provided by the Folio text occurs in the lines immediately preceding the bringing on of the dead bodies of Goneril and Regan. Albany says to Edgar: 'Let sorrow split my heart, if euer I / Did hate thee, or thy Father.' (5.3.168–9) Edgar tells Albany how he has known the miseries of his father and says: 'List a breefe tale, / And when 'tis told, O that my heart would burst.' (5.3.173–4) Edgar goes on to tell how Gloucester died: 'But his flaw'd heart / (Alacke too weake the conflict to support) / Twixt two extremes of passion, ioy and greefe, / Burst smilingly' (5.3.188–191). So far as I can trace, Shakespeare nowhere uses the expression 'broken heart' in the poetic sense generally evident in the period, and subsequently evident in John Ford's play *The Broken Heart*. Passages in *King Lear* nevertheless suggest that his poetics of the broken heart involve a conception of the way in which a heart can split, break or burst from the weight of too much grief, and in particular from the dynamic conflict of two extremes of passion, such as joy and grief.

F. David Hoeniger offers some contextual resources for understanding Shakespeare's vocabulary, not least the vocabulary of 'heart-strings', which moves awkwardly between metaphorical strings, like those of a musical instrument whose physical forms are made from guts, and a more literal physiology of the heart. According to Hoeniger, 'The notion that extreme grief makes the heart-strings "crack" occurs especially often in Elizabethan Literature.'[22] This conception of heart-strings can be related to Galen's conception of the fibres and bands of the heart.[23] The expression 'heart-strings' is used in various places in Shakespeare's work, including *Two Gentlemen of Verona*, *The Rape of Lucrece* and *Othello*. The breaking of such strings is related to broken hearts. Consider the following lines spoken by King John:

The tackle of my heart, is crack'd and burnt,
And all the shrowds wherewith my life should saile,

Are turned to one thred, one little haire:
My heart hath one poore string to stay it by,
Which holds but till thy newes be vttered,
And then all this thou seest, is but a clod,
And module of confounded royalty.

(*King John* 5.7.52–8)

In *Richard III*, when Elizabeth's rebuke to Richard concludes: 'Harpe on it still shall I, till heart-strings breake', he responds, 'Harpe not on that string, Madam, that is past,' (4.4.295–6), as if to shift from heart-rending physicality to the metaphor of the harpy with only one note. In the Quarto text of *King Lear*, Edgar talks of how 'the strings of life, / Began to cracke' from the power of grief. Hoeniger summarizes the awkward medical evidence by suggesting that:

What Shakespeare does refer to more than once is two quite different notions that likewise were developed during the Middle Ages: the first is that passions like extreme grief, which produce excess of melancholy humor, cause the heart to contract by its cold, so that being in urgent need of blood and spirit, the heart draws them away from the body's extremities and the face grows pale as a result. The other notion is that shortly before death, the blood and spirits rush back into the heart in order to aid it in its battle against the cold.[24]

These issues are significant in *King Lear*, not least because, as Hoeniger argues, 'Nowhere else in Jacobean drama or the whole of English Renaissance literature is the emotional turmoil leading to madness presented with anything like the seriousness and understanding Shakespeare shows in *King Lear*.'[25] In the light of Lear's references to his heart and 'hysterica passio' Hoeniger amplifies his claim regarding Shakespeare's specific emphasis on medical conditions in *King Lear* by suggesting that: 'These are not, like the passage previously discussed, metaphorical statements, and the

---

22 F. David Hoeniger, *Medicine and Shakespeare in the English Renaissance* (London and Toronto, 1992), p. 146.

23 See for example, Charles Singer, *Galen on Anatomical Procedures: Translation of the Surviving Books* (Oxford, 1956), pp. 178–9.

24 Hoeniger, *Medicine and Shakespeare*, p. 149.

25 Ibid., p. 307.

commentaries on them by the play's editors prove unsatisfactory . . . Lear alludes to distressing physical sensations. The upset in his emotional state is now accompanied by turmoil and pain in his body.'[26] The unsatisfactory nature of existing commentary on physical as opposed to metaphorical, metaphysical or psychological symptoms is particularly acute in discussions of the end of *King Lear*.

A plausible interpretation of the dynamics of Lear's death involves the swift oscillation between his joy that Cordelia may still live, and his grief for her death. Although there are similarities between Gloucester and Lear, Gloucester dies despite or perhaps even because of the recognition that Edgar still lives and has been helping him. Lear explicitly states that if Cordelia were to live this might redeem all his sorrows. Two important features of the report of Gloucester's death contrast with Lear's death. Gloucester has been blinded and his heart is flawed and weak, whereas Shakespeare goes to some lengths to suggest that Lear's heart is strong. Gloucester's flawed heart, we are told, 'burst smilingly'. There is much compressed in this remarkable image, combining difficulties already sketched relating mind and grief in the breaking of a heart. Gloucester's sorrow is partially redeemed, and the image 'burst smilingly' suggests both the joining of joy and grief and an identity between physical suffering and Gloucester's emotional state. The suggestion that Gloucester smiles in death suggests a violent death which might nevertheless be reconciled with death from natural causes. The image seems designed to highlight the greater tragedy of Lear's death from more psychologically internal wounds and in a state of passionate strength. However beautiful the image of a heart that 'burst smilingly', it would be difficult for an actor to perform. The image is best left to the imagination. This is illustrated by the difficulty of staging the end of Ford's play *The Broken Heart*, where the actor playing Calantha somehow has to act sufficient to warrant the description offered by Bassanes of 'her smile in death' (5.3). The actor playing Antony, by comparison, is called on to perform extremes of heart-ache without dying, but is allowed recourse to words rather than gestures to convey his emotional and physical

state on hearing news of Cleopatra's death: 'The seuen-fold shield of *Aiax* cannot keepe / The battery from my heart. Oh cleaue my sides. / Heart, once be stronger then thy Continent, / Crack thy fraile Case' (4.15.38–41). Lear himself verbalizes his rages against Regan: 'you thinke Ile weepe, / No, Ile not weepe, I haue full cause of weeping, [*Storme and Tempest.*] But this heart shal break into a hundred thousand flawes / Or ere Ile weepe; O Foole, I shall go mad.' (2.4.456–9). Lear goes mad rather than weep or let his heart break into a hundred thousand flaws, but in the movement from Act 3 to 5, he comes through madness to reach the point where although he does not weep, his heart nevertheless breaks. Within these intimations of Jacobean physiology, Shakespeare distinguishes how different passions affect the heart. The final breaking of Lear's body reveals not the breaking of a weak heart, but of a tragically strong heart which will not weep.

By way of illustrating medical conceptions of the heart Shakespeare might have known, Thomas Wright's *The Passions of the Minde in Generall* (1604) provides the following striking description of the way the imagination sends data to the heart:

[When the imagination conceives the form of some object] by sense or memory . . . convenient or disconvenient to Nature, presently the purer spirits flocke from the brayne by certaine secret channels to the heart, where they pitch at the dore, signifying what an object was presented, conuenient or disconuenient for it. The heart immediately bendeth, either to prosecute it, or to eschew it: and the better to effect that affection, draweth other humours to helpe him, and so in pleasure concurre great store of pure spirits; in paine and sadnesses, much melancholy blood; in ire, blood and choller; and not onely (as I said) the heart draweth, but also the same soule that informeth the heart residing in other parts, sendeth the humours vnto the heart, to performe their seruice in such a worthie place . . . [27]

Further minor indications in the final scene of *King Lear* suggest that Lear's heart is finally broken as the

---

[26] Ibid., p. 320.
[27] Quoted in Ibid., p. 156.

passionate conflicts of his soul become too great for his heart. Hoeniger even suggests that his final moments could be diagnosed medically according to Jacobean physiology: 'in persons close to death, the spirit of the eye grows weak, so that the sight becomes dim or fuzzy. Hippocrates already noted that this is a sign of approaching death. Shakespeare alludes to it more than once, notably near the end of *Lear*, when the King, having difficulty recognizing Kent, refers to his "dull sight" and tells him, "Mine eyes are not o'the best".'[28] A similar semiotics of dying informs the death of King John, from his declaration that his 'heart is sicke' (5.3.4) to Prince Henry's explanation that: 'the life of all his blood / Is touch'd, corruptibly: and his pure braine / (Which some suppose the soules fraile dwelling house) / Doth by the idle Comments that it makes, / Fore-tell the ending of mortality.' (5.7.1–5). Much of the detailed description of the causes of King John's death can be read into the implied gestures and physicality reworked in the staging of Lear's death.

Understanding the playtexts of *King Lear* involves, then, a careful consideration of the implied acting of the tragic body and Shakespeare's choreography of death. The historically specific condition revealed by analysis is that the play suggests a carefully worked identity between the metaphorical sense of what it means to die of a broken heart and a more literal sense of the breaking of the heart within Elizabethan and Jacobean psychology and medicine. The interactions of body, text and performance cannot be separated without losing sight of the play's dynamics. Moreover, despite the tendency of modern medicine to believe in the objective qualities of diagnosis, this analysis begins to suggest how diagnosis of phenomena such as heart-attacks depends on a performative understanding of the body in which we are trained to recognize gestures as signs. If the body is performative to a degree that is tragic, then there is a kind of poetic theatricality at the heart of medical diagnosis. Theatre in this sense is a condition of the possibility of understanding what a heart-attack is and looks like. Although Shakespeare's tragedy of the body can be read and performed through a

poetics of the tragic body which is psychologically plausible, Shakespeare is also concerned to support the metaphors of psychological drama with a pathology of physical symptoms. These symptoms are part of the way the drama is enacted through the actions of bodies and cannot easily be brought into line with modern medical conceptions, particularly for passions of the mind and affairs of the heart. The historical specificity of the body in Shakespeare's drama poses difficult questions about the viability of the historicizing approaches of modern performance. This begins to suggest how the historical differences of Shakespeare's tragedies have been romanticized by poeticizing and dissociating the sensibilities dramatized by Shakespeare.

Shakespeare died on 23 April 1616. A few days before, on 16, 17 and 18 April, William Harvey gave his first set of lectures setting forth in public his view of the circulation of the blood. Harvey's account of the circulation of the blood was first published in Latin in 1628. His view of blood circulation and the heart as a mechanical pump which pumps blood around the body is broadly the same as that of modern medicine. Harvey's view, however, was initially greeted with considerable scepticism, not least because it overturned traditions of thought which traced their authority back to Galen and Aristotle. Challenges to the Aristotelian and Ptolemaic view of astral bodies suggested by Copernicus, Kepler and Galileo provoked comparable difficulties for the traditions of natural philosophy. Shakespeare appears not to have known of Harvey's work. Their near contemporaneity specifies the way Shakespeare's conception of physiology, especially of the heart and blood, involves a world-view different from those familiar to modern readers and audiences of Shakespeare. 'World-view' here is no exaggeration. Harvey's conception of the circulation of the blood shifted a range of political metaphors associated with the heart and with blood. Harvey, for example, dedicated his work *De Motu Cordis*, to Charles I, and in a translation

---

[28] Ibid., p. 96.

published in 1653 the opening words declare:

The Heart of creatures is the foundation of life, the Prince of all, the Sun of their Microcosm, on which all vegetation does depend, from whence all vigor and strength does flow. Likewise the King is the foundation of his Kingdoms, and the Sun of his Microcosm, the Heart of his Commonwealth, from whence all power and mercy proceeds . . . [29]

Four years after the execution of Charles I and seven years before the restoration of monarchy, the relation between king and commonwealth suggests the politically charged metaphors associated with hereditary principles and the physiology of the heart. The political symbolism involved is perhaps most familiar from the fable of the belly in Shakespeare's *Coriolanus* (1.1). As many of Shakespeare's tragedies show, the affairs of a king's heart are affairs of state. The special metaphorical and physical importance of the king's heart is also evident in Queen Elizabeth's famous if apocryphal remark about having the weak and feeble body of a woman, but the heart of a king, by implication the heart of her father Henry VIII. Although a staunch Royalist, Harvey challenged the prevailing scientific ignorance regarding the body, criticising poetic accounts of blood and spirit.[30] In *De Circulatione Sanguinis*, translated into English in 1653, Harvey argued, for example:

commonly ignorant persons when they cannot give a reason for any thing, they say presently, that it is done by Spirits, and bring in Spirits as performers in all cases; and like as bad Poets do bring in the gods upon the Scene by head and ears, to make the *Exit* and *Catastrophe* of their play.[31]

Harvey need not have looked far in the drama produced between 1580 up to the closure of the theatres in 1642 for instances where spirits are deployed as mysterious performers within a poetics of the body. The hindsight provided by Harvey highlights important historical dynamics regarding the tragic body in Shakespeare's theatre. Modern conceptions of the blood-stream and heart-attacks were not available to Shakespeare. There is a significant historical gulf between the imaginary bodies of Shakespearian society and subsequent scientific understandings of the body. Soon after Shakespeare's death, the poetics of the body in Jacobean drama was challenged, not only by the religious lobby, but also by new scientific conceptions of the body, conceptions which brought science and poetry into a conflict from which poetic drama has struggled to survive. Thomas Browne's *Pseudodoxia Epidemica,* for example, takes issue with the medical evidence regarding the death of Cleopatra in a spirit of inquiry which undermines the poetry of the asp.[32] The conflict between science and tragic drama might once have informed new ways of understanding the relation between physical and emotional suffering, but the poetics of the body offered by drama has become increasingly subservient to pseudo-scientific rhetoric and diagnosis.

Such problems can seem peripheral to Shakespearian tragedy, but Shakespeare's tragedies look different if the spiritual physiology of the body and its humours is foregrounded. The implied gestural repertoire in *Hamlet* requires some understanding of how Elizabethan and Jacobean audiences would have understood the states of mind and body experienced by Hamlet and Ophelia. Medical potions of various kinds are central to many Elizabethan and Jacobean tragic dramas, perhaps most notably in the strange and risky drugs which simulate death in *Romeo and Juliet*. Awkwardly physiological and psychological states of mind and body are central to *Macbeth* involving both Macbeth's

[29] William Harvey, *The Anatomical Exercises*: De Motu Cordis *and* De Circulatione Sanguinis *in English Translation*, ed. Geoffrey Keynes (New York, 1995), p. vii.

[30] For some discussion of Harvey's impact and reception, see Robert G. Frank, 'The Image of Harvey in Commonwealth and Restoration England', *William Harvey and his Age*, ed. Jerome J. Bylebyl (Baltimore and London, 1979), pp. 103–43.

[31] William Harvey, *The Anatomical Exercises*, p. 155.

[32] Thomas Browne, 'Of the Picture Describing the Death of Cleopatra', *Pseudodoxia Epidemica*, *The Works of Sir Thomas Browne*, ed. Charles Sayle (Edinburgh, 1927), 3 volumes, vol. 2, pp. 235–6 (Book 5, chapter 12).

hallucinations and Lady Macbeth's fate. *Julius Caesar* and *Othello* foreground physical states awkwardly analogous with modern conceptions of epilepsy. In Othello's case the unhinging of his mind and body works according to a physiology and psychology which is poetically plausible in terms of jealousy, but for which modern conceptions of psycho-sexual desire are profoundly anachronistic. In most of Shakespeare's tragic dramas, a combination of extreme mental and physical states is endured by the central tragic heroes, states which involve conceptions of the body which are alien to modern medicine. Shakespeare's plays are in part responsible for developing theatrical conventions which make it possible for the tragic body to become a public performance. The trials of kings are dramatized as mental and physical conditions afflicting the body of an actor in a cognitive arena which is also politically charged. The way the drama of the body is rendered plausible for modern audiences allows beliefs in the psychology and physiology of troubled spirits, ghosts and unhinged minds or hearts to be romanticized within poetics of performance and theatricality.

The medical and political dynamics of Shakespeare's playtexts and his dramatization of the tragic body are too often ignored. The specificity of Shakespeare's dramatic purposes can be measured against earlier representations of heartbreaking scenes. Some of the most intriguing dramatic precursors for the dynamics sketched here can be found in the final scene of Seneca's *Hercules Furens*, as Amphitryon and Hercules contemplate the heart-rending situation in which Hercules has killed his own children. The terms found for raging and wrathful hearts in Jasper Heywood's translation obscure the shifting physiology of 'pectus' and 'cor'. Amphitryon's cry: 'Ecce quam miserum metu / cor palpitat pectusque sollicitum ferit' (1298–9) becomes 'loe see how leaps with feare afright / My wretched harte, and how it doth my careful body smight.'[33] In the strange world of Thomas Preston's *Cambises* (*c.* 1569), the literalism of a heart-piercing arrow shot by Cambises is matched by the more metaphorical but no less

lethal arrows of Cupid, a mixture of lamentation and mirth captured in Ambidexter's immortal lines:

A, a, a, a! I cannot chuse but weepe for the queene! / Nothing but mourning now at the court there is seene. / Oh, oh, my hart, my hart! O, my bum will break! / Very greefe so torments me that scarce I can speake. (1133–6).[34]

The end of the second part of *Tamburlaine* provides more substantive material for comparison, not least through the medical description of Tamburlaine's sickness provided by the Physician:

>   my lord, this day is Criticall,
> Dangerous to those, whose Chrisis is as yours:
> Your Artiers which alongst the vaines conuey
> The liuely spirits which the heart ingenders
> Art partcht and void of spirit, that the soule
> Wanting those Organons by which it mooues,
> Can not indure by argument of art.[35]

Amid talk of bleeding, wounded and broken hearts, Amyras ascends to the chariot, saying lines rich with dramatic, physical and metaphysical ambiguity:

Heauens witnes me, with what a broken hart
And damned spirit I ascend this seat,
And send my soule before my father die,
His anguish and his burning agony.
(4591–4602 / 5.3.206–9)

Marlowe's drama sets the medical against the emotional significance of broken hearts to provoke political and theological reflection. Broken hearts figure in the final moments of many subsequent plays, but by the time of John Ford's plays *'Tis Pity She's A Whore* and *The Broken Heart*, the

---

[33] Citing the Loeb Classical Library edition, Seneca, *Tragedies* vol. 1, trans. Frank Justus Miller (Cambridge, 1979); and *Seneca: His Tenne Tragedies*, trans. Thomas Newton (1581) (London and New York, 1927), 2 vols., vol. 1, p. 51.

[34] Thomas Preston, *Cambises*, quoted from *Specimens of Pre-Shakesperean Drama*, ed. John Matthews Manly (Boston, 1897), 2 vols., vol. 2, p. 207.

[35] Christopher Marlowe, *Tamburlaine the Greate*, the second part, *The Works of Christopher Marlowe*, ed. C. F. Tucker Brooke (Oxford, 1910), p. 134, 4483–9. (5.3.91–7 in the Oxford edition edited by David Bevington and Eric Rasmussen.)

dramatic components are dissociated to the point of becoming mannered theatrical effects rather than searching provocations. In *'Tis Pity She's A Whore*, the sight of Annabella's heart on a dagger is so mournful as to break the heart of Florio, her father, but the contrast between the stage spectacle of an actual heart and Florio's sudden death from internal wounds lacks the intensity or purpose of *King Lear*. Similarly, at the end of *The Broken Heart*, what appears to be offered as a homage to the pathos of the final moments in *King Lear* comes close to burlesque as the emblematic significance of broken hearts is milked for one too many moral tag. Such moments in Ford nevertheless serve both to suggest the memorable specificity of the final moments of *King Lear* and to indicate how quickly Shakespeare's dramatic association of sensibilities became subject to a logic of dissociation.

What might seem like poetic licence in Shakespeare's tragedies can be understood, accordingly, as a critical and historical moment in the conflict between theatrical and medical dramatizations of the body and death. The historicity of the tragic body shows how the historical imagination of tragedy dramatizes the body as an embodiment of conflicts between nature and history. Unnatural death provides an allegory of history. Once the body and its physiology are subjected to historical shifts in our knowledge of biology, the human body of the tragic actor can no longer contain the physical and metaphysical extremes of nature and history in the same way. A conflict between poetic justice and scientific realism previously focused on the performance of a breaking heart becomes dissociated. The tragic implications that link this broken heart with the broken family and the broken state are no longer so resonant. This suggests a need for a healthy hermeneutics of suspicion when regarding what is living and dead in the playtexts of Shakespeare.

LEAR'S AFTERLIFE

JOHN J. JOUGHIN

I

It is true that, with respect to the disaster, one dies too late.   (Maurice Blanchot, *The Writing of the Disaster*)[1]

What does it mean to speak of the afterlife of a literary text? And why do some texts retain an enduring significance while others simply fade away? The survival of one text over another clearly depends on its sustained ability to unsettle existing conventions and to defamiliarize habitual perceptions, and in the case of canonical texts, such as Shakespeare, this is clearly a transformative potential which is retained over a considerable period of time. In this respect, of course, the afterlife of any given text is directly dependent on its critical life, its ability to draw generations of readers back to crucial points of analysis or interpretative ambiguity. In tracking back across Shakespeare's critical heritage and dipping into the closely contested editorial squabbles of years gone by, one unearths a series of textual disputes and dilemmas which open out into questions which remain unanswered to this day. In confronting the unlikely resurrection of Hermione at the end of *The Winter's Tale*, or the confusion surrounding the whereabouts of Lady Macbeth's 'missing children', the critic encounters a form of inexplicable alterity or otherness which exceeds his or her intellectual grasp, rather than providing the grounded repleteness of a 'meaningful' solution.[2] In the case of a dramatic text, the qualitative newness of a play's afterlife is clearly also linked in quite complex ways to our experience of a play in performance; often these are moments of affective intensity which linger on after the play and force us to re-evaluate our preconceptions concerning how an individual scene might be construed. In these and a multitude of other ways then, there is clearly an implicit *recognition* that the value of a literary text is that it serves to remind us of the limits of our comprehension even as it functions to sharpen our response. Yet the question remains: why do some literary afterlives prove more enduring than others? And if a key aspect of our engagement with literary and dramatic texts is the sense in which they continue to resist a definitive explanation, then why, or in what sense, can this aspect of literary experience still be said to remain distinctive or meaningful?

In some respects *Lear* remains the exemplary text through which to explore precisely these types of issues, insofar as our enduring fascination with the play seems to be inextricably linked to a sense of incomprehension and anxiety concerning its transgression of most conventional thresholds of taste and decorum. In other words, *Lear*'s position as a text which takes us beyond conventional

---

[1] Maurice Blanchot, *The Writing of the Disaster*, trans. Ann Smock (Lincoln and London, 1995), p. 4.

[2] Indeed, as I have argued elsewhere, it is precisely in escaping 'reasonable explanation' that Shakespeare's open-ended resistance to conceptual control might finally prove to be a far more crucial resource for critical thought, providing a form of access to the 'literary conditions' of philosophical questioning itself. See John J. Joughin, 'Philosophical Shakespeares: an introduction', in John J. Joughin, ed., *Philosophical Shakespeares* (London and New York, 2000), pp. 1–17.

expectations – sometimes to the point of in-credulity – has the merit of offering us a type of critical degree zero against which to press *any* claims to meaningful interpretation. Such is the extent of the 'wildness' of the play's formal disintegration that for many critics there is something simulta-neously implausible and unactable about Shake-speare's text which borders on barbarism. For the nineteenth-century critic Charles Lamb, *Lear* ap-proximates to a type of disaster 'painful and disgust-ing', 'beyond all art' and 'essentially impossible to be represented on a stage'.[3] And Lamb's disparage-ment is already hinted at in the Preface to Samuel Johnson's edition of the play, where he is compul-sively drawn back to *Lear*'s unreality, and repeat-edly confronts the dilemma of 'proving' its excep-tions. Here, for example, is Johnson on Gloucester's blinding:

I am not able to apologize with equal plausibility for the extrusion of Gloucester's eyes, which seems an act too horrid to be endured in dramatic exhibition, and such as must always compel the mind to relieve its distress by incredulity.[4]

For Johnson the fascination of witnessing these and other improbabilities is that from the very outset they transfix us *even as* they keep the audience in a state of perpetual tumult:

General Observation. The tragedy of *Lear* is deservedly celebrated among the dramas of Shakespeare. There is perhaps no play which keeps the attention so strongly fixed; which so much agitates our passions and interests our curiosity. The artful involutions of distinct interests, the striking opposition of contrary characters, the sudden changes of fortune, and the quick succession of events, fill the mind with a perpetual tumult of indignation, pity, and hope.[5]

Here and elsewhere in his Preface to the play, some-thing clearly snags on Johnson's reading conscious-ness as he witnesses a series of events which in their 'artful involution' defy 'reasonable explanation', even as they then serve to heighten his perception of the drama to the point of extreme discomfort. Well over a century later, A. C. Bradley confirms *Lear*'s surplus effect in similar terms, observing that the play is simply

too huge for the stage ... the immense scope of the work; the mass and variety of intense experience which it contains; the interpenetration of sublime imagination, piercing pathos, and humour almost as moving as the pathos; the vastness of the convulsion both of nature and of human passion.[6]

As Philip Armstrong comments, these and other critical encounters with the play testify to an 'ex-cess that overflows generic boundaries'; it is as if 'there must be in the play something more than the play, which returns upon the spectator'[7] – and here perhaps Johnson's use of the term '*involution*', both in the process of 'involving', but also in the literal sense of 'involute' – suggesting a 'tight coil' or 'curled spiral' waiting to recoil upon the spec-tator – might betray more than it could possibly know.

In this article I want to try to unpack the signif-icance of one such after-effect: the '*pietà*-like' im-age of Lear holding the dead Cordelia in his arms, a scene of 'pity and hope' which has continued to haunt critics, editors and spectators of the play alike. Such is the affective intensity of the scene

---

[3] Charles Lamb, 'On the Tragedies of Shakespeare (1810–11)', in Frank Kermode, ed., *Shakespeare: King Lear* (Basingstoke, 1992), pp. 42–3.

[4] Samuel Johnson, 'Preface and Notes to *King Lear* (1765)', in Kermode, ed., *Shakespeare: King Lear*, p. 28.

[5] Johnson, 'Preface', p. 27.

[6] A. C. Bradley, *Shakespearean Tragedy: Lectures on Hamlet, Oth-ello, King Lear, Macbeth* (Basingstoke, 1992), p. 211.

[7] See Philip Armstrong, 'Uncanny Spectacles: Psychoanalysis and the Texts of *King Lear*', *Textual Practice*, 8: 3 (1994), 414–34; p. 416. I'm grateful to Armstrong for alerting me to Bradley's comments. As Armstrong's essay demonstrates there is a clear link to psychoanalytic theory here, particularly in relation to the play's staging of 'excessive affect'. I do not pursue that line of enquiry myself, although I will want to follow Armstrong in touching briefly upon Freud's sense of the 'uncanny'. For the time being though I would want to note that a more explicit link could be established between psychoanalytical criticism and the province of aesthetics; Freud himself makes the connection clear enough when he argues in the open-ing lines of his essay that: 'aesthetics is understood to mean not merely the theory of beauty but the theory of the quali-ties of feeling'; see Sigmund Freud, 'The Uncanny', in James Strachey, ed., *Complete Psychological Works*, vol. 17, Standard Edition (London, 1963), pp. 217–56, p. 219.

that it seems to retain an almost totemic significance, particularly for directors of the play, who invariably recall the incident in their programme notes, as if to somehow exorcise its affect. Here, for example, is Barrie Rutter, founder and director of the Northern Broadsides theatre company, offering a 'behind the scenes' glimpse of the genesis of his recent touring production of the play:

So there we were in Salts Mills in 1993, rehearsing *Merry Wives*: pigeons flying around the wooden beams of the spinning lobby on the fifth floor, and Shakespeare's comedy giving us all a lot of fun. Suddenly, I stop rehearsals and say, 'Wouldn't it be terrific if Lear walked the whole length of this room carrying the dead Cordelia, saying "Howl, howl howl"?' I turned round and the merry wives with Mistress Quickly (Polly Hemingway, Elizabeth Estensen and Ishia Bennison) all had tears rolling down their cheeks. 'Yes', they croaked in unison.

I've hung on to that image for six years, and now have a chance to use it. As a touring company, of course, we have to adapt to different venues and each theatre or space will see the equivalent of 'the long walk'.[8]

Rutter's comments testify to the fact that in performance (even, indeed, in rehearsal), there is something 'out of joint', ob-scene or extra about the 'unbearable spectacle' of Lear carrying Cordelia across the stage at the end of the play. Rutter's 'advance recollection' of the scene confirms a type of 'spectral effect' insofar as Derrida reminds us that: 'a specter is always a *revenant*. One cannot control its comings and goings because *it begins by coming back*'.[9] An analogous form of temporal dislocation is already anticipated by the position of the scene in the play itself, so that, as R. A. Foakes reminds us, strictly speaking Cordelia's death comes '*after* the end' of the play (or at least follows the formal completion of the drama with the deaths of Goneril, Regan and Edmund);[10] on the other hand, without the episode that comes after and disrupts the play's formal unity, *Lear* would somehow be incomplete. These and other types of disturbance that 'add only to replace' confirm the contradictory logic of what Derrida would term the scene's supplementarity.[11] In the process, as Foakes observes: 'the final scene stretches out Lear's suffering beyond the point at

which to have died would have been fitting'.[12] Repeated but always singular, the recurring agony of Cordelia's death confirms *Lear* as a tale that can never be told but is in some sense crucial to our experience of the play.[13] The untimeliness of the scene and its excessive affect, as well as its proximity to death and the compulsion of critics to repeat their engagement with the scene ever since, clearly takes us into the territory of Freud's notion of the *Unheimlich* or uncanny.[14] It is quite simply a spectacle of 'inexpressible horror' or, as Lear himself puts it: 'Howl, howl, howl . . .'.

One should hardly be surprised, then, that in confronting the unendurable excess of the scene and in an attempt to make the play 'fit' for consumption, the solution of early editors and adaptors was to 'regularize' the ending of the play in order to confirm *Lear* as a formal comedy more in keeping with its original source material. Nahum Tate's 'New-modelling' of the story with Edgar and Cordelia married off as a 'celestial Pair' and Lear living on into happy retirement is the obvious example. Yet traditionally, from Tate's 1681 production onwards, even in its absence, the scene troubled critics and editors of the play. For Samuel

---

[8] Barrie Rutter, 'Rutter Writes', in programme notes for Northern Broadsides touring production of *King Lear* (1999), no pagination.

[9] Jacques Derrida, *Specters of Marx: The State of the Debt, the Work of Mourning and the New International*, trans. Peggy Kamuf (New York and London, 1994), p. 11 (Derrida's emphasis).

[10] R. A. Foakes, 'Introduction', in W. Shakespeare, *King Lear*, ed. R. A. Foakes (Walton-on-Thames, 1997), p. 72; also compare Stephen Booth, *King Lear, Macbeth, Indefinition and Tragedy* (New Haven, 1983), p. 11.

[11] Jacques Derrida, *Of Grammatology*, trans. Gayatri Chakravorty Spivak (Baltimore and London, 1976), pp. 141–64, and compare Andrew Bennett and Nicholas Royle who offer an accessible and provocative overview of the paradoxical logic of literary endings in their *Introduction to Literature, Criticism and Theory* (Hemel Hempstead, 1999), pp. 251–9; see esp. pp. 253–4.

[12] R. A. Foakes, *Hamlet versus Lear: Cultural Politics and Shakespeare's Art* (Cambridge, 1993), p. 211.

[13] Again compare Bennett and Royle, *Introduction to Literature*, p. 254.

[14] Freud, 'The Uncanny', *passim*.

Johnson, for example, there is a lasting sense of injustice surrounding Cordelia's death, the reverberations of which carry far beyond the theatrical experience itself:

Shakespeare has suffered the virtue of Cordelia to perish in a just cause, contrary to the natural ideas of justice, to the hope of the reader, and, what is yet more strange, to the faith of the chronicles . . . A play in which the wicked prosper and the virtuous miscarry may doubtless be good, because it is a just representation of the common events of human life; but since all reasonable beings naturally love justice, I cannot be easily persuaded that the observation of justice makes a play worse; or that, if other excellencies are equal, the audience will not always rise better pleased from the final triumph of persecuted virtue.

In the present case the public has decided. Cordelia, from the time of Tate, has always retired with victory and felicity. And, if my sensations could add anything to the general suffrage, I might relate, I was many years ago so shocked by Cordelia's death that I know not whether I ever endured to read again the last scenes of the play till I undertook to revise them as editor.[15]

In teasing out the implications of Johnson's response I would want to argue that something like the residue of the supplementary affect we noted above now re-surfaces in a critical context, and that as a consequence Johnson's appeal to 'the natural idea of justice' begins to sound a bit strained. The moment comes when Johnson the critic adopts the position of a spectator. Crucially, the critic cannot help conceding that in performance, just as the scene is unfit, it fits – so even as Cordelia's death scene flouts any 'justifiable' moral schema, it remains 'a *just* representation of the common events of human life'. In some respects, then, the episode constitutes a potentially transgressive or 'critical' location precisely *because* of its lack of fit or indeterminacy. In the process it is as if the disjointure between moral ideal and dramatic practice itself remarks a type of discordant 'truth' about the actual predicament of moral life. Of course the predictable disavowal follows, insofar as Johnson is quick to remind the reader that 'all reasonable beings naturally love justice'; yet in the course of attempting to

justify his own position Johnson feels bound to concede that:

this conduct [suffering the virtue of Cordelia to perish in a just cause, contrary to the natural ideas of justice] is justified by the Spectator, who blames Tate for giving Cordelia success and happiness in his alteration and declares that, in his opinion, *the tragedy has lost half its beauty.*[16]

Somewhat confusingly, then, it might be said that there are two types of 'truth' to be had here: the idealized 'truth' which depends on the formalized convention of Cordelia's recovery; and the disconcerting authenticity of the unfit yet somehow more 'just' spectacle of her 'perish [-ing] in a just cause'. The reference to the justification 'by the Spectator' is now made even more explicit, and as soon as Johnson switches to this perspective he finds himself admitting that the playwright's work sustains its relative exclusivity (its 'tragic beauty' if you like), by 'authenticating' a claim to validity that is somehow unique. The fact that this truth claim simultaneously also exceeds the restrictive demands of empirical truth which governed the neo-classical criticism of the period is, I would want to argue, precisely the point. Johnson's remarks serve to remind us that, in performance, Cordelia's death presents us with a type of untheorizable excess; such moments threaten the critic with a relinquishment of intellectual control – the mind full of 'perpetual torment' no doubt – yet it is precisely here that the ethical demand of the play is finally disclosed. The event-like relation of performance constitutes an irruptive excess – something that 'happens' outside an a priori grid of expectations and refuses the foreclosure of conventional attempts to explain it away. As a result 'justice' is revealed as a type of acategorical category: one which at once complies with and deviates from the formal aesthetics of which it is part.

As we have seen, witnessed in performance the force of this encountered otherness ensures that the

[15] Johnson, 'Preface', 27–9; p. 28.
[16] Johnson, 'Preface'., 28, (Johnson's emphasis).

viewing subject experiences a sense of ungrounding and disorientation, so that for Rutter we might recall that the dislocation of the 'long walk' recurs outside of the rehearsal space ('Suddenly I stop rehearsals'), though still somehow within it, as – 'in character' but beside themselves with pity – the 'merry wives' shed tears and croak their affirmation of witness. As Robert Eaglestone observes: 'It is in these [uncanny] moments when our sense of our selves and our relation to the *logos* is interrupted and put into question that the ethics of literature are at their clearest.'[17] In occupying the same time as the characters, we effectively 'live through' a sequence of moments with them, and while we cannot actually put ourselves in the 'presence' of characters during performance, in acknowledging their specificity as particular individuals, as Stanley Cavell reminds us: 'we are in, or can put ourselves in, their *present*'.[18] Characters and audience confront this form of the encountered other on an almost nightly basis. Moreover, in performance, the unendurable excess of incidents like Cordelia's death retains a 'complex and shaming power': a sense of witness, for the audience that views them.

We might begin to speak here then of the ethics of interpretation, in a twofold sense: not just in the sense of our encounter with otherness in performance where we are presented with what we might term after Levinas and Derrida 'the irreducible otherness of the other', but also in terms of the act of criticism itself, insofar as it demonstrates a willingness to 'promote' the unexpected or the *unheimlich* 'within the material it examines'.[19] Alert to those same 'artful involutions' that continue to disrupt and plague philosophical idealism with the very impossibility of their representation – in endlessly repositioning us and in being open to a form of otherness which both attracts and defies our comprehension – this process of interpretation is necessarily open-ended, for as Eaglestone puts it: 'There can be no final reading, no last word.'[20] In this regard, an ethical reading is also, as Maurice Blanchot reminds us, an act of testimony, a form of reading which is no longer passive, but is passivity's reading:

Finally, there is the reading that is no longer passive, but is passivity's reading. It is without pleasure, without joy; it escapes both comprehension and desire. It is like the nocturnal vigil, that 'inspiring' insomnia when, all having been said, 'Saying' is heard, and the testimony of the last witness pronounced.[21]

Blanchot's incomprehension in the face of disaster is, perhaps, not so far removed from Johnson's 'perpetual tumult of indignation, pity, and hope', yet even as we live on *after*, or survive the disaster itself, we might ask what type of justice would actually be possible in such a violently unjust world? In the case of Cordelia's death, the ethical demand of the scene seems to lurk within the uncanniness of the acts of testimony we have briefly reviewed above, even as they then serve as a palpable reminder that in some profound sense in being drawn back as witnesses we are both absent and present – this is doubtless why the scene continues to transfix us so powerfully. Yet is it possible that our continued *fascination* with *Lear*'s closing scene – its haunting afterlife, if you like – almost sustains a 'micrology' of our relation to the play itself, that each time the scene is performed, it secretes the truth of an ethical exigency – a 'felt contact at a distance' – that offers, and then refuses us, the chance of redemption? These moments of affective intensity clearly 'live on' in performance and thus in a fundamental sense constitute the 'afterlife' of Shakespeare's play. Yet in merely testifying to the fact that we continue to survive the unendurable, can *Lear*'s 'artful involutions' then still be said to retain their transformative

---

17 Robert Eaglestone, *Ethical Criticism: Reading After Levinas* (Edinburgh, 1997), p. 175.

18 See Stanley Cavell, *Disowning Knowledge in Six Plays of Shakespeare* (Cambridge, 1987), p. 108, Cavell's emphasis. I'm also directly indebted here to Stephen Mulhall's exposition of Cavell in *Stanley Cavell: Philosophy's Recounting of the Ordinary* (Oxford, 1994), esp. pp. 198–9.

19 I am grateful to Terence Hawkes for clarifying this distinction; compare his incisive account of 'The Heimlich Manoeuvre', *Textual Practice*, 8: 2 (1994), 302–16; cf. esp. p. 312.

20 Eaglestone, *Ethical Criticism*, p. 179.

21 Maurice Blanchot, *The Writing of the Disaster*, trans. Ann Smock (Lincoln and London, 1995), p. 101; also cited in Eaglestone, *Ethical Criticism*, p. 175.

potential against all the odds, or is there simply a limit to the play's afterlife? And – to return to the question I opened with – how, in these circumstances, can *Lear* then still be said to remain distinctive or meaningful?

II

We come after, and that is the nerve of our condition.
(George Steiner, *Language and Silence*)[22]

These questions arguably become even more pressing for a modern audience, who 'live on' after the horrific events of the twentieth century. After all, in this context, as R. A. Foakes reminds us, *Lear*'s apparently 'passive indifference to suffering' is all too depressingly familiar:

Its [*King Lear*'s] exposure of the horror of torture and suffering no longer seems outrageous in the context of concentration camps, napalm bombs, anti-personnel mines, and acts of terrorism such as have become familiar in report to everyone . . . It has seemed to some the play of our time in being open to nihilistic interpretation as showing not the potentially heroic journey or pilgrimage of Man through life, but rather a progression towards despair or mere nothingness.[23]

From Foakes's perspective then, the danger is that by now, however sympathetically we might view the play, we are simply inured to *Lear*'s displays of cruelty. Yet ultimately, this seems to me to be a rather complacent position to take. In a certain sense Foakes is clearly right to remind us that *Lear* is 'to some the play of our time in being open to nihilistic interpretation', but might this not also run the risk of universalizing an encounter which finally resists universalization? While there has been a tendency for critics to suggest that our culture could be 'valued' according to the nature of our engagement with this play alone – and here of course Foakes's sense of *Lear* as our contemporary consciously echoes Jan Kott's hugely influential *Shakespeare Our Contemporary* – I would want to argue that this actually oversimplifies the nature of our relation to the play. Paradoxically of course, as I've already suggested above, the fact is that Shakespeare's

play constitutes a type of exemplary text precisely *because* it continues to remind us of the limits of our attempts to engage in meaningful interpretation. In teasing out the implications of this, we might push the argument on a stage further and say that the paradox is that *Lear* can still remain 'valuable' for us *only* in its wider perception that modern culture is increasingly found to be lacking in value; and thus, in the same process, *Lear*'s 'value' is somehow simultaneously to survive the experience of outliving its own utility. In this respect the notion of *Lear* being 'our contemporary' clearly stands in need of some fuller interrogation, especially insofar as it echoes recent philosophical debates concerning the problem of nihilism. There are several possible ways of responding to nihilism, yet *Lear*'s delineation of the problem comes uncannily close to the experience of those philosophers who suffer a sense of belatedness in surviving the catastrophic history in which they continue to find themselves implicated. For thinkers such as Theodor Adorno for example, 'living on' after events such as the Holocaust, is bound up with a sense of unjustifiable survivorhood and in such a context there is something inhuman, not just in surviving disaster, but in attempting to theorize it. In the opening section of his 'Meditations on metaphysics' in *Negative Dialectics* Adorno is forced to wonder

whether after Auschwitz you can go on living – especially whether one who escaped by accident, one who by rights should have been killed, may go on living.[24]

For Adorno then, the 'despair and or mere nothingness' to which Foakes alludes is at once a tangible yet still somehow 'unreal' feature of our modern existence. In these circumstances, 'survival' is directly complicit with an epistemological regime it outlives, but which it now also in some sense necessarily continues to inhabit. For those

---

[22] George Steiner, *Language and Silence* (London, 1985), p. 22.
[23] Foakes, 'Introduction', 2.
[24] Theodor W. Adorno, *Negative Dialectics*, trans. E. B. Ashton (London, 1990), p. 363.

who practise philosophy this means negotiating the realization that philosophy was always already non-redemptive; it 'lives on', we live on (precisely) because 'the moment to realise it was missed'. Or as Adorno puts it:

survival calls for the coldness, the basic principles of bourgeois subjectivity, without which there could have been no Auschwitz; this is the drastic guilt of him who was spared. By way of atonement he will be plagued by dreams such as that he is no longer living at all, that he was sent to the ovens in 1944 and his whole existence since has been imaginary, an emanation of the insane wish of a man killed twenty years earlier.

Thinking men and artists have not infrequently described a sense of being not quite there, of not playing along, a feeling as if they were not themselves at all, but a kind of spectator.[25]

For those who 'come after', then, bearing witness once again confirms the uncanny sense 'of being not quite there'. And again of course, it is difficult not to hear in these lines the key trope of Lear's own journey, a character who also crucially in some sense lives life belatedly, and for whom enduring finitude entails the discovery of an identity which is now directly predicated on the loss of identity:

LEAR...Who is it that can tell me who I am?
FOOL Lear's shadow.[26]

In either form, survival constitutes a type of haunting and Lear is a shadow or a shade of what he once was. Fittingly enough, of course, in *Lear* characters reside 'out o'th'grave' having long outstayed their welcome. In such a world as this, the only wonder is that, as Kent puts it on the king's eventual demise: 'he hath endured so long; / He but usurped his life' (5. 3. 315–16). Indeed, in some sense, as Francis Barker reminds us, under the conditions existing in the play: 'one is never more truly oneself than when speaking of oneself as not oneself'.[27] In 'coming after' we are confronted with a play which refuses the comfort of narrative continuity and settled identity, and in a world lacking the 'existential balm' of religion Shakespearian tragedy already offers us a shadow narrative of the despair and nihilism of late modernity.[28] The

shared 'disappointment' of a post-religious world and of a post-metaphysical philosophy is one of a spectral afterlife where there is an inability to reconcile metaphysical speculation with experience.[29] We are presented instead with a world of acute discontinuity and self-misrecognition and the failure of religion or philosophy to make any significant or practical difference. The lack of an antidote to this situation takes us to the precipice of what Nietzsche would term 'the last form of nihilism' which: 'includes disbelief in any metaphysical world and forbids itself any belief in a *true* world', in having reached this standpoint:

one grants the reality of becoming as the *only* reality, forbids oneself every kind of clandestine access to afterworlds and false divinities – but *cannot endure this world though one does not want to deny it*.[30]

In this climate, as the British philosopher Simon Critchley puts it, the challenge for a newly

---

[25] *Ibid.*

[26] William Shakespeare, *King Lear*, ed. Foakes, 1. 4. 221–2. All subsequent quotations from the play are taken from this edition.

[27] Francis Barker, *The Culture of Violence: Essays on Tragedy and History* (Manchester, 1993), p. 15.

[28] Though of course, 'historicizing' *Lear*'s percipient untimeliness presents us with another set of problems. In 'coming after' we are clearly confronted with a memory which refuses sequential narrativization. As such, we are confronted with what Lyotard terms an 'improper achronolgical effect', one which is nonetheless entirely contemporary in that it results from the *continued shock* of 'unassimilated traumatic experience'; see Jean-François Lyotard, *Heidegger and 'The Jews'*, trans. Andreas Michel and Mark Roberts (Minneapolis, 1990), p. 16. For a fuller explication of Lyotard, to which I am directly indebted here, compare Nicola King, ' "We come after": Remembering the Holocaust', in Roger Luckhurst and Peter Marks, eds., *Literature and the Contemporary: Fictions and Theories of the Present* (Harlow, 1999), pp. 94-108, p. 97; I am also grateful to King for suggesting the epigraph for this section of the paper.

[29] See Simon Critchley, *Very Little . . . Almost Nothing* (London and New York, 1997), pp. 1–28, esp. p. 2, I am indebted here and above to Critchley for providing some key distinctions concerning the problem of nihilism.

[30] Friedrich Nietzsche, *The Will to Power*, trans. W. Kaufmann and R. J. Hollingdale (New York, 1968), p. 13; also cited by Critchley in *Very Little*, pp. 7–8.

attenuated philosophical enterprise is to locate 'a meaning to human finitude without recourse to anything that transcends that finitude'.[31] Baldly stated, there is no redemption, nor can there be, at least not for us, not yet . . .

Yet enduring finitude means that there is always an unsettled moment of the 'post' or an aftermath and in raising contemporary questions concerning our disenchantment with metaphysics, even the most recent adaptations of the play continue to confirm Foakes's sense of *Lear*'s 'openness' to nihilistic interpretation. Unsurprisingly perhaps, these reworkings of the Lear myth are often tales of survival and traumatic memory too. In Jane Smiley's *A Thousand Acres*, for example, amidst a revisionist reading which transports Lear to the mid-West of America we are offered a sub-text concerning the 'recovered memory' of paternal abuse and incest,[32] while in the recent Dogme 95 film *The King is Alive* (2000) directed by Kristian Levring, a group of tourists find themselves abandoned in a disused mining village in the middle of the Namibian desert. In a setting which aptly evokes a sense of depletion and exhausted resource, the survivors attempt a memorial reconstruction of *Lear*, presumably in an attempt to utilize drama in order to sustain a mutually recognizing community. Yet the power of performance is reduced, as one unwilling participant is told: 'You don't have to worry, you know. Nobody has to fall in love and everybody gets to die in the end.' Digitally shot with hand-held cameras according to Dogme house-rules, the film's visual feel accentuates intimacy but also conveys the alienation and distance of docudrama. And in a further twist we are confronted with a group of recognizably Shakespearian actors, including David Calder and Janet McTeer, in the process of learning to unlearn their parts, characters who literally might be said to play along 'by not playing along'.

In several recent reviews *The King is Alive* is cast as resembling Beckett, thus indirectly substantiating Foakes's observation that Shakespearian tragedy might still more properly be construed as 'a kind of parallel' to the twentieth-century Theatre of the Absurd. For, as Foakes rightly implies, not the least

disconcerting aspect of *Lear*'s timely untimeliness is that it could just as easily be read alongside plays like *Waiting for Godot* and *Endgame*.[33] Shakespeare's dramaturgy, like Beckett's, is littered with characters that seem to teeter on the abyss of survival, endlessly enduring an 'experience of the limit': characters who are 'unable to go on, unable not to go on',[34] and where the need to confront an unreconciled gap between theory and practice, action and word, in part also closely mirrors the practical failure of philosophy or art to change or transform the world. Moreover, in the case of each playwright – Beckett and Shakespeare – we might say that we are faced with the possibility that drama has lost its therapeutic function and its ability to rekindle community.

In the course of contemplating these questions in their Shakespearian context one is inevitably drawn back here to the seminal work of Stanley Cavell (another early reader of Beckett's *Endgame*) who in the very midst of his groundbreaking analysis of *Lear* offers the following despairing aside on the relation that 'currently' obtains between tragedy and modern life:

Since we are ineluctably actors in what is happening, nothing can be present to us to which we are not present. Of course we can still know, more than ever, what is going on. But then we always could, more or less. What we do not now know is what there is to acknowledge, what it is I am to make present, what I am to make myself present to. I know there is inexplicable pain and death everywhere, and now if I ask myself why I do nothing the answer must be, I choose not to.[35]

---

[31] See Critchley, *Very Little, passim.*

[32] For a fuller exposition see Roger Luckhurst, 'Memory Recovered / Recovered Memory', in Luckhurst and Marks, eds, *Literature and the Contemporary*, pp. 80–93, esp. 86–7.

[33] Foakes, in Foakes, ed., *King Lear*, p. 2.

[34] Again compare Critchley, *Very Little*, p. 23.

[35] Cavell, *Disowning Knowledge*, pp. 116–17, also cited in Richard Halpern, *Shakespeare Among the Moderns* (Ithaca and London, 1997), p. 108. Elsewhere in the *Lear* essay of course Cavell draws a rather different distinction between spectatorship and character and the ability of the theatre to disclose the uneven (and potentially redemptive relationship) between the theatricalization and literalization of our relations with others. What though, I wonder, would Cavell

Caught up (at a distance) in the same cold-war hostilities as Beckett and Kott, in its original form, as Richard Halpern reminds us, Cavell's *Lear* essay inevitably 'bears the marks of its historical moment (1967)' as 'the death and suffering to which Cavell refers is exemplified primarily, as he makes clear, in the Vietnam War'[36] – scenes of suffering which, we might remember at the time, appeared on television screens on an almost nightly basis, and to which, as Halpern adds: 'as citizen and intellectual he [Cavell] feels opposed – yet in regard to which he finds himself choosing the course of paralysis or inaction'.[37]

Yet curiously, of course, insofar as the problem of 'spectatorship' to which Cavell alludes here relates to a form of distance, it is simultaneously a form of distance which results from 'our' almost omnipresent proximity to suffering – a proximity which in its very intimacy breeds a type of passivity. In such a context there is something indifferent in the encounter itself. And the tragedy of course is that, in the very act of watching, as Cavell reminds us, 'we absent ourselves' from incidents of pain and death. In short, even in 'seeing' we could ultimately be said to avoid the confusion of contact, for as Cavell himself puts it: 'What we do not now know is what there is to acknowledge, what it is I am to make present, what I am to make myself present to.'[38] In glossing the fuller drift of this passage from Cavell, Richard Halpern offers the following summation:

Modernity, Cavell argues, has inverted the traditional relation between tragic theatre and the world. Theater used to be a privileged place in which we could witness human suffering without actually being obliged to intervene in it; we could be, as Cavell puts it, ethically 'present' to tragic characters without actually being in their presence. Now, however, passive indifference to suffering has become the norm, and so theatrical spectatorship is no longer a special case but depressingly ubiquitous.[39]

There is no simple outside to this situation, even as we continue to inhabit it. Yet for a culture which is in some sense post-metaphysical the key problem remains that, as Cavell's comments imply (and as we saw earlier with Adorno), philosophy and art are now inevitably complicit with the very process they would otherwise be expected to overcome. During his reading of *Lear* Cavell maintains his own complex sense of individual indictment, maintaining a watchful almost Adornian-like vigilance over the fact that in this context there is something inhuman not just in surviving disaster, but in surviving disaster and failing to confront it.[40] In this respect then, as Jay Bernstein notes, Adorno, Cavell, Beckett (*and* I would want to add *Lear*) each indirectly circle around similar problems:

How can art stop being a pain-killer yet be appropriate to what makes all response inappropriate and still, still authenticate the call of the things of this unworldly world? How can it make a promise that is not complicit with what has undone all promises or kept them too well?[41]

If actual events have now shattered the basis upon which the task of thinking might be reconciled with experience,[42] and if theatre in its modernity falls short of empathy, the problem remains that if we choose the path of paralysis and inaction we must also finally absent ourselves from pain and death. I would simply wish to counter that, in pushing this oscillation between contact and distance to another kind of ultimate limit, in these circumstances Cordelia's death nevertheless remains a 'special case'.

---

make of Levring's *The King is Alive* which, in self-consciously aping the so called reality-TV format of survival shows like *Big Brother* and *Survivor*, is already all too literally implicated in dramatizing the theatricalization of its relationships with others. This makes for a particularly complex turn of Cavell's sense of the theatricalization of existence which I have not got time to examine here.

36 Halpern, *Shakespeare Among the Moderns*, p. 108.
37 Halpern, *Shakespeare Among the Moderns*, p. 108.
38 Cavell, *Disowning Knowledge*, pp. 116–17.
39 Halpern, *Shakespeare Among the Moderns*, p. 108.
40 Although Halpern insists that 'Cavell's use of "we"... both indicts him as an individual and absolves him as a mere participant in a generalized abdication', see Halpern, *Shakespeare Among the Moderns*, p. 109.
41 See Jay Bernstein, 'Philosophy's Refuge: Adorno in Beckett', in David Wood, ed., *Philosophers' Poets* (London and New York, 1990), pp. 177–91; p. 183.
42 Compare Critchley, *Very Little*, passim

III

Last witness, end of history, close of a period, turning point, crisis – or, end of (metaphysical) philosophy.
(Maurice Blanchot, *The Writing of the Disaster*)[43]

In the course of 'opposing' a redemptive reading of *Lear* Stanley Cavell offers the following observation:

Is this a Christian play? The question is very equivocal. When it is answered affirmatively, Cordelia is viewed as a Christ figure whose love redeems nature and transfigures Lear. So far as this is intelligible to me, I find it false both to the experience of the play and to the fact that it *is* a play. *King Lear* is not illustrated theology (anyway, which theology is thought to be illustrated, what understanding of atonement, redemption, etc., is thought to be figured?), and nature and Lear are not touched, but run out. If Cordelia exemplifies Christ, it is at the moment of crucifixion, not resurrection.[44]

Without wanting to reinstall a theological component to suffering (although, doubtless, as Cavell's comments suggest, there almost always inevitably is one), I would want to argue that in the face of contemporary 'indifference to suffering', our enduring fascination with the image of Cordelia in Lear's arms is that, against all the odds, it continues to sustain a form of (secular) transfiguration from which there is no option of turning away, and which still seems to touch us with what Blanchot evocatively terms a 'grasping contact':

The image
    Why fascination? Seeing implies distance, the decision that causes separation, the power not to be in contact and to avoid the confusion of contact. Seeing means that this separation has nonetheless become an encounter. But what happens when what you see, even though from a distance, seems to touch you with a grasping contact, when the manner of seeing is a sort of touch, when seeing is a *contact* at a distance? What happens when what is seen imposes itself on your gaze, as though the gaze had been seized, touched, put in contact with appearance? Not an active contact, not the initiative and action that might still remain in a true touch; rather, the gaze is drawn, absorbed into an immobile movement and a depth without depth. What is given to us by contact at a distance is the image, and fascination is passion for the image.

What fascinates us, takes away our power to give it meaning, abandons its 'perceptible' nature, abandons the world, withdraws to the near side of the world and attracts us there, no longer reveals itself to us and yet asserts itself in a presence alien to the present in time and to presence in space . . . Fascination is . . . vision that is no longer the possibility of seeing, but the impossibility of not seeing, impossibility that turns into seeing, that preserves – always and always – in a vision that does not end: a dead gaze, a gaze that has become the ghost of an eternal vision.[45]

Blanchot's 'contact at a distance' is not an 'active contact' but neither is it the passive proximity of indifference rehearsed in Cavell's sense of our own individual participation in a 'generalized abdication' from responsibility. Crucially, as Jay Bernstein reminds us, for Blanchot, in yielding 'a passion for the image', fascination confronts us with 'the precedence of the object' or, as Blanchot himself puts it, 'seeing is a sort of touch'.[46] In its very duration the image of Lear holding Cordelia yields something of this complex phenomenology to its audience, manifesting 'a depth without depth' which only in the actual process of closing unfolds itself on uncertain surfaces, as a series of pressing intangibles which barely disclose themselves as: 'breath, mist and stain(ing)' or the 'chance' of a 'feather stirring' (cf. 5. 3. 260, 264). Such is the auratic potential of the scene that it fixes our gaze, yet insofar as it demands our attention, it does so without ever quite relinquishing itself to us, and in doing so it 'imposes itself on the gaze' as an enduring image.

43 Blanchot, *The Writing of the Disaster*, p. 101.
44 Cavell, *Disowning Knowledge*, p. 73.
45 Maurice Blanchot, *The Gaze of Orpheus* in *The Station Hill Blanchot Reader: Fiction and Literary Essays*, ed. George Quasha (Barrytown, New York, 1998), pp. 412–13; also cited in Jay Bernstein, 'Fragment, Fascination, Damaged Life: "The Truth about Hedda Gabler" ', in Max Pensky, ed., *The Actuality of Adorno: Critical Essays on Adorno and the Postmodern* (Albany, New York, 1997), pp. 154–82; pp. 156–7. I should note that my understanding of Blanchot (though not my reading of *Lear*) is considerably indebted to Jay Bernstein at this point and in the arguments that follow, cf. esp. pp. 156–8.
46 Bernstein, 'Fragment, Fascination, Damaged Life', p. 157.

In the process it is as though 'the gaze had been seized, touched, put in contact with appearance'.[47]

Of course, in some sense the scene offers us a distorted perspective, and in the process of breathing life into a stone, the brutal fact of the matter might well be that she dies and he lives. Yet Lear's preoccupation with Cordelia's corpse also confirms an 'aestheticization of suffering' which, whilst it is barely recoverable, and remains beyond comprehension, still exists in such close proximity and in such extreme circumstances that the manner of 'seeing' itself asserts an irreducible alterity which in its partial redemption sustains the 'touch' of the other. And the distinction between 'seeing' and reading remains crucial here, as in performance, beyond the detached objectivities of editorial hindsight, what fixes us is precisely the memory of what Samuel Johnson protests himself unable to rewitness and yet is bound to disavow: 'I was many years ago so shocked by Cordelia's death that I know not whether I ever endured to read again the last scenes of the play till I undertook to revise them as editor.' We might say that Cordelia's death confirms what Blanchot terms 'the impossibility of not seeing', so that however much Johnson opts for it, the 'choice' of turning away does not ever really enter into the equation. Even as fascination maintains its endless recurring 'contact at a distance', then, it is also inextricably intertwined with what Blanchot elsewhere terms last-witness, and which in the present extract confirms itself as a form of spectatorship which 'asserts itself in a presence alien to the present in time and to presence in space', from which finally there is no absenting oneself. In short, our fascination with Cordelia's death confirms the 'conduct' of turning and last witness as an incessant testament which is just and fitting though never quite *justified* by the spectator. It preserves 'a vision that does not end', an image which Rutter 'hangs on to for six years'. Its moment of memorial is momentous, and it remains a compulsive trope both in terms of the decisive or critical point it retains in the play's overall dramatic structure, but also in its confirmation of an 'ethical exigency' which eventually proves impossible to avoid or eliminate.

IV

Finished, it's finished, nearly finished, it must be nearly finished . . .   (Samuel Beckett, *Endgame*)[48]

Art or philosophy, or any form of practice is bound to be inadequate, an inappropriate response to the now infinite disaster . . . but we are always standing somewhere, talking; so winding up, having done with art and meaning is less easy than it appears: the habit of meaning is hard to break. Maybe, but who are we to say, the task of ending meaning is infinite too (maybe that is the disaster – too), an uncompletable task; perhaps we can be stopped, but not finish.   (Jay Bernstein on *Endgame*)[49]

In some form, one might say that *Lear*'s Theatre of the Absurd, like Beckett's, ends as it begins, by eking out its own utter sense of incompletion. The untimeliness of Beckett's world, and of 'our' world, is almost wholly in keeping with *Lear*'s. In the case of *Endgame* we are confronted with an apocalyptic terrain to rival *Lear*'s, as we witness a 'master' and his 'servant' entombed in what appears to be a type of nuclear bunker where the survivors hang on to the last vestiges of 'human contact'. And in Beckett's drama, as in Shakespeare's, while writing the disaster maintains its endless unendurability, it also sustains its own form of 'waning intensity'.[50] Amidst their overwhelming sense of disenchantment the plays somehow retain an ethical impulse, so that a utopian glimmer that things could be otherwise, however paltry, just about remains intact. In this respect, at least, as Bernstein observes: 'having done with art and meaning is less easy than it appears: the habit of meaning is hard to break'.

For my part though, the strain at the end of *Lear* also sustains a utopian impulse and in doing so is eventually probably more Adornian than Cavellian in terms of its overall ethical trajectory. Adorno's thought, like Beckett's, is often caricatured as securing nothing more or less than a fatalistic pessimism of the intellect, yet even amidst

---

47 Again compare Bernstein, 'Fragment'.
48 Samuel Beckett, *Endgame* (London, 1964), p. 12.
49 Bernstein, 'Philosophy's Refuge', p. 183
50 I owe this phrase to Critchley, *Very Little*, p. 27.

disenchantment and indifference, the 'seismic' potential of Adorno's philosophy resides in its willingness to sustain a 'standpoint of redemption' against all the odds.[51] For Adorno, as for Cavell, it is true to say that there is eventually 'no conceivable standpoint from which the disaster might be named or articulated',[52] yet as Max Pensky reminds us, in addressing those things that fall by the wayside Adorno's work simultaneously responds to 'an ethical intuition, according to which the repressed other – the nonidentical – can reappear within the ruins of a dominant discourse' and the wreckage of its unassimilated material.[53] Eventually then we might say that Beckett's art, like Adorno's philosophy, 'survives its own apocalypse' in that, although art and philosophy will always come too late, in the very process of witnessing its own demise it holds on to the possibility that 'one day it will arrive in time'.[54] In this respect, for Adorno, as Simon Critchley puts it:

the reality or unreality of redemption hardly matters. What is important is the messianic demand [of redemption] and not whether this demand is underwritten by some guarantee of redemption.[55]

Adorno of course does not attempt a reading of *Lear*, yet if we were to extend the logic of his position, in reading the runes of Shakespeare's play in the face of despair but also from a 'standpoint of redemption', we could say that, even in death, *Lear*'s 'messianic demand' is maintained. In no small part, as I have intimated above, it continues to be sustained by the ungraspable image of Cordelia, of which there is no letting go. Of course such a reading would expose us only to 'a universe of greys', a type of future past which oscillates between the despair of being 'too late' in the 'hope against hope' of affirmation, and in holding on to a 'not yet' which is finally unfulfillable.[56] There is evidently no straightforward sense in which this finally underwrites either an act of overcoming or a form of restoration. Yet by the final scene of Shakespeare's play, of course, this is precisely Lear's 'place'. And, when they are culled from their original theatrical context, it is perhaps unsurprising that his own 'last'

words read very much like a fragmented series of recalcitrant one liners from Beckett:

not yet
'Why then she lives.'
'if it be so . . .'
'stay a little. Ha?'
'What is't thou sayst?'
'Do you see this?'   (5. 3. 261, 263, 269, 270, 308)

too late
'she's gone for ever'
'She's dead as earth'
'now she's gone for ever'
'No, no, no life!'
'Never, never, never, never, never'
                              (5. 3. 257, 259, 268, 304, 307)

Caught between hope and despair, Lear holding Cordelia confirms the broken halves of a type of dialectical image that will never finally add up. Or as Lear puts it:

'I might have saved her; now she's gone for ever'
                              (5. 3. 268)

Fittingly of course it is an 'image of horror' and as such it remains constitutively incomplete and unfulfillable in its very failure to reconcile a felt discrepancy between thought and experience. Yet just as *Lear*'s closing scene necessarily remains

---

51 For a more detailed unpacking of the full paradox of Adorno's 'standpoint' in this respect see Critchley, *Very Little*, pp. 18–23.

52 See Theodor Adorno, *Aesthetic Theory*, trans. C. Lenhardt (London, 1984), p. 354, but also compare the 'finale' to Adorno's *Minima Moralia: Reflections from Damaged Life* (London, 1978), p. 247.

53 See Max Pensky, 'Editor's Introduction: Adorno's Actuality', in Max Pensky, ed., *The Actuality of Adorno: Critical Essays on Adorno and the Postmodern* (Albany, New York, 1997), pp. 1–21, see esp. p. 6 and p. 19, n. 8.

54 See Pensky, 'Editor's Introduction', p. 10; and compare Eva Geulen, 'Theodor Adorno on Tradition', in Pensky, ed., *The Actuality of Adorno*, pp. 183–93, esp. p. 186.

55 Critchley, *Very Little*, p. 19.

56 Again of course the register here is also Adornian. For a fuller explication of these 'temporal vocabularies' and for an explication of their significance for Adorno's work to which I'm indebted see Pensky, 'Editor's Introduction', p. 10 and Guelen, 'Theodor Adorno on Tradition', p. 186.

incomprehensible, it also retains its ethical imperative in sustaining its evocative demand that it must somehow still be construed for the sake of future action.[57] In this sense, at least, the play's ultimate scene of departure maintains its currency. And the line '*now* she's gone forever' might just as easily be turned back against itself, in being said to 'forever' occupy the moment of the '*now*'. Alongside Lear, each one of us hangs on to this. Nothing more and nothing less. It is the play's endlessly recurring after-image – a moment of last witness which suddenly unexpectedly resurrects its close contact at a distance:

> Do you see this? Look on her: look, her lips,
> Look there, look there! *He dies*　　　(5. 3. 308–9)

V

Metaphysics must know how to wish.[58]
　　　　　(Theodor Adorno, *Negative Dialectics*)

So where does this leave those who come after? How does one go on? And what form might that future action take? Fittingly of course *Lear* remains equivocal to the last:

> EDGAR: The weight of this sad time we must obey,
> 　　Speak what we feel, not what we ought to say.
> 　　The oldest hath borne most; we that are young
> 　　Shall never see so much, nor live so long.
> 　　　　　　*Exeunt with a dead march.* (5.3. 322–5)

In the closing lines of the play 'feeling' and 'speaking', rather than feeling and seeing, are cast in tantalizing proximity. Perhaps then it is a form of obligation, a 'speaking' that eventually comes from learning by heart? Let me expand briefly on what it might mean to say this.

When I worked with a group of students on these lines recently, several of them noticed a resemblance to the well-known fourth stanza of Laurence Binyon's poem 'For the Fallen':

> They shall grow not old, as we that are left grow old:
> Age shall not weary them, nor the years condemn.
> At the going down of the sun and in the morning
> We will remember them.[59]

Doubtless it was the time of year, as we were studying the play just after the Remembrance Sunday services commemorating the anniversary of Armistice Day and held annually across Britain in memory of those who have sacrificed their lives for peace. Of course, in Binyon's stanza, in surviving the disaster, it is we who come after, we who are left to grow old and weary while our predecessors are forever young and immortalized as a consequence. In Edgar's speech, however long we have got left, in outliving those that 'we' survive, those who are left will never live so long as those who are now also in some sense immortalized. So on an intuitive level at least the students' sense of a correspondence between the two stanzas seems absolutely right. Yet something continues to trouble me in the comparison.

Even in the short term of growing old, can we never live up to our elders who are old but forever young? And even while they remain beyond reproof, as Binyon implies, will the unlived lives of our ancestors in turn effectively condemn us? Does this mean that there is no learning from experience? In suggesting that: 'we that are young / Shall never see so much, nor live so long', Edgar's speech is earthbound in that it constitutes a reflection from within experience that inaugurates a degree of responsibility for those who come after. And we need to live the conditionality of our inheritance, however fraught with difficulty that 'living' might be. Perhaps a clue resides in the words of the obligation that precede *Lear's* last testament?

> The weight of this sad time we must obey,
> Speak what we feel, not what we ought to say.

As Foakes reminds us in his gloss on the line, there seems to be a conscious echo of *Lear's* opening scene here: 'in 1.1, Goneril and Regan spoke dutifully what they *ought to say*'.[60] But now we might

---

[57] Again compare Critchley, *Very Little*, p. 19.
[58] Adorno, *Negative Dialectics*, p. 407.
[59] Laurence Binyon, 'For the Fallen' in Helen Gardner, ed., *The New Oxford Book of English Verse* (Oxford, 1972), p. 831.
[60] Foakes, in Foakes, ed., *King Lear*, p. 392; Foakes's emphasis.

notice that in closing there is also the more sub-stantial temporal duty or 'obedience', which pre-cedes what we merely 'ought' to say: 'The weight of this sad time *we must obey*' – a duty, that is to say, which is beyond mere public duty, and one which arguably marks an ethical turning point in com-ing after but now lying beyond the empty rhetoric which attended the official investment of power and responsibility at the beginning of the play. The outcome is discordant; yet it also arguably re-marks the recognition that 'the obligations imposed by the dead *are* the obligations we discover and re-negotiate in life'[61] – a form of ethical demand that lives on in our day-to-day commitments and con-tinues to inform our relations with others in its development beyond the unredeemable lament of Binyon's in memoriam.

Of course, as Foakes observes elsewhere:

The last line [of the play] remains enigmatic, since say-ing what one feels (Lear in his rages? Goneril and Regan expressing their lust for Edmund?) may be just as damag-ing as saying what one ought to say (Goneril and Regan speaking by the rules in the opening scene?).[62]

For her part, we might remember that, during the opening scene, Cordelia effectively enacted an 'ar-ticulated silence',[63] rehearsing what she felt by opt-ing out of linguistic exchange in taking the side of things against language; thereby indirectly ac-knowledging the inequality of those speech acts which are based on dissimulation, and where even in speaking 'true', people will say anything – the 'dutiful ought' of Goneril and Regan in pledging their allegiance. In contrast the articulated silence of loving and being silent is one which in refusing justification and suffering false accusation is willing to risk the consequence:

LEAR But goes thy heart with this?
CORDELIA Ay, my good lord.
LEAR So young and so untender?
CORDELIA So young, my lord, and true.
LEAR Well, let it be so. Thy truth then be thy dower
(1.1. 105–9)

It is not merely that, as Foakes suggests, Cordelia 'thought she had to conceal her feelings' in the opening scene.[64] Rather, to love and to suffer the love of dutiful silence, which is still to be felt as such and to be dutiful, is a type of learning by heart which despite its unhappiness refuses to heave its heart into its mouth (1.1. 91–2).

This is not to hypostasize the experience of suf-fering or to universalize its significance, but rather to suggest that the facticity of suffering 'makes a virtue out of limitation' and resides in an open-ness to corrigibility. Here the difference between thinking and saying cannot be merely anticipated, so that – as the philosopher Gillian Rose puts it:

To grow in love-ability is to accept the boundaries of oneself and others, while remaining vulnerable, wound-able, around the bounds[65]

– an ability that Cordelia exhibits from the start. And, unlikely as it seems, a morsel of this senti-ment still survives in the play's closing stanza, even after the enduring memory of her death at the end of the play. As a consequence, we are bound to acknowledge it, for its obligation is an ob-ligature, a binding-up, or bond, to which we are still bound.[66]

However constrictive and unrelenting it might now seem to be, this is 'true' even of Tate's imposed

---

[61] I borrow this formulation directly from Wendy Wheeler who makes use of it in an intriguing discussion of Graham's Swift's, *Last Orders*. See Wendy Wheeler, 'Melancholic Modernity and Contemporary Grief: The Novels of Graham Swift', in Luckhurst and Marks, eds., *Literature and the Contemporary*, pp. 63–79, p. 78. Though I should note that both Wheeler and I are indebted in turn to the work of the philosopher Gillian Rose. Compare especially Gillian Rose, *Mourning Becomes the Law: Philosophy and Representation* (Cambridge, 1996).

[62] Foakes, 'Introduction', p. 79.

[63] I borrow this phrase from Barker, *The Culture of Violence*, p. 11.

[64] Foakes, in Foakes, ed., *King Lear*, p. 392.

[65] Gillian Rose, *Love's Work* (London, 1995), p. 98.

[66] Again I'm grateful to Wendy Wheeler for pointing out the 'tie' between obligation and ligature, see Wheeler, 'Melan-cholic Modernity', in Luckhurst and Marks, eds., *Literature and the Contemporary*, p. 76.

comedic ending to the play, which unwittingly secretes its own testament to provisionality and improvization even as it strives to forget the fact of that which will not be forgotten. After all, Tate's original Dedication actually hinges on its own admission of an impossible juggling act. In the course of defending his 'New-modelling of this story . . . whereof I had no Ground in my Author' he protests that he was 'wract with no small Fears for so bold a change', and although he locates his main justification for the 're-modelling' of the play in its performance, protesting the change 'well received by the audience', he feels bound to add one further 'theoretical' disclaimer:

Neither is it of so Trivial an Undertaking to make a Tragedy end happily, for 'tis more difficult to save than 'tis to Kill: The Dagger and Cup of Poison are always in Readiness; but to bring the Action to the last Extremity, and then by probable means to recover All, will require the Art and Judgement of a Writer, and cost him many a Pang in the Performance.[67]

Is it too fanciful to hear a trace of regretful overcompensation in Tate's account of his 'accomplishment'? In 'hindsight', perhaps the trick will be in preserving the spirit of Tate's ethical intuition – his acknowledgement that *''tis more difficult to save than 'tis to Kill'* – against the formal reconciliation that he finally opts for. Yet the admission of *'probable means'* remains improbable. Faced with discordancy Tate opts for resolution, but the trace of protestation – *''tis more difficult to save. . . to bring the Action to the last Extremity, and then by probable means to recover All'* – almost saves Tate's wishful thinking as a wishful need, acknowledging a part of truth which exceeds his grasp yet remains tantalising within reach. I would want to re-style Tate's 'improvement' of *Lear* as a comedy finally recast as a drama of misrecognition, where, to read Tate in the spirit of Gillian Rose reading Hegel,

the drama of misrecognition . . . ensues at every stage and transition of the work – a ceaseless comedy, according to which our aims and outcomes constantly mismatch each other, and provoke yet another revised aim, action and discordant outcome.[68]

If we accept the comic possibility of the impossible recursion that admits that it is more difficult to save than it is to kill, even as Tate would rather save us from doing so, then it – the comic possibility – still potentially saves us. For then we uphold 'ceaseless comedy' against mere comic closure. And if we do not, we deny any attempt to imagine it otherwise.

In some ways *Lear*'s aesthetic, like Beckett's and Adorno's, still undoubtedly presents us with a universe of greys. And this means that those who survive are left to express the unimaginable. In this respect art and philosophy can only offer some small consolation, so that, as Adorno observes,

Perennial suffering has as much right to expression as a tortured man has to scream; hence it may have been wrong to say that after Auschwitz you could no longer write poems.[69]

To which *Lear* responds:

Howl, howl, howl, howl! (5. 3. 255)

Yet only once the formal propriety of *Lear*'s comedy is measured in the totality of its non-fulfilment can a responsible criticism also then begin to contemplate things as they actually 'are'. The trick of course will be in preserving this ethical demand without reconciling ourselves to the barbarism which would deny vulnerability (even in its partial admission of truth) and then merely confirm *Lear* as a formal comedy and have done with the rest.

---

[67] Nathum Tate, 'Dedication and Prologue to *King Lear* (1681)', in Kermode, ed., *Shakespeare: King Lear*, pp. 25–6.

[68] Rose, *Mourning Becomes the Law*, p. 72.

[69] Adorno, *Negative Dialectics*, p. 362.

SONGS OF MADNESS: THE LYRIC AFTERLIFE OF SHAKESPEARE'S POOR TOM

WILLIAM C. CARROLL

'To sing publikely, is by a kinde of tolleration, permitted only to beggars'

Henry Chettle, *Kind-Hartes Dreame*[1]

In Izaak Walton's *The Compleat Angler* (1653), written nearly five decades after the first appearance, in 1605, of Shakespeare's Poor Tom in *King Lear*, Piscator promises Coridon that 'I'll sing a song that was lately made at my request, by Mr *William Basse*, one that hath made the choice songs of the *Hunter in his cariere*, and of *Tom of Bedlam*, and many others of note'.[2] In the nineteenth century, Isaac Disraeli claimed that 'Poems composed in the character of a Tom-o'-Bedlam appear to have formed a fashionable class of poetry among the wits; they seem to have held together their poetical contests, and some of these writers became celebrated for their successful efforts [here he cites Walton]'.[3] And writing after Disraeli, William Chappell observed of one ballad, 'This is the song which, under the name of Mad Tom, was much sung in theatres, and in other public places ... until within about thirty years ago [i.e. the 1840s]'.[4] In this article, I want to examine how, and why, the destitute figure of Poor Tom of Bedlam – in Shakespeare, a complex emblem of suffering, poverty, displacement, and, in part, histrionic counterfeiting – was transformed into a music-hall entertainer, a subject of 'poetical contests' for fashionable 'wits'.

The type of beggar known as a Poor Tom of Bedlam was especially flamboyant. Also known as an Abraham or Abram Man, Poor Tom was a lunatic beggar, supposedly an escaped or released inmate of Bedlam Hospital. Such beggars were widely believed to be licensed to beg (and therefore not subject to arrest), but there is no evidence, according to A. L. Beier, to support this belief.[5] In fact, the Poor Tom figure was often understood as a stereotype of the con-man.[6] There was a standard Bedlam 'look', moreover, as described by John Awdeley in 1561: 'An Abraham man is he that walketh bare armed, and bare legged, and faineth him selfe mad, and caryeth a packe of wool, or a sticke with baken on it, or such like toy, and nameth himselfe poore Tom'.[7] Poor Tom has 'shag haire, and staring eyes',[8] and some Poor Toms, according to another writer, were said to wear a metal plate around their arm with an inscription identifying Bedlam Hospital;[9] John Aubrey remarked that Poor Toms carried 'a great horn of an ox in a string ... which when they

---

[1] Henry Chettle, *Kind-Hartes Dreame 1592*, ed. G. B. Harrison. (1922; reprint New York, 1966).

[2] Izaak Walton, *The Compleat Angler* (London, 1935), pp. 86–7.

[3] Isaac Disraeli, *Curiosities of Literature*, vol. 3 (New York, 1881), p. 50.

[4] William Chappell, ed., *The Roxburghe Ballads* (Hertford, 1874), vol. 2, p. 259.

[5] A. L. Beier, *Masterless Men: The Vagrancy Problem in England 1560–1640* (London, 1985), p. 115.

[6] See William C. Carroll, *Fat King, Lean Beggar: Representations of Poverty in the Age of Shakespeare* (Ithaca, 1996) and Beier for the history of beggars in this period.

[7] John Awdeley, *The Fraternity of Vacabondes*, in *The Rogues and Vagabonds of Shakspere's Youth*, eds. Edward Viles and F. J. Furnivall (London, 1880), p. 3.

[8] Samuel Rowlands, *The Complete Works of Samuel Rowlands* (1880; reprint New York, 1966), vol. 2, p. 32.

[9] Gamini Salgado, ed., *The Elizabethan Underworld* (London, 1977), p. 198.

came to an house for alms, they did wind, and they did put the drink given them into this horn'.[10] One of Poor Tom's most distinctive traits, finally, was his penchant for self-mutilation. Shakespeare picks up all these characteristics of the Poor Tom figure in *King Lear*, when he makes Edgar disguise himself in 2.2 (2.3 in conflated editions):

> Whiles I may scape
> I will preserve myself, and am bethought
> To take the basest and most poorest shape
> That every penury in contempt of man
> Brought near to beast. My face I'll grime with filth,
> Blanket my loins, elf all my hairs in knots,
> And with presented nakedness outface
> The winds and persecutions of the sky.
> The country gives me proof and precedent
> Of Bedlam beggars who with roaring voices
> Strike in their numbed and mortifièd arms
> Pins, wooden pricks, nails, sprigs of rosemary,
> And with this horrible object from low farms,
> Poor pelting villages, sheep-cotes and mills,
> Sometime with lunatic bans, sometime with prayers
> Enforce their charity. 'Poor Tuelygod, Poor Tom.'
> That's something yet. Edgar I nothing am.
>
> (2.2.168–84)

I have argued elsewhere that Shakespeare's Poor Tom represents a watershed in the cultural representation of the type of madman beggar; here I wish to extend that argument in other directions. I now want to shift our attention from Poor Tom's appearance, important as it is, to Poor Tom's voice. I want to argue here that the most notorious beggar-figure in early modern English culture is as distinctively described, and perhaps more so, by his voice as by his appearance, and that his voice, after 1605, was radically transformed. Early modern and contemporary accounts of beggars have naturally been concentrated on their appearances, since it will not be possible to reproduce voices for another three centuries;[11] still, there is a surprising amount of information about Poor Tom's voice. What makes his voice so distinctive, after *King Lear*, is his singing; yet prior to 1605, Poor Tom's voice was understood as anything but one of harmony.

The earliest references to the Poor Tom figure, or to bedlamites more generally, say little or nothing

about Tom's singing. John Skelton (1522) refers to Wolsey as 'Such a madde bedleme' because 'he rayles and he ratis',[12] while Sir Thomas More remarks (*c.* 1522) that 'thou shalt in Bedlam see one laugh at the knocking of his own head against a post'.[13] John Awdeley, as we saw, reported that Poor Tom 'nameth himselfe poore Tom',[14] but neither the quality of his voice nor his singing is mentioned. In his amplification of Awdeley, however, Thomas Harman (1567) says of the type, 'some of these be merye and verye pleasant, they will daunce and sing; some others be as colde and reasonable to talke with all'.[15] In a poem published about a year after *Lear*'s first performance, Richard West says of the counterfeit madman-beggars that 'They, / Doe rage with furie as if they were so frantique... One calls her selfe poore Besse the other Tom'.[16] (Poor Bess was the female equivalent of Poor Tom.) Of the relatively few references to the type prior to *King Lear*, then, the stress, in terms of voice, is on Poor Tom's rage,[17] his railing, his mad laughter, and

---

[10] John Aubrey, quoted in H. B. Wheatley, *London Past and Present* (London, 1891), vol. 1, p. 176. Margaret Cavendish describes a beggars' marriage (in *Natures Picture*, London, 1671) at which '*Tom-a-Bedlam* wound his Horn, at best; / Their Trumpet now, to bring away the Feast' (Oo2ʳ).

[11] Early modern visual representations are, in the end, of limited value. There is a generic sameness to these pictures across a great span of time, and some ballad pictures are simply recycled from other ballads. However, it should not be so surprising that such representations are similar, for beggars are always known only through representation: they themselves do not write, draw, or even read; rather, they are written about, drawn, and read by a higher class, which can never quite *see* them.

[12] John Skelton, *The Complete English Poems*, ed. John Scattergood (New Haven, 1983), p. 295.

[13] Thomas More, *The Four Last Things*, ed. D. O'Connor (London, 1903), p. 7.

[14] John Awdeley, *The Fraternity of Vacabondes*, p. 3.

[15] Thomas Harman, *A Caveat or Warening for Commen Cursetors Vulgarely Called Vagabones*, in *The Rogues and Vagabonds of Shakspere's Youth*, p. 47.

[16] Richard West, *The Court of Conscience or Dick Whippers Sessions* (London, 1607), F3ᵛ.

[17] E.g. the demonic figure in Gervase Markham's *Rodomonths Infernall* (London, 1607) who 'Thunders his bedlam wrath in dead mens eares' (B1ᵛ).

his self-naming as 'Poor Tom';[18] Harman's is the only pre-1605 reference I have been able to find which refers to Poor Tom as potentially 'merye' or even capable of dancing and singing. After the appearance of Shakespeare's Poor Tom, however, many accounts of the figure change considerably: Poor Tom's identification with song becomes a prominent feature, and eventually he is associated with a particular voice and with particular songs.[19]

Thomas Dekker's appropriation of Harman's rogue book in *The Bellman of London* (1608) begins a new process of amplification in the accounts of the various rogue types. Dekker's key addition to the sketch of the Poor Tom figure is the development of his voice: he 'will talke franticklly of purpose', we are told, 'he calls himselfe by the name of *Poore Tom*, and comming neere any body, *cryes* out, *Poore Tom* is a cold. Of these *Abraham-men*, some be exceeding mery, and doe nothing but sing *songs*, fashioned out of their owne braines'.[20] By the time of his third rewrite of Harman, in *O per se O* (1612), Dekker says that 'Some made an horrid noise hollowly sounding, some whoop, some holler, some show only a kind of wild distracted ugly look, uttering a simple kind of *maunding* [begging] . . . Then will he dance and sing or use some other antic and ridiculous gesture, shutting up his counterfeit puppet-play with this epilogue or conclusion: "Good dame, give poor Tom one cup of the best drink! Well and wisely! God save the King and his Council and the governor of this place, etc." '.[21] Dekker offers other examples of Poor Tom's verbal begging appeals (too long to quote here), all of which, like the 'epilogue' above, are extremely rational and highly conventional; readerly interest in the type of the Poor Tom figure has evidently required Dekker to borrow (or simply invent) beggars' appeals from other types in order to satisfy the demand. By the time of Ben Jonson's *The Devil Is An Ass* (1616), the link between Poor Tom and singing is so strong that Jonson can simply allude to it, even to a specific song, when one character puts off another with several irrelevant comments, including 'Your best song's *Thom. o' Bet'lem*' (5.2.35).[22] Editors of Jonson invariably refer to four songs entitled 'Tom

of Bedlam' in Chappell's great collection, but as we shall see, most, and probably all of them, postdate Jonson's play. A few years later, in *The Lover's Melancholy* (1628), John Ford has a stage direction, '*Enter Cuculus like a bedlam, singing*' a ballad in defence of using tobacco, followed by two other songs in illustration of his melancholy;[23] in *Perkin Warbeck* (c. 1625–34), Ford links the chaos of the Scottish court to the voices of the mad in Bedlam ('The rare discord of bells, pipes, and tabors, / Hotchpotch of Scotch and Irish twingle-twangles, / Like to so many choristers of Bedlam / Trolling a catch' [3.2.4–7]).[24] In *The Changeling* (1622), the madmen's voices are said to be 'the chimes of Bedlam' (1.2.192),[25] and in Fletcher's *The Pilgrim* (1622), the voices of the mad are 'like bels rung backward /

---

18 Richard Brathwait, in *Natures Embassie* (London, 1621), describes those affected by the winter's cold: 'poore *Tom*, though he be mad; / "Cold makes *Tom a Bedlam* sad" ' (p. 254). Cf. *King Lear*: 'Poor Tom's a-cold' (3.4.137).

19 Many post-*Lear* allusions to Poor Tom of course continue the earlier traditions of his description: John Andrewes equates the allegorical figure of a 'Detracter' (in *The Anatomie of Basenesse*, London, 1615) with Poor Tom: 'So strange is the distraction of this *Tom* / of *Bedlam*, that all places, times, and men / without distinction seeme alike: for when / The furious rayling fit comes on him, from / His stinking stomacke, hee'le belch forth such geere, / such filth; and with such violence, as though / he meant to cast his rotten garbage: so / He ioyes to make his loathsomnesse appeare' (E 1ᵛ). Thomas Brewer, in *The Life and Death of the merry Deuill of Edmonton* (London, 1631), describes a husband locked in his room by his wife: 'he walked up and downe in his chamber, chafing, fretting and mumbling like poore Tom of Bedlam in his barne or bowsing Inne' (F 2ʳ).

20 Thomas Dekker, *The Non-Dramatic Works of Thomas Dekker*, ed. A. B. Grosart (1885; reprint New York, 1963), vol. 3, p. 101.

21 E. D. Pendry, *Thomas Dekker* (Cambridge, MA, 1968), p. 292.

22 *Ben Jonson*, ed. C. H. Herford and Percy and Evelyn Simpson (Oxford, 1925–52).

23 John Ford, *The Lover's Melancholy*, ed. R. F. Hill (Glasgow, 1985).

24 John Ford, *Perkin Warbeck*, ed. Donald K. Anderson, Jr. (Lincoln, Nebraska, 1965).

25 Thomas Middleton and William Rowley, *The Changeling*, ed. George Walton Williams (Lincoln, Nebraska, 1966).

They are nothing but confusion, and meer noyses' (4.3.5–6).[26] In Thomas Lupton's description of Bedlam (1632), the equation seems complete: 'the men [in Bedlam] may be said to be faire Instruments of Musicke, but either they want strings, or else though being strung are out of tune'.[27]

These last few references, to be sure, are more generic than specific to Poor Tom: in a conventional but powerful trope, the voices of the mad are understood as equivalent to broken or dissonant music; words without reason are like notes without harmony. As Ben Jonson observed, 'For what is so furious, and *Bethl'em*-like, as a vaine sound of chosen and excellent words, without any subject of *sentence*, or *science* mix'd?'.[28] What makes such dissonance so disturbing is its closeness to but its violation of larger schemes of order; the harmony of sweet music, in particular, was frequently invoked as a signifier of divine order. Thus the 'choristers' and 'chimes' of Bedlam in their very chaos invoke the possibility and desirability of cosmic order, of a higher state from which a fall has occurred. (Cf. Ophelia's lament over Hamlet's 'noble and most sovereign reason / Like sweet bells jangled out of tune and harsh' (3.1.160–1)). The yoking of music and madness is quite logical, then, and since Bedlam was the most (in)famous madhouse in early modern England, it is also quite logical that its name be associated with the 'confusion, and meer noyses' of madness. Yet this general nexus of associations still does not fully account for the *singing* Poor Tom figure.

It is my contention that the ease of Jonson's allusion to 'Your best song's *Thom. o' Bedlam*', and the subsequent history of such ballads, to which I will turn in a moment, is really enabled by the appearance of Shakespeare's Poor Tom eleven years earlier. Two other plays just prior to or contemporaneous with *King Lear* may help us calibrate the impact of Shakespeare's Poor Tom more precisely. In Dekker's *The Honest Whore, Part 1* (1604), much of the fifth act takes place in Bedlam, but the list of inhabitants there (5.2.153–66) does not include a Poor Tom – there are, instead, two old men and a married man who was too jealous – nor is there

any singing. In the madhouse scenes in *Northward Ho* (1605; printed 1607), again there is no Poor Tom figure, but there is a bawd who sings a song. But after *King Lear*, Poor Tom's singing becomes conventional, and other singing beggars proliferate. By the time of Richard Brome's *A Jovial Crew; or, The Merry Beggars* in 1641, the singing beggar was a dramatic stereotype, the play itself closer to a Broadway musical than Shakespeare's tragedy. Indeed, the subsequent stage history of this play, in the Restoration and eighteenth century, shows it being turned into an astonishingly successful comic opera, with the addition of more and more songs. The original songs in Brome's play, as his subtitle suggests, reflect the tradition of the merry beggar, in which poverty is highly romanticized, and the usual binaries are inverted:

> From hunger and cold, who lives more free,
> Or who more richly clad than we?
> Our bellies are full; our flesh is warm;
> And, against pride, our rags are a charm.
> Enough is our feast, and for tomorrow
> Let rich men care; we feel no sorrow.
> No sorrow, no sorrow, no sorrow, no sorrow.
> Let rich men care; we feel no sorrow.
>
> (1.1.339–46)[29]

Shakespeare's Edgar, then, establishes the emblematic figure of Poor Tom as a dramatic character in 1605, but he also originates Poor Tom's voice as an instrument of song. Yet in Shakespeare's play, Poor Tom's songs, and his voice generally, are anything but merry: to the contrary, they are cries of pain and despair, scraps of old ballads, curses, and broken fragments of the Ten Commandments and Seven Deadly Sins. To his father Gloucester's query, 'What are you there? Your names?', Edgar

---

[26] *The Dramatic Works in the Beaumont and Fletcher Canon*, ed. Fredson Bowers (Cambridge, 1985).

[27] Donald Lupton, *London and the Countrey Carbonadoed and Quartred into Severall Characters* (London, 1632), p. 78.

[28] *Ben Jonson*, vol. VIII, p. 574.

[29] Richard Brome, *A Jovial Crew*, ed. Ann Haaker (Lincoln, 1968). See Haaker's brief stage history, pp. xi–xii, for an account of later versions of the play.

offers a self-definition as Tom of utter debasement and self-loathing:

Poor Tom, that eats the swimming frog, the toad, the tadpole, the wall-newt and the water; that in the fury of his heart, when the foul fiend rages, eats cowdung for salads, swallows the old rat and the ditch-dog, drinks the green mantle of the standing pool; who is whipped from tithing to tithing, and stocked, punished, and imprisoned; who hath had three suits to his back, six shirts to his body,

> Horse to ride, and weapon to wear;
> But mice and rats and such small deer
> Have been Tom's food for seven long year.
>
> (3.4.121–31)

His is truly one of the 'roaring voices', full of pain and humiliation. Edgar's voice of pain in *King Lear* is the voice of suffering, of madness, and of poverty; but what is absolutely distinctive about Shakespeare's Poor Tom is, as we will see, finally inimitable. Later versions of the Poor Tom figure – to oversimplify – will pick up the fact of Tom's singing, but not his voice, not his pain, not his poverty.

Yet Shakespeare's Poor Tom, surprisingly, does sing a fair amount in the play, far more than most critics have realized; indeed, most accounts of song in the play refer to the Fool (in part because so few of Edgar's sung allusions can be identified). I count eight different moments when Poor Tom seems to sing, almost all of them echoes or quotations from ballads. Some of these ballads are lost, but some, like 'Come o'er the burn, Bessy, to me' (Q Sc. 13.21; 3.6 in conflated texts) are quoted in other plays, and both an early broadside ballad (1564) and the music for it exist.[30] Similarly, the ballad behind Poor Tom's 'Thorough the sharp hawthorn blow the winds' (3.4.44–5) is also known.[31] It is important to note again, however, that Shakespeare's Poor Tom never sings anything like the later ballads which bear his name. Ironically, the Poor Tom who quoted scraps from old ballads later became the source and object of sophisticated and polished ballads himself.

To what song, then, is Jonson's Pug referring in 1616, when he says, 'Your best song *Thom. o' Bedlam*?' It is not necessarily the same one to which Walton refers, since there were several such songs by the 1650s. Perhaps I should now distinguish between the music, on the one hand, and the song, or words, on the other. The earliest printed version of the tune known as 'Mad Tom' is in John Playford's *The English Dancing Master* (1651); in the first edition, it is called 'Graies Inne Maske', while in later editions it is 'Grayes-Inn Mask, or (Mad Tom)' (see illustration 1).[32] Chappell connects this tune to the licensed revels at the Inns of Court during the reign of James I, and suggests that it was composed by John Cooper, one of the music-masters to King James's children.[33] It is perhaps 'a popular version of an instrumental piece originally composed for Beaumont's *The Masque of the Inner Temple and Gray's Inn* (1613)', according to John H. Long.[34] In any event, the tune of 'Mad Tom' became very well known and was used for a number of different ballads in the seventeenth century and later, many of which had nothing to do with Bedlam beggars or even poverty.[35] In these ballads Shakespeare's Poor

---

[30] It also appears in W. Wager's *The Longer Thou Livest* (*c.* 1569), where Moros sings the refrain of many songs 'as fools were wont' (1.1.94–6; R. Mark Benbow, ed., *The Longer Thou Livest and Enough Is As Good As A Feast* (Lincoln, 1967)). Only this refrain of the actual song survives.

[31] 'The Friar of Orders Grey', in Thomas Percy, *Reliques of Ancient English Poetry* (London, 1765), l. 95. The Quarto *Lear* reads 'blows the cold wind' (Sc. 11, 41).

[32] John Playford, *Playford's English Dancing Master 1651*, ed. Margaret Dean-Smith (London, 1957); *The Dancing-Master... The Fifth Edition* (London, 1675).

[33] Chappell, *Roxburghe Ballads*, vol. 2, p. 259.

[34] John H. Long, *Shakespeare's Use of Music: The Histories and Tragedies* (Gainesville, Florida, 1971), p. 52.

[35] Such as a song 'To the tune of, *Wellcome to Towne mad Tom*', in the collection of jests, *The Pinder of Wakefield* (London, 1632), C 3; 'News from Colchester' (*c.* 1660), by John Denham (*The Poetical Works of Sir John Denham*, ed. T. H. Banks (New Haven, 1928)); 'The Cock-Crowing at the Approach of a Free Parliament... And Mad Tom of Bedlam the Tune is' and 'A New Ballad. To an Old Tune, *Tom of Bedlam*', in *Rump: Or an Exact Collection of the Choycest Poems and Songs* (London, 1662); 'Upon Bringing in the Plate' (1662; printed in Robert Graves, *Loving Mad Tom: Bedlamite Verses of the XVI and XVII Centuries* (1927; reprint New York, 1970), p. 73; much later, 'Air X' in Gabriel Odingsells' *Bays's Opera* (London, 1730) is 'to the tune of Mad Tom' (p. 14). A variant of this tune in lute

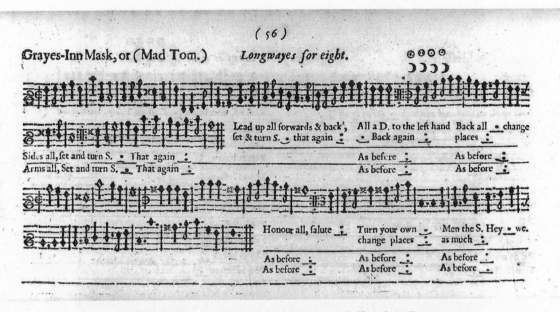

1 John Playford, *The Dancing-Master*. London, 1670. Shelf-Mark: M K. 1.a.11.

Tom has now become, in the standard reference, *Mad* Tom; the privileging of one category of his nature – his madness – over the other – his poverty – reflects the whole history of the character, as we shall see.

But what of the song of Mad Tom? What were the words, and their origin? The earliest known version of a Mad Tom song is that found in a manuscript collection written between 1615 and 1623; a later manuscript version, dated probably after 1650, has also been identified. This song was printed as well in the later collections, *Wit and Drollery* (1659) and *Le Prince D'Amour* (1660). I quote the first of eight stanzas:

From ye hagg & hungry Goblin,
yt into raggs would rend yee,
& ye spirit yt stand's by ye naked man,
in ye booke of moones defend yee
That of your fiue sounde sences,
you neuer be forsaken,
Nor travel from your selues with Tom,
abroad to begg your bacon
    while I doe sing any foode any feeding,
    feeding – drinke or clothing,

Come dame or maid, be not afraid,
poore Tom will iniure nothing.[36]

Tom has been 'in durance soundlie caged, / On ye lordlie loftes of Bedlam / with stubble softe and daintie, / braue braceletts strong, sweet whips ding dong / with wholsome hunger plenty'. In this poem, Tom is still poor as well as mad, but even at this early date, his madness is more prominent.

The best-known Mad Tom song appeared in *Le Prince d'Amour* (1660), and in earlier black-letter copies of the ballad, as well as in one manuscript; Playford included it in the second edition (1675) of his *Choice Ayres, Songs, and Dialogues* (see illustration 2). Precise dating of all this material is difficult, but certainly every known version postdates 1605.

tablature also dates from *c.* 1613–1616 (Claude M. Simpson, *The British Broadside Ballad and Its Music* (New Brunswick, 1966), pp. 263–6, 710–13).

36 *Le Prince d'Amour* (London, 1660), p. 167; the poem's title here is simply '*Tom of Bedlam*'. See Stanley Wells's transcription of the same song from the commonplace book compiled by Archbishop Sancroft (1619–93), in 'Tom O'Bedlam's Song and *King Lear*', *Shakespeare Quarterly* 12 (1961), 311–15.

2 John Playford, *Choice Ayres, Songs and Dialogues . . . The Second Edition Corrected and Enlarged*. London, 1675.

The first lines of this song are justly famous:

> Forth from my sad and darksome cell,
> From the deep abyss of Hell,
> Mad Tom is come to view the world again,
> To see if he can ease his distemper'd brain.
> Fear and despair pursue my soul.
> Hark! how the angry Furies howl!
> Pluto laughs, and Prosperine is glad,
> To see poor naked Tom of Bedlam mad.
> Through the woods I wander night and day
> To find my straggling senses.[37]

This Tom is still poor as well as mad, his destitution at least articulated: 'In vain with crys I rend the skies, / For pity is not common. / Cold and comfortless I lie, / Help! O help! or else I die'.[38] This song is the most popular and frequently reprinted of all the Mad Tom songs; it appeared in collections throughout the Restoration and into the eighteenth century. Indeed, it was so recognizable that it became subject to parody, as in John Mottley and Thomas Cooke's *Penelope, a Dramatic Opera* (1728), when Tom Thimble the tailor (who is in love) sings: 'Forth from my Shopboard am I come, / To try the Force of Love again; / Poor Tom can neither work, nor keep at Home, / Till Pen will deign to cure his distemper'd Brain. / O! Alas! I'm all forlorn, / I am become the Neighbour's Scorn'.[39]

The printed versions of other Mad Tom songs found in various collections date from 1660 into the eighteenth century.[40] The range of these songs expands to include the voices of women – for example, Mad Maudlin (in an echo of Tom's song) – 'From forth th' *Elisian* Fields, / A place of restlesse souls, / Mad *Maulkin* is come, to seek her naked *Tom*'[41] – and of course Mad Bess of Bedlam –

> Poor *Bess* will return to the place whence she came,
> since the World is so mad, she can hope for no Cure;
> for Love's grown a Bubble, a Shadow, a Name,
> which Fools do admire, and wise Men endure.[42]

One of the continuing stories embedded in these other songs is the quest of Maudlin or Bess to find Tom, the lover who has rejected her;[43] Tom's madness will therefore also become partly attributable to love-madness, his poverty sliding even further away from the figure. One of the Restoration songs

(1656) is simply titled 'Loving Mad Tom': 'I'le bark against the Dog-Star, / And crow away the Morning; / I'le chase the Moon / Till it be Noon, / And I'll make her leave her Horning. / *And seek what e're betides her, / Yet I will love / Beneath or above, / That dirty Earth that hides her*'.[44]

The Tom o' Bedlam songs which stem from the popularity of the Poor Tom figure thus increasingly diverge from Edgar's voice in *King Lear*. The jagged madness of Edgar/Poor Tom's voice was reproduced as a new commodity, and conventionalized. This stanza from the 'hagg and hungry Goblin' song reflects how quickly the suffering voice of Tom has been transformed into the poetical:

> with an hoast of furious fancies
> whereof I am comaunder,
> with a burning speare, & a horse of the aire,
> to the wildernesse I wander.
> With a knight of ghostes & shadowes,
> I sumon'd am to Tourney.
> ten leagues beyond the wide worlds end
> mee thinkes it is noe journey.[45]

This stanza became a kind of touchstone of romantic madness; it was quoted by Edgar Allan Poe

---

37 Chappell, *Roxburghe Ballads*, vol. 2, pp. 259–60; the tune is 'Gray's-Inn Mask'. In *Le Prince d'Amour*, l. 3 still reads 'Poor Tom' rather than 'Mad Tom'; the *Roxburghe* text is from 1673.

38 Chappell, *Roxburghe Ballads*, vol. 2, p. 260. Another song, not of Mad Tom but set to the same music, took its title from lines near the end of Tom's song: 'The man in the moon drinks clarret, / With powder-beef, turnep, and carret' (*Roxburghe Ballads*, vol. 2, p. 261). The ballad sheet on which this other song was printed says that it is 'as it was lately sung at the Curtain, Holywell' (*Roxburghe Ballads*, vol. 2, p. 256); this reference establishes the music as prior to 1625, when the Curtain theatre seems to have ceased life as a theatrical venue.

39 John Mottley and Thomas Cooke, *Penelope, a Dramatic Opera* (London, 1728), p. 24.

40 E.g. 1660 (*Le Prince d'Amour*), 1661 (*Westminster Drollery, Merry Drollerie, Wit and Drollery*), 1672 (*Covent Garden Drollery*), 1699 (*Wit and Mirth*).

41 Robert Graves, *Loving Mad Tom*, p. 37; text from 1682.

42 Ibid., p. 54; text from Playford.

43 Among the titles: 'Love's Lunacie; or, Mad Bessie's Fegary [i.e. Vagary]'; 'Bess of Bedlam'; 'Mad Maudlin is Come'; 'To Find my Tom of Bedlam'.

44 Robert Graves, *Loving Mad Tom*, p. 26; text is from 1682.

45 *Le Prince d'Amour*, p. 169.

(epigraph to 'The Unparalleled Adventure of One Hans Pfaall', 1835), Rudyard Kipling (epigraph to chapter 15, *The Light That Failed*, 1899), and Walter de la Mare (in chapter 21, *Memoirs of a Midget*, 1922).

Thus the voice of Tom (or Bess or Maudlin, or yet other vagabonds) became part of the picturesque and the poetical. In the eighteenth century, for example, Jacob Hildebrand invokes 'Phantasia' in his 'Bedlam', linking the 'airy Pow'r' (l.3) with its 'thousand restless Forms... [and] thousand busy Dreams' (lines 7–8) to 'The wretched, wandring Lunatick's Retreat... Bedlam' (lines 14–15) which 'in the gaudy Fields of Fancy range' (line 40).[46] Similarly, in James Wilson's 'The wonderful Adventures and heroic Atchievements of Mad Tom' (1771), 'The dog-star now rages, and Bedlam's broke out, / The madmen all run thro' our streets with a shout: / 'Tis full moon and full sea, full tide in their head, / They threaten the poets, and fill them with dread!' (lines 1–4). After recounting several dangerous actions by 'Mad Tom' (line 9), the narrator proposes to 'Sing him to his senses' (line 42).[47] George Stevens, in 'Tom O'Bedlam' (1788), depicts a similarly pathetic but more sentimentalized figure:

> Bare-foot and Head-bare, his Blanket tight skewer'd,
> *Tom o' Bedlam* paraded, erect as my Lord;
> The Boys left their play, at his raggedness scar'd,
> The Mob pity struck, at his misery star'd.
> Girls laugh'd, and the Fops, fashion form'd for the day,
> Shrill screaming on tiptoe stole trembling away;
> While Infants crept close, in their mothers arms hid,
> Tom, Beauty-like mov'd, heedless what harm he did.[48]

Disraeli might very well have had Stevens' poem in mind when he summed up this tradition: 'An itinerant lunatic, chanting wild ditties, fancifully attired, gay with the simplicity of childhood, yet often moaning with the sorrows of a troubled man, a mixture of character at once grotesque and plaintive, became an interesting object to poetical minds.' The last stanza of one song, Disraeli noted, 'contains the seeds of exquisite romance'.[49]

William Henry Ireland (1803), like many other writers, linked Tom's madness with the tradition of the mad lover:

> Sing, pretty warblers of the grove!
> Chaunt strains melodious, strains of love;
>   Poor Tom grows sick at heart:
> Shrill scream thy song, fell bird of night!
>   The bat and raven's my delight;
> I've snapp'd the rankling dart.
> Who's now so free, so gay as I?
>   Who tastes such heavenly joys?
> Tush, tush! poor love-sick Tom will die,
>   And leave the Bedlam boys.[50]

The apotheosis of this increasingly sentimentalized tradition is no doubt Ernest Dowson's 'To One in Bedlam':

> With delicate, mad hands, behind his sordid bars,
> Surely he hath his posies, which they tear and twine;
> Those scentless wisps of straw that, miserably, line
> His strait, caged universe, whereat the dull world stares,
> Pedant and pitiful. O, how his rapt gaze wars
> With their stupidity! Know they what dreams divine
> Lift his long, laughing reveries like enchaunted wine,
> And make his melancholy germane to the stars'?

Dowson ends in a kind of paroxysm of envy: 'better than love or sleep, / The star-crowned solitude of thine oblivious hours!' (lines 13–14).[51]

The commodification of the beggar's voice can be seen from another perspective as well, that of the economic history of the broadside ballad, revolving around the conditions of purchase and sale. In Henry Chettle's *Kind-Hartes Dreame* (1592), one of the apparitions, Anthony Now-now, laments the increase in the number of ballad-mongers, those

[46] Jacob Hildebrand, *Works* (London, 1735), pp. 12–13.
[47] James Wilson, *Miscellanies in Prose and Verse* (London, 1771).
[48] George Alexander Stevens, *Songs, Comic, and Satyrical* (Oxford, 1772), lines 1–8, p. 228.
[49] Disraeli, *Curiosities of Literature*, pp. 50, 53.
[50] William Henry Ireland, 'Crazy Tom, the Bedlamite', lines 21–30, in *Rhapsodies* (London, 1803), p. 118.
[51] Ernest Dowson, 'To One in Bedlam', in *The Poems of Ernest Dowson* (London, 1905), lines 1–8 (p. 10).

itinerant pedlars/vagrants who comprised a national distribution system of household commodities ranging from pots and pans and items of clothing, to broadside ballads; Shakespeare's Autolycus (in *The Winter's Tale*, 1610) and Jonson's Nightingale (in *Bartholomew Fair*, 1614) are flamboyant examples. The increase that Anthony Now-now mentions is predominantly one of youth, and he laments that 'boyes of able strength, and agreeable capacity, should bee suffered to wrest from the miserable Aged, the last refuge in their life (beggery excepted) the poore helpe of Ballad-singing'. The basis of this lament is that 'to sing publikely, is by a kinde of tolleration, permitted only to beggars'[52] – i.e. by real beggars, and by ballad-mongers, whose poverty and itinerancy made them, legally as well as practically speaking, vagrants. There are numerous complaints in the century 1550–1650 of the dangers posed by wandering ballad-mongers, from their alleged links to crime and their supposed smuggling of Catholic relics and trinkets, to their general economic status – a threatening, free-floating status as entrepreneurial precursors of an emergent capitalism. Ultimately, these 'mercuries' would even be linked to sedition; a 1647 ordinance against 'the many Seditious, False and Scandalous Papers and Pamphlets daily printed and published' prohibited the writing, printing or sale of any work not officially licensed. The punishment of 'the Hawker, Pedler or Ballad-singer' who violates the ordinance will be 'to forfeit and lose all his Books, Pamphlets and printed Papers exposed to sale, and also to be whipt as a Common Rogue'.[53]

Ballad-mongers sang in order to sell; their voices were their chief means of advertising.[54] Most broadside ballads were third-person stories, the truth of which was authenticated, in part, by the singer's distance from the narrative, and therefore his objectivity. When Autolycus, in *The Winter's Tale*, tells of the ballad of the 'fish that appeared upon the coast ... forty thousand fathom above water, and sung this ballad against the hard hearts of maids', the gullible countrymen ask 'Is it true?' and are reassured by the con-man's assertion of supposed empirical evidence and authority: 'Five justices' hands at it, and witnesses more than my

pack will hold' (*Winter's Tale* 4.4.273–82).[55] But in that minority of ballads which are told in the first person, the singer/presenter must become, or represent, the speaker, at least in his or her voice. In the even more special case of the Mad Tom ballads which emerge after Shakespeare's *King Lear*, the ballad-monger, himself a specimen of poverty and vagrancy, now performs the role of poverty, vagrancy, and madness. The irony is that the Poor Tom figure is at times already a performance, a role with its own costume, actions and voice. There was therefore a special and unique link between the ballad-monger who hawked Poor Tom ballads in the streets, and the Poor Tom figures encountered in the streets; in some ways, they were the same figure. Indeed, one anonymous author in 1641 observed that of the street hawkers or 'wandring Stationers ... one of you came out of a hedge, another out of New-gate, a third out of the New-prison, and the fourth not beeing a moneth out of Bedlam, roundly, profoundly, and soundly cries out with a voyce made of cannon proofe, *Come buy a new Booke, a new Booke, newly come forth*'.[56]

The popularity of the Mad Tom ballads, and of the music to which they were set, led in at least two directions. First, the music itself became dissociated from the words, and served as the tune of many other songs, some of them not at all related to the character. Secondly, and conversely, the words were dissociated from the music, and the specific social conditions of performance were lost. As the songs were written down as broadside ballads, then later collected in Restoration and seventeenth-century royalist drolleries and collections of wit and

---

[52] Henry Chettle, *Kind-Hartes Dream*, p. 21.

[53] C. H. Firth and R. S. Rait, eds., *Acts and Ordinances of the Interregnum, 1642–1660* (London, 1911), vol. 1, pp. 1021–3.

[54] See Bruce Smith, *The Acoustic World of Early Modern England* (Chicago, 1999), on the 'soundscape' of street vendors and peddlers hawking ballads in early modern London, pp. 64–5.

[55] On the ballad-monger's pretence of authenticity, see Natascha Würzbach, *The Rise of the English Street Ballad, 1550–1650* (Cambridge, 1990), pp. 47–52.

[56] *The Downefall of Temporizing Poets, unlicenst Printers, upstart Booksellers, trotting Mercuries, and bawling Hawkers* (London, 1641), A2[r–v].

ingenuity, they became poems, the oral became the written, the pain of poverty became the pleasure of the picturesque and sublime. The mechanical reproduction of the performed voice led to its commodification as entertainment. Inevitably, this process of commodification enacted a parallel ascent of text and audience up the generic and social hierarchies.[57] Poor Tom's fragmented voice became polished songs, then literary ballads, then whole collections of *poems*, while the audience shifted from the public marketplace to the men 'of note' mentioned by Walton, and then sophisticated readers; the site of the voice likewise shifted from the street to the salon, and then to the mental privacy of the single reader. Already by 1675, as Natascha Würzbach has noted, 'street ballads had long become institutionalized as entertainment literature, alongside the recently established 'drollery' and printed play, so that Mrs Pinchwife [in Wycherley's *The Country Wife*] could expect and ask for them from the bookseller'.[58]

Even before their incorporation into different forms of what we would now call bourgeois culture, the broadside ballads only rarely portrayed the poor, and many of those instances represented them as either fraudulent, such as 'The Vagabond', 'The Cunning Northerne Beggar' (*c.* 1626), and 'The Begger-Boy of the North',[59] or as contented and leading a superior life, as in 'Ragged, and torn, and true' (*c.* 1618–30). It is true that an older, Christian tradition of social criticism exalted the poor and denounced the rich, as in 'London Lickpenny' (*c.* 1500), with its refrain, 'for lacke of money, I may not spede',[60] or 'The Poore Man Payes for All', with its perception of 'how wealthy men / Did grind the poore men's faces, / And greedily did prey on them'.[61] Even the earliest of the Mad Tom ballads, however, seem generations removed from the abjection of the Shakespeare character, Poor Tom. Moreover, Edgar/Poor Tom's place in *King Lear*'s critique of the court and monarchical ignorance (or worse) of the kingdom's 'Poor naked wretches' (3.4.28) is crucial; as an inversion of the reason of the sovereign, the madness of the beggar both reflects and undermines it, just as the beggar's poverty inverts the sovereign's wealth, calling into question the very principle of equity.[62] Yet few of the later ballads retain any trace of this political vein of potentially radical social critique.[63] Poor Tom's lyric afterlife was predominantly that of the poetical ballad, shaping a pre-Romantic figure of the naif associated with romance and the imagination.

Perhaps the most ironic appropriation of Poor Tom's voice in a political cause was by Sir Francis Wortley, in a ballad dated 27 June 1648, 'Mad Tom A Bedlams Desires of Peace', which strongly supports the royalist position:

> Poor Tom hath been imprison'd,
> With strange oppressions vexed;
> He dares boldly say, they try'd each way,
> Wherewith Job was perplexed.
> Yet still he cries for the king, for the good king,
> Tom loves brave confessors,

---

57 The broadside ballads themselves originally seemed aimed at a lower-to-middling urban public and a relatively uneducated rural audience, but Watt has shown that higher social ranks collected them as well. See Tessa Watt, *Cheap Print and Popular Piety 1550–1640* (Cambridge, 1991), pp. 1–7, and Natascha Würzbach, *The Rise of the English Street Ballad, 1550–1650*, p. 26. On the commodification of culture in this period, see Robert Weimann, *Authority and Representation in Early Modern Discourse* (Baltimore, 1996), pp. 113–19, and Michael Bristol, *Big-time Shakespeare* (London, 1996), pp. 31–41. Weimann locates the beginnings of this process in the 1590s.
58 Natascha Würzbach, *The Rise of the English Street Ballad, 1550–1650*, p. 248.
59 Chappell, *Roxburghe Ballads*, vol. 3, pp. 323–5.
60 Vivian de Sola Pinto and Allen E. Rodway, eds., *The Common Muse* (London, 1957), p. 96.
61 Chappell, *Roxburghe Ballads*, vol. 2, pp. 334–8.
62 See Judy Kronenfeld's *King Lear and the Naked Truth* (Durham, NC, 1998) for more on the question of charity and distribution; see Margot Heinemann, ' "Demystifying the Mystery of State": *King Lear* and the World Upside Down', *Shakespeare Survey* 44 (1992), pp. 75–83, for a discussion of the inversion trope.
63 Among the generic beggar ballads, several are satires written during the reign of James, attacking the influx of Scots into English society: 'Too many *Scottish* beggars in *England* doe dwell…A page at the first, of a page grewe a knight, / a Lord and a vicounte, an Eirle by this light) / by begging, by begging' ('Let bare-footed beggars still walk in the street', in Hyder E. Rollins, ed., *Old English Ballads 1553–1625* (Cambridge, 1920), pp. 376–8).

But he curses those dare their king depose,
Committees and oppressors.

After blessing and praying for various royalist supporters ('the hopefull duke of Gloster', 'the reverent suffering bishops', 'the loyall hearted gentry'), Poor Tom, in his final stanza, asks to 'Blesse the printer from the searcher \ And from the houses takers! \ Blesse Tom from the slash; from Bridewel's lash, \ Blesse all poore ballad-makers!'.[64] Poor Tom and the anti-parliamentary printers and ballad-makers are now virtually the same. Mad Tom is thus linked to the larger history of the ballad in English, particularly, as Rollins showed,[65] in the important role ballads played in political opposition during the interregnum, and increasing government attempts to suppress their publication. Such printers were indeed subject to 'the searcher'. But surely royalist supporters of the monarchy were among the very last people in England with the moral right to appropriate Tom's voice in their cause.

Poor Tom's final indignity was to become a comic bit-part. In Peter Hausted's university drama, *The Rivall Friends* (performed at Cambridge before the King and Queen in 1632), 'A Bedlam' is brought on stage in Act 5, Scene 5, to play the part of 'Oberon' in a complicated deception plot. At first less than cooperative ('Let braue *Tom* alone'), he sings two prepared songs designed to convince a gull that Tom is Oberon (even though he is observed to have 'a *horne* like a *Tom* of *Bedlam*'); the Bedlam departs the play immediately, shoved out 'the back dore', speaking again his only autonomous words, 'Let braue *Tom* alone'.[66] Tom's name, but little else, crossed the Atlantic to appear in a political satire, *Androboros* (1714), by Robert Hunter. 'Tom of Bedlam', who has been appointed 'Clerk of the Senate', is in the mold of the Plautine tricky servant, speaking witty prose throughout the play, occasionally singing a snatch of a song.[67] His connection to Shakespeare's figure is minimal. Poor Tom would eventually become a comic weapon in satire, as seen in John Henley's poem, 'Tom o'Bedlam's Dunciad: or, Pope, Alexander the pig' (1729) and Francis Tolson's 'Tom of Bedlam: or, a mad poem, writ by a mad author. Reflecting on

the madness of some persons' (1701) and 'Tom of Bedlam's New Medley' (1720).[68]

Yet prior to the Restoration the domestication of Poor Tom's voice was by no means complete, as three final incidents will indicate. On 9 January 1618, just ten years after the publication of Shakespeare's play, King James witnessed a performance of an entire 'Play . . . of Tom of Bedlem, the Tincker and such other mad stuffe'. One of the notorious features of this performance was 'a certain song sunge by Sir John Finet, (wherin the rest bare the bourdon [refrain]) of such scurrilous and base stuffe that it put the King out of his goode humor, and all the rest that heard it'. John Chamberlain, who wrote of this incident, marvels that no one seemed to understand 'how unfit it was to bring such beastly geare in publike before a Prince'.[69] Indeed, even in his post-Shakespearian manifestations, Poor Tom is 'beastly geare'.[70]

The second incident is a case decided in Star Chamber, 8 June 1632, in which Micha Smith and

---

64 Thomas Wright, *Political Ballads Published in England During the Commonwealth* (London, 1841), pp. 102, 106.

65 Hyder E. Rollins, ed., *Cavalier and Puritan: Ballads and Broadsides Illustrating the Period of the Great Rebellion 1640–1660* (New York, 1923).

66 Peter Hausted, *The Rivall Friends* (London, 1632), L4ʳ⁻ᵛ.

67 Robert Hunter, *Androboros. A B[i]ographical Farce in Three Acts* (New York, 1714).

68 Cited in D. F. Foxon, *English Verse 1701–1750* (London, 1975).

69 N. E. McClure, ed., *The Letters of John Chamberlain* (Philadelphia, 1939), vol. 2, pp. 129, 131. According to Anthony Weldon, Sir Edward Zouche's part was 'to sing bawdy songs; and tell bawdy tales', while Finet was 'to compose these Songs', and George Goring 'was master of the game for Fooleries' (Anthony Weldon, *The Court and Character of King James* (London, 1817), pp. 28–9). Finet was apparently not in serious trouble, however, because he became Master of Ceremonies for the Court in March 1627; he had received the reversion of the office in September 1618 (Albert J. Loomie, S. J., *Ceremonies of Charles I: The Note Books of John Finet (1628–1641)* (New York, 1987), p. 10).

70 Stanley Wells suggests, in 'Tom O'Bedlam's Song and *King Lear*', that the 'hagg and hungry Goblin' song might well be the one sung at Theobalds; the earliest version of the song is in a manuscript collection headed 'Giles Earle his booke, 1615', predating the incident, but Wells points out that the collection also included some material dated as late as 1623.

the married couple, A. and Martha Osmonton, brought an action for libel against five men, chief among them one Benjamin Martin. Their offence was 'with malice among themselves' to have

framed and contryved a false and scandalous lybell in meeter or verses against the said Martha Osmonton and Micha Smith. The verses were sett to the tune of Tom of Bedlam, and to this effect: There is a report of a cryme committed betweene some of the holie Brotherhood [i.e. Puritans], ending with a scurrilous verse, wench lye still, &c. and none did suspect that they were the elect, up the hill they came tripping with nimble bodies bending, and upon her he nymblie skipped: and so when he had instructed her, he said Yonder cometh a sinner. Her husband then like an heavy headed man came up the hill lamenting, the bell ringing away they hast to sermon. Her face is long, her browes are black, her high woodden heeles they are in the fault, they made her catch a fall, and as for the man soe holie he is, that he will speake to noe bodie he meets, &c. That these verses were meant of the Plaintiffs Micha and Martha, and her said husband, and the defendants did afterwards maliciouslie scatter and publish the same verses, to the great scandall of the complainants and of religion, &c.

The judges quickly agreed that the claims were false, and therefore it was a libel, but Lord Heath was especially exercised against Martin, who set 'the tune of it, to the tune of the Watch Currants and Tom of Bedlam. It is a wicked and profane libell against such as go to Church carefullie . . . I say they are Atheists that scoffe at religion in others'.[71]

Finally, one of the strangest manifestations of the bedlam's voice occurred in Thomas Jordan's *A Diurnall of Dangers*, a survey of one week's apocalyptic events during the political upheavals of 1642. On the Saturday, 'there was a combustion amongst the *Bedlamites*; insomuch that the Keeper and his strong assistance could scarce restraine them. One (above the rest) cryed, cryed, He would have Justice, or he would pul the house down: and swore he was committed for a mad man, because he had the audacious impudence to demand his owne at the hands of his betters. Four or five other cryed out, *They make us mad, They make us mad*, and our onely way is to petition that we have no more new moones.' The 'combustion' spirals further out of control, Jordan

relates, becoming literal as well as figurative: 'one of the maddest sort, with three or foure mad women, had set fire of the straw, which were seconded by most of the rest'. At this point, 'by a strange miracle [the Bedlamites] were reclaimed, with Musick, and a Song, made and sung by a Gentleman that was almost recovered from his lunacie; and while the fire slacked, thus went on his Ditty'. As this song has never, to my knowledge, been reprinted, I quote it in its entirety:

SONG Tune Tom of Bedlam.
The world is all but madnesse,
　　Then why are we confined
To live by Law, and lie in straw,
　　With hunger almost pined?
　　But then give me way
　　　　Take my locks, take my bolts off,
　　　　Wee'le be free as they be,
　　　　who keepe such state, that none dare prate,
　　　　Yet are as mad as may be.
The State is in distraction;
　　Can any man deny it?
But her[e]'s the curse attends it worse,
　　Ther's none can make it quiet.
　　Then give, &c.
The Trojan Siege was tedious,
　　I'th' dayes of old King Priam,
The sword did stand in the mad mans hand,
　　Who was as mad as I am.
　　Then give, &c.
To armes I heare the drum beat,
　　Let me my Captains pay have:
Why should they goe and leave me so?
　　I have as much cause as they have.
　　Then give, &c.
Alas ther's none obeyes me,
　　'Tis power prevails on all things:
The World is bad, and dangerous mad,
　　Whilst we lye here for small things.
　　Then let me stay,
　　Keepe the doores, let me sleepe here.
　　Abroad I shall be sadder,
　　Should I but goe, they'le use me so,
　　I feare 'twill make me madder.

---

[71] S. R. Gardiner, ed., *Reports of Cases in the Courts of Star Chamber and High Commission* (London, 1886), pp. 149, 152.

'*With this conclusion*', Jordan reports, '*all was quiet, and thus ends this weekes disasters with the strange remedies; thinke of them, and let it be a faire warning to us*'.[72]

Although the song and music of Poor Tom were appropriated, transformed, and domesticated after 1605, then, they could at times still be associated, as they are in Shakespeare's play, with subversion, mockery and social critique. What vanishes from the later manifestations, however, is poverty itself. Poor Tom's poverty *and* his madness are essential, intertwined aspects of his nature. Indeed, his poverty is in many ways prior to his madness; his mental disturbance functions more as a sign of other disorders. But after *King Lear*, other, irresistible cultural forces romanticized or idealized the figure, emphasizing his madness while simultaneously erasing his poverty. Of all the transgressive social categories embodied in the destitute figure of Poor Tom, it is social class which is most effaced, perhaps because class was and still remains the most threatening of categories. Tom's madness, by contrast, which was often counterfeit in the earliest descriptions, became his defining characteristic after *King Lear*, and even his madness at times took the form of love-madness. Finally, *Poor* Tom's voice – something jagged, strange, and pathetic in Shakespeare – turned into *Mad* Tom's voice – something lyric, harmonious, and pleasing; and after 1649, when it became illegal to sell ballads in the streets, Tom's voice became completely domesticated. It is a curious fate indeed for the roaring voice.

---

[72] Thomas Jordan, *A Diurnall of Dangers* (London, 1642), A4^{r-v}.

SECULARIZING *KING LEAR*: SHAKESPEARE, TATE, AND THE SACRED

PETER WOMACK

Drama and religion, having lived in holy matrimony for some five hundred years, are given a decree of divorce nisi at the Reformation, which, under the pressures of the Renaissance, is made absolute shortly after the Restoration.

(Glynne Wickham)[1]

I

Nahum Tate's *King Lear* was first seen in the winter of 1680–1, and it was in his adaptation, or in further adaptations of it, that the play was always performed until Macready went back to a (heavily cut) Shakespearian text in 1838. For over 150 years, then – half its post-Restoration stage life – *Lear* appeared on the English stage without the Fool, with a happy ending, and usually with an added love story leading to the marriage of Edgar and Cordelia. Moreover, it was during the years when this travesty held sway that the play secured its leading place in the canon. It had been revived between 1660 and 1680, but not often. It was Tate's version that established itself as a stock play in the early eighteenth century; it was Tate's King Lear that Garrick took up in 1742 and made into his greatest role; by the time he retired in 1776 it was one of the acknowledged mountain peaks of the English repertoire, undertaken as such by Kemble in 1788 and Kean in 1820. Ironically, it was just this exalted reputation which eventually brought Tate's theatrical reign to an end: to literary Romantic playgoers such as Lamb and Keats, the adaptation now seemed a vulgar affront to the sublimity of the true play. Sentiment swung against the happy ending, Macready's experiment was accepted as a success,

and for Victorian bardolatry Tate was already, as he has remained, a derisory footnote to the history of a masterpiece.[2]

This easy dismissal doesn't deal with the fact of Tate's resilience. The extraordinary longevity of his version is not a simple case of cultural absent-mindedness: repeatedly, we can see theatres *deciding* to keep it. It was attacked many times, throughout the eighteenth century, from Addison to Genest,[3] and within the theatre there were several inconclusive signs of dissatisfaction. Garrick kept tinkering with the text but never broke with Tate's structure.[4] George Colman staged, and published, a partially restored text in 1768, but it only lasted until 1773.[5] In 1823 Kean attempted to reinstate

---

[1] Glynne Wickham, *Early English Stages 1300 to 1660*, vol. 2, part 1, (London, 1963), p. 40.

[2] My outline of this (quite familiar) story is drawn from William Shakespeare, *The Tragedy of King Lear*, ed. Jay L. Halio (Cambridge, 1992); *Plays in Performance: King Lear*, ed. J. S. Bratton (Bristol, 1987); Nahum Tate, *The History of King Lear*, ed. James Black (London, 1976); Christopher Spencer, *Nahum Tate* (New York, 1972).

[3] Addison: *Spectator* No. 40 (1711), in *Shakespeare: The Critical Heritage*, ed. Brian Vickers, 6 vols. (London, 1974–81), vol. 2, p. 273. Genest: John Genest, *Some Account of the English Stage*, 10 vols. (Bath, 1832), vol. 8, pp. 131–4.

[4] G. W. Stone, 'Garrick's Production of *King Lear*: A Study in the Temper of the Eighteenth-Century Mind', *Studies in Philology* 45 (1948), 89–103; H. W. Pedicord, 'Shakespeare, Tate and Garrick: New Light on Alterations of *King Lear*', *Theatre Notebook* 36 (1982), 14.

[5] Published as *The History of King Lear, As it is Performed at The Theatre Royal in Covent Garden*, 1768, Cornmarket Press reprint (London, 1969). The performance history is traceable

the tragic ending, but gave up, probably after three performances.[6] It is as if a sort of gravitational pull returned people to Tate's solutions even if they wanted to get away. Nor was this a simple case of theatrical practice triumphing over literary judgement. The happy ending continued to find critical supporters, most famously including Samuel Johnson in his revered edition of 1765.[7] What was it that Tate was doing right? There are two well-established ways of answering that question, neither of them wholly satisfactory.

One is to say that Tate was bringing the play into conformity with the taste of his age. Critics from Dryden onwards, after all, were very conscious of their own neoclassical refinement; they looked back at Elizabethan drama across a historical gulf which had been opened up by classical scholarship and French cultural hegemony;[8] Shakespeare's ignorance of 'the rules' was the object of interminable discussion among eighteenth-century editors. It is not surprising, then, if the acting editions of such a period sought to elevate Shakespeare to its own standards of regularity and decorum. And it is true that Tate's local rewriting reflects this kind of intention: he smooths out the versification, spells out the ellipses, and reduces (particularly by cutting the Fool) the text's extreme stylistic heterogeneity. The verbal texture ends up more polite, consistent, transparent and flat – more 'Augustan', one could impressionistically say.

However, the theory of adaptation as enlightenment correction is less convincing at the level of structure and action. Although, as we shall see, Tate is serious about the play's unity of action, he does nothing to mitigate its chronicle-like looseness of time and place. And he retains both the blinding of Gloucester and the illusory suicide at Dover Cliff, incidents which the critics of the following century or so would repeatedly condemn as obscene and improbable respectively. Tom o' Bedlam, with all the extravagance of his disguise and the grotesque comedy of his idiom, is also preserved fairly complete. There is not much here to meet the criteria of John Dennis or Charles Gildon; rather, the script belongs to the actual tragic theatre of the 1680s, which included the neo-Shakespearian

experiments of Otway and the lurid excesses of Nathaniel Lee[9] – just that English stage whose barbarism aroused Voltaire's quizzical dismay in the 1720s.[10] 'Refining' *Lear* is not exactly what Tate is doing after all.

The other current account of his project, and his success, refers it to political history. His *Lear* was one of ten Shakespeare adaptations or revivals that appeared in a sudden cluster between late 1677 and early 1682 – that is, it was part of the theatre's response to the long-drawn-out political crisis prompted by anti-Catholic attempts to control the succession to Charles II's throne. The reading this invites is not difficult to construct: Tate moves both Edmund and Edgar closer to the national centre of events than they are in Shakespeare, and so offers to turn the play's conflict into a straightforward shoot-out between heroized legitimate successor (the Duke of York) and demonized illegitimate successor (the Duke of Monmouth), general happiness being secured by the eventual victory of the former. The play becomes a legitimist fable.[11]

The trouble with this very localized reading is that it grounds Tate's structure in circumstances that

---

in *The London Stage 1660–1800*, Part 4, ed. G. W. Stone, Jr (Carbondale, Illinois, 1962).

[6] The slightly uncertain evidence is reviewed in the preface to the Cornmarket reprint *King Lear: Cumberland's Edition*, *c*.1830 (London, 1970).

[7] *Johnson on Shakespeare*, ed. Arthur Sherbo (New Haven and London, 1969), p. 704.

[8] Classically expressed by Dryden in, for example, 'Essay on the Dramatique Poetry of the Last Age' (1672), in Vickers, vol. 1, pp. 143–52.

[9] Lee's *The Rival Queens* (1677) and Otway's *Venice Preserv'd* (1682) were both popular star vehicles for much of the eighteenth century.

[10] Voltaire, *Letters on England*, tr. Leonard Tancock (Harmondsworth, 1980), Letter 18, 'On Tragedy'.

[11] This reading is persuasively presented by Nancy Klein Maguire, 'Nahum Tate's *King Lear*: "the king's blest restoration"', in *The Appropriation of Shakespeare*, ed. Jean I. Marsden (Hemel Hempstead, 1991), pp. 29–42. She is seconded in, for instance, Michael Dobson, *The Making of the National Poet: Shakespeare, Adaptation and Authorship*, (Oxford, 1992,) pp. 81–5, and Susan J. Owen, *Restoration Theatre and Crisis* (Oxford, 1996), pp. 225–8.

would cease to be topical within a decade, and so fails to account for the remaining century and a half of his adaptation's currency. And even within the immediate framework, it entails a somewhat paranoid reading of Tate's own account of his intentions. What he says is that, admiring Shakespeare's play but finding it irregular and improbable, he has sought to improve its coherence so as to please a modern audience. While this may indeed be no more than a cover story for Tate's darker purpose, it is not clear why he should be so disingenuous.

I think it may be more revealing to choose naivety – to take it that Tate's intentions were as he describes them, and that he owed his lasting place in the repertoire to his success in carrying them out. This involves looking more closely at what he did in fact do to the script, and asking: what exactly was *wrong* with *King Lear* the way it was before?

II

Tate's own diagnosis is well known: he found Shakespeare's play to be

a heap of jewels, unstrung and unpolished, yet so dazzling in their disorder that I soon perceived I had seized a treasure. 'Twas my good fortune to light on one expedient to rectify what was wanting in the regularity and probability of the tale, which was to run through the whole a love betwixt Edgar and Cordelia, that never changed word with each other in the original.[12]

The love of Edgar and Cordelia, then, is first and foremost not a sentimental decoration, but a structural 'expedient', the string on which to arrange the scattered jewels. It works like this. The Duke of Burgundy rejects the disinherited Cordelia, as in Shakespeare, but the King of France has been cut: so she remains unmarried in Britain. She is therefore present when Lear leaves Gloucester's castle for the heath, and goes out herself to try to find him; however, Edmund, who is a much more explicit sexual predator than in the original, sends villains to capture her so that he can rape her. She is rescued from this peril by the disguised Edgar, who reveals himself to her, and they exchange declarations of love. Subsequently, the old king's supporters, led

primarily by Kent, assemble an army against the sisters: Cordelia is with this army, is reunited with Lear, and shares in his defeat, much as in Shakespeare. Edmund attempts to have Lear and Cordelia murdered in prison, but in this version Edgar is in time to save them; Edgar and Cordelia marry and become king and queen of a restored realm.

It is really surprising how many incoherences are resolved by this device. It 'renders Cordelia's indifference and her father's passion in the first scene probable' (p. 1). It transforms Edgar's disguise from 'a poor shift to save his life' to 'a generous design' to stay close to Cordelia and watch over her interests. It makes the military opposition to Goneril and Regan a patriotic insurrection rather than a foreign invasion, and so removes the need for Shakespeare's evasiveness about the French King. This in turn gives Kent an active role in the denouement, rather than the ineffectual hanging about into which Shakespeare allows him to drift after his robust beginning. It counteracts the disintegrative effects of the double plot by literally uniting the interests of the two families. It gives the ending a morally satisfying shape, saving the lives not only of Lear and Cordelia, but also of Gloucester and Kent, whom Shakespeare adds to the death toll for reasons, and even by mechanisms, which are not readily understandable. And it triumphantly settles the succession, the very question which set the plot in motion to begin with.

We can summarize this sevenfold improvement by saying that Tate has made the play newly *purposeful*. Cordelia has a purpose when she offends her father, Edgar and Kent have purposes when they adopt their disguises, the nation has the purpose of throwing off the usurpers, the play as a whole moves purposefully towards the crowning of Lear's successor. The 'heap of jewels' Tate found in the Folio is brought into order in the sense that the play's events are arranged in a set of relations of means to ends.

[12] Dedication, in Tate, *The History of King Lear*, ed. Black, p. 1. Subsequent references to the dedication and the text are to this edition.

To reconstruct Tate's success, we need to enter this network of instrumental relationships and feel how *pleasing* it is – to register its intelligibility, its compelling consonance of character and action, the concentrated energy with which one consideration leads to another and propels the story forward. Shakespeare's *King Lear*, by these standards, appears as a structure disabled by passivity. In Acts 3 and 4 particularly, the theatrical interest is perversely invested in a collection of characters – Lear himself, the Fool, Gloucester, Edgar, Kent – who are no longer, or not yet, the subjects of any recognizable dramatic action. Cut off from real interaction by madness, blindness or pretence, they wander in an empty landscape, absorbed in their own suffering or exchanging fragmentary messages about actions which may be taking place elsewhere. The atmosphere engenders small, irritating enigmas: why does Edgar adopt such an uncomfortable alias instead of simply running away? why do both he and Kent retain their disguises after the need for them has passed? why are Lear and Gloucester left straying about rather than being delivered to the French camp? what happens to the Fool? who is in command of the French army? Tate's reforms answer or abolish almost all of these questions, and so recover the dramatis personae as active subjects within a syntax of intelligible cause and effect.[13]

We are not, in short, to be left asking 'why?'. For example: why does Edgar not reveal his true identity to Gloucester? In both versions, when Gloucester is blinded he is also undeceived about his sons, at which point Edgar is, in theory, free to drop his disguise. In both versions, however, he continues to present himself to Gloucester as Poor Tom. Tate instantly tells us why. As soon as his Edgar hears Gloucester speak of his innocence, he responds, aside:

Alas, he's sensible that I was wronged;
And should I own myself, his tender heart
Would break between th'extremes of grief and joy.
(4.2.24–6)

Shakespeare, on the other hand, leaves the equivalent moment unclear. In the scene where father and son meet (4.1), Gloucester twice speaks of Edgar's innocence, but there is no sign that Edgar himself takes it in. Lost in his own thoughts, he neither abandons his disguise nor decides to retain it; he just carries opaquely on as he is.

Tate has not simply invented his rationalization. Its terms are taken from the story that Shakespeare's Edgar tells about Gloucester's death:

> his flawed heart –
> Alack, too weak the conflict to support! –
> 'Twixt two extremes of passion, joy and grief,
> Burst smilingly.[14]

But the difference between the two contexts for the same idea vividly marks the distance between the two dramaturgies. In Shakespeare, the narrative moment negates or even mocks the narrator's capacity to control events: after his long struggle to sustain his father's life, Edgar inadvertently precipitates his death. The event is not produced by anyone's will, and not exactly in opposition to anyone's will either. It happens, independently of any of the agencies visible on the stage. In Tate, on the other hand, the same words are taken out of the past tense of narrative and reset in the conditional tense of deliberate planning: rather than constituting a mystery which baffles intention, they now form part of the very mechanism of intention, articulating the power of consciousness to determine what happens. An *opaque event* is recontextualized as a *transparent motive*.

---

[13] At this point the canons of neoclassical criticism do illuminate Tate's poetics. For instance John Dennis, developing the familiar Aristotelian topos of the superiority of poetry to history, declares: 'in an Historical Relation we seldom are acquainted with the true Causes of Events; whereas in a feign'd Action which is duly constituted, that is, which has a just beginning, those Causes always appear' ('On the Genius and Writings of Shakespeare' (1712), in *Eighteenth-Century Essays on Shakespeare*, ed. D. Nichol Smith, 2nd edn (Oxford, 1963), p. 26). Thus when Shakespeare 'feigns an action' but leaves its causes as opaque as they were in the chronicle source, this suggests his 'complete ignorance of Poetical Art'.

[14] *King Lear* 5.3.195–8, in *The Norton Shakespeare*, ed. Stephen Greenblatt *et al.* (New York and London, 1997). Subsequent quotations from Shakespeare's *Lear* are from the 'conflated text' in this edition.

The new dramatic syntax is at odds with the old one, and it is when a collision produces anomalies that the incompatibility is most clearly visible. Take for example Cordelia's behaviour in the opening scene. Tate's Cordelia, like his Edgar, immediately explains why she acts as she does:

> How am I distressed,
> That must with cold speech tempt the choleric king
> Rather to leave me dowerless, than condemn me
> To loathed embraces!   (1.1.92–5)

This way of putting it means that when she says, 'Nothing, my lord', we know that her tone is deliberate ('cold speech'), and that her covert intention is to displease Lear so as not to have to marry the 'loathed' Burgundy. She is calculating the effect of her words in the same way as her sisters. Indeed, her conduct in the scene is if anything *more* hypocritical than theirs, since she says, as in Shakespeare, that the reason for her disappointing answer is her inability to speak anything but the truth – that is, she is passing off her chosen strategy as the inescapable effect of her personality. We thus get, astonishingly, a Cordelia who makes Goneril and Regan look comparatively naive. Of course she is still more likeable than they are, but that is only because her concealed aim is love, whereas theirs is wealth and power. All three are lying.

This casts a rather cold light on Tate's dramaturgy. He finds Cordelia's behaviour in Shakespeare's opening scene 'improbable' in the sense that he cannot see a reason for it; so he renders it probable by supplying one – that is, he adjusts its context so that it is *in Cordelia's interests* not to flatter the king. What that then highlights is the abrupt gratuitousness of the equivalent moment in Shakespeare. The authority and danger of Cordelia's refusal come just from its disinterestedness, which disconcerts the harmonious play of half-concealed interests that have informed the scene up to this point. Lear, Goneril, Regan and the audience have all been understanding one another well enough; now the dramatic syntax encounters an abyss. (That it is 'improbable' is the point.) Tate,

however, hastens to fill the abyss in, even at the cost of his heroine's integrity.

This can be put in more structural terms. Cordelia's speech about 'loathed embraces' replaces her first Shakespearian aside: 'What shall Cordelia speak? Love, and be silent.' Tate's Cordelia cannot intelligibly say that, because her acquisition of a motive means precisely that she is no longer 'silent'; her dramatic situation is articulate, reasoned, explanatory. The same is obviously true of the other end of the role: whereas Shakespeare's Lear ends where he began, seeking in vain to coax a sound from Cordelia's lips, Tate's Cordelia is naturally included in the normal discursive circle of a stage happy ending. The adaptation shows by contrast, then, how Shakespeare's Cordelia is a role which moves from silence to silence. The paradox which strikes every actress who does it – that it is absolutely central to the play but hardly has any lines – reflects the sense in which it is fundamentally non-discursive.[15] By filling this essential stillness up with talk, Tate effaces the subtle disjunction between Cordelia and the rest of the play: throughout, as in the first scene, she is rewritten so that she inhabits *the same speech world* as everybody else, however corrupt that is.

The insistence on 'probable' motivation has an even more drastic effect on Gloucester. In a new soliloquy immediately after the blinding scene, Tate's Gloucester first determines to end his miserable life, but then adds

> Must I then tamely die, and unrevenged?
> So Lear may fall: no, with these bleeding rings
> I will present me to the pitying crowd,
> And with the rhetoric of these dropping veins
> Enflame 'em to revenge their king and me.
>
>   (3.5.83–7)

---

[15] In many types of theatre, including that of the 1680s, this is an immediate casting problem. Structurally, Cordelia is the heroine, but in practice the part offers so little that it is difficult to offer it to the star. This is surely one contributory reason for the longevity of Tate's version: by augmenting the role with a love interest and a good deal of supplementary 'distress', he built it up into a plausible female lead.

This startling discourse has been assembled from several sources in the Shakespearian text. Shakespeare's Regan briefly commented that it was unwise to have let him live on after his blinding, because 'where he arrives he moves / All hearts against us' (4.5.1–12); the new speech picks up her machiavellian diagnosis and appropriates it as Gloucester's plan, once again redeploying ironic contingency as sophisticated intention. By the same logic, the 'bleeding rings' are borrowed from Edgar's narrative in Shakespeare's final scene: as part of Gloucester's own speech, the notation of the son's horror and pity becomes, bizarrely, a newly blind man's calculation about the heart-rending impact of his own appearance in the future. Exactly like Cordelia's truthfulness, Gloucester's blindness loses its silent character and becomes a deliberate 'rhetoric'.

Gloucester's plan, like most plans in Tate's consequential world, takes effect. He is twice described as making public speeches to rouse the people against the usurpers' rule (4.1.37–44 and 5.2.16–20). Moreover, the scene in which he engages Poor Tom to lead him is interrupted by a chance meeting with Kent and Cordelia. Gloucester gives Cordelia his blessing, urges Kent to lead the forces of resistance, ringingly hopes that his cause will prove 'as prosperous as 'tis just' (4.2.110) – and then resumes his melancholy journey to the cliff-edge. Thus the role becomes seriously incoherent: Gloucester is the orator and elder statesman of a national rebellion, but at the same time he is a deracinated outcast with no one to look after him except a poor lunatic. Unable to reconcile Shakespeare's lost and isolated Gloucester with his own purposeful and patriotic one, Tate helplessly alternates them from one scene to the next.

The source of the muddle, I think, is that the blinding of Shakespeare's Gloucester has the effect of cutting him off from the logic of probability. He has gone beyond advantage and disadvantage; he fluctuates between wanting to die and indifference; like Cordelia, though in a wholly different way, he is disinterested. To the common-sense observation that he cannot go off by himself because he cannot see his way he replies, 'I have no way, and

therefore want no eyes' (4.1.19). A character who can say that seriously is no longer amenable to the syntax of cause and effect. Tate keeps the line, but in his context it is merely the emphatic expression of an emotion. In reality his Gloucester does have a 'way': it is to contribute to his own revenge and the restoration of the rightful king. Tate is resisting the idea of a state of total *outsideness* to the action of the play; the tenacity of the resistance can be measured by his readiness to incur, for the sake of it, radical inconsistency in the role of Gloucester, despite the fact that consistency of character is a leading canon of the dramatic regularity in whose name the adaptation was undertaken in the first place. At almost any cost, Gloucester has to remain connected with the plot.

At this point it becomes fairly simple to say what Tate's adaptation is most fundamentally rejecting in the Shakespearian text. All these examples suggest that what Tate will not allow into the text is silence, opacity, disjunction. Edgar, Cordelia, Gloucester must all explain themselves, all speak the prevailing language and acknowledge the prevailing principles of action. In a way, it *is* a matter of unity after all – not the externally policed 'rules' of neoclassical criticism, but the underlying rule that everything must hang together, so that every part of the text is subject to the same discursive regime of cause and effect. Formally and ideologically, there is to be *one world*, with no no-go areas, no blocks on the circulation of meaning, no enclaves where the writ of instrumental rationality does not run. With, to put it another way, no transcendence.

III

Transcendence is excluded by the most influential of all eighteenth-century eulogies of Shakespeare:

Other dramatists can only gain attention by hyperbolical or aggravated characters, by fabulous and unexampled excellence or depravity, as the writers of barbarous romances invigorated the reader by a giant and a dwarf; and he that should form his expectations of human affairs from the play, or from the tale, should be equally deceived. *Shakespeare* has no heroes; his scenes are occupied only by men, who act and speak as the reader thinks that he should himself have spoken or acted on the same occasion. Even where the agency is supernatural the dialogue is level with life. Other writers disguise the most natural passions and most frequent incidents; so that he who contemplates them in the book will not know them in the world: *Shakespeare* approximates the remote, and familiarizes the wonderful; the event which he represents will not happen, but if it were possible, its effects would probably be such as he has assigned; and it may be said, that he has not only shewn human nature as it acts in real exigences, but as it would be found in trials, to which it cannot be exposed.

This therefore is the praise of *Shakespeare*, that his drama is the mirrour of life; that he who has mazed his imagination, in following the phantoms which other writers raise up before him, may here be cured of his delirious extasies, by reading human sentiments in human language: by scenes from which a hermit may estimate the transactions of the world, and a confessor predict the progress of the passions.[16]

Johnson's magisterial formulation grounds Shakespeare's reputation in the idea of the *real* – 'men', 'life', 'the world', the 'probable', 'human nature'. Clearly this idea is too general to stand alone as a positive value: if it is not to be vacuous, it needs something which is *not* 'the world' against which it can define itself. And in fact the whole passage depends for its force on the hapless 'other writers' who fail to do what Shakespeare paradigmatically does. They deal in the fabulous, the unexampled and the unrecognizable; Shakespeare, the poet of nature, is then substantiated as the dramatist who is not only free of their errors but can actually be used to correct them.

Who are they meant to be? The wider context of the Preface, and of the tradition of praising Shakespeare it inherits, makes it clear that Johnson's target is modern playwriting, allegedly in thrall to the rules and conventions of the neoclassical French stage, entangling its characters in the formulaic vicissitudes of love and filling their mouths with 'hyperbolical joy and outrageous sorrow'. Whereas Shakespeare is steadily in touch with real life and common humanity, modern drama is cut off from these things because of its fatal artificiality, which elevates critical canons, generic shibboleths and literary models at the expense of nature.

This is not an ideologically innocent contrast. A typical deployment of it by John Upton, writing in the 1740s, traces the rot back to 1660:

> when we brought home our frenchified king we did then, and have even to this day continued to, bring from France our models not only of letters but (O shame to free-born Englishmen!) of morals and manners... It seems no wonder that the masculine and nervous Shakespeare and Milton should so little please our effeminate taste, and the more I consider our studies and amusements the greater is the wonder they should ever please at all. The childish fancy and love of false ornaments follow us thro' life, nothing being so displeasing to us as nature and simplicity.[17]

And a reviewer of Johnson, disappointed at his conceding as much as he does to 'the French academy', regards the whole idea of 'taste' as an un-British innovation: 'Shakespeare is to be tried by a more sure criterion, that of feeling, which is the same in all ages and all climates. To talk of trying Shakespeare by the rules of *taste* is speaking like the spindle-shanked beau who *languished* to thresh a brawny coachman.'[18]

The aggression of these formulations is in part defensive.[19] The criteria of the 'French academy' had often been invoked, by both French and English critics, to convict Shakespeare's plays of improbability, absurdity, and unnaturalness. To condemn neoclassical drama for just these vices by a standard of 'nature and simplicity' derived from

---

[16] Samuel Johnson, Preface to Shakespeare (1765), *Johnson on Shakespeare*, pp. 64–5.

[17] John Upton, *Critical Observations on Shakespeare*, 2nd edn, 1748, extracted in Vickers, *The Critical Heritage*, vol. 3, p. 291.

[18] William Guthrie, reviewing Johnson in *Critical Review*, November 1765, extracted in Vickers, *The Critical Heritage*, vol. 5, p. 212.

[19] One context of the literary attacking and defending is the contemporary struggle between France and Britain for global domination. The prestige of Johnson's Shakespeare reflected not only its own merits, but also its appearance in the aftermath of the war of 1756–63: the spindle-shanked beau had just been threshed by the brawny coachman in a fracas extending from Calcutta to Quebec. A world-historical future awaited the winner of Shakespeare *v.* Corneille.

Shakespeare pointedly reverses the direction of the attack. Johnson's management of this reversal is less overtly nationalistic, but more deadly. He suggests an analogy between the 'aggravated' characters of fashionable tragedy and the giants and dwarfs of 'barbarous romances', and comments that as representations of real life they are as bad as each other: 'he that should form his expectations of human affairs from the play, or from the tale, should be equally deceived'. So the dramatic correctness which dismisses Shakespeare as barbarous romance is placed as *indistinguishable from* romance itself when judged by the solid touchstone of Shakespearian reality. The Gallic hyper-cultivation of 'art' is allied to barbarism because both are in flight from – what therefore becomes the crucial valorizing term – nature.[20]

It is a far-reaching move. It makes Shakespeare into the founding exemplar of a robustly English and empirical poetics which can resist the cultural hegemony of French theory, while still sustaining critical discriminations capable of excluding the vulgar and the uncivilized. As the necessary oppositions are rolled out – art and nature, the rules and liberty, refinement and solidity, the fantastic and the human – we can watch the twin-birth of Shakespeare and English criticism. Criticism is needed to articulate the values embodied in Shakespeare, and Shakespeare is needed as the embodiment of the values articulated in the criticism. Together they set about the making of English Literature. The power of this project to shape both Englishness and the literary curriculum could be amply documented from the following two centuries and more. What concerns us here, though, is its shaping of Shakespeare. He is the originating occasion and emblem of the whole mission – and this role calls for a particular *kind* of Shakespeare.

We can see it in the long quotation from the Preface, and its characterization of those necessary others. Shakespeare's identification with life and human nature is defined by its opposition to a consistent set of negative signs: the fabulous; heroes, giants and dwarfs; disguise; the remote and wonderful; mazes; phantoms; delirious ecstasies. It is oddly in keeping with this dimly back-projected landscape that the argument concludes by somewhat whimsically introducing a hermit and a confessor. They too are part of the catalogue of negations, because their seclusion from the world is understood as an ignorance of the ordinary business of life – that is, a lack of precisely that knowledge which Shakespeare's plays uniquely and richly contain.

Johnson's confidently named reality, that is to say, has as its 'other' something more culturally specific than his universalizing terminology at first suggests. There exists, across the tracks from the judiciously seen 'transactions of the world', a Gothic space of magic and deception, of solitude, illusion and other-worldliness. It is as the opposite of all these things that the father of the English drama confirms us in our common human nature. But at the same time, reading this passage in the light of Tate's struggles with *King Lear*, we can't help noticing that Johnson's non-nature, with its disguises, its remoteness and its delirious ecstasies, looks rather familiar. When the characters of *Lear* become detached from the transactions of *their* world – Lear and the Fool, Edgar, Kent, Gloucester – it is into just this negative space that they maze our imaginations by withdrawing.

As we saw, Shakespeare's Cordelia does not inhabit the probable world. Her truth and love are unconditional; they have 'no cause' (4.7.76). Ordinary heredity cannot explain her difference from her sisters, 'Else one self mate and make could not beget / Such different issues' (4.3.33–4). From her temporary absence in France she returns as if from another world: so far from being 'natural', she is now the daughter 'Who redeems nature from the general curse / That twain have brought her to' (4.6.200–1), adorned with fantastically wrought hagiographical description (4.3. 9–31) and verbal echoes of Christ (4.4.24–5), and appearing to the ruined king as a soul in bliss to lead him out of

---

[20] G. F. Parker is categorical: 'Johnson's experience of Shakespeare as the poet of nature animates the whole of his account . . . ; on that central perception he rests his claim for Shakespeare's abiding greatness, and from it all his other observations flow.' *Johnson's Shakespeare* (Oxford, 1989), p. 1.

purgatory (4.7.45–8).[21] In short, the conventions by which the role works are partly medieval: Shakespeare's complicated dramatic texture includes the stage image of a saint.[22] Gloucester, in the context this suggests, can be seen to withdraw not only from the plot but from the world: luridly maimed and wandering in the wilderness, accompanied by a mysterious beggar who is part demon and part friendly animal, he is both a kind of martyr and a kind of ascetic, moving via a spectacular miracle and an obscurely purgative process to a death which is also a blissful reunion. His trajectory too is a kind of displaced sanctification; a whole area of the play is being made out of hagiographic material.

Conversely, the world from which these characters absent themselves seems from their retrospective point of view to be both fallen and illusory: it is Lear's great stage of fools, which those who have left it watch with angelic tears and laughter, as if they were God's spies. This radical disjunction of worlds is dramatised, for example, in the staging of the battle in 5.2. According to the story, this is the climax of the action – the moment when the forces of good and evil come together to fight it out and settle the fate of the kingdom. But the audience is made to share Gloucester's point of view; so the decisive battle is diminished to a brief noise heard, or dreamt, by an old blind man resting under a tree.[23] A comparable remoteness is produced by the unrelieved viciousness of the vestigial 'transactions of the world', as the only characters who remain in it – Goneril, Regan, Edmund, Oswald – are reduced to interchangeable ciphers of competition and lust. In the end, they are no less alien to us than the saints and martyrs: they are the damned. Johnson's 'mirrour of life' is shivered, its unitary image criss-crossed by the lines that divide heaven from hell, the sacred from the profane, 'the world' from the unworldly spaces inhabited by mendicants, madmen and devils.

Putting it like that comes close to placing *King Lear* on a kind of sacred stage, as if Shakespeare were reinventing the religious drama which the English Reformation had just brought to an end. What needs to be added to that context, though, is that if this is sacred theatre, it is also a particularly theatrical kind of sacredness. Cordelia comes from Heaven, but also only from France. Edgar seems to converse with Hoppedance and Frateretto, but breaks off to remind the audience that he is pretending. Gloucester's miracle is a trick; he only thinks he jumped off a cliff. As the Fool points out, a night of bad weather is not really the apocalypse. But these ambiguities, while they deflect the play's supernaturalism in one sense, if anything move the dramaturgy still further away from the level rendition of life. The theatrical images are unnatural not only in the sense that they are sacred, but also in the sense that they are fakes. The expansive view of general human nature is obscured by a murky mixture of theophany and showmanship, the generic Protestant term for which is superstition.

So the ecstasies and delusions which it is Shakespeare's historic mission to put to flight turn out to be *also* Shakespeare. The vindication of the down-to-earth English poet against the cavils of frenchified critics entails his extrication, not simply from pedantic rules of drama, but more intimately from the metaphysics of his own stage. Johnson's authoritative promulgation of the poet of nature is tacitly founded on the suppression of the sacred dimension of early modern theatre. It was this decatholicized and empirical Shakespeare that Tate delivered: the 'one world' which he imposes upon the layered artifice and denaturing mysteries of *King Lear* is the

---

[21] Of these six citations, Tate keeps 'thou art a soul in bliss', but cuts the other five.

[22] The Catholic dimension of *King Lear* has been discussed in the light of the play's appearance in the repertoire of the recusant players who were examined for performing a saint play in Yorkshire in 1610. See John L. Murphy, *Darkness and Devils: Exorcism and 'King Lear'* (Athens, Ohio, 1986), pp. 93–118, and Stephen Greenblatt, 'Shakespeare and the Exorcists', in *Shakespearean Negotiations* (Berkeley, California, 1988), pp. 94–128. I discussed the saint-play element in the Yorkshire players' other show, *Pericles*, in 'Shakespeare and the Sea of Stories', *Journal of Medieval and Early Modern Studies*, 29:1 (1999), 169–88.

[23] Tate keeps the scene (5.3), but adds a soliloquy for Gloucester which connects him emotionally with the battle he cannot be part of. Always, in detail, Tate can be seen repairing disjunctions, stitching the dramatic world together.

same as 'the world' in whose irreducible actuality Johnson grounds Shakespeare's reputation.[24]

In the longer run, of course, the secularization of Shakespeare was accomplished not by scissors and paste but by literary criticism. Once this more refined and ambitious 'adaptation' was under way, Tate was redundant; in fact he became an unsightly reminder of the iconoclastic violence that had once been needed. Perhaps that is why literary critics are so rude about him. But the worst we can say about his crassness and incompetence only makes his resilience the more remarkable, and testifies the more

impressively to the urgency of the ideological demands he transitionally satisfied.

---

[24] Several mid eighteenth-century champions of *Lear* (though not of course Johnson) illustrate Shakespeare's knowledge of human nature with lines that are in fact Tate's – e.g. Samuel Foote in 1747 (Vickers, *The Critical Heritage*, vol. 3, pp. 211–15), or John Shebbeare in 1755 (Vickers, *The Critical Heritage*, vol. 4, p. 184). On the stage, in particular, what counted as *King Lear* was an incompletely distinguished mixture of Shakespeare, Tate, and Garrick; here we see Tate contributing very directly to Shakespeare's cultural triumph.

'LOOK ON HER, LOOK': THE APOTHEOSIS OF CORDELIA

JANET BOTTOMS

The 'after-life' of any Shakespeare play is lived through a variety of media – stage performance, critical analysis, translation and adapatation – but it is at least arguable that such life and popular accessibility as 'Shakespeare' continues to enjoy owes much to his preservation in the educational system. Bowdlerized, moralized, weighed down with notes or expanded into 'tales', still the Shakespeare they met in school has been for many people the only one they know, and deserves at least a footnote in the story. A special place should also be reserved for those editors and adapters by whom 'the attention of young females, both in schools and families' was 'carefully directed to the study of our English Classics'[1] at a time when the classical languages still ruled boys' education, since without their efforts, and those of the women's reading groups and literary societies, Shakespeare might have ceased to have any 'after-life' outside a small coterie of intellectuals. Particular interest therefore attaches to their appropriation of *King Lear*, a play which presented a unique problem to young women in the nineteenth century.

It is something of a critical commonplace to say that for the 'Romantics' *Hamlet* and *Lear* were the greatest of all Shakespeare's plays – and this in contrast to views expressed in the eighteenth century, when *Lear* was seen as an imperfect play liberally sprinkled with moral tropes. By 'the Romantics', in such contexts, of course, we mean the male Romantic author-critics of the early nineteenth century for whom, as Lamb put it, 'the greatness of Lear is not in corporal dimension, but in individual... While we read it, we see not Lear, but

we are Lear, – we are in his mind, we are sustained by a grandeur which baffles the malice of daughters and storms.' The absence even of Tate's version from the London stage during the Regency years encouraged such imaginative appropriation, undisturbed by visible reminders of the old king's 'corporal infirmities and weakness, the impotence of rage'.[2] For women – linked in Lamb's dithyramb with storms – the position was somewhat different. Who were they to identify with – to 'be'? In marked contrast to Charlotte Lennox's eighteenth century view that Lear's reaction to the 'noble Disinterestedness' of Cordelia's answer had 'all the Appearance of a Judgment totally depraved' even before he ran mad,[3] Lamb's magnification of the King entailed a corresponding diminution of Cordelia. Even in the *Tales from Shakespear*, written primarily for girls, Lamb had already (1807) commented that her 'plainness of speech, which Lear called pride' was hardly 'daughter-like' and 'did indeed sound a little ungracious'. By contrast, the 'honest freedom' of Kent, though it also stirred the king to anger, was proof of his 'courage', and Lamb enlarged his role in the story to make him

---

1 J. R. Pitman, 'Advertisement', *The School Shakspeare: or Plays and Scenes from Shakspeare, Illustrated For the Use of Schools* (London, 1822), np.

2 Charles Lamb, 'On the Tragedies of Shakspeare, Considered with Reference to their fitness for Stage Representation', *The Works of Charles and Mary Lamb*, ed. T. Hutchinson, 2 vols. (London, 1924), vol. 1, p. 136.

3 Charlotte Lennox, *Shakespeare Illustrated* (London, 1754), p. 287.

Lear's protector in his madness and instrumental in persuading Cordelia to return from France to succour her father.[4] Lamb authorized Lear's perspective on events,[5] and Hazlitt and Coleridge followed his lead – Hazlitt seeing in Cordelia an 'indiscreet simplicity', with 'a little of her father's obstinacy in it,' quite different from Kent's 'manly plainness',[6] while Coleridge criticized a 'little faulty admixture of pride and sullenness in Cordelia's "Nothing" '. Regan and Goneril were, for him, pictures of 'the pure unnatural . . . unsoftened or diversified by a single line of goodness or common human frailty,' though 'some plausible excuses' could be found for Edmund. As for Lear, 'all [his] faults increase our pity. We refuse to know them otherwise than as means and aggravations of his sufferings and his daughters' ingratitude'.[7]

What place could there be for the female reader in such a reconstituted play? Judith Hawley has argued that the nineteenth century saw a critical division along gendered lines; and that while the male Romantic critics tended to 'aestheticise and psychologise Shakespeare', women showed a persistent concern with, even 'a violent attachment to morality'.[8] This is true only up to a point, however, since the clearly gendered judgements of Hazlitt and Coleridge show that morality was an issue for them as well. The story of King Lear and his daughters focused a moral issue which was seen as of key importance to both men and women in the nineteenth century. Its subject, said Hazlitt, 'is that which strikes its root deepest into the human heart; of which the bond is hardest to be unloosed; and the cancelling and tearing to pieces of which gives the greatest revulsion to the frame'. A 'firm faith in filial piety' was the 'prop' whose failure brought 'giddy anarchy and whirling tumult'.[9] This was a theme which continued to touch nineteenth century sensibilities deeply, even growing in importance as the century progressed. The 'deep' law 'that children must obey their parents' was eternal and universal, declared the reverend schoolmaster–editor of one school edition in 1876:

All governments appeal to us in its name; Rome ruled through the vigour derived from its performance;

Germany now builds her homely domestic life upon it; France still clings to it as her one fixed point amid revolutions; and we ourselves are anxiously thinking how it may be most firmly maintained amongst us, in spite of adverse influences.[10]

And on the domestic front, 'the peace of home love, the very stronghold of right battle in the world,' commented Henry Morley, in Cassell's threepenny National Library edition of *Lear*,

is so familiar, so full of playful ease, that we are apt to think little of its force. But let there be but the suspicion of a chill look, or a harsh word, where home love should be, and we wince, as we wince at nothing else that is in itself so trivial. Here Shakspeare puts for the chill look extremest cruelty, and shows life in its wildest storm of suffering.[11]

While not dissenting from the moral, some women began also to feel a need to 'aestheticise

---

[4] See the comment by Jonathan Bate, 'Lamb on Shakespeare', *Charles Lamb Bulletin* n.s. 51 (1985), 76–85; p. 84.

[5] Lamb consistently turns into apparently reliable narrative form the content of Lear's self-exculpatory speeches of denunciation; e.g. 'and [Lear] said that she spoke an untruth; *and so indeed she did* [my italics], for the hundred knights were all men of choice behaviour and sobriety of manners, skilled in all particulars of duty, and not given to rioting or feasting, as she said'. Charles Lamb, 'King Lear', in Charles and Mary Lamb, 'Tales from Shakespear', *Works*, ed. Hutchinson, vol. 2, p. 105.

[6] William Hazlitt, 'Characters of Shakespear's Plays' (1817), *Lectures on the Literature of the Age of Elizabeth and Characters of Shakespear's Plays* (London, 1909), p. 109.

[7] Terence Hawkes, ed., *Coleridge on Shakespeare* (Harmondsworth, 1969), pp. 203, 197, 206.

[8] Judith Hawley, 'Shakespearean Sensibilities: Women Writers Reading Shakespeare', in J. Batchelor, T. Cain and C. Lamont, eds., *Shakespearean Continuities* (London, 1997), pp. 293, 301.

[9] Hazlitt, 'Characters', pp. 108–9.

[10] Charles Moberly, ed., Introduction, *King Lear. Select Plays of Shakspere* (London, Oxford and Cambridge, 1876), p. 5.

[11] Henry Morley, ed., Introduction, *King Lear* (London, 1888), p. 21. Morley was Professor of English Language and Literature at Queen's College, London, and the introductions to his cheap and popular editions of the English classics were widely circulated. Alfonzo Gardiner also quotes them in his school edition of the Lambs' *Tales from Shakespeare* (Manchester and London, 1888).

and psychologise'. In this context it is important to recall that, for many, their first introduction to *Lear* would have been in that very site of 'home love' which the play so dramatically threatened, probably read to them by the *pater* himself, while his family 'pursued their several occupations; the mother and girls at their sewing; the boys with their slate or their sketching'.[12] This was a a scene replicated in many households, and it could not but influence the way in which girls and women interpreted the play. Where were their sympathies to be directed? Who was to be deemed responsible for that first 'chill look'? If even the most well-intentioned deviation from absolute submission could produce such anarchy, must not unquestioning filial obedience obviously be a girl's first duty? Dorothea Beale, whose father read Shakespeare to her in her childhood, would later preach the value of great literature to women in teaching them 'habits of obedience to duty, of self restraint' and 'the true woman's ornament of a meek and quiet spirit'.[13] As Alan Sinfield puts it, 'Ideology makes sense for us – of us – because it is already proceeding when we arrive in the world...If we come to consciousness within a language that is continuous with the power structures that sustain the social order, how can we conceive, let alone organize, resistance.'[14]

Nineteenth-century commentaries on *Lear*, by both women and men, were certainly conceived within an ethic of filial duty and devotion; yet it is also true that 'women as well as men have been extremely efficient at propagating their own versions of patriarchal and bourgeois ideology',[15] and in some of these commentaries we find women developing their own 'take' on the issues, choosing their own aesthetic perspective, and – while remaining within the moral constructs of their day – creating their own 'story' of Cordelia. The process began with the publication of anthologies and abridged texts. As knowledge of Shakespeare by 'young females' in 'polite society' rose in importance, the need for texts which would enable them 'to examine [his] excellences in a *compendious mode*' (italics original) became increasingly apparent, while the standard works, such as Dodd's *Beauties of Shakespeare* or Enfield's *Speaker*, were seen as 'enfeebled in effect, from the total want of connexion; it being impossible duly to appreciate the excellencies of Shakspeare, without close and immediate reference to the characters and situations of his personages'.[16] 'The "art" of other times and places that we "appreciate" is, ipso facto, that upon which we can gain some kind of purchase from our own time and place, mediated through our particular institutions,' and 'we select and assemble' it to suit our needs.[17] Girls, it was felt, needed stories, and stories, moreover, which featured characters and themes appropriate to their own condition. In 1789 Joseph Johnson, the publisher of Enfield's work, brought out *The Female Reader*, edited pseudonymously by Mary Wollstonecraft, in which all the extracts were 'carefully disposed in a series that tends to make them illustrate each other', since 'linking the detached pieces seemed to give an interest to the whole, which even the slightest connexion will not fail to produce.'[18] The connecting themes were also those considered most appropriate to girls, so that whereas Enfield's only extract from *King Lear* was the 'Blow winds' speech, *The Female Reader* included three 'pathetic pieces' from the play, two of them focusing on Cordelia, while the third presented a similar example of filial virtue in the care of Gloucester by his son Edgar. It was the first sign of a marked change of emphasis in succeeding anthologies.

In 1811 Anna Laetitia Barbauld brought out *The Female Speaker*, also modelled on Enfield but with

---

[12] Charles and Mary Cowden Clarke, Preface, *Cassells Illustrated Shakespeare*, 3 vols. (London, 1868), vol. 3, p. ix.

[13] Dorothea Beale, speaking in 1865; quoted in Elizabeth Raikes, *Dorothea Beale of Cheltenham* (London, 1908), p. 147.

[14] Alan Sinfield, *Faultlines: Cultural Materialism and the Politics of Dissident Readings* (Oxford, 1992), pp. 32, 35.

[15] Kate Flint, *The Woman Reader 1837–1914* (Oxford, 1993), p. 10, n. 5.

[16] Pitman, *'Advertisement'*.

[17] R. Samuel, E. MacColl and S. Cosgrove, *Theatres of the Left* (London, 1985), p. 28.

[18] Mary Wollstonecraft, 'The Female Reader...by Mr Cresswick', *The Works of Mary Wollstonecraft*, ed. J. Todd and M. Butler (London, 1989), vol. 4, p. 55.

'subjects more particularly appropriate to the duties, the employments and the dispositions of the softer sex'.[19] Here Shakespeare was represented by a select group of heroines comprising Imogen, Cordelia, Rosalind, Miranda, Brutus's Portia, and 'Katherine Summoned before the High Commission Court'. For the first time, it seemed, a specifically female, if not feminist, canon was beginning to develop, with which girls and young women were invited to identify. It was to influence even those collections not exclusively aimed at girls, as we can see from the mid-century anthology of *Extracts from Shakspere For the Use of Schools*, 'adapted to the youth of both sexes, and for use in the family circle',[20] and avowedly based on Dodd's famous and much reproduced *Beauties* of a century earlier. This departs from Dodd, however, first in providing brief narrative introductions to the extracts from each play, and secondly in the addition or the suppression of certain passages. The *King Lear* section now focuses much more strongly on 'the unjust exclusion of Cordelia' from her inheritance, and, while still including her father's speeches on ingratitude and his raging on the heath, adds 'The King of France's approval of Cordelia's conduct'. A passage called simply 'Patience and Sorrow' in Dodd, is explicitly retitled 'Cordelia's emotion on hearing of her Sister's cruelty'; and Dodd's 'Cordelia on the Ingratitude of her sisters' ('O my dear father...') becomes the much longer 'Scene between Lear and Cordelia', the sole extended passage of actual dialogue.

Such refocusing on Cordelia's role, and emphasis on 'story', inevitably diminished Lear, whose 'grandeur', as the male Romantics recognized, was in language rather than action. By bringing Cordelia's scenes into closer conjunction it also created a need to find some consistency between them – something which would reconcile the girl who could speak with 'a coldness, a curtness not quite suitable from a child to a parent', with the icon of 'feminine softness and grace... the representative of all that is lovely and virtuous'.[21] Though in 1836 the editor of *Select Plays from Shakspeare... for Schools and Young Persons* failed to include her in his list of Shakespeare's feminine

models 'of courtesy, gentleness, grace, and every combination of moral beauty',[22] change was already on the way as a result of Anna Jameson's *Characteristics of Women, Moral, Poetical and Historical*. Appearing first in 1832, this was succeeded almost immediately by a second, enlarged edition, and under its later title, *Shakspeare's Heroines*, would shape the attitudes of several generations of women. Jameson removed her subjects from their immediate dramatic contexts, but drew together every scattered reference to them to create her own imaginative projections. To counter the Romantic belief that 'the greatest strength of genius is shown in describing the strongest passions; for the power of the imagination in works of invention, must be in the force of the natural impressions, which are the subject of them',[23] she undertook to show that 'in truth, in variety, in power' Shakespeare's women were equal to his men; and that those 'in whom the virtuous and calm affections predominate and triumph over shame, fear, pride, resentment, vanity, jealousy, – are perfect in their kind, because so quiet in their effect'.

Eminent among these was Cordelia, within whose heart was 'a fathomless well of purest affection', even though, to the casual eye, its waters might seem to 'sleep in silence and obscurity'. The very slightness of her role now became a positive feature.

The character appears to have no surface, no salient points upon which the fancy can readily seize: there is

---

[19] Anna Laetitia Barbauld, Preface, *The Female Speaker* (London, 1811), p. v.

[20] Anon, Preface, *Extracts From Shakspere, For the Use of Schools* (London, 1862).

[21] William Young, 'On the Character of the Religious Belief and Feeling which pervade the Tragedy of King Lear', in J. R. Seeley et al., *Three Essays on Shakespeare's Tragedy of King Lear* (London, 1851), pp. 80, 81. These prize winning essays by boys of the City of London School are interesting for their mixture of Coleridge's criticism with the romanticization of Cordelia.

[22] Edward Slater, ed., *Select Plays From Shakspeare; adapted chiefly for the Use of Schools and Young Persons. With notes from the best Commentators* (London, 1836), p. xi.

[23] Hazlitt, 'Characters', p. 126.

3   King Lear rejects his daughter, illustrated by Herbert Sidney, in Charles Alias, *Scenes from Shakespear For the Young* (1885).

little of external development of intellect, less of passion, and still less of imagination. It is completely made out in the course of a few scenes, and we are surprised to find that in those few scenes there is matter for a life of reflection, and materials enough for twenty heroines . . . [but] is not, however, to be comprehended at once, or easily.

Jameson will have no truck with Nahum Tate's 'puling love heroine' – such cheap sentimentalism is 'absurd'; 'discordant with all our previous impressions, and with the character as unfolded to us' – but it is important that her Cordelia be absolved of the faults attributed to her by Coleridge and other influential critics. Obviously, a character as 'generous, delicate, but shy' as Cordelia, was bound to be struck dumb by Lear's apparent 'holding out

a bribe for professions' of love. 'If Cordelia were not thus portrayed, this deliberate coolness would strike us as verging on harshness or obstinacy; but it is beautifully represented as a certain modification of character', as 'a natural reserve, . . . a subdued quietness of deportment and expression, a veiled shyness thrown over all her emotions, her language and her manner, making the outward demonstration invariably fall short of what we *know* [my italics] to be the feeling within'.[24] Terms such as

---

[24] Anna Jameson, *Characteristics of Women, Moral, Poetical and Historical*, 2 vols. (London, 1832), vol. 1, p. lii; vol. 2, pp. 88–9, 101, 97.

'veiled loveliness', 'delicacy', 'tender' and 'gentleness' recur in Jameson's account. Cordelia is compared with Antigone, but where the latter's love of truth and sense of duty 'are apt to strike us as severe and cold', Cordelia's heroism is 'more passive and tender – it melts our heart'. Her truly 'feminine nature' is proved by her power of 'feeling and inspiring affection', shown not only in her own actions in the second half of the play but by the testimony of Lear himself, Kent, France, and even the Fool, who pined away after she went into France.

Cordelia was vindicated. 'It is a woman's right _not_ to be forced to say how she loves, even by a father and king', declared one editor. 'Has she not her rights, as indefeasible as her father's?'[25] It is noticeable that nineteenth-century commentators lay stress on her inability to heave her heart into her mouth while avoiding the uncomfortable clarity of her next speech, and particularly the mutuality comprehended in her choice of the word 'bond'. Instead they substitute the term 'duty', a word of almost more than religious significance to the Victorians.[26] In fact, she is Shakespeare's embodiment of 'the ideal Englishwoman', combining 'faithfulness, strong will and transparent candour' with her ' "gentle and low" voice' to make her 'the most gracious and gentle vision that ever floated before a poet's mind'.[27] The emphasis is not on anything she 'says or does', but what she is in herself, what she feels, thinks and suffers'.[28] As pictured in _Cassell's Illustrated Shakespeare_ or in the book of _Scenes_ or tableaux for staging by children,[29] she kneels before her father in a spirit of devoted humility, 'not to beg for pity, but ready to bear whatever punishment he should lay upon her'.[30] This tableau is accompanied by France's summary commendation:

Fairest Cordelia, that art most rich, being poor;
Most choice, forsaken; and most lov'd, despis'd.

According to Jameson, 'In early youth, and more particularly if we are gifted with a lively imagination, such a character as that of Cordelia is calculated above every other to impress and captivate us ... We are won more by what we half perceive and half create than by what is openly expressed and freely bestowed.'[31] In the latter part of the century a great deal of creative effort went into turning Cordelia into a heroine for girls. The inadequacies of Shakespeare's text were supplied by the various narrative versions which described her fair beauty, 'wonderful eyes', and transparent goodness. 'Cordelia! the very name breathes of tenderness and peace.' With 'hands meekly folded upon her aching heart' she accepts her father's unjust judgement, repays his cruelty with loyalty,[32] and finally redeems him through her 'tender and faithful' love, for though Lear 'expires in an agony of grief, he has been delivered from his pride and passionate wilfulness'.[33] The 'living martyrdom' that, according to Charles Lamb, Lear himself suffers in 'the flaying of his feelings alive',[34] is replaced by the redemptive martyrdom of Cordelia, 'whose body may be stretched out on the rack of this rough world, but whose soul remains unsullied, clear, triumphant over death',[35] and is seen ascending to heaven in 'a momentary glimpse of a bright celestial vision ... which made the king cry, "Look there, look there!" '.[36]

Such a 'fantasy of martyrdom and posthumous vindication', giving vent, as it may, to 'egotism,

---

[25] Moberley, _Lear_, p. 7.

[26] See George Eliot's comment on 'the words, God, Immortality, Duty ... How inconceivable was the first, how unbelievable the second, and yet how peremptory and absolute the third', quoted in _Oxford Dictionary of Quotations_ (London, 1981), p. 201.

[27] Moberley, _Lear_, p. 11.

[28] Jameson, _Characteristics of Women,_ vol. 2, p. 115.

[29] Charles and Mary Cowden Clarke, eds., _Cassell's Illustrated Shakespeare_, 3 vols. (London, 1868), vol. 3, p. 456. Charles Alias, ed., _Scenes From Shakespear For the Young_, Illustrated by Herbert Sidney (London, 1885), p. iv.

[30] Alice Hoffman, _The Story of King Lear: from the play of Shakespeare_ (London, 1905), p. 11. Hoffman's story is only one of the many narrative versions of the plays written in the decades just before and soon after the turn of the century.

[31] Jameson, _Characteristics_, vol. 2, p. 98.

[32] Hoffman, _The Story of King Lear_, pp. 3, 7.

[33] Morley, _King Lear_, p. 21.

[34] Charles Lamb, 'On the Tragedies of Shakspeare', p. 137.

[35] S. P. B. Mais, ed., _Shakespeare's King Lear_ (London, 1914), p. v.

[36] Thomas Carter, _Stories from Shakespeare_ (London, 1910), p. 50.

desire for admiration, for power, for violence, for other qualities which are not socially approved', holds a strong attraction for women in a patriarchal society. As Sally Mitchell has shown in an article on women's recreational reading, popular mid-Victorian novels 'all shared the same patterns of feeling; they created a world of suffering, inhabited by women who were morally superior, though often miserable, and men who needed their help and came to recognize this need'. The woman reader's psychological need for recognition took pseudo-masochistic form in 'a strong association of the tender emotions with scenes of pain and suffering', or scenes where onlookers would sympathetically remark on both the beauty and 'the depth of suffering revealed in [the heroine's] face'. Love, also, was strongly identified 'with the nurturing, caritative qualities of maternal femininity, i.e. with that aspect of the sexual urge which woman could, acceptably, be thought to feel'.[37] The suffering Cordelia, who sacrifices her personal security and happiness with France to devote, after all, *all* her 'care and duty' to her unkind father, and redeem him by her 'kind nursery', was well suited to the psychological fantasy needs of dutiful Victorian daughters.

In some instances this may, perhaps, have led to that subversive, 'cathartic identification' defined by Hans Robert Jauss, and offered the outwardly quiet daughter an 'inner liberation' leading to 'free reflection' and the use of her own 'judgment rather than the adoption of specific patterns of activity', though it is more likely to have produced the 'reverse side of cathartic identification' by which she simply succumbed to 'the magical power of illusion', and lost herself in passive fantasy. The response which parents and teachers wanted was neither of these, but rather an 'admiring' or 'norm-creating admiration' with a figure of perfect womanliness. While Cordelia remained tainted with the suggestion of coldness or pride – while her forthright statement of obligation suggested uncomfortably independent powers of reasoning – she could not fulfil this role, for, as Jauss indicates, such 'admiring identification' must always be with the space *gestalt*, 'the "undivided whole" which ignites our affective relationship to a model' rather than with

4 'King Lear'. Illustration by H. C. Selous for *Cassell's Illustrated Shakespeare*, vol. 3 (1868) edited by Charles and Mary Cowden Clarke.

'the indeterminate individual wholeness of a person'.[38] Once her individual qualities had been decently obscured under a veil of feminine delicacy and modest reserve, however, Cordelia could take her place as 'the impersonation and the symbol of perfect love, that hopes all things, endures all things, and is ready to forgive all things'.[39] She was ready for

---

37 Sally Mitchell, 'Sentiment and Suffering: Women's Recreational Reading in the 1860s', *Victorian Studies* 21 (1977), 29–45; pp. 32, 45, 36, 34, 37.

38 Hans Robert Jauss, 'Levels of Identification of Hero and Audience', *New Literary History*, 5 (1974), 283–317; pp. 298, 297, 303.

39 J. M. D. Meiklejohn, *Shakespeare's King Lear* (London and Edinburgh, 1879), p. vii.

love and emulation as the 'sweetest and noblest' – and least talkative – 'of Shakespeare's heroines'.[40] As the Principal of Lady Margaret Hall declared, the first step in the education of girls must be to place 'a high ideal' before them, 'giving them, early in life, what may be called a poet's view of their own sex', so that by the time they reached twelve or fifteen they would be 'in love with Miranda, Cordelia, Desdemona', and catch something of their 'beautiful feeling, their dignity, . . . their eternity'.[41]

The importance of such love, such a 'pre-reflective affirmation',[42] seemed even to increase as the century drew to its close. 'In this age of feminine eagerness and prominence', wrote one woman teacher in an open letter to a 'Girl-Friend' in 1895, it was all the more important that the 'would-be "new woman"' should study Shakespeare; for let her 'dear Dorothy' be assured that 'without the deep heart of Cordelia, the devotion of Imogen, the patience of Hermione, the generosity of Portia, the gentleness of Desdemona, the joyousness of Rosalind, and the grace of Perdita, all the enlightenment and freedom of the nineteenth century will but serve to make you a byword in your generation'.[43] This was not the climax of Cordelia's 'story', however. The conditions which nurtured it – the patriarchal home circle, and the small, non-academic girls' school – were giving way to an education and examination system designed more for boys than for girls. Twentieth-century school editions show a return to criticism of Cordelia's 'misplaced obstinacy',[44] a 'defect not uncommon in women'.[45] Essay subjects change from inviting comments on the statement that 'Cordelia is the noblest creation of Shakespeare' to questioning the extent to which she was 'responsible for the tragedy of *King Lear*'. Cordelia had become again 'a real woman' – the term as used is implicitly derogatory – who, 'by her actions, some might say "imperfections"' is largely to blame for the

catastrophe, since 'had she humoured her old father, just to please him, things would have been different'.[46] Even today many students instinctively react in the same way, and Cordelia's clear statement of the nature of the patriarchal system goes unrecognized. On the other hand, recent feminist argument, while granting more dignity to her resistance, tends equally to deny merit to her 'saving love', which 'works in the action less as a redemption for womankind than as an example of patriarchy restored'.[47] Perhaps the character of Cordelia is too radically discontinuous, too much an absence rather than a presence, given too few words to serve as an adequate counterweight to Lear's more vocal anguish. The way in which the Victorians filled the gaps no longer satisfies or convinces; yet if, as Kathleen McLuskie says, a text may be made to 'reveal the conditions in which a particular ideology of femininity functions' and 'the hold which such an ideology has for its readers both female and male,'[48] the same may be surely be said of Cordelia's story as it was written, took life, and died, over the course of a century.

---

40 Mais, *Shakespeare's King Lear*, p. v.
41 Elizabeth Wordsworth, *First Principles in Women's Education* (Oxford, 1894), p. 9.
42 Jauss, 'Levels of Identification', p. 304.
43 Kathleen Knox, 'On the study of Shakespeare for Girls. A Letter to a Girl-Friend', *The Journal of Education*, n.s.XVII (1895), p. 223.
44 Mais, *Shakespeare's King Lear*, p. iv.
45 F. W. Robinson, *A Commentary and Questionnaire on King Lear* (London, 1927), p. 10.
46 Norman T. Carrington, ed., *Shakespeare: King Lear* (Bath, 1963), p. 24.
47 Kathleen McLuskie, 'The Patriarchal Bard: Feminist Criticism and Shakespeare', in J. Dollimore and A. Sinfield, eds., *Political Shakespeare: New Essays in Cultural Materialism* (Manchester, 1985), pp. 99, 101.
48 'The Patriarchal Bard', p. 106.

JACOB GORDIN'S *MIRELE EFROS*:
KING LEAR AS JEWISH MOTHER

ISKA ALTER

Confronted by the complex, unruly, and finally destructive processes of history which would eradicate their presence from the human narrative, generations of Jews since the 1880s have come, by necessity perhaps, to view the family as the primary agent to secure communal and religious survival. In the face of the destabilizing changes brought by modernity to the cities, towns, and *shtetlakh* of eastern Europe and the Russian Pale of Settlement, the persecution and dispersal of nearly one-third of the area's Jewish population, the near-annihilation of European Jewry, and the threat of erasure implicit in assimilation, there emerged a domestic ideology compounded in unequal measure of nostalgia, idealization and fact to validate and sustain this radically empowered vision of family as the single most important vehicle of cultural transmission and ethnic continuity. It should not surprise, therefore, given the pervasive, if ambivalent, stereotypes of Jewish family life that abound and are the consequences of such an historically determined ideological construction, that *King Lear*, shaped in no small measure by a kind of apocalyptic familialism, occupies a special place in Yiddish theatrical and cinematic history in its various re-formations. It was one of two Shakespearian texts to remain consistently in the performed repertory (the other being *The Merchant of Venice*).

SHUND, SHAKESPEARE, AND
JACOB GORDIN

In 1892, and again in 1898, the Russian–Jewish playwright Jacob Gordin (often denounced by his critics as more Russian than Jewish in politics, practice, and self-presentation), whose dramatic experiments would liberate the Yiddish stage from charges of aesthetic (not to say moral) triviality, fashioned two strikingly different variants of *King Lear*. Although both adaptations translated Shakespeare's fearsome tragedy into the pattern of domestic melodrama, each used its common theatrical source to remake the figure of King Lear and his kingdom in particularly distinctive ways, and in so doing uncover the faultlines in the domestic mythologies that sought to rationalize late-nineteenth-century eastern European Jewish family culture, even as the plays themselves move toward inevitable, albeit sentimental, reconciliation dictated by the claims of mutual loss, collective memory, and individual need.

The first effort, which Gordin entitled *The Jewish King Lear* with deliberate and overdetermined calculation, uses Shakespeare's original in a more conventional and self-consciously specific manner. Gordin would go so far as to have one of the characters in Act 1 rehearse King Lear's story as a warning to the play's unwise protagonist. Gordin thereby exposed to scrutiny the pressing, disruptive issues confronting the various Diaspora communities, such as secularization, religious repressiveness, intolerance, hypocrisy, women's rights, filial obligation, parental responsibility, family breakdown (the play does indeed contain, just barely, all these fractious, jostling elements). He was not simply concerned to make available to his audiences the classics of world literature in versions they might find accessible, an instructional strategy the dramatist would employ throughout his career, introducing the Jewish playgoer to the work of Hugo, Tolstoy, Ibsen, Schiller, Lessing, Gogol, and Hauptmann, as well as Shakespeare. Gordin had also come to believe in the theatre's transformative authority as an instrument which 'socializes great ideas and brings men of widely different social ranks to one intellectual level',[1] and wished to exploit its potential to effect social and political change.

However, it is Gordin's second re-creation of his Shakespearian model that is my concern here.[2] Initially called *The Jewish Queen Lear*, an intended, if obvious, reminder of both literary prototype and authorial variant, it was ultimately renamed *Mirele Efros*, an equally clear indicator for the spectator of how to situate its crucial difference – the feminization of power, family, and dramatic energy – in the new play's cultural economy as well as in its theatrical history. Like its predecessor, which was written for the great tragedian Jacob Adler, *Mirele Efros,* too, was ostensibly devised for a particular player (Keni Liptzen). And, as with *The Jewish King Lear*, it soon entered the general repertory of the Yiddish stage across the Diaspora, providing a starring role to test the skill of every major actress through several performing generations. But unlike the earlier work, *Mirele Efros* continued to be a staple of what remained of the tradition as recently as 1996 when it was performed in Montreal at the Saidye Bronfman Centre for the Performing Arts under the direction of Bryna Wasserman. Commenting on the vitality of Gordin's (melo)drama, Esther Rachel Kaminska, the doyenne of the European Yiddish stage until her death in 1925, would tell her daughter Ida, who first played the grandchild Shloime to her mother's Mirele in 1905, and who herself would be playing Mirele with her daughter Ruth well into the 1970s: 'My daughter, you'll have performed a lifetime and you'll have presented more than a hundred different plays, but you'll have to endlessly repeat *Mirele.*'[3]

What, then, accounts for the continued viability of a playscript so firmly rooted in the particularities of a world very nearly lost to the events of history? Irving Howe contends that

In some deep way *Mirele Efros* spoke to the common Jewish perception, grounded in a sufficiency of historical experience, that the survival of a persecuted minority required an iron adherence to the traditional patterns of family life. Mirele represents the conserving strength of the past which alone has enabled the Jews to hold together in time.[4]

I would argue, however, that Howe's comments represent not only a circumstantial oversimplification of the conditions that may have compelled Gordin's second reimagining of the Lear story, but also that they reveal a serious misunderstanding of the text's dramatic narrative as well. Nor can I fully endorse Lulla Rosenfeld's assertion that for the first time, in *Mirele Efros*, an author depicts the looming stage presence of the mother figure 'as the *ethical* head of her home', instead of as a character always 'operating *outside* the moral code'.[5] Rather I contend that some attempt should be made to read *Mirele Efros* against the prevailing customary assumptions. The shifting demands of three occasionally incompatible forces – the requirements of the Yiddish stage at a certain moment in its development as a popular communal institution, the not-quite-effaced claims of the Shakespearian subtext, and, most important perhaps, the playwright's own ambivalent relation to and understanding of the sociocultural environments of the *shtetl*-dwellers of eastern Europe and their immigrant counterparts – produce a less comforting, more unstable text than has been recognized heretofore.

Although I have written elsewhere about the Yiddish theatre and the ways in which it employed

---

[1] Jacob Gordin, quoted in Irving Howe, *World of Our Fathers*. With the assistance of Kenneth Libo (New York, 1976), p. 469.

[2] In lieu of rehearsing the entire plot of *Mirele Efros* in the body of my essay, I have supplied a synopsis in Appendix B.

[3] Ida Kaminska, *My Life, My Theatre*, edited and translated by Curt Leviant (New York, 1973), p. 280.

[4] Howe, *World of Our Fathers*, p. 495.

[5] Lulla Rosenfeld, quoted in *Jacob Adler, A Life in the Theatre: A Memoir*, edited, translated, and with commentary by Lulla Rosenfeld (New York, 1999), p. 259.

the Shakespearian canon throughout its short-lived but intense existence,[6] it is nevertheless worthwhile to repeat some of that past and to summarize briefly the history of what is, after all, an eccentric histrionic alliance, given the extraordinary cultural significance that has been assigned to the iconic Will. From its inception in 1876 to its decline into dismissive sentimentalism, the Yiddish stage collapses into a bare century the generic pattern of theatrical evolution: beginning as the quasi-religious Purim play performed in synagogue courtyards and private homes, emerging next into a kind of vaudeville sketch, song and interlude, before erupting in an Elizabethan flourish of creative energy during the 1890s and the turn of the century, followed by an expansion to include modernist experimentalism from the teens to the early 1930s, and finally dying into irrelevance as the population that once sustained its communal purpose is reabsorbed, assimilated if you will, into the larger society.

Shakespeare is introduced into this process in response to increasingly noisy criticism from those who had become convinced of the drama's capacity, not to say its responsibility, to transform or even to revolutionize the cultural aspirations of the masses (as Jacob Gordin most assuredly believed), a civilizing gesture, taming the excesses of *shund* (trash) that had come to dominate the stage. Not only could Shakespeare provide the elaborate plots and extravagant action so beloved of Jewish audiences, but also he could satisfy the demand for aesthetic and intellectual seriousness, or, as it might be dubbed, 'Art'. Between 1890 and 1905 at least ten of Shakespeare's plays were offered in New York City's Yiddish theatres,[7] either in crude literal translations or in *ibergesezt und varbessert* ('translated and made better'), that is, altered to incorporate the remembered experiences of the *shtetls*, towns and cities left behind. However, few of these productions became a permanent part of a company's repertory. Indeed, after 1905 Shakespeare virtually disappeared from the performing tradition, to be replaced by original Yiddish drama and, eventually, by the new European *avant garde*, especially the theatrical innovations from pre- and post-Revolutionary Russia. No longer was Shakespeare

regarded as the presumptive sign of cultural sophistication, if he ever had served such a function for the Jewish community; nor was his theatrical appropriation considered to be a means of gaining cultural acceptability in those societies which continued to marginalize the Jew, if it ever had been such an instrument – save, of course, for those insistent exceptions, *King Lear* and *The Merchant of Venice*.

The ruinous domestic politics pursued by Lear, his daughters, and their husbands, which conspicuously provide the aesthetic spine and ideological support for the action of *The Jewish King Lear*, is necessarily a more elusive presence in the matriarchal setting of *Mirele Efros* where it functions much like *pentimento* does for the visual artist, as 'an old conception, replaced by a later choice . . . a way of seeing and then seeing again'.[8] Indeed, Zalmen Zylbercwaig in his monumental *Lexicon of the Yiddish Theatre* would disregard even such a tenuous relationship to an assumed Shakespearean progenitor: 'In *The Jewish King Lear* Gordin is afraid to express his own feelings and visions; he holds fast to Shakespeare's coattails. In *Mirele*, he stands proudly on his own feet. The events and the characters have no similarity to Shakespeare's tragic drama.'[9]

Notwithstanding this observation, Gordin's adaptation remains linked to its Jacobean antecedents in the observations of American critics and reviewers who have commented on productions, if not always on the work of their Yiddish-speaking

---

[6] Iska Alter, 'When the Audience Called "Author! Author!": Shakespeare on the Yiddish Stage', *Theatre History Studies*, x (1990), 141–61.

[7] The ten plays recorded by Nahma Sandrow in her most valuable, not to say essential, *Vagabond Stars: A World History of the Yiddish Theatre* (New York, 1977; repr. New York, 1986) are *The Taming of the Shrew, Romeo and Juliet, Hamlet, Othello, Julius Caesar, Macbeth, Coriolanus* (believe it or not; of course, it is a play with another 'Jewish' mother), *King Lear, The Merchant of Venice*, and *Richard III*.

[8] Lillian Hellman, *Pentimento: A Book of Portraits* (Boston, 1973), p. 3.

[9] Zalmen Zylbercwaig, compiler and editor, *The Lexicon of the Yiddish Theatre*, assisted by Jacob Mestel. Vol. 1 (New York, 1931), columns 411–14, transl. Sylvia Alter Protter.

counterparts.[10] In fact, *Mirele Efros* does contain analogous *dramatis personae*, in addition to the central role of the eponymous Jewish Queen Lear: Machla, the devoted servant, the female Kent; Shalman, the steward, undoubtedly a version of Gloucester; Shaindel, the daughter-in-law, into whose character Regan, Goneril, and Edmund have been more or less merged; Reb Nuchum, the father-in-law, the Fool who is truly a fool; and Joseph – Yosele – the 'good son', more Edgar, perhaps than Cordelia, without the principles of either. And certainly Gordin's drama contains a number of verbal allusions to the ideas embedded in the poetry of the source-text, usually spoken by the ruling voice of Mirele Efros herself:

> An ill-match can't be the will of Providence.
> Men create their own unhappiness and then blame Providence. No, I shall have no reproaches for Heaven.   (Act 1, p. 9)

I am going. My old friends are leading me. Perhaps it would have been nicer and better, if I were taken from here in a hearse. It is a great misfortune when a person outlives himself.   (Act 3, p. 49)[11]

That these lines, a translation of a translation, do not have the emotional or figurative resonance of the original playscript is not simply a function of the limitations of literary Yiddish at a particular historical moment; or the (in)ability of Jacob Gordin to exploit effectively a language in whose written form he was not always comfortable; or even of the talent of A. J. Gordin (the playwright's son) as translator, although surely these factors must be taken into account. The very assignment of these speeches to Mirele evokes wisdom rather than villainy, pathos rather than tragic irony, while their situational placement in the generic configuration of melodrama diminishes their theatrical power: to give the revision of Kent's terse, anguished 'The wonder is he hath endured so long; / He but usurped his life' (5.3. 315–16)[12] to the still-living protagonist, and to locate the lines at the end of the third act of a four-act work instead of in the bleak emptiness of the conclusion is to sentimentalize both meaning and affect.

However, the more vexed issue for any reimagined *King Lear* is neither the depth of characterological analogy nor the extent of referential allusion, but whether it is necessary, or even possible, to stage effectively the correspondence between the imperium of the patriarchal state and the tyranny of the patriarchal family Shakespeare so carefully establishes and out of which he builds the desolation of tragedy once history has dissolved such connections. For Jacob Gordin, the theatrical response to this question is constructed out of the multiple intersecting requirements of dramaturgy, the imperatives of melodrama, and the circumstances of the Jewish experiences in late-nineteenth-century eastern Europe, the historical landscape and the cultural terrain that provides the setting for *The Jewish King Lear* and *Mirele Efros*.

The position of the Jews as marginal, defined by host societies as irritants to the body politic, with limited authority to control civic existence, virtually dictates the domestication of Shakespeare's merciless theatre. While it is too obviously the case, as Coppélia Kahn long ago observed, that 'the family is both the first scene of individual development and the primary agent of socialization ... a link between psychic and social structures and ... the crucible in which gender identity is formed',[13] for many of the Jewish inhabitants of eastern Europe,

---

[10] Reviewers from such disparate publications as *Variety* (October 25, 1967), the New York *Daily News* (20 October 1967), *The Jerusalem Post* (26 December 1994), and the Montreal *Gazette* (12 October 1996) note, for various reasons, the supposedly absent generative text.

[11] Jacob Gordin, *Mirele Efros*, typescript, transl. A. J. Gordin, 'Jacob Gordin Papers, 1893–1910', Folder No. 97, Record Group No. 530, Microfilm No. MK 511. YIVO Institute for Jewish Research, New York. A. J. Gordin, the playwright's son, seems to have produced this not always legible typescript in 1924 and, so far as I know, it is the only translation presently available for research purposes.

[12] William Shakespeare, *King Lear*, ed. R. A. Foakes, The Arden Shakespeare, Third Edition (Walton-on-Thames, 1997), p. 391.

[13] Coppélia Kahn, 'The Absent Mother in *King Lear*', in *Rewriting the Renaissance: The Discourses of Sexual Difference in Early Modern Europe*, eds. Margaret W. Ferguson, Maureen Quilligan, and Nancy Vickers (Chicago, 1986), p. 35.

and certainly for Jacob Gordin, the family is the *only* available kingdom over which the contending forces of psyche and society are permitted to battle in the drama of power. What further compliments the matter of revision in *Mirele Efros* is the transference of dominion from male prerogative to female regency.

MIRELE EFROS: THE RETURN OF THE MOTHER

That maternal absence, in part or in full, explains the defensive patriarchy of Lear's mythic Britain, the unstable masculinity of its ruler, and the subsequent behaviour of his unmothered daughters is a position that has been frequently argued in recent scholarship, most notably by Coppélia Kahn.[14] In *Mirele Efros*, the Mother is not simply reinstated in the *Lear* plot, she becomes Lear: Jacob Gordin's text represents a domestic space under feminine jurisdiction, located within a culturally specific, theatrically particular eastern European Jewish environment heavily reliant on forms of maternal governance for its survival.

When *King Lear* opens, he has been exercising sovereignty as father and monarch over a long reign. He claims that weariness and age have persuaded him to divide his kingdom among his three daughters, their husbands and, in Cordelia's case, her soon-to-be-husband (this ceremony is also the final stage in the division of the family domain for it is to be the occasion of his youngest daughter's betrothal), and surrender power on the condition that his daughters pass a test that would recognize publicly their continued allegiance to his paternal status. It is the case, however, that whatever the outcome of the I-love-Lear-the-most competition, he does not really mean to surrender power but, rather, responsibility. In a sense, he wishes, at what he defines to be the end of his life, to return to childhood, if not childishness, where fantasies of omnipotence are coupled with the evasion of blame, consequence, and accountability. The ritual concludes for Lear in unexpected humiliation, then rage, eroding the constituents of both his social and personal identities – kingship, fatherhood and

masculinity – as Cordelia rejects his paternal demands and he must, perforce, punish her by denying his paternity. Others call into question his excessive response – although it is, perhaps, not so excessive, if we acknowledge the emotional as well as the political consequences for Lear – and his actions are seen as a sign that he is, in fact, exactly what he purported to be in his performed desire to remove himself from dominion: a weary, aging monarch. And thus does the tragedy begin to spiral toward cataclysm.

Mirele Efros, on the other hand, presents us with the alternative dramatic situation in which patriarchal majesty has become matriarchy, and the landscape of authority over which Mirele exercises control is itself divided into two territories of differing, even contradictory, imperatives in what could be argued is an eastern European Jewish variant of the queen's two bodies: a domestic sphere, where she as Mother not only regulates the lives of her sons but also directs the household, authorized to do so by culture and religion and an economic 'kingdom', which can be construed by orthodoxy as the locus of illegitimate, but certainly informal or, at the very least, unrecognized female power. The Efros fortune and all that goes with it in the social hierarchy of Grodno, presumably acquired, maintained and increased by the late Reb Solomon has, in fact, been re-created by Mirele's business acumen because her long-dead husband died a bankrupt. Only Shalman, her steward, knows that it is Mirele's hard work, ability and discretion that have kept the prosperity and the family standing intact.

Although Jewish tradition, historical necessity and even the occasional rabbinic commentary have allowed women to enter the commercial marketplace, it is presented as a function of their inferiority, lesser creatures who exist to serve husband, children and an ideal/ideology of domesticity within a community continually under external threat. It is not without its own special irony that the considerable informal power that such access confers

---

[14] Kahn, 'The Absent Mother in *King Lear*', pp. 33–49.

is equally the sign of diminished status.[15] Mirele nonetheless is justifiably proud of her accomplishments:

I tried my best that the House of Solomon Efros should be run as before. I tried to make the men see how foolish they are when they think a woman is weaker than a man and can only act like a servant or a wife. All his creditors I paid back ruble for ruble ... All of you have been raised the way Solomon Efros's children should be raised. With teachers, with music instruction, with all the pleasures. What I suffered nobody knew ... Nobody noticed ... Now we are again wealthy, but all of this belongs to me.   (Act 2, p. 30)[16]

But to possess personal ambition that transgresses the boundaries of domesticity, to take satisfaction in such 'illicit' accomplishments, however secretly that pride has been harboured, to act will-fully in precisely those areas where female will-lessness is mandated, is to court quite a different kind of disaster than the annihilating catastrophe that Lear created for his kingdom and his family. Employing the expressive, if manipulating, rhetoric of the maternal caregiver, she yields financial control to the children she has infantilized:

Now you want to be the leaders; now you feel unhappy, good. I'm not going to make it worse. My happiness will be when you are happy. And my satisfaction will be your satisfaction. Tomorrow morning I will give you all the books, all the documents, and everything in the safe.   (Act 2, p. 30)

Mirele Efros begins in Sluzk, a small *shtetl* some distance from the town of Grodno where her rule, her reputation and her wealth shape the circumstances of communal life. Removed from the sources of her power in a known and familiar world, she becomes vulnerable from the outset to challenges to her double imperium. Unlike the initial action of *King Lear*, the occasion which introduces the events of the play is solely a betrothal which, during the course of Act I, becomes a marriage, the rite which enacts the variable and slippery nature of domestic authority, made more so because Jewish identity is matrilineal, and the one who owns the bride's allegiance can, perhaps, manage the future.

Mirele seems to have chosen her eldest son's fiancée not unaware of the issues involved. Joseph is known throughout much of the play by the diminutive and diminishing Yossele — it is his mother's desire to keep him a child, for if he remains the Child, then she remains the Mother. He had wanted to marry an educated city girl (a too-apparent challenge to maternal dominance). Mirele insists on locating a poor young woman from an impoverished rabbinical family living in an unprepossessing village, who would necessarily accept her mother-in-law as the site of both economic and domestic order. And once again unlike Lear, Mirele does not as yet want to concede any territory or divide her kingdom. She does not realize that marriage-as-institution already and inevitably has divided the kingdom. Rather, Mirele wishes to extend her preeminence by absorbing the newly constituted 'family' within her own. Even were Shaindel (also regressively called Shaindele) exactly what Mirele assumes her to be, this familial imperialism is doomed, just as Lear's extension of monarchical rule into the family imperils all.

But Shaindel is not what Mirele's assumptions about her would suggest. Neither passive nor obedient, equally aware of the value of her rabbinic lineage (not surprisingly transmitted through her mother's genealogy) and the absence of the monetary resources to sustain its worth, she is an appropriate adversary, a rare combination of Cordelia's

---

[15] Considerable work has been done at this point on the lives of eastern European Jewish women in the cities, towns, and *shtetls* of that now vanished world. I will cite only three of those many that have proved especially useful: Susan A. Glenn, *Daughters of the Shtetle: Life and Labor in the Immigrant Generation* (Ithaca and London, 1990); Paula Hyman, 'The Modern Jewish Family: Image and Reality', in *The Jewish Family: Metaphor and Memory*, ed. David Kraemer (New York, 1989), pp. 179–93; and Paula Hyman 'Eastern European Jewish Women in the Age of Transition, 1880–1930', in *Jewish Women in Historical Perspective*, Second Edition, ed. Judith Baskin (Detroit, 1998), pp. 270–86.

[16] I wish to thank Sylvia Alter Protter (1914–2000) for her translation of these two speeches. The page containing this dialogue was missing in A. J. Gordin's typescript; so Mrs Protter read the original Yiddish text.

(self-)righteousness, Goneril/Regan's deviousness, and Edmund's capacity for resentment; '. . . I did spitefully cross you and your friends because I felt that you despise me, that you look down on me as unworthy' (Act 4, p. 55).

She knows that, as the progenitor of the next generation of Jews, she will be able to defy her mother-in-law's maternal warrant. However, it is only when the ritual of marriage incorporates Shaindel and her confrontational family into Mirele's household that she can actively become a source of oppositional authority. Certainly, too, the entire institutional and emotive weight of marriage – the love that follows upon marriage, the urgent claims of sexuality that are sacralized by marriage, the child(ren) that are born within marriage, the personal and social consequences of heterosexual culture, if you will – establish seductive, imprisoning bonds that rival those forged by maternity.

If the excesses of patriarchy and uncertain masculinity determine the aggressive brutality of Regan and Goneril, then the matriarchal supremacy embodied in Mirele Efros devalues and/or feminizes all the males who are members of her extended community save Shalman, whose eventual financial success erases dependency, making it possible for him to support his former employer when she chooses to reject both her family and the Family as determinants of her continuous identity. Joseph, Daniel, and Reb Nuchum, on the other hand, are ineffectual men, weak, foolish and malleable, to a greater or lesser degree, made so by their submission to the multiple incarnations of the matriarch as she appears in the play: Mirele, the maternal governor, source of economic as well as affective nature; Hanah Dwoire, the combative wife of a poor, incompetent *rebbe*, engineer of the match that will ensure her family's well-being; and Shaindel, the usurper, empowered by her sexuality and marital status.

Given the nature of the cultural situation that creates the action of *Mirele Efros*, given the characterological shift that the cultural situation engenders in the Shakespearian play-text, and given the structural (or perhaps the aesthetic) demands that such cultural and characterological factors

need to satisfy, what generic choices become available other than the unavoidable movement away from tragedy? Since female power of any sort – whether it be the drive for self-definition, or the familial dominance, or, more particularly, financial influence and control – can be neither assumed nor assured, the playwright will need to establish both the history and the tenuousness of Mirele's ascendancy before it can be renounced or taken away. Hence, the 'division of the kingdom' must occur much later than Act 1 in the play's unfolding dramatic action. Nor can the surrender be an especially willing one because the acquisition of authority has been so hard-won.

If Lear is abandoned to the storm within and without, deprived of his retinue of knights, the last remaining vestige of kingship's power, by his daughters and his rage, then the process of matriarchal expulsion is studied, deliberate, and, in part, chosen in response to quite other forms of gendered public and domestic humiliation. Mirele's reluctant capitulation, managed by Shaindel in collusion with her family, especially her mother, occurs over a three-year period in which Mirele first must relinquish the purse strings, then untie the apron strings.

Departure, when it finally transpires, is precipitated on the one hand by an enforced inability to complete a promised act of communal charity and on the other by Shaindel's physical abuse of the faithful Machla (much as Kent is treated), and is absolute, although, unlike the maddened king, Mirele abandons the strife-ridden household supported by servant and steward. This abdication is theatrically as well as ideologically justified by two disparate but related circumstances: first, the 'love' Mirele claims for her son which ratifies the sacrifice she is willing to make in his name, in an environment where 'love' can be another name for exploitation and, quite unlike Lear's test in which the appropriately expressed formula of a child's 'love', becomes the instrument of concession; and, second, the challenge staged by marital 'love' as Shaindel takes what she believes is hers by right of the marriage bed.

It is important to observe in this context that the requirements of structure and the needs of culture coincidentally demand that no one participating in this drama be 'punished' – even Shaindel's resentful belligerence is permitted to remain a fact of her character rather than eliminated or elided away, although she surely has been humbled. Of course, money has been lost and the Efros business, now administered primarily by Shaindel, has fallen on hard times; but in the ideological configuration that sustains the play, the loss is neither apocalyptic nor especially catastrophic.

And what of Mirele? Unable to retain her position as domestic matriarch, she has, in the ten years that have passed since she closed the door on her family in a gesture more reminiscent of Nora Helmer than of King Lear, become a singular economic force in the community at large, as Shalman reports: 'She has remained a ministerial head. The merchants have justly named her "the Napoleon in Pettycoats [sic]"' (Act 4, Scene 1, p. 51). While her only psychological and social validation seems to be self-willed achievement – we watch her continue to conduct business in the face of family pleas to return home – there are, nevertheless, clear indications that she is ready to resume maternal authority, if, indeed, she ever had truly relinquished that majesty.

Although physically deprived of her family, Mirele's sacrificial departure inevitably inserts her presence in familial memory, just as it surely reinstates her within the more general idea of Family. More practically and more ironically, she assists the family financially, not only underwriting the efforts of the family firm through occasional secret loans negotiated by Shalman, no longer her employee, now her partner, but also honouring her promise that 'Mirele Efros will not compete against the firm of Joseph and Daniel Efros. No.' (Act 3, p. 47). Most important in this litany of retained power, however, is the assumption of the role of Grandmother, a recognition of her ability to use the future as well as of her commitment to the familial ethos of Jewish survival. In the unavoidable gesture of reconciliation so common in the dramaturgy of the Yiddish theatre, Mirele returns home to celebrate her grandson's barmitzvah, the ritual moment of renewed possibility, as the boy named after Reb Solomon Efros takes his place

within the adult community linking the past with the time to come. The desolation of Lear's end has been replaced by promise, sentimental, no doubt, but hard-won nonetheless.

MIRELE EFROS: THEATRE PRACTICE AND PERFORMANCE HISTORY

Mirele Efros emerged into stage history during the fractious beginnings of the Yiddish theatre's golden age, not simply as the product of a particular reformist playwright's volatile imagination, for whom the theatre as a creative space and a communal place was as much (or perhaps more) a political instrument as it might have been an aesthetic choice. As playscript, a document for performance rather than a literary text, a social form contingent on institutional realization and popular response, it was shaped by various contending, occasionally contradictory, dramatic claims whose insistent performative demands release the emotive energies in text as well as spectator that sustain the play's vitality.

In 1898, when Jacob Gordin fashioned his second version of the Lear narrative, Yiddish theatre practice had become a veritable grab-bag of dramatic history, a haphazard, untidy accumulation of attitudes, conventions, and techniques derived from its roots in the ludic *purimshpiel* and cabaret to near-vaudeville skits and interludes developing into melodramatic operetta and operatic melodrama, *tsaytbilder* (contemporary scenes of the day), and including elements of Gordin's own adaptive realism, any or all of which could, and frequently did, appear in a single given production. Although quintessentially a drama constructed out of types, archetypes and anti-types, it nonetheless encouraged improvisation and spontaneity, so long as they could be contained within clearly drawn characterological limits (as is the case with a number of genres that originate in modes of popular entertainment, such as *commedia dell' arte*).

Reliance on type was further made a condition of dramatic structure because the Yiddish stage was an institution that devoured plays, whose clamorous audiences required a continually changing repertory. In order to satisfy this ongoing pressure for the new, authors regularly 'baked' plays; that is, 'turn[ed] them out like trays of individual buns shaped from the same batch of dough and shoveled in and out of a hot oven' by 'add[ing] a superficially Yiddish flavor to somebody else's play, by giving it a Yiddish title, by giving the characters Yiddish names, and by setting them down in Eastern Europe or the Lower East Side or ancient Palestine'.[17]

Given such presentational necessities and representational disorderliness, it can hardly surprise that Gordin's commitment to textual integrity was greeted with considerable scepticism; scripts, after all, had been formulated loosely and treated casually precisely in order to open performative discontinuities which players could fill with bombast, the exaggerated gesture or sentimental song, and the ad lib. As one actor explained to Hutchins Hapgood, in his discussion of the Yiddish theatre that appeared in his *The Spirit of the Ghetto* (1902), 'that when he is cast in a [Joseph] Latteiner[18] play he does not need to learn his part. He needs only to understand the general situation, the character and the words he already knows from having appeared in many other Latteiner plays.'[19]

Because in this kind of histrionic olio roles had been conceived as 'loose, expansive outlines of characteristic behavior... no more than a rough sketch... just sufficiently outlined',[20] and existed within a system of theatrical practices that devalued the written text as the primary source of dramatic energy, the actor became the generative instrument driving performance. It was through his/her physical body, voice, gesture, presence, personality, imaginative dexterity, and verbal flair that the play, whoever its author, ultimately was realized.

Until Gordin attempted, with qualified success, to discipline – make 'real', if you will – the more than baroque acting styles that prevailed on the Yiddish stage, voices remained loud (as they needed to be in order to compete successfully with audiences who treated the space/place as an extension of family), gestures extravagant, presence imposing, and personality charismatic. Yet notwithstanding such manifold excesses, spectators as well as non-Yiddish-speaking, and often non-Jewish, critics, who found in the Yiddish theatre a vibrancy sorely lacking in its American counterpart, experienced, instead, performances they named as 'natural', by which they seemed to have meant sincere, unselfconscious and emotionally intense:

It is the acting which gives even to the plays having no intrinsic relation to reality a frequent quality of naturalness. The Yiddish players, even the poorer among them, act with remarkable sincerity. Entirely lacking in self-consciousness, they attain almost from the outset to a direct and forcible expressiveness... To be true to nature is their strongest passion, and even in a conventional melodrama their sincerity, or their characterization in the comic episodes, often redeem the play from utter barrenness.[21]

That these particular patterns of Yiddish stage procedure, method, and communal purpose also may reinvoke the development of Tudor/Stuart dramaturgy are circumstances recognized by journalists and reviewers as early as the turn of the twentieth century. John Corbin would write of just such a connection in *The New York Times*, April 26, 1903, employing a romanticized critical vocabulary that should not sound entirely unfamiliar:

In its naive and unabashed expression of the popular taste the Yiddish plays of the Bowery are on the precise plane of the plays that delighted the Bankside under Elizabeth.[22]

---

[17] Nahma Sandrow, *Vagabond Stars*, pp. 105–8.

[18] During the 1890s, Joseph Latteiner and Moishe Hurwitz were the leading playwrights for the Yiddish stage in New York. Over the years, Latteiner wrote approximately 150 plays, while Hurwitz wrote some 90 works. I have made *no* attempt to regularize the multiple and variant spellings of authors', actors', and characters' names as they appear throughout the text.

[19] Hutchins Hapgood, *The Spirit of the Ghetto* (1902; rpt. New York, 1976), p. 124.

[20] Howe, *World of Our Fathers*, p. 471.

[21] Hapgood, *The Spirit of the Ghetto*, p. 137.

[22] Quoted in Faina Burko, 'The American Yiddish Theatre and Its Audience Before World War I', in *The Legacy of Jewish Migration: 1881 and Its Impact*, ed. David Berger, Social Science Monographs (New York, 1983), p. 88.

Some seventy years later, the more sophisticated, and certainly less sentimental scholar, Dr Gerald Pinciss would observe:

Many of the early Elizabethan and early Yiddish plays were short-lived and hastily written combinations of genres and styles. The rivalry between acting companies, the boisterousness of the audience, the postlude of jigs and songs and prayers, and even the high productivity and generally low literary merits of men like Peele, Greene, and Dekker, with their heroes full of bombast and rodomontade, remind one of the early Yiddish theatre on the East Side. The Elizabethan and the Yiddish theatre clearly had both actors and audiences delighting in what Bottom was hoping for, a part to tear a cat in.[23]

In order to force this neo-Renaissance theatre into modernity, Gordin not only sought to revise its representational content, translating his belief in the superiority of European realism into dramatic narrative, but also acted to reorganize its unruly stagecraft by stabilizing text, fixing the importance of authorship, and ordering the business of production. However, as *Mirele Efros* surely indicates, Gordin's work inevitably retains substantial evidence of the collateral and older tradition: 'there are clownish and operatic intrusions inserted as a constant condition of success'.[24]

That *Mirele Efros* is fundamentally shaped by generic requirements of the playwright's notional realism is obvious enough; therefore, any production must be anchored in that now-lost material world of late-nineteenth-century Eastern European Jewry. These twin claims certainly will condition stage action, as Rena Wasserman, Shaindel in Bryna Wasserman's 1996 version for the Saidye Bronfman Centre in Montreal, found in the consequences for movement and interpretation of wearing the traditional corset: ' . . . the first time I tried mine on, I thought I couldn't breathe. It puts you back to an era when women were confined, structured in a certain way. You can't plop in a chair. Every movement is a statement. It does something to your mind to be physically trapped in'.[25]

Nevertheless, the playscript remains an open text, sufficiently flexible to be adapted and revised over the years to satisfy the needs or abilities of

a particular company, the technique or talent of a particular actor, and/or the demands of a particular audience at a given cultural moment. Each modification, however necessary it is alleged to be, increasingly simplifies character (already a danger in a play reliant on forms of structural melodrama) and further removes the events of plot from their emotional and historical sources. Nahma Sandrow notes, for example, the effects of merely condensing *Mirele* from Gordin's four hours to the more comfortable two in her review of a 1994 Folksbiene production (again directed by Bryna Wasserman): 'it meant sacrificing much of the verbal cleverness. Gordin's violent highs and lows have been tamed, the broad, even grotesque, comedy is lighter, the tirades and the tears more restrained'.[26]

But other kinds of alteration have more serious implications for audiences attempting to read/experience these reconfigured stage or screen adaptations. In 1939, Joseph Berne and Roman Rebush made a film version of *Mirele Efros*. Yiddish playwright Ossip Dymow wrote the screenplay and, in so doing, inevitably perhaps, rewrote Gordin's play. Notwithstanding the inherent differences between media, it is instructive to examine the new reading produced by Dymow's transformed text. Of course, transferring the work from the theatre to the screen multiplies textual opportunity: we are entertained at the wedding by the parodic *badkhen* (a jester whose specialty is weddings) chanting his cautionary sermon to the bride and her guests in which he describes the responsibilities of married life; we are allowed to laugh more heartily at Reb Nuchum's drunken incompetence because we see him being cheated by the local peasantry, thus even further diminishing his position in a female-centred household; and we are permitted to weep more bitterly as Mirele leaves her home in the snow of winter with only memories encircling

---

[23] Howe, *World of Our Fathers*, p. 467.

[24] Hapgood, *The Spirit of the Ghetto*, p. 137.

[25] Quoted in Heather Solomon, 'Arts Scene', *Canadian Jewish News*, 3 October 1996.

[26] *Jewish Daily Forward*, 2 December 1994, p. 9. I want to thank Bryna Wasserman for all her kindness and all her help.

a close-up of her unhappy countenance, thereby bringing the image of rejected maternity close to bathos.

However, these visual comments, interpolated into the primary text, are elaborations made possible by the expanded technical resources provided by the camera. Within the unfolding cinematic narrative, Dymow has contrived additional, more significant variations which continue to dilute what many critics already regard as a tenuous link between Gordin's script and its presumptive Shakespearian analogue. Younger son Daniel, who heroically offers Mirele his share of the family fortune, becomes a successful doctor, rather than the feckless wastrel Gordin created; Machla, Mirele's faithful servant–companion–defender, dies off-screen (Gordin carefully kept her alive to the end); Shalman is assigned the role of unrequited and unacknowledged love interest for Mirele, instead of remaining simply steward, then business partner, and married man; a sister is invented for Shalman so that propriety is maintained when Mirele moves into his house; and, of course, most important, Mirele herself, too quickly and too easily deprived of her sharp, demanding supremacy, is rendered as more sinned against than sinning, more victim than Queen Lear.[27]

The interpretive *effect* of these changes, a number of which also appear in stage adaptations, such as Ida Kaminska's for the Jewish State Theatre of Poland, is two-fold: first, the qualified normalization of the Efros family, whom Gordin, with some undeniable ambivalence, portrays as collapsing under the combined pressures of status disaffection, acquisitive greed and disabling male inadequacy, manufactured and enforced by aggressive female authority; second, in a strategy increasingly employed by the immigrant generation and their children to validate the receding past, the substitution of sentimentality and nostalgia for the edgy, uncomfortable threat posed by Gordin's acid-tongued, sometimes hostile, often angry, but always imperious matriarch.

If Yiddish stagecraft was dependent upon roles frequently devised for specific actors to inhabit and make live, as well as a highly elastic concept of the dramatic text, then few authors were so adept at creating these performed identities as Jacob Gordin, whose work the playwright David Pinski would judge to be 'semiart. . . . He doesn't really write plays, he writes roles'.[28] Although conceived for Keni Liptzen, who claimed to have portrayed Mirele over 1500 times and who was described as 'liv[ing] only for the theatre and [while] working on a role forgot everything, walked around in a daze, her eyes looking into another world',[29] *Mirele Efros* exemplifies Gordin's special talent in designing a part that claimed the ambitions of innumerable actresses over the years of the play's history, character and play becoming particularly identified with the Kaminskas – mother, daughter, granddaughter, and even great-granddaughter.

That it is a drama of roles, as the Yiddish theatre traditionally constructed them, was disparagingly noted by Abraham Cahan, editor of the *Jewish Daily Forward*, who commented on a Liptzen performance that 'One should read the book, not see how Mrs. Liptzen smoothes over his work on stage in order to make us forget what a mishmash "Mirele" is',[30] and seconded tersely some ninety years later by a reviewer writing of Bryna Wasserman's 1996 production in Montreal, 'Only Mirele and Shayndele appear to be fully written characters'.[31] As various players undertook the part, Mirele Efros became a kind of performative anthology testifying to the ways in which altered acting styles not only reconstituted the very nature of the protagonist as she appeared on stage but

---

[27] Of course, this list does not exhaust the changes made from script to screenplay, but the problem hardly can be unfamiliar to the scholar of Elizabethan–Jacobean–Caroline drama.

[28] Quoted in Howe, *World of Our Fathers*, p. 471.

[29] Lulla Rosenfeld, *Bright Star of Exile: Jacob Adler and the Jewish Theatre* (New York, 1977), p. 309.

[30] Quoted in Zylbercwaig, *Lexicon of the Yiddish Theatre*, columns 1115–16. Translated by Sy Barasch who has my thanks.

[31] Pat Donnelly, *The Gazette*, October 12, 1996. This information was provided in a publicity packet kindly sent me by Bryna Wasserman.

also reflected the changed cultural position of the Yiddish theatre in the increasingly dispersed, no longer Yiddish-speaking Jewish communities.

A case in point: in 1911,[32] Esther Rachel Kaminska was invited to perform the role in New York at the request of Keni Liptzen's husband, theatre manager Michael Mintz, perhaps in order 'to discredit [her] in the Gordin repertoire, especially *Mirele Efros*', or so reports her daughter Ida.[33] The competition between the two actresses whose radically differing approaches to the role exposed the widening fractures separating an older, more histrionic tradition from a technique that valued restrained verisimilitude is vividly described by Abraham Cahan. Note too, that it is Liptzen's grandiose intensity that is associated with Shakespeare and *King Lear*.

Liptzen's pride, her humor, her shrewdness came not from Lithuania, but from Shakespeare . . . She was not proud like an ordinary woman, but like a Lear. She did not go about the stage like a rich housewife from Grodno or Berdichev, but like a queen. On the mechanical means that help a melodramatic performance, Liptzen was more expert than Kaminska. Melodrama was the core of Mirele Efros, but whatever one may say about the faults of her playing, her Mirele Efros was an outstanding interpretation of the Yiddish stage.[34]

The emotional, melodramatic Liptzen may have won this theatrical battle, if Cahan's observations are to be trusted, but her aesthetic victory and popular triumph proved temporary in the face of time and changing taste. Ida Kaminska would write, 'After her death in 1925, an American writer remarked, "Esther Rachel came much too soon to us in America. Only now, after the Yiddish Art Theatre has been performing for several years, are they acting in the style Esther Rachel utilized years ago." '[35] And, indeed, contemporary performance practice assuredly underwrites this contained and disciplined version of the natural, as Richard F. Shepard, reviewing Ida Kaminska's depiction of Mirele Efros in 1967, makes clear:

Miss Kaminska, in the title role, gives a glowing performance, underplayed with taste despite all the obvious

opportunities to shriek and weep . . . Miss Kaminska never grovels, but [acts] with little mannerisms . . . her hands tremble, her face contorts and she radiates a sad smile of self-sacrifice. It is great acting.[36]

But, of course, Richard Shepard mentions neither William Shakespeare nor *King Lear*. For the family narrative which Shakespeare cast as apocalyptic patriarchal tragedy and Jacob Gordin recast as the melodrama of matriarchal power, exile and reunion, has limited social use or value as theatrical experience for the assimilated heirs of the Jewish community that first claimed Gordin's vision. They go elsewhere to confront the emotional dynamics released by *Mirele Efros*. The spectators who 'took children to see *The Jewish King Lear* and *Mirele Efros* to teach them the consequences of treating their parents badly' and those 'guilty sons and daughters mailing money orders to their parents in the old country'[37] after witnessing the fall and rise of the Efros family, have become the 'mostly middle-aged and elderly . . . remnants . . . [who] applauded speeches in favor of honor [and] sniffed at momentary triumphs of selfishness',[38] watching Ida Kaminska in 1969. In the 1990s, their children, grandchildren, and even great-grandchildren, who come to see Bryna Wasserman's productions in New York and Montreal, must listen to Gordin's dialogue through simultaneous translation and encounter the emotions of familial disintegration through the screen of distance, curiosity, alienation, and perhaps longing.

---

[32] This date is a contentious one. Ida Kaminska assigns her mother's second tour to New York to 1909; Nahma Sandrow to 1911; Zalmen Zylbercwaig putatively to 1911; and the late Lulla Rosenfeld to 1912.

[33] Kaminska, *My Life*, p. 12.

[34] Quoted in Jacob Adler, *A Life on the Stage: A Memoir*, pp. 260–1.

[35] Kaminska, *My Life*, p. 12.

[36] *The New York Times*, 'Yiddish Troupe of Warsaw', 20 October 1967, p. 55.

[37] Sandrow, *Vagabond Stars*, p. 158.

[38] Murray Schumach, 'Theatre: The Nostalgia of Gordin's *Mirele Efros*', *The New York Times*, 26 December 1969, p. 41.

APPENDIX A

Cast list provided by A. J. Gordin for his translation.

Persons in the play		Age
Mirele Efros		50
Joseph (Yossele)	her older son	20
Daniel (Donie)	her younger son	18
Machla	her maid	50
Mr Shalman	her manager	50
Mr Nuchum (Nuchumtze)	Shaindel's father	50
Hanah Dwoire	his wife	50
Shaindel (Shaindele)	their daughter	18
Shloime	Joseph's son	13

Musicians, Guests (Jewish Men and Women), Expressmen (Russians), etc.

APPENDIX B

[Synopsis]

Act 1: In Sluzk, a Polish *shtetl*

The end of the nineteenth century: Mirele Efros, a rich and powerful widow from the small town of Grodno, arrives in the small town of Sluzk with her two sons, Joseph (Yossele) and Daniel (Donie), her retinue of servants, her personal maid/companion, Machla, and her steward Reb Shalman to solemnize the marriage of Yossele to Shaindel (Shaindele), daughter of a poor but respectable family. Yossele, who had initially hoped to marry an educated city girl, has fallen in love with Shaindele's photograph. Prior to the ceremonies, the soon-to-be in-laws, Hanah Dwoire, herself the daughter of a famous rabbi, and her foolish husband Reb Nuchum (Nuchumtze) attempt to extort additional money for the privilege of marrying their daughter. Mirele is so angry that she almost calls off the wedding to the chagrin and embarrassment of Hanah Dwoire and Reb Nuchum and the near-tears of Yossele. Mirele, who has always tried to make her children happy, reconsiders and asks for an immediate

wedding. Preparations are made and large donations are made, as Shalman shows Nuchumtze how to make a tidy little something extra by padding the charity list, with Mirele's unspoken awareness. The wedding is held in Mirele's rooms and the whole village is invited.

Act 2: In Grodno, three years later

Mirele tells Machla that she is indulgent toward Shaindele and accepts her hostile behavior because of Yossele's great love for her. Hanah Dwoire insinuates that Shalman is cheating the family because Mirele is not only too old and too unpredictable in her conduct but also too trusting, and is an "old woman" no longer capable of running the business; so she suggests that the young people assume control. Shaindele enlists the aid of Donie, Yossele's brash, more Europeanized younger brother, to help make her demands of Mirele. Shalman acknowledges that he has made a good deal of money, but always with Mirele's approval as she herself admits, a confession which only increases the tension. An investigation as to the estate left by Reb Solomon Efros leads to the admission that the business was completely bankrupt at his death. It has been Mirele's astuteness, ingenuity, and hard work for eighteen years that have rebuilt the family fortune. Ceding authority, Mirele is disturbed by her children's distrust and while alone reads her Bible for comfort.

Act 3: In Grodno

Nuchumtze, now the family administrator, has returned drunk from a business trip, incoherent about receipts, and cheated by the peasants. Donie, still more Europeanized, has returned drunk from Riga unwilling to explain his vast expenditures, but suggesting that Shalman once again run the business. As charges of theft ring in the air and the noisy, ugly quarrel continues, with considerable physical violence between the brothers, Mirele arrives appalled at the state of her once stable family. She is further shocked to see Shaindele wearing her jewels and as Shaindele is reprimanded for this, she retorts 'Of what use is jewelry to an old person like you'. During this ongoing dispute, the planning committee for the new hospital arrives expecting Mirele's promised donation. Shaindele, now fully in charge of the family business, refuses to give her mother-in-law the funds, further humiliating her, this time publicly, even as Machla and Shalman attempt to offer their financial help to underwrite her contribution. As Machla tells Shalman of the decay and corruption in the Efros house, Shaindele overhears and strikes her. This is as much as Mirele can bear. She asks Shalman if she can live at his home and help him with his business. As Mirele leaves her own home, she says 'some thirty odd years ago, I came to this house with a great many things, with many bright hopes, many good prospects. Now I am going away with just this little bundle of things, and the dress on my back.'

Act 4: In Grodno, ten years later

Yossele comes to Shalman's house to plead with Mirele, once again a powerful economic force in the community, to return for the occasion of his son Shloime's barmitzvah. Shaindele, too, comes to plead and tries to explain to Mirele that from the moment she entered the Efros home she felt humiliated because of her own poverty and upbringing, which caused her deplorable behavior toward Mirele. Mirele refuses to return from her voluntary 'exile', for she is not yet ready to forgive, even though she did go to the synagogue to see her grandson read from the Torah. Where his parents have failed, Shloime succeeds in winning his way to his grandmother's heart. She returns to her home in time for the celebration, agrees to remain with her children, and all are happy about the reconciliation.

'HOW FINE A PLAY WAS MRS LEAR': THE CASE FOR GORDON BOTTOMLEY'S *KING LEAR'S WIFE*

RICHARD FOULKES

'[H]ow fine a play was Mrs Lear' recalled the artist and stage designer Paul Nash when he wrote to its author Gordon Bottomley on 17 January 1917.[1] A few years later Nash was to make a significant contribution to the afterlife of Bottomley's *King Lear's Wife* – and consequently to that of Shakespeare's *King Lear* upon which it was based – when his costume and set designs, created for the Amsterdam Theatre Exhibition, were shown at the International Theatre Exhibition in London in 1922, by which time his reputation was established as an outstanding war artist. The correspondence between the two men had begun in 1910 when Nash, born in 1889, was a student at the Slade School of Fine Art and Bottomley, fifteen years his senior, had already made his mark in literary circles. The son of a cashier in a worsted mill in Keighley, where he attended the local grammar school, Bottomley fought a lifelong battle against ill health despite which he produced a steady output of poetry which was highly regarded by discriminating admirers amongst whom was Edward Marsh.

In 1912 Marsh – civil servant, scholar and patron of the arts – edited the first volume of *Georgian Poetry* the success of which eventually resulted in four further volumes. Marsh's attitude to the inclusion of *King Lear's Wife* in the second volume of *Georgian Poetry* was indicative of his high regard for the poet. As soon as Marsh heard in July 1913 that Bottomley had started work on the play he wrote to him 'asking to see the work as soon as it was done',[2] but progress was desperately slow because of the author's physical condition, living in constant fear of (lung) haemorrhages. He described his method as working up his 'daily limit of a dozen lines before thinking of writing down even one . . . In the end I could do as much as twenty lines a day if I did not forget to be cautious. By the end of the summer of 1913 I had finished *King Lear's Wife*; throughout that fragmentary, interrupted process of composition the theme had held me intently, and I cannot see that the slow irregular work is anywhere apparent in the result'.[3] Though they shared a common theme, Bottomley and Shakespeare practised very different methods of composition.

Bottomley was mistaken in his recollection that he finished *King Lear's Wife* by the end of the summer of 1913 since his letter to Marsh accompanying the manuscript of the play was dated 16 April 1914. Marsh's response was rapturous. He wrote to Rupert Brooke, then in Tahiti:

There is only one really great literary event – Gordon Bottomley's play *King Lear's Wife* of which he sent me the MS last week. I don't want to dethrone Lascelles [Abercrombie] but I must say that I think this is as good as anything of his – the poetic drama is born again, of that

---

[1] Claude Colleer Abbott and Anthony Bertram eds., *Poet and Painter Being the Correspondence Between Gordon Bottomley and Paul Nash 1910–1946* (London, 1955), p. 81. Nash recalled his first encounter with Bottomley's work (*Crier by Night*) and – three years later – the man himself in *Outlines. An Autobiography* (London, 1949), pp. 84–5 and pp. 161–3.

[2] In Christopher Hassall, *Edward Marsh Patron of the Arts* (London, 1959), p. 247.

[3] In Gordon Bottomley, *Poems and Plays*, ed. Claude Colleer Abbott (London, 1953), p. 15.

there is no doubt. It is short, but the action, the character drawing, and the verses are all the work of a master. There are lines that are like nothing, but the famous things in Webster.[4]

To Bottomley himself Marsh dispatched a telegram: 'It is a masterpiece'[5] and subsequently, having read the play aloud to Paul Nash, wrote:

I expected a great deal – but it has surpassed all that I had hoped or imagined – it is one of the great things . . . It seemed hardly possible beforehand that a play about Lear should not find itself in a slightly false position! But yours can hold up its head against any such thought.[6]

Marsh had already offered Bottomley 'twice the profits which would normally have accrued to him if the poet would permit the initial publication of "King Lear's Wife" in *Georgian Poetry* II'.[7] In his Prefatory Note to that volume, having referred regretfully to the deaths of Rupert Brooke and James Elroy Flecker, both of whom had contributed to the previous volume, Marsh wrote: 'The alphabetical arrangement has been modified in order to recognise the honour which Mr Gordon Bottomley has done by allowing his play to be first published here'.[8] The only point on which Marsh took issue with Bottomley was the name of the title character Hygd (pronounced 'Higg'), but the dramatist stood firm saying that Hygd had 'a kind of gaunt monolithic dignity which rather satisfies me'.[9] Since she of course was entirely his own creation, Bottomley understandably felt no inclination to defer to others.

King Lear's Wife is what would now be called a prequel, filling in incidents which occurred before the beginning of Shakespeare's play. Lear's bedridden wife Hygd is attended by two waiting-women Merryn and Gormflaith, with the latter of whom Lear is having an affair. After observing her husband and Gormflaith together, Hygd suffers a relapse and dies. Goneril, the only one of her three daughters to appear, avenges her mother's death by killing Gormflaith, but when he realises that his mistress has been unfaithful to him Lear suppresses his protest. The play ends macabrely with two old women laying out Hygd's body.

5 *King Lear's Wife* by Paul Nash. Pencil and colour wash from his own model.

Although Marsh organized a reading of the play with Henry Ainley as Lear and approached Harley Granville Barker and Basil Dean about staging it,[10] it was exposed to fullest critical comment on the page rather than the stage. As the reviews assembled in *Georgian Poetry 1911–1922: The Critical Heritage*[11] reveal, many of them devoted much of (the generous amount of) space available to them to Bottomley's play. The unsigned review in the *Times Literary Supplement* (9 December 1915) objected to Bottomley's indulgence in ugliness 'for the sake of ugliness, as if it were interesting in itself'. Similarly in the *New Statesman* (25 December 1915) J. C. Squire remarked on the recurrence of 'horror' so that one feels 'that he is *putting* it there all the time', most excessively in the concluding episode with the corpse-washers. More positively Arthur Waugh in

4 In Hassall, *Edward Marsh*, p. 277.
5 Ibid., p. 278.
6 Ibid., p. 278.
7 Robert H. Ross, *The Georgian Revolt Rise and Fall of A Poetic Ideal 1910–22* (London, 1967), p. 154.
8 Edward Marsh ed., *Georgian Poetry 1913–15* (London, 1915).
9 In Hassall, *Edward Marsh*, p. 279.
10 Ross, *The Georgian Revolt*, p. 153.
11 Timothy Rogers ed., *Georgian Poetry 1911–1922: The Critical Heritage* (London, 1977).

the *Quarterly Review* (1916, pp. 365–86) considered that the play served 'very reasonably to explain the inhuman treatment meted out to their father by Goneril and Regan at a later stage of his history' and S. P. B. Mais in the *Nineteenth Century* (November 1916 pp. 1008–22) wrote:

In point of fact, anyone who has for years been troubled by the earlier play will recognize at once how much the new one clears up the ground. It is impossible to re-read 'King Lear' after finishing 'King Lear's Wife' without noticing again and again points that used to puzzle the imagination, now made perfectly plain.

In fact Bottomley's achievement exceeds offering plausible incidents and characters, he absorbs the themes, imagery and atmosphere of Shakespeare's play. As Ernest Reynolds argued when comparing Bottomley's *King Lear's Wife* and *Gruach* (1922), which recounts Lady Macbeth's first encounter with her future husband,[12] with other re-workings of Shakespeare such as St John Ervine's *The Lady of Belmont* (1925): 'With Gordon Bottomley (1874–1948) we are on a different plane ... More than any of the poets so far discussed here Bottomley understands the power of poetic suggestion'.[13]

Narrative and character issues aside, any dramatist or novelist essaying the challenge of recreating the Lear story has to postulate a moral framework in which the action unfolds. By setting his play in pre-Christian times, Shakespeare was able to present a wide spectrum of attitudes to god/the gods, ranging from the implicitly Christian embodied by Albany and Edgar to the outright scepticism of Edmund, from the despair of Gloucester's 'As flies to wanton boys are we to th' gods;/ They kill us for their sport' (*The History of King Lear*, Scene 14, lines 35–6) to Kent's simple trust 'It is the stars' (Scene 16, line 33) and the elementalism of Lear's 'Blow, wind, and crack your cheeks!' (Scene 9, line 1). Nahum Tate's facilely optimistic resolution in *The History of King Lear* (1681) ('*Cordelia*: Then there are gods, and virtue is their care.'[14]) long proved to be more palatable than Shakespeare. Bottomley, who was of course writing post-Darwin, seems to have intentionally maintained Shakespeare's ambiguity. Thus at the beginning of the play he depicts the waiting-woman Merryn as follows:

Taking her beads from her girdle, she kneels at the foot of the bed
O sweet Saint Cleer, and sweet Saint Elid too,
Shield me from rooting cancers and from madness:
Shield me from sudden death ... [15]

In contrast Goneril, 'a virgin huntress' (p. 12), witnesses 'the first tips of light,/On Raven Crag near by the Druid Stones' in the circle of which she 'raised up' her 'shining hand in cold stern adoration' (p. 14). Hygd approves her 'worship on that height' and continues:

And you do well to worship harsh men-gods,
God Wind and Those who built his Stones with him;
All gods are cruel, bitter and to be bribed,
But women-gods are mean and cunning as well,
That fierce old virgin, Cornish Merryn, prays
To a young woman, yes and even a virgin –
The poorest kind of woman – and she says
That is to be a Christian: avoid then
Her worship most, for men hate such denials,
And any woman scorns her unwed daughter. (p. 14)

Goneril is a child of nature, the huntress who sings lyrically about owlets and baby otters (pp. 19–20), but who has no compunction in killing Gormflaith with her hunting knife, an act which passes unreproved: 'The filth is suitably dead' says Lear (p. 47).

In his address at the Memorial Service for Bottomley in St Martin-in-the Fields on 28 September 1948 John Masefield said: 'His mind created a fair system, showing the final and infallible working-out of a great justice, and the utter final forgiveness of sins sorrowed-for'.[16] Whether or not it is

[12] Gordon Bottomley, *Plays and Poems*.
[13] Ernest Reynolds, *Modern English Drama: A Survey of the Theatre from 1900* (London, 1950), p. 76.
[14] Nahum Tate, *The History of King Lear*, ed. James Black (London, 1976), p. 92.
[15] Gordon Bottomley, *King Lear's Wife and other plays* (London, 1922). Subsequent page references are given in the text.
[16] John Masefield, *Words Spoken by John Masefield at a Memorial Service in the Church of St Martin-in-the-Fields September 28 1948* (London, 1948).

dependent upon an external deity, this 'great justice' is certainly demonstrated in *King Lear's Wife*. Lear stands guilty of adultery and what amounts to the mental cruelty of Hygd. He reaps a grim harvest for both, not only in Bottomley's play, but also by implication in Shakespeare's. Gloucester is of course the face of overt adultery, but, as S. P. B. Mais noted, Lear's speech 'Adultery? Thou shalt not die for adultery' (Scene 20, line 108) reaches such a frenzied pitch that his own culpability might plausibly be inferred. In Bottomley's play Hygd's illness is fundamentally mental, as the Physician asks Merryn if she knows of 'Some bitterness or burden in the mind . . . it may be/ Some wound in her affection will not heal' (p. 9) and Goneril accuses her father 'Now you have done murder with your mind.'(p.38) Those who live by the sword die by the sword and those who damage the minds of others eventually suffer the same fate.

In Bottomley's scenario Lear's treatment of Hygd stems from her failure to bear him a son, producing instead a third daughter Cordeil/Cordelia:

HYGD Because a woman gives herself for ever
    Cordeil the useless had to be conceived
    (Like an after-thought that deceives nobody)
    To keep her father from another woman.   (p. 18)

Hygd deeply resents Cordeil ('My little curse. Send her away-away . . . ' (p. 17)) who, rejected by her mother, craves her father's love, beating (unseen) on the door and calling out 'Father . . . O, father, father . . . I want my father' (p. 17) in a manner somewhat reminiscent of the tiresome Violet-Elizabeth Bott in Richmal Crompton's 'William' stories. Between the end of Bottomley's play and the beginning of Shakespeare's Lear's relationship with Cordelia must have changed from indifference to guilt-induced doting, with her refusal to declare her love for him triggering a reversion to his earlier antipathy.

With Cordeil heard but not seen and Regan dispatched by her elder sister in four lines, describing her as sidling amongst the 'sweaty half-clad cook-maids' rendering lard after a pig killing (p. 14), Lear's progeny are primarily represented

by Goneril. In *King Lear* Lear's proposal 'Then let them anatomise Regan; see what breeds about her heart. Is there any cause in nature that makes this hardness?' (Scene 13, lines 70–2) is based on the supposition that the root of Reagan's evil lies within her, a view which Edward Bond directly counters in Act 2 Scene 6 of *Lear* in which an autopsy of Fontanelle's (Regan's counterpart) womb reveals only beauty as Lear acknowledges in amazement 'I have never seen anything so beautiful'.[17] In *King Lear's Wife* Bottomley's exploration of the origins of filial ingratitude is perforce confined to Goneril, who accuses herself to her mother as follows:

Dearest, I am an evil daughter to you:
I never thought of you – O, never once –
Until I heard a moor-bird cry like you.
I am wicked, rapt in joys of breath and life,
And I must force myself to think of you.

                                        (pp. 12–13)

That Goneril should categorize passing negligence as wickedness suggests that, far from having a propensity to evil, she is extremely self-censorious about relatively minor shortcomings. In a touching role reversal she sings a lullaby to her mother. Her subsequent treatment of her father therefore stems from his of her and in one particularly powerful speech she seems to anticipate his curse ('Into her womb convey sterility', Scene 4, line 27):

GONERIL, *after a silence.*
    Hard and unjust my father has been to me;
    Yet that has knitted up within my mind
    A love of coldness and a love of him
    Who makes me firm, wary, swift and secret,
    Until I feel if I become a mother
    I shall at need be cruel to my children,
    And ever cold, to string their natures harder
    And make them able to endure men's deeds;
    But now I wonder if injustice
    Keeps house with baseness, taught by kinship –
    I never thought a king could be untrue,
    I never thought my father was unclean . . .

                                        (pp. 18–19)

---

[17] Edward Bond, *Lear* (London, 1983), p. 59.

Lear's own attitude towards Goneril also fore-shadows the sequence of events between Bottomley's play and Shakespeare's when he says 'I thought she [Goneril] had been broken long ago:/ She must be wedded and broken, I cannot do it' (p.48), though it has to be said that Albany hardly seems to possess the obvious qualities for the task.

Although he was working in a different tradition from the Ibsenite new woman drama, Bottomley's play with its strong (Goneril) and sympathetic (Hygd) women was no more immune from that influence than it can have been from the women's suffrage movement, which was at its height when Bottomley was engaged in the slow and painful process of composition. Hygd's lament 'We are good human currency, like gold,/ For men to pass among them when they choose' (p. 16) no doubt struck a chord with many female readers at the time. In writing a play about King Lear's wife, Bottomley was opening up a subject which was to absorb authors late in the twentieth century: *Lear's Daughters* (1987) by Elaine Feinstein and the Women's Theatre Group in which Lear wants a son and the Queen (played by the Fool) dies;[18] Howard Barker's *Seven Lears: The Pursuit of Good* (1990) in which Lear is married to the insufferably virtuous Clarissa whom he and his three daughters conspire to be rid of;[19] and Jane Smiley's *A Thousand Acres* (1991) in which Larry's (Lear) wife has died of cancer to which their daughter Rose (Regan) also falls victim, as she and her elder sister Ginny (Goneril), the novel's narrator, do to sexual abuse by their father.[20]

By the end of the twentieth century poetry had ceased to be the accepted vehicle in which to revisit Shakespearian subjects. The verse drama movement, which had been hailed as such a promising prospect between the wars, had faded away. Bottomley, as one of the few and by far the most effective of the Georgians to adopt the dramatic form, might properly be regarded as a harbinger of T. S. Eliot, Christopher Fry and their like. Indeed his essay *A Note on Poetry and the Stage* was reprinted as a pamphlet by the Religious Drama Society,

of which E. Martin Browne, the first director of Eliot's plays, was the leading figure.[21] Bottomley discoursed on poetry in the theatre as he had done in an earlier piece 'Poetry and the Contemporary Theatre' in which he wrote:

The poetic drama is, indeed, not so much a representation of a theme as a meditation upon it or a distillation from it; its business is far less the simulation of life than the evocation and isolation of our delight of the elements of beauty and spiritual illumination in the perhaps terrible and serious theme chosen.[22]

This conjunction of the 'terrible' subject matter and the 'spiritual' treatment of it, which was the hallmark of Bottomley's work (and much Georgian poetry), took an extreme form in the concluding section of *King Lear's Wife*. The play's principal source and inspiration was of course Shakespeare's *King Lear*, but Bottomley did not confine himself to that play. When Hygd observes Lear and Gormflaith together, the king's mistress is trying on his wife's crown, which is reminiscent of Prince Hal in *2 Henry IV*. The Physician, to whom reference has already been made, suggests the Doctor of Physic in *Macbeth* to which *King Lear's Wife* is further indebted for the 'two elderly women . . . wear[ing] black hoods and shapeless black gowns with large sleeves that flap like ungainly birds: between them they carry a heavy cauldron of hot water' (p. 41). Though victims of the same down-sizing that had reduced Lear's daughters to one, the two elderly women are manifestly counterparts to the three witches. Bottomley has the gift of investing key words with a resonance that irresistibly recalls their use in Shakespeare. Thus in the Elder Woman's

---

18 In Daniel Fischlin and Mark Fortier eds., *Adaptations of Shakespeare: A critical anthology of plays from the seventeenth century to the present* (London, 2000).

19 Howard Barker, *Seven Lears: The Pursuit of Good* (London, 1990).

20 Jane Smiley, *A Thousand Acres* (London, 1992).

21 Gordon Bottomley, *A Note on Poetry and the Stage* (London, 1944).

22 In Myron Simon, *The Georgian Poetic* (Berkeley, Los Angeles, London, 1975), p. 52.

6 Gormflaith by Paul Nash.

opening lines to Hygd's corpse,

Saving your presence, Madam, we are come
To make you sweeter than you'll be hereafter,
And then be done with you   (p. 41)

'hereafter' invokes two uses in *Macbeth*: the Third Witch's 'All hail, Macbeth, that shalt be king hereafter!' (1.3.48) and Macbeth's 'She should have died hereafter.' (5.5.16). During the process of laying out the body ('A little blood is lightly washed away' p. 45; 'the Queen is setting' p.48) the two women squabble and even fight over the deceased's possessions, but even more disturbing is the song sung (three times) by the Elder Woman:

> A louse crept out of my lady's shift –
> Ahumm, Ahumm, Ahee –
> Crying 'Oi! Oi! We are turned adrift;
> The lady's bosom is cold and stiffed,
> And her arm-pit's cold for me.'   (p. 43)

By the time the play appeared in print the impact of this chillingly graphic illustration of the processes of human mortality was no doubt intensified by readers' awareness of the carnage of the First World War. Though he had written *King Lear's Wife* with publication rather than performance in prospect, Bottomley nevertheless conceived his plays in terms of their effect in the theatre:

If some of my critics maintain that my poems are not dramas and have no place on the stage, nevertheless I claim a platform for them on which they can live, more abundantly than in a printed book, as performed poetry.[23]

Such was the power of poetry in performance that through its utterance the characters ascended to a spiritual plane where 'the words become the action', an effect in which the 'sound of the words' became 'part of their meaning'. There could be little doubt about the impact of the Elder Woman's song on the stage, but before that could be proved *King Lear's Wife* had to be licensed by the Lord Chamberlain as Examiner of Plays.

The play, which was to be premiered at Barry Jackson's Birmingham Repertory Theatre on 25 September 1915, was duly submitted for approval. The reader was G. S. Street, who from 1914

---

[23] Gordon Bottomley, *A Stage for Poetry: My Purpose with My Plays* (Kendal, 1948), p. xiii.

7 King Lear by Paul Nash.

which he says 'ends with two horrible old women laying out the corpse', summing up as follows:

It is serious poetic play and being so, and having the theme it has, the author must be allowed some plainness of phrase. This he does not abuse and though the primitive issues of love and marriage are put plainly there is no word used which (though allowed to Shakespeare) is now forbidden nor is there anything to complain of in the main part of the play. But at the end one of the old women sings a revolting ditty at intervals – pp. 22, 23 and 24 – beginning 'a louse crept out of my lady's shift', which I dare say can be permitted in Shakespeare, but seems to me, in a new play, needlessly offensive to modern taste. I think this might be cut out. I also think that the audience might be spared any gruesome details in the business of laying the corpse out and that a caution might be given to this effect. Otherwise the play, which is a strong thing on the whole, is Recommended for licence.[26]

Accordingly the Lord Chamberlain's Register records: 'This licence is granted subject to the undertaking given that the following shall be omitted: – (1) The Dirge sung by the "Elder Woman" at the Conclusion of the Play. (2) All references to a louse crawling out of a lady's shift, "armpits" and "savour" associated with a corpse on pages 22, 23 and 25'.[27]

The promptbook for John Drinkwater's production does not incorporate these deletions.[28] There is a vertical line in the (left) margin by each of the three places in which the offending dirge appears, but far from crossing it out, Drinkwater has added stage business for the performers. It is possible that Drinkwater prepared his promptbook whilst awaiting the licence, though even so he might be expected to have incorporated its stipulations.

worked alongside Ernest Bendall, succeeding him as senior examiner in 1920.[24] Street's report dated 17 September 1915 is a balanced and perceptive critique of the play, which he begins by describing as 'A study of barbaric passion, written in blank verse which, though unequal, is good and strong on the whole'.[25] He then proceeds to summarise the work,

[24] John Johnston, *The Lord Chamberlain's Blue Pencil* (London, 1990), p. 265.
[25] The Lord Chamberlain's Collection of Plays in the Manuscript Room, The British Library. Ref. 61954.
[26] Ibid.
[27] The Lord Chamberlain's Register vol. x, 1915–17. Licence number 3741.
[28] In the Birmingham Repertory Theatre Archive in the Birmingham Central Library.

Enclosed in the promptbook is a sheet music MS for the song and this was reproduced as Appendix A in a subsequent edition of *King Lear's Wife*, preceded by this note:

In the course of the production the song of the Elder Woman, toward the close of the play, was fitted with so appropriate a melody, by a fortunate modification of a folk-tune, that it seems well to continue the connexion by printing the arrangement here.[29]

Reviews, though they found the content of the plays distasteful ('unpleasant' chimed the *Era* and the *Stage*)[30] and remarked on the terrible old hags (played by Betty Pinchard and Maud Gill), did not refer specifically to the song. The evidence about its inclusion therefore falls short of certainty.

The unenthusiastic reception in Birmingham, as part of an ill-assorted triple bill with two comedies (*The Battle of the Pump* by C. A. Castell and Samuel Foote's *The Liar*), was partly because – with the exception of Ion Swinley as Lear – it was inadequately acted, but mainly because of the play itself. One critic found it utterly ill-suited to the time: 'In these days of sorrow we cannot tolerate those callous old hags of the death chamber, the least horrible of whose remarks is that the corpse will soon be as "stiff as a straw mattress," which evoked a burst of untimely laughter',[31] though another did recognize what Bottomley was trying to do: 'He has fulfilled a paradox – he has written something full of beauty in expression without any loveliness in its subject'.[32]

The Georgians rallied around Bottomley, who was carried upstairs for the first performance and 'planted in a box, supported by bolsters with his feet resting on a purple cushion'.[33] Marsh, by then a close associate of Winston Churchill, was prevented by other duties from attending the first night, but was later caught by the camera outside the theatre alongside Drinkwater and Lascelles Abercrombie.[34] Edward Thomas, who had written to Bottomley wishing '*Mrs Lear*' the kind of success you would like',[35] had to content himself with reading about the performance.

In May 1916 *King Lear's Wife* reappeared in London in what might be considered more fitting company as part of Viola Tree's fund-raising matinee of so-called 'Georgian Plays' at His Majesty's Theatre, together with Wilfred Wilson Gibson's 'verse-fantasy "Hoops"' (about a circus clown) and Rupert Brooke's *Lithuania*, a piece of ultra-realistic prose in which 'horrors piled on horror's head'.[36] This time Maud (Lady) Tree played Hygd, Viola Tree was Goneril and Murray Carrington Lear. This was one of those comfortable and cultured occasions in which the great and good of wartime London rallied somewhat self-indulgently for the benefit of a worthy cause (in this case a Day Nursery for the children of soldiers and sailors). The literary critic H. A. Saintsbury appeared as the Physician; Ivor Novello, with whom Marsh had formed what was to be a lifelong friendship, composed two settings for songs to be sung by Viola Tree[37]; Lady Diana Manners (later Duff-Cooper) 'solved' the 'problems of the bed' with 'a great embroidered curtain'[38] and 'Among the audience were Mr. Asquith and the members of his family'.[39] Viola Tree had wanted 'to cut out the finale of the corpse-washers', which she presumably regarded as too harrowing for this august assembly, but when Bottomley refused 'she cut out half of it all by herself'.[40] Paul Nash was not present. May 1916 found him training as a map instructor (and meeting Edward Thomas in the process), prior to being gazetted as Second Lieutenant in the Hampshire Regiment. His absence did not prevent him from passing judgement (in a letter to Bottomley) on the 'miserable inefectualities [sic] of that performance'.[41]

---

[29] Bottomley, *King Lear's Wife*, p. 207.

[30] *Era* 29 September 1915; *Stage* 30 September 1915.

[31] *Birmingham Daily Post*, 27 September 1915.

[32] *Birmingham Daily Mail*, 27 September 1915.

[33] Hassall, *Edward Marsh*, p. 368.

[34] Ross, *The Georgian Revolt*, opposite p. 160.

[35] R. George Thomas ed., *Letters from Edward Thomas to Gordon Bottomley* (London, 1968), p. 255–6.

[36] *Illustrated London News*, 27 May 1916.

[37] Hassall, *Edward Marsh*, p. 393.

[38] Bottomley, *A Stage for Poetry*, p. 14.

[39] *The Times*, 20 May 1916.

[40] Abbott and Bertram eds., *Poet and Painter*, p. 133.

[41] *Poet and Painter*, p. 81.

8 Goneril by Paul Nash.

9 The Corpse Washer (Elder Woman) by Paul Nash.

During the closing months of 1921 and the first half of 1922 Nash and Bottomley were in frequent correspondence about the former's creative response to *King Lear's Wife*, which he described as 'a very inspirational drama' to which its author replied 'I agree with you altogether that something more was set free when I came to Mrs Lear'.[42] In November 1921 Nash wrote to Bottomley that he was 'busy designing a scene and costumes for King Lear's Wife' and that he proposed to 'send them on with some others to the great Theatre Exhibition at Amsterdam to which I have been invited to contribute'.[43] In creating the model set Nash paid particular attention to the bed, which by 16 December he declared 'a great triumph', constructed out of 'rather indifferent PreRaphaelite postcards . . . In colour . . . greyish pink brown with curtains of an

[42] *Poet and Painter*, pp. 131–2.
[43] *Poet and Painter*, p. 127.

136

10   Queen Hygd by Paul Nash.

orange tint . . . [and] in perfect proportion for the model', though in a theatre with a wide stage ('such as the Haymarket') 'you would have to make it longer to preserve the present significance'.[44]

Concurrently with the Amsterdam Theatre Exhibition there were, as the Victoria and Albert Museum's director Cecil Harcourt Smith put it, 'suggestions in the press and elsewhere that the Museum should hold an Exhibition of Theatrical Art', in response to which he dispatched 'Mr. Martin Hardie (Keeper of the Department of Engraving, Illustration and Design) . . . to inspect the Exhibition' in Amsterdam.[45] As a result from 3 June to 16 July 1922 the Victoria and Albert Museum hosted the International Theatre Exhibition Designs and Models for The Modern Stage, which was essentially the Amsterdam exhibition. Inevitably being transported around Europe had taken its toll on the

fragile models and in mid-May 1922 Nash wrote to Bottomley 'Mrs Lear is now *secotined* down, so the death chamber is positively realistic if you put your nose inside the curtains'.[46] On 2 June he reported with evident pride: ' So far as I could see, our models [*King Lear's Wife* and *Gruach*] out-top all the

---

[44] *Poet and Painter*, pp. 128–9.
[45] *International Theatre Exhibition Designs and Models for The Modern Stage* (London, 1922), p. 5.
[46] Abbott and Bertram eds., *Poet and Painter*, p. 145. Nash (*Outlines*, p. 219) refers to building 'theatre models . . . for two plays by Gordon Bottomley'. As his letter to Bottomley of 22 April 1925 shows, Nash used the same method for his illustrations of Shakespeare's *King Lear*: 'I spent the Easter holidays building models and drawing from them – 5 scenes' (Abbott and Bertram eds., *Poet and Painter*, p. 183). See *Shakespeare's The Tragedy of King Lear: newly printed from the first folio* (London, 1927).

others; and, so far as I could hear, everybody says so. Hardie has chosen Mrs Lear for reproduction in the catalogue, and there are only sixteen plates altogether'.[47] Edward Gordon Craig, who opened the exhibition, reviewed it for *The Times* where he found 'Nash's model for *King Lear's Wife* the best in this major international show'.[48] As with the second volume of *Georgian Poetry*, *King Lear's Wife* was again accorded pre-eminence amongst contemporary work.[49]

As Claude Colleer Abbott wrote 'the dramatist had found an interpreter beyond his hopes and the artist plays that excited him . . . yet their gifts were never seen together on the stage'.[50] Nash died in 1946, Bottomley in 1948, the year in which his *A Stage for Poetry My Purpose with My Plays* was privately published. There he wrote of Nash's designs for *King Lear's Wife*: 'I still hope to see them carried out'.[51] This is still possible as Nash's original designs for *King Lear's Wife* have survived as part of the Emily and Gordon Bottomley Collection at Tullie House Museum, Carlisle.[52] The prospect of staging a Shakespeare play alongside another or others on the same theme has often been advanced, but rarely achieved. Uniquely *King Lear's Wife* offers the opportunity of realizing a remarkable partnership between two rare talents: Bottomley's with the poet's pen, Nash's with the artist's brush. Is there a theatre company that will give this distinguished contribution to the afterlife of *King Lear* an afterlife of its own?

---

[47] *Poet and Painter*, p. 146.

[48] Andrew Causey in his introduction to the re-issue of the Bottomley-Nash correspondence: *Poet and Painter: Letters between Gordon Bottomley and Paul Nash 1910–1946* (Bristol, 1990), p. xix.

[49] In (the catalogue) *International Theatre Exhibition* Nash's designs for costumes for *King Lear's Wife* appear as number 84 (p. 12) and are followed by four other entries for the artist. Nash was represented by two models: 254 *King Lear's Wife* and 255 *Gruach* (p. 19).

[50] Abbott and Bertram eds., *Poet and Painter*, p. xviii.

[51] Bottomley, *A Stage for Poetry*, p. 14.

[52] The Emily and Gordon Bottomley Bequest has been part of the art collection at Tullie House Museum, Carlisle since 1949. The Bottomley Collection consists of six hundred paintings, prints and drawings including original work by Ford Madox Brown, Arthur Hughes, Dante Gabriel Rossetti and Charles Ricketts, as well as many fine examples (two portraits of Bottomley) of Nash. In summer 2001, Melanie Gardner, Keeper of Fine and Decorative Arts, mounted an exhibition entitled 'Pre-Raphaelites and Beyond: The Emily and Gordon Bottomley Bequest'. *King Lear's Wife* was represented by three of the eleven designs in the collection: the stage set, the Corpse Washer and the costumes for Goneril and Gormflaith. I gratefully acknowledge Melanie Gardner's assistance with the preparation of this article.

SOME LEARS

RICHARD PROUDFOOT

I

'In Goethe's view, every old man knows what it is to be King Lear. "Ein alter Mann", he dolefully remarked, "ist stets ein König Lear!" ' I quote Peter Conrad's extended and subtle discussion of *King Lear* offshoots – novels, plays and films – in 'Expatriating Lear', the third chapter of *To be Continued*.[1] That *King Lear* may offer a paradigm of old age is a comment congruous with the view of Shakespeare as universal genius, speaking from the height of poetic imagination to the heart of every man (we notice already the absence of women from the formulation).

When we turn to literature the proposition that every old man is a King Lear is both enticing and challenging.

> There was an Old Man with a beard,
> Who said, 'It is just as I feared! –
> Two Owls and a Hen,
> Four Larks and a Wren,
> Have all built their nests in my beard!'[2]

The collocation of an old man with a beard and the name of Lear does not, alas, allow me to add Edward Lear's old man to the inexhaustible search for the cultural traces of *King Lear* in the nineteenth century – though with a little ingenuity and a little straining it would no doubt be possible to relate the bird-loud beard to the trauma of Shakespeare's King Lear in the storm of Act 3 and the madness of Act 4. Certainly searchers for King Lear in nineteenth-century fiction should carry an identikit portrait of an old man in which a beard (white, long and either wind-swept or restored to order by a daughter's loving care) would constitute an important identifying mark.

The pursuit of Lear through a number of nineteenth- and twentieth-century rewritings, or revisions, or appropriations, or adumbrations, signals the start of the reappraisal of Shakespeare's tragedy during a period which saw it emerge at least as the most powerful rival to the nineteenth-century dominance of *Hamlet* on the way to its later role as paradigmatic Shakespearian tragedy, or the play which spoke most directly and most powerfully to the late twentieth century. This period was, ironically, also one in which the questioning of earlier critical assumptions about 'Shakespearian tragedy' was to lead to energetic subversion of orthodox readings of King Lear as tragic hero and to the superseding of the Old Man with a beard by an increasingly intolerant roster of daughters and others as the central figures in derivative fictions.

In the course of my short discussion of these large topics I shall expose some of my own perplexity in face of a mushrooming scholarly interest in

---

A first version of this paper was delivered at the inaugural meeting of the Polish Shakespeare Association in Gdansk, November 1992. In a radically revised version it was delivered, in substantially this form, on 29 April 2000 at the *Shakespeare Tage* of the Deutsche Shakespeare Gesellschaft, Bochum.

[1] (Oxford, 1995), p. 97.

[2] E. Lear, *A Book of Nonsense* (London, 1863); reprinted in E. Rhys, ed., *A Book of Nonsense by Edward Lear, Lewis Carroll, The Author of Lilliput Levee and other Writers* (London, 1927), p. 3.

what Ruby Cohn in her pioneering study in 1976 called 'modern Shakespeare offshoots'.[3] As well as Peter Conrad I must acknowledge at the outset the stimulus of the work of R. A. Foakes, both in *Hamlet versus Lear: Cultural Politics and Shakespeare's Art* (1993) and in his innovative and wide-ranging edition of *King Lear* for the third series of the Arden Shakespeare (1997).[4] As will be all too apparent, I have made no attempt to keep track of the full range of publications on the topic in the 1990s.

My first source of perplexity is simple. How do we know when we are reading an 'appropriation'? Sometimes, of course, the answer may be clear. Its author may make the connection explicit. When Ivan Sergeivich Turgenev, in 1870, gave one of his long short stories the title 'A Lear of the Steppes', he invited a response instantly reinforced by the opening sentences of the story. Readers are placed at once in the self-conscious position of testing the story – or at least its central figure, 'a certain Martyn Petrovich Kharlov' – against their memories of Shakespeare's character and the play in which he appears.[5]

The novella soon reveals its affinity with *King Lear*: not only does Kharlov, prompted by a dream, renounce his property in the interests of his two daughters, but the episodes include his being turned out of the house in a storm and a powerfully climactic death scene. Where it mainly diverges from Shakespeare is in sustaining the father's relation with his ungrateful daughters as its central concern. Kharlov's dying words are addressed to his younger daughter, Evlampia: ' "I will not p–..." '. Riding home, the narrator asks himself: ' "What was he trying to say to her as he was dying?"... "I will not – put my curse on you"? or "pardon you"?[6] At least in the young narrator's eyes Kharlov remains a male victim of female malice and duplicity. *King Lear* may provide a useful, though hardly indispensable, point of access to 'A Lear of the Steppes', but Turgenev's story hardly provides a reciprocal stimulus to return to Shakespeare nor does reading it much challenge received interpretations of Shakespeare's play.

Another explicit derivative of *King Lear*, the one-act verse drama 'King Lear's Wife' by the minor English poet Gordon Bottomley, stands in a rather different relation to Shakespeare's tragedy.[7] Published in 1915 and professionally staged in London in the same year, Bottomley's play has a cast list which includes King Lear and two of his daughters, Goneril and Cordelia (although the latter figures only as the off-stage voice of a neglected and complaining child). Ruby Cohn suggests that Bottomley set himself the task of answering one of King Lear's most memorable questions: 'Is there any cause in nature that makes these hard hearts?'[8] Bottomley's answer, in her view, was his title, 'King Lear's *Wife*'.[9] This may seem, however, too reductive a formula for a play that represents a radical departure from such then current readings of Shakespeare's tragedy as A. C. Bradley's 'redemption of King Lear'.[10] *King Lear* is remarkable, even by the usual standards of Shakespearian drama, in its lack of reference to the past life of its characters. In 'King Lear's Wife' (as in his later 'Gruach', which invents an episode from the early life of Lady Macbeth[11]), Bottomley indulged in fictional psychology, imagining formative moments adequate to account for the unanalysed and unexplained relationship between Shakespeare's Goneril and her father.

The action takes place in the bedchamber of the dying Queen Hygd, reaching its major climax with her death and concluding as two cynical serving women prepare her corpse for burial. But the play shows Hygd not merely as the sexually frigid source of the infidelities of her apparently much younger

---

[3] *Modern Shakespeare Offshoots* (Princeton, 1976).

[4] (Cambridge, 1993); (Walton-on-Thames, 1997). References to quotations from *King Lear* are to this edition.

[5] I. S. Turgenev, tr. Jessie Coulson, 'A Lear of the Steppes', in *A Nest of Gentlefolk and other Stories* (London, New York, Toronto, 1919), p. 371.

[6] Turgenev, 'A Lear of the Steppes', p. 452.

[7] C. C. Abbott, ed., *Gordon Bottomley: Poems and Plays* (London, 1953), pp. 129–63.

[8] *King Lear* 3.6.74–5.

[9] Cohn, *Modern Shakespeare Offshoots*, p. 251.

[10] A. C. Bradley, *Shakespearian Tragedy* (London, 1904), pp. 197–263.

[11] Abbott, *Gordon Bottomley*, pp. 165–210.

and certainly virile husband. Hygd is quite as much a victim as a cause of Lear's philandering. Lear has taken as his mistress Gormflaith (a name that occurs in the Danish source-material for *Hamlet*[12]), a young woman in the queen's service, to the dismay not only of Hygd herself but of her daughter Goneril, a chilly and athletic young Amazon with a sharp appetite for the hunt and the kill. It is Goneril who avenges her mother, by first stabbing Gormflaith and then devaluing Lear's infatuation by showing him evidence of her infidelity to him.

The play does indeed exhibit a tidiness in its psychologically explanatory action that goes some way towards justifying Cohn's dismissal of it as 'neat, comprehensible, and too simply credible'.[13] Where, however, it does cast light on Shakespeare's tragedy — or at least prompt thought about it — is in its displacement of Lear from the centre of the action, showing him as a weak man ruled by his passions and surrounded by women whose strength, ambition and firmness of purpose he can overcome only by arbitrary assertion of his power as king, husband and father. Goneril's murder of his mistress provokes him to the play's sharpest and least predictable response, 'I thought she had been broken long ago: / She must be wedded and broken, I cannot do it.'[14] We may wonder how he supposed Albany up to the job, but that, of course, is hardly the point, which is rather to reveal the total constriction of even so militant a suffragette as Goneril in a world in which male power is still unassailable.

It would doubtless be an exaggeration to hail Bottomley as either an early luminary of the Freudian school of criticism or a notable prophet of feminism, and yet his play opens up a vista on *King Lear* not wholly congruous with the received view of his period as one of complacent bardolatry in the twilight of Empire. For all his prolixity, slack versification and old-fashioned melodramatic dramaturgy, he does open up gaps in Shakespeare's rendering of the Lear story and contrives — if nothing else — to sharpen our sense of the extent to which the very absence of the explanatory family history he supplies imparts dangerous intensity to the clash between Shakespeare's Lear and his daughters.

When is a Lear not a Lear? Tracing the allusions to Shakespeare's plot or characters in the works of later writers is a pursuit as inexhaustible as it is often likely to prove at last trivial, yielding a mixed bag of red herrings and wild geese. As in the case of Turgenev's novella, a later fiction may depend heavily on *King Lear* without throwing much retrospective light on its source by the nature and quality of its engagement. Conversely, a text that announces no such connection, either explicitly or through immediately recognizable correspondence of character or event, may reveal itself as drawing on and reciprocally defining some aspect of the submerged original.

The situation at the beginning of Jane Austen's *Sense and Sensibility* concerns wills and inheritance. Two deaths in unexpectedly close succession, those of his wealthy great-uncle and of his father, leave young Mr John Dashwood heir to the estate where his father had lived with his second wife and three daughters in the lifetime of the elderly uncle who has chosen as his heirs the males in his family, his nephew, his great-nephew John, and John's four-year-old son Harry. Though 'a steady, respectable man' John Dashwood is also 'rather cold-hearted, and rather selfish'.[15] However, he is affected by his father's deathbed plea 'to do everything in his power' to make his stepmother and half-sisters comfortable.

When he gave his promise to his father, he meditated within himself to increase the fortunes of his sisters by the present of a thousand pounds a-piece. He then really thought himself equal to it. The prospect of four thousand a-year, in addition to his present income, besides the remaining half of his own mother's fortune, warmed

---

[12] The poetess Gormflaith, daughter of Cearbhall, Lord of Ossory, King of Dublin (*c*. 887), was 'wife of three kings' but was 'forced at last to beg for bread from door to door': see I. Gollancz, *The Sources of 'Hamlet': with Essay on the Legend by Sir Israel Gollancz* (Oxford, 1926), pp. 9–10 and family tree opposite p. 56.

[13] Cohn, *Modern Shakespeare Offshoots*, p. 252.

[14] Abbott, *Gordon Bottomley*, p. 163.

[15] J. Austen, *Sense and Sensibility*, ed. C. Lamont (London, New York, Toronto, 1970), pp. 1, 3.

his heart and made him feel capable of generosity. – 'Yes, he would give them three thousand pounds: it would be liberal and handsome! It would be enough to make them completely easy. Three thousand pounds! he could spare so considerable a sum with little inconvenience.' – He thought of it all day long, and for many days successively, and he did not repent.[16]

The second chapter is a scene between John and his rich wife, who is 'a strong caricature of himself; – more narrow-minded and selfish'.[17] The appalling comedy of her progressive dissuasion of her husband from his vision of munificence sets the scene and establishes some of the social and moral values for the ensuing narrative. Its dynamic may recall equally the acquiescence of Macbeth in face of his wife's forceful persuasions to the murder of Duncan and the coldly calculating reduction of Lear's hundred knights to none by Goneril and Regan. Though neither, of course, corresponds with the circumstances of the Dashwoods, both reminiscences nourish a sense of the inhumanity of the selfish argument. That *King Lear* may indeed have been active in Jane Austen's imagination is urged by a succession of resonances released by the language of her dialogue.

Mrs John Dashwood did not at all approve of what her husband intended to do for his sisters. To take three thousand pounds from the fortune of their dear little boy, would be impoverishing him to the most dreadful degree. She begged him to think again on the subject. How could he answer it to himself to rob his child, and his only child too, of so large a sum? And what possible claim could the Miss Dashwoods, who were related to him only by half blood, which she considered as no relationship at all, have on his generosity to so large an amount. It was very well known that no affection was ever supposed to exist between the children of any man by different marriages; and why was he to ruin himself, and their poor little Harry, by giving away all his money to his half sisters? 'It was my father's last request to me,' replied her husband, 'that I should assist his widow and daughters.'[18]

The words 'half blood' will set the ears of Lear-hunters aquiver with its echo of Albany's 'half-blooded fellow', addressed to Edmund – Shakespeare's only use of the word.[19] The word is

rare enough to attract attention, and Jane Austen repeats it a page later. Her usage points to no more than the sharing of only one parent, and legitimacy of birth is not an issue in the social world of her novel. However, the ties of kinship are, and the implicit analogy with Gloucester's sons serves to reinforce the injustice of a selfishness which has no imaginable excuse in family history. When John Dashwood toys with the less costly alternative of settling an annuity on his stepmother, his wife is quick with an answer.

I have known a great deal of the trouble of annuities; for my mother was clogged with the payment of three to old superannuated servants by my father's will ['Age is unnecessary'?[20]], and it is amazing how disagreeable she found it. Twice every year these annuities were to be paid; ... My mother was quite sick of it. Her income was not her own, she said, with such perpetual claims on it.[21]

Mrs John Dashwood's final argument clinches the matter – and totally subverts the point of Mr Dashwood's dying plea to his son.

'Your father thought only of *them*. And I must say this: that you owe no particular gratitude to him, nor attention to his wishes, for we very well know that if he could, he would have left almost every thing in the world to *them*.' This argument was irresistible. It gave to his intentions whatever of decision was wanting before; and he finally resolved, that it would be absolutely unnecessary, if not highly indecorous, to do more for the widow and children of his father, than such kind of neighbourly acts as his own wife pointed out.[22]

Like Goneril and Regan, Mrs John Dashwood has acted: and 'i'the heat'.[23]

To count *King Lear* as among the literary sources of *Sense and Sensibility* might seem to be

---

[16] Ibid., p. 3.
[17] Ibid., p. 3.
[18] Ibid., p. 6.
[19] *King Lear* 5.3.81.
[20] *King Lear* 2.2.344.
[21] Austen, *Sense and Sensibility*, p. 8.
[22] Ibid., p. 10.
[23] *King Lear* 1.1.309.

a confession of lack of both qualities, but the connection, once suggested, is hard to forget and it can at least be said that it helps to contextualize the civilized inhumanity of the Dashwoods in a broader moral vision. For Jane Austen's Henry Crawford in *Mansfield Park*, familiarity with Shakespeare was 'part of an Englishman's constitution. His thoughts and beauties are so spread abroad that one touches him every where, one is intimate with him by instinct'.[24] Jane Austen's intimacy with him, as it is implied in the opening chapters of *Sense and Sensibility*, is less a matter of reminiscence of detail than of imaginative incorporation.

II

In England in the nineteenth century, as indeed elsewhere in Europe, the Shakespearian tragedy most likely to promote imitation or variation was *Hamlet*, most famously, perhaps, in Goethe's *Wilhelm Meister*. *Hamlet* likewise haunts the pages of Dickens, never more than in *Great Expectations*, which is pervaded by the uneasy relations of Pip to his 'ghost' and surrogate father Magwitch and to the unattainable Estella. When called upon by Bulwer Lytton to rewrite the authentically inconclusive ending of the novel which confirms the impossibility of any rapprochement between Pip and Estella, Dickens came up with an alternative ending in which they meet again at the ruins of Satis House. As close reading reveals, Dickens imagined that scene (like the initial encounter of Pip with Magwitch in the graveyard) in terms of the language and imagery of Hamlet's encounter with the Ghost of his father, imparting to the purportedly 'happy' alternative ending an undefined sense of unease and lack of true resolution.[25] Though Hamlet is a dominant presence in Dickens, Lear and Cordelia, father (or grandfather) and daughter (or grand-daughter) can also be glimpsed sporadically – in *The Old Curiosity Shop*, in *Dombey and Son*, or in *Little Dorrit*. Near the end of the nineteenth century in England *Hamlet* continued to raise his indecisive or suicidal head in fictions as diverse as George Meredith's *The Tragic Comedians*[26] and Marie Corelli's *The Mighty Atom*.[27]

Meanwhile, two substantial and radical appropriations of *King Lear* had been published in France: Balzac's *Le Père Goriot* and Zola's *La Terre*.[28] Balzac's thorough familiarity with several of Shakespeare's plays, and in particular the pervasive influence throughout his work of *King Lear*, is well documented.[29] His own mother's repudiation of her merchant parents after her socially climbing marriage may well have helped to attract her son's attention to the cruelties of family life as portrayed in *King Lear*. The young Zola, having sent his first two successful novels for comment to the critic Hippolyte Taine, was advised to broaden his canvas and to take as his models both Balzac and Shakespeare. He took the advice, and *King Lear* duly figures in his notebooks for *La Terre*.[30]

Le Père Goriot, published in 1834, is set in the Paris of 1819. Despite the initial prominence given to other characters, Balzac soon reveals that 'old Goriot' is to be his protagonist (the inadequate

---

[24] Jane Austen, *Mansfield Park*, ed. J. Lucas (London, Oxford, New York, 1975), p. 306.

[25] C. Dickens, *Great Expectations*, ed. A. Calder (Harmondsworth, 1985), ch. 59, pp. 491–3. I owe this perception to my colleague at King's College London, Dr George Myerson.

[26] (London, 1880).

[27] (London, 1896).

[28] *Le Père Goriot* (1834), *La Terre* (1887).

[29] E.g., Pierre-Georges Castex, ed., *Le Père Goriot* (Paris, 1960), p. xiv, records Balzac's acknowledgement of the influence of *Othello* on *La Gina* and of *Macbeth* on *Le Cousin Pons* and adds: 'Le Roi Lear *ne pouvait être loin de sa pensée, alors qu'il travaillait au* Père *Goriot*'; another commentator on *Le Père Goriot*, Pierre Citron, finds 'Rien d'invraisemblable à ce que Balzac ait pensé au *Roi Lear*' (Paris, 1996), p. 7.

[30] Guy Robert, *'La Terre' d'Émile Zola: étude historique et critique* (Paris, 1952), assumes that the collapse of Fouan was inspired by three models, among them *King Lear*, to which there is an explicit reference in Zola's notebook for the novel, easily accounted for by Zola's knowledge and admiration of Shakespeare from his youth. Taine's advice, in a letter declining Zola's invitation to review *Thérèse Raquin*, to broaden his social canvas and to take as his models Balzac and Shakespeare, oddly overlooks the strong traces of *Macbeth* in this early work of Zola (see F. W. J. Hemmings, *Émile Zola*, second edition, corrected (London, Oxford, New York, 1970), pp. 48–9).

English translation loses the double sense of *père*, but it is still an improvement on the infelicitous *Daddy Goriot* adopted by an early English translator in the 1860s). The setting, in a 'family boarding house in the Rue Neuve-Sainte-Geneviève between the Latin Quarter and the Faubourg Saint-Marcel' which has been run 'for the last forty years' by 'the elderly Madame Vauquer, *née* de Conflans',[31] both constitutes the tidal shelf of impecunious respectability on which the central characters are washed up on their slow journeys to or from financial and social success and affords a varied chorus of unsympathetic commentators on the chief events.

That old Goriot derives from Lear is abundantly evident once his true relations with his two daughters emerge from the hostile gossip and salacious imaginings of his landlady and fellow-lodgers. Balancing the social comedy and meticulously detailed surface of the narrative is an underlying structure of drama. The role of Goriot is announced at the outset: he is a tragic hero of common life, an impressive and memorable human victim of the advance of a 'civilization' whose pursuit of money, sex and social status constitutes the principal activity of the other characters – he was also to Balzac 'Christ-like father'.[32] Balzac places his Lear within his vision of a human comedy, a comedy of social and economic life. With a further, unexpected, nod at Shakespeare, he confirms the veracity of his narrative with the English phrase '*All Is True*'.[33]

Readers of *Le Père Goriot* familiar with *King Lear* will only gradually recognize the connection and, having done so, will then begin to perceive that Balzac's response to Lear extends beyond mere narrative connection and the implicit rejection of any aristocratic or cathartic vision of tragedy. With only two daughters, Goriot lacks a Cordelia (always a tricky role in appropriations of *King Lear*). As his progressive impoverishment accentuates his role as butt and scorn of the Maison Vauquer, he begins to attract the sympathetic attention of the southern law-student Eugène de Rastignac. In terms of *Lear*, Rastignac sets out as an Edmund: his social and amatory ambitions lead him to neglect his studies, to incur heavy debts and eventually to engage in a love affair with Goriot's younger daughter, the Baroness Delphine de Nucingen. The suicidal self-sacrifice of Goriot in supporting the extravagance of his daughters ends, however, by turning Rastignac into his most loyal friend and supporter. By now more Edgar than Edmund, it is he who cares for the dying man and makes the last efforts to bring his daughters to his deathbed.

The allusions to Lear mount and become more particular at the climax of the novel, as Goriot lies dying (in a crisis brought on by his daughters' having quarrelled in his presence). In his ramblings he covers many of the topics of Lear's enquiry into the sources of authority and the obligations of nature. His attempts to summon his daughters to his deathbed are unavailing: they echo with thematic, at times nearly verbal, reminiscence of the speeches of Lear.

'To think that neither of his daughters is coming!' Rastignac exclaimed. 'I'll write to them both.'
'Neither of them!' cried the old man, sitting up. 'They are busy, they are sleeping, they will not come. I knew it. You have to die to know what your children are ... Ah! If I were rich, if I had kept my money, if I had not given it all to them, they would be here now; they would fawn on me, and cover my cheeks with their kisses!'[34]

He interprets his own destruction.

'The county will go to ruin if the fathers are trampled underfoot ... Society, the whole world, turns on fatherly love, everything falls to pieces if children do not love their fathers.' ... 'There is a God in Heaven, and we fathers are avenged whether we wish it or not.' ... 'The law demands that they should come to see their father die; the law is on my side ... Go and tell them that not to come is parricide!' ... 'Oh! They are vile, stony-hearted women, my curse upon them; I abhor them! I shall rise from the grave at night to curse them again'.[35]

---

[31] *Old Goriot*, tr. M. A. Crawford (Harmondsworth, 1951), p. 27.
[32] Ibid., p. 15.
[33] Ibid., p. 28.
[34] Ibid., p. 284.
[35] Ibid., pp. 287–9.

But these complaints alternate with an awareness of his own responsibility, not, like Lear, for begetting his daughters, but for spoiling them.

'I have expiated to the full the sin of loving them too much. They themselves have been the instruments of vengeance, they have tortured me like executioners ... I returned to them as a gambler does to the gaming-table. They were my own particular vice; they took the place another man fills with his mistresses, that's the whole story!' ... 'It is all my fault; I taught them to trample me underfoot. That was how I liked it to be, and it's nobody's business but mine, it's no concern of human justice or God's justice. God would be unjust if he condemned them for their behaviour towards me. I did not know how to treat them; I was stupid enough to resign my rights'.[36]

Where Lear is restored by music, Goriot's agony is attended by the medical student Bianchon, a man whose interpretation is wholly mechanistic. A typical comment is 'The mechanism still works; but in his case it's a pity; it would be far better if he died'[37] ('The wonder is he hath endured so long'; 'He hates him / That would upon the rack of this rough world / Stretch him out longer'[38]). Thus the ravings of Goriot are rendered doubly impotent. The ironies of what follows demand reference back to Shakespeare for full appreciation of their effect. Goriot does eventually die in the presence of his elder daughter, but he has lost consciousness before her arrival. In a reversal of Shakespeare's conclusion it is she, not he, who seeks in vain for evidence of continuing life: 'Just then Goriot opened his eyes; but it was only the effect of a muscular contraction. The Countess's quick movement of awakened hope was a sight no less terrible than the sight of the dying man's eye'.[39]

Certainly the narratives, and their interpretation, diverge: Lear is not destroyed by love of Goneril and Regan. But I am aware of no critical account of the end of Shakespeare's tragedy dating from before 1834 which begins to show the sensitivity to the death of Lear implied by Balzac's variation on it, a sensitivity not to words alone but to the whole imagined impact of the scene as staged – which, of course, it was not, until Macready rejected Tate's rewritten ending at Drury Lane in 1838.

Of 2532 entries in a substantial two-volume bibliography of *King Lear* by Larry Champion, only three relate to *Le Père Goriot* (two of them perfunctorily – 'Students exposed to both of these works come to understand how deeply complex are the duties and responsibilities of parenthood'.[40] One documents Balzac's knowledge of Shakespeare in general[41]; one conducts a brief but sensible search for Lear beyond the obvious similarities in *Le Père Goriot*.[42] Zola rates a single entry that relates to a public lecture delivered on the 19 January 1889 by the eminent French scholar of English literature Emile Legouis when he was a young lecturer at the University of Lyons. It was published in a text prepared by his son, Pierre Legouis, on the fiftieth anniversary of the death of Zola.[43] *La Terre* achieved such a *succès de scandale* in 1887 as to make it an obvious route by which to introduce *King Lear* to a non-specialist French lecture audience two years later.

In such a context it comes as no surprise to find Legouis at once celebrating Zola's skill in transposing the Lear story to the farmlands of the Beauce in the 1860s and using him as whipping-boy in arguing for a transcendent and redemptive reading of Shakespeare's tragedy. He heads his comparison 'A Lear without Cordelia' and concludes by charging Zola, the self-professed realist, with a personally biased and satirical pessimism. The connection between the two texts is clearly if briefly established. Legouis outlines the fortunes of the

---

36 Ibid., pp. 286–7.
37 Ibid., p. 291.
38 *King Lear* 5.3.315, 313–14.
39 *Old Goriot*, p. 299.
40 Golata, John, ''Père Goriot' and *King Lear*', *English Journal*, 56 (1967), pp. 1288–9: item 2417 in ''King Lear': An Annotated Bibliography*, compiled by Larry S. Champion, 2 vols. (New York and London, 1980).
41 Champion, item 625: Hamblen, Abigail Ann, 'Lear the Universal', *The Cresset*, 30 (March, 1967), pp. 15–18.
42 Champion, item 2455: Besser, Gretchen, 'Lear and Goriot: A Re-evaluation', *Orbis Litterarum*, 27 (1972), pp. 28–36.
43 Champion, item 2354: Legouis, Pierre. '*La Terre* de Zola et le *Roi Lear*', *Revue de Littérature Comparée*, 27 (1953), pp. 417–27.

old farmer, Fouan, from his reluctant division of the land that he is too old, at sixty-nine, to go on farming unaided between his daughter Fanny and his two sons, Hyacinthe and Buteau, through the gradations of humiliation he suffers at the hands of each of his children in turn, to his final brutal murder by Buteau and his wife Lise. He then charges Zola with a lapse from veracity: 'Are Goneril and Regan, Buteau and Hyacinthe, more real than Kent and Cordelia?'[44]

Several responses suggest themselves. Even if one represses a reflex rejection of the question as, if not meaningless, at least uncritical, one can proceed to challenge the perception of the novel that generated it. *La Terre* is not simply the tragedy of Fouan: it portrays a community, centred indeed on the extended family of the Fouans and on their village. It displays both the inherited and traditional meanness and brutality of men and women whose life is virtually 'cheap as beasts',[45] but it also defines the threat to their existence posed by political, economic and technological change. Like *King Lear*, *La Terre* is the product of a period of rapidly changing values and of challenge to received ways of perceiving the world. But it also differs from *Lear*, of which it is as much subversion as version.

Bourgeois propriety doubtless motivated the reticence of Legouis about the motives and circumstances of the murder of Fouan. The old farmer and his three children may correspond in some sense to Lear and his daughters, but the youngest, Buteau – in this schema an unlikely Cordelia – turns out to be more of an Edmund. Having married Lise (whom he has impregnated) for opportunistic reasons, he continues to lust after her adolescent sister, Françoise. Throughout the eight years of the narrative, Françoise resists Buteau's crude importunities (though physically roused by him) and marries the novel's honest man, Jean Macquart (though without loving him). The climax of violence and brutality is reached with the rape of the heavily pregnant Françoise by Buteau on the piece of land that is the source of their contention. The consequent attack on Françoise by her jealous sister, Lise, ends with the infliction of a mortal wound with a scythe. Françoise, ruled by the

imperative of retaining the family's hold on its land, dies stoically, never revealing even to her husband the guilt of her sister and brother-in-law. Fouan, having witnessed the attacks on Françoise, must be silenced. He in turn is brutally murdered by Buteau and Lise, who succeed in disguising his death as an accident. At this point, the Shakespearian reader will register not only an extension of Shakespeare's Lear story to its logical conclusion but a gearshift into *Macbeth* (a play whose presence in Zola is even more clearly perceptible in the early *Thérèse Raquin* and the late *La Bête Humaine*).[46]

Narrative pattern may clinch the connection between *La Terre* and Shakespeare – a connection made fully explicit in a note among Zola's sketches for the novel: 'They must finally rob him: King Lear'[47] – but congratulating Zola on the skill of his transposition is hardly to the point. True, the children's haggling over the allowance to be paid to their parents recalls the calculation of Goneril and Regan over Lear's hundred knights; true, Fouan is turned out in a storm by Buteau and Lise, eventually finding refuge in the warm filth of a pig-sty (before at last returning to their house, silent and defeated). *La Terre*, like most of Zola's novels in the Rougon–Macquart cycle, creates its human action in a specific and minutely realized setting. The rich farmlands of the Beauce provide a beautiful setting, shown in the succession of the seasons, for a barely human life from which in the end the protagonist, Jean Macquart, withdraws in horror and sorrow after the loss of his wife. As in *King Lear*, all sources of value and authority are questioned, but unlike Shakespeare's tragedy, Zola's novel offers at the end not even an ambiguous or mistaken hope of consolation for 'the poor creature of earth'.[48] It is no part of Zola's purpose to celebrate

---

44 Legouis, '*La Terre*', p. 427: 'Goneril et Régane, Buteau et Hyacinthe sont-ils plus vrais que Kent et Cordélie?'

45 *King Lear* 2.2.456.

46 *Thérèse Raquin* (1867); *La Bête Humaine* (1890).

47 Cited by Legouis, *La Terre*, p. 418, on the authority of Guy Robert, 'Zola et le classicisme', *Revue des sciences humaines* (1948) and '*La Terre*' d'Émile Zola (Paris, 1952).

48 *King Lear* 3.4.115–16.

Shakespeare: for him, as for Balzac, Shakespeare's *King Lear* becomes a model not by reason of any national or cultural investment in 'Shakespeare', but because in it Shakespeare confronts issues, personal, social, political and philosophical, which continued to concern these French and Russian writers of the nineteenth century. Their creative responses to Lear represent reactions of a complexity and sensitivity far in advance both of the theatrical practice of their time and of most formal critical comment on the play. What traditional myopia confined them to the neglect reflected by Champion's *Bibliography*? The twenty years since it was published have begun to change the picture by exploring the insight into Shakespeare's tragedy to be found in creative responses to it as well as in stage history and formal criticism.

The 'Lears' I have considered so far have, once identified, shown clear signs of their relation to Shakespeare's play, whether in terms of narrative structure, correspondence of individual character or engagement with identifiable issues. If 'King Lear's Wife' may indeed be read as an answer to the question 'What cause is there in nature that makes these hard hearts?' – engaging with a gap in Shakespeare's narrative to offer an answer – equally the theme of divided inheritance launches *La Terre* into its more explicitly political engagement with the same issue and its exploration of whether the denial to nature of 'more than nature needs' devalues human life to a bestial rate.[49] The relation of both to *King Lear* is overt.

Even more overt is the connection with *King Lear* of Jane Smiley's *A Thousand Acres* (1991).[50] And yet this claim might be challenged, as the novel never makes explicit a connection without which it cannot be fully relished or even, perhaps, understood. As Peter Conrad perceptively remarks, 'The lives of Smiley's characters have been predetermined by a Shakespearean text they know nothing about'.[51] A similarly unknowing reader might find much in the novel hard to understand, not least the actions of its King Lear figure, Larry Cook, whose erratic behaviour, fully intelligible to readers of Shakespeare, who can see how those actions follow the predictable pattern of Shakespeare's

sequence of events, can hardly be accounted for in the novel except in terms of the onset of senility; nor can the choice of Ginny (Goneril) as narrator and the ways in which her actions in the last two sections of the book rewrite Act 5 of *King Lear* make full sense unless they are set against Goneril's successful poisoning of her sister Regan and subsequent suicide. Smiley's novel is in six sections, in the sixth of which Ginny, surviving Act 5, as it were, escapes from the world of the family and the farm to build a new life and to bring up the children of her dead sister Rose (Regan). It is the detailed allusiveness of the novel, a feature fully intended and expounded in public by its author, which most detracts from its exceptional power and imagination in transposing the plot and many major concerns of the play into the alien world of Iowa in the late 1970s. The personal lives of the characters are caught up in the onset of an ecological and financial disaster, whose symptoms in the novel include Ginny's repeated miscarriages and the cancer that kills her mother and her sister. The implication of Larry in creating both the toxicity of the water supply, by his use of chemicals on the farm, and the psychological trauma of the daughters, by his sexual abuse of them after their mother's death, is thematically coherent but overloads the novel in the direction of too many good causes at once. Starting with the avowed aim of writing a novel which, if read before Shakespeare, might serve adolescent girls as 'a prophylactic against the guilt about proper daughterhood that I knew *King Lear* could induce', Smiley ends by revealing the power of her antagonist by the sheer weight of the artillery she finds it necessary to mount against him.[52]

---

49 *King Lear* 2.2.455.

50 J. Smiley, *Thousand Acres* (New York, 1991).

51 Conrad, *To Be Continued*, p. 131.

52 J. Smiley, 'Shakespeare in Iceland' (delivered at the World Shakespeare Congress in Los Angeles in April, 1996), in M. Novy, ed., *Transforming Shakespeare: Contemporary Women's Re-Visions in Literature and Performance* (New York, Basingstoke, 1999), pp. 159–79, p. 173. In an appendix (first published on 21 June 1998 in the *Washington Post Book World*, p. 1)

III

The last texts I shall consider stand in more equivocal relation to *Lear*, although a case can be made for reading them as very different manifestations of a similar response to the play, which questions its assumptions about power structures, self-images and gender roles. They are *An Unsuitable Job for a Woman* by P. D. James[53] and *Late Call* by Angus Wilson.[54]

P. D. James is a popular and widely read writer of detective fiction. Her book announces its possible relation to Shakespeare by giving its young female private detective heroine the name Cordelia Gray. Cordelia's occupation provokes disapproving comment from a succession of other characters, both men and women, who stress its unsuitability for a woman. The Shakespeare connection is highlighted by the following exchange, about a third of the way into the book.

> Cordelia had come up to the group and had stood over them for a few seconds before they took any notice of her. She said:
> 'I'm looking for Hugo and Sophia Tilling. My name is Cordelia Gray.' Hugo Tilling looked up:
> 'What shall Cordelia do, love and be silent.'
> Cordelia said:
> 'People who feel the need to joke about my name usually enquire after my sisters. It gets very boring.'
> 'It must do. I'm sorry . . .'[55]

By this point in the story Cordelia has revealed both her affinity with her namesake's directness and lack of tact, and her isolation in a male world.

To summarize a detective novel is problematic, as an outline of its events entails a subversion of its narrative method. However, I must try, without skewing it too unfairly in the direction of my argument, to describe *An Unsuitable Job for a Woman*. The main narrative is of Cordelia's investigation of the circumstances in which Mark Callender, son of Sir Ronald Callender, the celebrated director of a state-of-the-art private research laboratory, has committed suicide in a village outside Cambridge. Sir Ronald employs Cordelia to carry out the investigation (assuming, as later emerges, her incompetence and inability to succeed in it). This narrative,

which leads to the unorthodox outcome expected by readers of P. D. James, is framed by two episodes in London.

Cordelia graduated from casual employment as a temporary typist ('a suitable job for a woman') to assistant, and then to partner, of Bernie Pryde, a private detective and former police officer who left the police force under a cloud. Her own haphazard education, after early loss of her mother, was in England, while her communist–anarchist father lived on the Continent. Her hopes of entry to Cambridge from her Catholic Convent School were dashed when her father decided that a teenage daughter would be an asset and called her out to join him in Italy. His death left her without roots, and without a higher education.

The novel's first event is Cordelia's discovery of Bernie Pryde dead. He has killed himself rather than face an inoperable cancer. In its conclusion, Cordelia is called in by Scotland Yard and interrogated about her investigation by Superintendent Adam Dalgliesh (well known to her readers as James's detective in many earlier novels). Dalgliesh was Bernie's superior and hero, but he was also responsible for his dismissal from the police force.

Cordelia's case involves two murders, both passed off as suicides. Mark was killed by his father, Sir Ronald, and then left as if he had hanged himself (Edmund's plan for Cordelia in *King Lear*). The point at issue is money. The *King Lear* connection centres on Sir Ronald. Mark is indeed his son, but not, as the world supposes, 'honest madam's issue'.[56] In youth, Ronnie Callender had a lover, Emma Leeming. With her collusion, he married a

---

to this essay Smiley distances herself from *A Thousand Acres*, observing 'I think Shakespeare wrote *The Winter's Tale* to answer *King Lear* with hope' (Novy, *Transforming Shakespeare*, p. 178).

53 P. D. James (London, 1972): my attention was drawn to this novel by my colleague at King's College London, Dr Paul Kenny. Quotations are taken from the reprint by Penguin Books (Harmondsworth, 1989).

54 (London, 1964).

55 James, *An Unsuitable Job for a Woman*, p. 73.

56 *King Lear* 1.2.9.

wealthy woman who, being unable to bear a child, agreed in turn to pose as the mother of Emma's son, Mark, conveniently dying soon afterwards. Ronnie, using so much of her money as he inherited directly, built his career and his research centre. Mark, learning (by means too elaborate for brief summary) of his true maternity, dropped out of his university studies to take a job as resident gardener in a village near Cambridge. He tells his father that so far from securing his own share of his 'mother's' inheritance for the research centre, he will renounce it and will acknowledge Miss Leeming (still Sir Ronald's companion and Personal Assistant) as his true mother. His father kills him.

Cordelia untangles the web and confronts Sir Ronald. Unknown to her, Miss Leeming can hear them. She shoots the father (and murderer) of her son, using the unlicensed gun Cordelia inherited from Bernie to do it. Cordelia takes charge, rigs this new murder as another 'suicide' and, in a notable act of female bonding, colludes with Miss Leeming in the cover-up. 'What shall Cordelia speak? Love and be silent'.[57] Deducing the extent of Cordelia's involvement, Dalgliesh and his own superior, sitting in Olympian conclave at Scotland Yard, agree to let the truth remain concealed. But even now they will concede no success to a female investigator. Dalgliesh reflects: 'I find it ironic and oddly satisfying that Pryde took his revenge. Whatever mischief that child was up to in Cambridge, she was working under his direction'.[58]

Is there a King Lear in this text, so overtly connected with some of the issues of Shakespeare's tragedy? If so, it must, I suppose, be Sir Ronald – a Lear who launches the action by murdering his own 'Cordelia' (or should it rather be 'Edmund'?) and trying to pass it off as a suicide, though he is perhaps more Gloucester than Lear. As in Shakespeare the clash is between the disparate values of a selfish and self-absorbed father and an honest and altruistic child. But Cordelia Gray, for all the apparent success of her conspiracy to protect the murderess of Sir Ronald, remains subject to higher male authority (and to the legacies of a dead father and a dead male colleague). Whether or not she is in a suitable job for a woman remains in question when,

at the end of the book, she returns to her London office.

Outside the office a man was waiting, a middle-aged man in a tight blue suit, pig eyes sharp as flint among the fleshy folds of the face.
'Miss Gray? I'd nearly given you up. My name's Fielding. I saw your plate and just came up by chance, don't you know.'
His eyes were avaricious, prurient.
'Well now, you're not quite what I expected, not the usual kind of Private Eye.'
'Is there anything I can do for you, Mr Fielding?'
He gazed furtively round the landing, seeming to find its sordidness reassuring.
'It's my lady friend. I've reason to suspect that she's getting a bit on the side. Well – a man likes to know where he stands. You get me?'
Cordelia fitted the key into the lock.
'I understand, Mr Fielding. Won't you come in?'[59]

Why should Shakespeare be brought into any discussion of this detective novel? And again, why not, given the open invitation of Cordelia's name? *An Unsuitable Job for a Woman* is set in Cambridge; a literary group of characters validates the wide range of allusive reference characteristic of the more sophisticated kind of English detective novel (even the fake suicide note is a quotation from Blake's 'Marriage of Heaven and Hell'). More to the point, however, even within the confines and conventions of its genre, this book may be described as dwelling more than casually on two serious concerns of *King Lear*: the limited power of women in traditional areas of male dominance, here represented by criminal detection, scientific research and the older English universities; and the danger incurred by a child of independent mind who chooses to oppose paternal will.

The relation to Shakespeare of the *Lear* offshoots I have mentioned may, perhaps fancifully, be likened to the musical form of theme and variations. *King Lear* – like 'La Follia', or that

---

[57] *King Lear* 1.1.62.
[58] James, *Unsuitable Job*, p. 204.
[59] Ibid., pp. 204–5.

over-familiar tune by Paganini, or the theme delivered to Beethoven by Diabelli – remains in view, sometimes clearly perceptible in melodic contour; sometimes submerged as no more than a rhythmic motif or harmonic progression; inverted, augmented or diminished, but still affording a point of reference for the revelatory novelty of the variation.

My final example invites a slight modification of the musical analogy. Angus Wilson's *Late Call* is a variation that never states its theme, even vestigially. Nonetheless I would wish to propose both that reference to *King Lear* accounts for very much of what we find in the novel and that reciprocally *Late Call* constitutes a far-reaching meditation or fantasia on *Lear*, from the sharply particularized perspective of the English Midlands in the early 1960s – the period of Harold Macmillan, secondary modern schools, Butlin's holiday camps, New Towns, sociology, the public acceptance of John Osborne's *Look Back in Anger*, and the Wolfenden report on the law relating to homosexual behaviour. By the time he wrote *Late Call*, Angus Wilson was well known for his short stories and novels, especially for *Anglo-Saxon Attitudes*, a work of Dickensian scope in which he exercised a keen eye and ear and a sharply witty pen on the social snobberies and moral duplicities of the English middle classes and academia.

Late Call is in various ways the most problematic of my exhibits in relation to *King Lear*, in that the relation of father to daughter, though arguably fundamental to it, is confined to a brief two pages in its 'Prologue'. The protagonist (and principal consciousness) of the novel is Sylvia Calvert, *née* Tuffield. The story of her retirement is set very exactly in the years 1963–4 and most of it takes place in the New Town in the South Midlands (perhaps based on Milton Keynes?) where she goes to live with her son Harold. She is 63 at the time of her retirement and the action extends to include her 65th birthday. The Prologue, subtitled 'The Hot Summer of 1911', is a third-person narrative of the day whose memory Sylvia treasures for a lifetime as a moment of true happiness – the day when she played truant from domestic chores on her father's farm for an escapade in the fields and woods with little Myra Longmore, the daughter of her

parents' summer lodger, Mrs Longmore. The children's idyll, from which they return (Lear-like?) wet and dirty and with clothes torn or lost, ends with the irate departure of Mrs Longmore and the beating of Sylvia by her brutal father 'Till the blood run'.[60] Throughout this prologue, Sylvia is unnamed: to middle-class Mrs Longmore she remains simply 'the Tuffield girl' in a strong initial statement of the class hierarchies which remain an important concern throughout the novel. Her anonymity is also an indicator of Sylvia's total lack of egotism, even perhaps of a stable sense of identity – later, when asked to describe herself, she will reply 'I'm very fat', then, 'I was a manageress, but I'm nothing now', and finally, 'it's really true, you know, I'm a nobody. I always have been'.[61]

'Nothing will come of nothing'.[62] *Late Call* tells the story of Sylvia's further loss, in retirement, of a succession of sustaining roles and relationships. So far an analogy with the experience of Lear (at least in one reading of the play) holds, but unlike *King Lear* Wilson's novel ends with renewed optimism as Sylvia determines, after her husband's death, to live alone and to make a new life for herself. Sylvia Calvert's story is thus both a negative image and a revision of Lear's. As in *King Lear*, the family is central.

In respect of the character of Lear my musical image may still serve. Wilson's novel may be seen as a canonic variation in three voices, of which the top vocal line is inverted. Lear's role is divided between three members of the Calvert family. First comes the grandmother, Sylvia ('Who is Silvia? What is she . . . ?'[63]). Her retirement from a job as a hotel manageress is the starting point of the main narrative. No mere 'King Lear's Wife' but a female protagonist, a Queen Lear, Sylvia's 'late call' is to a belated, fumbling and painful journey from loss of roles to acquisition (or recovery) of a personality. The second 'Lear' is her husband,

[60] Wilson, *Late Call*, p. 33.
[61] Ibid., pp. 132–3.
[62] *King Lear* 1.1.90.
[63] *The Two Gentlemen of Verona* 4.2.38.

Captain Arthur Calvert, who retains from his finest hour, the first World War, only 'the name and all th'addition'[64] to a commissioned rank (for which he lacked the social background and to which he was promoted only in wartime circumstances) and the ruined lungs of a victim of poison gas. His death is the climactic event of the novel. The third 'Lear' is their son Harold, sole survivor of their three children, whose sister and brother died, respectively, in a childhood accident and in World War II. Harold, very recently widowed, offers his parents a home, in Sylvia's retirement, in his new house in a New Town. His share of Lear's role is as father and as man in authority. He is headmaster of a secondary modern school and author of a successful series of textbooks for backward readers. He has three children, Ray, Mark and Judy.

Once the analogy with *King Lear* is detected, detail after detail confirms it, inviting – even imposing – the desire to compare and contrast. Sylvia renounces the identity and authority vested in her as a hotel manageress; she goes to live with her widowed son, in a household still dominated by memories of the recently dead Beth, where she has no natural role and where her familiar furniture looks merely shabby and out of place; isolation from her son and cultural distance from her grandchildren reduce her to near-suicidal depression; her recovery starts when she rescues a child from danger in a violent thunderstorm and survives a consequent mild stroke. Wilson's inversion of *King Lear* entails not merely casting Lear as a woman, but as a woman who starts from a depressed self-effacement diametrically opposite to Lear's ignorant self-assurance.

The case of his other 'Lears' is simpler. Arthur's story is of a slow crawl towards death, tended not by a daughter or grand-daughter, but by his wife. His only potential Cordelia is his socially snobbish grand-daughter Judy, whose dealings with him have been minimal and awkward, especially when, early in her grand-parents' stay, she is shocked to encounter 'unaccommodated man'[65] in the shape of her naked grand-father on the landing as he leaves the bathroom. This young lady is absent from his funeral, having gone 'into France'[66] with one of her posh school-friends. If Sylvia experiences

an emotional and spiritual pilgrimage, and Arthur is Lear as Old Man, the case of Harold is different. Tormented by sexual deprivation after the loss of his wife, he proceeds in the course of the novel to lose his authority as the father of his sons and to see his mother withdraw decisively from his attempts to manage her life for her. Where *King Lear* finds the breakdown of family relationships symptomatic of a wider descent from order to chaos, *Late Call* finds its contrasting focus in the need to escape the constricting duties and unspoken assumptions of domestic life. As Sylvia reflects during Arthur's final illness, 'Why do we all have to be so much each others' jobs?'[67] Her emotional education, whose catalyst is the young American girl she saves in the storm, is won by experience. Sylvia is a great reader of escapist fiction: 'in novels you read of family feuds that went deep enough to kill young love for ever, and that the brush of a hand roused tenderness enough to mend the fiercest quarrel. But books and life were not the same; there was no sense in expecting such a thing'.[68]

Nineteenth-century novelists effected the transposition of tragedy into bourgeois or peasant life. But for Goriot or Fouan, as for Lear, loss of the love and solidarity of family life remains a catastrophe. Conversely, for Sylvia Calvert, freedom consists precisely in shedding the obligations to others, parents, husband, hotel-residents, children and grandchildren, which have occupied her life and restricted, even prevented, her own growth and understanding. The tragic theme is reversed: here, convincingly, is a Lear redeemed – more convincingly, we might agree, than in Bradley's famous reading of Shakespeare's tragedy, whose demolition was completed in the 1980s and 1990s by a new textual criticism which resists the conflation of the Quarto and Folio accounts of Lear's death. The novel ends with these words:

---

[64] *King Lear* 1.1.137.
[65] *King Lear* 3.4.105.
[66] *King Lear* 1.4.71.
[67] Wilson, *Late Call*, p. 303.
[68] Ibid., p. 33.

Now for the last move but one. She only looked forward to finding a place of her own. Somewhere near Town Centre, if she could get it. That would be a good centre for operations. Operations! What a gloom she could be! She chuckled aloud. Harold looked up.

'You're in good form these days, Mother.'

'Yes, dear, I think I am,' she said.[69]

Stage productions and adaptations of Shakespeare's plays are established areas of research and investigation. As is increasingly apparent derivative fictions can also offer historical commentary on the text from which they derive. Novelists too can be interpreters: their work constitutes a potentially important resource that is at last receiving something of the attention it deserves.[70]

Of course, Shakespeare's own place in the story isn't quite what I've seemed to imply. 'Variations on a Theme by Shakespeare' would not have served me as an alternative title. Shakespeare's *King Lear* is itself a variation – in many ways the most radical of all variations – on a narrative that was already, in its received form, four hundred years old when he used it as the basis of his play. Far behind that form, as shaped by Geoffrey of Monmouth, lie the folktales which impart so much of

its mythic quality to the story of King Lear and his three daughters – or two daughters – or two sons and daughter – or of 'Queen Lear' and her son and three grandchildren. The 'complex...duties and responsibilities of parenthood'[71] were, and remain, one source of the story's 'surplus of signifier', (in Frank Kermode's memorable phrase[72]), but so too do the questions of age and retirement, the struggle for power inside and outside the family and, as became increasingly apparent in the twentieth century, the many questions surrounding the role and position of women in society and in fiction.

---

[69] Ibid., p. 316.

[70] See, e.g., M. Novy, ed., *Transforming Shakespeare: Contemporary Women's Re-Visions in Literature and Performance* (New York, Basingstoke, 1999).

[71] See note 40 above.

[72] F. Kermode, *The Classic* (London, 1975), p. 140: 'The survival of the classic must therefore depend upon its possession of a surplus of signifier; as in *King Lear* and *Wuthering Heights* this may expose them to the charge of confusion, for they must always signify more than is needed, by any one interpreter or any one generation of interpreters.'

KING LEAR AND ENDGAME

R. A. FOAKES

In *Shakespeare our Contemporary* (translated 1964), Jan Kott headed one chapter '*King Lear* or *Endgame*'. In so doing, he invited readers to think of Shakespeare's play in terms of Samuel Beckett's absurdist drama, first performed in 1957. He argued that in the 'new theatre' of Beckett, Dürenmatt, and Ionesco, tragedy had been replaced by the grotesque: 'Grotesque means tragedy re-written in different terms'[1]; the hero still loses his 'struggle against the absolute', an absolute that is confirmed in tragedy but mocked and desecrated in the grotesque. Kott's example of such tragedy is Sophocles' *Antigone*, where the heroine 'is doomed to choose between human and divine order', and, he says, 'The tragic situation becomes grotesque when both alternatives of the choice imposed are absurd, irrelevant, or compromising' (p. 108). Hence 'Tragedy is the theatre of priests, grotesque is the theatre of clowns' (p. 113). Kott leaps from this definition into an account of the scene of Gloucester's mock suicide in *King Lear*, identifying Gloucester as Everyman wandering through a world in which 'both the medieval and renaissance orders of established values disintegrate' (p. 118), and we are left with the earth, bleeding and empty. So the theme of *King Lear* 'is the decay and fall of the world' (p. 123), and is focused in the relationship in this scene between Edgar and Gloucester, which he links with that of Pozzo and Lucky in *Waiting for Godot*. Kott cites Gloucester's line, ''Tis the time's plague when madmen lead the blind' (4.1.49), and goes on:

This is Edgar leading the blind Gloster to the precipice at Dover. This is just the theme of *Endgame*; Beckett was the first to see it in *King Lear*; he eliminated all action, everything external, and repeated it in its skeleton form.

(p. 127)

The Fool embodies the idea of the grotesque for Kott in rejecting 'all appearances, of law, justice, moral order. He sees brute force, cruelty and lust. He has no illusions ...' (p. 136), and so exposes the absurdity of the absolute (p. 137).

Kott's persuasive rhetoric influenced Peter Brook's nihilistic treatment of *King Lear* in his 1962 production (film version 1970), which in turn influenced critical readings of a play that had been commonly perceived as a play of redemption. From this time on it came more to be viewed as offering a bleak vision in which 'every source of consolation with which we might greet the final disaster' is repudiated.[2] Jan Kott and Peter Brook had been anticipated by Herbert Blau in his San Francisco Workshop production (1961), on which he comments in his book, *The Impossible Theater* (1964).[3] But Blau rooted his absurdist version of *King Lear* not in metaphysics but in history, in his concern with the political situation at the time, the tensions of the Cold War, the proliferation of missiles and threat of war provoked by the Cuban crisis of 1961–2, and the building of the Berlin Wall (1961). The effects of the atom bomb on Japan that were brought back to notice in the film *Hiroshima mon*

---

[1] *Shakespeare our Contemporary* (1962), trans. Boleslaw Taborski (London, 1964), p. 105.
[2] N. S. Brooke, *King Lear* (London, 1963), p. 57.
[3] (New York, 1964).

Amour (1959) also influenced Blau, who made explicit the political circumstances that underlie Kott's essay. And Blau's consciousness of what seemed a political madness that might doom the world I think was shared by Beckett who, when writing *Endgame* (French 1957, published 1958 in English), can hardly not have been conscious of the explosion of the first hydrogen bomb on Bikini atoll in 1954, and the uprisings in Poland and Hungary that were crushed by the Soviet Union in 1956.

Kott seems to have transposed the political into the metaphysical, so that in his account both *Endgame* and *King Lear* become 'a criticism of the absolute in the name of frail human experience' (p. 105), and a 'universal *reductio ad absurdum*' (p. 137); he saw them as philosophical and quasi-mythical plays about the end of the world. His account is basically rather solemn and portentous, in keeping with many other commentaries on Beckett's plays, such as Jonas Barish's on *Waiting for Godot*: the personae, he says, are 'cut off from past and future, home and family, education and occupation, and all the other reassurances of quotidian daily life. What remains is simply the universe in its brute incomprehensibility, its stubborn refusal to speak to man, the desolation produced in us by our feeble efforts to interrogate it, and the struggle to survive even when all the familiar guideposts have been swept away'.[4] Such accounts miss out the element of humour, even when they see the importance of the clown figure; Kott does see this, but only in order to emphasize that even the buffoonery is metaphysical, and that Clov's 'gabble is eschatological' (p. 130). If Shakespeare's play offers any purchase on *Endgame*, it may be necessary to begin from the apparent differences rather than the links between them. Kott's imaginative coupling of the two plays ignores the grounding of *King Lear* in strong plots, in the family, in rule, and in a rich interplay of fully developed characters. It is not a play about the rituals of killing time in an incomprehensible world; but then, is it sufficient to account for *Endgame* in this way? Are there other reasons for linking the two plays?

Beckett himself, as is well known, directed the French version of the play, *Fin de Partie*, in Berlin in 1967, when he told the actor Ernst Schroeder that Hamm is a King in a chess game that is lost, and makes 'senseless moves' as 'only a bad player would. A good one would have given up long ago. He is only trying to delay the inevitable end'.[5] Apart from this advice to an actor, Beckett refused 'to be involved in exegesis of any kind'.[6] So his one explanatory comment has been very influential in encouraging critics to regard *Endgame* as a play about the end of the world and the end of life. The removal of what Barish called 'familiar guideposts' forces us to construct meanings, and one possibility may be that the room in which the action takes place is a last refuge after some (nuclear?) disaster that has devastated the earth. One of the two windows looks out on a desolate land where Mother Pegg's light is out, and the other looks out to sea, where the beacon light has failed; so all signs of light and life are extinguished. Hamm and Clov like to say, 'There's no one else / There's nowhere else',[7] so at times they regard themselves as the last survivors of the human race.

The image of an endgame at chess provides a superficial frame for the action, but the moment Hamm begins to speak, 'Me to play', a range of other meanings opens up. 'To play' may, for instance, be to engage in a game, to behave frivolously or jokingly, to indulge in wordplay, to perform for amusement or in order to deceive (as in 'play dead'). All of these are vital human activities, and the games with words that construct whatever 'reality' the play deals in are much more important than chess, so that the play is not simply about things coming to an end. It is true that various losses are reported in the course of the action, – there is no more pap, bicycles or rugs, Nagg loses a tooth, they run out of sugar-plums and pain-killers, – and that a general sense of deterioration is conveyed. At the same

---

[4] Jonas Barish, *The Anti-theatrical Prejudice* (Berkeley and Los Angeles, 1981), p. 457.

[5] Ruby Cohn, *Back to Beckett* (Princeton, 1974), p. 152.

[6] In a letter to Alan Schneider written in December, 1957, and printed in Beckett's *Disjecta* (London, 1983), 109.

[7] *Endgame* (New York, 1958), p. 6.

time, change marks the process of life:

HAMM Nature has forgotten us.

CLOV There's no more nature.

HAMM No more nature! You exaggerate.

CLOV In the vicinity.

HAMM But we breathe, we change! We lose our hair, our teeth! Our bloom! Our ideals!

CLOV Then she hasn't forgotten us.   (p. 11)

Their byplay at once conveys the sense of intense life, which means change as people grow older and face death, and a sense of stasis, since all the moves could be repeated. Clov asks, 'Why this farce, day after day?' (p. 32), and all we see could happen again – the tableau at the end is not much different from that at the beginning.

The idea of 'game' contains a paradox, for if Hamm and Clov are playing a game they are bound to lose, the game of life, at the same time what makes that life is the act of playing or performing, to the audience on and off the stage. Hamm consciously behaves as a ham actor in his self-dramatizing, misquoting Shakespeare's *Richard III* (p. 22), conducting an audition (p. 35), citing Prospero (p. 39), making an aside (p. 49), and he is troubled by an underplot while warming up for his last soliloquy (p. 78), while Clov goes off saying, 'This is what we call making an exit' (p. 81). So on one level Hamm and Clov are performing their own play with farcical interludes and music-hall routines, and everything they say may be part of their method for passing the time, or indeed for creating the world in which they appear to exist. They are not simply playing out hopeless final moves that lead to death. The contradiction between the series of losses or losing moves and the series of 'turns' or performances by which Hamm and Clov create their life with much comic vitality tends to confirm Wolfgang Iser's comment that *Endgame* 'compels its reader to reject the "meanings" it stimulates'.[8] No one meaning or set of meanings satisfies. The play is not so much about an end as about continually postponing an ending: 'It's a day like any other day', says Hamm (p. 45), and Clov responds, 'All life long the same inanities'. They

consciously replay routines that have momentary validity but no final meaning.

It could be said that *Endgame*, like other works by Beckett, abandons a traditional sense of closure or order – abandons traditional formal structures, and treats the concept of order, both order as what Frank Kermode calls the 'Christian paradigm'[9] and as orderliness, with irony, even amused contempt; Hamm prays to a God who doesn't exist (p. 55), while Clov notably fails to achieve the order he loves, and which he can only imagine as universal oblivion (p. 57). In abandoning traditional plot development the play would seem to be a rejection of tragedy. The death of tragedy in the twentieth century, anticipated by Nietzsche, foreseen by Joseph Wood Krutch (1929), and described by George Steiner,[10] was related to the notion that there is no room for a hero in mass societies governed by bureaucracies, and no significant role for an individual. Politics was seen as discredited by corruption, and war as played out horrifically by remote controls. A process begun in World War 1 gathered pace in World War 2, and the succeeding age of nuclear weapons confirmed the uselessness of heroic action. *Endgame* fitted this state of affairs as a new art form in which characters are cut adrift from the 'real' world and create an internalized world of their own – gesture displaces action and scuttles meaning. On a metaphysical plane this may be regarded as nihilistic; on a more mundane level, it can be seen as a reflection of what life has become for many people, a repetition of routines that have no overall meaning, an anticipation of the television sitcom such as the enormously successful 'Seinfeld', which avoided any content, any concern with issues outside the misunderstandings and pratfalls of home and coffee shop. The routines are what keep Hamm and Clov, Nagg and

---

[8] *The Implied Reader* (Baltimore, 1974), p. 273.

[9] *The Sense of an Ending* (Oxford University Press, 1966), pp. 115–16.

[10] See Frederick Nietzsche's *The Birth of Tragedy* (1872), Krutch's *The Modern Temper* (New York, 1929), and Steiner's *The Death of Tragedy* (London, 1967).

Nell alive, which is why Hamm insists, 'Outside of here it's death' (pp. 9, 70).

At the same time, *Endgame* is not simply a denial of tragedy. In an early and influential essay on the play and its relation to existentialism, Theodor Adorno affirmed that 'History is excluded' from it,[11] but this is not so; Hamm, Clov and Nagg either have or make up a past for themselves, a past when something other than what is taking place on the stage happened. Hamm has parents who speak about their past, when they sailed on Lake Como and when they crashed their tandem in the Ardennes on the road to Sedan (pp. 16, 21); and Hamm once took Clov, who may be his child, into his house (p. 38). A feature of their routines is to exchange 'the old questions, the old answers, there's nothing like them!' (p. 38). A preliminary version of the play, 'Avant Fin de Partie', a manuscript of 1952–3, is set, with realistic detail, in Picardy after World War 1. Late in World War 2 Beckett served as an ambulance driver in Normandy, and was appalled by the destruction of St Lô, the shortages of food and pain-killers, the rats roaming the streets, and the general desolation.[12] Echoes of this wartime experience survive in *Endgame*, in the shortages of necessities, the desolate world outside of sea on one side and land on the other, in the references to Sedan and the Ardennes, where so many soldiers lost their lives in battle and Nagg and Nell lost their shanks (p. 16): 'HAMM The whole place stinks of corpses. CLOV The whole universe' (p. 46). By the time Beckett was composing *Endgame* the development of fusion devices and the threat of mutual assured destruction, of apocalypse, had become a keystone of policy for the Soviet Union and the United States in the cold war.[13]

I think Beckett's involvement in war and in the political situation of the early 1950s is reflected in the play, if indirectly. Hamm is a potentate of a sort, wearing a 'toque' or brimless hat in place of a crown, and he appears to think of himself as a ruler in his Shakespearian allusions to *Richard III*, 'My kingdom for a nightman', and to *The Tempest*, 'Our revels now are ended.' He has exercised power in the past, sending Clov to inspect his 'paupers'

(p. 8), as he still does in his room, which may be his 'kingdom' (p. 23) or the 'world' (p. 25). That world is now a place of desolation, as suggested in Hamm's anecdote of the mad painter he once used to visit in an asylum:

HAMM I once knew a madman who thought the end of the world had come. He was a painter – and engraver. I had a great fondness for him. I used to go and see him, in the asylum. I'd take him by the hand and drag him to the window. Look! There! All that rising corn! And there! Look! The sails of the herring fleet! All that loveliness!

(*Pause.*)

He'd snatch away his hand and go back into his corner. Appalled. All he had seen was ashes.

(*Pause.*)

He alone had been spared.

(*Pause.*)

It appears the case is . . . was not so . . . so unusual. (p. 44)

In the allied bombing raids on St Lô an asylum was burned and all its inmates destroyed in the fire. It may not be too fanciful to suppose Beckett's war experiences in St Lô and Dieppe fed into the imagery here. Hamm and Clov seem now to be in a world of ashes in which they and Hamm's parents are alone. Yet Hamm remains a figure of power, who makes Clov suffer, is cruel to Nagg and Nell, and has killed Mother Pegg by denying her oil for her lamp. If the world is coming to an end because of some cataclysm, perhaps in the ashes left after a nuclear war, at the same time Hamm as a figure of authority appears in some sense to have responsibility for the state of affairs in the play. In spite of his dependence on Clov he takes power for granted as if he has always held sway, and we catch a glimpse into his past in his story of his refusal to help the starving man and boy who crawled to him in winter, apparently in wartime, since he asks them 'what is the object of this invasion?' (p. 51). The man has

---

[11] *Twentieth Century Interpretations of Endgame*, edited Bell Gale Chevigny (Englewood Cliffs, 1969), p. 106.
[12] S. E. Gontarski, *The Intent of Undoing in Samuel Beckett's Dramatic Texts* (Bloomington, Indiana, 1985), pp. 33–5.
[13] Spencer R. Weart, *Nuclear Fear* (Cambridge, Mass., 1988), p. 235.

come from 'Kov', suggesting a Russian place (Kiev? Kovno? Kharkov? – a location from World War 2?) now uninhabited, and Hamm denies him bread or corn, offers to take him into service but apparently rejects the child, and abandons the tale with the man on his knees begging. The story is briefly continued in dialogue with Clov (pp. 59–61) and again in Hamm's last soliloquy, where Hamm confronts the man with his 'responsibilities' (p. 83), denying his appeal.

Hamm puts on a special voice for his narratives, and seeks Clov's praise for his 'technique' (p. 59), but at the same time the 'chronicle' (p. 58) he constructs is told as a chunk of autobiography, and relates to the moment when, with Clov off stage, he begins 'to grieve' for all those he might have helped or saved: 'The place was crawling with them' (p. 68). In Hamm's story the play contains a sketch of a tragic fable in which he brutally denies help to others, concerned only to maintain his control and authority. He has been the cause of death and pain to others in the play, and his story points to a past in which he has had great power and abused it, a power signalled in his name, the hammer of Clov, Nagg and Nell, all nails in French (clou), German (nagel) and English. The play that contains Hamm's story is at the same time implicated in it,[14] and it should not surprise us to find that Roger Blin, to whom *Fin de Partie* was dedicated, and who played Hamm in the first production in London in 1957, thought of it as a 'tragic play':

I saw in *Fin de Partie* the theme of the death of kings. Perhaps unduly but nevertheless deliberately I slanted Hamm towards King Lear. From set designer Jaques Noel I asked an armchair evoking a Gothic cathedral, a bathrobe of crimson velvet with strips of fur, and a scepter like a gaff for Hamm. Whatever was regal in the text, imperious in the character, was taken as Shakespearian. Beckett was not opposed to it.[15]

Blind to the sufferings of others, Hamm's selfish tyranny, his cruelty, and his failure to help those he might have saved, have reduced him to his present condition, dependent on Clov and in a condition where he can only 'play and lose and have done with losing' (p. 82). Here can be seen an analogy with King Lear, whose blindness to the nature and feelings of others and habit of exercising arbitrary power are instrumental in bringing him to a condition in which he has lost everything, even the will to live. In Hamm's story is buried a potential tragic fable, and like *King Lear*, it is 'loaded with political resonances',[16] not in showing us a tyrant progressively marginalized as he is stripped of all his followers and possessions, but rather as a 'work of art directly promoted by the existence of first the atomic and then the hydrogen bomb'.[17] The difference is that in Shakespeare's play it is Lear's patriarchal regime that is destroyed, a matter of huge significance and emotional power, which Kent sees as an image of 'the promised end' (5.3.261) or doomsday, whereas in *Endgame* the whole world appears to be coming to an end as a matter of utter meaninglessness. Whatever latent tragedy is buried in Hamm's story is left as gesture, narrated for effect ('Technique, you know', as Hamm says to Clov, p. 59), for the story remains on that level unfinished; but on another level, the play itself is the end of the story, as suggested in Hamm's final comment on it, 'Well, there we are, there I am, that's enough' (p. 83). In this larger perspective, Hamm's actions seem trivial in relation to the destruction of life itself as if after some nuclear war: 'Outside of here it's death' says Hamm (pp. 9, 70) and Clov refers to 'all these dying of their wounds' (p. 80).

There has been much debate about the small boy Clov thinks he sees from the window facing land towards the end of the play, if only because this episode shows the one major change from the text of *Fin de Partie*. In the French version the boy is described in more detail as sitting down contemplating his navel like a Buddha, and there is

---

[14] As argued by H. Porter Abbott in *Beckett Writing Beckett. The Author in the Autograph* (Ithaca, New York, 1996), p. 143.

[15] Dougald McMillan and Martha Fehsenfeld, *Beckett in the Theatre* (London and New York, 1988), p. 171.

[16] H. Porter Abbott. *Beckett Writing Beckett*, p. 130.

[17] Anthony Cronin, *Samuel Beckett The Last Modernist* (London, 1996), p. 467, citing Vivian Mercier's *Beckett/Beckett* (London, 1977).

other quasi-religious symbolism, with references to Moses and possibly to Dante:[18]

CLOV Il a l'air assis par terre, adosse a quelquechose.
HAMM La pierre levée . . . Ta vue s'améliore. Il regarde la maison sans doute, avec les yeux de Moïse mourant.
CLOV Non.
HAMM Qu'est-ce qu'il regarde?
CLOV Je ne sais pas ce qu'il regarde . . . Son nombril.

In *Endgame* these allusions have disappeared, and we are left uncertain whether the boy 'exists' or not. It seems to me more in keeping with the totality of the play if we suppose the boy does not exist. In *King Lear*, ostensibly a play set in pagan times, Christian echoes serve to lend a special grace to the character of Cordelia, enhancing the pathos of the ending, in which the entrance of Lear carrying her dead body may be thought of as shadowed by the image of a pietà. In *Endgame* by contrast Christian allusions are undercut. When Hamm first tries to tell his story about the man who came begging for help on Christmas Eve, he breaks off to call for a prayer before denying Nagg a sugar plum, but for him there is no God: 'The bastard! He doesn't exist!' The effect of this is comic in relation to the absence of an immediate sign from God, but of a piece with the rest of the play, for instance, with the joke about the tailor who takes three months to make a pair of trousers, and meets the complaint of the customer that God made the world in six days with the comment, 'But my dear Sir, look –

(*disdainful gesture, disgustedly*) – at the world, and look – (*loving gesture, proudly*) – at my TROUSERS'. Clov's words that open the play are 'Finished, it's finished, nearly finished, it must be nearly finished', echoing the last words of Christ on the cross according to John 19.30, 'It is finished: and he bowed his head and gave up the ghost.' But in the play nothing is finished, and this, like other Christian allusions is subverted, turned into a joke; it is as if the history of the first part of the twentieth century has for Beckett made religion itself pointless in an empty and meaningless universe. Whereas such allusions in *King Lear* contribute to a tragic effect, and hint at metaphysical implications ('Is this the promised end?'), those in *Endgame* are deliberately emptied of significance. Shakespeare could make tragedy out of the decline of a monarch corrupted and blinded by his absolute power, but for Beckett, whose *Endgame* has historical roots in two world wars and the possibility of total annihilation in a third, the rubble of tragedy alone remains in Hamm's unfinished story; the only way to make drama out of such disaster was through irony and farce.

---

[18] See the comments by Martin Esslin and Hugh Kenner in *Samuel Beckett, Twentieth Century Views*, ed. Martin Esslin (Englewood Cliffs, New Jersey, 1965), pp. 29–30, 53–6, and McMillan and Fehsenfeld, *Beckett in the Theatre*, p. 194.

SHAKESPEARE IN PAIN: EDWARD BOND'S *LEAR* AND THE GHOSTS OF HISTORY

THOMAS CARTELLI

Like ghosts we teach a dead religion, build a few more prisons to worship Caesar in, and leave it at that.
Edward Bond[1]

We haven't arrived where we live as long as Shakespeare writes our plays.
Heiner Müller[2]

There can be no starker alternative – or harsher antidote – to the Shakespearian afterlife concocted by the makers of *Shakespeare in Love* than Edward Bond's *Lear*, which was first produced in London in 1971 (unless, of course, we include in the mix Bond's later play *Bingo*, which had its first production in 1973). Though very differently situated, both works are studies in pain: in the social and political pathologies that produce it and the emotional pathologies produced by it. As such, they return us to a period in postwar cultural history when Shakespeare's status as 'our contemporary' was figured very differently than it is today, when a play like *King Lear* drew to itself correspondences to everything from the Holocaust to philosophical and theological assessments of the absurdity of the human condition and of man's inhumanity to man. Probably the most prominent manifestation of that moment's approach to *King Lear* is the punishing black-and-white austerity of Peter Brook's 1971 film, which in many ways served to illustrate Jan Kott's influential assessment of the play as Shakespeare's *Endgame* in *Shakespeare Our Contemporary* (1964).

The popularity of *Shakespeare in Love* in so many quarters of today's playgoing and filmgoing public (even in the scholarly community itself), with its explicit privileging of youthfully romantic plays like *Romeo and Juliet* and *Twelfth Night*, and the vogue for fast-paced, high-tech refashionings of tragedies like *Hamlet* and *Titus Andronicus*, indicate the need for an historicized assessment of this earlier, comparatively more sombre moment in the Shakespearian afterlife. The postwar cultural and intellectual climate that informed Kott's and Brook's existentializing of *King Lear*, and the Cold War strains and tensions that inform Bond's decidedly more brutal but avowedly more hopeful politicizing of the play, have all but faded from the consciousness and concerns of Shakespeare's audiences. Though the world continues to explode with tribal rivalries and religious tensions that have naturalized ethnic-cleansing and indiscriminate acts of terrorism as established forms of political expression, the metaphoric curtain (and materially attendant wall) that divided our houses for some forty years – and that serves as something like an organizing principle in Bond's play – has also begun to drift out of memory. It is, perhaps, for this reason alone – as a cautionary reminder or warning – that I choose to bring back into focus Edward Bond's *Lear*.

Though many have tried, beginning with Nahum Tate's notorious rewriting of the play's ending, it is harder to imagine an afterlife for *King Lear* than it is for any other play in the canon, short of

---

[1] Edward Bond, 'Author's Preface', *Lear* (London, 1983), p. lxv. All quotations from *Lear* will be cited in the body of this essay by act, scene, and page number.

[2] 'Shakespeare a Departure', *Theatremachine*, tr. and ed., Marc von Hening (London, 1995), p. 101.

Timon of Athens. This is, after all, a play that concludes with an unmediated vision of the afterlife itself – 'Is this the promised end? / Or image of that horror?' – and that leaves no question about the unendurable prospects of enduring in a world shorn of all its bright prospects and illusions. Bond, however, approaches this existential dead-end, amid all the 'endgame' obsequies lavished on it by Kott and others in the late sixties, less as an obstacle than as an opportunity to attack the assumptions that had effectively naturalized *King Lear*'s closing dispensation as an accurate representation of the conditions of existence as they always and ever obtain, regardless of existing social or political arrangements.

Like many British playwrights of his generation (whose number included John Arden, Arnold Wesker, David Storey, and Ann Jellicoe, among others), Bond served his apprenticeship working in the immediate shadow of John Osborne and the so-called 'angry young men' and under the broader, joint influence of Beckett and Brecht.[3] Possibly discerning their incompatibility in a way that other writers and directors of his generation did not (Bond writes at a later date, 'I don't like the Absurdists. I am an optimist. I believe in the survival of mankind. I don't believe in an "Endgame" or "Waiting for Godot"'), Bond takes his stand with Brecht: a position that becomes dramatically pronounced both in his composition of *Lear* and in the notes, poems, and commentary he composed both before and after its production.[4] He does so, as I contend above, in part to correct a prevailing misrepresentation of history as reflective of a changeless and essentially absurd human condition, but mainly to make a case for the space of human agency and the viability of intervention in history. As Bond writes:

Shakespeare took this character and I wished to correct it so that it would become a viable model for me and, I would like to think, for our society. Shakespeare does not arrive at an answer to the problems of his particular society, and that was the idea of total resignation, accepting what comes, and discovering that a human being can accept an enormous lot and survive it. He can come through the storm. What I want to say is that this model is inadequate now, that it just does not work.

Acceptance is not enough. Anybody can accept. You can go quietly into your gas chamber . . . Shakespeare had time. He must have thought that in time certain changes would be made. But time has speeded up enormously, and for us, time is running out.[5]

Though Bond makes a strong case here for the pressure imposed by historic contingency ('You can go quietly into your gas chamber') on his appropriation of Shakespeare, one could just as well use Bond's corrective to isolate and exemplify an obvious problem with Bond's conceptualization of both Shakespeare's play and *Lear* itself: a problem solved by the 'Absurdists' by reading and reproducing the play as an early modern version of *Endgame*. Invested as he is in the idea of rationally ordered social change (and in the idea of a 'rational theatre' as one of the media of social change), Bond writes in the wake of failed solutions and of revolutions that do no more than reproduce – and often exceed – the depredations of the political orders they seek to supplant. Bond is, of course, keenly aware of our century's history of failed social experiments and of the horrors perpetrated by governing systems avowedly based on the most scientific principles. Indeed, he stages a version of just such a corrupted revolution in the reign of terror his

---

3 According to William Gaskill, commenting on two of Bond's contributions to the Writer's Group of the Royal Court Theatre in the late fifties, one 'was rather Beckett-like and the other rather Brecht-like in style'. Quoted in Malcolm Hay and Philip Roberts, *Edward Bond: A Companion to the Plays* (London, 1978), p. 8. As John Elsom remarks of this 'second wave' of British dramatists: 'Unlike Osborne, they were surrounded by technical alternatives. They could write in the style of Brecht and no director would quail. They could write Absurdist plays without necessarily being accused of meaningless obscurity . . . They could write for three basic types of stage – arena, thrust and proscenium – or for no formal stage at all' (*Post-War British Theatre*, London, 1976, p. 178).

4 Hay and Roberts, *Edward Bond*, p. 26. For informed accounts of Brecht's influence on postwar British theatre, see Peter Davison, *Contemporary Drama and the Popular Dramatic Tradition in England* (Totowa, NJ, 1982), particularly chapter 3, and John Elsom, *Post-War British Theatre* (London, 1976), chapter 7.

5 Hay and Roberts, *Edward Bond*, p. 18.

character Cordelia orchestrates in the second and third acts of his play, and in the renewed urgency she brings to the rebuilding of a wall that earlier served as site and symbol of the divisiveness, and deludedness, of Lear's own political regime. Possibly out of reluctance to give any firm shape to the rational social change he envisions, Bond restricts his identification of a morally reformed and politically refined consciousness to a single, imminently doomed individual.[6] But by having this character (Lear himself) engage at play's end in the solitary labour of digging *out* a wall he has, himself, first caused to be erected and then die in the attempt, Bond arguably dissipates any hope for the social change he envisions in an all too recognizable image of absurdist futility. In at least one respect, then, Bond's play seems to end in the same conflation of Brecht and Beckett that Bond seemed intent on disavowing and dissolving, and which Alan Sinfield considers (in a telling observation on Brook's 1962 RSC production of *King Lear*) not only incompatible but 'politically and artistically incoherent'.[7]

Bond, however, claims otherwise in an essay entitled 'Saving Our Necks', published in the program notes of the 1975 Liverpool Everyman Theatre's production of *Lear*, in which he expressly defends Lear's gesture against the charge of absurdism:

My Lear makes a gesture in which he accepts responsibility for his life and commits himself to action . . . My Lear's gesture mustn't be seen as final. That would make the play a part of the theatre of the absurd and that, like perverted science, is a reflection of no-culture. The human condition isn't absurd; it's only our society which is absurd. Lear's very old and has to die anyway. He makes his gesture only to those who are learning to live.[8]

This passage is doubly significant insofar as it communicates Bond's intention to have Lear's closing act of defiance constitute more of a signal or gesture made on behalf of its witnesses (one of whom, cued by Bond's stage-direction, would be prompted to 'look back' on the dead Lear and on his shovel stuck 'upright in the earth' before being hurried along offstage) than an action complete in itself, as well as Bond's claim to possession/ownership of a Lear ('My Lear') that must be held distinct from

Shakespeare's Lear whose 'suffering and partial, ineffective illumination represent the fallible condition of all human goodness'.[9] From this perspective, Bond's *Lear* clearly points more in the direction of Brecht's *Mother Courage* – which correspondingly ends with the daughter of Mother Courage beating a drum to warn soldiers in a neighbouring village of an imminent attack – than it does in that of Beckett's *Endgame*.

Bond's preference for Brecht over Beckett is not, of course, a mere accident of influence. It no doubt followed from Bond's participation in what Alan Sinfield calls 'the rise of Left-culturism' in Great Britain in the sixties and seventies, and from an avowed commitment to political activism and social change that placed him in the vanguard of a

---

[6] It is worth wondering whether Bond's failure to commit himself to a more firmly shaped social or political alternative was affected by the political climate of his times. As John Elsom writes: 'For most of the 1960s, a Labour government was in power, and it was hard for left-wing writers to generate the same degree of self-righteous outrage against (say) the Labour government's tacit support for the American involvement in Vietnam, as had previously been aroused against Suez.' Although, as Elsom remarks, some writers and directors (Elsom specifically names Peter Brook; I would, for obvious reasons, also nominate Bond) 'did their best' to express such outrage, 'left-wing writers [in general] showed a reluctance to attack the Labour Party and government directly, though they might attack a System which somehow existed above, beyond and surrounding the government' (*Post-War British Theatre*, London, 1976, pp. 179–80). Bond's depiction of Shakespeare's implication in a non-historically-specific 'Goneril-society – with its prisons, work-houses, whipping, starvation, mutilation, pulpit-hysteria and all the rest of it,' in his Introduction to *Bingo* (Woodstock, IL, 1976, p. 7), suggests his working deployment of just such an all-embracing 'System' in *Lear* as well.

[7] Sinfield, '*King Lear* versus *Lear* at Stratford', *Critical Quarterly*, 24:4 (1982), p. 12. For his part, Perry Nodelman applauds what he takes to be this apparent disparity between Bond's practice as a dramatist and his theoretical aims and intentions. Nodelman construes Lear's act of digging out the wall as 'a personal gesture Lear makes for himself, a stand taken against the wall-building tendencies of all political philosophies – including Edward Bond's' ('Beyond Politics in Bond's *Lear*', *Modern Drama*, 23 (1980), p. 275).

[8] Quoted in Hay and Roberts, *Edward Bond*, p. 54.

[9] Bond, 'Types of Drama,' *The Worlds, with The Activists Papers* (London, 1980), p. 126.

generation of other politically committed dramatists.[10] Moreover, as John Elsom observes, Brecht not only 'influenced many British dramatists of the 1960s', but his influence on the determination of the content and style of British theatre arguably 'made him the most dominant single personality to affect drama since the decline of Shaw'.[11] Apart from their obvious political affinities, possibly the most prominent sign of Brecht's influence on Bond is the latter's responsiveness to Brecht's development of what was, for all rights and purposes, a highly innovative way of writing dialogue that synthesized colloquialism and an unusual plainness of address with an insidiously effective parody/imitation of bureaucratic jargon or 'officialese'. Elsom writes that '[t]he suppleness with which Brecht used his new proletarian language, with its prim exactness, its slang, deliberate roughness and officialese, fascinated his disciples and caught on with his public in Germany. But it also caused problems in Britain' where playwrights found it difficult to reproduce the 'estrangement' (or alienation) effect achieved by 'Brecht's verbal style'. He adds that '[l]acking Brecht's language, British actors had to work towards "estrangement" by other means, often contorted and unnecessary ones'.[12] For his part, the arguably 'contorted' means Bond employed to supplement the 'pointed, austere and polished language' he managed to shape in a more effective manner than did Brecht's other British disciples, was 'his use of violent images' and penchant for 'building his political cases from extreme examples', both of which are put on prominent and provocative display in *Lear*, to which we must now turn.[13]

Before beginning an examination of representative sections of the play itself, it would be useful to provide a brief summary of how Bond's *Lear* differentiates itself from Shakespeare's tragedy. Bond's play is set in an unspecific space and time but at a slight evolutionary remove from the feudal order of Shakespeare's play in which radical political change was effected by abdication or usurpation. In Bond, Lear's two elder daughters are renamed Bodice and Fontanelle, and wilfully marry themselves off to

Lear's enemies, the Duke of Cornwall and Duke of North, respectively, against whom Lear has built and defended his wall. Lear soon finds himself at war with his daughters and their husbands and, in short order, is defeated and made a refugee. Bond's Cordelia is a woman whose husband (identified simply as the Gravedigger's Boy) gives the outcast Lear temporary haven and who is subsequently raped and widowed onstage by an act of officially sanctioned state terror. Prompted in part by motives of vengeance to take up arms against the daughters and their armies, Cordelia and her consort, John, soon assume the roles of no-nonsense revolutionary ideologues who successively subdue the daughters and initiate their own reign of terror whose site and symbol is the rebuilt wall.

Almost all the other characters from Shakespeare's play are excluded from Bond's script – most notably the Gloucester family and Kent – though several residually survive in the form of new characters who may be said to distill them. The Gravedigger's Boy, for example, maintains after his murder a ghostly presence in companionship with Lear that recalls Edgar in his guise as Poor Tom, while the character Warrington, a composite of Gloucester and Kent, is made to suffer much the same kind of vengeful, arbitrary violence at the hands of Lear's daughters as Gloucester does in *King Lear*. Bond reserves for Lear the burden of having his eyes surgically removed (as opposed to having them more spontaneously gouged out) which may be said to exceed in brutality what is generally considered the most horrific moment in Shakespeare's play, but for reasons that are different than some have assumed. Bond's dramatic disposition of Warrington, which leads on to the brutal treatment lavished on Lear, may provide us with a convenient bridge back to a consideration of the claims made against, and on behalf of, Bond's construction of violence in his play.

[10] See Sinfield, *Literature, Politics, and Culture in Postwar Britain* (Berkeley, 1989), pp. 241–5.
[11] Elsom, *Post-War British Theatre* (London, 1976), pp. 123, 125.
[12] Elsom, *Post-War British Theatre*, p. 117.
[13] Elsom, *Post-War British Theatre*, pp. 188, 191.

After having his tongue cut out offstage, and suffering a savage beating at the hands of Fontanelle and a casually officious torturer named Soldier A ('Yer wan 'im done in a fancy way?...I once 'ad t' cut a throat for some ladies t' see once' (*Lear*, 2.4/13)), Warrington is treated to the following indignity before being let loose and allowed to 'flap round the battlefield':

BODICE...He can't talk or write, but he's cunning – he'll find some way of telling his lies. We must shut him up inside himself. (*She pokes the needles into* WARRINGTON's *ears*.) I'll just jog these in and out a little. Doodee, doodee, doodee, doo.   (*Lear*, 2.4/15)

Critical commentary on *Lear* has fastened less on Bond's effort to remake *King Lear* as a highly charged political parable for his time than on its prominent trafficking in violent effects. As Stanley Wells observed of a 1982 production of *Lear*: 'What with rape, mutilation, ghosts and mental tortures, this might well seem more like *Titus Andronicus* than *King Lear*'.[14] Although I acknowledge the validity of the comparison to *Titus*, I think Bond's orchestration of violent acts and effects in *Lear* is considerably more complicated than Wells allows, and operates more to 'shock us out of a casual acceptance of violence' than to invite us to revel in it.[15] (It is, in passing, hard to see how Cornwall's 'Out, vile jelly! / Where is thy lustre now?' [3.7.81–2]) and unusual use of his boot in *King Lear* are less objectionable than Bodice's use of words like 'flap' and 'jog' and unusual use of her needles in *Lear*.) Indeed, apart from Bond's depiction of Bodice's infantilized delight in poking her knitting needles through Warrington's ears, which has its own dramatic logic however repellent or excessive we may find it, Bond's crafting of violent effects in *Lear* is not only dramatically coherent, but adheres closely to the grain of the extra-dramatic points he is trying to make. The scenes of violence in Bond's *Lear*, particularly those of Act 2 which record the executions of Bodice and Fontanelle, the autopsy of Fontanelle, and the 'scientific' removal of Lear's eyes, operate both as graphic manifestations of modern state-sponsored violence and as purposeful efforts to bring Bond's playgoers

into direct contact with scenes of their most studied avoidance.

What Bond most wants to address and correct is the assumed exceptionality of this kind of violence: the idea that it wildly deviates from established structures of normative behavior and that some over-arching standard of humaneness must always qualify or hover over scenes of inhuman brutality. As he famously writes in the 'Author's Preface' to *Lear*:

I write about violence as naturally as Jane Austen wrote about manners. Violence shapes and obsesses our society, and if we do not stop being violent we have no future. People who do not want writers to write about violence want to stop them writing about us and our time. It would be immoral not to write about violence.

(*Lear*, p. lvii)

At the same time, Bond wants to claim that the normative itself is the product of an informing set of social and political conditions that effectively enables or precludes specific kinds of behaviour. While it is no doubt the glee and studied callousness of Bodice's behaviour, and the cold officiousness of the character (hereafter called the Fourth Prisoner or 'prison doctor') who surgically removes Lear's eyes, that will most disturb playgoers, Bond calculatedly stages these scenes in the absence of any visible or viable indication or indicator of onstage resistance. In so doing, he takes direct aim at a much-noted moment in Shakespeare's play when a servant of Cornwall's verbally objects to, and physically intervenes in, Cornwall's blinding of Gloucester. While the servant's resistance arguably supplies a surrogate form of humane agency for an audience otherwise compelled passively to submit to an intolerable action, Bond considers this act of surrogation false to the picture of power

---

14 Review of *Lear*, *TLS*, 16:7 (1982).
15 Elsom, *Post-War British Theatre*, p. 188. As Elsom goes on to remark, Bond's 'violent scenes provoked two contrasting reactions [in Bond's original audiences]: one was that Bond simply likes blood...and the other was that Bond hated cruelty so much that he was determined to bring home to his audiences the full horror of it' (pp. 188–9). It is the latter view that 'I happen to share' with Elsom.

relations Shakespeare has put into play. As Bond writes:

In [Shakespeare's] *Lear* there's the very telling scene where the servant kills one of the dukes who is putting out Gloucester's eyes. Servants don't do that – that's a feudal myth he's going back to. [Shakespeare] wants very much to believe that sort of thing, and it's not true. If the man's paid to stand by, he will stand by – there's nothing else he can do.[16]

Bond's quarrel with Shakespeare turns mainly on Bond's own privileging of what human nature is or is not capable of within the terms of a feudal reality (as opposed to feudal myth), and suggests that in his effort to 'de-mythify' Shakespeare, he may well be applying an article of faith in social determinism that contradicts his well-advertised commitment to the intervention of individual agency. After all, one *can* imagine (and Shakespeare surely did) even the lowliest subordinate acting against his own best interest to satisfy what he takes to be a higher or prior obligation (though, writing as he was in the long shadow of the Holocaust and Hiroshima, and in more immediate relation to Cold War orthodoxies and the perpetration of atrocities in Vietnam by avowedly God-fearing young men, it might have been more difficult for Bond to imagine this).[17]

But what mainly drives Bond in his own play is the refusal to provide the audience with any easy access to escape or relief from the sense of guilt or responsibility it might experience at having effectively *allowed* these, or similar, actions to occur. As Bond writes in 'To the Audience', a poem composed as one of his working papers during his drafting of *Lear*:

You sit and watch the stage
Your back is turned –
To what?

The firing squad
Shoots in the back of the neck
Whole nations have been caught
Looking the wrong way

I want to remind you
Of what you forgot to see

On the way here
To listen to what
You were too busy to hear
To ask you to believe
What you were too ashamed to admit

If what you see on the stage displeases
You run away
Lucky audience!
Is there no innocence in chains
In the world you run to?
No child starving
Because your world's too weak
And all the rich too poor
To feed it?

On the stage actors talk of life and imitate death
You must solve their problems in your life
I remind you
They show future deaths[18]

Writing in tune with the contemporaneous penchant of his fellow dramatists to confront or, even, offend the audience, Bond seeks, in this poem, to theorize a dramatic practice that is designed to put the audience itself on trial for its sins of omission and crimes of silence, and to have it acknowledge the quiet violence of its characteristic obliviousness and neglect.[19] Where Shakespeare enables playgoers to feel that they have, in fact, mounted a form of vicarious resistance against Regan and Cornwall through the medium of the defiant servant, Bond wants playgoers to witness and recognize their own cowed permissiveness and passivity in the unresisting matter-of-factness of characters who willingly act out their roles as torturers.

---

[16] Conversation with Howard Davies, November, 1976. Quoted in Hay and Roberts, *Edward Bond*, p. 60.

[17] Richard Strier persuasively claims, in *Resistant Structures: Particularity, Radicalism, and Renaissance Texts* (Berkeley and London, 1995), that this is exactly what Shakespeare is doing in this scene. Strier identifies the servant's resistance to Cornwall as 'the clearest articulation and most extreme case in the play of the paradox of service through resistance' (p. 194).

[18] *Theatre Poems and Songs* (London, 1978), p. 4.

[19] For a wide-ranging account of this phenomenon, see Peter Davison, *Contemporary Drama and the Popular Dramatic Tradition in England* (Totowa, NJ, 1982), pp. 128–51.

The poem and the crescendo of violent acts in *Lear's* second act that starts with Fontanelle's assassination and subsequent evisceration, and concludes with Lear's blinding, indicate that Bond sees such scenes as an opportunity to bring inside the theatre what the audience chooses to avoid seeing outside it, not, I would submit, merely to offend them but to confront them with the consequences of their presumed indifference. And, as noted above, there is in Bond's conceptualization of a passively permissive audience more than a residual shadow cast by the comparatively recent history of the unresisting and, in many cases, willing collaboration of 'good Germans' in the Final Solution and of 'good Europeans' in the successive subjugations of Eastern Europe by Hitler and Stalin ('Whole nations have been caught / Looking the wrong way').

These 'ghosts of history' are given a different form of embodiment onstage in the character of the Gravedigger's Boy who 'survives' his own murder in part to dramatize the personal costs of the overarching, and continuous, social catastrophe that Bond's play dramatizes. A composite Edgar/Poor Tom figure, the Gravedigger's Boy affiliates himself with Lear after his death and maintains a fawning, childlike dependency relationship with him thereafter that models the kind of relationship Shakespeare's Lear would have liked to maintain with Cordelia. The Boy effectively operates as the sentimentally charged ghost of suffering humanity of Shakespeare's *King Lear*, as the affective locus of that play's history or afterlife, as well as of history itself insofar as history, as heretofore constructed, constitutes a sentimental education in human pain and endurance.

The ghost of the Gravedigger's Boy first appears to Lear in the cell to which he is initially consigned by his daughters, and finds Lear in a disoriented state of mind in which Lear responds favourably to the Boy's claim that he can 'fetch' Lear's daughters 'here' (2.2/38). However, the daughters that the Boy summons are themselves 'ghosts' of the Lear family history, not the daughters as they are now but as they once were, or might have been, when Lear's was the law of the land:

FONTANELLE Do my hair...Father comes home today.
BODICE I must put on my dress.
FONTANELLE O you dress so quickly! Do my hair.
    (BODICE *attends to her hair.*)
LEAR My daughters!
BODICE They're burying soldiers in the churchyard. Father's brought the coffins on carts. The palls are covered with snow...   (2.2/38)

In a revealing convergence of past and present, the ghosts of his daughters past provide Lear with an education in the damaging consequences of the schooling in the normalization of pain he has given them. This education, in turn, leads Lear to a revelation that is rooted in *King* Lear's powerful jeremiads ('None does offend, I say, none'), but that also operates as a site-specific response to the European postwar dispensation – 'We won't chain ourselves to the dead, or send our children to school in the graveyard. The torturers and ministers and priests will lose their office. And we'll pass each other in the street without shuddering at what we've done to each other' – that becomes positively Blakean as it proceeds: 'The animal will slip out of its cage, and lie in the fields, and run by the river, and groom itself in the sun, and sleep in its hole from night to morning' (2.2/40).

This utopian resolve, however, dissolves as soon as the ghosts of the daughters depart, leaving Lear alone with their surrogate, the Gravedigger's Boy, with whom he achieves a more modest (and residually Shakespearian) embrace of humanity: 'Here. I'll hold you. We'll help each other. Cry while I sleep, and I'll cry and watch while you sleep. We'll take turns' (2.2/42). The later, second killing of the 'ghost' of the Gravedigger's Boy, whose body has been rapidly deteriorating at any rate, significantly occurs at a moment in the play when Lear has rejected this consolation of mutual dependency in favour of engaging in the kind of direct action discussed earlier. Although Lear's decision to dig out the rebuilt wall soon makes a ghost of him as well, it also reconfigures what we recall of him and how we recall it. The terminal demise of the Gravedigger's Boy, and Lear's rejection of a sentimentalized attachment to him as a desired destination, effectively frees Lear to pursue an alternative provoked but not ghosted by history, to move into a position of dignity and defiance (of dignity *via* defiance) as opposed to one of calmness and acceptance.[20] As Bond writes in 'The Activists Papers':

Shakespeare says that Lear's suffering and partial, ineffective illumination represent the fallible condition of all human goodness. The problem is seen to be political but the solution given isn't – it recommends calmness and acceptance. Shakespeare tries to give the public problem a private solution. Lear finds his own peace and dies. This means that he finally relates to the audience in the way all characters in bourgeois theatre relate to it. He's an individual with buttons on his jacket who resolves an epic problem – in a private way. This sort of drama was still possible when Shakespeare wrote.[21]

'This sort of drama was still possible when Shakespeare wrote', but is not, Bond implies, for those of us who live in the wake of world-historical events like those Bond repeatedly evokes in the concentration-camp atmosphere of the prison where both of Lear's daughter's are murdered, one is eviscerated, and Lear himself is blinded by a would-be Joseph Mengele. Or so Bond indicates both in *Lear* itself and in other places like his programme notes to the 1975 production where he writes that 'We have to have a culture . . . that isn't a way of learning how to endure our problems – but a way of solving them'.[22]

Bond is doing considerably more here than quibbling with Shakespeare's dramatic choices, which do not, in any event, land entirely on the side of 'calmness and acceptance' as the servant's resistance to Cornwall and King Lear's physical struggle to defend Cordelia plainly indicate. He is also doing more than mere Shakespeare-bashing, as his choice of subject matter alone should suggest. Like Heiner Müller, he is explicitly recognizing that 'We haven't arrived where we live as long as Shakespeare is writing our plays', unless, that is, we firmly believe that the privately negotiated solutions to political problems at the beginning of the seventeenth century can be so generalized as to speak to the problems that beset us today or, more specifically,

to the problems Bond was specifically addressing at *Lear*'s moment of production. But how do we 'arrive where we live', how do we arrive at ourselves, if we continue to employ Shakespeare as our dramatic medium? In the following passage, Alan Sinfield incisively restates the logic that often informs the thinking behind contemporary productions of *King Lear*:

Since *King Lear* is a great play . . . it must speak to our condition. And if our condition seems to involve brutally destructive political systems and profound inner compulsions which threaten a general apocalypse, then the play must be seen to address such issues. The text as we have received it tends to encourage certain ways of seeing the world and to inhibit others and does not, of course, envisage modern society. Therefore the play and current concerns must, by one means or another, be brought into line.[23]

As Sinfield goes on to observe, the play is more often than not 'brought into line' by cutting, changes of emphasis in characterization or line readings, resettings of time and place, etc., all pursued in the effort to 'make it work'. By way of contrast, he remarks that 'If, instead, the company reworked the play explicitly, the interpretation would lose the apparent authority of Shakespeare, and Shakespeare's apparently conservative oeuvre would lose the apparent authority of speaking to all conditions.' He concludes that 'This is the great collusion in which most productions of Shakespeare have become involved. The shuffles commonly conducted maintain both these dubious authorities, and more adventurous treatments – like Bond's and Charles Marowitz's – become objects of suspicion'.[24]

The crucial word here is 'authority'. Do 'more adventurous treatments' of Shakespeare by writers

---

[20] In a rather brilliant term paper on this subject, a student of mine, Tyler Ault, contends that the ghost of the Gravedigger's Boy 'represents social morality's grip on Lear' and is, in the end, 'revealed as the thing that must die' so that Lear's reformed consciousness may live.

[21] Bond, *The Worlds with The Activists Papers* (London, 1980), p. 126.

[22] Hay and Roberts, *Edward Bond*, p. 53.

[23] Sinfield, '*King Lear* versus *Lear*', p. 12.

[24] Sinfield, '*King Lear* versus *Lear*', p. 13.

like Bond necessarily lack the authority of Shakespeare? Don't they continue to feed off it either to their benefit or detriment? Alternatively, might there be more at stake than authority in choosing to model one's play on so influential a precedent? Do even the most radical departures from the Shakespearian original not keep us stuck in the same circle of meaning and reference?[25] If so, why does Bond choose to remake/renovate *King Lear* in the first place? What is gained, what is lost, in the process?

As Sinfield elsewhere observes, *Lear* is one of several examples of the reworking of Shakespearian texts that are consistent with Jonathan Dollimore's notion of 'creative vandalism'. As described by Sinfield, creative vandalism involves 'blatantly reworking the authoritative text so that it is forced to yield, against the grain, explicitly oppositional kinds of understanding'.[26] But oppositional to what or to whom? In a provocative interview with Howard Davies prior to his production of *Bingo* at The Other Place in November 1976, Bond observes that Shakespeare

is not God and that he is not somebody who provides a total blueprint for the way people should live. What is dangerous about him is that he is such a good artist, of course. I mean, the Germans don't have this hang-up about Goethe, because Goethe is not such a good artist as Shakespeare by any means and so they are able to arrive at some sort of judgment about him. You know, we think that two people went up to the mountain and got things written on tablets, one was Moses and the other one was Shakespeare. He's the sort of great idol of the humanist West or whatever, and it's not true. As a guide to conduct, or to attitudes to work, he's not so good for us. I object to the idea of him being for all ages in that particular sense.[27]

Bond's point here is considerably more subtle and suggestive than it may appear at first blush. Unlike critics of the last twenty years who are committed to the wholesale debunking of 'the Shakespeare myth', Bond is not specifically concerned with the idea that Shakespeare's work has been so thoroughly appropriated by the British political/cultural establishment (imperial and domestic) that his influence must be held to be suspect, if not downright

pernicious. Rather, he contends that Shakespeare's artistry is 'dangerous' only insofar as it lends a spurious authority to the idea that the plays continue to provide 'a guide to conduct' or 'blueprint for human behavior'. Bond's quarrel with Shakespeare fastens on the tendency to confuse the quality of the art with the variety of behaviour the art would appear to advocate or encourage. While the one may well be as transcendent as bardolaters claim it is, the other remains profoundly tied to its place and moment of production. As Heiner Müller suggestively observes, 'Shakespeare is a mirror through the ages, our hope a world that he doesn't reflect anymore'.[28]

A Shakespeare for *our* time must, by extension, be redirected, deployed in a manner that offers *different* guides to conduct and blueprints for behaviour than served in his own time. In both *Lear* and *Bingo*, Bond effectively applies this kind of presentist understanding of what was personally at stake for Shakespeare in his composition of *King Lear*, and explores the implications of positions taken by Shakespeare's Lear to actions allegedly taken by Shakespeare himself. But in so doing he seeks to hold Shakespeare accountable for the positions he takes less to redress him for his failures than to establish the necessity of such accountability today. As Bond states during the same conversation with Davies, in a comment prompted by a question regarding Shakespeare's suicide at the end of *Bingo*, Shakespeare had

written this play about Lear, who went mad on the heath, and standing on the heath insisted on certain moral insights, certain moral priorities for conduct, and you did those things even if it meant *your* death and even if

---

25 I raise (and explore) this same question with specific application to Aimé Césaire's *Une Tempête* in my book, *Repositioning Shakespeare: National Formations, Postcolonial Appropriations* (London, 1999). My second chapter, 'Shakespeare at Hull House: Jane Addams's "A Modern Lear" and the 1894 Pullman Strike', may also be of interest to students of the *King Lear* afterlife.

26 Sinfield, *Faultlines: Cultural Materialism and the Politics of Dissident Reading* (Berkeley and London, 1992), p. 22.

27 Quoted in Hay and Roberts, *Edward Bond*, pp. 57–9.

28 'Shakespeare a Departure', pp. 100–1.

it meant the destruction of your family. You did these things because there is no other life that is bearable. For Lear. And Shakespeare must have known that, otherwise he couldn't have written the play. That's what Shakespeare wanted, you know, otherwise you don't invent somebody like Lear as a fantasy, do you? You're saying something essential about what you demand and what you insist on, as the price or cost . . . for being on this earth.[29]

And as Elsom writes of Bond's treatment of Shakespeare in *Bingo*: 'Bond's argument is an extreme extension of that voiced by Brecht; that private virtue, private heroism, private morality is not enough: even Shakespeare was corrupt because he lived in a corrupt society . . . Only political action to change that society is worth considering'.[30]

It is for such reasons among others that Bond stages what is arguably the most unsettling scene in *Lear*, that is, the sequence wherein Lear plays witness to the 'little autopsy' the opportunistic Fourth Prisoner performs on the body of Fontanelle. This scene (which effectively revisits Lear's earlier reunion with the ghosts of his daughters past) bears reproducing in some detail:

LEAR Is that my daughter . . . ? (*Points.*) That's . . . ?
FOURTH PRISONER The stomach.
LEAR (*points*) That?
FOURTH PRISONER The lungs. You can see how she died. The bullet track goes through the lady's lungs.
LEAR But where is the . . . She was cruel and angry and hard . . .
FOURTH PRISONER (*points*) The womb.
LEAR So much blood and bits and pieces packed in with all that care. Where is the . . . where . . . ?
FOURTH PRISONER What is the question?
LEAR Where is the beast? The blood is as still as a lake. Where . . . ? Where . . . ?
FOURTH PRISONER (*to* SOLDIER O) What's the man asking? (*No response.*)
LEAR She sleeps inside like a lion and a lamb and a child. The things are so beautiful. I am astonished. I have never seen anything so beautiful. If I had known she was so beautiful . . . Her body was made by the hand of a child, so sure and nothing unclean . . . If I had known this beauty and patience and care, how I would have loved her.

The GHOST *starts to cry but remains perfectly still.*
Did I make this – and destroy it?   (2.6/59)

Two different kinds of materialism are in competition here: the cold, technical materialism of the self-styled prison doctor whose interest in the body is purely functional (he wants to know how it died), and the aroused moral materialism of Lear who starts out wanting to know where in her physical being the evil of Fontanelle can be found, but ends up locating the source of her misdirected life in his own actions. Though it was clearly a bullet that undid what Lear now discerns as Fontanelle's glorious creation, a prior cause has brought Lear into this one-sided reunion with what was Fontanelle around this table. With a logic that sustains Bond's play, and its difference from Shakespeare's, throughout, Lear discovers that there is no beast within, only beastly behaviours that mar the beauty of creation for which he now finds himself accountable.[31]

Possibly to disrupt this moving and oddly idealized encounter with his daughter, Bond next has Lear put *his hands into* FONTANELLE *and [bring] them out covered with dark blood and smeared with viscera* (stage-direction) as he announces:

Look! I killed her! Her blood is on my hands! Destroyer! Murderer! And now I must begin again. I must walk through my life, step after step, I must walk in weariness and bitterness, I must become a child, hungry and stripped and shivering in blood, I must open my eyes and see.   (2.6/61)

Within the brutal economy of Bond's production, this bloody prospect is but prelude to his staging of a second daughter's execution and Lear's own

---

29 Hay and Roberts, *Edward Bond*, p. 59.
30 Elsom *Post-War British Theatre*, p. 190.
31 Perry Nodelman cogently, but differently, contends that 'Lear understands [here] what he did not understand all along – that the world as it is and the people in it are more wonderful than anything one might make them.' In 'Beyond Politics in Bond's *Lear*', *Modern Drama*, 23 (1980), p. 274.

blinding. But if Bond's staging suffers from a commitment to excess that brings *Lear* back into the circuit of reference to *Titus Andronicus*, it has the virtue of immersing Lear himself in the viscera of a pained moral accountability that cannot be easily mystified or sublimed away, and of doing much the same to his audience. And this, I take it, is how Bond brings *King Lear* back into the circuit of 'where we live', or, more accurately, where we *lived* when the prospect of going 'quietly into your gas chamber' was considerably more vivid than it is today.

'THINK ABOUT SHAKESPEARE': *KING LEAR* ON PACIFIC CLIFFS

MARK HOULAHAN

'Think about Shakespeare', admonishes the garrulous 'Academic Woman' in Toa Fraser's acclaimed play *Bare*, 'and perhaps if he had known about the Pacific, what might have been his interpretation of it? I mean, these are pretty complex issues, but I'm sure you can get your heads down and start thinking about it. And while I think of it, see you next week, All right.'[1] The question is both haunting and hilarious: Fraser catches perfectly the concatenating logic which can easily attend weakly formulated studies of Shakespeare's texts and imperial discourse; yet haunting because, as Fraser clearly also knows, there are no direct Shakespearian representations of the Pacific. Shakespeare has been present in the Pacific since at least 1769 when a copy of the *Complete Works* sailed on Cook's 'Endeavour' in the luggage of the artist Sydney Parkinson. For Shakespearians, of course, 1769 marks Garrick's famous Shakespeare Jubilee, and its signal announcement of the canonization of the bard. Australasians remember 1769 instead for the epochal voyage during which Cook claimed both New Zealand and Australia as English possessions. The conjunction of that famous voyage and Garrick's jubilee means that these territories have been, over the last two hundred years, inescapably Shakespearized, as have the more tropical islands, such as Samoa, which Cook's voyages also helped to bring to the attention of Europe. The force of cultural and colonial history, then, has assured that Pacific artists have responded to Shakespeare's silence on Pacific topics by devising a number of responses to Fraser's initial question. Unable or unwilling as yet to dispense with Shakespeare's books they have tried to interpret themselves and their cultures in Shakespearian terms.

In this they are scarcely alone. A brace of modern studies has underlined attempts throughout the English speaking world and well beyond to rewrite and re-enact Shakespeare in such ways. The print and performance cultures of the South Pacific have received much less attention in these terms than other areas of the world, particularly in the Northern Hemisphere. Pacific Shakespeare, then, can scarcely be said yet to exist. This article is an attempt to imagine what such Shakespeares would be like. Specifically, since *Lear*'s afterlives have extended from the London of 1605 where the play was first performed as far in space and time as the New Zealand of the 1990s, is there anything distinctive about such far-flung *Lear*s? Does geographical translation demand also antipodean mutation? This article examines four possible answers to the question: Ngaio Marsh's 1956 production of *Lear* in Christchurch, New Zealand; followed in turn by three antipodean novels which rework *Lear* within radically different fictional worlds: Randolph Stow's *To the Islands* (1958); Albert Wendt's

My thanks to Jane Ledwell, Catherine Silverstone, Michelle Keown, Linda Keith, Peter Holland and his *Shakespeare Survey* assessors. Their comments have all strengthened this chapter. My attendance at Montreal SAA 2000 meeting for which the first draft was prepared was funded by the Faculty of Arts and Social Sciences at the University of Waikato. This 'final' version was prepared during a semester of research leave, granted by the Leave Committee of the University of Waikato.
[1] Toa Fraser, *Bare* (Wellington, 1998), p. 13.

Pouliuli (1977) and the charged fragments of *Lear* dispersed through many of Janet Frame's works. In location these *Lears* range from Western Australia through Samoa to New Zealand, the geographical spread designed to suggest, tentatively, the breadth of possibility in Pacific *Lears*. I will consider the approaches to *Lear* opened out, in turn, by all of the above, and then assess what might, collectively, be made of them. The *Lears* are presented here in, roughly, chronological order. This is a narrative convenience, and should not be taken to represent a simplistic chronological pattern, breaking from the chains of anglophilic traditionalism into a brave new Pacific world of post-colonial freedom. At the same time, it will become clear what strain of Pacific *Lear* I find more engaging: 'all of us have our preferences' as Christopher Hill trenchantly puts it, 'the reader will no doubt soon discover mine'.[2]

MARSH

Marsh, of course, is well known internationally for her classical detective novels, themselves saturated in Shakespeare references. In New Zealand Marsh is renowned also as a Shakespearian director. From 1943 to 1972 she staged fifteen of Shakespeare's plays. The casts were largely amateur (usually drawn from students of the local university), but the productions were hugely successful, several of them touring through New Zealand and to Australia. This was partly because, in the 1940s and 1950s, touring British companies had ceased to present Shakespeare; and local professional theatre was still in its infancy. If local audiences were to see live performances at all, amateur and semi-professional would have to suffice.[3]

In 1956, Marsh staged *King Lear* in Christchurch's Civic Theatre. The nature of the production can be assessed from the promptbook, surviving photos and the enthusiastic coverage of the local press, all lodged in the Marsh archives in the Alexander Turnbull Library in Wellington.[4]

The Civic Theatre, a standard nineteenth-century colonial performance space, has, of course, a proscenium stage. Beyond its arch, Marsh constructed an apron stage thrusting into the audience

on which most of the action was staged, while still using the main curtains to effect scene changes.[5] In the archives only the second half of the promptbook survives, allowing a glimpse of the production from the first storm scene until the end. The stage was set with two monumental-looking flights of stairs, connected by a rampart. In the sketches, the effect is like looking at some outcrop of Stonehenge.[6] This was the set throughout the final three acts of the play. When necessary, location changes would be signalled by furniture and props. For example, the scenes in Poor Tom's hovel were marked by a 'brazier and benches'; this was then replaced by a chair for the blinding of Gloucester in 3.7. Gloucester's subsequent 'leap' in 4.5 took place against the background of a 'dead Tree' mounted on top of the central rostrum, a resonant sign of the ruin of Albion. Marsh's *Lear* was staged a year after Peter Hall's first English language production of *Waiting for Godot*, so that this tree may be intended as an echo of Beckett's more famous one which acquires leaves between the acts. Gloucester of course, could not see them, but his sighted colleagues were helped on their way to Dover by a sign-post, pointing stage right, bearing the legend 'Dover'. Further stage right (should you have missed the sign) a milestone proclaimed also 'to Dover': this was the backdrop to the King's preaching in 4.6. These are a telling reminder that Marsh saw it as her main business, as a director, to sign-post for her actors as well as her audience precisely what was happening on stage. She planned her productions well in advance, and in meticulous detail. Her production, for

---

[2] *The World Turned Upside Down* (Harmondsworth, 1978), p. 17.

[3] The best guide to Marsh's life (and addiction to Shakespeare) is Margaret Lewis's *Ngaio Marsh: A Life* (Wellington, 1991).

[4] The production details which follow are taken from the promptbook, Alexander Turnbull Library MS papers 1397–4/15.

[5] An effect praised by C. E. S., the local reviewer in *The Christchurch Press* (Friday 24 August 1956), p. 7.

[6] Marsh trained as a painter. The sketches throughout the promptbooks are in her hand. Her acute visual skills led to the creation on stage of strikingly painterly and sculptural tableaux. The promptbook lists a cast of forty-seven, which would indeed require careful placement on stage.

example, greatly extends the Folio's resonant instruction: 'storm still'. Throughout the heath scenes, numerous moments are marked by either 'wind' or 'thunder' or both. Even the King's great question: 'What is the cause of thunder?' (3.4.145)[7] was underscored by the stage direction: 'Thunder', as if thunder itself was answering the question asked of it.

Marsh's precision extended to choreographing her actors in balletic formation. From the end of 3.2, for example we get the following sequence:

LEAR I am a man more sinned against than sinning
                                [Kneel, huddle with fool]
KENT Alack, bareheaded?   [Up to Lear]
Gracious my Lord, hard by here is a hovel   [Raise Lear]
...   [Fool coughing, prompts
                                King's concern]
LEAR...Come, your hovel   [Move towards prompt
                                side].
        [Then halt & take Fools face in his hands]
        Poor fool, and knave.   (3.2, 59–72)[8]

The stage directions here, typical of Marsh's meticulousness suggest the precision of a storyboard for a screenplay. Each moment here is seen, as it were, in extreme close up, for 'Marsh was a powerful orchestrator, pulling the disparate elements of production together that impressed her audiences, getting her casts to think and work together'.[9]

The local reviewer has an apt phrase for the production. The characters were costumed in a simplified version of medieval livery, with symbolic crests for the ruling houses. Lear was adorned, the reviewer says, with the 'Dragon of the Great Pendragonship'.[10] Pendragonship, effectively, is what Marsh was practising. The production was doubtless fluent and effective, nicely judged to the tastes of her audiences. Overall the staging was poetic with precise attention to small details, such as the Dover sign and the King holding the Fool's head. The production transported us to a fantastical neo-medieval space. It is designed not to reflect upon the islands where the play was performed but rather to abandon them in imaginative flight. Marsh travelled frequently to England and was well briefed on staging practices of the 1940s and 1950s, the

successes of Olivier, Gielgud and Ralph Richardson. Here in Christchurch, with limited means and budget she simulates what she had seen on her theatrical grand tours. The elimination of Pacific location was matched by her determination, often remarked, to eliminate the New Zealand accent, which Marsh despised and whose flat inexpressiveness she was merciless at satirizing. As a consequence many of her actors, as one of them (the playwright and director Mervyn Thompson) bitterly put it, 'detested the sound of [their] own voices / strangled them in the cradle of [Marsh]'s desire'.[11] The production is then interesting not because it was innovative but precisely because it was not, bearing surely the features of Shakespeare staged throughout the English-speaking world in the 1940s and 1950s, 'positioned between the alkaline of a colonial past, and the acid of a postcolonial future'.[12] It makes no concession, in other words, to the latitudes in which it was staged. For this essay, let Marsh's *Lear* then stand as a late imperial groundbase from which later Pacific *Lears* might depart, enacting, as we shall see, increasingly eccentric (or de-centred) fictive versions of the play.

STOW

Two years after Marsh's production, Randolph Stow published his third novel, *To the Islands*.

---

[7] Unless otherwise stated, quotations from the play come from the Oxford Shakespeare's *Tragedy of King Lear*.

[8] The lines quoted here are as typed up in the promptbook.

[9] Paul Bushnell, 'The Most Ephemeral of the Arts', *Return to Black Beech: Papers from a Centenary Symposium of Ngaio Marsh 1895–1995,* eds. Carol Acheson and Carolyn Lidgard (Christchurch, 1996), p. 86.

[10] C.E.S., *The Christchurch Press*, p. 7.

[11] Mervyn Thompson, 'On the Death of Ngaio Marsh', *Landfall* 144 (December 1982), p. 445. Bushnell remarks on this in his essay cited above, as does Lauris Edmond in her contribution to the *Return to Black Beech* volume, 'Immortal Longings: Ngaio Marsh's Voice in New Zealand History', pp. 1–6. For the similar dilemmas of the Canadian actor's confrontation with Shakespeare, see Dennis Salter's 'Acting Shakespeare in Postcolonial Space', in *Shakespeare, Theory and Performance*, ed. James C. Bulman (London, 1996), pp. 113–32.

[12] Bushnell, 'The Most Ephemeral of the Arts', 84.

A prefatory note warns readers that this 'is not, by intention, a realistic novel'.[13] In his revised edition of the novel Stow (in a striking yoking of the author figure with the Lear pilgrim at the novel's centre) describes himself further as a 'fanatical realist'.[14] That is, perhaps, that by paying it very close attention a known, carefully evoked landscape will be transformed as a site for an allegorical and poetic drama which proceeds far beyond realism. 'Fanatical' novelist and 'fanatical' main character merge. In part the novel celebrates the terrain around Wyndham in Western Australia; part of Stow's ambition is to construct this landscape as an appropriate landscape for fictions. He evokes the splendour of this space, unfolding the story 'between the rocky ridge and the far blue ranges, dotted with white gums, yellow flowering green-trees, baobab yet in full possession of their foliage'.[15] Here Stow locates his main narrative: the decline and triumph of Heriot a white missionary who, aged sixty-seven, has come to the end of his evangelizing life. Traumatized by guilt he goes 'walkabout' accompanied by Justin, an aboriginal from his mission station. Together they head toward the islands of the novel's title; in local belief, these are islands of the dead, hovering just off shore.

Heriot needs no literary critic to tell him that he has become a Lear figure, complete with matching fool; nor that his odyssey across the plain to the sea matches Lear's trek towards Dover: 'literary influences there certainly were, and the text confesses them'.[16] For Heriot himself frequently quotes the play, and Stow's densely poetic narration is suffused with a range of allusions to the text.[17] Heriot looks like a classical Lear, 'a big man with his wild white hair, his face carved and calm', and he sounds like one too: ' "Why do you stay here listening to me? I've got nothing to say. A very foolish fond old man. I can sit here all day happily complaining to myself about unhappiness" '. Like Lear, Heriot has plenty to say about 'nothing', one of the *Lear* code words which echo through the book. Like Lear also, Heriot is not finally content to 'sit here all day' so he embarks on his final journey.[18]

The trek across the external landscape is also, like Lear's, passage across more psychic territory as

well: 'He saw himself as a great red cliff, rising from the rocks of his own ruin'.[19] In landscape terms, Heriot combines the functions of Gloucester and Lear, for Stow leads his main character to something very like Gloucester's Dover cliff:

He was staggering then to the top of a rocky rise, and when he came there he stood suddenly still, his white hair blowing against the sky, his eyes dazzled with the sea... He came forward to the edge of the cliffs, where they dropped, vast red walls, to the faraway sea below. And the sea, where the light was not on it, was the blue green of opals and endlessly rearing, smashed into white at the foot of the rock.[20]

Heriot seeks to evade both Lear's and Gloucester's fates: 'he would work a change on the world before it blinded him'. Transformation, rather than death, overtakes him. In his last moment, the narration tells us the 'old man kneeled among the bones and stared into the light'. What follows is an epiphany of self-insight: ' "My soul", he whispered, over the sea-surge, "my soul is a strange country." '[21] These last lines are enigmatic; but they do suggest that his journey to the 'undiscovered country' beyond the shore has begun. Stow provides Heriot, in other words, with a specific vision where, on stage we hear Lear's cryptic and surely delusional 'Look, her lips. / Look there, look there' (5.3.286–7).

In a preface to the revised edition of the novel, Stow comments on the boldness of his strategies. Ironically, given the novel's Lear-obsessed, death-inflected observations of ageing and failing, he

---

13 Randolph Stow, *To the Islands* (Harmondsworth, 1971 (1958)), n.p.
14 Randolph Stow, *To the Islands* (London, 1983), p. xi.
15 Stow, *Islands* (1971), p. 12. Unless otherwise stated, references are from the first edition of the novel.
16 Stow, *Islands* (1983), p. xi.
17 John P. Beston explores the Lear connections in 'The Theme of Reconciliation in Stow's *To the Islands*', *Modern Fiction Studies* 27 (Spring 1981), 104–5.
18 Stow, *Islands* (1971), p. 12, 75.
19 Ibid., p. 35.
20 Ibid., p. 206.
21 Ibid., p. 206.

notes the youthful confidence which made his intertextual strategy possible. 'Nowadays I should hardly dare to tackle such a *King Lear*-like theme; but I do not regret having raised the large questions asked here, and so wisely left unanswered'.[22] An older novelist might not be so extreme. Ten years after publishing his Lear novel, Stow created another Lear figure in his libretto of George III songs for Peter Maxwell Davies' *Eight Songs for a Mad King*, where the presence of Lear is much more conservative, a precursor to the amusements of Alan Bennett's *The Madness of King George. To the Islands'* poetic brashness is a mark of the print culture from which it springs. Geologically, the landscape Stow describes is among the oldest in the world; and the Aborigine peoples whom Heriot tends have lived in Australia for 40,000 years. In the 1950s, however, white settler culture in Australia was effectively just emerging. Accounts by famous exiles from that culture (by Germaine Greer, Robert Hughes and Clive James, for example) attest to the crushing force of its 1950s conformity. Heriot's flight is in part a rejection of that culture too.

In Australia, Shakespeare is of course often invoked as the source and guardian of metropolitan norms.[23] Here, in a sense, he becomes instead Stow's ally. The extravagance of Lear's language, the fantasticality of his flight in Acts 3 and 4, help justify Stow's breaking with realist narrative, providing an authority for the novel's leap from its specific terrain into allegorical and philosophical territory. Western Australia becomes an appropriate space for a metaphysical adventure towards the 'soul...strange country'[24] with which the novel ends. Stow thus seeks for his country a philosophical sophistication Patrick White sought also in his quest fictions from the 1950s and 1960s. In his revised preface Stow denies any direct influence, yet acknowledges the similarity of his and White's approach: to move away from 'the tyranny...of social realism',[25] at the same time as moving away from the tyrannies of the society that realism had been designed to describe. In particular, through his allegory Stow draws attention to the plight of the tribes of Western Australia, dispossessed from

their mission stations and sent to a nearby town, immersed in 'drink, prostitution, violence and gaol'.[26] As Lear does with his outrageous entourage of fool, madman and fugitive, Heriot makes common cause with his aboriginal retainer, Justin. In his own work on mission stations, Stow had known both dedicated missionaries and their loyal indigenous followers, on which his characters are based.[27]

However 'Australian', these strategies link the novel with international cultural currents. For Heriot's quest is clearly existential; he rejects the God he had previously served. This seems comparable to the pilgrims in White's Australian novels. Stow's existential Lear, moreover, accords with wider mid-century patterns both of interpretation and performance. Like Beckett's Hamm, Stow's Heriot plays out a Lear-like endgame. Heriot's quest takes him from the oasis-like setting of the mission station, 'across huge desolations... appearing and disappearing through a curtain of dust...'[28]: something close, then, to the terrain Clov describes from the high windows of his *Endgame* prison cell. Stow's climax anticipates also the extraordinary final moments of Brook's filmed *Lear* where Paul Scofield falls diagonally from right to left across the frame of the screen, dropping, finally, below the screen and thus apparently beyond the frame of the world. His passing is followed by a blaze of white on the screen. What this means

---

[22] Stow, *Islands* (1983), p. ix.

[23] Connections between Shakespeare and Australian culture are explored in Philip Mead and Marion Campbell eds., *Shakespeare's Books: Contemporary Cultural Politics and the Persistence of Empire* (Melbourne, 1993).

[24] Stow, *Islands* (1971), p. 175.

[25] Stow, *Islands* (1983), p. xi. Connections between White and Stow's 'predilection for the metaphysical (in relation to both landscape and personalities)' are traced by Carole Ferrier, 'Fiction in Transition', in Bruce Bennett and Jennifer Strauss eds. *The Oxford Literary History of Australia* (Melbourne, 1998), pp. 215–16.

[26] Stow, *Islands* (1983), p. x.

[27] A useful summary of Stow's life and writings may be found in Anthony J. Hassall's *Strange Country* (St Lucia, Queensland, 1990), pp. xiii–xix. Hassall uses Heriot's last words to evoke, in his title, Stow's general approach to issues of Australian identity.

[28] Stow, *Islands* (1971), p. 83.

is quite opaque. A companion film of Stow's Lear could readily borrow the same imagery to enact Heriot's island transfiguration, 'and out again', to borrow in turn from John Fowles' famous peroration 'upon the unplumb'd, salt, estranging sea',[29] living out Stow's desire both to reject the 'strange country' of Australia and, contradictorily, to transform it as well.

WENDT

Where Stow's Heriot draws on the philosophy of Lear's quest, Faleasa, the mock-heroic chief (*ali'i*) of Albert Wendt's novel *Pouliuli*, draws on Lear's manic energy, his wilful madness and scabrous rage against the world he has helped create and which he has ruled. Like many of Wendt's characters, Faleasa reflects on the enormous changes wrought in the Pacific throughout the twentieth century by the economic and cultural pressures of European and American power. Wendt grew up in Western Samoa, and was educated, like many Samoans, in New Zealand, an experience of migration vividly described in his first novel, *Sons for the Return Home*.[30] Wendt now teaches Pacific writing at the University of Auckland. His recent fiction oscillates between evocations of life in Samoa itself and fictions set in New Zealand and elsewhere. Wendt's address to Shakespeare in *Pouliuli* lacks the arch self-consciousness which some would find too cumbersome in Stow, but in his later writing, Wendt's use of Shakespeare becomes more overt. In the story 'Hamlet' a shy schoolboy commits Hamlet's speeches to memory, connecting with the words in a series of epiphanies; the more recent 'Heat' describes a Samoan production of *Antony and Cleopatra* which integrated local dances and love songs.[31] Most strikingly, Wendt's first play, *The Songmaker's Chair*, returns aggressively to the themes of *Lear*: here a Samoan elder, in exile in Auckland, New Zealand, prepares for death by summoning his family to settle, before he dies, issues of status and inheritance. The play draws directly on *Lear*, and in the manner of several recent Shakespeares in New Zealand, integrates elements of Samoan and Maori protocol.[32]

Unlike Stow's Heriot, or the more recent Wendt characters described above, Faleasa never quotes Shakespeare directly (though many of his thoughts are close paraphrases of Lear's), but he wakes in the first chapter of *Pouliuli* energized by Lear's impulse to 'Unburdened crawl toward death' (1.1.41). Faleasa finds himself filled 'with an almost unbearable feeling of revulsion – yes that was the only word for it, revulsion' at 'everything and everybody that he was used to and had enjoyed'.[33] He feigns madness, literally vomiting over his house and his extended family who sleep inside it. 'When [Faleasa] started vomiting', Wendt explains, 'he was actually vomiting out this novel'.[34] From within his cloak of ungovernable rage and unpredictable behaviour Faleasa is able to observe his children and watch the battle for succession unfold around him. He returns to lucidity to announce his withdrawal from the world:

'...I am too old and too sick. Someone else, someone younger and healthier, has to assume the leadership. All I want for the remaining years of my life is peace and quiet to prepare for my final journey to God.'[35]

Only his childhood friend and life-long confidante, the fool-like Laaumatua, and Wendt's reader are privy to the inner meaning of Faleasa's retreat.

---

29 *The French Lieutenant's Woman* (London, 1971), p. 447.

30 Wendt's life and writing career are concisely summarized in Briar Wood's essay, 'Wendt, Albert' in *The Oxford Companion to New Zealand Literature in English*, eds. Roger Robinson and Nelson Wattie (Auckland, 1998), p. 581–2.

31 Both stories in *The Best of Albert Wendt's Short Stories* (Auckland, 1999)

32 The play has been workshopped and given a well-received public performance/reading on 31 May 2000. Currently it is under further development, and has been scheduled for full performance by the Auckland Theatre Company in 2003. For comparable attempts to weave Shakespeare with Pacific performance, see Pacific Underground's *Romeo & Tusi* (Wellington, 2000), where events in Verona are translated to 'Sorry Street', somewhere in Auckland and where the two households are Maori and Samoan, respectively.

33 Albert Wendt, *Pouliuli* (Auckland, 1977), p. 1.

34 Juniper Ellis, '"The Techniques of Storytelling": An Interview with Albert Wendt', *Ariel* 28:3 (1997), p. 88.

35 Wendt, *Pouliuli*, p. 35.

In a conversation early in the novel, Faleasa expresses lucidly the cosmic rage which Lear discovers in Acts 3 and 4:

Perhaps in our insane world in which terror and violence feed on the heart's sinews, what we call insanity or, rather those people we brand as insane are really the only sane creatures among us. Who knows. For seventy-six years I lived what I now see as an insane existence. I was easy meat for all the cannibals; and the worst, the most rapacious of all, were my own aiga and village.[36]

Through his staged madness Faleasa declares war on the most rapacious of those around him: his eldest son and his two eldest daughters, 'both prodigious breeders, gossips and relentless schemers'[37] placing his faith in his gentle and strong son Moaula. He appoints Moaula to succeed him. Together with Laaumatua, they then conspire to defeat a local politician, Malaga. Previously, Malaga had received Faleasa's patronage. With the new insights of his seventy-sixth year, Faleasa realises that Malaga has become hopelessly corrupt and will have to be defeated at the next election. He tricks Malaga into thinking he still has his support, whilst lobbying for a rival candidate.

Faleasa, then, finds himself cleft in Lear's double bind. For how can you renounce the world and retain at the same time 'all th'addition to a king' (1.1.136)? How can you abandon your power base/mana and still expect that those to whom you have bequeathed it will treat you as if you still had that power? Like Lear, Faleasa derives considerable pleasure from denouncing his world; and demonstrates also a mischievous glee in his strategic bouts of madness. Yet, like Lear, he finds himself increasingly impotent, unable to change a world which, from his new perspective as external observer, he can see stands in desperate need of change. Like Gloucester and Lear, Faleasa comes to understand this in a cliff-top epiphany:

... he would stroll to the western end of the village and, in the small palm grove over-looking the sea, sit at the edge of the cliffs and let the smell and sight and feel of the sea's mystery wash out his pain. ... he was still trapped in his own juices, odour, excrement; he was simply an old

man nobody needed anymore; he was valueless – that was the truth of the matter.[38]

Yet, like Lear, Faleasa clings to the hope that he might reassert his power. In striving for that hope, he loses like Lear the only child who loves him. The politician Malaga is duly defeated. In the street brawl which follows the election Faleasa's beloved son and heir Moaula kills two opponents and is jailed for life. The children Faleasa despises take over his village. In the play, of course, Cordelia's death is enough finally to destroy the king. Wendt denies his hero any such grandeur, though as his son is about to kill he offers a version of the pathos of Lear's anguished final negatives:

Desperately he stepped forward to try to stop his son who, except for Laaumatua, was the only person he had ever genuinely and deeply loved. 'No! No!' he called to Moaula. He tripped and fell forward.[39]

Instead the arrest of his son drives him truly into the madness he had previously been so skilled at feigning. We last see him being jeered at outside the village church 'his arms outstretched to the dazzling sky, his mouth fixed in a soundless scream, his long hair and beard as brilliantly white as the whitewashed church walls',[40] his only solace now his fool-friend Laaumatua, who will tend him in his senility.

Faleasa's descent into madness and silence has the power and pathos of many fine stage Lears. The novel begins 'early on a drizzly Saturday morning'[41] with the crisis of Faleasa's seventy-sixth year. Wendt then uses the novel form to fill in the back story. Chapters in the present alternate with Faleasa's previous life. He remembers his own past, and the mythological, pre-European past of Samoa. It is to that past, the 'pouliuli' of the novel's title, that Faleasa is trying to return, the time, as the

---

36 Ibid., p. 17.
37 Ibid., p. 6.
38 Ibid., p. 94.
39 Ibid., p. 142.
40 Ibid., p. 144.
41 Ibid., p. 1.

Samoan historian Damon Salesa puts it, of 'darkness, heathenism, ignorance'.[42] This 'pouliuli' 'or the colour black' is also 'a fertile colour, a fecund darkness',[43] a colour, as Wendt puts it in a recent poem, that 'lives . . . in all its magic plumage'.[44] The simplistic impugning of that 'darkness' by European missonaries is something that Wendt seeks to qualify, as do the new generation of Samoan historians, such as Salesa.[45]

Like Lear's, Faleasa's quest is futile, for during the personal past he remembers, that older Samoa has been changed utterly. He has lived through the First War (after which Western Samoa was made a New Zealand protectorate) and the Second War, when the base at PagoPago on Tutuila, in American Samoa, was used by the American forces in the Pacific.[46] American penetration of course continues to be a fact of South Pacific life. Faleasa prospers because he can harness the new economic power Americans and New Zealanders bring with them. He thrives in the competition this new world brings about. Yet his final attempts to manoeuvre in that world prove catastrophic as well. Through madness he hoped to escape to freedom: instead he becomes trapped in himself, while the venal world around him refuses to end. Salesa makes the distinction in Samoan terms between the darkness of heathen ignorance and the time of *malamalama* ('understanding, light, Christianity').[47] Wendt's sombre comedy shows that perhaps the real darkness is the engulfing of Faleasa's family in tides of modern greed and venality.

For Samoa, then, *Lear* allows Wendt to adumbrate themes he pursued in much of his early fiction. He grew up in Samoa in the 1930s and 1940s, and has written frequently of the great changes wrought on his homeland in that time, vividly fictionalizing clashes between Christian and pre-Christian values, between Samoan values and those of various invading cultures: German, English, American, New Zealand. These clashes between traditional and emergent cultures he frequently depicts as a dynastic struggle, as chiefly families strive to define the world in which they will live. These struggles have allowed Wendt to demonstrate 'the manipulation of power, who suffers from it, and how that affects the people in power. I have been writing about that in all of my books'.[48] Like Shakespeare, Wendt finds the family romance a powerful narrative for such themes. The kingdom Faleasa divides is geographically far smaller than Lear's: one village in a small South Pacific nation. Yet that division, as in Shakespeare, has drastic (and moving) personal and societal consequences.

FRAME

Wendt was the first Samoan novelist, although he has lived and worked in New Zealand for many years, writing both for a Samoan as well as a wider Pacific audience. He reworks a canonical text to evoke a Samoan world in ways which will generally be familiar to readers of post-independence fictions from, say, Africa and the West Indies. Janet Frame, held by many to be New Zealand's greatest living writer, has been bound by no such direct impulse toward writing her nation, although, as her autobiography makes clear, she made a conscious decision to remain in New Zealand, where the 'prospect of exploring a new country with not so many layers of mapmakers, particularly the country where one first saw daylight and the sun and the dark, was too tantalising to resist'.[49] Yet, like so many colonial artists, especially those in

---

[42] Damon Salesa, *Off the Record: the Magazine of the Friends of the Turnbull Library* 8 (2001), p. 5.

[43] Ellis, 'The Techniques of Storytelling', p. 87.

[44] Albert Wendt, *Photographs* (Auckland, 1995), p. 7.

[45] In turn, this section of the essay has profited from the generously attentive reading given several drafts by Michelle Keown from the University of Stirling, part of a new generation of scholars of Pacific literatures.

[46] In 1899, Germany and the United States divided the archipelago which makes up Samoa between them. Western Samoa was then allocated to New Zealand as part of Germany's punishment for losing the First World War. For its part, New Zealand was rewarded for its customary loyalty in times of war to Great Britain.

[47] Salesa, *off The Record*, p. 5.

[48] Ellis, 'The Techniques of Storytelling', pp. 82–83.

[49] Janet Frame, *The Envoy from Mirror City* (Auckland, 1985), p. 151.

white settler colonies (such as Marsh and Stow also) she has been highly conscious of the heritage of British culture. The first volume of her autobiography *To the Is-Land* tracks, among other things, a series of literary epiphanies, as the world of words came both to describe the world she lived in and, in a post-romantic gesture, to allow Frame to escape from 'facts and truths and memories of truths...always toward the Third Place, where the starting point is myth'.[50] Her autobiography traces her quest for the 'power of words...a constant search and need for what was, after all, "only a word" – imagination'.[51] Schooled in New Zealand in the 1930s and 1940s, Frame was of course exposed to Shakespeare's works.[52] Her autobiography is telling evidence of the conventionality of her culture's immersion in Shakespeare at this time. More powerfully she also shows an epiphany through which she emerged into a more powerful engagement with Shakespeare. Cast as Lady Macbeth in a classroom exercise, she committed the role to memory. She never got to perform her scene, she recalls. 'I lost my chance to be Lady Macbeth. Even so I gained Shakespeare'.[53] From then the *Complete Works* became her solace. When, years later, she was in a series of mental institutions, her Shakespeare followed her, 'in a little rose-embroidered bag'. Even when she was not stable enough to read, she imagined that 'when no one was reading him he invariably read himself'.[54]

Unlike Marsh, Stow and Wendt, Frame nowhere directly rewrites *Lear*. None of her fictions is such a direct counter to any of Shakespeare's texts. Rather, like the mother creature in *Aliens*, Shakespeare is reticulated everywhere in Frame, rising to the textual consciousness both of Frame (in her memoirs) and her characters. Many of them are endowed with her knowledge of Shakespeare. Theirs is not a scholar's Shakespeare, anxiously checking citations for their accuracy. Rather it is a Shakespeare deeply recalled, a Shakespeare of isolated fragments of words which float into Frame's worlds to radiate their textual power. In this way she investigates, as it were, not so much the after-life of *Lear* as its

radioactive half-life, for, as Frame puts it:

even at night when most of the city of tragedy is quiet one can hear the inner explosions of Shakespeare's unattended works as new layers of meaning are cast spontaneously from their context.[55]

In the third volume of her autobiography, Frame records her quest in London to be accurately diagnosed, discovering that she had 'never suffered from schizophrenia',[56] having spent several years in institutions being constructed (and constructing herself) as mentally disturbed. She compares the result of this quest to Lear's play-long realization. 'Like King Lear I had gone in search of "the truth" and I now had nothing. "Nothing will come out of nothing"'.[57] Yet out of those years of nothing, as the autobiographies show, came the beginnings of her prolific creative output. Likewise her poetic and fictional voices strive to remember the 'something' that come out of *Lear*'s nothings. The confused exile Godfrey Rainbird, for example, in *Yellow Flowers in the Antipodean Room*, finds

himself repeating the words he remembered from some play he'd seen.

'No cause. No cause.'

---

[50] Janet Frame, *To the Is-Land* (London, 1983), p. 11.

[51] Ibid., p. 203.

[52] The autobiographies should be read alongside Michael King's authoritative *Wrestling with the Angel: A Life of Janet Frame* (Auckland, 2000). King clarifies Frame's life in institutions and her obsessive wandering since then throughout New Zealand. She shares both predilections with the Lear and Gloucester avatars explored in this section.

[53] Frame, *Is-Land*, p. 206.

[54] Janet Frame 'Memory and a Pocketful of Words', *TLS* (4 June 1964), p. 487.

[55] 'The half-life of a reaction...is the time required for the concentration of a reactant to decrease to half its initial value...Carbon-14 is continuously produced in the upper atmosphere and has a half-life of 5,770 years', *Macmillan Encyclopedia of Chemistry*, vol. 2, ed. Joseph J. Lagowski (New York, 1997), pp. 711–12; Frame, 'Memory', p. 487. In terms of cultural radioactivity, then, Shakespeare's works are well within their first half-life, hence *Lear*'s ongoing explosive power.

[56] Frame, *Envoy*, p. 102.

[57] Frame, *Envoy*, p. 110.

What was the play? Wasn't there an old man on a heath in a storm?[58]

And it is to the experiences of Lear and Gloucester on the heath and Dover Cliff that Frame obsessively returns, drawn by the play's most extreme location and its investigation there of extremes among the marginalized and the punished. Thus 'Miss Zoe Bryce, school-teacher, usherette, engaged in private research, plunged from the small cliff-area where she lived at the edge of the alphabet.'[59] Effectively many of Frame's voices are conducting such alphabet research, and hence their repeated returning to Lear's cliff, where so many aspects of social and personal relations are renegotiated. Istina Mavet, for example, the narrator of *Faces in the Water*, is endowed with many of Frame's own memories of her time in institutions. Like Frame, Mavet draws consolation from a copy of Shakespeare's works. Even when Mavet herself is not well enough to read, she knows the copy 'had decided to read itself'. Then, in a key passage, Mavet draws on her memory of *Lear* to characterize her plight and those of her fellow inmates:

Yet at night . . . I would remember to say to myself, thinking of the people of Lawn Lodge, and the desperate season of their lives,

> *Poor naked wretches wheresoe'er you are*
> *That bide the pelting of this pitiless storm,*
> *How shall your houseless heads and unfed sides,*
> *Your looped and windowed raggedness defend you*
> *From seasons such as these.*

And I thought of the confusion of people, like Gloucester, being led near the cliffs,

> *Methinks the ground is even.*
> *Horrible steep . . .*
> *Hark, do you hear the sea?*

And over and over in my mind I saw King Lear wandering on the moor and I remembered the old men at Cliffhaven sitting outside their dreary ward, and nobody at home, not in themselves or anywhere.[60]

Spiritually these old men descend also from the houseless wanderers in Dickens.[61] The empathy here extends from Lear to Gloucester; his plight provides another recurring set of images. 'What if men/should pluck out your eyes' wonders Frame's poem of a 'Skid Row No-Hoper', and then, in a gesture towards Goneril and Regan, what would happen if 'women wear them/as beads in a necklace'. Or why, the voice asks in 'The Sun Speaks at Perihelion': 'Why did spies gouge out my eyes.'[62] This might be avoided, suggests the narrator of the semi-autobiographical *Owls Do Cry*, but only by taking charge of the process in advance: 'Take . . . your eyes out, like Gloucester, to save your sight of the cliff and the greater gods . . . Your life out as a precaution against living.'[63] This fatalism is shared by the paranoid young voice in *The Adaptable Man*, who at twenty one knows already the harsh truth that 'eyes have to be plucked out before they meet' as youth prepares for the 'narrowing of the main stream to a single obsession of age' when 'men are like flies to be exterminated'.[64] Frame's many *Lear* echoes keep returning to Dover Cliff, as insistently as the sign in Marsh's 1956 production. Yet the effect is radically different. Marsh's *Lear* seems preoccupied with affirming traditional values, leaving unquestioned the values of the society the production was designed to entertain. Frame instead takes the tradition-bound Shakespeare she inherited and uses him as a rhetorical weapon against that society. Her attack is never frontal, hence she attempts no rewrite of the *Lear* narrative. Rather her fragmented *Lear* sustains a

---

[58] Janet Frame, *Yellow Flowers in the Antipodean Room* (New York, 1969), p. 189.

[59] Janet Frame, *The Edge of the Alphabet* (Christchurch, NZ, 1962), p. 205.

[60] Janet Frame, *Faces in the Water* (London, 1961), p. 114. The passage from *Lear* is as Mavet quotes it.

[61] As Adrian Poole evokes them in his eloquent 'Shadow of Lear's "Houseless" in Dickens', *Shakespeare Survey 53* (2000), pp. 103–13.

[62] Janet Frame, *The Pocket Mirror* (New York, 1967), pp. 101, 33.

[63] Janet Frame, *Owls Do Cry* (Melbourne, 1976), p. 45.

[64] Janet Frame, *The Adaptable Man* (New York, 1965), pp. 66, 78.

guerilla style war against the restrictions of New Zealand's cultural practices. Frame climbs the hill, then, as do Stow and Wendt, with something like Susan Traherne's aim in David Hare's great post-Second War play *Plenty*: 'I climbed the hill to get a better view.'[65] From their various Pacific cliffs, they use Shakespeare to 'see better'.

Yet their visions are as disparate as the polities from which their authors and producers come and which their *Lear*s strive to address. There could be no single Pacific *Lear*, given the diversity of this region. Rather the remappings of the play I have traced respond to Albert Wendt's call for a plurality of artistic maps of this region:

maps emerging out of the Pacific, maps brought in and imposed, maps combining the two . . . maps which reveal the rivers, mountains and geographies of a people's agaga/psyche . . . new maps, new fusions and interweavings . . . [66]

Here Wendt's focus is on the indigenous peoples of the Pacific, whose collective identity is frequently addressed under the term 'Oceania', a term which rejects the false romance of the term 'South Seas' on the one hand, and the Anglo-American imperialism sometimes implied by the use of the term 'Pacific'.[67] In these terms, writing from Samoa jostles uneasily with fictions from the white settler cultures of New Zealand and Australia. And yet, as a new history of the region reminds us: 'Broad and deep ties draw these polities and peoples together.'[68] Wendt himself, for example, has studied in New Zealand, where he has taught for many years, and from where he continues to publish his fiction and poetry for a New Zealand, Samoan and wider international audience. Toa Fraser, cited at the beginning of this essay, writes that his 'work continues to be informed by his Fijian–British heritage'.[69] He grew up in London: and all his Pacific plays have premiered in New Zealand. Such overlaying of journeys and locations, of identities expressed through a welter of maps is characteristic of Pacific writers in their works and in their lives. Hence to map Pacific Shakespeares we would need to begin with a reach as heterogeneous as this essay attempts.

Chronologically I have traced a movement from Marsh's 'mimic men' production of 1956 through the revisionary fictions of Stow (1958) and Wendt (1977) to Frame's free-wheeling implosions. This suggests the utopian closure of some post-imperial romance: from craven imitation to artistic freedom. It would be fairer, I think, to construe these versions as tendencies or possibilities within 'Lear's Afterlife'; synchronically still available, no matter how diachronically invented in the first instance. These *Lear*s are sufficiently inventive to suggest that we will be thinking about Shakespeare and his place in the Pacific imaginary for some time to come. In these terms, there has been Shakespeare aplenty in the Pacific since 1769, but as yet little sense of how, in general, Pacific Shakespeares ought to be described. In those terms, as Andrea Sarti remarks at the end of *Galileo*, as readers, writers, actors, audiences, and teachers: 'We don't know nearly enough . . . We are really only at the beginning'.[70]

---

[65] David Hare, *Plenty* (London, 1986), p. 86.

[66] Albert Wendt, 'Pacific Maps and Fiction(s): A Personal Journey', *Asian and Pacific Inscriptions:Identities, Ethnicities, Nationalities*, ed. Suvendrini Perera (Melbourne, 1995), p. 15.

[67] See, for example, Wendt's 'Towards a New Oceania', *Writers in East–West Encounter: New Cultural Bearings*, ed. Guy Amirthanayagan (London, 1985), pp. 201–15. The valence of these various terms is eloquently explored also in Epeli Hau'ofa's 'Our Sea of Islands', *Inside Out: Literature, Cultural Politics and Identity in the New Pacific*, eds. Vilsoni Hereniko and Rob Wilson (New York, 1999), pp. 27–39. O. K.Spate explores the history of such terms in his '"South Sea" to "Pacific Ocean": a Note on Nomenclature', *Journal of Pacific Studies* 7 (1977), pp. 205–12. Spate notes that both terms were in use from the sixteenth century onwards; after 1850, Pacific came to dominate, while South Sea was increasingly reserved for the highly coloured world of romance and tourist promotion.

[68] Donald Denoon, Philippa Mein-Smith and Marivic Wyndham, *A History of Australia, New Zealand and the Pacific* (Oxford, 2000), p. 1.

[69] Programme note for Fraser's new Pacific play *Paradise*, Circa Theatre Wellington, April 2001.

[70] Bertolt Brecht, *The Life of Galileo*, trans. Desmond I. Vezey (London, 1968), p. 122.

ACTORS, EDITORS, AND THE ANNOTATION OF SHAKESPEARIAN PLAYSCRIPTS

MICHAEL CORDNER

In recent years, Shakespearian editing – long conducted in a quiet intellectual backwater, undisturbed by larger culture wars – has itself become a key battleground for current theoretical controversy. Debate has, however, tended to focus on the handling of the texts themselves, especially the practices of emendation and modernization, while other key aspects of editorial responsibility have received scant attention. The work of annotation, in particular, remains effectively unscrutinized.

This selectivity of vision has left undisturbed the traditional assumption that the rationale and aims of Shakespearian annotation are self-evident and therefore easily defined – so easily, in fact, that no one need devote energy to defining, or debating, them in print. R. A. Foakes has noted, with regret, the complete absence of 'guides to making a commentary on a Shakespeare play', a situation rendered more disturbing, since 'in editions like those in the Arden series the commentary, which is on the same page as the text, may well be the editorial contribution that is most useful and most studied'.[1] Editors themselves generally remain silent about the principles or preferences that shape their style of annotation. Similarly, reviewers of new editions, though they may on an *ad hoc* basis query this or that piece of annotation, rarely mount a broader challenge to the rationale (or lack of it) discernible in the overall pattern of annotation in a particular edition; and too often they confine their comments to generalities, pausing only to remark that a particular editor's notes are 'judicious' or that another's 'are copious, perhaps sometimes even excessive',

but also 'thoughtful and unintimidating'.[2] In neither of the reviews from which those comments are taken is a single illustration offered in support of these judgements.

Yet the most cursory comparison of recent editions of the same Shakespeare play is likely to reveal major discrepancies in the decisions different editors have made about which aspects of the text require their intervention as annotators.[3] In the absence of systematic debate about what might

---

[1] R. A. Foakes, 'On Finishing a Commentary on *King Lear*', in John Batchelor, Tom Cain and Claire Lamont (eds.), *Shakespearean Continuities: Essays in Honour of E. A. J. Honigmann* (Basingstoke, 1997), p. 238. Cp. Marvin Spevack's assertion that 'For the editor of Shakespeare they [i.e. the notes on the text] may constitute the most important challenge; for the great majority of readers they are the most important source of information' ('A New Shakespeare Dictionary (SHAD) and the Notes on Language in Editions of Shakespeare', in Herbert Mainusch and Dietrich Rolle (eds.), *Stüdien zur Englischen Philologie* (Frankfurt, 1979), p. 123).

[2] Barry Gaines, reviewing the Arden 3 *Antony and Cleopatra*, and Jeanne Addison Roberts, reviewing the New Cambridge *The Merry Wives of Windsor*, in *Shakespeare Quarterly*, 50 (1999), pp. 207 and 376 respectively.

[3] Akihiro Yamada – in 'Editions of Shakespeare in the Twentieth Century', *Analytical and Enumerative Bibliography*, 10 (1999), pp. 72–5 – has helpfully exemplified 'how arbitrary the editorial practice has been' by comparing the annotation of six lines from *The Merchant of Venice*, 3.2, in six modern editions, and sixteen lines from *Antony and Cleopatra*, 2.2, in seven modern editions. In the case of the latter, seven words or phrases were singled out for comment across the sampled editions, but only one of these was annotated by all seven editors, while three others were each glossed by only one of the editors.

constitute a good commentary, such discrepancies grow naturally from the improvisatory way in which the work of annotation will in many cases have been carried out. In an article published as long ago as 1942, Arthur Friedman noted the paradox that, while many an editor possessed a clear set of criteria to guide his collation of texts, the same editor would often, even when his annotation was complete, 'find it difficult to state exactly why he has annotated certain passages and not others'.[4] Such paradoxes live on in modern Shakespearian editing.

The absence of rigorous scholarly scrutiny of annotation procedures can also create problems when Shakespearian editing attempts to respond to new or revised agendas. All our ongoing series of Shakespeare editions proclaim, in obedience to current fashion, that they aim to be more performance-oriented. But, without explicit discussion of what this might entail for the line-by-line drafting of the annotation in individual editions, what certainty can we have that these conversions are more than skin-deep?

Older definitions of the Shakespearian annotator's duties, on the rare occasions when a scholar attempted one, tended simply to specify the provision of 'glosses for difficult, obscure, or archaic words and phrases'. (Samuel Schoenbaum, who produced that list, added that doing anything more was 'in effect having a free ride at the expense of a captive audience that has paid its money for the plays'!)[5] Other attempts at definition may have been more detailed, but they did not extend in any significant way the range of activities demanded of the annotator. In 1993, for example, Brian Vickers's list of key desiderata required the Shakespearian editor 'to explain words or expressions that are no longer current, historical allusions, technical terms in such disciplines as philosophy, law, medicine – to supply cogently, in other words, the basic information needed to understand the play and to guide the reader in ways of interpreting and evaluating it'.[6] Vickers's list assumes that annotating a playscript imposes no generically specific demands distinct from those involved in annotating novels, poems or discursive prose.

In contrast, the General Editors' Preface to Arden 3 editions proclaims different priorities in its assertion that its editions' 'notes and introductions' will 'focus on the conditions and possibilities of meaning that editors, critics and performers (on stage and screen) have discovered in the play'. Yet confidence dwindles when the same Preface goes on to remark that the Arden 3 notes 'will offer glossarial and other explication of verbal difficulties', and that they '*may* also include discussion of points of theatrical interpretation' (my emphasis).[7] So, addressing 'points of theatrical interpretation' becomes optional, not obligatory. It also appears to be assumed that this final category of activity can be added to the list as a logically separate responsibility, the addition of which need not significantly affect the established procedures for handling 'verbal difficulties'. Accordingly, change can proceed aggregatively and does not need to involve radical rethinking of established practice.

This seems to me to be a serious misconception. Rendering our Shakespeare editions convincingly performance-friendly must entail recognizing that the 'explication of verbal difficulties' is itself frequently bound to raise crucial and complex issues of 'theatrical interpretation'. In Shakespearian theatre, in Keir Elam's words, 'the principal mode of *praxis* . . . lies in what Pirandello called 'spoken action', that is in direct acts of language rather than in some verbally decorated extra-linguistic substance'.[8] Exploring Shakespearian dialogue, Lynne

---

[4] Arthur Friedman, 'Principles of Historical Annotation in Critical Editions of Modern Texts', *English Institute Annual 1941* (New York, 1942), pp. 116–17.

[5] Samuel Schoenbaum, 'Editing English Dramatic Texts', in R. J. Schoeck (ed.), *Editing Sixteenth Century Texts* (Toronto, 1966), p. 20.

[6] Brian Vickers, reviewing the Oxford Shakespeare editions of *Love's Labour's Lost* and *Macbeth*, *Renaissance Studies*, 7 (1993), p. 229. For another list of the annotator's duties which displays a similarly narrow focus on linguistic exegesis, see David Bevington, 'Editing Renaissance Drama in Paperback', *Renaissance Drama*, N. S., 19 (1988), p. 134.

[7] William Shakespeare, *King Lear*, ed. R. A. Foakes (Walton-on-Thames, 1997), pp. xiii–xiv.

[8] Keir Elam, *Shakespeare's Universe of Discourse: Language Games in the Comedies* (Cambridge, 1984), p. 6.

Magnusson has recently emphasized that 'People *do* things to one another with words, whether they command, request, criticize, apologize, insult, vow, promise, or simply fail to respond.'[9] As the voice coach Cicely Berry has phrased it, 'words change both the situation, the speaker and the listener', and 'After words are spoken, nothing is quite the same again.'[10] To date, what little discussion there has been of how to achieve a more stage-centred style of annotation has predominantly concerned itself with questions of physical action.[11] The fact that dialogue is itself a form of action, and one which raises fundamental interpretative issues for both reader and performer, has not yet been directly confronted.

Annotation, as traditionally practised, has been a semi-clandestine craft. In his 1942 article Arthur Friedman mused that the paucity of theorizing in the field might be 'because so many of the annotator's problems seem purely particular questions of research'.[12] Thus, annotation implicitly presents itself as, in Anne Middleton's sceptical characterization, 'an ordinary practical activity', which labours, incident-by-incident, to solve problems and remove obstructions which might defeat other, less experienced or well-informed, readers. Middleton does not wish us to be deceived by such appearances. In her view, annotation is clearly not merely a neutral provision of historical, cultural, linguistic, or critical 'facts' indispensable to understanding the text's implications.[13] Instead, it is frequently guided by its own concealed or undeclared agendas. Though it may appear to provide in each instance of its operations a neutral and objective transfer of authoritative information, its choice of what information to convey, and how to convey it, will often presuppose a prior interpretation of the text, to which convincing alternatives may well exist, but which may nowhere be adequately acknowledged in the process of annotation.[14] The impulse to control and circumscribe meaning can be a powerful impulse in scholarly activity, and devising the annotation for an ambitious text provides many opportunities and temptations for an editor to indulge that impulse. This can prove especially misleading when the text in question is a playscript.

In what follows I will not attempt to draw up comprehensive guidelines for a more performance-responsive style of annotation. It seems to me that the immediate need is simpler – i.e. to establish clearly that serious problems in this respect do repeatedly arise in Shakespearian annotation as it is currently practised. My method will be to scrutinize a number of passages from recent editions which seem to me questionable and misleading. My conviction is that in each case these difficulties have arisen because insufficient attention has been paid by the annotator to the performance challenges and potentiality of the scripts. This examination will, I hope, both offer detailed exemplification of some recurrent fallibilities in scholarly practice and identify some, at least, of the areas where systematic rethinking is urgently needed.[15] This project

---

9 Lynne Magnusson, 'Dialogue', in Sylvia Adamson, Lynette Hunter, Lynne Magnusson, Ann Thompson and Katie Wales (eds.), *Reading Shakespeare's Dramatic Language: A Guide* (London, 2001), p. 135.

10 Cicely Berry, *The Actor and his Text* (London, 1987), p. 20

11 See Ros King's comments on the current state of play in 'Staging the Globe', in W. R. Elton and John M Mucciolo (eds.), *The Shakespearean International Yearbook I: Where Are We Now in Shakespearean Studies?* (Aldershot, 1999), p. 131. A provocative contribution to the debate on editors' treatment of stage action has recently been made by Margaret Jane Kidnie, 'Text, Performance, and the Editors: Staging Shakespearean Drama', *Shakespeare Quarterly* 51 (2000), 456–73.

12 Arthur Friedman, 'Principles of Historical Annotation', 116

13 Anne Middleton, 'Life in the Margins, or, What's an Annotator to Do?', in Dave Oliphant and Robin Bradford (eds.), *New Directions in Textual Studies* (Austin, 1990), p. 169. See D. C. Greetham, 'Enlarging the Text', *Review* 14 (1992), 27–9.

14 See the claim by Ralph Hanna III – in 'Annotating *Piers Plowman*', *TEXT* 6 (1994), p. 159 – that annotation 'does not form a continuous argument – as the essay does – but is textually dispersed, responds to an appropriate lemma and must be rejoined by the reader to create an argument. But it nonetheless strives for a total interpretative view of the text and presupposes that no detail "makes sense" apart from the commentator's take on the whole.'

15 See my earlier preliminary explorations in this area in 'Annotation and Performance in Shakespeare', *Essays in Criticism* 46 (1996), pp. 289–301. Laurie E. Maguire has also recently given some attention to annotation in editions of early modern drama in her 'Feminist Editing and the Body of the

inevitably demands the use of examples from recent editions. I wish therefore to stress that the choice of sources for these examples is arbitrary, in as much as it reflects the pattern of my recent re-reading of Shakespeare plays. It would be easy to multiply comparable examples from editions of other plays. I would also stress that these local objections to particular pieces of annotation in no way imply a larger judgement upon the editions from which they are taken.

My first example concerns recent editorial responses to a brief exchange from the extended sparring-match between Falstaff and the Lord Chief Justice in *2 Henry IV* 1.2:

LORD CHIEF JUSTICE Well, the King hath severed you and Prince Harry. I hear you are going with Lord John of Lancaster against the Archbishop and the Earl of Northumberland.
FALSTAFF Yea, I thank your pretty sweet wit for it.

(lines 203–7)[16]

Giorgio Melchiori's 1989 New Cambridge edition provides this observation on Falstaff's riposte: 'Implying that the separation was promoted by the Lord Chief Justice'. In his 1998 Oxford Shakespeare edition René Weis begs to differ: 'Probably a mildly sarcastic general remark, meaning something like "Thank you for so shrewdly reminding me of what is all too obvious to me", rather than a specific connecting of the Lord Chief Justice's severing of Falstaff and Hal, or his commission.' What concerns me here is the dubious rhetorical work performed by that opening 'Probably'. Weis offers no evidence in support of his preferred reading. The words in themselves are clearly susceptible of Melchiori's interpretation, and nothing I can see in the surrounding dialogue militates against that interpretation. If Weis's own discourse analysis, say, of the larger sequence has led him to query this, then he owes it to his readers to spell out his thinking; but he offers no hint of such evidence. His own alternative account is also perfectly playable. But, as far as I can see, this is not a situation where, on the available evidence, one of the two readings can claim superior authority. If he had simply added another alternative to the one Melchiori offered,

Weis would have performed a helpful service for his readers and alerted them to the possibility that the interaction between the two characters at this point can legitimately be performed in different ways. Melchiori's reading, for example, is predicated on a Falstaff who believes that the Lord Chief Justice is actively working against him; in Weis's reading, Falstaff is merely riled by the Lord Chief Justice's rubbing salt in his wound. In succumbing, however, to the desire to affirm one version as being more plausible and authentic than the other, Weis asks his readers to accept, without question, the authority of his own preferences, without himself observing the normal protocols requiring the presentation of evidence in such circumstances of scholarly disagreement. In the process, Weis misleads his readers about the potential range of the performance meanings logically educible from the playscript before them.

A parallel example can be found in the handling of a passage from Claudius's anguished soliloquy in *Hamlet*, 3.3, 68–70, in Philip Edwards's 1985 New Cambridge edition of the play. The relevant lines appear in the Second Quarto in the following form:

O limed soule, that struggling to be free,
Art more ingaged; helpe Angels make assay,
Bow stubborn knees, and hart with strings of steale,

The First Folio version reads:

Oh limed soule, that struggling to be free,
Art more ingag'd: Helpe Angels, make assay:
Bow stubborne knees, and heart with strings of Steele,

These lines have provoked an extended history of scholarly dispute, about, for instance, the meaning of 'assay' and about whether 'make assay' should be addressed to the 'limed soul' or the 'angels'. The punctuation in both Second Quarto and First Folio supports the latter option; and modernized editions

Text', in Dympna Callaghan (ed.), *A Feminist Companion to Shakespeare* (Oxford, 2000), pp. 59–79.
[16] This modernized version comes from William Shakespeare, *The Complete Works*, ed. Stanley Wells and Gary Taylor (Oxford, 1986), p. 579.

which favour the other interpretation must therefore decisively repunctuate at this point. Edwards belongs in that camp, and his version of these lines accordingly takes this form:

> Oh limèd soul that struggling to be free
> Art more engaged! Help, angels! – Make assay:
> Bow stubborn knees, and heart with strings of steel

He buttresses this with the following note: 'I think it is more likely that Claudius is addressing himself than the angels. After his appeal, "Help, angels!" there is a silence, and then in a quieter tone he turns to himself, knowing that it is he who must make the effort.'

Edwards's 'likely', like Weis's 'Probably', on the face of it concedes the possibility of differing opinions; but Edwards then moves even more firmly than Weis to legislate in favour of his own preferences. He provides his readers with no information about the arguments advanced by others in favour of alternative hypotheses, nor does he offer any evidence in support of his own reading, merely the assertion that one addressee is more likely than the other. There then follows an account of the key lines which prescribes the 'correct' way of playing them, including desired phrasing, emphatic and carefully positioned use of pause, and apt choice of relative tonalities. As we have seen, enforcing Edwards's preferred phrasing entails radical repunctuation of the earliest printings. The dash, for instance, which conveys in Edwards's version that indispensable, pregnant pause is entirely his own invention, a fact unacknowledged in his note. It is difficult to conceive of an argument which would convincingly demonstrate that such a pause is metrically indispensable here, while the Second Quarto and First Folio versions both indicate a different, totally plausible, positioning for the caesura in that line.[17] Edwards's reading offers an intelligent and interesting surmise about *one* way in which the passage might be, and indeed has been, performed.[18] But rival versions of equal plausibility exist, and they too have been staged successfully. In such circumstances, it has to be illegitimate for an editor simply to decree the superior likelihood of his own interpretative preference.

Such practices would be questionable in annotating any kind of text. In a playscript, their consequences are especially damaging, since they seek to impose upon stage dialogue a fixity of meaning it can never in practice possess. In theatrical performance, verbal action is partly an effect of an intricate array of interpretative choices taken by the player concerning intonation, emphasis, rhythm, inflection, use of pause, vocal colour, relative tempi, and so on. Subtle adjustments in any of these may profoundly alter the nature of the communication effected. Melchiori's and Weis's versions of Falstaff's retort can both be conveyed in performance using the nine words Shakespeare has provided, but the different readings would require from their respective players totally distinct vocal characterizations of those words. The surviving text, however, provides us with no evidence on the basis of which we might seek to adjudicate between the claims of these rival versions to authorial authenticity. Even if we were to imagine Shakespeare in the process of composition hearing each phrase in a precise performance version, no notational system has ever existed which would allow him to commit such a detailed interpretative scenario to paper. Compared with musical notation, the traditional methods of

---

[17] Michael Warren – in 'Repunctuation as Interpretation in Editions of Shakespeare', *English Literary Renaissance*, 7 (1977), p. 168 – has pointed out how, in altering copy-text punctuation, 'each editor, far from presenting to the public a reading or acting text as close as possible to the Shakespearean original, has created a distinctive "Shakespeare" who has been filtered through the editor's individual consciousness, and who reflects that editor's presuppositions about the play's interpretation, especially in relation to performance'. Agreeing with this does not entail ignoring the fact that Quarto and Folio punctuation will often – or, indeed, usually – be scribal or compositorial rather than authorial. Appropriate caution about what the original printed punctuation can tell us does not, however, license a modern editor to substitute his or her own punctuation for that in the earliest printings and then to behave as if the interpretation thus insinuated were self-evidently the best or only authoritative one.

[18] Peter McEnery, for instance, phrased this segment of Claudius's soliloquy in a manner very similar to that prescribed by Edwards in John Caird's 2000 Royal National Theatre production of the play.

recording theatrical dialogue are exceedingly primitive. The bare words – without any markings to indicate, for example, significant emphasis, tonal shading, or ironic pointing – are all we are usually given. Accordingly, nothing survives to enable us to say authoritatively how Shakespeare may have intended Falstaff's line to be delivered, since the words by themselves, however sharply etched they may be, are insufficient to supply that information.[19] Annotation which seeks to deny this fact in effect indulges in a form of literary wish-fulfilment.

It also ignores the exigencies under which Shakespeare worked. We do not know what exchanges of information he may have had with his fellow players as they prepared to introduce, say, *Hamlet* to Globe audiences: but the pressured timetable by which new plays were made ready for the stage in the early modern period is unlikely to have permitted an effective line-by-line exegesis by the author of 'correct' ways of handling each word spoken, and the scarce punctuation in surviving play manuscripts and cue-scripts does not suggest that the latter were designed to be prescriptive even about such a fundamental issue as phrasing. Many key decisions about how to play substantial portions of a script must perforce have been delegated to the players' craft skills and inventiveness.

In any case, theatrical performance is such a complex and mobile signifying system that Shakespeare, like any other writer for the medium, must have needed to accommodate himself to the probability that the performance results derived from his words upon the page would inevitably generate meanings he had not predicted (and might even have been astonished by). Changes in the relative proximity of two bodies on stage can transform the implications of an exchange. An unanticipated intensity of audience laughter on a particular line can inspire players to find new possibilities in the dialogue which follows. An actor's discovery of a new way to shape and focus a speech can provoke from his fellows, if they are capable of it, an instinctive re-imagining of their own responses to that speech. Drama is an art which exists in the present tense, and in small ways as well as large each performance

of a script will differ from its predecessors and successors, even if only because audiences differ and players must negotiate anew each day the best way of securing and holding the attention of the accidental assembly of heterogeneous spectators whom they must now entertain. Short of bestowing upon him the implausible gift of total omniscience, there is no way in which a playwright can be credited with the capacity to foresee the variant meanings such volatile circumstances of communication will spark into life. The contract between playwright and performer must accordingly assume that creative input in this partnership is not solely the prerogative of the former. Indeed, one definition of a dramatist's responsibilities might be that he or she should provide writing of an effective, distinctive, and novel kind, which is yet not so prescriptive that it deprives the player of the freedom to react fluently and decisively to changing circumstances of performance or of the ability to carve new possibilities, apposite to this present moment of performance, from the dialogue provided.[20]

It is also true, as Jonathan Miller has argued, that an 'actor's performance as a particular character requires hypothesis'.[21] Working from the proposition

---

[19] A crucial turn of the plot in Ian McEwan's *Amsterdam* (London, 1998), pp. 148–9, hinges on this ambiguous quality of written English: 'In a language as idiomatically stressed as English, opportunities for misreadings are bound to arise. By a mere backward movement of stress, a verb can become a noun, an act a thing. To refuse – to insist on saying no to what you believe is wrong – becomes at a stroke, refuse – an insurmountable pile of garbage. As with words, so with sentences. What Clive had intended on Thursday and posted on Friday was, You deserve to be *sacked*. What Vernon was bound to understand on Tuesday in the aftermath of his dismissal was, You *deserve* to be sacked. Had the card arrived on Monday, he might have read it differently. This was the comic nature of their fate; a first-class stamp would have served both men well. On the other hand, perhaps no other outcomes were available to them, and this was the nature of their tragedy.'

[20] Some scholars, of course, accord yet further power to early modern actors *vis-à-vis* the playwrights they employed. See, for instance, Stephen Orgel, 'What is a Text?', *Research Opportunities in Renaissance Drama*, 24 (1981), p. 3.

[21] Jonathan Miller, *Subsequent Performances* (London, 1986), p. 43.

that 'it is *people* who mean and not *expressions*; so that it is possible for two people to mean different things *by* the same expression', Miller observes how little information playscripts usually provide about the dispositions and designs of the characters who are intended to communicate meanings via the dialogue the dramatist provides for them. He presumes that playwrights, in composing speeches, are likely to 'conceive them in the mouths of a more or less distinct individual person', but he then notes that, 'more often than not, the only thing that survives in the written script is the lines themselves – like the skeleton of a prehistoric creature – leaving the actors and directors free to reconstruct the soft parts of the role, in a way that may be at odds with the creature that once lived as a whole within the writer's imagination'. Consequently, 'as everyone knows', he concludes, 'it is possible to perform the lines assigned to Hamlet, say, in a hundred different ways, all of which are at least *compatible* with the basic semantic references of the script'.[22]

The remarkable diversity of the actors who have successfully forged their personal incarnations of Hamlet from the words Shakespeare invented for the character amply confirms Miller's assertion. Yet this truth which 'everyone knows' is effectively disregarded every time an editor invents a note of the kind we have seen Weis and Edwards composing. A real advance in rendering our editions more performance-responsive would have been achieved if it could be accepted that any such move by an editor of a Shakespeare play is likely to represent an illegitimate imposition of personal preferences upon a potentially unsuspecting reader. The urge to insist on a single 'correct' interpretation must be resisted, in the interests of responding flexibly to the multifarious potentialities of the dialogue. Annotation cannot, of course, track all the possible, plausible, performance extrapolations which have been, and could be, made from Shakespearian scripts; but, in offering explanatory help which many readers may well find indispensable in negotiating the texts' complexities, editors need to avoid prematurely delimiting that rich field of potentiality.

My next three instances provide further examples of the biasing effect preconceptions about the nature of the character speaking a particular line can have on editorial practice. As Philip Edwards insists that Claudius should pause at one particular point in line 69 of his soliloquy, so Anthony Hammond in his 1981 Arden 2 *Richard III* is equally confident about the apt performance of a debated piece of wordplay in 4.2. He modernizes the relevant passage as follows:

RICHARD Ha, am I King? 'Tis so – but Edward lives.
BUCKINGHAM True, noble Prince.
RICHARD   O bitter consequence,
  That Edward still should live – true noble prince!
  Cousin, thou wast not wont to be so dull.

(lines 14–17)

Neither First Quarto nor First Folio provides any punctuation in line 16 between 'live' and 'true noble prince'. The possibilities here have been variously debated. Ernst Honigmann in his 1968 Penguin edition, for instance, left the First Quarto/First Folio punctuation unaltered and commented: 'Whether taken as an interjected repetition ("live! – 'True, noble prince'! – ") or as part of Richard's sentence (live a true noble prince), we cannot miss his impatience.' As his repunctuation implies, Hammond is not content with such fence-sitting. He offers the following gloss: 'There seems to be no way to make Richard's meaning clear by punctuation alone: Alexander's has been adopted here, though NCS calls it "obscure". Richard picks up Buckingham's vague reply, and turns its meaning, to make it clear that Edward, while he lives, is still the true Prince.' This note puzzlingly claims certainty about a true meaning, which punctuation, however, is unable to convey, and which the First Quarto/First Folio punctuation clearly does not convey. But from what source of authority then is this certainty about the line's true meaning derived, if all existing means of notation have proved inadequate to the task of communicating it? Once again it is probable that Shakespeare will have had

---

[22] Jonathan Miller, 'Plays and Players', in R. A. Hinde (ed.), *Non-Verbal Communication* (Cambridge, 1972), pp. 362–3.

a clear view on this matter as he composed the speech, and he may well have instructed Richard Burbage in the reading he intended. But the only forms in which the text has come down to us provide no way of recovering that hypothetical interpretative preference. Hammond's claim to certainty can, one presumes, only derive from undeclared assumptions about what *his* Richard would mean by this line. Once again an editor's subjective preference is being dressed up as a passage's authentic meaning.

A matching instance occurs in the 1994 Oxford Shakespeare edition of *Twelfth Night* by Roger Warren and Stanley Wells. In 1.2, Viola responds to the Sea Captain's account of Olivia and her mourning of the recent deaths of her father and brother with these words:

> O that I served that lady,
> And might not be delivered to the world
> Till I had made mine own occasion mellow,
> What my estate is. (lines 38–41)

Warren and Wells comment on this sequence: 'Shakespeare presents both his heroines in the same emotional situation, bereaved of their brothers, partly to contrast their reactions to that loss. Viola's interest in Olivia, and urge to serve her in the next line, derives partly from sympathy for someone who has suffered a similar bereavement.' The first sentence of this note is fair enough, though its inclusion in the annotation may be questionable, since the point it makes does not clarify any difficulty in the dialogue and might therefore more naturally be dealt with in the Introduction. The second sentence, however, is problematic. Nothing in this speech – or at any other point in the play's dialogue, as far as I am aware – establishes that Viola feels such empathetic 'sympathy' for the countess because the latter's bereavement parallels her own.[23] The kind of feeling invoked in this comment is often displayed by modern actresses in the role, and the note is presumably influenced by experience of that performance tradition. But, as an observation designed to explicate this passage of dialogue, it is misleading, since it supplies a motivation nowhere invoked in these speeches,

which can easily be performed without any such idea being brought into play. It is indeed possible to discern an exactly opposite logic in Viola's speech – i.e. Olivia's having suffered two recent bereavements makes her a mistress whose mood may chime well with a voyager burdened, as Viola is, by the experience of her own recent loss. It could be valuable for an edition to provide a note recording the fact that many Violas perform this set of lines, and the role in general, in ways which make such empathetic emotions central to their presentation of the character. But the Oxford note appears to be written from so far within this tradition of performance that it fails to acknowledge that other ways of conceiving the role are also possible.

Preconceptions about who is likely to have the upper hand in particular relationships can similarly lead editors to insist on interpretations which reify a text into suspect patterns. In his 1993 New Oxford *Much Ado About Nothing*, 1.1, Sheldon P. Zitner singles out the following passage for comment:

> BENEDICK If Signor Leonato be her father, she would not have his head on her shoulders for all Messina, as like him as she is.
> BEATRICE I wonder that you will still be talking, Signor Benedick; nobody marks you.
> BENEDICK What, my dear Lady Disdain! Are you yet living? (lines 109–15)

Zitner comments on 'head' in Benedick's first speech: 'Apparently this refers to Leonato's grey hair, but there is also a covert reference to the cuckold's proverbial horns and thus to Hero's possible objections. This provokes Beatrice's reply, which may have been Benedick's aim.' I am unconvinced, ubiquitous though allusions to cuckold's horns are in the period, that this passage, in fact, contains one. But I am more interested for the present in the concluding hint that Benedick's meandering remarks on Leonato and Hero may be deliberate provocation aimed at Beatrice. The speech is clearly

---

[23] At a later moment in the action, Viola does empathetically imagine Olivia's feelings; but here the trigger is her realization that Olivia has fallen in love with her in her male disguise: 'Poor lady, she were better love a dream!' (2.2. 26).

not one of Benedick's most energized and witty efforts, and discerning a sub-textual motivation in it helps save his face. It also restores the initiative to him. But is that justified? A literal reading of the exchange might suggest exactly the opposite – i.e. that Benedick has gone on labouring at being funny long after his audience has tired of him and that Beatrice's interjection is therefore woundingly accurate. Zitner's note does not acknowledge that the interpretation he proposes involves reversing what will, to many, seem to be the common-sense logic of the exchange. This is not to say that his solution is unplayable, merely that making it the sole possibility identified in his note privileges it unduly. One might deduce that Zitner instinctively favours a Benedick of high adrenalin who would not lose momentum so lamentably soon after his first appearance. But performance history demonstrates that the scene can indeed be played persuasively in ways which confirm the truth of Beatrice's barb. Here, as in the preceding examples from *Richard III* and *Twelfth Night*, a greater alertness to the variegated array of Richard IIIs, Violas and Benedicks which interpreters can plausibly generate from Shakespeare's dialogue would have produced annotation less legislative and restrictive in its attitude to the three scripts' performance potentialities.

My remaining examples focus upon the explication of verbal cruxes. The first two concern the challenge represented by the repetition, with significant variation, of key phrases or patterns of speech – a dramatic resource of which Shakespeare makes frequent use. The intricacies of such patterning may easily ensnare the annotator. It can, for example, be crucial not to assume that a repeated phrase will register in the same way on each of its appearances. Gary Taylor, in his 1982 Oxford Shakespeare *Henry V*, argued that some Quarto readings should be admitted into the emended Folio text. These included Pistol repeating his tagline, 'Coup' la gorge', in 4.6, after Henry's command that 'every soldier kill his prisoners' (line 38), an instruction reinforced in Taylor's edition by the interpolated stage direction, '*The soldiers kill their prisoners*'. So, even if we are not to imagine Pistol

himself immediately executing his own prisoner (which, in Taylor's reading, is offered as a real possibility), it is yet crystal clear what the sequel to his farcical encounter with Le Fer in 4.4 is now fated to be. Taylor's argument has proved contentious, and subsequent editors have not always been prepared to follow his lead. I do not intend to offer an opinion on the strictly bibliographical merits of his case. What interests me is the position taken in his 1992 New Cambridge edition by Andrew Gurr, who opposes Taylor on this issue: 'Pistol's added 'Couple gorge' in Q is a comic catchphrase insertion which would lose all its comedy if immediately enacted with blood on stage. Q is not a good guide to the original staging here.' Gurr's logic seems flawed to me. It depends on an unacceptably rigid notion of the 'comic' and assumes that a phrase used initially as a 'comic catchphrase' cannot, later in a performance, acquire different resonances for the audience. The three most recent Royal Shakespeare Company productions of *Henry V* have all, in varying ways, acted on Taylor's suggestion, precisely because directors and actors are drawn by its enticing theatrical potential. For a *miles gloriosus*, flamboyantly boastful, but of extremely doubtful soldiership, suddenly to find his bluff called on the battlefield by his king is in itself a promising dramatic idea; but for that crisis to be cued by his recurrent catchphrase turning in a second from words almost devoid of meaning into ones carrying literal significance – Pistol is required to cut Le Fer's throat – offers the possibility of a brilliant piece of theatrical prestidigitation. There may be other, juster, grounds for challenging Taylor's theory, but Gurr's unconvincing response to it only serves to highlight the provocative nature of the performance possibilities it opens up.

A related difficulty can arise when a sequence of repeated word-uses lures editors into glossing early deployments of the key term or terms in the light of meanings they are only likely to acquire later in the action. An example of this can be found in the handling of a passage in *The Comedy of Errors* 1.2, in the 1962 Arden 2 edition by R. A. Foakes. In his modernization the key lines appear as follows:

ANTIPHOLUS OF SYRACUSE
Farewell till then: I will go lose myself,
And wander up and down to view the city.
FIRST MERCHANT
Sir, I commend you to your own content. *Exit.*
ANTIPHOLUS OF SYRACUSE
He that commends me to mine own content
Commends me to the thing I cannot get.
I to the world am like a drop of water
That in the ocean seeks another drop,
Who, falling there to find his fellow forth,
(Unseen, inquisitive) confounds himself.
So I, to find a mother and a brother,
In quest of them, unhappy, lose myself.

(lines 30–40)

Foakes glosses 'lose myself' in line 30 as follows: 'roam at random, but perhaps suggesting also the sense "lose my wits", cf. line 40 and n.' The promised note at line 40 is more expansive:

foreshadowing main themes of the play, confusion of mind, produced by the 'errors' of meeting the wrong twin, cf. l.95 below, II. ii.11, 184, etc., and confusion of identity (see Introduction, p. xliii). Antipholus, who feels he has no identity, is given one in Ephesus, where everyone claims acquaintance of him, and discovers another in falling in love with Luciana (see III. ii. 39–40 and n.), before 'finding' himself at the end of the play in meeting his parents and brother. For the extension of the sense of 'lose' here, cf. *Ant.*, I. ii. 114, 'Or lose myself in dotage'.

Foakes is not unique in looking beyond line 30 while seeking to explain it. Perhaps following his lead, T. S. Dorsch in his 1988 New Cambridge edition comments on the same phrase in that line in the following terms: 'wander about at random (as at 11–14). It may, as also at 40, imply "lose my wits", in anticipation of the errors and confusions of the day'. Foakes, however, in his note on line 40 goes further than his fellows in tying the whole play into a neat thematic package. In the process, he risks coming adrift from the probable performance meanings of these lines at this early point in the play. His god's-eye-view of the comedy's overall progress may contain much that is valid; but what is the evidence that 'lose myself' in line 30 has as

one of its meanings 'lose my wits'? Foakes presents none, but lets it rest merely as an unsupported surmise. Dorsch sensibly refers the phrase back to earlier lines in 1.2 in which Antipholus has catalogued the exploration of Ephesus he intends to make; and one meaning of the phrase here clearly has to be a humorous reference to the likelihood that Antipholus' roaming will at some point result in his becoming lost in a strange town. It can also plausibly be read as alluding to the Merchant's advice earlier in the scene that, in the interests of his survival, Antipholus should pass himself off as 'of Epidamnum' (line 1). Accordingly he will 'lose' himself by disguising his Syracusan origins (a meaning neither Dorsch nor Foakes observes). But nothing he has so far said prepares an audience to interpret him as meaning that he runs the risk (or courts the possibility) of losing his wits during his sight-seeing trip. To a spectator already acquainted with the play, the phrase may acquire proleptic irony, given the strange experiences which await the character, and which will in due course lead him to doubt both his own and the Ephesians' sanity. But that is a layer of dramatic implication quite distinct from anything the actor of the Syracusan Antipholus can here represent his character as consciously intending; and those layers should be systematically distinguished by the annotator. No current edition of the play recognizes the need to do this.

A similar scepticism applies to the belief of both editors that 'lose myself' in line 40 certainly means 'lose my wits'. I see no evidence of this. The immediate context twins it with 'confounds himself' in line 38, which Foakes, following C. T. Onions's *Shakespeare Glossary* (London, 1911), glosses as 'mingles indiscriminately with the rest'. The primary meaning of 'lose myself' in line 40 consequently looks to me to be 'lose all sense of my individual identity or personal existence', which is a more precise meaning than, and quite distinct from, the generalized 'lose my wits' our two annotators favour. Being mistaken for another will in due course impose great stress on both brothers' sanity; but that lies some way ahead. Foakes's thematic preoccupations have made him leap too many fences at once and load these early exchanges with meanings they are unlikely to carry in performance at this point. In the process, they also lead him to lose sight of one of the inherent theatrical pleasures of such repetition. It is open to the player of the Syracusan Antipholus to voice 'lose myself' in line 40 in a way which directly recollects his prior use of it in line 30, but which also indicates that the phrase has now gained added resonance and fresh significance. Alone, Antipholus speaks of things he would not share with the Merchant – a development neatly paralleled by this shift in the meanings which can be discerned in his repeated use of 'lose myself'. Alertness to the possibility of such verbal metamorphoses has to be fundamental to any aptly theatrical annotation of a Shakespearian playscript.

Glossing can detach words from their immediate dramatic context in other ways also. In their first encounter in *The Taming of the Shrew*, 2.1, Petruchio and Katherina share this exchange (in the modernized text of H. J. Oliver's 1982 Oxford Shakespeare edition):

PETRUCHIO ...
 Hearing thy mildness praised in every town,
 Thy virtues spoke of, and thy beauty sounded,
 Yet not so deeply as to thee belongs,
 Myself am moved to woo thee for my wife.
KATHERINA 'Moved', in good time! Let him that
  moved you hither
 Remove you hence. I knew you at the first
 You were a movable.   (lines 190–6)

To explain the exclamatory 'in good time' in line 194 Oliver provides the following gloss:

Best explained by Schmidt, as equivalent to *à la bonne heure*: an exclamation 'used either to express acquiescence, or astonishment and indignation'. Katherine, punning on 'moved', is expressing all three.

In doing so Oliver follows the consensus among the play's modern editors, who agree in accepting the accuracy of Schmidt's interpretation, though they differ in how they employ modernised punctuation to reflect it. Ann Thompson in her 1984 New Cambridge text, for instance, reads ' "Moved" – in good time!', while the Riverside edition offers 'Mov'd! in good time!', and Brian Morris's 1981

Arden 2 favours 'Mov'd, in good time!' All, however, concur in accompanying 'in good time' with an exclamation mark, while either (like Oliver) transcribing Schmidt's own phrases of explanation in an accompanying note or providing a briefer gloss on the lines of Riverside's 'indeed, forsooth'. Thompson, alone, puzzlingly, sees no need for a note here.

This scholarly agreement confronts Katherina's modern stage interpreters with a tricky technical challenge. That 'in good time' here means 'indeed!' is not a conclusion which most contemporary auditors will reach unaided. As a result, I have heard accomplished actresses phrase those three simple monosyllables in unavailingly emphatic ways as they laboured to convey the required information to their audiences. Performing four hundred-year-old scripts on twenty-first century stages will inevitably pose such problems. But, in this case, is the burden scholars have united in imposing on performers a textually valid one?

Obedience to Schmidt's authority involves in these modernised editions substantial alteration of the First Folio punctuation, which in this line and a half reads: 'Mou'd, in good time, let him that mou'd you hether / Remoue you hence'. The exclamation marks so beloved of modern scholars are therefore an editorial interpolation. In addition, the First Folio's non-committal use of commas leaves open the question of whether 'in good time' is most naturally or most plausibly to be grouped with 'Mou'd' or with the clause that succeeds it. In the light of the First Folio punctuation, the modern conviction that the first of these options is self-evidently correct looks questionable, especially if we go on to ask whether we should accept Schmidt's gloss as the only possible meaning of that key phrase in this speech.

Schmidt's interpretation is paralleled by *OED*'s fourth entry for 'in good time', which explains it 'As an expression of ironical acquiescence, incredulity, amazement, or the like: To be sure! indeed! very well! (Cf. Fr. *à la bonne heure*). *Obs.*' *OED* does offer a Shakespearian exemplification of this sense, but from *The Tempest*, not *The Taming of the Shrew*. In deciding that this meaning is the apposite one for Katherina's line here, Schmidt did not invoke in connection with it three other early modern meanings of the phrase which *OED* documents, all of which were current in the 1590s: (1) 'After the lapse of a suitable interval; in due course or process of time; at a proper time, when it seems good'; (2) 'Soon or early; quickly'; and (3) 'At a right or a seasonable moment; luckily'.[24] If 'in good time' is grouped with the phrase which follows it in Katherina's speech, then the performer can bring one or more of these further meanings tellingly into play. Katherina can then, for example, be rendered as sarcastically demanding: 'let those who brought you here remove you from my sight (and life) as swiftly as possible' (meaning no. 2); and, in addition, it would be easy for an actress simultaneously to invoke meaning no. 1 (i.e. the 'suitable interval' would in this case be as brief as possible) and meaning no. 3 (i.e. such a speedy departure would in her eyes be indeed fortunate and seasonable).

It is not my prime purpose here to argue for the superiority of these other meanings, though I have little doubt that they offer the player more theatrically stimulating fare. What interests me more is the way in which Schmidt's choice of gloss has distorted subsequent commentary on this speech. Schmidt made a debatable decision in favour of the exclusive aptness to the *Shrew* line of one late sixteenth-century meaning of the phrase. The acceptance of that judgement then generated an editorial fixation with the imputed dependence of 'in good time' on the preceding 'Mou'd'. This then blinded scholars to the other phrasing possibilities implicit in the First Folio punctuation (and in the information readily available in *OED*), with the result that all current editions of the play mislead the reader about the performance options implicit in Katherina's retort.

Sophistication in benefiting from the knowledge and skill of lexicographers is one of the foundation-stones on which any major edition of an early modern playscript must be built. But unquestioning reliance upon a particular lexicographer's conclusions is clearly unwise. Similarly, a distinction needs to be drawn between the work of a lexicographer in compiling a dictionary entry and the task of an ed-

itor in designing a note to a passage of dialogue.[25] The lexicographer deals either with single words or brief phrases and must fashion glosses which, while sufficiently precise, have in many instances to answer to a potentially vast range of individual uses of the lemma material. The play editor addresses the specific deployment and potentiality of a word or phrase in an idiosyncratic context within a carefully crafted fictional narrative, the theatrical interpretation of that word or phrase often being susceptible to widely differing performance outcomes. Too often the activity of annotation in modern Shakespeare editions atomizes the text into tiny verbal fragments,[26] which are then treated in isolation from the rest of the dialogue, and which receive glosses, often transcribed with too little caution directly from dictionaries and reference works, which

---

[24] Schmidt records and illustrates, but does not link to this *Shrew* passage, two further Shakespearean meanings for the phrase, which overlap with *OED*'s definitions. These are: 'at the right moment, in good season, not too early and not too late' and 'fortunately, happily, upon a wish' (Alexander Schmidt, *Shakespeare-Lexicon: A Complete Dictionary of All the English Words, Phrases and Constructions in the Works of the Poet*, revised and enlarged by Gregor Sarrazin (Berlin, 1962), vol. 2, p. 1230).

[25] Some commentators come uncomfortably close to conflating the two roles. See, for example, Marvin Spevack's assertion – in 'The Editor as Philologist', *TEXT* 3 (1987), pp. 91–2 – that 'We are editors, but we were not editors, to begin with. We come from no Department of Editing. We are philologists by profession, editors by choice or chance, by nature or necessity. As philologists and editors we practice philology; we deal with language in texts.'

[26] See the comment by Anne Middleton, 'Life in The Margins', pp. 169–170, that 'The very grammar of annotation is strangely evasive: it is phrasal, not clausal, eschewing open predication, and largely confined to the appositive mode. In other words, it is insistently anti-narrative (or counter-narrative) in discursive form, tending to occlude the horizontal coherence of the text for the vertical plenitude of superimposed or parallel forms of information: it adduces endlessly, but it does not explain itself – or, finally, its text.' She goes on to observe that annotation 'lends to the text it elucidates a rich *vertical* density, a thickness of possible referentiality to the "life-world," to other texts, to other discrete points in the text itself, at the cost of repeatedly cutting across the *horizontal* strands of development along which poetic invention and rhetorical development proceed'.

narrow down unacceptably the range of meaning those words can in practice carry on the lips of actors.

Another passage a little later in 2.1 of *The Taming of the Shrew* merits attention. In Oliver's modernization it reads:

PETRUCHIO Thou hast hit it. Come sit on me.
KATHERINA Asses are made to bear, and so are you.
PETRUCHIO Women are made to bear, and so are you.
KATHERINA No such jade as you, if me you mean.
PETRUCHIO Alas, good Kate, I will not burden thee,
 For knowing thee to be but young and light.
KATHERINA Too light for such a swain as you to catch, ...   (lines 199–205)

Annotation clearly needs to alert readers to the multiple meanings some key words bear here. Thompson in her New Cambridge edition, for example, informs us that 'bear' in line 200 means 'bear loads', while in line 201 she identifies 'children' as the implicit object of 'bear'. But more senses of the verb are in play here than this pair of notes acknowledges. In line 201, for instance, a relevant meaning for 'bear' has to be 'carry a man's weight during sexual intercourse'. Brian Morris in the 1981 Arden 2 edition essentially agrees with Thompson on line 200, where he offers 'carry burdens' as his paraphrase, but copes better than she does with line 201, where he offers: 'bear children (with a second sexual sense evidenced by Petruchio's "burden" in l.203)'. Oliver essentially echoes Morris by providing at line 201: 'Petruchio adds two further senses to the one used by Katherine: (i) bear children; (ii) bear the weight of a lover (as in the Nurse's characteristic would-be jest, *Romeo*, 2. 5. 76)'. Frances Dolan in her 1996 edition follows this pattern, but conveys the information via a note on line 200: 'carry (with puns in the following lines suggesting "bear children" and "support a man during sexual intercourse")'.[27]

The three annotators who identify the sexual meaning of 'bear' here agree that it is only active from line 201 onwards, and that it is therefore the man who introduces it into the sparring. What would justify such a belief? Why would we agree to rule out the possibility that Katherina could also be invoking it in line 200? There are numerous ways in which her 'Asses are made to bear, and so are you' line could be inflected on stage so as to invoke the 'woman on top' topos[28] – i.e. she is asserting that in any relationship between them, including the sexual one Petruchio may have in mind, nature has ensured that she will unfailingly be the dominant partner (or will, in a multitude of senses, always be astride him). If a performer of the role chose that option, then Petruchio's reply might open up further possibilities in his use of 'bear' than any of our editors have recognized. He would be both reasserting male sexual dominance and insisting that it is woman's assigned fate to cope with, and submit to, male supremacy in general. In other words, 'bear' meaning 'endure, tolerate, reconcile oneself to' (*OED*, *v*, 8) must also be relevant to this exchange.

So current annotation of the passage both unnecessarily restricts the range of the verb's potential meanings and is also inappropriately doctrinaire in legislating about when particular meanings might or, indeed, must be brought into play. At some level implicit assumptions may be at work here about Petruchio's exploiting male prerogatives to be the looser-tongued of the two. But nothing in the words themselves rules out the possibility that Katherina could be playing on the sexual meaning of 'bear' from her first use of it. Annotation which seeks to tie down the line-by-line meaning of the punning in passages like this is likely to go astray in this way. This scene will work in one way, if Katherina in line 200 intends only to insult Petruchio's intelligence, but then discovers that by her unwary use of 'bear' she has allowed him the chance to shift the dialogue into sex talk, and quite differently, if Katherina is from the beginning a self-aware punster, fully in control of the verb's sexual register as well as one or more of its other meanings. The printed text tolerates both of

---

27 Frances E. Dolan (ed.), *William Shakespeare, 'The Taming of the Shrew': Texts and Contexts* (Boston and New York, 1996), p. 79.
28 See Natalie Zemon Davis, *Society and Culture in Early Modern France* (Oxford, 1987), pp. 124–51.

these performance options, as well as others. The theatrically astute tactic here would be to provide a single note which explores, for the complete exchange, the range of meanings available for 'bear', but then makes it clear that deciding exactly when different combinations of these are in play is not something about which it is possible to legislate conclusively, but about which firm, inventive decisions will need to be taken in order to produce a performance of the scene. Clinging to the desire to be decisive line-by-line risks radically misrepresenting the true situation to an edition's readers and potentially deprives them of some of the key, pro-active, imaginative pleasures which exploring a playscript, in rehearsal or in an armchair, can otherwise offer them.

Two further moments in this scene, both involving stage directions, are worth pausing over. The first appears as follows in the Wells/Taylor *Complete Works*:[29]

BAPTISTA (*to Hortensio*)
Well, go with me, and be not so discomfited.
Proceed in practice with my younger daughter.
She's apt to learn, and thankful for good turns.
Signor Petruccio, will you go with us,
Or shall I send my daughter Kate to you?
PETRUCCIO
I pray you do.   *Exeunt all but Petruccio*
            I'll attend her here,
And woo her with some spirit when she comes.
                                    (lines 160–9)

As the *Textual Companion*[30] to the *Complete Works* records, the '*Exeunt*' direction has been adjusted from the First Folio's '*Exit. Manet Petruchio.*' It has also been repositioned. The equivalent direction in the First Folio is placed before 'I pray you do'. This is clearly unsatisfactory, since, if interpreted literally, it makes Baptista ask a question and then not pause to hear the reply. The First Folio, of course, includes numerous instances where stage directions are positioned, often because of lay-out considerations, in ways which are not logical in performance terms. Deciding on the best alternative positioning for this stage direction is, however, more difficult. The *Complete Works* solution is playable, but so also

are the two following alternatives (both to be found in modern editions):

I pray you do. I'll attend her here,
And woo her with some spirit when she comes.
                        Exeunt all but Petruccio

I pray you do. I'll attend her here –
                        Exeunt all but Petruccio
And woo her with some spirit when she comes.

In his Oxford Shakespeare edition H. J. Oliver strongly favours the second of these, underpinning his reorganization of the text with this comment: 'Petruchio speaks the words "I pray you do. I'll attend her here" as Baptista leaves, and completes the second sentence when Baptista is out of hearing.' That his version is an alteration of the First Folio lay-out is recorded in the edition's textual collation, but not mentioned in this note, which consequently does not explicitly admit the possibility of other views. As so often, one is left wondering what could justify such editorial confidence. Each of the three versions above is likely to generate somewhat different effects in performance. If the complete couplet, for instance, is spoken to Baptista, then it is most likely that its tone will remain confident, even boastful. If the last line and a half of it are spoken as part of the soliloquy, then it is open to the actor, among other possibilities, to begin to adopt a more ruminative tone, and even, as some modern actors do, suggest a character needing to improvise a fireproof strategy quickly in order to cope with a challenge for which he feels less than fully prepared – something Petruchio has not allowed Baptista to glimpse.[31] Once again, editors

29 Stanley Wells and Gary Taylor (eds). *Complete Works*, p. 41.
30 Stanley Wells and Gary Taylor with John Jowett and William Montgomery, *William Shakespeare: A Textual Companion* (Oxford, 1987), p. 173.
31 Ralph Alan Cohen also comments on this stage direction, but raises a different query about it, in 'Looking for Cousin Ferdinand: The Value of F1 Stage Directions for a Production of *The Taming of the Shrew*', in Laurie E. Maguire and Thomas L. Berger (eds.), *Textual Formations and Reformations* (Newark, 1998), pp. 275–6. Elsewhere in his article, Cohen makes a series of important points about the ways in which editorial

should respect the text's openness and not seek to impose their own preferences as if they were the only legitimate interpretation.

A more intricate set of performance choices arises from the positioning of a stage direction later in the scene. This is the sequence in the Wells/Taylor version:

PETRUCCIO
> Come, come, you wasp, i'faith you are too angry.

KATHERINE
> If I be waspish, best beware my sting.

PETRUCCIO
> My remedy is then to pluck it out.

KATHERINE
> Ay, if the fool could find it where it lies.

PETRUCCIO
> Who knows not where a wasp does its sting?
> In his tail.

KATHERINE
>   In his tongue.

PETRUCCIO
>   Whose tongue?

KATHERINE
> Yours, if you talk of tales, and so farewell.

PETRUCCIO
> What, with my tongue in your tail? Nay, come again,
> Good Kate, I am a gentleman.

KATHERINE
>   That I'll try.
>   *She strikes him*

PETRUCCIO
> I swear I'll cuff you if you strike again.

>   (lines 209–18)

This reproduces, as do all recent editions, the First Folio positioning of this stage direction. In 1623 the key passage was printed as follows:

> *Kate.* Yours if you talke of tales, and so farewell.
> *Pet.* What with my tongue in your taile.
> Nay, come again, good *Kate,* I am a Gentleman,
> *Kate.* That Ile trie.   *she strikes him*
> *Pet.* I sweare Ile cuffe you, if you strike againe.

This makes perfectly good performance sense and interestingly separates the moment of maximum provocation by Petruchio – his lewd 'What, with my tongue in your tail?' – by a line and a half from the moment at which she strikes him. One ex-

trapolation from this might be a Katherina who, allowed a little thinking time, only decides to revenge herself with a blow once apparently reassured by Petruchio's 'Good Kate, I am a gentleman' that she can do so with impunity, since gentlemen do not strike ladies – a deduction swiftly proved false by his next speech. The First Folio's lay-out, however, with characteristic economy positions the stage direction in a space towards the right-hand margin which would otherwise be empty. We may wonder, therefore, whether it is a totally reliable guide to the only or best moment at which Katherina should strike Petruchio. If an exit earlier in the scene arrives, as we have seen, too soon in the First Folio text, might a blow at this point be cued too late? Certainly the play's performance history records other solutions here. I will sketch just one of them. In this version Petruchio's aggressive 'tongue in your tail' line leaves Katherina speechless and only able to express her outraged feelings by lashing out at him. She then begins to leave, and he attempts to prevent this happening ('Nay, come again') by reassuring her that she need not fear he will retaliate with a blow of his own ('Good Kate, I am a gentleman'). Emboldened by this reassurance, Katherina returns, but only to test his promise by striking again ('That I'll try') – a possibility he had not foreseen and which he heads off by swiftly rescinding his previous promise. The verbal form in which he does this acquires added meaning in this reading. His statement that 'I swear I'll cuff you if you strike *again*' specifically wards off a repetition of the aggression in which she has already indulged once. No edition I have consulted sees any need to comment here. But silence means that it is taken as read that the 1623 siting of the stage direction is incontestably correct. This has to be an unsatisfactory state of affairs.

The final category of problem I wish to highlight can be illustrated by recent editors' annotation of the opening movement of 5.1 of *Measure for Measure*. The opening speeches run as follows in the Wells/Taylor *Complete Works*:

---

tradition has mishandled stage directions in this play through a lack of careful thought about their performance implications.

DUKE (*to Angelo*)
　My very worthy cousin, fairly met.
　(*To Escalus*) Our old and faithful friend, we are glad
　　to see you.
ANGELO *and* ESCALUS
　Happy return be to your royal grace.
DUKE
　Many and hearty thankings to you both.
　We have made enquiry of you, and we hear
　Such goodness of your justice that our soul
　Cannot but yield you forth to public thanks,
　Forerunning more requital.
ANGELO　　　　　　　　You make my bonds still greater.
DUKE
　O, your desert speaks loud, and I should wrong it
　To lock it in the wards of covert bosom,
　When it deserves with characters of brass
　A forted residence 'gainst the tooth of time
　And razure of oblivion.　　　　　　　(lines 1–13)

The Duke's 'our soul/Cannot but yield you forth to public thanks,/Forerunning more requital' (6–8) prompts a minimalist response from J. M. Nosworthy in his 1969 New Penguin edition. He singles out 'Forerunning more requital' and paraphrases it as 'preceding other rewards', while offering no other interventions. Brian Gibbons in his 1991 New Cambridge edition finds the passage as a whole perplexing and accordingly comments on it at slightly greater length: 'Contorted expression presumably meaning "cannot but concede to public demand by handing you over to be thanked by them, before I myself give you further reward"'. N. W. Bawcutt, in his 1991 Oxford Shakespeare text, is also more interventionist than Nosworthy. He offers two notes, the first of which takes as its lemma 'yield...thanks' and reads: 'This seems a slightly cumbersome way of saying 'thank you in public', but the formality may be deliberate: their merit is so great that he is compelled to make a public affirmation although it may embarrass their modesty'. He then also glosses 'Forerunning more requital' as 'preceding a greater reward to be made later'.

The puzzle here is that none of our annotators responds to the equivocating ironies in the Duke's speech. In effect, they gloss it as Angelo and Escalus might decode it. But the audience possesses knowledge neither of these characters is privy to,

and the fact of that 'discrepant awareness'[32] has to be central to the task of explicating the theatrical power of the Duke's language here and throughout this final act. We know that the Duke is fully acquainted with the extent of Angelo's duplicity and have been led to expect a culminating confrontation between them as the Duke resumes his powers and unmasks offenders. What we do not yet know is how and when that confrontation will be brought about. In such circumstances spectators are likely to be alert to undercurrents and hints in the Duke's words which none of the characters on stage will be able to identify. For instance, 'Forerunning more requital' may suggest to Angelo and Escalus the promise of greater rewards to come; but, since 'requital' also meant 'punishment' in early modern English, the phrase contains another, darker layer of implication which only the audience can discern.

Intricacies of this kind form the characteristic currency of the Duke's speech here. When, for instance, he informs Angelo that his proven qualities warrant being recorded 'with characters of brass' so that they will never be forgotten, more is involved than any recent annotator manages to convey. Bawcutt, for instance, glosses 'characters of brass' as 'bronze letters (of the sort found on a tomb or monument)', while J. W. Lever in the 1965 Arden 2 edition comments on lines 11–13: 'The inspiration is Horace, *Odes*, III. xxx: '*Exegi monumentum aere perennius*', and Ovid, *Metam.*, xv. 871 ff.; a Renaissance commonplace for eternal fame'. Gibbons synthesizes their efforts by annotating 'deserves...oblivion' thus: 'deserves to be fortified against the assaults of time and fallible human

---

[32] The term was introduced by Bertrand Evans, *Shakespeare's Comedies* (Oxford, 1960), pp. viii–ix. (It was subsequently adopted, with due acknowledgement to Evans, by Manfred Pfister, *The Theory and Analysis of Drama* (Cambridge, 1988), translated by John Halliday, pp. 49–55.) In his chapter on the play, Evans, p. 207, identifies the key fact about Act 5 which our editors neglect: 'Dependent upon discrepancies in awareness for its very existence, the denouement of *Measure for Measure*, in both its workmanship and its effects achieved by workmanship, has few peers and no superiors in Shakespearian comedy.'

memory by being recorded in engraved brass (with allusions to Horace, *Odes* III. 30, Ovid, *Metamorphoses* XV. 871ff.)'. But this misses the real performance riches here. The key question is what these long-lived inscriptions will record. As only the audience is positioned to recognize, they promise to be the perfectly fitting memorialization for Angelo's misdeeds, since brass was already, as *OED* (*n.* and *a*, A1b) informs us, 'taken as a type of hardness or insensitivity; impudence, effrontery, nerve' – qualities comprehensively incarnated by a deputy, who has proven commandingly corrupt in his discharge of the supreme power entrusted to him and confident of exploiting his reputation for probity and icy virtue to mask the true nature of his deeds, when others try to bring him to account. Such extremity of corruption does indeed, as the Duke insists, deserve to be recorded in a manner which can never be erased (lines 12–13), but as an instance of infamy, and not (as Angelo and Escalus will hear it) as a merited tribute to Angelo's exemplary discharge of supreme authority. Glossing 'razure' (line 13), therefore, as simply 'obliteration, effacement' (Lever) or 'act of effacement or obliteration. See Sonnet 122. 7' (Gibbons) does not begin to address what is really dramatically at issue here.

At this point Bawcutt proves more active than elsewhere. His note on 'razure of oblivion' reads: 'erasure or loss of reputation brought about because the person concerned is no longer remembered. In lines 12–14 the Duke echoes the language of Renaissance poets who promise to immortalize their subjects (see Sonnets 19 and 55). The lines are addressed specifically to Angelo, and are heavily ironic.' He thus cues his readers that, at least in these lines, the Duke's language is registering on a number of levels simultaneously. But, given his ignoring of identical phenomena earlier, this comment might, for a literal-minded reader, prove misleading – i.e. Bawcutt could be read as saying that only in those three lines is this kind of irony at work, whereas in fact it is a sustained feature of the Duke's verbal manoeuvring throughout this section of the final act.

The stage history of *Measure for Measure* over the last century has brought us a bewildering array of different readings of the Duke – from figures touched with divine authority via earnestly self-doubting refugees from power to suavely duplicitous authoritarian despots. Each actor of the role, in performing the opening of Act 5, has had to negotiate his own way of turning the 'discrepant awarenesses' built into the script to the advantage of his interpretation. There have been versions in which these ironic counter-currents which Angelo and Escalus cannot detect have been only lightly and teasingly touched on by the player, leaving the spectator unsure as to their ultimate significance. There have been other performances in which they have been inflected with a sense of threat and an apparent promise that an eye will be exacted for an eye, so that the eventual ending in forgiveness emerges unexpectedly for first-time viewers. And, in yet others, the predominant impression has been of a Duke delighted to have this degree of covert superiority of knowledge – and, therefore, political and moral advantage – over his chief ministers. Whatever the particular actors' agendas, all have had to work out their own solutions about how to manage and exploit the gap between how their fellow characters are positioned to respond to them and the ways in which spectators will be hearing and deciphering their words. It is therefore puzzling to find that the editions we have sampled remain deaf to this fundamental aspect of Act 5's language and plotting. But, to map such a theatrical phenomenon adequately, annotators would need to be in the habit of distinguishing systematically between these two levels of communication, and that is not the case in any recent scholarly edition of *Measure for Measure*.[33]

---

[33] A recent schools edition, dedicated to enabling schoolchildren to experiment with the translation of Shakespearian scripts into performance, proves more responsive in this respect than its more august rivals. The Cambridge School Shakespeare text of the play, edited by Jane Coles and Rex Gibson (Cambridge, 1993), heads Act 5 (p. 140) with the comment that 'The Duke's language in Act 5 is rich in dramatic irony. His words carry a deeper meaning for the audience than is perceived by Angelo.' It then suggests the following class exercise:

Traditional annotation of Shakespearian playscripts has remained closely tied to the lexicographer's skills, and resistance to a serious change in its priorities is often based on the claim that the inexperienced reader's first need is the decoding of everything in the language which will appear archaic, obscure or rebarbative to them. My central contention here is that an adequate performance of that task indispensably requires a kind of theatrical literacy and sophistication from editors which has not always been in evidence. Unless annotators take fully on board the need to be alert to the theatrical implications and potentialities of these playscripts, they will often seriously mislead their readers as to the significance and reverberations of the words and passages they single out for attention. We have three major single-play series – Arden 3, the New Cambridge Shakespeare, and the Oxford Shakespeare – currently in energetic competition with one another, and at times it is difficult to tell them conclusively apart.[34] But a series which set out, as a key priority, to provide a truly theatrical annotation of the plays' language could achieve real distinctiveness and finally, in the process, tackle a task which should be absolutely central to scholarly engagement with these scripts.

One last thought. John Kerrigan has recently argued that 'Editions of the *Sonnets* differ because they are produced by particular readers, with different thoughts about other readers.'[35] In the words of Stephen A. Barney, 'Commentary accommodates a text to a presumed audience.'[36] A long-settled scholarly tradition ensures that major editions of Shakespeare are primarily targeted at an audience of readers, not actors or directors. The new interest in performance issues proclaimed by our current Shakespeare series means that some care is now taken in most editions to chronicle, query, criticize – and even, occasionally, celebrate – some of the realizations the stage has conjured from the texts across the centuries. But the editions, and the annotation they offer, are not themselves designed in any concerted way to be, in one of their dimensions, a dialogue with potential performers and directors, aiming to stimulate and facilitate fresh

performances, whether in real auditoria or in theatres of the imagination. Philip Brett has complained, in terms similar to much of my argument here, that editorial treatment of early modern music is often too doctrinaire and prescriptive and that 'what the performer needs from the editor is surely an open discussion of the possibilities and a measured judgement as to which courses of action are preferable'.[37] In the case of the music of Byrd and Tallis, Lawes and Tomkins, Purcell and Blow, however, editors at least take it as given that part of their mission is to encourage and influence new performances of the compositions on which they labour. It is a bizarre anomaly that this should so emphatically not be the case with the editing of early modern drama. Correspondingly, we will know that our editions have become truly performance-alert, when it is clear that annotators regard themselves as communicating, not just with armchair readers and desk-bound students, but with people interested in realizing afresh the potentiality in performance of these much-debated words upon the page.

'One person reads the Duke's lines 1–18, pausing at each punctuation mark. At each pause, a second person, as Angelo, interprets the remark. The third person states the Duke's hidden meaning, for example:

Person 1 (The Duke): 'My very worthy cousin'.

Person 2 (Angelo): 'He thinks highly of me, like a close relative.'

Person 3 (the Duke's secret thoughts): 'Worthy – of little worth!''

In my earlier essay on this subject (see note 16 *supra*), p. 300, the Cambridge School Shakespeare edition of *All's Well That Ends Wells* was found to be comparably superior to its competitors in its responsiveness to a staging difficulty in that play.

[34] For further thoughts on this subject, see my 'An End to Shakespearean Editing?', *Cambridge Quarterly*, forthcoming.

[35] John Kerrigan, 'The Editor as Reader: Constructing Renaissance Texts', in James Raven, Helen Small and Naomi Tadmor (eds.), *The Practice and Representation of Reading in England* (Cambridge, 1996), p. 120.

[36] Stephen A. Barney, 'Introduction', in Stephen A. Barney (ed.), *Annotation and Its Texts* (Oxford, 1991), p. viii.

[37] Philip Brett, 'Text, Context, and the Early Music Editor', in Nicholas Kenyon (ed.), *Authenticity and Early Music: A Symposium* (Oxford, 1988), p. 98.

TITUS ANDRONICUS:
THE CLASSICAL PRESENCE

NIALL RUDD

This paper has to do with the play's *Romanitas*. By that I mean, not its tenuous relation to historical fact, but rather the characters' awareness of Rome's cultural traditions.[1] The plural is needed, because there were two such traditions. When, as Horace said, 'Captive Greece made her rough conqueror captive' (*Epistles* 2.1.156), she brought to Latium her poetry and mythology (along with much else). The point is so familiar that one tends to forget its exceptional nature. In the annals of imperialism how many victors have learned the language of the vanquished and set about acquiring their culture? From Homer and his successors the Romans learned about Priam, Hecuba, and the rest; and when, with their growing sense of power, they looked for a pedigree that would rival the Greeks' in age and prestige, they found it in Troy. The link was supplied by the story of Aeneas, that was eventually given its classic form by Virgil. But first the contribution of Aeneas had to be reconciled with the other, native, tradition that Rome was founded by her eponymous ancestor Romulus.[2] This was achieved by making Aeneas' descendant Ilia ('Trojan woman') Romulus' mother. Rome's subsequent fortunes, as they passed gradually from legend to history, were recounted by Livy, and the two traditions together were presented by Ovid and Plutarch.

As a result, when Titus makes his entry in the play, he can salute Jupiter Capitolinus – the central symbol of Rome's power (1.1.80), and then, without any sense of incongruity, go on to speak of his own 'five and twenty valiant sons, / Half of the number that King Priam had' (82–3). We have

already heard something of the moral context in which he is expected to operate. The senatorial order is seen as the noble defender of justice (1.1.2), and its members are addressed as the guardians of virtue, justice, continence, and nobility to which Jupiter's temple is consecrated (1.1.14–15). The speeches of Saturninus and Bassianus are, of course, pieces of undisguised flattery. But they do reflect the standards which the senate was supposed to uphold[3] – standards that form an ironic background to what is about to happen.

We have also been told something about Titus. His surname is Pius, and he has been chosen Emperor 'For many good and great deserts to Rome' (1.1.23–4). In view of the numerous Virgilian

---

[1] In the Introduction to his commentary (Cambridge 1994), p. 37 Alan Hughes speaks of 'a modern audience's resentment of classical allusions'. Perhaps he's right; but here we are concerned with the young Shakespeare, who was still in his twenties and was doubtless showing off. Greene called him 'an upstart crow'; but the taunt was something of a boomerang, because it was filched from Horace, who had warned Celsus about the danger of stolen plumage (*Epist*.1.3.15–20). Horace himself had raided the capacious wardrobe of Aesop (Phaedrus 1.3; Babrius 72). I am not qualified to judge how far the allusions, especially in Act 1, indicate the influence of Peele.
For the unhistorical history see T. J. B. Spencer, 'Shakespeare and the Elizabethan Romans', *Shakespeare Survey 10*, 1957, 27–38.

[2] The English pronunciation of 'Romulus' tends to disguise the meaning of his name , i.e. 'Roman'; English also reverses the quantity of the e in 'Remus', which was short.

[3] Cicero, e.g. laid it down that 'the order should be morally faultless and an example to the rest of the citizens' (*Laws* 3.28). For Rome's moral vocabulary see the index of D. C. Earl, *The Moral and Political Tradition of Rome* (London, 1967).

analogies that follow it is fair to see 'Pius' as a reminiscence of *pius Aeneas*, but the use of Pius as an emperor's *surname* is made easier by the fact that from AD 138–61 Rome was ruled by Antoninus Pius. The origins of 'Andronicus' are less clear, but perhaps the important thing to remember is that 'Conqueror of men' was a suitable name for a victorious general.[4]

Before taking any political action, however, Titus must discharge a religious duty: he must bury his dead sons. As he has just compared himself to Priam, one recalls that Priam's last achievement in the *Iliad* was to recover the body of Hector for decent burial. Likewise in Virgil's epic, before entering the underworld Aeneas must bury his comrade Misenus (6.149–235). Later the Sibyl explains that, unless they have been buried, the souls of the dead cannot be transported across the Styx: *centum errant annos volitantque haec litora circum* (329) – 'They wander for a hundred years and *hover* about these *shores*'. That is what Titus has in mind when he says 'Why suffer'st thou thy sons unburied yet / To *hover* on the dreadful *shore* of Styx?' The theme of burial points forward to the altercation about the dead Mutius (352–95), and ultimately to the fate of Tamora at the end of the play.

Respect for the dead takes a more sinister form when Lucius demands that Tamora's son, Alarbus, be hacked to pieces and sacrificed *Ad manes fratrum* (101) – 'to the spirits of our brothers... / That so the *shadows* be not unappeas'd' (103). George Hunter[5] refers us to an early precedent, related in Livy 1.25.12, where the last of the Horatii kills the last of the Curiatii, saying 'Duos *fratrum manibus* dedi: tertium causae belli huiusce, ut Romanus Albano imperet, dabo' ('I have offered two *to the spirits of my brothers*, I shall offer the third to the purpose of this war, that Roman should rule over Alban'). Ovid (*Met.*13.443ff.) tells how earlier still Achilles' ghost demanded that Polyxena, Hecuba's daughter, be sacrificed to his *spirit* (*manes*); the Greeks duly obeyed the pitiless *shadow* (*umbrae*). The words 'spirit' and 'shadow' are not in Golding's version (529–39). As Lucius indicated, there might be harmful consequences if the shadows were not appeased;[6] but his demand is made in

excessively bloodthirsty terms. When Titus consents, Tamora makes a passionate and reasoned protest in words that foreshadow Portia's speech in *The Merchant of Venice*. Titus is somewhat uneasy, and with half an apology ('pardon me') he insists that Lucius and his brothers are asking 'religiously' for a sacrifice 'T'appease the groaning *shadows* that are gone' (129). This and Lucius' impatient pressure justify Tamora's bitter response 'O cruel, irreligious piety!' Andronicus has disgraced his name. Chiron adds 'Was never *Scythia* half so barbarous!' In Seneca's *Troades* Andromache, hearing of Astyanax's death, cries 'What Colchian, what *Scythian* with his shifting home has committed such a crime?' (1104–5). This is the verdict of one of 'the barbarous Goths' (28), whose hands so far are clean. Demetrius, however, now makes a step on the downward path, reminding his mother of Hecuba who took a 'sharp revenge / Upon the *Thracian tyrant* in his tent' (140f.). 'Sharp revenge' is a pregnant phrase, for Golding, describing Hecuba's revenge on Polymestor for murdering her son, says she 'Did in the traitor's face bestowe *her nayles*, and scratched out / His eyes' (*Met.* 13.673–4).[7] 'The *Thracian tyrant*' also comes from Golding, who at v. 678 translates Ovid (565) quite literally: 'The *Thracians* at theyr *Tyrannes* harme for anger waxing wood'. Like Shakespeare's Goths, the Thracian race is also *pronum... in Venerem* (Ovid, *Met.*6.459–60).

As his sons are buried Titus delivers a short but noble speech of committal (151–9). Soon after, he is greeted by Marcus, who speaks of 'this funeral

---

[4] For other observations on the names see R. A. Law, 'The Roman Background to *Titus Andronicus*', *Studies in Philology* 40, 1943, 145–53, and J. Bate in his admirable commentary (London 1995) pp. 93–4. In what follows I adopt Bate's lineation. All line references are to Bate's edition.

[5] G. K. Hunter in J. C. Gray (ed.), *Mirror up to Shakespeare* (Toronto, 1984), pp. 184–5.

[6] See Ovid, *Fasti* 2.533ff. with J. G. Frazer's notes (vol. 2 of his great commentary, pp. 431ff.).

[7] The episode is referred to in Euripides, *Hecuba* 37–41, 188–90; see also Seneca, *Troades* 191–96. E. Jones maintains that Shakespeare knew Euripides through Erasmus' Latin translation (*The Origins of Shakespeare* (Oxford, 1977), pp. 90–105).

pomp [presumably in the sense of the Latin *pompa* 'procession'] / That hath aspired to Solon's happiness' (179–80). In Herodotus 1.32 Solon tells Croesus that a fortunate man should not be called 'blessed' until his life is finished. Shakespeare could have found this in Plutarch's *Life of Solon* (North's translation) 'When the goddes have continued a man's good fortune to his end, then we think that man happy and blessed, and never before' (Nonesuch ed. 1929, vol. 1, p. 270). Marcus' elliptical reference shows his erudition and his wish to console Titus, but it rather misrepresents Solon; for it suggests that the sons have achieved happiness simply in virtue of being killed. Solon's dictum applies only to those who have been fortunate throughout life and in their death.[8]

When Saturninus declares he will marry Titus' daughter, Lavinia (244–7), he bids Tamora, who is obviously glowering, to brighten up: 'Thou com'st not to be made a scorn in Rome' (269). Bearing in mind that Tamora has already said 'We are brought to Rome / To beautify thy triumphs' (112–13), one suspects that Shakespeare is thinking of Cleopatra, who was determined not to be displayed in a triumph (Livy, fr.54 *non triumphabor*, reflected in Plutarch's *Life of Antony* 84.4; cf. Horace, *Odes* 1.37.30–2 with Porphyrion's Greek note); one thinks of her defiant speech in *Antony and Cleopatra* 5.2.55ff. 'Shall they hoist me up, / And show me to the shouting varletry / Of censuring Rome?' (cf. ibid. 209–13). Saturninus then makes a noble gesture '*Ransomeless* here we set our prisoners free' (278). A similar gesture was made by Scipio as recorded in Plutarch, *Life of Scipio Africanus*: 'Scipio gave them [all the Spanish prisoners] libertie to depart *without* paying of *ransome*' (North, 1603, p. 1088).

In consenting to the marriage of Lavinia to Saturninus, Titus has taken no account of Bassianus, who breaks in 'Lord Titus, by your leave, this maid is mine' (280). Marcus supports him, appealing to one of the fundamental principles of Roman law, viz. *suum cuique* 'to each his own'[9] – a phrase that, like several other references to law and justice, sounds an ironical note in a play where the only law is the *lex talionis*. This interchange recalls

a much earlier dispute in which another Lavinia had been betrothed to Turnus (*Aen*.7.366) but was then assigned by her father to Aeneas (*Aen*.7.268–73; cf. *coniuge praerepta* in 9.138) – an action which precipitated a full-scale war: '*pactaque* furit pro *coniuge* Turnus' as Ovid says in *Met*.14.451 ('And Turnus fights furiously for his *promised bride*'). Doubtless the Virgilian precedent was responsible for the name of Titus' daughter, who was '*betroth'd*' to Bassianus (290). As Lavinia is dragged away, Mutius tries to prevent pursuit and is killed by Titus for dishonouring his father. The episode may be set beside a famous case at the beginning of the republic. Brutus, the first consul, superintended the execution of his two sons, who had plotted to restore the Tarquins. Livy (2.5.8) mentions the anguish on the father's face, but does not suggest for a moment that he had any choice.[10] Titus' action, however, was committed in a fit of rage arising from wounded *amour-propre*.

After this fracas Saturninus decides that he doesn't want Lavinia after all, and turns to 'lovely Tamora, queen of the Goths / That like the stately *Phoebe* 'mongst her *nymphs* / Dost *overshine* the gallant'st dames of Rome' (320–2). It has been noticed that in *Aen*.1.498ff. (in Phaer's translation, first published in 1573) the lovely Dido is 'most like vnto *Diana bright* when she to hunt goth out ... / Whom thousands of the lady *Nimphes* await to do her will, / She on her armes her quiuer beares, and all them *overshines*'.[11] But Virgil in turn is indebted to Homer, who says that Nausicaa, like Artemis, outshone her attendants (*Odyssey* 6.109).

Lucius now begs that Mutius be buried with his brothers in the family tomb (352–3). Titus angrily refuses – the tomb is for 'none basely slain in brawls' (358). He seems unaware that it takes

---

[8] The usual form of the dictum in modern times is 'Call no man happy until he is dead'.

[9] See, e.g., Cicero, *De Natura Deorum* 3.38 (*Iustitia, quae suum cuique distribuit*), Justinian, *Digest* (Ulpian) 1.1.10.

[10] The gentle Virgil shows his unease: see *Aen*.6.819–23. A less famous case is that of Titus Manlius, who had his son executed for disobeying orders (Livy 8.7).

[11] Diana (Phoebe) was also, of course, the Moon goddess.

two to make a brawl. As the wrangle continues, Marcus appeals to Titus as 'more than *half my soul*' (378). The phrase comes, directly or otherwise, from Horace, who in *Odes* 1.3.8 addresses Virgil as *animae dimidium meae*. As so often, the imitator goes one step further than his source: '*more than half my soul*'; similarly Lavinia loses hands as well as tongue. Marcus then pleads 'Thou art a Roman, be not barbarous' (383), and finally he cites the action of the Greeks who on Ulysses' advice buried Ajax (384–6). This information could have come from Lambinus' note on Horace, *Satires* 2.3.187: 'Ulysses . . . Agamemnonem . . . exoravit ut Aiacem sineret sepeliri' – 'Ulysses prevailed on Agamemnon to allow Ajax to be buried'. Given the focus of this paper, it is fair to point out that the appeals to Titus' Graeco-Roman heritage are placed at the climax of the speech and succeed in tipping the scales. Saturninus, cast in the role of Agamemnon, agrees with ill grace.

In the short scene that follows Saturninus accuses his brother of 'rape' in the sense of 'abduction' (409), as in Claudian's *De Raptu Proserpinae*. This somewhat absurd overstatement prefaces the theme of 'rape' in the full sense, acted out in the rape of Lavinia. The ensuing altercation is stilled by 'the subtle Queen of Goths', who excuses Titus for not dissembling his fury and then urges Saturninus to dissemble his, whispering 'I'll find a day to massacre them all' (455). As a result, the hunt scheduled for the morrow arouses feelings of foreboding, whether or not one remembers *Aeneid* 4.

In 1.1.500 Aaron speaks for the first time. He proves to be quite at ease in Graeco-Roman culture, declaring in Marlovian hyperbole that his mistress is climbing Olympus' top, and that she is bound to him as tightly as Prometheus is to Caucasus (516) – a rather odd simile, foreshadowing the brutal instances of bondage that are to follow. Tamora is likened to a goddess, Semiramis, a nymph, and a siren – all alluring females, and the last, at least, potentially murderous.[12] Aaron then separates Chiron and Demetrius who are quarrelling over Lavinia. He does so by diverting them from adulterous seduction (for Lavinia is as chaste as Lucrece) to joint rape, Lavinia being seen as

'a dainty doe' (617; cf.593 and 2.1.26). Secrecy must be observed, but as 'The Emperor's court is like the house of Fame' (626) – Ovid, *Met.*12.39ff. *via* Chaucer[13] – the youths are to take Lavinia quietly into a wood, where they will be 'shadow'd from heaven's *eye*' (630). This, of course, is quite intelligible in itself, but it also represents the remnant of an earlier allusion in which Bassianus is visualized as wearing 'Vulcan's badge' (589), i.e. horns. The adultery of Mars and Venus was reported to Vulcan (Venus' husband) by the sun who, as the original spy in the sky, sees everything – a famous story from the *Odyssey* 8.266ff. recounted by Ovid in *Met.*4.171ff. Ovid does not refer to an eye, but Golding (206–8) does: 'It is reported how this god [i.e. the Sunne] did first of all espie, / (For everie thing in Heaven and Earth is open to his *eie*) / How Venus with the warlike Mars advoutrie did commit'.

Demetrius claims that until (right or wrong) he satisfies his lust he is going through hell. 'Be it right or wrong' seems to be the intended meaning of *Sit fas aut nefas* (633).The normal Latin for this would be *sive fas sit sive nefas*, and a trawl through CD Rom PHI has produced no example of the phrase given in the text; so the writer may be improvising. In the words *per Stygia, per manes vehor* (635) *Stygia* seems intelligible enough, though I have not noticed this neuter plural adjective being used as a noun = 'the Stygian regions'. The reading of F4 (*Per Styga*) 'through the Styx' deserves consideration. The words will then be scanned quite regularly as the beginning of an English iambic pentameter, like the shorter phrase *Sit fas aut nefas* in 633. The source is acknowledged to be Seneca's iambic trimeter *per Styga, per amnes igneos, amens sequar* ('Through the Styx, through the river of fire, I will follow in my madness') from *Phaedra* 1180, spoken by the heroine in an agony of guilt. A copyist unfamiliar with the Greek accusative singular

---

[12] Goddesses could be cruel; Semiramis was a half-legendary Assyrian queen who used to murder her lovers (Diodorus Siculus 2.13.4); nymphs could also be dangerous, as Hylas found (Apollonius, *Argonautica* 1.1207ff.); the Sirens need no comment.

[13] Virgil, *Aen.*4.173ff., the original source, mentions no house.

might have altered *Styga* into a Latin neuter plural (cf. the misprint in Hughes's note), whereas the opposite process would have been most unlikely. It seems more probable, however, that the change was made deliberately by Shakespeare; for the general *Stygia* would have combined with the general *manes* ('spirits'), which he substituted for the other river (i.e. Phlegethon).

In 2.2 Tamora, who is now the emperor's wife, conveniently forgets her pledge of devotion in 1.1.334–7, and tries to seduce Aaron: 'let us sit, / And whilst the *babbling* echo mocks the hounds...' (16–17). Echo was called a *vocalis nymphe* in Ovid, *Met*.3.357; Golding (443) rendered this as 'a *babling* nymph'. (One recalls that for such babbling Echo had been deprived of speech.) Tamora proposes that they follow the example of Aeneas and Dido in the cave (*Aen*.4.165ff.); Aaron, however, declines, for 'Blood and revenge are hammering in my head' (39). He looks forward to Bassianus' death and the violation of Lavinia: 'His Philomel must lose her tongue today, / Thy sons make pillage of her chastity' (43–4). This is the first sign that Ovid's story is about to be woven into the action of the play.

There follows an exchange of discourtesies. Bassianus opens: 'Who have we here? Rome's royal empress... Or is it Dian, habited like her...?' (55ff.). In the Greek romances it was common for a young man, on meeting a young woman, to ask in admiration whether she was a goddess. The earliest example comes in the source of all romances, where Odysseus addresses Nausicaa (*Odyssey* 6.151–2). More to the point, in *Aeneid* 1 Aeneas encounters a female figure dressed in hunting garb and wonders if it is Diana (329); actually it is Venus in disguise. To Bassianus' sarcastic question Tamora retorts 'Had I the pow'r that some say Dian had, / Thy temples should be planted presently / With horns, as was Actaeon's'. At this Lavinia reveals an unexpectedly coarse side of her character: ' 'Tis thought you have a goodly gift in horning', i.e. making men cuckolds; Saturninus will surely have horns now; let's hope his hounds don't catch sight of him. The horrifying story of Actaeon was to be found in Ovid, *Met*.3.138ff. As A. B. Taylor remarks, 'The invocation of Actaeon is ominous in a play where men and women are about to turn predators'.[14] Bassianus then refers insultingly to Aaron's colour, despising as 'a barbarous Moor'(78) the man whom Tamora had called her 'sweet Moor' (51). As Shakespeare has been thinking of the *Aeneid*, it is possible that he has in mind Virgil's Iarbas, another member of 'the Moorish race' (*Aen*.4.206–7), who is motivated by malevolence towards another leader, viz. Aeneas. Virgil never mentions his colour, but the phrase *Gaetulus Iarbas* (4.326) has connotations of wildness and savagery.

Tamora now tells her sons that Bassianus and Lavinia have enticed her to 'A barren detested vale' (93). As her account develops it becomes harder to remember that this is the *locus amoenus* described in such idyllic terms to Aaron (12–18). She alleges that they intended to tie her to a tree (the bondage theme again) and leave her to die. Her sons therefore murder Bassianus and make to drag Lavinia away, telling Tamora to ignore her pleas. Lavinia then cries 'When did the tiger's young ones teach the dam?' – a clever adaptation of Ovid's straightforward comparison of Procne to a tigress (*Met*.6.637). Bassianus' body is then flung into a pit, as Aaron had instructed. In describing the pit Shakespeare's imagination runs riot.[15] Just a few points are relevant here. First, the place is 'As hateful as Cocytus' misty mouth' (236). The mist may owe something to the sulphurous vapour (*halitus*) that issued from the cave at the entrance to the underworld in *Aeneid* 6.240. Again, Shakespeare is thinking of hell in terms of its rivers; for not only does he use 'Cocytus' but also, with the adjective 'hateful', he alludes to 'abhorred Styx'. Later the pit is a '*gaping* hollow of the earth' (249); likewise Virgil's cave yawns 'with a vast *gape*' (*vasto hiatu* in v.237). Finally, with 'a swallowing womb' we have a grotesque inversion of *Terra Mater*. Housman had something similar in mind when he wrote 'Now to her lap the incestuous earth / The son

---

[14] A. B. Taylor, *Shakespeare's Ovid* (Cambridge, 2001), p. 66.
[15] D. Willbern's paper in *English Literary Renaissance* 8, 1978, 159–82 (cited by Bate, p. 9 n.1) was not available to me; but see H. James, *Themes in Drama* 13 (1991), 128–9.

she bore has ta'en' (*Additional Poems* VIII). Inside the pit the dim light given out by the carbuncle ring on Bassianus' corpse reminds Martius of Pyramus 'When he by night lay bathed in *maiden blood*' (232). This is the view that Thisbe had of the dead Pyramus by moonlight. It comes, not directly from Ovid, but from Golding: 'And there bewevltred in his *maiden bloud* hir lover she espide' (4.162).

As Shakespeare could not represent the rape and mutilation on stage, the atrocities are described in 2.3, first brutally by Demetrius and Chiron, and then sympathetically by Marcus, but the sympathy rings false as Marcus dwells in loving detail on the girl's injuries (especially in 23–5). Equally false in this situation are his Ovidian allusions. He infers that 'some Tereus hath deflowered thee' (26) and then describes her blood coming 'As from a *conduit* with three issuing spouts' (30). This goes beyond what Ovid had said about the bleeding Pyramus: 'As when a *Conduite* pipe is crackt, the water bursting out / Doth shote it selfe a great way off and pierce the Ayre about' (Golding 4.148–9). As the story was supposed to explain how the berries of the mulberry tree became red; the blood *had* to spurt into the air. Yet the image of the cracked pipe has been much criticized as a lapse of taste. Gower left it out (*Confessio Amantis*, 3.4.2); Chaucer took it in his stride: 'The blod out of the wounde as brode sterte / As water, whan the *condit* broken is' (*The Legend of Good Women*, 851–2); but Shakespeare multiplied it by three.

Marcus also notices that the loss of Lavinia's hands prevented her from revealing the crime in the manner employed by Philomel, who 'in a tedious sampler sewed her mind' (39). Had Lavinia's tongue not been cut out, she could have charmed her attacker, who would have fallen asleep 'As *Cerberus* at the Thracian poet's feet' (51). As often, Shakespeare is blending two passages. In the story of Orpheus ('the Thracian poet') and Eurydice, Cerberus, on hearing Orpheus' song, ceases to bark (Virgil, *Georgics* 4.483), but does not fall asleep. In *Aeneid* 6, however, he does fall asleep after devouring the drugged cake thrown to him by another *vates* – not a poet, but a prophetess (419–23). When Marcus leads in the wounded Lavinia he compares her to

a wounded deer (3.1.90–1) – a simile taken up by Titus in one of those puns that make the modern reader uncomfortable.[16] The figure itself picks up the 'dainty doe' mentioned by Aaron (1.1.617) and Demetrius (2.1.26). Dido, too, had been likened to a stricken doe (*Aen*.4.68–73), and the immediate cause of the war in Italy was the wounding of a pet stag (*Aen*.7.483ff.).

In 3.1 Titus tries to save his sons' life by allowing Aaron to chop off his hand, but the hand is returned to him along with the young men's heads. Here, as the editors point out, Shakespeare is indebted to Bandello, *Novelle* 3.21. The severed heads, however, come from Seneca's *Thyestes*, in which Atreus removes the cover of a dish, revealing the heads of the sons whom Thyestes has just eaten (1004–5). In both plays the moment is a terrific *coup de théâtre*; but by using the severed heads here at this halfway point Shakespeare forfeited the chance of using them later on, and had to fall back on a less plausible alternative.

After 3.1 Lucius departs to persuade the Goths to attack Rome 'And make proud Saturnine and his empress / Beg at the gates like Tarquin and his queen' (298–9). According to Livy 1.59.1, following the death of Lucretia, Brutus swears 'to hunt down L. Tarquinius Superbus along with his wicked wife'; in 1.60.2 he adds that 'the gates were closed against Tarquinius'; and in 2.6.2 Tarquin pleads to the Etruscans that he is an exile and 'in poverty' (*egentem*). Shakespeare has combined these elements to form a picture of the royal pair begging at the gate.[17]

In 3.2.52ff. comes the scene where Marcus kills a fly with his knife. Titus exclaims 'Out on thee, murderer! thou kill'st my heart; / Mine eyes are cloy'd with view of tyranny.' The combination of

---

[16] Other examples are the plays on 'hand' in 3.1; one is reminded of Dryden's complaint that Ovid was 'frequently witty out of season' (*Essays of John Dryden*, ed. W. P. Ker, (Oxford, 1900), vol. 1.234; cf. vol. 2.256–7).

[17] P. Legouis, *Shakespeare Survey 28*, 1975, 73 cites a Latin translation of Dionysius of Halicarnassus, *The Roman Antiquities* 5.3.2, which had *omnium rerum necessarium indigens* (lacking all necessities). But the idea was already in Livy.

sharp instrument, fly, and tyranny raises the possibility that Shakespeare may have half remembered how the tyrant Domitian 'at the beginning of his reign . . . used to do nothing more than catch flies and run them through with a sharp pen' (Suetonius, *Life of Domitian* 3.1). Shakespeare's scene, of course, may be entirely original – one thinks of 'As willingly as one would kill a fly' (5.1.142) and 'As flies to wanton boys'. But although Philemon Holland's translation of Suetonius (1606) was probably too late, Domitian's behaviour was so odd that Shakespeare might have heard of it through another channel – perhaps even his schoolmaster. However that may be, he builds this trivial scene into a vicious attack on the Moor (67–79). As the act closes, Titus leads Lavinia and the boy Lucius away to read 'Sad stories chanced in the times of old' (84).

This is immediately taken up in 4.1, where young Lucius is told that 'Cornelia never with more *care* / Read to her sons than she hath read to thee / Sweet poetry and Tully's Orator' (12–14). Cornelia's care in educating the Gracchi is recorded at the beginning of Plutarch's *Life of Tiberius Gracchus*; North uses the phrase 'so *carefully*'. The commentaries may be right in referring to Cicero's *Orator* and *De Oratore*, but it is worth mentioning that in another rhetorical work, the *Brutus*, Cicero twice reports Cornelia's activities as a mother (104 and 211). Of these passages the former is the more interesting in that it too refers to her *care* (*diligentia*).

Lavinia is now in a highly agitated condition – so much so that Lucius recalls reading how 'Hecuba of Troy / Ran *mad* for sorrow' (20–1) – perhaps a rather distant echo of Golding, who speaks of Hecuba being 'dumb for sorrow' (13.645), but Nørgaard (see note 24) may be right in pointing to Cooper's Thesaurus, where '[Hecuba] finally waxed *madde*, and did bite and strike all men she met'. Lavinia now seizes a copy of the 'Metamorphosis' (so entitled by Golding), and manages, with some help, to find 'the tragic tale of Philomel' (47). From this we infer that the 'sweet poetry' which she used to read to Lucius included Ovid's masterpiece. Titus, beginning to understand what has happened, suspects she was 'Forc'd in the ruthless, vast, and

gloomy woods'. Ovid had written *in stabula alta trahit, silvis obscura vetustis* (*Met.*6.521) – 'drags her into deep *stabula*, darkly hidden by ancient *woods*'; there he was using *stabula* in the sense of 'dens', as Virgil did in *Aen.*6.179, where Aeneas made his way *in antiquam silvam, stabula alta ferarum* ('into an ancient forest, the deep *dens* of wild beasts'). In view of this it is perhaps significant that Marcus asks 'O why should nature build so foul a *den*?' (59). Golding (6.663) mistranslates *alta stabula* as 'a pelting graunge' – a small barn. Yet he has some excuse, for unlike Shakespeare Ovid later says that Philomela was locked up in a building: *structa rigent solido stabulorum moenia saxo* (573, cf. 596) – 'the walls of the building (*stabulorum*) were firmly constructed out of solid stone'. Titus now urges Lavinia to indicate in some way who did the deed. Could it have been Saturnine, 'as Tarquin erst / That left the camp to sin in Lucrece' bed?' (63–4). This, of course, was not Tarquinius Superbus, but his son Sextus, whose crime was recounted in Livy 1.57.6–58.12 and described in *The Rape of Lucrece* (512ff.). Marcus traces his own name in a sandy plot.[18] And now comes the moment of recognition (Aristotle's *anagnorisis*). Fulfilling Chiron's taunt 'And if thy stumps will let thee, play the scribe' (2.3.4), Lavinia writes (in Latin, one notes) '*Stuprum*. Chiron. Demetrius' (78). The dramatic impact of this can be assessed when we contrast it with the chapbook, in which Lavinia succeeds in composing a rhyming couplet: 'The lustful Sons of the proud Emperess / Are doers of this hateful wickedness'.

At the sight of the names Titus, according to the transmitted text, exclaims: *Magni dominator poli, / Tam lentus audis scelera? tam lentus vides?* – 'Ruler of great heaven, are you so insensitive when you hear of crimes? So insensitive when you witness them?' *Magni*, however, is a misquotation, as Theobald

---

18 Maxwell points out that here Shakespeare is drawing on Ovid's description of the bovine Io, 'who *printed* her name in the *sande* with her foote' (Golding, 1.804–5; Ovid, 1.649 had *in pulvere* 'in the dust'). A little earlier (1.635–6) Ovid's Io tried to stretch out her arms (*bracchia*) but had no arms to stretch out. Golding, significantly, has 'handes' (1.788–9); cf. *TA* 2.3.6–7.

saw; for Seneca does not admit a long syllable at that point in the line. The second verse undoubtedly comes from Seneca, *Phaedra* 672, and line 671 ends *Magne* (sic) *regnator deum*; similarly in *Thyestes* 1077 Jupiter is addressed as *summe caeli rector* ('Highest ruler of heaven', not 'Ruler of highest heaven'), and in the very next line we find *dominator*. Again one wonders whether it is Shakespeare's change or that of a copyist.[19]

Marcus kneels down with Titus, Lavinia, and young Lucius who is now 'the Roman Hector's hope' (88), his father, who has gone to enlist the help of the Goths in saving the city, being now 'the Roman Hector'. They swear an oath of vengeance which Titus wishes to engrave on 'a leaf of brass' (102). This phrase has nothing to do with the myth of the ages. It refers to the durability of brass (cf. Horace, *Odes*.3.30.1 *monumentum aere perennius*). Titus mentions this material, because the sands on which Marcus and Lavinia have just written will be blown by the *wind* 'like Sibyl's *leaves* abroad' (105); in *Aen*.6.74–5 Aeneas begs the Sibyl not to entrust her prophecies to *leaves* that will be scattered by the *winds*.

In 4.2.20 young Lucius delivers to Chiron and Demetrius weapons sent by Titus ostensibly for their protection (15–16). The accompanying scroll reads *Integer vitae scelerisque purus / Non eget Mauri iaculis nec arcu* ('The man who is unblemished in his life and free from crime has no need of a Moor's javelins or bow'). Spelt out, the message means, I take it, 'An *honest* man needs no weapons, least of all those of a Moor'. Chiron recalls reading Horace's verse (*Odes* 1.22.1–2) 'in the grammar', but fails to see its significance. Aaron, however, does see the point and comments, in an aside, on Chiron's stupidity ('Now, what a thing it is to be an ass!').

Tamora's black baby is now brought in, and Aaron in high style refuses to allow Demetrius kill it, casting himself as Jupiter against the giant Enceladus and 'Typhon's brood'[20] – even, if need be, against Hercules and Mars (97). He sets about ensuring the baby's safety by murdering its nurse, and then carries it away for protection to the Goths, remarking good-humouredly: 'I'll make you ··· suck the goat, / And cabin in a cave' (179–81). This only

makes sense if we remember that in Greek mythology the infant Zeus was hidden in a Cretan cave to prevent Cronus (the original child-eater) from devouring him; there he was suckled by the goat Amalthea.[21] (One thinks of Poussin's beautiful picture in the Dulwich Gallery.[22]) The parallel gains relevance from the fact that the Italian counterpart of Cronus was Saturn, and this baby is being smuggled away to escape the wrath of Saturninus.

In the myth of the metals Astraea (Justice) eventually tired of men's wickedness and rose to the skies, where she became the constellation Virgo. In Aratus' account (*Phaenomena* 129–36) this happened with the arrival of the bronze age; Ovid (*Met*.1.141–50) says it was in the age of iron that *terras Astraea reliquit*. When in 4.3.4 Titus quoted the phrase, no doubt the more learned would have remembered Ovid's context. Yet it is the *consequences* of Astraea's departure that are emphasized. In what follows, the main concern is absent Justice; between 4.3.9 and 4.4.23 the word itself occurs eleven times. So (at the risk of being 'reductive') it seems a mistake to give too much attention to the myth, which is not actually mentioned.[23]

---

[19] In another work (*Epistles* 107.11) Seneca translates some lines of the Stoic Cleanthes beginning '*Duc, o parens celsique dominator poli*' (Lead me o Father, ruler of high heaven). This was not part of a play, and both thought and context were quite different. Yet in view of *dominator poli* one ought not to rule out a possible influence on our passage.

[20] The Giant Enceladus' part in the revolt against Jupiter is mentioned in Horace, *Odes* 3.4.56; he was struck down by a thunderbolt and imprisoned under Sicily (Apollodorus, 1.6.2 in Frazer's Loeb edition) or Etna (Virgil, *Aen*.3.578–80). Typhon, offspring of Tartarus and Earth, also took part in the attack (Apollodorus 1.6.3). He fathered various monsters, e.g. the Chimaera and the Sphinx (see Apollodorus, vol. 2, Index). He is said to have suffered the same fate as Enceladus.

[21] Apollodorus 1.1.5–7 with Frazer's notes.

[22] For other representations see J. D. Reid, *The Oxford Guide to Classical Mythology in the Arts, 1300–1900* (Oxford, 1993), vol. 2, pp. 1068–70.

[23] In 3.1.16–22 Titus is explicitly referring to the sequence of the seasons, not to the myth of metals; so 'eternal springtime' (21) can be no more than an ironical glance at Ovid's *ver erat aeternum* (*Met*.1.107).

In 4.3.48 the sequence, I take it, is 'We are not large like cedars or giants, but in our determination we are solid steel,

In 4.3.54ff. Titus distributes arrows destined for half a dozen divinities. The conceits about hitting Virgo, Taurus, Aries and the rest (which were perhaps thought of as being represented on the wall of the court) are based, as Maxwell says, on Seneca, *Thyestes* 844ff., where the chorus predicts that the signs of the zodiac will fall down. Later (4.4.61ff.) news comes that Lucius is leading an army against Rome, as Coriolanus had done so long before . In 5.1 he makes a noble entry, but before long is clamouring that Aaron and his baby be hanged (47–8, 51–2). In return for the safety of the child Aaron proceeds to tell all that has happened. He treats the rape and mutilation of Lavinia as acts of entertainment (91–6), whereupon Lucius cries out that her two attackers were '*barbarous beastly* villains like thyself' (97). (Golding in 6.655 calls the intention of Tereus '*barbrous* and *beastly*'.) Finally Lucius orders Aaron to be gagged (151).

Taking a hint from Ovid's Procne who disguises herself as a Bacchanal (*Met.*6.589ff.), Tamora now dresses herself as Revenge (5.2.3); Chiron and Demetrius are Rape and Murder. Titus is not deceived, but Tamora thinks he is mad and plans to use him 'to scatter and disperse the giddy Goths' (78). In due course Titus orders Chiron and Demetrius to be tied up and gagged (160–1). After rehearsing their crimes, he proceeds to tell them his grisly plans: 'For worse than Philomel you used my daughter, / And worse than Progne I will be revenged' (194–5); the banquet will prove 'More stern and bloody than the Centaurs' feast' (203) – an ambitious claim, for at that feast, recounted by Ovid in the most gruesome detail (*Met.*12.210–535), well over fifty lives were lost.

In the preparation and description of the meal Shakespeare diverged from his sources, as noted above. Unlike Ovid and Seneca, he included the sons' heads in the dish (189 and 200) (we are to imagine the skulls being ground into dust and then made into a paste.) In Ovid, when Tereus sends for his son, Procne says 'You have within the one whom you want' (*Met.*6.655). When he asks again, Philomela bursts in and hurls the child's head at his father, who immediately pursues the women; before he can catch them they are transformed into birds. In Seneca, when Thyestes calls for his sons, Atreus with a flourish uncovers the dish, revealing their heads (1005). In Shakespeare, Titus serves the meal dressed as a chef (5.3.30). Before it begins he asks Saturninus if Virginius was right to kill his daughter. Livy (3.44) tells how Appius Claudius was seized with a desire to debauch Verginius' daughter (*virginis . . . stuprandae libido*). By employing a legalistic device he was about to succeed in doing so when her father, Verginius, intervened and killed the girl. Shakespeare draws on a later version which says she was actually 'enforced, stained, and deflowered' (38).[24] Saturninus says Virginius' action was justified, whereupon Titus kills Lavinia (45–6), explaining that she had been raped by Chiron and Demetrius. Saturninus: 'Go fetch them hither to us presently'. Titus: 'Why, there they are, both baked in this pie; / Whereof their mother daintily hath *fed*, / Eating the flesh that she herself hath *bred*' (60–1). The rhyme seems to come from Golding: 'King Tereus . . . *fed* / And swallowed downe the selfsame flesh that of his bowels *bred*' (6.824–5). Yet the picture of a mother eating her own children is doubly revolting, because she seems to be taking them back into her body. The point is made by Shakespeare himself when he makes Titus say 'and bid that strumpet . . . , / Like to the earth, swallow her own increase' (5.2.190–91). Instead of gloating over Tamora's horror, Titus kills her. In Seneca the victim reacts with a typical flight of rhetoric:

---

though our sufferings are intolerable. And since there's no justice here, we will approach heaven.' The phrase 'metal, steel to the very back' is a boast (see Lyly, *Euphues*, ed. R.W. Bond, *Complete Works* (Oxford, 1902), vol. 1, p. 207 and all the passages noted in Tilley s 842, also *OED steel* 1a and 1f.). The reference to the power of shrubs *vis-à-vis* cedars is straightforward, as in *Luc.* 664–5 (even though Tilley's references at C 208 show that paradoxically the shrub was sometimes judged the stronger). The expression, then, is surely favourable; so it cannot refer to the iron age. Undue emphasis (I think) is given to the myth by R. S. Miola (*Shakespeare's Rome*, Cambridge 1983) in his otherwise perceptive third chapter.

[24] This version, *pace* Maxwell, is not in Florus 1.17.24, which says only that Appius *intended* to debauch the girl (*stupro destinaret*); for further evidence see H. Nørgaard, *English Studies* 45 (1964), 140.

addressing Jupiter as *tu, summe caeli rector, aetheriae potens / dominator aulae* ('Thou, highest ruler of heaven, powerful master of the celestial court'), Thyestes urges the god to bring cosmic chaos.

With Tamora, Titus, and Saturninus all dead, a speaker urges Marcus to re-enact the role of Aeneas recounting the fall of Priam's Troy to Dido; he is to tell what new Sinon has bewitched the citizens (for Sinon see *Aen.*2.57–198, especially the reference to his tricks and craftiness in 195–6), and who has brought 'the *fatal engine* in [*fatalis machina* describes the horse in *Aen.*2.237] / That gives our Troy, our Rome, the fatal wound' (5.3.79–86). 'Our Troy, our Rome' – the presence of the past could not be more concisely explicit. Marcus at first sight complies: like Aeneas, he cannot *utter* all the bitter *grief* (5.3.88) – *Infandum, regina, iubes renovare dolorem* in *Aen.*2.3 (*Unutterable*, o queen, is *the grief* that you bid me recall); but unlike Aeneas he really *is* unable to face the task and passes it on to Lucius, who summarizes the events, speaking of his own part once again in terms that recall Coriolanus.[25]

After being hailed as emperor, he promises to bring reconciliation; but first he passes a cruel sentence on the defiant Aaron: 'Set him breast-deep in earth and famish him; / There let him stand and rave and cry for food' (178–9). Many listeners, no doubt, would have recalled the fate of Tantalus. In Homer (*Odyssey* 11.582ff.) he stands in a pool and is plagued by thirst; he is also 'tantalized' by fruit, figs, and olives. In Horace (*Epodes* 17.66) he is tortured by the sight of an ample meal; and in a similar passage a young boy is to be buried up to his neck and starved within the sight of food (*Epodes* 5.31ff.). But how is Tantalus connected with the play? In Seneca's *Thyestes* Tantalus' ghost appears in the opening scene, complaining about the tortures of both hunger and thirst (1–6; cf.152ff.). He is, we are reminded, the grandfather of Atreus and Thyestes. And his crime? He carved up his son Pelops and served him as food to the gods. So there seems ample reason why he should have occurred to Shakespeare at this point in the play. Moreover, one of Thyestes' murdered sons was also called Tantalus.

As for Tamora, she is to be denied burial; instead she will be thrown 'to *beasts* and *birds* to prey' (197). Such a fate is mentioned several times in ancient literature, but since we know that Shakespeare had been reading the *Thyestes*, it is reasonable to cite vv.1032–3 of that play. There, realizing that his sons are dead, but not that he has eaten them, Thyestes asks Atreus: *Utrumne saevis pabulum alitibus iacent, / an beluis servantur, an pascunt feris?* ('Do they lie there as *prey* for cruel *birds*, or are they reserved for sea-monsters? Or are they food for *beasts*?'). Such, then, is the fate in store for Tamora. The last word of the play is 'pity', but it is the kind of pity associated with vultures.

Although there have been various attempts to moralize the *Metamorphoses*, it is now generally accepted that the various effects – comic, pathetic, horrific, bizarre – are all parts of an ever-moving narrative, all facets of the poet's iridescent imagination. Occasionally we find his brutality sensational or even absurd, and his sentimental descriptions of cruelty repellent; but Ovid himself is not deeply involved, and does not invite us to pause and ponder. Unlike Virgil, he has little to offer the earnest. This cast of mind is surely what appealed to Shakespeare at this stage of his career. Opinion about Seneca's tragedies is still divided. Can they be seen, not just as an orgy of horrors, but as a Stoic's attempt to show what happens when reason is overthrown by lawless passions? And are their emotional passages noble rhetoric or overblown bombast? The various controversies surrounding *Titus Andronicus* also seem set to continue. But as we watch the writer's memory at work – taking now from Virgil, Ovid, or Plutarch, now from Livy, Horace, or Seneca, and combining or altering what is taken to suit his dramatic purpose – we can hardly deny that, in addition to much else, the play is a brilliant display of creative reminiscence.

---

[25] So Bate 13–15, rightly; but 'unkindly banished, / The gates shut on me, and turned weeping out / To beg relief among Rome's enemies' (103–5) also reminds us disturbingly of an earlier exile (3.1.299).

JULIUS CAESAR, MACHIAVELLI, AND THE USES OF HISTORY

ROBIN HEADLAM WELLS

Why did Shakespeare use stories from the Graeco-Roman world? Machiavelli went to Roman history because he believed that Livy's narratives provided political lessons that could be applied to the modern world. It has traditionally been supposed that Shakespeare dramatized stories from Plutarch and other historians for similar reasons. For the new 'politic' historiographers, and, it used to be generally assumed, for Shakespeare as well, the importance of ancient history lay in its ability to illuminate modern events.[1] In recent years these assumptions have been challenged by materialist and postmodern scholars who have argued that the supposedly essentialist view of humanity underpinning this rational historiography is an invention of pre-theoretical literary scholarship. Shakespeare, it is claimed, was a precursor of our own disillusioned postmodern view of 'man' and history. *Julius Caesar* certainly suggests that Shakespeare took a sceptical view of politics. But evidence in the play in support of the claim that he shared the anti-humanist theories of the postmodern historiographers he is said to anticipate is less strong.

I

In *Radical Tragedy* Jonathan Dollimore claims that Machiavelli was an anti-essentialist.[2] This could hardly be further from the truth. Machiavelli believed that if the past contains a lesson for the present it is because human nature is fundamentally the same in all ages. Informing his pragmatic view of history was a belief in human universals. Both in *The Prince* and in the *Discourses* we repeat-

edly find such phrases as these: 'men almost always follow in the footsteps of others, imitation being a leading principle of human nature'; 'men generally ... are ungrateful, fickle, feigners and dissemblers'; 'men never do good unless necessity drives them to it'; 'nature has so constituted men that ...'; 'the human mind is perpetually ...'; and so forth.[3] By observing the way men behaved in the past and noting the consequences of their actions you could predict what outcome similar actions might have in the present. In the *Discourses* Machiavelli wrote: 'If the present be compared with the remote past, it is easily seen that in all cities and in all peoples there are the same desires and the same passions as there always were. So that, if one examines with diligence the past, it is easy to foresee the future of any commonwealth, and to apply those remedies that were used of old' (p. 302).

Was Machiavelli's rational historiography fatally flawed by its essentialist premises? Postmodern historiographers are sceptical about the political value of history. If there is no transhistorical essence of

---

[1] For discussion of the influence of the new 'politic' historiography in early modern England see F. J. Levy, *Tudor Historical Thought* (San Marino, 1967), pp. 237–85; Arthur B. Ferguson, *Clio Unbound: Perception of the Social and Cultural Past in Renaissance England* (Durham, NC, 1979), pp. 3–27.

[2] *Radical Tragedy: Religion, Ideology and Power in the Drama of Shakespeare and his Contemporaries* (Brighton, 1984), pp. 170–1.

[3] *The Prince*, ed. Quentin Skinner and Russell Price (Cambridge, 1988), pp. 19, 59; *The Discourses of Niccolò Machiavelli*, ed. and trans. Leslie J. Walker, 2 vols. (London, 1950), 1. 217, 295, 356.

human nature and no universal passions and follies, history can have limited meaning for the present. In an essay on Foucault Hayden White suggests that, insofar as Foucault rejected all the conventional categories of historical description and explanation, he could best be described as an 'anti-historian'. 'Foucault,' he explains, 'writes "history" in order to destroy it.' Unlike the traditional historian, who sought to understand the past and to make it intelligible to his readers, partly by revealing the sequence of cause and effect in the unfolding of events, and partly by appealing to those constant elements in human nature that survive from one age to another, Foucault wanted to disrupt our false sense of coherence and defamiliarise the past. Because there is in reality no continuity in history, and no universal *humanitas*, the past can have no more meaning for us than a theatre of the absurd. Foucault, writes White, 'sought to show how we are isolated within our peculiar modalities of experience, so much so that *we could not hope to find analogues and models for the solution of the problems facing us, and thereby to enlighten us to the peculiar elements in our present situation*'. White argued that, insofar as Foucault tried to show how all systems of thought are 'little more than terminological formalisations of poetic closures with the world of words, rather than with the "things" they purport to represent and explain', he had more in common with the poet than the traditional historian.[4]

Over the past two decades it has been widely assumed that Shakespeare too was an anti-essentialist. It is said that, like most leading intellectuals of the time, he recognized that human nature, with its apparently unique sense of interiority and self-determination, was merely an illusory effect of discourse; in reality 'man' was a radically decentred being with no universal characteristics and no inner being. The historical moment that gave birth to the self was the emergence of a bourgeois capitalist economy at the beginning of the early-modern period. Though some postmodernists are willing to cede limited powers of agency, it is still widely accepted that it is 'incorrect', as Dollimore puts it, to read the period 'through the grid of an essentialist humanism'.[5] If this argument is right it

should follow that for Shakespeare history would have had little more meaning than it did for Foucault: no attempt to understand the past and relate it to our own age could be anything more than a tale told by an idiot, full of sound and fury, signifying nothing.

II

If Shakespeare did anticipate Foucault's belief that it is pointless looking to history for instructive analogues of modern events, it is puzzling that he should have built into his play so many coded allusions to his own world. The parallels between Shakespeare's Rome and Elizabethan England are well known.[6] With its ailing, autocratic ruler toppled by a Machiavellian rebel who looks back to an heroic age when men were more warlike (1.3.80–4), and its talk of a group of 'noblest-minded' aristocrats (121) 'factious for redress of [personal] griefs' (117),[7] *Julius Caesar* would inevitably have put contemporary audiences in mind of the beliefs and ideals of the Sidney-Essex alliance. Essex's querulous *Apologie* – written at a time when rivalry between the two main factions in the Privy Council was at crisis point[8] – was published only just before Shakespeare wrote *Julius Caesar*. Like Cassius, Essex was a man with a grievance.[9]

---

4 'Foucault Decoded: Notes from Underground', *Tropics of Discourse: Essays in Cultural Criticism* (Baltimore, 1985), pp. 239, 234, 257, 259. 'Foucault Decoded' was first published in *History and Theory*, 12 (1973) (my italics).

5 Dollimore, *Radical Tragedy*, p. 155.

6 See for example Tom McAlindon, *Shakespeare's Tragic Cosmos* (Cambridge, 1991), pp. 76–8; David Daniell, ed., *Julius Caesar*, The Arden Shakespeare (Walton-on-Thames, 1998), pp. 23–4.

7 Quotations from Shakespeare are from *The Complete Works*, ed. Stanley Wells and Gary Taylor (Oxford, 1986).

8 See Wallace T. MacCaffrey, *Elizabeth I: War and Politics 1588–1603* (Princeton, 1992), pp. 453ff.; see also Wernham, *The Making of Elizabethan Foreign Policy*, passim; John Guy, *Tudor England* (Oxford and New York, 1988), pp. 439ff; Penry Williams, *The Later Tudors: England 1547–1603. The New Oxford History of England* (Oxford, 1995), p. 364.

9 Underlying Essex's quarrel with Elizabeth was a sense of personal grievance. While he feigned helpless susceptibility to

He surrounded himself with discontented nobles who shared his desire to remove what seemed to him a tyrannical ruler and reform government. His watchword was honour. And that meant a willingness to use violence in defence of personal or national reputation. In a pamphlet in praise of the aristocratic leaders of the Essex faction Gervase Markham described honour as 'the food of every great spirit, and the very god which creates in high minds Heroical actions'.[10] For Cassius too honour is a word that has talismanic significance. 'Honour is the subject of my story,' he tells Brutus (1.2.94).

These parallels are familiar to modern scholars. If Shakespeare takes care to avoid committing himself to one side or the other, that is understandable. Essex was a figure of whom, in Markham's words, 'it behove[d] every man to be careful how to write'.[11] But it has not been noticed that the parallels go further than a general resemblance between the political situation of Rome before Caesar's assassination and London in 1598/9. Shakespeare makes verbal allusion to the militant-Protestant faction and their values. For Essex's supporters, words like 'heroic', 'virtuous' and 'honourable', were a code that signalled commitment to an aggressively militarist political agenda.[12] The counterpart of these heroic epithets was a cluster of words to do with sleep, dreams, enchantment and idleness. 'Sleep' was widely used by members of the militant-Protestant faction as a metaphor for the false sense of security which they believed was blinding the government to political dangers at home and abroad.[13] In *Julius Caesar* there is much talk of heroic action. Cassius is an admirer of 'any bold or noble enterprise' (1.2.298) and incites his supporters to 'undergo with me an enterprise / Of honourable-dangerous consequence' (1.3.122–3); Ligarius welcomes an 'exploit worthy the name of honour' (2.1.316). But the anonymous letter that Lucius finds in the window speaks of the need for Brutus to rouse himself from the 'sleep' of inaction: 'Brutus, thou sleep'st. Awake, and see thyself. / Shall Rome, et cetera? Speak, strike, redress'. Brutus then rereads the letter's key phrase: 'thou sleep'st. Awake' (2.1.46–8).[14] It is the combination of imagery of 'bloody, fiery, and most

terrible' deeds (1.3.129) on the one hand, and the exhortation to awake from the sleep of 'security' (2.3.7) on the other that makes these allusions so pointed.

Such topical allusions would be meaningless if we were not expected to see analogies between the final years of republican Rome and fin-de-siècle England. But what are we meant to deduce from them? As many critics have pointed out, it is impossible to say for certain whether Shakespeare is for or against Caesar. 'After all the clear balancing of this against that, and for all the power of the figures on stage to move us,' writes David Daniell in his recent Arden edition of the play, 'there comes into view no alternative basis of authority at all, either divine or popular. There is only possession of power, the politics of the school playground'.[15] In the last century a long line of critics going back to A. P. Rossiter in the 1950s emphasised the dialectical nature of Shakespeare's plays. For critics like Rabkin, Elton, McElroy, Jones and Grudin, they were best seen as, in W. R. Elton's words, 'a dialect of ironies and ambivalences, avoiding in its complex movement and dialogue the simplification of direct statement and reductive resolution'.[16]

Elizabeth's beauty, in reality he deeply resented being subject to a woman's authority (see Mervyn James, *Society, Politics and Culture: Studies in Early Modern England* (1978; repr. Cambridge, 1986), p. 444).

[10] Markham *Honour in his Perfection* (London, 1624), p. 4).

[11] Ibid., p. 26.

[12] See James, *Society, Politics and Culture*, pp. 308–415. For discussion of the politically nuanced use of these terms by Shakespeare and his contemporaries see Robin Headlam Wells, *Shakespeare on Masculinity* (Cambridge, 2000), pp. 7–10 and passim.

[13] Blair Worden, *The Sound of Virtue: Philip Sidney's Arcadia and Elizabethan Politics* (New Haven and London, 1996), p. 62.

[14] Shakespeare takes the phrase 'Brutus, thou sleep'st' from Plutarch. It occurs, in slightly different forms, in the lives both of Brutus and Julius Caesar (*Plutarch's Lives of the Noble Grecians and Romans*, trans. Sir Thomas North, 6 vols. (London, 1895–6), 5.63; 6.190).

[15] *Julius Caesar*, p. 38. See also Robert S. Miola, '*Julius Caesar* and the Tyrannicide Debate', *Renaissance Quarterly* 38 (1985), 271–89.

[16] 'Shakespeare and the Thought of his Age' (1971), *The Cambridge Companion to Shakespeare Studies*, ed. Stanley

But if, as Daniell says, Shakespeare 'does not endorse anyone' (p. 34), what are we expected to learn from this dramatization of the most momentous event in Roman history? That Republican politics is simply a power game from which we can deduce nothing of value? That history has no more to offer than a poet's fiction? This would be a truly Foucauldian view of history and literature.

The fact that Shakespeare is careful to avoid taking sides doesn't mean that the play has no view to offer on the historical event it dramatizes. One of the central ironies of *Julius Caesar* is the fact that an action designed to deflect a feared event hastens that very outcome.[17] There is a similar structural irony in *Macbeth*. By attempting to avert destiny, Macbeth himself is instrumental in ensuring that the ancient prophecy of a re-united kingdom would be realized.[18] In *Julius Caesar* too the fulfilment of prophecy is accelerated by an action that is intended to forestall it. Despite his republican sympathies, Plutarch considered Caesar to be a providential figure 'whom God had ordeyned of special grace to be Governor of the Empire of Rome, and to set all thinges againe at quiet stay, the which required the counsell and authoritie of an absolute Prince'.[19] Shakespeare doesn't refer in *Julius Caesar* to the 'time of universal peace' (*Antony and Cleopatra* 4.6.4) that was to follow the third stage of Rome's civil wars. Nor is there any proof that the many supernatural signs in the play apparently betokening divine displeasure are anything more than coincidence. However, contemporary audiences would have known perfectly well that Octavius' supremacy and the transformation of Rome into a dictatorship was brought forward by Caesar's murder. Instead of averting these events, the assassination hastened them.

On the question of whether or not there is a 'providence of some high powers / That govern us below' (5.1.106–7) the play is non-commital. But looked at from a purely pragmatic point of view there is an inescapable irony in the fact that the immediate consequence of an action carried out in the name of 'Liberty, freedom, and enfranchisement!' (3.1.80) is 'Domestic fury and fierce civil strife' (3.1.266), followed by the deaths of all the conspirators. Cassius imagines the celebratory re-enactment of their 'lofty scene' (3.1.113) in future times. Has he read no history? Doesn't he know that conspiracies almost always end in disaster? 'There have been many conspiracies, but history has shown that few have succeeded', wrote Machiavelli in *The Prince* (p. 65). Machiavelli was not a monarchist defending the divine right of hereditary rulers. He was simply pointing out what works and what doesn't work in politics. *The Prince* considers the consequences of conspiracies in principalities; the *Discourses* looks at them from a republican point of view. But the message is the same: 'there is . . . no enterprise . . . more dangerous or more rash than is this . . . those [who involve themselves in conspiracies] usually bring disaster both upon themselves and upon their country' (*Discourses*, pp. 470–1). Plutarch dwells on the brutality of the way in which Caesar was 'hacked and mangeled amonge them, as a wilde beaste taken of hunters'.[20] But Machiavelli, also writing

---

Wells (Cambridge, 1986), p. 32. See also Norman Rabkin, *Shakespeare and the Common Understanding* (1967; repr. Chicago and London, 1984); Bernard McElroy, *Shakespeare's Mature Tragedies* (Princeton, 1973); Emrys Jones, *The Origins of Shakespeare* (Oxford, 1977); Robert Grudin, *Mighty Opposites: Shakespeare and Renaissance Contrariety* (Berkeley, Los Angeles and London, 1979).

[17] Joseph S. M. J. Chang notes that, by joining the conspiracy Brutus 'incites the civil war which destroys the very Republic he seeks to preserve' ('*Julius Caesar* in the Light of Renaissance Historiography', *Journal of English and Germanic Philology* 69 (1970), 63–71; p. 70). However, in taking Brutus' protestations of honesty at face value, Chang does not allow for the fact that Shakespeare may be hinting ironically on Brutus' political naivety. I discuss this question below.

[18] In *Poly-Olbion* Drayton explains how, by murdering Banquo and causing Fleanch (Shakespeare's Fleance) to flee to Wales, Macbeth was indirectly responsible for bringing about a marriage that would unite the houses of Plantagenet and Tudor. For Fleanch married the daughter of Llewellin, the Prince of Wales. His descendant, Henry VII, married Elizabeth of York, and it was their eldest daughter, Margaret, who married James IV. James VI and I could thus claim both to unite the houses of York and Lancaster, and also to restore the ancient British line. (*The Works of Michael Drayton*, 5 vols., ed. J. William Hebel (Oxford, 1931–41), 4 (1933), 167).

[19] *Plutarch's Lives*, 6.237.

[20] Ibid., 5.68.

from a republican point of view, makes no appeal to the emotions, and no reference to heaven's will. His interest in the subject is pragmatic: conspiracies seldom achieve their intended effect. Describing how Caesar's death was avenged, he simply says: 'of the conspirators, after they had been driven out of Rome, one and all were killed at various times and in various places' (*Discourses*, p. 487).

Machiavelli also considers the consequences of unconstitutional action in his discussion of the Coriolanus story. As we know from Plutarch, Coriolanus was not noted for his diplomacy. So incensed were the plebeians by his contempt for them that, had it not been for the intervention of the tribunes, and their insistence that he appear before the senate, Coriolanus would probably have been murdered by the mob. But crisis was avoided because there was a legal outlet for public anger. Summing up the significance of these events, Machiavelli wrote:

all should reflect on the evils that might have ensued in the Roman republic had he been tumultuously put to death, for this would have been an act of private vengeance, which would have aroused fear; and fear would have led to defensive action; this to the procuring of partisans; partisans would have meant the formation of factions in the city; and factions would have brought about its downfall.

Thus far Machiavelli might almost have been describing Caesar's murder. But he continues:

As, however, the matter was settled by persons vested with the requisite authority, no opening was provided for the evils that might have resulted had the matter been settled by private authority.   (*Discourses*, p. 228)

Machiavelli's observations on unconstitutional action had a particular significance for English readers in 1599. *Julius Caesar* was written and performed while Essex was out of the country. Until news began to filter back to London of the truce that he had been forced to conclude with Tyrone in September 1599, no one could have predicted with certainty the outcome of the earl's mission to suppress the Irish rebellion. Success might lead to a reconciliation with the Queen and the rehabilitation

of his own reputation as crusading national hero; failure would in all probability mean the end of his political career, at least while Elizabeth was alive. Given these uncertainties, it is difficult to imagine any intelligent Elizabethan watching a performance of *Julius Caesar* and not pondering the possible outcomes of a political coup. In his treatise on kingship St Thomas Aquinas wrote: 'to proceed against the cruelty of tyrants is an action to be undertaken, not through the private presumption of a few, but rather by public authority'.[21] Was this also Shakespeare's view? In *Macbeth* he presents us with the paradox of men resorting to extreme violence to restore civilized values. But *Julius Caesar* appears to confirm one of the central themes of the English history plays. Without giving away its author's political sympathies, it makes it clear that unconstitutional action is all too likely to be followed by 'Domestic fury and fierce civil strife'.

III

Had Shakespeare been reading *The Prince* and the *Discourses* in 1599? Probably, but not necessarily. Machiavelli was so well known in sixteenth-century England that traces of his ideas in literary works and political treatises are not necessarily a sign of direct debt.[22] In *The Jew of Malta*

---

[21] Thomas Aquinas, *On Kingship: To the King of Cyprus*, trans. Gerald B. Phelan, revised by I. Th. Eschmann (Toronto, 1949), p. 27.

[22] Although there were no printed English translations of *The Discourses* and *The Prince* until 1636 and 1640 respectively, several manuscript translations of both texts were available in Elizabethan England. Printed Italian editions were also in circulation from the 1580s (see Felix Raab, *The English Face of Machiavelli: A Changing Interpretation 1500–1700* (London, 1964), p. 53). Raab writes: 'everything indicates that, at least from the middle 'eighties onwards, Machiavelli was being quite widely read in England and was no longer the sole preserve of "Italianate" Englishmen and their personal contacts' (p. 53). On Machiavelli's influence in early modern England see also Levy, *Tudor Historical Thought*, pp. 238–42; Anne Barton, 'Livy, Machiavelli, and Shakespeare's *Coriolanus*', *Shakespeare Survey 38* (1985), pp. 115–29; Victoria Kahn, *Machiavellian Rhetoric: From the Counter-Reformation to Milton* (Princeton, 1994).

Marlowe capitalized unashamedly on the popular stereotype of the cunning schemer who takes a malicious delight in the spectacle of his own cruelty. *Julius Caesar* is Machiavellian in a different sense. Though Cassius has elements of the Machiavel of popular myth and uses systematic deception to realise his personal ambitions, he has little in common with Marlowe's buffoonish villain. Shakespeare's play is Machiavellian in the sense that it dramatises a pragmatic and sceptical view of politics which recognizes that virtue and utility are not always compatible.[23]

Shakespeare's Brutus is a man who prides himself on his own integrity. 'Believe me for mine honour, and have respect to mine honour, that you may believe', he tells the plebeians at Caesar's funeral (3.2.14–16). During one of the childish arguments that break out on both sides after the assassination, Cassius complains that Brutus has done him wrong. Brutus replies that he would never wrong an enemy, much less a friend: 'Judge me, you gods: wrong I mine enemies? / And if not so, how should I wrong a brother?' (4.2.38–9). In response to Cassius' angry words later in the same scene he tells him that such threats mean nothing to him: 'I am armed so strong in honesty / That they pass by me as the idle wind' (122–3). Brutus believes that integrity is the only true guide to conduct: if you display honesty in all your actions you will be repaid in kind. In the moving final scene of the play he tells his audience: 'Countrymen, / My heart doth joy that yet in all my life / I found no man but he was true to me' (5.5.33–5). These are generous words and they help to explain why Brutus is regarded by friends and enemies alike as 'the noblest Roman of them all' (67). But noble as his intention may be, what Brutus is saying simply isn't true. Throughout the play he has been surrounded by deceivers. Indeed, though Cassius admires his honesty, he knows that not even Brutus himself is incorruptible:

> Well, Brutus, thou art noble; yet I see
> Thy honourable mettle may be wrought
> From that it is disposed. Therefore it is meet

That noble minds keep ever with their likes;
For who so firm that cannot be seduced?

> (1.2.308–12)

Cassius is not a likeable character. But he is a much shrewder judge of human nature than Brutus is. In the space of two short scenes we see the truth of that judgement as Brutus allows himself to be persuaded that he must betray the man who loves him (1.2.313). But though Brutus speaks of the 'even virtue' of the rebel cause (2.1.132) as justification for the deception he has always claimed he is above, the imagery he uses tells another story:

> O conspiracy,
> Sham'st thou to show thy dang'rous brow by night,
> When evils are most free? O then by day
> Where wilt thou find a cavern dark enough
> To mask thy monstrous visage? Seek none, conspiracy.
> Hide it in smiles and affability;
> For if thou put thy native semblance on,
> Not Erebus itself were dim enough
> To hide thee from prevention. (2.1.77–85)

It is a measure of the confusion in Brutus' mind that he should tell Cassius that those engaged in what he himself describes as a 'monstrous' act of political treachery need no 'other oath / Than honesty to honesty engaged' (2.1.125–6). Later he tells his fellow conspirators they must disguise their true intention and act their parts with 'untired spirits and formal constancy' (223–6). That Cassius should urge his friends to act like 'true Romans' (222) is not out of character: as a Machiavel he has no scruples about using trickery to achieve his political ends. But Brutus has always proclaimed his belief in honesty as the paramount value in public life. For such a man to represent unswerving commitment to treachery as 'formal constancy' is either hypocrisy or self-deception. What Brutus says in soliloquy suggests the latter. In a kind of Freudian slip

---

[23] Machiavelli wrote: 'how men live is so different from how they should live that a ruler who does not do what is generally done, but persists in doing what ought to be done, will undermine his power rather than maintain it' (*The Prince*, p. 54).

he uses the traditional simile of political rebellion (compare Sidney's *Astrophil and Stella*, no. 5) to describe to himself his own mental confusion:

> Since Cassius first did whet me against Caesar
> I have not slept.
> Between the acting of a dreadful thing
> And the first motion, all the interim is
> Like a phantasma or a hideous dream.
> The genius and the mortal instruments
> Are then in counsel, and the state of man,
> Like to a little kingdom, suffers then
> The nature of an insurrection.   (2.1.61–9)

But it is not just self-deception that Brutus is guilty of. A Machiavel would probably say that his greatest crime is his political naivety. Whether or not Brutus should have listened to Cassius' warning about Caesar's ambitions is a matter of opinion: a contemporary monarchist would probably say he was wrong; a republican might feel that he was right. What is indefensible, from whichever position you view his actions, is the credulity he shows in the decisions he makes after the assassination. His first mistake is to take Antony's offers of friendship at face value and allow him to speak at Caesar's funeral. His second is to suppose that the plebeians can be trusted to make responsible judgements based on reason. Knowing how easily swayed the plebeians are, Cassius is horrified at the prospect of so consummate a politician as Antony being allowed to address them (3.1.234–7). But Brutus is determined to be fair and honest with the enemy he has just created. The result is summed up in the short symbolic scene that follows Antony's oration. The murder of Cinna is a powerful piece of stage symbolism. Rome is now controlled by the mob. It has become a tyranny.

Tom McAlindon has recently argued that in the English history plays Machiavellian deception never works to the benefit of the state; Shakespeare, he claims, endorses the humanist belief in truth as the only basis of justice and social order.[24] In an ideal world where 'noble minds keep ever with their likes' (1.2.311), politicians would no doubt be able to dispense with any 'other oath / Than

honesty to honesty engaged' and rely on mutual trust. But the world of *Julius Caesar* is far removed from that ideal. It is a world in which patricians employ systematic treachery, and plebeians are incapable of rational judgement. In such a world trust in the integrity of one's fellow politicians is the height of naivety.

IV

If *Julius Caesar* is thoroughly Machiavellian in its disillusioned view of politics, so too is it in its view of history. As many critics have noted, the play seems to be preoccupied with questions of meaning, interpretation and judgement.[25] A problem that occupies the minds of most of the major actors in this pivotal episode in Roman history is that of unnatural phenomena. Are these events a sign of divine displeasure at sacrilegious acts? Or are the gods indifferent to human affairs? Though Cassius and Caesar both change their minds on this question (1.3.61–71; 2.1.195–7; 5.1.76–8), we are no nearer to a definitive answer at the end of the play than we were at the beginning. The disasters that befall Rome after the assassination certainly make the unnatural events reported in the play look like 'instruments of fear and warning' (1.3.70). But since the gods themselves make no appearance, we cannot know whether they were warning men against Caesar's ambition or Cassius' planned coup, or indeed whether they exist at all. Similarly with Calpurnia's dream: though her own interpretation seems to be borne out by events, and that of Decius exposed as intentionally misleading, there is no proven connection between the dream and the events it appears to prophesy.

---

[24] 'Swearing and forswearing in Shakespeare's Histories: The Playwright as Contra-Machiavel', *Review of English Studies* 51 (2000), 208–29.

[25] See for example, Chang, '*Julius Caesar* in the Light of Renaissance Historiography', 63–71; René E. Fortin, '*Julius Caesar*: An Experiment in Point of View', *Shakespeare Quarterly* 19 (1976), 341–7; Robert S. Miola, *Shakespeare's Rome* (Cambridge, 1983), pp. 76–115.

Cicero (Shakespeare's character) claims that, when it comes to interpreting omens, 'men may construe things after their fashion / Clean from the purpose of the things themselves' (1.3.34–5). This is to suppose that, given the right information, it should be possible to arrive at a correct answer. But the play does not give us this information; it offers us no way of determining which interpretation is correct. In the absence of any certainties, the 'true cause' (1.3.62) of these portents can never be more than speculation and opinion. Is Shakespeare saying that the same is true of history, and that in the absence of determinate facts one interpretation has as much value as another? Is history, like poetry, merely representation? The play does not support this view.

In 2.1 there is a short episode that is striking in its seeming pointlessness. At the beginning of the scene Shakespeare gives us a marvellously convincing picture of an honest man wrestling with his conscience as he ponders the problem of whether or not to take action against a politician he thinks may become a tyrant. Then the conspirators arrive. The atmosphere is tense. Cassius draws Brutus aside. As they whisper together, Casca, Cinna and Decius talk amongst themselves. Since they are about to embark on an action that will transform Rome, you might expect them to reassure each other of the justice of their cause, or perhaps to reaffirm their resolve, or at least to run through their plans. But they talk of none of these things. Instead they argue about something completely inconsequential. Peering out at the night sky Decius says 'Here lies the east. Doth not the day break here?' Casca says bluntly, 'No'. Cinna joins in: 'O pardon, sir, it doth; and yon grey lines / That fret the clouds are messengers of day'. Casca replies:

> You shall confess that you are both deceived.
> (*He points his sword*)
> Here, as I point my sword, the sun arises.
>
> (2.1.100–5)

You could explain the scene in psychological terms – three men showing the pressure they are

under by quarrelling about trivia. But it's more than just a piece of psychological realism. The episode forms part of a pattern of opinion and counter-opinion that we have already glimpsed in Act 1. However, this dispute is quite different from the discussion about the significance of omens. The latter is a question of belief; the former is about facts. One is fluid and open ended; the other is determinate. It is true that Decius and Casca interpret the signs in the night sky in different ways. But that doesn't mean that the points of the compass are a matter of opinion. Either Casca is right or he is not, and no amount of debate can alter the fact. Sunrise will soon show who interpreted the signs correctly. Insignificant in itself, the dispute anticipates the motif of conflicting evidence and misinterpretation in the last two acts.

After their second quarrel (during which Cassius discovers that he has grievously misjudged Brutus), the two men receive conflicting reports of the actions of the Antony–Octavius alliance (4.2.225–30). They then discuss tactics (248–77). Brutus proposes that they march on the enemy immediately. Cassius disagrees. Brutus tells him they must cooperate with fortune when she is clearly working to their advantage ('There is a tide in the affairs of men') or suffer the consequences. Cassius reluctantly accepts Brutus' plan. But his misgivings are well founded. Once more Brutus has misjudged the situation. An immediate infantry attack is exactly what Octavius had hoped for: by initiating the engagement the enemy has sacrificed the advantage of higher ground (5.1.1–3).

Antony and Octavius too squabble about tactics: 'You said the enemy would not come down, / But keep the hills and upper regions. / It proves not so,' (5.1.2–4) Octavius tells Antony. 'Tut, I am in their bosoms, and I know / Wherefore they do it' replies Antony irritably (7–8). When Brutus and Cassius join them for a military conference, the two sides quarrel with each other. Only Octavius remains calm, coolly warning his enemies that he will never rest until every one of Caesar's wounds has been avenged. Once the battle of Philippi is under way, it is, contrary to Brutus' belief, misjudgement rather than fortune that determines the course of events. Believing that Titinius has been captured and that their situation is hopeless, Cassius falls on his sword. No sooner is he dead than Titinius enters wearing a wreath of victory. When he and Messala find Cassius' body, Messala comments on the irony of their predicament:

> Mistrust of good success hath done this deed.
> O hateful Error, Melancholy's child,
> Why dost thou show to the apt thoughts of men
> The things that are not? (5.3.65–8)

Titinius shares Messala's sense of the irony of the situation: 'Why didst thou send me forth, brave Cassius?' he says when Messala has gone, 'Alas, thou hast misconstrued everything' (5.3.79; 83).

As with the earlier debates over dreams and omens, and the arguments about political action, there is in Act 5 a mixture of conjecture, misjudgement and factual error. Was Cassius right to argue against taking the initiative at Philippi? There is no way of telling. Allowing the enemy to seek them out might have proved equally disastrous. But when Cassius commits suicide in the belief that their cause was lost, he was misinformed. This was not a matter of opinion. It was simple error. Pindarus was wrong; Titinius had not been captured. By returning repeatedly to the question of evidence and interpretation, *Julius Caesar* invites us to consider the problem that any historian must deal with in reconstructing the past. How reliable is our knowledge of the facts, and is our interpretation of them justified?

Postmodern historiographers argue that there is no essential difference between fact and interpretation. According to postmodernists Ellen Somekawa and Elizabeth Smith, 'within whatever rules historians can articulate, all interpretations are equally valid'.[26] Shakespeare does not appear to share this view. If, as Messala and Titinius observe, people often misinterpret the evidence, this presupposes that there are discoverable facts and that people are capable of getting them either right or wrong. There is no *a priori* reason for assuming that any

character, major or minor, is voicing Shakespeare's own views. But in this case Messala and Titinius happen to be right. The short-sighted Cassius (5.3.21) was wrongly advised that Titinius had been captured by the enemy. No sooner had he killed himself than the truth was revealed. Titinius had been surrounded by friends, not enemies. This is no more a matter of opinion than the argument in Brutus' house about sunrise. In both cases Error was showing men's thoughts 'the things that are not'.

Julius Caesar is an imaginative retelling of one of the most important events in Roman history. With its metadramatic concern with truth, interpretation and judgement it is also an invitation to reflect on the value of history. It may be true that, unlike the historian, the poet, in Sidney's words, 'nothing affirms, and therefore never lieth'.[27] Nevertheless, without a clear understanding of the difference between fact and interpretation, history, as Hayden White rightly argues, can have little meaning for the present. In *Julius Caesar* Shakespeare goes out of his way to emphasize that difference. While carefully avoiding commitment to either a monarchist or a republican point of view, he makes it clear that the story of Cassius' coup offers an instructive analogue for the present. But that analogue would only be meaningful if it told us something about human behaviour. The Earl of Essex's followers admired their leader for his virility; so strong was his sense of masculine pride that he was even prepared to quarrel with his sovereign when honour was at the stake. In a passage that could not help but strike a chord with contemporary readers of Essex's *Apologie*, Machiavelli warns that, when faced with the potential threat of tyranny, it is usually better to temporise than to risk violent action. If you do act precipitately you are likely to hasten the very evil you are seeking to avoid; the problem, as Essex

---

[26] Ellen Somekawa and Elizabeth A. Smith, 'Theorizing the Writing of History', *Journal of Social History* 22 (1988), 154.

[27] Sir Philip Sidney, *An Apology for Poetry*, ed. Geoffrey Shepherd (London, 1965), p. 123.

watchers could see all too well, is that 'men are by nature inclined to look with favour ... on enterprises which seem to have in them a certain virility'.[28] Without an understanding of those human universals which Machiavelli comes back to time and again in his political writings, we would indeed be, as White puts it, 'isolated within our peculiar modalities of experience'. Though it has been fashionable for some two decades to claim that most leading intellectuals of the time were radical anti-essentialists, the historical evidence points overwhelmingly in the opposite direction. Major and minor writers in this period are united in their belief in a transhistorical core of human nature, one of whose defining features is something that poets and dramatists refer to as 'the inward self'.[29] It is this essentialist view of humanity that forms the basis of their view of history.

[28] *The Discourses*, 1.287.

[29] So deeply rooted in neo-Stoic thought is the distinction between what Claudius calls the 'exterior' and the 'inward man' (*Hamlet*, 2.2.6) that it becomes an almost formulaic way of praising integrity. For example, when Sidney cites Aeneas as a model of virtue, he commends Virgil's hero for the control he shows both 'in his inward self, and ... in his outward government' (*An Apology for Poetry*, p. 120.). The first scholar to respond to materialism's anti-essentialist Shakespeare with a sustained reading of the plays as encoding a transhistorical view of human nature was Tom McAlindon. See *English Renaissance Tragedy* (Basingstoke, 1986), pp. 46–8; *Shakespeare's Tragic Cosmos* (Cambridge, 1991), pp. 21–4, 256–7; 'Coriolanus: an Essentialist Tragedy', *Review of English Studies* 44 (1993), 502–20; 'Cultural Materialism and the Ethics of Reading: or the Radicalizing of Jacobean Tragedy', *Modern Language Review* 90 (1995), 830–46. See also Robin Headlam Wells, *Elizabethan Mythologies: Studies in Poetry, Drama and Music* (Cambridge, 1994), pp. 11–16; Katharine Eisaman Maus, *Inwardness and Theater in the English Renaissance* (Chicago, 1995), pp. 1–34.

SCEPTICISM AND THEATRE IN *MACBETH*

KENT CARTWRIGHT

What is the cultural power of theatre? Defenders of the English Renaissance stage insisted on its instructional utility, but a more radical and unsettling idea had also begun to emerge by the late sixteenth century, that theatre can be, in an almost literal sense, true. That idea animates Thomas Heywood's *An Apology for Actors* (1612), which tells the story of a woman who, having previously killed her spouse, watches the on-stage ghost of a murdered husband and blurts out, 'Oh my husband, my husband! I see the ghost of my husband fiercely threatning and menacing me'.[1] For this guilty spectator, the uncanny vividness of the stage ghost transforms it into far more than a moral reminder. Rather, the ghost acquires an immediate, personal reality: 'so bewitching a thing is liuely and well spirited action', says Heywood, 'that it hath power to new mold the harts of the spectators' (B4ʳ). Qualities such as liveliness, well-spiritedness, and bewitchment express theatre's virtual life; rhetorically, they recall the sense of vividness evoked in the Renaissance concept of *energia*, a term applied to an image, often visual, so striking that it conveys a special liveliness and memorability, the impression of its own reality.[2] Thus the vivid claims proximity to the real.

I invoke *An Apology*, *energia*, and vividness as context for arguing that *Macbeth* (c. 1606) treats theatrical events as believable exactly – even only – because they are powerfully experienced.[3] One of Shakespeare's most psychological and spectacular dramas – the conjunction is no accident – *Macbeth*, of course, is replete with visions, such as the air-drawn dagger, so intense that they affect

[1] Thomas Heywood, *An Apology for Actors*; I. G., *A Refutation of the Apology for Actors*, intro. J. W. Binns (New York, 1972), sig. G2ᵛ. Although the *Apology* was published in 1612, scholars agree that it was likely written in 1607 or 1608.

[2] *Energia*, according to Erasmus, occurs when a description places an event 'before the reader painted with all the colors of rhetoric, so that at length it draws the hearer or reader outside himself as in the theatre ... this type of description consists chiefly in an exposition of details, of those in particular that most forcefully bring a thing before one's eyes, and produce an arresting narrative' (Desiderius Erasmus of Rotterdam, *On Copia of Words and Ideas* (*De Utraque Verborum ac Rerum Copia*), trans. Donald A. King and H. David Rix (Milwaukee, 1963), pp. 47–9). Erasmus is noting a principle earlier described by Quintilian: 'There are certain experiences which ... the Romans [call] *visions*, whereby things absent are presented to our imagination with such extreme vividness that they seem actually to be before our very eyes' (*The Institution Oratoria of Quintilian, with an English Translation by H. E. Butler, M. A.*, 4 vols. (Cambridge, 1921), 6.2.32); Quintilian argues (27–35) that the orator himself must feel the emotions that he wishes to arouse in his hearers. Stephen Greenblatt discusses the above passage, along with the views of Aristotle and Cicero, in regards to *enargeia* and witchcraft; 'Shakespeare Betwitched', in Tetsuo Kishi, Roger Pringle, and Stanley Wells, eds., *Shakespeare and Cultural Traditions: The Selected Proceedings of the International Shakespeare Association World Congress, Tokyo, 1991* (Newark, 1994), pp. 17–42, on pp. 29–30; see also pp. 39–40 n. 25. On *energia* and *enargeia*, see also Richard A. Lanham, *A Handbook of Rhetorical Terms*, 2nd edn (Berkeley, 1991), pp. 64–5.

[3] Greenblatt touches of this matter when he argues that in *Macbeth*, 'Shakespeare is staging the epistemological and ontological dilemmas that ... haunted virtually all attempts to determine the status of witchcraft beliefs and practices. And he is at the same time and by the same means staging the insistent, unresolved questions that haunt the practice of the theatre. For *Macbeth* manifests a deep, intuitive recognition that the theatre and witchcraft are both constructed on the boundary between fantasy and reality' ('Shakespeare Bewitched', p. 32).

characters as if real.[4] The notion that theatrical intensity can foster credibility introduces a strange hint of Protestant justification, of the psychology behind 'newness of life' turned to peculiar use. Moral implications notwithstanding, *Macbeth* takes as an overarching concern the authenticity of vivid experience, whether of the world or of the imagination and, in doing so, dramatizes a juncture in Renaissance epistemology.

The problem of knowledge – its erotic desirability, its dreadfulness, its elusiveness – haunts every corner of *Macbeth*. An obsession with knowing saturates its language: 'knowledge', 'judgment', 'thought', 'memory', 'doubt', 'trust', 'report', 'instruction', 'conclusion', 'prophecy', 'equivocation', and the life 'signifying nothing.' Yet despite the attention that *Macbeth* concentrates on understanding, little can be known. Stephen Booth concludes that 'it is almost impossible to find the source of any idea in *Macbeth*'; none of its conceptual categories will 'stay closed'; its words 'will not define'.[5] Such 'indefinition' recalls the kinds of arguments posed by the Greek sceptic Sextus Empiricus, whose influential works had become newly available in the 1560s and whose favourite line of argument is the demonstration that any truth-claim depends upon an endless regression of prior assumptions.[6] Sceptical questioning of what for certain can be known played an increasingly prominent role in Renaissance thought, provoking religious doubt in some and fideism in others.[7] The late sixteenth century marks an important moment in the rise of scepticism, Richard Popkin explains, because 'the intellectual crisis brought on by the Reformation coincided with the discovery and revival of the arguments of the ancient Greek sceptics' (xvi). Erasmus early in the century was influenced by scepticism, apparent in his debate with Luther, and Montaigne's *An Apology for Raymond Sebond* explores the vanity of mankind's faith in reason.[8] Montaigne's scepticism, of course, impressed itself on Shakespeare; likewise, other English playwrights, from Kyd to Marlowe to Marston, explored sceptical ideas.[9] More specifically, *Macbeth*, argues Stanley Cavell, helps to identify 'the catastrophe of the modern

advent of scepticism', expressed in 'a new intimacy, . . . [a] privacy shared (shared not with the public, but from it)'.[10] 'What scepticism threatens', according to Cavell, 'is precisely irretrievable outsideness, an uncrossable line, a position from which it is *obvious* (without argument) that the world is unknowable'.[11] If *Macbeth*'s political events originate in the 'unsayable privacy' of the Macbeths' marriage; if, that is, public action derives from what is occluded to knowledge; then the play demonstrates, for Cavell, the modern 'sceptical problematic', understood as the impossibility of knowing the basis on which we can know anything.[12]

---

4 Stephen Orgel notes the seeming paradox of *Macbeth*'s 'striking theatricality' yet its intense inwardness; 'Macbeth and the Antic Round', *Shakespeare Survey 52* (Cambridge, 1999), pp. 143–53, esp. p. 148. On *Macbeth* as a play about the problems of interpreting the visual, see Huston Diehl, 'Horrid Image, Sorry Sight, Fatal Vision: The Visual Rhetoric of *Macbeth*', *Shakespeare Studies*, 16 (New York, 1983), pp. 191–203.

5 Stephen Booth, *King Lear, Macbeth, Indefinition, and Tragedy* (New Haven, 1983), pp. 94, 96, 97. On doubleness, doubt, and confusion as aspects of the world of *Macbeth*, see T. McAlindon, *Shakespeare's Tragic Cosmos* (Cambridge, 1991), pp. 197–219, esp. 197–208.

6 See, for example, Sextus Empiricus, *Outlines of Pyrrhonism*, trans. R. G. Bury (Cambridge, MA, 1933).

7 On Renaissance scepticism, see, among others, Richard H. Popkin, *The History of Scepticism from Erasmus to Spinoza* (Berkeley, 1979); and Don Cameron Allen, *Doubt's Boundless Sea: Scepticism and Faith in the Renaissance* (Baltimore, 1964).

8 On Erasmus and Luther, see Victoria Kahn, *Rhetoric, Prudence, and Scepticism in the Renaissance* (Ithaca, NY, 1985), pp. 92–102.

9 See Geoffrey Aggeler, *Nobler in Mind: The Stoic-Sceptic Dialectic in English Renaissance Tragedy* (Newark, 1998); and Sukanta Chaudhuri, *Infirm of Glory: Shakespeare and the Renaissance Image of Man* (Oxford, 1981).

10 Stanley Cavell, 'Macbeth Appalled (I)', *Raritan* (Fall 1992): 1–15, on p. 2.

11 Stanley Cavell *Disowning Knowledge in Six Plays of Shakespeare* (Cambridge, 1987), p. 29.

12 Stanley Cavell, 'Macbeth Appalled (II)', *Raritan* (Winter 1993): 1–15, on p. 15. In *Disowning Knowledge* Cavell further describes scepticism and Shakespeare's relation to it: 'My intuition is that the advent of scepticism as manifested in Descartes's *Meditations* is already in full existence in Shakespeare, from the time of the great tragedies in the first years of the seventeenth century . . . The issue posed is no longer,

Macbeth responds to that problem of scepticism, I would argue, with a heightened sense of theatre's reality, an attitude inflected by Reformation psychology. Plays, of course, have always borne witness, paradoxically, to what is not there; medieval theatre, after all, has been thought to originate in the *Visitatio Sepulchri* (c. 970), the dramatization of Christ's absence at the tomb: '*Quem quaeritis?*,' asks the angel.[13] St Augustine, a theologian deeply in search of the real and also influenced by scepticism, was himself a lover of theatre in his youth; early in Book III of his *Confessions*, he ruminates on its uncanny power:

I was captivated by theatrical shows. They were full of representations of my own miseries and fuelled my fire. Why is it that a person should wish to experience suffering by watching grievous and tragic events which he himself would not wish to endure? . . . That was my kind of life. Surely, my God, it was no real life at all?[14]

In these lines, Augustine confronts the riddle of vicarious experience that drove Renaissance observers such as Stephen Gosson to oppose drama. 'Playes are no images of trueth', contends Gosson, who catalogues their falsehoods and stigmatizes their delights as devilish.[15] Although theatre can be compulsively attractive, surely it is not 'real life' – is it? An observation by Richard Lanham bears upon this problem: 'Man has a "motive", an urge, just to be alive, to reenact his own existence, and thus bolster, intensify it'.[16] By re-enacting our existence, that is, an art form such as theatre can confirm and heighten our sense of being alive; it verifies by reflection our experience of ourselves, to return to Augustine's quandary, as 'real'.

In modern philosophy, the term *realism* attaches to the view that mind-independent phenomena can exist, that a reality occurs 'out there' that may (or may not) correspond to our inferences.[17] The problem of the real figured prominently, of course, in the sixteenth-century debates between Protestants and Catholics over the Real Presence of Christ in the Eucharist.[18] From an experiential perspective, what we often mean by *real* differs from what we mean by a word such as *actual*, in that all actual experiences do not share equal degrees of realness: I stop writing on my computer, leave the library, and walk to the Metro station – events that are actual but not terribly real. They require little attention; tomorrow I will hardly bother to remember them. The philosopher Robert Nozick argues that people experience themselves as more 'real' in some circumstances than in others and regard some individuals as more real than others, just as some literary characters seem unusually real.[19] A realistic character projects something beyond the quotidian tenor of life: 'The reality of these characters consists in their vividness, their sharpness of detail, the integrated way in which they function toward or are tortured over a goal . . . They are intensely concentrated portions of reality'.[20] Likewise, Augustine's search for the real – the implicit subject of the *Confessions* – is real to us, transcends the limitations of time and place, because we recognize his passionate urgency. As Augustine's anecdote suggests, theatre seems a particularly apt and disturbing locus for questions of the real to arise,

---

or not alone, as with earlier scepticism, how to conduct oneself best in an uncertain world; the issue suggested is how to live at all in a groundless world' (p. 3).

13 On the religious origins of medieval drama see the classic study by O. B. Hardison, Jr, *Christian Rite and Christian Drama in the Middle Ages: Essays in the Origin and Early History of Modern Drama* (Baltimore, 1965).

14 Saint Augustine, *Confessions*, trans. Henry Chadwick (Oxford, 1991), pp. 35–7. Chadwick's translation, 'real life', captures neatly the contrast in Augustine's two uses of *vita*: '*talis vita mea numquid vita erat*' (Latin quoted from *St Augustine's Confessions, with an English Translation*, trans. William Watts (London, 1912), p. 104).

15 Stephen Gosson, *Playes Confuted in Fiue Actions* (1582), in Arthur F. Kinney, ed., *Markets of Bawdrie: The Dramatic Criticism of Stephen Gosson* (Salzburg, 1974), p. 169.

16 Richard A. Lanham, *The Motives of Eloquence: Literary Rhetoric in the Renaissance* (New Haven, 1976), p. 48.

17 On the realism/antirealism debate, see, for example, Christopher B. Kulp, ed., *Realism/Antirealism and Epistemology* (Lanhan, Md., 1997).

18 On theological issues of the Reformation, see Bernard M. G. Reardon, *Religious Thought in the Reformation*, 2nd edn (London, 1995).

19 Robert Nozick, 'Being More Real', *The Examined Life: Philosophical Meditations* (New York, 1989), pp. 128–40.

20 Nozick, *The Examined Life*, p. 130.

placed as it is between the corporal and the symbolic, performed by living actors comprehended as other than themselves, inspiring real emotions toward illusory objects. For the Renaissance, given the rise of scepticism, the Puritan condemnation of drama, and the Protestant emphasis on 'invisible' truth and its attendant doubts, those conundrums become intense.[21]

Macbeth addresses the problem of scepticism by turning theatre into a way of knowing: to argue so is to put scepticism and theatricality in a dynamic but paradoxical relationship, in which, although the premises of knowledge or action may recede before us, certain events can stand forth as compelling and authentic. Theatre's sense of lost certitude, of 'indefinition', is redeemed, at least in part, by its heightened sense of vividness. Indeed, *Macbeth* has often seemed to generate effects so vivid as to have a disturbing reality, as in the curse that presumably haunts productions or in the sense of uncanniness that some performers have experienced.[22] I shall consider the tension of scepticism and theatrical knowing in four aspects of *Macbeth*: (1) the credibility of Lady Macbeth's self-theatricalizing in the persuasion scene; (2) the uncanny reality of 'telepathic' character entrances; (3) the grotesque 'newness of life' called forth by Macbeth's murder of Duncan; and (4) the presentation of Macbeth's decline in terms of his recession into simulacra, theatrical representations of himself. At its extreme a curious relationship is at work in the play: representation, displacing actuality, becomes itself intensely real.

DECIDING TO MURDER DUNCAN

The experience of the real in *Macbeth* can be approached through two scenes involving decisions to murder: in reverse order, the conspiracy scene between Macbeth and the murderers (3.1) and the persuasion scene between Macbeth and Lady Macbeth (1.7). Although scenes of decision typically reveal a character's nature and motives, the couple's decision to kill Duncan is strangely unintelligible yet emotionally believable: the opaqueness of married privacy illustrates Cavell's 'sceptical

problematic', but the action convinces theatrically. How could such a momentous decision be intellectually occluded yet also credible and real?

To answer, it will help to examine Macbeth's behaviour in the later scene (3.1) in which he undertakes to persuade the murderers to assassinate Banquo and Fleance. In a previous meeting with the two thugs Macbeth had named Banquo as their tormentor and allowed a day for the men's grievance to fester; now he would orchestrate their anger to a crescendo and secure their agreement to murder. But, surprisingly, at every stage this rhetorical exercise turns anti-climactic. First Macbeth allows the murderers to demand additional proof, but they neither embrace his previous showings nor request more ('You made it known to us' (3.1.84)).[23] Second Macbeth attempts to goad them personally, but they reply in generalizations ('We are men, my liege' (90)). Third Macbeth promotes Banquo as their particular 'enemy' (104, 114), but the killers, 'weary with disasters' (111), answer only that they would hazard their lives on any chance. Finally Macbeth offers the murderers time to 'resolve' themselves apart, but they dismiss the invitation ('We are resolved, my lord' (138)). Overall, while Macbeth labours in careful stages to convince, challenge, enrage, and harden the two men so as to overcome any reluctance, they require no convincing at all.[24] While Macbeth strains needlessly,

---

[21] On the stage and Protestant 'invisible' truth, see Huston Diehl, *Staging Reform, Reforming the Stage: Protestantism and Popular Theatre in Early Modern England* (Ithaca, NY, 1997); on the stage and Protestant anxieties about inward mental states, see Katharine Eisaman Maus, *Inwardness and Theatre in the English Renaissance* (Chicago, 1995).

[22] On the *Macbeth*-curse, see Marjorie Garber, *Shakespeare's Ghost Writers: Literature as Uncanny Causality* (New York, 1987), pp. 87–123.; on acting in *Macbeth*, see Bernice W. Kliman, *Shakespeare in Performance: Macbeth* (Manchester, 1992), pp. 29–39.

[23] Citations of *Macbeth* will follow A. R. Braunmuller, ed., *Macbeth* (Cambridge, 1997).

[24] Joan Hartwig also observes that Macbeth's 'lengthy persuasion of the murderers is totally unnecessary' (p. 52), and she analyses the parodic parallels between this scene and the early persuasion scene; *Shakespeare's Analogical Scene: Parody as Structural Syntax* (Lincoln, 1983), pp. 52–7. For a related

dramatic tension between the rhetor and his hearers fizzles.

If this scene is not really about persuasion, what is it about? Two answers arise, both involving acts of displacement. One answer – perhaps the more conventional – is that the murderers' scene exhibits the extent to which Macbeth now embodies the spirit of his wife. By challenging the murderers' manhood and by taunting them as beasts ('hounds and wolves', 'dogs' (93, 94)), as Lady Macbeth had done with him, Macbeth may be displacing his still-unallayed doubts about his own manliness onto his auditors. He is performing Lady Macbeth: she has filled his psyche with an anxiety that he must assuage by acting out, imitating, her scorn. Yet the difference between Macbeth's urgency and the murderers' reserve also points to a second – perhaps less conventional – answer about the functioning of the murderers' scene. Macbeth's efforts to arouse the murderers suggest that he may seek from them a fervour commensurate with his own earlier passion. He desires not only their agreement but also their emotion, whether in hatred toward Banquo or in fear for children 'beggared' (89) by a heavy hand – this latter image recalling his own distress about a barren scepter (see 64–5). Macbeth identifies his cause with that of the murderers ('Banquo was your enemy . . . So is he mine' (114–15)), and invites a curious – and superfluous – bonding: the deed, 'Grapples you to the heart and love of us'; 'I to your assistance do make love' (105, 123). Hovering in the background of this language is a pseudo-marriage. Macbeth, that is, seems to be urging upon the murderers something of the complex, highly wrought emotional engagement that had been characteristic of him in the persuasion scene. He is re-dramatizing himself. That Macbeth would need to recreate the excited pitch of the earlier scene, where passion swept him toward action, points toward something insubstantial or unstable in his prior conviction.

Macbeth's claimed kinship with the assassins implies that his efforts to convince them to kill are attempts to convince himself – all over again, or, perhaps more to the point, for the first time. By instigating new murders, Macbeth would explain to himself why he undertook the first; he would make sense of his own previous actions, the unresolved emotion of the earlier scene displaced now into the later one. The idea is attractive: at this advanced stage in the play, Macbeth's behaviour can be viewed partly as an effort to authenticate, to clarify, or to make real his earlier decisions, for a quality of recuperation has infiltrated much of what he does: 'To be thus is nothing, / But to be safely thus' (49–50). That Macbeth might seek to identify or make real his motives for killing Duncan highlights the elusiveness of the past, with its half-done hero poised forever equidistantly between opposite shores: 'should I wade no more, / Returning were as tedious as go o'er' (3.3.137–8). What may repeat itself in *Macbeth* is not only the action of the past but also the original problem of motive[25] – and that pertains whether, with the assassins, Macbeth re-enacts his wife or imitates himself. In attempting to convince the murderers by reformulating his own experiences, Macbeth performs a theatrical act in which representation becomes his access to the experience of what is real. Debating with the murderers as with doubled versions of himself, Macbeth seeks to recapture and thus confirm the vividness and emotional power, the *energia*, of the persuasion scene.

The earlier scene becomes, then, the event that Macbeth must re-enact and explain – perhaps again and again – until he exhausts the possibility of meaning: 'It is a tale / Told by an idiot, full of sound and fury / Signifying nothing' (5.5.25–7). Paradoxically, the persuasion scene charts not one but two decisions by Macbeth that express two co-existing but mutually exclusive modes of human identity in

---

view, see also Jan H. Blits, *The Insufficiency of Virtue: Macbeth and the Natural Order* (Lanham, Md., 1996), pp. 101–5.

[25] James L. Calderwood argues that 'the murder of Duncan, of Banquo, and of Macduff's family is in a sense one deed tripled . . . [T]he second is a displaced version of the first, and the third a displaced version of both. By the same token the second is an attempt to perfect the first, and the third is an attempt to complete the second' (*If It Were Done: Macbeth and Tragic Action* (Amherst, 1986), p. 39). See also Robert Ornstein, *The Moral Vision of Jacobean Tragedy* (Madison, 1963), p. 232.

the play: the autonomous and the corporate selves. By corporate identity, I mean the sense of the self as so intensely in communion with someone else that the two seem to be sharing the same mental processes. In the conspiracy scene, the corporate model triumphs by manifesting itself through a theatrical vividness, even an uncanniness, that makes it convincing. Macbeth decides first, by himself, not to murder Duncan. His opening lines, 'If it were done when 'tis done . . . ' (1.7.1–10), pulse with interior life: the retrospective, unanchored 'it'; the shifting meanings of 'done'; the hissing sibilants and beating plosives; the sudden lingering of 'th'assassination'; the arhythmic stops and starts; the restless repetition of ideas; and the almost inarticulate longing ('the be-all and the end-all' (5)). His words express an unmediated gushing forth of thought and feeling as if from a true inner self. But moments later, after announcing to his wife, 'We will proceed no further in this business' (31), Macbeth reverses his initial decision and decides that he will kill Duncan, after all. This second decision possesses characteristics opposite to the previous one: while the first was made alone, the second is in conversation; while Macbeth's soliloquy had poured forth, here Lady Macbeth delivers most of the lines; while Macbeth had marshalled reasons in his soliloquy, here he decides without a compelling logic; while he had announced his first decision ('I have no spur . . . '(25)), here he betrays no definitive moment of choice. A final decision happens, but not as an emanation from some unmediated and authentic inwardness. Where does it take place?

Macbeth's decision to commit the murder occurs in the interval between his two lines: 'Who dares do more is none' (47) and 'If we should fail?' (59), a space filled by Lady Macbeth's soliciting and his listening. Her speech divides into two parts. The first part continues her challenging of Macbeth's manhood: 'When you durst do it, then you were a man' (49); the second part mutates from an argument into a kind of modelling, a demonstration of self-transformation, meant to be exemplary: 'I have given suck . . . ' (54). Until that speech, Lady Macbeth's questioning of her husband's manhood has failed to win him: the difference in her crucial

monologue is not so much her argument's reiteration as its speaker's monstrous self-fashioning.[26] She will inspire by her performance, but her speech poses daunting challenges that the actor must overcome. For example, as Lady Macbeth makes good on her earlier call to be unsexed, transformed into a thing of direst cruelty, she may bring to mind, as in 1.5, that well-known, self-metamorphosing infanticide, Seneca's Medea, whose majestic composure sets a high standard for comparison. Lady Macbeth postures, furthermore, in language notably blunt and graphic: one could speculate that a Renaissance boy-actor might have felt some awkwardness about delivering the lines or some anxiety about being convincing. In addition, Lady Macbeth must sound maternal, imperious, and demonic – contradictory effects whose proximity requires virtuosity of acting. Her speech also risks self-parody and auditorial alienation, for the image of plucking a baby from one's breast and smashing its brains out is melodramatic and repellent.[27] Lady Macbeth's sudden assurance might also register as facile, particularly if one remembers that Medea spends a play's length working herself up emotionally for infanticide. The abrupt deviation, moreover, from regicide to infanticide can appear gratuitous, even strange. Similarly,

---

[26] A distinguished line of criticism, of course, has viewed Lady Macbeth's attack on her husband's manhood as essential to her success in convincing him to assassinate Duncan: 'In this scene', says Janet Adelman, 'Lady Macbeth notoriously makes the murder of Duncan the test of Macbeth's virility' (*Suffocating Mothers: Fantasies of Maternal Origin in Shakespeare's Plays, Hamlet to The Tempest* (New York, 1992), pp. 130–46, on p. 138; see also p. 318 n. 21). Without contesting that view, I would yet draw attention to the pivotal importance of Lady Macbeth's shift from argumentation to self-representation.

[27] Marvin Rosenberg cites the following comment on the nineteenth-century Italian actress Adelaide Ristori's delivery of the infanticide speech: '"She seemed to tear the infant from her nipple and dash it to the earth. In any but a genius", the *Daily News* marvelled, "such an act, instead of startling, must have shocked an audience"' (*The Masks of Macbeth* (Berkeley, 1978), p. 274). From a psychoanalytic perspective, Janet Adelman calls Lady Macbeth's speech 'horrifying' because it activates 'the horror of the maternal function' latent within the play and within the culture; *Suffocating Mothers*, pp. 134–5.

the difference between the nature of the proposed act, symbolically a deicide, and the nature of the incentive, proof of manhood, is potentially farcical. Both character and performer, then, must draw themselves up grandly before the challenge of the speech, while spectators – including Macbeth – will have the pleasure of watching the character/actor confront and surmount the role's difficulties.[28]

No wonder, then, that onstage delivery of the infanticide speech 'is usually marked by an abrupt change of tone, expression, and movement', as Marvin Rosenberg notes, and that performers have often achieved, in the course of the speech, a 'hyperexcitement', sometimes even a 'kind of ecstasy' or 'strained exaltation'.[29] The effect can work so powerfully that it 'jolt[s]' both characters (p. 275). Lady Macbeth's speech thus comes to mirror Heywood's lively, well-spirited, and bewitching acting, an exemplum of vividness and realism. Lady Macbeth succeeds by changing the terms of the debate from manly daring to thespian daring; indeed, she would make the second term interchangeable with the first. If Lady Macbeth's modelling constitutes an 'argument', moreover, it is one made completely visible to spectators and, in that sense, not secret or 'shared from' them at all. Yet Lady Macbeth's argument-by-example remains opaque, because its complex tones and risky dynamics mean that the speech can be validated only according to its auditorial effect.

Lady Macbeth's effort works on at least one hearer, for Macbeth gushes with appreciation: 'Bring forth men-children only' (72). As Lady Macbeth has drawn up her body, inhabited her imperious vision, become theatre, she has also turned suddenly more real and believable to Macbeth. His reaction is convincing because it occurs as play-watching, something culturally familiar, potent and credible. But no audience's reaction will go so far as Macbeth's. While spectators watch Lady Macbeth's modelling exactly as does Macbeth, they are left to understand his wholesale change by means not of empathy but of imagination. Macbeth's response is unreproduceable – thus touched with the 'sceptical problematic' – and his motivation for the murder is revealed as a form of idiosyncratic spectatorship.

Macbeth functions as audience to Lady Macbeth's theatrical gesture; she captures his gaze, his intense looking, just as she captures that of the playgoers, so that the moment is almost voyeuristic. Her self-mimicry grips Macbeth, bewitches him, 'new mold[s]' him; his decision to kill expresses an imitative desire for something that he experiences through her, something outside himself. The very fact of theatre encourages this performative credibility; Macbeth believes Lady Macbeth because she successfully theatricalizes herself; she commands a vividness, a reality by reflection that is unavailable to the autonomous self. Macbeth's dialogue with Lady Macbeth displaces choice beyond the isolated self and into the psychic space occurring between it and another. That space is destabilizing, for Macbeth makes his fateful decision as the desire to imitate in his own life what he knows to be, even as he watches it, an imaginative enactment. The advent of modern scepticism in the Renaissance thus seems to encourage a paradoxical theatre, one in which vividness can become a form of knowledge and performance a virtual reality.

TELEPATHIC ENTRANCES

From the question of agency in decision scenes, I turn to a question of agency in dramaturgy: why do characters enter scenes when they do? Certain entrances in *Macbeth* support the impression that a corporate and theatrical agency is at work; their uncanny impact can enlarge our sense of how theatricality invites belief. *Macbeth* employs what might be called 'telepathic entrances', a device that exacerbates the sceptical dilemma. I use 'telepathic entrances' to describe occasions when a character appears as a virtual response to the statements or implicit thoughts of another character onstage. We are accustomed, of course, to a certain appositeness

---

[28] Different actresses, of course, have approached Lady Macbeth's speech differently; see Rosenberg, *The Masks of Macbeth*, pp. 273–7. On surmounting the difficulties of acting in Shakespeare, see Michael Goldman, *Acting and Action in Shakespearean Tragedy* (Princeton, 1985).

[29] Rosenberg, *The Masks of Macbeth*, pp. 273–4.

in entrances in early drama: 'Pat he comes like the catastrophe of the old comedy' (1.2.117), says *King Lear*'s Edmund, as his brother Edgar enters at the moment that the bastard wishes to dupe him.[30] Such entrances of convenience had long been common in English drama, but *Macbeth* employs them with a frequency that deserves remark and with a complexity that exceeds expediency. In *Macbeth* telepathic entrances are spectatorially thrilling because they offer metatheatrical evidence regarding a main question of the play, whether thoughts can have power over reality. That question reaches past the play's treatment of Edward the Confessor's healing hands to touch the new Stuart occupant of the English throne. James I was troubled by the idea of the king's cure, as is well known, and his 1605 visit to Oxford University (sometimes associated with *Macbeth*) featured a medical disputation, apparently much enjoyed by the king, on the topic: '*An imaginatio possit producere reales effectus?*' ('Whether the imagination can produce real effects?').[31] In *Macbeth* one version of that question is whether a character's thoughts can call another to him or her. To accord real effects to thoughts is to grant them a disturbing power that breeches the sceptical divide between self and world, altering the boundaries of what can be known.[32]

'You shall be king' (1.3.84), reflects Banquo to Macbeth, after the weird sisters vanish, to which Macbeth replies, 'And Thane of Cawdor too; went it not so?' (85). And one line later Ross and Angus enter to greet Macbeth as 'Thane of Cawdor' (103), apparently pulled to the stage magnetically by Macbeth's concealed desire. The entry of Ross and Angus initiates a series of entrances by characters who seem called forth by some preternatural power inside the play-world, some intensity of thought, statement or longing. Such entrances invest the mind with a fantastical, childlike power over others, creating moments of uncanny drama, the vivid working beyond mere colourfulness. But telepathic entrances are not unambiguous. Their problems are foreshadowed in Banquo's earlier response to the witches: 'Were such things here as we do speak about? / Or have we eaten on the insane root, / That takes the reason prisoner?' (81–3). The

authenticity of the weird sisters appears irrefutable yet naggingly dubious; were they quotidian presences or a joint fantasy so vivid as to be indistinguishable from reality – or something of both? The sisters inspire Macbeth's rapture without obviating Banquo's doubt.

In the case of Ross and Angus, the audience knows that their entrance, however telepathic, also had its commencement in an exit a scene earlier when Duncan sent the pair to 'pronounce the present death' of the current thane of Cawdor and 'with his former title greet Macbeth' (1.2.64, 65). Thus two orders of causation deploy themselves here and through much of the play, one from the realm of wish-fulfilment, the other from the realm of narrative exigency. How do we weigh these two possibilities? Although the telepathic explanation may never wholly negate the mechanical one, its surprise, uncanniness, and immediacy tend, I would argue, to give it authority. A certain *frisson* haunts these stage entrances, held slightly in check by the doubt activated in the recollection of an anterior agency. We recall that Ross and Angus's

---

[30] *King Lear*, ed. Jay L. Halio (Cambridge, 1992).

[31] John Nichols, *The Progresses of James the First*, vol. 1 (London, 1828), p. 536. Other of the disputations for James feature various questions about the viability of alchemy, the accessibility of human thoughts to heavenly creatures, and the conflict between public and private knowledge: '*An opera artis possit aurum conflari?*' (p. 536); '*An Sancti et Angeli cognoscunt cogitationes cordium?*' (p. 533); '*An Judex in judicando teneatur sequi legitimas probationes in judicio deductas, contra veritatem sibi privatim cognitam?*' (p. 535).

[32] The effect in question draws *Macbeth* toward the romances. When Leontes, for example, encourages Paulina to make Hermione's statue move, she responds, 'It is requir'd / You do awake your faith' (5.3.94–5); cited from G. Blakemore Evans, et al., *The Riverside Shakespeare* 2nd edn (Boston, 1997). Likewise, in Spenser's *The Fairie Queene*, Book I, Redcrosse's inappropriate thoughts and desires seem immediately to call forth real antagonists who embody them.

In an interesting essay on the problems of causality in *Macbeth*, James L. O'Rourke notes, 'There is an old English proverb about the operation of Wyrd which says "After word comes weird" – as the OED glosses it, "The mention of a thing is followed by its occurrence"' ('The Subversive Metaphysics of *Macbeth*', *Shakespeare Studies*, 21 (1993), pp. 213–27, on p. 216).

arrival in the third scene completes their exit from the second, like a stitch in the fabric of the story, but the precise moment of their entrance remains so apposite to Macbeth's thoughts as to be striking and mysterious, telepathic. Thus the thanes' arrival invokes a spectatorial surprise that validates Macbeth's 'rapt' (141) response to being named thane of Cawdor. His horrified thrill at the idea of murder, whose image unfixes his hair and makes his heart knock (133–4), confirms a visceral energy upon thought itself.

Moments later, *Macbeth* employs a telepathic entrance differently complex. 'There is no art / To find the mind's construction in the face', muses Duncan about the now-executed Cawdor, 'He was a gentleman on whom I built / An absolute trust' (1.4.11–14), at which words Macbeth enters. The new thane of Cawdor, of course, his presence demanded by Duncan, has simply reemerged from the previous scene, along with Banquo, Ross, and Angus. Yet the appositeness of this entrance overshadows its narrative rationale. What agency is at work? Macbeth does not enter because Duncan was thinking of him in particular; rather, the idea of duplicitous treachery calls Macbeth forth – ironically, of course, for Duncan considers Macbeth the opposite, the antidote, to misplaced trust. The causal agent is not Duncan's shocked insight but a reflexive energy or spirit of the play by which thoughts, desires, fears, and feelings receive direct responses – but not always those one might have consciously wished. By, in effect, making dramaturgy mystical, telepathic entrances hint at a special, partially hidden knowledge.

Macbeth has other entrances where a telepathic explanation registers strongly, but shadowed by a narrative one. No sooner has Lady Macbeth imagined herself chastising with the valor of her tongue all that impedes Macbeth from the crown (1.5.25–26) than a messenger enters with tidings that 'The king comes here tonight' (29). 'Thou'rt mad to say it', recoils Lady Macbeth, as if 'fate and metaphysical aid' (27) had suddenly made themselves manifest. Her desire to instigate murder commands telepathic power, it seems, even though the audience knows that Macbeth is hurrying hither from the

last scene with the news of Duncan's visit. One of the play's most obvious telepathic entrances comes in the persuasion scene when Macbeth confesses, 'I have no spur / To prick the sides of my intent', words that cue Lady Macbeth, as spur, to enter inquiring why Macbeth has 'left the chamber' (1.8.29).[33] A scene later, in the disarming tranquillity of night, Banquo asks, 'Merciful powers, / Restrain in me the cursèd thoughts that nature / Gives way to in repose', and the merciful powers answer him with '*Enter Macbeth . . .*' (s.d. at 2.1.10), the very character who might double in this play as 'cursèd thought'. Banquo, we gather, suffers from his own dishonourable fantasies, and Macbeth's entrance as Temptation identifies Banquo's susceptibility, even at the moment that he struggles to resist it. Thus Banquo's words show a telepathic power, although we know, too, that Macbeth has his own immediate business with Banquo and the night. Additional telepathic effects pepper the play: 'Sweet remembrancer!' (3.4.37), salutes Macbeth to his wife, as the not-so-sweet remembrancer, the bloody ghost of Banquo, slides into the king's place at the banquet table, that psychosomatically induced presence now subconsciously provoking Macbeth to name him before he sees him: 'Were the graced person of our Banquo present' (41). Later, in a scene with various telepathic signs, Macbeth vows to the witches that he will 'sleep in spite of thunder' (4.1.85), and a stage direction immediately intercedes challengingly with '*Thunder*.' Under assault, Lady Macduff flees from the stage '*crying 'Murder'*' (s.d. at 4.2.82), and thereupon Malcolm leads her husband into the next scene seeking to 'Weep our sad bosoms empty' (4.3.1–2), as if drawn across the stage by the lady's pathetic cry.

Telepathic entrances suggest that thoughts have an external valence, a conductivity in the world that obliterates its unknowability (the gulf between you and me), yet the play sprinkles its narrative explanations, too, like crumbs through the cave of the Minotaur. Telepathic entrances want to engulf

---

[33] Her probable entrance on 'spur' is made further likely by Duncan's earlier image, 'And his great love, sharp as his spur . . .' (1.6.24).

characters and spectators both; they register with a sudden emotional effect. Yet the narrative perspective has staying power, even if experienced at a low pitch and as an after-thought. The effect, then, is of an overarching engulfment and a flickering doubt. The potential estrangement, however, may actually help to make the telepathic explanation compelling, piquant. Some of Shakespearian drama's strongest impressions are created by the surmounting of impediments, as we have noted with Lady Macbeth,[34] and the narrative explanation provides just enough doubt to be an obstacle pleasurably overcome, so that the alternative acquires desirability. These moments encapsulate the play of scepticism and theatrical vividness, the sense of characters engaged intimately in ways that remain slightly elusive yet intuitively real. In their uncanniness, telepathic entrances point toward a corporate agency, as with Lady Macbeth, and they invite along the spectatorial spine a tingle that supports the play's relocating of authenticity and credibility.

'NEWNESS OF LIFE'

Saint Augustine, in his search for God, describes a seminal experience of being filled with an extraordinary, unearthly light that 'transcended' his mind.[35] Suddenly experiencing God 'within the heart', Augustine says, 'all doubt left me', and that assurance overwhelms his otherwise sceptical perception that things beneath God cannot 'be said absolutely to be or absolutely not to be'.[36] Augustine's certainty of the reality of God comes as an inner realization; it does not depend on the dubious external world, even though it changes utterly his perceptions of that world. Rather, his sense of new truth is enhanced – even confirmed – by its prior inaccessibility and unknowability. The world of Macbeth can provoke for characters moments of experiential certainty and hyper-realism – a new sense of authenticity – even though the play-world retains an opaqueness and instability of meaning over time. At work are opposing effects, for experiences can lose their potency as they recede from memory, yet they also can radically refashion one's sense of what has been and will come. In the latter

effect, Macbeth, during and after the murder of Duncan, passes into a new domain of consciousness in which the past and the present are changed and oddly animated. The vividness that seizes Macbeth in the murder scene, I want to suggest, reveals traces of Protestant 'newness of life' (Rom. 6.4), particularly as reflected by John Calvin and English Puritans such as William Perkins.[37] In a curious analogy to the Protestant sense of justification by God's grace, Macbeth becomes infused with an inchoate sense of the spiritual that gives depth, profundity, and a certain reality to Macbeth's vividly haunted life.[38]

Macbeth's new domain of experience resembles that of Senecan tragedy, but in a way that also enhances its Protestant colouring. Macbeth's 'new life' recalls the transformation that Senecan protagonists experience after committing an unspeakable crime. In Medea, to which Macbeth may allude, the eponymous heroine, after killing her elder son, recognizes a metamorphosis in herself: 'Everything's back, restored to me now . . . / I am a virgin again, newborn, unsullied. / This is the first moment of my new life' (1003–6).[39] Medea's sense of recuperated selfhood and power entails regret as well as joy: 'I'm sad, / deeply sorry for what I have done. But it is done, / . . . I have reached a truth, / . . . from

---

34 Michael Goldman has argued, for example, that great Shakespearian acting often involves a triumph over the difficulties structured into a role; see his *Acting and Action in Shakespearean Tragedy*.

35 Augustine, *Confessions*, trans. Chadwick, p. 123.

36 Augustine, *Confessions*, trans. Chadwick, p. 124.

37 English Protestantism, of course, is centrally concerned with inner Presence and its attendant problems. In understanding these matters, I have been much assisted by Debora Kuller Shuger's *Habits of Thought in the English Renaissance* (Berkeley, 1990).

38 An anxiety over inner truth touches the Renaissance variously, as in the public shock at the hidden malice of the conspirators in the Gunpowder Plot, or the accusation that Catholicism traffics in the fantastical, or the doubt about one's own election to salvation. On this subject, see Maus, *Inwardness and Theatre in the English Renaissance*.

39 *Medea*, from *Seneca: The Tragedies*, vol. 1, ed. and trans. David R. Slavitt (Baltimore, Md., 1992). All subsequent references will be to this edition.

which – I confess – I take a kind of joy' (1008–12). Fully cognisant of her crime, Medea passes into a new dimension of reality beyond prior comprehension. The Senecan narrative of transgression certainly differs from the Protestant narrative of salvation, but both suggest the gathering power in Elizabethan culture of a special epistemology of feeling, the sense of being so infused or consumed by an experience that one's perceptions, knowledge and self-awareness become radically reformed.

For Protestantism, the Pauline idea of an authenticating self-awareness, understood as newness of life, became a cornerstone of psychology. (An emphasis on personal transformation can also be traced in the Catholic counter-Reformation in England.[40]) In a typical passage, Calvin describes how the 'mind' and the 'heart' put on 'the inclination to righteousness, judgment, and mercy' in obedience to spiritual law: 'That comes to pass when the Spirit of God so imbues our souls, steeped in holiness, with both new thoughts and new feelings, that they can be rightly considered new'.[41] Calvin does not presume, predestination notwithstanding, that a person is transformed all at once through the grace made available to faith, since humanity's thoughts and works are inevitably tainted by the corruption of flesh and since the workings of grace can proceed slowly. The action of grace, nonetheless, acquires psychological markers, indicated by the kind of language that traverses the *Institutes*: 'inflamed', 'zeal', 'longing', 'inmost affection of the heart', 'inner feeling of the mind', and, of course, 'newness of life'.[42] William Perkins, in a work of the same year as *Macbeth*, emphasizes the link between grace and inner experience. According to Perkins, the 'work of sanctification' commences 'when God beginnes to kindle in the heart, any sparkes of faith'.[43] That imagery of kindling and sparks characterizes the tendency to grant justification a basis in psychological and emotional experience, and Perkins' treatise, like Calvin's, is peppered with a phraseology of inner action: 'breede in the heart', 'hunger and thirst after Christ', 'touched in conscience', 'stirre vp and exercise the inward man', 'joy of spirit'. According to Perkins, when a person finds 'new obedience' to Christ, that

surrender suffuses 'his minde, will, affections, and all the faculties of soule and bodie'.[44] Two decades earlier, attacking theatre's un-Godliness, Stephen Gosson also drew attention to how grace is identified by its energizing effects: 'The worde of God is liuelie, and mightie in operation: being liuelie, if it doe not quicken and stirre vs vp to a newenesse of life, it is a token that we haue no life, but are alreadie stone deade, in the workes of darkenes'.[45] Newness of life, by its very nature, cannot be fully understood until experienced.

Protestant psychology has implications for *Macbeth*. Its emphasis upon spiritual Presence as an inward experience, upon faith as not 'propositional belief but a theocentric emotionality', inevitably confers special privileges on feeling and consciousness (as does Senecan tragedy) – especially since the workings of God upon the heart

---

40 See, for example, the Jesuit Robert Persons's *The First Booke of The Christian Exercise, Appertaying to Resolution* (1582), ed. Victor Houliston (Leiden, 1998). Based on St. Ignatius's *Spiritual Exercises*, Persons's *Resolution* encourages the individual's meditation and reflection so as to achieve 'a radical and permanent inner change' (xxiv). According to Persons, such change is marked by 'a new spirit and a new heart' in the individual, who acquires energy, clarity, pleasure, and a new and revisionary 'light of understanding' through the workings of grace (pp. 145, 152; see pp. 143–59). Persons's *Resolution* was the most popular devotional book of the English Renaissance and was read widely by Protestants. Thus, while the present argument emphasizes the deep interest in 'newness of life' in Protestant psychology, it is important to remember that reformed Catholicism shared much with English Protestantism.

41 John Calvin, *Institutes of the Christian Religion*, ed. John T. McNeill, trans. Ford Lewis Battles (Philadelphia, 1960), in 2 vols. (vols. 20 and 21 of *The Library of Christian Classics*), vol. 20, p. 600.

42 On desire and longing as key Protestant markers of the Spirit at work in us, see Shuger, *Habits of Thought*, passim, e.g., pp. 41–4.

43 William Perkins, *The Whole Treatise of the Cases of Conscience* (Cambridge, 1606), number 482 of *The English Experience: Its Record in Earl Printed Books Published in Facsimile* (New York, 1972), pp. 51–2.

44 Perkins, *Cases of Conscience*, p. 64; see also pp. 75–7.

45 Gosson, *Playes Confuted in Fiue Actions*, pp. 149–50. It is striking how Gosson's language intersects with Heywood's in *An Apology for Actors*.

can be mysterious.[46] Thus the authority of inner experience runs the danger of drifting beyond its originary religious and moral coordinates.[47] Indeed, quasi-religious longing forms the emotional penumbra of Macbeth's 'If it were done' soliloquy, as in his desire to perform an act of almost religious consummation, 'the be-all and end-all – here'. The sense of inwardness and authenticity in Macbeth's soliloquy reflects the power that private fantasies can acquire when suffused with subjective religious desire. In Renaissance theatre, such language assumes a virtually self-confirming sense of reality.

As part of that tendency, *Macbeth* employs a psychology of personal transformation. Although Macbeth expresses a vivid imagination early in the play, his perception of the murder of Duncan changes, becomes, after the fact, more crystalline, comprehending, and moving. Duncan's murder takes Macbeth into a new domain of feeling and recognition, a macabre 'new life', that could not be foreseen or grasped before it happened.[48] As critics note, the murder recreates Macbeth's castle, previously remarked for its pleasant seat and delicate air, into a Hell, the point driven home by its comic 'devil-porter' who holds the door to 'th'everlasting bonfire' (2.3.16,18). That sense of a new, even hellish locale is also expressed in Macbeth and Lady Macbeth's preternaturally heightened sensitivity to sound ('Didst thou not hear a noise? . . . Did not you speak?' (2.2.14–16)); in Macbeth's graphic witnessing of the sleepers, itself a displaced witnessing to the murder ('One cried "God bless us!" and "Amen" the other, / As they had seen me with these hangman's hands' (29–30)); in the spirit-voices of the night ('Methought I heard a voice cry, "Sleep no more"' (37)); and in the horrifying luminousness of Duncan's blood ('Will all great Neptune's ocean wash this blood / Clean from my hand?' (63–4)). These items constitute a kind of visitation, an inversion of Pentecostal experience, with Macbeth now saturated by not a Holy but a demonic spirit. Macbeth's hands drenched in unwashable blood have obvious and ironic religious associations, first, with Pilate's attempt to wash his hands clean of responsibility for the killing of Jesus, and second, with baptismal immersion,

paradigmatically that of Christ, in which are figured simultaneously his washing away of sin and his sacrifice of blood.[49] Macbeth, in his own way, undergoes a bloody baptism that forever changes his sense of his very identity. Present here is what Debora Shuger calls 'participatory consciousness', a pattern of thought typical of theologians such as Lancelot Andrewes, in which an object assumes anagogical meaning (the reflection of sacred history in private experience) and in which knowing 'is not a matter of evidence but the penetration of the knower by the known'.[50] Contrasting with Lady Macbeth's rationalism, Macbeth's new life of preternatural awareness is intensely 'participatory', as in his metonymic identification of his own hands with Duncan's blood: 'this my hand will rather / The multitudinous seas incarnadine' (64–5). Macbeth takes the deed into his innermost heart – 'To know my deed, 'twere best not know myself' (2.2.72) –, the knower now penetrated by the known.[51]

---

46 Shuger, *Habits of Thought*, p. 81; on the Protestant psychology of inner experience, see, pp. 17–69 and *passim*; on the possibility that personal doubt might show, paradoxically, the Spirit at work, see pp. 41–4, 69–70, and *passim*.

47 Richard Hooker acknowledges that danger in *The Laws of Ecclesiastical Polity*, as Shuger discusses, *Habits of Thought*, p. 27.

48 Peter Milward stresses the apocalyptic connotations of Macbeth's murder of Duncan, although from a different perspective; *Shakespeare's Apocalypse* (Tokyo, 2000), pp. 45–54. Milton also shows Adam and Eve, after they have eaten of the apple, experiencing a certain 'new life': 'As with new Wine intoxicated both / They swim in mirth, and fancy that they feel / Divinity within them breeding wings / Wherewith to scorn the Earth' (*John Milton: Complete Poems and Major Prose*, ed. Merritt Y. Hughes [New York, 1957], *Paradise Lost*, IX.1008–11).

49 As Calvin puts it, 'Ever since Christ cleansed us with the washing of his blood, and imparted this cleaning through baptism . . .' (*Institutes*, p. 687).

50 Shuger, *Habits of Thought*, pp. 63, 64; see pp. 47–68.

51 *Macbeth*'s concentration on the transformational nature of experience can be underscored by comparing the scene in question with Faustus's signing of his contract with Lucifer in Marlowe's play. Faustus dismisses all the warning signs and undergoes no inner change; instead, when he begins to question Mephostophilis, he discovers with some annoyance that he can learn only what he already knows.

The understanding of Duncan's murder as an act of 'deep damnation' had been present in Macbeth's soliloquy in the persuasion scene (1.7.1–23), where his language hinted at Judas's betrayal at the Last Supper,[52] but Macbeth's emphasis on a de-icide inaugurating a new time, intensifies appreciably after the event: 'Had I but died an hour before this chance, / I had lived a blessèd time … / … renown and grace is dead' (1.3.84–7). In similar language, often considered wistfully sincere, Macbeth adds, 'Here lay Duncan, / His silver skin laced with his golden blood / And his gashed stabs looked like a breach in nature, / For ruin's wasteful entrance' (104–7). Macbeth's regret and longing in both speeches, if taken as earnest, expand upon his amazement in the murder scene, just as his words amplify Macduff's earlier statement that 'Most sacrilegious murder hath broke ope / The Lord's anointed temple' (60–1).[53] If circumstances compel Macbeth to pretend grief in these speeches, the enactment has the effect of calling forth genuine sorrow – for his words have the ring of personal truth. Thus playacting and sincerity converge, as Macbeth's self-theatricalizing provides access to the real. Indeed, the act of murder electrifies Macbeth's sensations; flooded with images of deicide, he is spell-bound with apparent remorse – all signs that Duncan's murder has acquired a new meaning and power in his consciousness. These qualities were lacking, in intensity if not in kind, before the murder, where Macbeth had marshaled himself toward the deed by means of self-negation, through Tarquin's ravishing strides. With his crime, he may not have achieved 'the be-all and end-all', but in his sense of vividness and revelation, Macbeth does discover a terrible 'newness of life'.

The penumbra of Macbeth's new life shows in his re-imagining, even sentimentalizing, of Duncan.[54] 'Loved, loving, trusting, generous, surrounded with images of fertility and divine grace too numerous to count, he is presented to us … as the ideal king for an ideal world', concludes Maynard Mack of Duncan.[55] But the notion of the King as the epitome of a nostalgic, lost ideality may fit Duncan deceased better than Duncan alive. Against the view that the King is a teary-eyed,

out-of-touch ruler of a disappearing world, the director Peter Hall interprets Duncan, for all his courteousness, as 'adroit', 'clever', 'very much in command', and not eminently 'murderable'.[56] Evidence of that view comes in Duncan's deft, almost challenging, designation of Malcolm as his heir at the celebratory moment when he is dispensing the garlands of victory to his thanes. Courteous, yes, but Duncan is also playing dynastic hard-ball and stifling any fantasies of ambition, as Macbeth well realizes: 'that is a step / On which I must fall down, or else o'erleap' (1.4.48–9).[57] At the beginning of the play, furthermore, Duncan's kingdom is typified, according to Graham Bradshaw, by 'Acts of appalling savagery' that 'obliterate any steadying, sustaining sense of the values which are ostensibly being defended'.[58] Macbeth himself later refers to

---

[52] Peter Milward notes that Christ's statement to Judas at the Last Supper, 'That thou doest, do quickley' (*John* 13.27, quoted from *The Geneva Bible*) is echoed in Macbeth's emphasis, at Duncan's 'last supper', on an action that is best 'done quickly' (1.7.2); *Biblical Influences in Shakespeare's Great Tragedies* (Bloomington, 1987), pp. 112–13, 124.

[53] Evident here is the Pauline notion of the body as the temple of the Lord, but it is tempting also to hear in the lines a reference to the tearing, at Christ's crucifixion, of the curtain that hung before the *sanctum sanctorium* in the Second Temple, as reported in *The Gospel of Mark*. The rending of the curtain exposes the inner sactum and thus echoes and completes the opening of the heavens at Jesus's baptism; thus Macduff's lines may bear a distant trace of the image of baptism, deepening the new connotations of Duncan's death.

[54] For a similar perspective, see Wilbur Sanders, *The Dramatist and the Received Idea: Studies in the Plays of Marlowe and Shakespeare* (Cambridge, 1968), pp. 257–8.

[55] Maynard Mack, *Killing the King: Three Studies in Shakespeare's Tragic Structure* (New Haven, 1973), p. 150. Contrastingly, David Norbrook, in perhaps the best political analysis of the play, emphasizing its republican values, observes that 'critics tend to exaggerate his [i.e. Duncan's] sacramental character' ('*Macbeth* and the Politics of Historiography', in Kevin Sharpe and Steven N. Zwicker, eds., *Political Discourse: The Literature and History of Seventeenth-Century England* (Berkeley, 1987), pp. 78–116, on p. 94).

[56] Peter Hall, 'Directing *Macbeth*', in *Focus on Macbeth*, ed. John Russell Brown (London, 1982), pp. 231–53, on p. 234.

[57] See Hall, 'Directing *Macbeth*', pp. 233–4.

[58] Graham Bradshaw, *Shakespeare's Scepticism* (Brighton, 1987), p. 222; see pp. 219–22.

the 'fitful fever' of Duncan's life and his immunity in death from 'steel', 'poison', 'malice domestic', and 'foreign levy' (3.2.24–5). Duncan's reign was no Arcadia.[59] Even some critics who appreciate Duncan's nurturing side consider him a spurious ideal: 'Heavily idealized, this ideally protective father is nonetheless largely ineffectual'.[60] Yet 'renown and grace is dead', says Macbeth of the murdered Duncan, and he later laments that for the profit of others he has murdered 'the gracious Duncan' (3.1.65). The word *gracious* may dominate the play's view of Duncan after his fall, but that is a post-mortem emphasis. It occurs in the context of the murder's dastardly and pitiable nature and the hellishness of Macbeth's discovered world. It is true, but retrospectively so. Macbeth has entered a domain in which metaphoric and symbolic values can displace the previous fact, becoming themselves the new reality now defining his life.

'Newness of life' in *Macbeth* raises suspicions about the dangers of imagination and even reason, suspicions reminiscent of the scepticism that informs Montaigne's *Apology for Raymond Sebond* (and that sometimes occurs in early seventeenth-century Protestant treatises). For Montaigne, man is an inconstant and pathetic figure whose rational imagination is unique but self-subverting:

And if it be so that he alone above all other creatures hath this liberty of imagination and this license of thoughts which represent unto him both what is and what is not and what him pleaseth, falsehood and truth, it is an advantage bought at a very high rate and whereof he hath little reason to glory; for thence springs the chiefest source of all the mischiefs that oppress him, as sin, sickness, irresolution, trouble, and despair.[61]

As a moral fable, *Macbeth* confirms Montaigne's view; as a poetic and theatrical experience, *Macbeth* repudiates it. The play raises suspicions about the imagination and even sense impressions; it demonstrates the vanity of Macbeth's reason and of his reliance on the witches; but neither scepticism nor nihilism constitutes the truth upon which the action settles. Although Macbeth learns that he was mistaken to trust the witches, events tend nevertheless to reinforce the vividness and magnetism

of visions, dreams, and psychosomatic experiences. By making them aspects of crime, Shakespeare detaches the power of lively impressions from their ethical import. In that regard, despite its much-noted indebtedness to the morality tradition, *Macbeth* careens wildly away from morality values.[62] The play succeeds perhaps not so much by being a 'morality' or even by inspiring auditorial sympathy toward its protagonist as by activating culturally compelling, deeply felt, religious and literary models of inward authenticity, while harnessing them to a harrowing criminality. *Macbeth*, in that paradox, is genuinely frightening.[63] The contradiction is instructive because it isolates the epistemological stakes when, against the threat of scepticism, one attempts to affirm the possibility of knowledge by insisting that the vividness and realism of heightened moments of experience manifest a kind of truth. Macbeth's version of 'newness of life' is grotesque; simultaneously, he offers the most enlivened, authentic, and real consciousness in the play. In that paradox lies *Macbeth*'s own witchcraft.

BECOMING THE IMAGE OF ONESELF

While arguing that theatrical vividness constitutes a kind of epistemology, I have also been investigating the achievement of that effect through various acts of displacement: how corporate identity displaces individual identity and theatricality displaces reason; how telepathic agency displaces narrative logic; how post-murder visions displace prior

---

[59] Bradshaw, *Shakespeare's Scepticism*, p. 222; similarly, Stephen Orgel concludes that 'Duncan's rule is utterly chaotic' ('Macbeth and the Antic Round', p. 146).

[60] Adelman, *Suffocating Mothers*, p. 132.

[61] Michel de Montaigne, *Selected Essays of Montaigne, in the Translation of John Florio*, ed. Walter Kaiser (Boston, 1964), pp. 104–5.

[62] See also Howard Felperin, *Shakespearean Representation: Mimesis and Modernity in Elizabethan Tragedy* (Princeton, 1977), pp. 118–44.

[63] On *Macbeth* as a terrifying play, see Bradshaw, *Shakespeare's Scepticism*, pp. 219–56.

ones.[64] The play offers various other examples: Macbeth displaces the emotional repercussions that he feels toward the murder into his choked response to the praying sleepers; Lady Macbeth echoes the witches as she spurs Macbeth, displacement conferring on her an uncanny vividness.[65] Engagement with the real, as I suggested at the outset, can come through experiences that, oddly, are representational rather than actual. If in the first act, Lady Macbeth creates believability by theatricalizing herself, Macbeth's vividness in the last one arises from his acts of self-displacement, expressive of his urge to externalize thought into a finished event: 'The very firstlings of my heart shall be / The firstlings of my hand ... / ... be it thought and done' (4.1.146–8). Macbeth's essential act of self-theatricalization – correspondingly an act of self-negation – is to displace himself into characters, things, and symbols that come, in turn, to represent him.[66] By the play's end, he will achieve a metamorphosis – perhaps what he has wished – into something virtually exterior, the theatrical representation of himself. The last act lays the groundwork for Macbeth's self-displacement by emphasizing a new instability in his being. He enters crying, 'Bring me no more reports' (5.3.1), but suddenly seeks what he has rejected: 'What news more?' (30). He asks the doctor for medical information but then consigns 'physic to the dogs' (48). He claims that he can never 'sag with doubt' (10) yet admits to Seyton that 'this push / Will cheer me ever or disseat me now' (20–1), a judgement at least half full of sagging doubt. He then, contradictorily, punctures altogether any possibility of 'cheer': 'I have lived long enough' (22). But even that tentative position – the quiescence of old age, 'the sere, the yellow leaf' (23) – Macbeth immediately displaces with another, the absence of the consolations of life, which he 'must not look to have' (26). What began as confidence in the witches vacillates until it sounds like its reverse, despair.

As the dialogue turns to matters of sickness, other people and things begin to appear as simulacra for Macbeth. 'How does your patient, doctor?', Macbeth queries about Lady Macbeth (38), but the physician's depiction of restlessness and

'thick-coming fancies' (39) fits Macbeth as well as her. When Macbeth speaks of a 'sweet oblivious antidote' for his wife that can 'Cleanse the stuffed bosom of that perilous stuff / Which weighs upon the heart' (44–6), his words bespeak a longing on his own behalf, and it is his resistance to healing himself that gives voltage to his condemnation of physic. At a deeper level of displacement, the image of weight upon the heart, which the Doctor takes as applying now strictly to the husband, pulls the dialogue toward a bedrock of Shakespearean *Weltschmertz* that seems no longer bound precisely to an occasion. Finally, the patient becomes not simply Lady Macbeth but the diseased land of Scotland itself (52), riddled with the Macbeth-infection (in implicit contrast to the English kingdom healed by the king's touch). The point that I would urge about this scene is that Macbeth's successive dilations on Lady Macbeth and Scotland turn into successive displacements of the self; the more he rages and declaims, the more he disappears into the things he has diseased. In Macbeth's curious instability lies much of the drama of the last act.

In self-displacement, Macbeth has sought 'To crown' his 'thoughts with acts' (4.1.148), deeds becoming the hallmark of his kingship. Remarkable in the last act is the physicality of Macbeth's thoughts. His emotions, feelings, and cogitations take on a curious externality, as if he had become a series of bodily perturbations: 'The mind I *sway* by

---

64 Stephen Booth offers a related example of displacement in *Macbeth*. Noting that Macbeth, when slain by Macduff, receives no death speech nor is otherwise 'labeled as dead', Booth argues that the acknowledgment lavished on young Siward furnishes a 'displaced fulfillment of the audience's need for certainty' regarding Macbeth (*King Lear, Macbeth, Indefinition, and Tragedy*, p. 93). Emotional needs generated in one domain are fulfilled in another.

65 On Lady Macbeth's displacement of the witches, see Peter Stallybrass, '*Macbeth* and Witchcraft', in *Focus on Macbeth*, ed. John Russell Brown (London, 1982), pp. 189–209, on pp. 196–8; for a compelling psychoanalytic version of that argument, see Adelman, *Suffocating Mothers*, pp. 134–8.

66 Even before the last act, Macbeth has become increasingly removed from his killings, his destructive impulse displaced into others: the murderers act as his factors; his implacable militia sweeps down upon Macduff's household.

and the heart I *bear* / Shall never *sag* with doubt nor *shake* with fear' (5.3.9–10; emphasis mine). Correspondingly, Macbeth perceives others psychosomatically and kinesthetically: 'those linen cheeks of thine / Are counsellors to fear'; 'Pluck from the memory a rooted sorrow, / Raze out the written troubles of the brain' (16–17, 42–3). Thought – 'thick-coming fancies' – takes on qualities of weight, colour, texture, and energy, perhaps even more so here than in most Shakespearian plays. Macbeth's inner experience has transmogrified into outward motion and sensation, as if his whole being were now strangely theatricalized. The thick-coming palpability of Macbeth's thoughts helps to make his instability understandable, for in some unexpected sense, the firstlings of his heart have indeed become the firstlings of his hand. Macbeth's physicality of thought constitutes an ironic expression of his newness of life, for his vividness and immediacy of mental experience have now reached the point of burden, one that he would escape – were there some 'sweet oblivious antidote'.

'Be it thought and done' becomes a cruel catchphrase. Macbeth's desire to have his thoughts translated instantly into deeds constitutes a parodic reduction of a central tenet of Catholicism in opposition to Protestant theology. In the debates about the Real Presence in the sixteenth century, the Catholic position toward '*Hoc est corpus meum*' (*Matt.* 26:26) was that 'Christ's word was his will', as Nathaniel Woodes expresses it in *The Conflict of Conscience* (1581), reproducing just such a debate (4.1.1120).[67] Anglicans refused to embrace the Catholic literalism that the will of Christ transubstantiates the host into flesh. This argument remained heated throughout the century, with one particular exchange of warring publications coming in the last two decades. The Catholics argued, as William Rainolds puts it, in a treatise dedicated to James VI of Scotland, that the Real Presence was 'wrought in the elements of bread and wine by the force of Christs words'.[68] Catholics emphasized the transforming 'force' and 'power' of Christ's intention. Macbeth's 'Be it thought and done' manifests just such a pseudo-Catholic vision made into blasphemous vanity and farce. The idea

of an omnipotent mentality underscores Macbeth's grotesque dream of self-deification. His condition constitutes a verdict, furthermore, on the desirability of the tempting hypothesis, aroused by the narrative structure, that thoughts might have uncanny power. As imaged in the heavy body-armour propelled on and off by his mood swings, Macbeth's virtual physicality of thought manifests itself in behaviour so restless and unstable as to be ineffectual. The human desire to merge thought and act becomes an untenable, even ridiculous, Catholic fantasy. For Macbeth, the final, ironic permutation of 'Be it thought and done' will be its lingering suggestion of an unconscious desire for relief, the emptying out of his freighted mind.

For better or worse, then, Macbeth's imagination has come to constitute his reality. Thus, in the final fighting before the castle, Macbeth can dispatch Young Siward almost effortlessly, since he believes himself invulnerable. When he encounters Macduff, his imagination destroys him. Before their fateful conversation, the two first "*Fight*" (s.d. at 5.8.8). In that skirmish, Macbeth evidently holds his own without difficulty, as his taunting of Macduff indicates: 'Thou losest labour, / As easy mayest thou the intrenchant air / With thy keen sword impress as make me bleed' (8–10). Yet after Macduff proffers his fantastical and lame explanation of how he was not 'born of woman', Macbeth finds that Macduff's words have 'cow'd my better part of man' (18). Given the play's dynamics, that line should induce thespian hesitating or shrinking,

---

[67] Quotations from *The Conflict of Conscience* refer to the edition in Edgar T. Schell and J. D. Shuchter, eds., *English Morality Plays and Moral Interludes* (New York, 1969). Part of the authority of the Catholic interpretation derives from *John* 1.1: 'In the beginning was the Word, and the Word was with God, and the Word was God.'

[68] William Rainolds, *A Treatise Conteyning the True Catholike and Apostolike Faith* (Antwerp, 1593; rept. Menston, 1970), p. 48; see pp. 48–53; see also John Hamilton, *Ane Catholik and Facile Traictise* (Paris, 1581; rept. Menston, 1971), e.g., p. 13. For an inventory of treatises in this dispute, see Peter Milward, *Religious Controversies of the Elizabethan Age: A Survey of Printed Sources* (London, 1977), p. 133.

Macbeth experiencing his imagination in his bodily capacities. Betrayed by the witches, so he thinks, and preferring not to fight Macduff at all, Macbeth now falls before Macduff's sword. Shakespeare gives us Macbeth's initial, successful skirmish followed by his emotional collapse to make the point clear: Macbeth can be defeated on the battlefield once he has been defeated in his imagination. Cowed in spirit, he has transformed from martial equal into Macduff's prey. The prophecies of the witches have so consumed Macbeth, so possessed his identity, that they are the only reality that he can live out. Thoughts have power, ironically so, as Macbeth becomes the puppet of his fantasy: be it thought and done.

If Macbeth is the most vivid personage in the last act, he also suffers the most extreme reduction, since, his valiant fury notwithstanding, he will end up as a theatrical sign. The play, of course, is permeated with theatrical imagery, notably of costuming. Macbeth and Lady Macbeth will assume masks or vizards to veil their true intent; later, Macbeth as king will resemble a player too small for his regal garments. Macbeth himself points up the play's theatrical imagery in his 'tomorrow' speech, and it needs only a backward glance to see in Lady Macbeth a walking shadow, a poor player, compulsively re-enacting the scenes she has played, witnessed by the audience of Gentlewoman and Doctor. In the spirit of costuming, Macbeth's garments are said not to fit him: his cause is too 'distempered' to 'buckle' 'within the belt of rule' and his title hangs 'loose about him, like a giant's robe' (5.2.15–16, 21). It will be in resistant armour that Macbeth finds comfort and identity: 'At least we'll die with harness on our back' (5.5.51). This sense of the theatricalized self is supported by other stage references: 'Why should I play the Roman fool and die / On mine own sword?' (1–2), asks Macbeth, treating his end as if it were a classical drama. When Macbeth imagines life–his own life–as a 'poor player / That struts and frets his hour upon the stage' (5.5.23–4), he recalls the bombastic, Tamburlainean acting then familiar at the rival northern playhouses, as if even Macbeth had come to see himself as a theatrical caricature.[69]

The vision of Macbeth's self refracted into stage figures culminates in the play's final theatrical image. Before they duel, Macduff chides Macbeth to 'live to be the show and gaze o'th'time. / We'll have thee, as our rarer monsters are, / Painted upon a pole and underwrit, / "Here may you see the tyrant"' (5.7.24–7). Macduff imagines Macbeth as an exhibition inside a tent or booth, probably at a fair, advertised at the entrance by a sign nailed upon a stick, with a motto and a painted likeness, inviting the commons to enter as gawkers. That is close to what Macbeth will become, for moments later the triumphant Macduff re-enters with a theatrical property, surely a wooden form of a head with a painted face, mounted on a stick. The property risks being deflating and parodic, since a generic head upon a pole will be striking not for how it resembles but for how it fails to resemble Macbeth or any living person. That impression will linger for the remainder of the scene if Macduff continues to display the head frowning down upon the close.

That Macbeth should become a painted wooden head is, on one level, unrealistic and unbelievable; it makes the tragic carnivalesque and introduces absurdity into the freeing of the time. On another level, Macbeth will be revealed as transformed into the kind of theatrical externalization or objectification of himself that he has long desired, and his icon will acquire the uncanny realism perhaps only available through theatre. Macbeth's desire for externalization is expressed early when, for example, he marshals his way toward the murder by play-acting a stagey, stalking Tarquin. It is expressed toward the end in Macbeth's displacement of his identity into other people, objects and images; in his theatrical metaphor of a walking shadow; in his encasing of his exterior with armour and shield; and even in his silence at death. Such is the ultimate revelation, that Macbeth's longing for transport constitutes a longing to empty out his churning interiority by

---

[69] On Marlovian heroic acting in the northern playhouses, 1599–1609, see Andrew Gurr, *Playgoing in Shakespeare's London* 2nd edn (Cambridge, 1996), p. 159 and pp. 158–64 *passim*.

becoming his theatrical sign. Here Macbeth arrives at the final displacement of selfhood begun in the persuasion scene.

The last scene has power because Macbeth is a theatrical sign of extraordinary resonance.[70] He broods over the ending like the eyes of Dr T. J. Eckleburg, but his spirit is also reticulated in the imagery and action of the scene; it is the absent Macbeth, not any present character, who gives uncanny vitality to the conclusion. To mention briefly some of the well-known internal allusions: Macbeth's mounted head repeats the decapitation of the rebel McDonwald from the play's beginning; Macduff now replaces Macbeth in the tempting position of curber of rebellion's lavish spirit; Malcolm, recalling Duncan, promises just rewards, surprises with title changes, and quickly departs for more celebration. A pattern suggests itself of restoration and further rebellion, a possibility made authentic by Macbeth's theatrical remains. Like the ghost-play of the *Apology for Actors* brought alive in an auditor's imagination by an alien spirit, like the uncanny agency adumbrated by telepathic entrances, the realm of Scotland is infused with its own displaced, vivifying spirit in the effigy of Macbeth. Ultimately, we might say that displacement serves *Macbeth* because its true effect is not of separation but of convergence, of shortened distances – between Macbeth and the other painted heads, between the object and its representation, between life and theatre.

CONCLUSION

In the early 1600s, observes Andrew Gurr, the northern London playhouses emphasized a drama of melodramatic engulfment, with considerable citizen appeal, while the Bankside playhouses opted for a more detached and ironic theatre, pleasing to sophisticates.[71] The exception was the Globe, which followed neither trend yet flourished in popularity among various classes. Shakespeare could certainly employ engulfment or estrangement, yet it would be typical of his innovative theatre to juxtapose those effects complexly.[72] Likewise, affirmation in *Macbeth* acquires a certain contiguousness with doubt. Scepticism, applied to drama, works surprisingly to bring attention to the texture of lived experience, to the sense impressions by which we construct understanding, to the intersection of materiality and consciousness. Hence the theatre of *Macbeth* lays claim to what is real in acts of displacement, whereby dramatic emotion becomes reified and validated in its own right. Incubating in *Macbeth* is the possibility of both the fascinated horror of Websterian tragedy and the wonder of late Renaissance romance. Indeed, the play constitutes a virtual parable of the transformation of the Elizabethan taste for action into the Jacobean interest in states of mind.[73] In cultivating these grounds, *Macbeth* demonstrates the degree to which a play's ideas and characters can become more believable and real by being successfully theatricalized, the degree to which, that is, drama had acquired a new cultural credibility and authenticating power.

---

[70] For Marjorie Garber, he becomes a kind of talisman; *Shakespeare's Ghost Writers*, p. 115.

[71] Gurr, *Playgoing in Shakespeare's London*, pp. 158–64.

[72] On engagement and detachment in Shakespearian tragedy, see Kent Cartwright, *Shakespearean Tragedy and Its Double: The Rhythms of Audience Response* (University Park, 1991).

[73] On this transformation, see G. K. Hunter, *English Drama 1586–1642: The Age of Shakespeare* (Oxford, 1997), p. 21.

REVELS END, AND THE GENTLE BODY STARTS

SIMON SHEPHERD

You can recognize the queen of the gods not by her face, nor by her clothing, but by her bearing. 'Great Juno comes', says Ceres in *The Tempest*, 'I know her by her gait'.[1]

In a production of the play that wanted to ensure, rather than estrange, the wonder of the masque, Juno's bearing would not work to establish personal idiosyncracy – a characteristic slouch, for instance – but would produce instead a sense of typical majesty and divinity. And an audience would probably have little problem in sharing Ceres' ability to recognize a person from the way she holds herself. They haven't seen Juno before, but she must be the one with the divinely queenly pose.

This seems commonsensical stuff. But it begins to unravel when we ask how a divine bearing actually holds itself. What makes it distinct from a mortal stance? And do queens move differently from ladies, from serving-women, from kings? These questions are not just relevant to actors, whose work is to make the representation. They are also relevant to those who watch and interpret the representation, in that modes of bodily organization don't only suggest social status, category or occupation, but at the same time imply qualities – seriousness, wastefulness, triviality, majesty, etc. An audience can be made to feel that a queen is dignified or that she is affected, that she has natural authority or unnatural pomp. In other words, insofar as it suggests that which is natural, right, proper, good, the movement of the body plays a key part in the ideological work done by a play.

The job of this chapter is to substantiate that assertion, by looking at how the text of *The Tempest*, in scripting its bodies, speaks its class attitudes without, it seems, breathing a word.

BODY SCRIPT

Before we get onto *The Tempest*, however, a little more needs to be said about this notion of scripting bodies. In a recent essay, 'Playing with a Difference', Robert Weimann attends to moments when the Renaissance playtext seems to suggest – or require – different modes of playing from actors. One of his examples is from *Hamlet* Q 1, where the performer slides between Renaissance prince and common player. From here Weimann goes on to talk about the distinction between 'representational acting and presentational playing'.[2]

While the identification of different modes of playing has been made by a number of authors,[3]

---

[1] William Shakespeare, *The Tempest* (1611), ed. S. Orgel (Oxford, 1987), 4.1.102. Hereafter line references to this edition are given in the body of the text.

[2] Robert Weimann, 'Playing with a Difference: Revisiting "Pen" and "Voice" in Shakespeare's Theater' *Shakespeare Quarterly* 50:4 (1999), 415–32; p. 420.

[3] See, among others, Bernard Beckerman, *Theatrical Presentation: Performer, Audience and Act*, ed. Gloria Brim Beckerman and William Coco (London, 1990); Martin White, *Renaissance Drama in Action: An Introduction to Aspects of Theatre Practice and Performance* (London, 1998); also Ashley Dukes, *Drama* (London, 1926); Elizabeth Burns, *Theatricality: A Study of Convention in the Theatre and in Social Life* (London, 1972); Susan Melrose, *A Semiotics of the Dramatic Text* (Basingstoke, 1994).

what interests me about Weimann's account is his attempt to show how mode of performance is produced by written text. But I think this demonstration can, and should, go a lot further. For a start, Weimann's essay limits its discussion to only two modes of playing, which is perhaps rather more restricted than we need to be. More importantly, although Weimann talks of a mutual engagement between body and text, at a crucial juncture he seems to simplify this relationship. This can be seen clearly when he emphasizes the materiality of performance: 'playing in the presence of spectators is an expense of irreducible physical energy'. Performance is never just a '*medium*', relaying the signifiers 'given in the words of the text', but an '*agency* in its own right', drawing on 'a unique and irreplaceable source of living strength that is inseparable from the transaction itself'.[4] While this is a proper insistence on productive effort, I think it simplifies at each binary pole. Energy may be irreducible, but it is not undifferentiated in its application and exhibition (the singer and acrobat both spend energy, but against different resistances). This expenditure of energy is also culturally valorized: some people find it necessary to avoid sweat. And, while what has come down to us from the Renaissance may be verbal texts, words comprise only one 'text' in the theatre. There are also visual and sound designs, and there is choreography. Words can perhaps be relayed, but a movement text ends up being inhabited.[5] So there are real problems with making a separation between body and verbal text. We need an approach which instead explores their modes of interrelation, the inscription of body and the bodiliness of text.

This exploration has to respect the specificity of the body both as biological presence and as cultural text. To this end, what could begin to open up the discussion is some consideration of performance phenomenology. This would firmly put the body back into the slightly disembodied notion of 'mode of performance' and perhaps reveal a range of bodily modes within the representational or performatory – or indeed any other – modes. It will then enable us to see how these physical modes, these scripted bodies, all produce different,

but concrete, relations in and to space, institution, audience. From here we can take further the work of defining the correlation between a specifically embodied performance practice and its precise historical moment. As a particular instance of that correlation I am concentrating here on the ideological work done by the performing body.

Rather than being a modern imposition, this approach to the body via performance phenomenology had a currency in Shakespeare's theatre. In the work of Elizabethan anti-theatricalists we encounter ideas as to how the mode of embodiment works on an audience and an awareness that this mechanism has ideological implications. Among generalizations about the stage's provocations to lust and licence, Stephen Gosson offers this specific example of how an audience responds to stage action: 'when Bacchus rose up . . . the beholders rose up'.[6] It is a model of muscular empathy that can still be observed, especially in sporting performances. A common instance is the excitement of the football match which energizes the bodies of the spectators. There's no rational need for the upper body to rise as your team gets close to the opposing goal. As Roger Caillois puts it in his wider discussion of games, 'A physical contagion leads them to assume the position of the men or animals in order to help them'.[7] This physical contagion, or kinaesthesia, is

---

For juxtaposed modes, or as he would say 'registers', of performance in *Hamlet*, see Mick Wallis, ' "To Be, or Not to Be" – What are the Questions?', in *Hamlet*. *Essays*, ed. Ian Clarke (Loughborough, 1994) – and thanks to Mick Wallis for the Dukes reference.

4 Weimann, 'Playing with a Difference', p. 427.
5 See Keir Elam, *The Semiotics of Theatre and Drama* (London, 1980) on texts; 'Like Meyerhold, reflexologists, and behavioural psychologists, Brecht believed that the mere imitation or copying of appropriate gestures and expressions could bring about desired mental states.' Jonathan Kalb, *The Theatre of Heiner Müller* (Cambridge, 1998), p. 27.
6 Stephen Gosson, *Playes Confuted in Five Actions* (London, 1582), sig. G 5.
7 Roger Caillois, *Man, Play, and Games* (1958), trs. M. Barash (New York, 1961). An example of the theoretical development of the idea is Michael Taussig's reflection on Freud's 'ideational mimetics': 'in which . . . bodily copying of the other is paramount: one tries out the very shape of a

possible in all performance-audience relationships, but it is most obvious where cultures of spectating assume – and construct – emotional expressivity. Awareness of this means that analysts of performance need in general to develop a less abstracted and monolithic idea of audience.

For my purposes here, in trying to develop a way of discussing the body in relation to ideology, the concept of kinaesthesia allows discussion of texts which don't engage in conspicuous meaning-making. The effects of dance, for example, are felt emotionally and, as it were, in the body, rather than being capable of verbal articulation: Alexandra Carter suggests that the kinaesthetic impact of ballet derives from 'a bodily response to the richness of colour and texture on stage, the complexity of patternings of large casts and the aesthetic values of classicism – clarity of line, formality of shape, virtuosity, harmony'.[8] One dance analyst connects the kinaesthetic impact to Kristeva's 'semiotic', which is characterized as 'pulsing, kinetic, heterogeneous space whose meanings are much more fluid and imprecise' than those of the 'symbolic' which has a logic and is 'translatable'.[9]

Kristeva's semiotic, and the model of kinaesthesia, have already found a place in analysis of Renaissance drama.[10] In *Shakespeare's Art of Orchestration*, Jean Howard suggests that in some circumstances the content of a speech matters rather less than its event or sound. Her analysis argues that the audience is taken up powerfully by such nonverbal phenomena as the rhythms of filling and emptying the stage.[11] When textures of sound and occupation of spaces are seen to produce excitement, performance is being thought of as social event, a gathering of bodies as much as minds: the audience 'is situated in the phenomenological continuum of space through physical proximity, linguistic inclusions, and the uniquely theatrical mirroring that links audience with performer in a kind of corporeal mimetic identification'.[12] The approach to performance of phenomenology is attentive to the effects produced in the spectator simply as a result of materially sharing the space with the performance. Many of these effects on the spectator by-pass the intellect; they are felt

in the body. Nevertheless they work powerfully to shape a spectator's sense of the performance. And in many cases non-cognitive effects are actually scripted by the performance-makers – Garner, for example, shows how Samuel Beckett's requirements for visual organization methodically disorient spectators.[13] Herein lies the force of Jean Howard's observations with regard to the patterns of filling and emptying of Shakespeare's stage.[14]

When phenomenology asks us to attend to the moved spectator it seems to offer a way into

---

perception in one's own body; the musculature of the body is physiologically connected to percepts'. Michael Taussig, *Mimesis and Alterity: A Particular History of the Senses* (London: Routledge, 1993), p. 46. See also Henry W. Sullivan, '*Mimesis Hysteresis*: What in the Audience is Moved when the Audience is Moved?', *Gestos* 7: 14 (1992), 45–57, for a Lacanian model.

[8] Alexandra Carter, 'Dying Swans or Sitting Ducks? A Critical Reflection on Feminist Gazes at Ballet', *Performance Research* 4: 3 (1999), 91–8. See also, on modern dance, S. Manning, 'The Female Dancer and the Male Gaze', in *Meaning in Motion: New Cultural Studies of Dance*, ed. J. Desmond (Durham, NC, 1997).

[9] Ann Daly, 'Dance History and Feminist Scholarship: Reconsidering Isadora Duncan and the Male Gaze', in *Gender in Performance: The Presentation of Difference in the Performing Arts*, ed. L. Senelick (Hanover, 1992), p. 244.

[10] Somewhat contentiously I use the adjective 'Renaissance' rather than the more generally preferred term 'early-modern'. I do this after having experienced various forms of puzzlement from scholars who work on the modern period, for whom 'early-modern' tends to refer to the years around 1900.

[11] Jean Howard, *Shakespeare's Art of Orchestration: Stage Technique and Audience Response* (Urbana, 1984), pp. 128, 103.

[12] Stanton B. Garner, Jr, *Bodied Spaces: Phenomenology and Performance in Contemporary Drama* (Ithaca, 1994), p. 4. See also Bert O. States, *Great Reckonings in Little Rooms: On the Phenomenology of Theater* (Berkeley, 1985) and 'The Phenomenological Attitude', in *Critical Theory and Performance*, ed. Janelle G. Reinelt and Joseph R. Roach (Ann Arbor, 1992); Bruce Wilshire, *Role Playing and Identity: The Limits of Theatre as Metaphor* (Bloomington, 1982).

[13] Garner, *Bodied Spaces*, pp. 76–7.

[14] See also Jarrett Walker, 'Voiceless Bodies and Bodiless Voices: The Drama of Human Perception in *Coriolanus*', *Shakespeare Quarterly* 43 (1992), 170–85: 'I use the categories of body and voice to refer to *phenomena*, prior to their assimilation into a perceived world or even their assimilation as metaphors' (172, n.6).

exploring the relationship between performance and historical moment: 'Lived bodies strain at the seams of a culture's ideological fabric . . . simultaneously registering, creating and subverting cultural conventions, embodied experience is necessarily complex and messy.'[15] Yet there is a problem in that terms such as 'lived' and 'embodied' are very generalized. They don't speak historical specificity. Phenomenology, then, only takes us so far. For more detailed historical information we need to turn to the rich stream of recent work on the cultural text of the body.[16] But in making this turn we encounter a new problem, in that much of this work, deriving ultimately from Bakhtin and Foucault,[17] seems to be more concerned with ideologies of body than with lived experience of body (which will yet always be partly a product of ideology even while exceeding it). As Gail Kern Paster says, for Bakhtin 'the body's concrete materiality – or lack of it – remains primarily symbolic. He is interested neither in actual bodily practices over time nor in the body's changing modes of self-experience'.[18] A similar point has been made about Foucault, in whose writings, says Bryan Turner, 'the discourse appears to be almost sociologically disembodied': 'there is a pronounced reluctance to reduce systematic thought to interests, especially the economic interests of social groups'.[19] If the abstraction is re-embodied, with relation to groups with their own interests, the image of the passive lived body is once again challenged. The Foucauldian one-way street is subverted: as Arthur Frank says, 'Disciplines not only make bodies productive in terms defined by some other, whether king or factory owner. Disciplines can also be used by bodies themselves to achieve productive ends of their own.'[20] Some of those disciplines may be theatrical.

A more precise historical focus on bodily practice seems to be offered by those who analyse texts designed to train the materiality of the body – preeminently Norbert Elias, with key contributions from Georges Vigarello, Frank Whigham, Anna Bryson and Tom Bishop.[21] Their various accounts tell of a steady increase in restraint and 'enclosure' of the body through dissemination of techniques of politeness and civil living. But, coherent

and detailed as it is, this history again has problems in relation to actual practice. Firstly, there is a difficulty with being precise about the point

---

[15] A. C. Albright, *Choreographing Difference: The Body and Identity in Contemporary Dance* (Hanover, 1997), p. 5.

[16] A number of these works will be referenced throughout, but the following are of central importance: Peter Stallybrass, 'Patriarchal Territories: The Body Enclosed', in *Rewriting the Renaissance: The Discourses of Sexual Difference in Early Modern England*, ed. Margaret W. Ferguson, Maureen Quilligan, Nancy J. Vickers (Chicago, 1986); Leonard Tennenhouse, *Power on Display: The Politics of Shakespearean Genres* (London, 1986); Gail Kern Paster, *The Body Embarrassed: Drama and the Disciplines of Shame in Early Modern England* (Ithaca, 1993).

[17] Mikhail Bakhtin, *Rabelais and his World*, trs. Helene Iswolsky (Bloomington, 1984); Michel Foucault, *Discipline and Punish: The Birth of the Prison*, trs. Alan Sheridan (New York, 1979) has perhaps been the most influential of his works in this field.

[18] Paster, *Body Embarrassed*, p. 15. Peter Stallybrass, 'Reading the Body: *The Revenger's Tragedy* and the Jacobean Theater of Consumption', *Renaissance Drama* 18 (1987), 137, suggests that Bakhtin is caught into an 'essentialist problematic'; the historian of food, Stephen Mennell, points out that it was the upper classes which gorged themselves, the gaping orifices were on the bodies of dukes and bishops: Stephen Mennell, 'On the Civilizing of Appetite' in *The Body: Social Process and Cultural Theory*, ed. Mike Featherstone, Mike Hepworth, Bryan S. Turner (London, 1995).

[19] Bryan S. Turner, 'The Government of the Body: Medical Regimens and the Rationalization of Diet', *British Journal of Sociology* 33:2 (1982), 254–69; p. 257.

[20] Arthur W. Frank, 'For a Sociology of the Body: An Analytical Review', in *The Body: Social Process and Cultural Theory*, ed. Mike Featherstone, Mike Hepworth, Bryan S. Turner (London, 1995), p. 58.

[21] Norbert Elias, *The Civilizing Process*, trs. Edmund Jephcott (Oxford, 1978, 1982), 2 volumes; Georges Vigarello, 'The Upward Training of the Body from the Age of Chivalry to Courtly Civility', in *Fragments for a History of the Human Body, Part 2*, ed. Michel Feher, with Ramona Neddaff and Nadia Tazi (New York, 1989); Frank Whigham, *Ambition and Privilege: The Social Tropes of Elizabethan Courtesy Theory* (Berkeley, 1984); Anna Bryson, 'The Rhetoric of Status: Gesture, Demeanour and the Image of the Gentleman in Sixteenth- and Seventeenth-Century England', in *Renaissance Bodies: The Human Figure in English Culture c. 1540–1660*, ed. Lucy Gent and Nigel Llewellyn (London, 1990); Tom Bishop, 'The Gingerbread Host: Tradition and Novelty in the Jacobean Masque', in *The Politics of the Stuart Court Masque*, ed. David Bevington and Peter Holbrook (Cambridge, 1998).

of emergence of the trained courtly body. Foucault's docile body is associated with the eighteenth century; most of the historians of Renaissance courtesy find it in the Renaissance. But historians of earlier periods, including Elias, find it earlier: Jean-Claude Schmitt highlights the transmission of restrained behavioural precepts from Cicero to Ambrose; Jan Bremner discovers the ethic of uprightness in ancient Greek culture.[22] Rather than a continuous evolution we have perhaps to think of negotiations and conflicts over bodily decorums at each period. For the prescriptions for restraint of the body are tropes regularly repeated by a set of dominant cultures. Which brings us to the second problem. Anna Bryson notes the quantity of evidence as to 'the roistering and thoroughly uncivil behaviour' of young gentlemen about town – which implies a 'less than complete' response to the courtesy manuals. Indeed, she suggests that social superiority may have manifested itself precisely as 'freedom from rules and restraints'.[23] Thus, insofar as it is concerned with written rules and prescriptions for the body, the history of courtly discipline is bound within its medium – written text. Sites of bodily negotiation are elsewhere.

Some of these sites, with their different ideas of bodily potential, are examined by a discipline that has run parallel with, and borrowed from, the study of courtliness. Dance history has proved itself such a potent area of enquiry in recent years because it is dealing with the body as an expressive medium.[24] Its primary sources are less legislative, ethical ideals, formulas for courtliness, than descriptions of the body in motion and instructions for movement. It was possible to be a young gentleman without following Castiglione to the letter, but it is not possible to dance a coranto without observing a particular arrangement of steps. These written instructions are in turn supplemented, for the historian, by musical texts, with their specific shapes, rhythms, speeds.[25] Together these materials give the impression (which might not be wholly illusory) that the operation of a historical body may be known in a way which is more direct, less mediated, than inferring it through descriptions of recommended civil behaviour (or indeed interpret-

ing woodcuts and paintings[26]). After all, a modern body – even allowing for biological and cultural differences – can still try out the steps and rhythms, can still encounter those balancing points where culture does battle with musculature; flesh can inhabit these texts. But, even here, the intellectual constraints of received orthodoxies make themselves felt, allowing abstract models to squeeze out the evidence of specific practices, replicating the theoretical text that the academy knows it ought to speak. Thus, although the work of the dance historian Skiles Howard contributed much to our understanding of the political meanings made by courtly dances, her work was, in the opinion of Barbara Ravelhofer, fatally flawed with respect to its commentary on gender. Howard describes how

22 Jean-Claude Schmitt, 'The Ethics of Gesture', in *Fragments for a History of the Human Body, Part 2*, ed. Michel Feher, with Ramona Neddaff and Nadia Tazi (New York, 1989); Jan Bremner, 'Walking, Standing, and Sitting in Ancient Greek Culture', in *A Cultural History of Gesture*, ed. Jan Bremner and Herman Roodenburg (Cambridge, 1993).

23 Bryson, 'Gesture', p. 152.

24 John Ward, 'Newly Devis'd Measures for Jacobean Masques', *Acta Musicologica* 60 (1988), 111–42; Mark Franko, *Dance as Text: Ideologies of the Baroque Body* (Cambridge, 1993); Skiles Howard, *The Politics of Courtly Dancing in Early Modern England* (Amherst, 1998); Barbara Ravelhofer, ' "Virgin Wax" and "Hairy Men-monsters": Unstable Movement Codes in the Stuart Masque', in *The Politics of the Stuart Court Masque*, ed. David Bevington and Peter Holbrook (Cambridge, 1998). See also Roy Strong, *Art and Power: Renaissance Festivals 1450–1650* (Woodbridge, 1984); John C. Meagher, *Method and Meaning in Jonson's Masques* (Notre Dame, 1966).

25 See, for example, Ward, 'Newly Devis'd Measures'; Susan McClary, 'Unruly Passions and Courtly Dances: Technologies of the Body in Baroque Music', in *From the Royal to the Republican Body: Incorporating the Political in Seventeenth- and Eighteenth-Century France*, ed. Sara E. Melzer and Kathryn Norberg (Berkeley, 1998).

26 The problems with inferring 'real-life' performance practices from paintings are spelled out by Shearer West, *The Image of the Actor* (New York, 1991). Skiles Howard tends to efface the impact of visual convention when she reads a woodcut of dancing couples in order to infer how the country dancers are less classically restrained than the courtly pair, whereas it can also be argued that bent bodies and physical closeness are shorthand graphic markers for countryfolk and clowns.

male power is restated in the dominance of male dancers over female partners; Ravelhofer finds evidence that suggests to her that dance steps produced more various, if not more flexible, ideas of gender, for example the Duke of Buckingham's feminine dance. Howard's work is vitiated, she feels, by an attempt to employ – or produce – a Foucauldian scenario at the 'expense of performance practice and historical fact'.[27]

I suspect that Howard found herself sucked into the symbolic domain of Foucault because she wanted to ask an entirely legitimate question: once we have identified the bodily practice, what does the body then mean? This brings us back to Weimann's problems with theatrical analysis. We have been faced either by an approach which aims to describe practice without addressing meaning,[28] or by a mode of semiotic 'reading' which disprivileges bodiliness.[29] By borrowing from performance phenomenology, I suggest, we are enabled to extend the range of ways in which Renaissance drama 'means' while at the same time not losing a grasp on it as an art of space, sound, flesh. In this way, accounts of body ideologies may be grounded in the materiality of staged practices. So, as a very brief example, in Peter Stallybrass's seminal essay, 'Patriarchal Territories', he suggests that in the second half of the play Desdemona is 'reformed within the problematic of the enclosed body'.[30] To which an analysis of bodied space might add that, whereas in the second half the dramaturgy produces Desdemona as alienated from the acting space, her displays of bodily discipline (as in the prayer before Iago, 4.2) suggested a potent self-control. Being enclosed has ambivalent value.

In seeking to ground body ideologies in stage practices, I am trying to avoid the model which assumes a separation between written text and performing body: where 'The body . . . does not speak for itself', or 'The body alone has no meaning'.[31] What interests me, as I said above, is the impact of the text on the flesh, the production of body by script, as part of ideological production. This comes about not only through the activities required by the text, but through the mode of performance it indicates. Insofar as the words invoke such things

as genre or intertextual reference or parodic quotation, they indicate a register of movement (like a register of language), suggesting how it is done. For although the stage may share with 'real life' views on correct civility, appropriate gender behaviour, physiological mechanisms, it is also citation – a quotation of these views and behaviours,[32] negotiating them, sometimes contesting them. The body on stage operates through, on one hand, a range

---

[27] Ravelhofer, ' "Virgin Wax" ', p. 247.

[28] B. L. Joseph, *Elizabethan Acting* rev. edn (London, 1964); John Russell Brown, 'On the Acting of Shakespeare's Plays', *Quarterly Journal of Speech* 34 (1953), 477–84; Marvin Rosenberg, 'Elizabethan Actors: Men or Marionettes?' *PMLA* 69 (1954), 915–27; Lise-Lone Marker, 'Nature and Decorum in the Theory of Elizabethan Acting', in *The Elizabethan Theatre*, vol. 2, ed. David Galloway (1970); Joseph R. Roach, *The Player's Passion: Studies in the Science of Acting* (Ann Arbor, 1993); Harold Frisch, 'Shakespeare and the Language of Gesture', *Shakespeare Studies* 19 (1987), 239–51.

[29] One of the most productive readings of stage pictures is David Bevington, *Action is Eloquence: Shakespeare's Language of Gesture* (Cambridge, Mass., 1984). See also, among many others, John H. Astington, 'Eye and Hand on Shakespeare's Stage', *Renaissance and Reformation* 10:1 (1986); Bernard Beckerman, *Shakespeare at the Globe, 1599–1609* (New York, 1962); Ronald J. Boling, 'Stage Images of Cressida's Portrayal', *Essays in Theatre* 14:2 (1996), 147–58; Alan C. Dessen, *Elizabethan Drama and the Viewer's Eye* (Chapel Hill, 1977) and 'Shakespeare's Patterns for the Viewer's Eye: Dramaturgy for the Open Stage', in *Shakespeare's More than Words can Witness: Essays on Visual and Nonverbal Enactment in the Plays*, ed. Sidney Homan (London, 1980); Barbara Hodgdon, 'Shakespeare's Directorial Eye: A Look at the Early History Plays', in *Shakespeare's More than Words can Witness: Essays on Visual and Nonverbal Enactment in the Plays*, ed. Sidney Homan (London, 1980); George R. Kernodle, *From Art to Theatre: Form and Convention in the Renaissance* (Chicago, 1944); Dieter Mehl, 'Emblems in English Renaissance Drama', *Renaissance Drama* n.s.2 (1969), 39–57; Ann Pasternak Slater, *Shakespeare the Director* (Hassocks, 1982); Glynne Wickham, *Early English Stages, 1300–1660* (London, 1963), vol. 2, 1576–1660.

[30] Stallybrass, 'Patriarchal Territories', p. 141.

[31] Stallybrass, 'Reading', p. 121; Susan J. Wiseman, ' '*Tis Pity She's a Whore*: Representing the Incestuous Body', in *Renaissance Bodies: The Human Figure in English Culture c. 1540–1660*, ed. Lucy Gent and Nigel Llewellyn (London, 1990), p. 195.

[32] See Stephen Orgel, 'The Spectacles of State', in *Persons in Groups: Social Behaviour as Identity Formation in Medieval and Renaissance Europe* (Binghampton, New York, 1985), p. 117, on the problems produced by the stage's miming of greatness.

of generic possibilities, and on the other a series of degrees of explicit quotedness. It may be made to 'speak' by the script, but when the body is speaking you can sometimes hear the characters' lines differently – as parody or quotation. In enacting a gait within a particular register, or in generically juxtaposing that gait with another, the stage may have the effect of estranging that which in another context seems natural, normal, proper. In this way the scripting of bodies may put pressure on culturally circulated ideas about, and especially valuations of, particular bodies.

Insofar as the scripting of bodies leads to effects which are kinaesthetic, the mobilization of bodily value is ideologically more successful in that it produces responses that are non-cognitively felt rather than explicitly discussed. In making that point, it also has to be noted that we are not necessarily dealing with conscious intention on the part of the makers of the work. They may be unconsciously operating within their own ideological constraints as to what is practical or proper. To illustrate how the produced text will indicate this residual ideological shape I shall borrow from Richard Dyer's analysis of the film *In the Heat of the Night*. Sidney Poitier and Rod Steiger have different acting styles; the difference is compounded by ideologically shaped conventions of film lighting which disprivilege black skin, so that Steiger 'can display a range of modulations of expression that indicate the character's complex turmoil of feelings and reminiscences. Poitier, by contrast, remains the emblematic, unindividualised, albeit admirable, black man'.[33] Alongside the film's liberal project, the materiality of the bodies tells a different story.

Thus in summary: the project is an attempt to read the body scripting of the Renaissance stage as a set of effects. These body effects, drawing from and running alongside the verbal aspects of the play, produce felt responses in spectators. These responses, far from being outside the ideological domain, are deeply part of it. In this way, by closely focusing on what actual performing bodies are required to do, we may develop an enhanced knowledge of the ideological practices of the play.

Which brings us back to that highly ideological thing, a divinely queenly pose.

In the analysis of *The Tempest* which follows I shall attempt not only to define the gait of goddesses and others, but also exemplify and substantiate the general argument whereby registers of movement and systems of physical difference act as fleshly disciplines which make cultural meanings.

COURTLY GEOMETRIES

Juno and her divine gait appear in the masque organized by Prospero to celebrate the betrothal of his daughter Miranda to Ferdinand. The entertainment consists of entrances and speeches by three goddesses, a song, and then a dance by nymphs and reapers. It is, of course, famously dispersed before it can reach the customary climax in the mingled dancing of masquers and spectators. Rather than blurring the distinction between masquing fantasy and daily life, the ending of this entertainment throws into high relief the contrast between the masque's way of inhabiting the stage and that of its on-stage spectators.

By contrast with the newly fashionable and lavish masques of the royal court, Prospero's is a rather simple affair, a quotation of the mode.[34] But it does enough to suggest the atmosphere and, most importantly for our purposes here, the physical regimes of the masque. These regimes were mostly focused on courtly dancing, which has been very well documented in some enthralling work by dance historians.[35] The masquing body would

---

[33] Richard Dyer, *White* (London, 1997), p. 99.

[34] For examples of recent work on Prospero's masque in relation to courtly masques, see *The Tempest*, ed. Orgel, introduction; Kevin R. McNamara, 'Golden Worlds at Court: *The Tempest* and Its Masque', *Shakespeare Studies* 19 (1987), 183–202; David Bevington, '*The Tempest* and the Jacobean Court Masque', in *The Politics of the Stuart Court Masque*, ed. David Bevington and Peter Holbrook (Cambridge, 1998). See also Alan Brissenden, *Shakespeare and the Dance* (London, 1981).

[35] Ward, 'Newly Devis'd Measures'; Mark Franko, *Dance as Text: Ideologies of the Baroque Body* (Cambridge, 1993); Howard, *Politics*; Ravelhofer, '"Virgin Wax"'. See also, Roy Strong, *Art and Power: Renaissance Festivals 1450–1650*

seem, to put it summarily, to exemplify control and balance. As Skiles Howard says, quoting Caroso (1600), 'The courtly body danced according to "the laws of symmetry and perfect theory", with geometry realized on the body by costume and choreographic design'.[36] That geometry may also be said to inhabit the musculature, insofar as gestures of arms and hands tended to be inhibited: with the emphasis being on the feet, the body's verticality is promoted. Thus with regard to the popular early Renaissance form of *basse dance* (or 'measures' in English), Arbeau (1588) recommended 'the steps should not be so big as to deform the erect posture of the upper body.'[37] Another restraint on the masquing body comes from the geometric choreography mentioned by Howard. This traced on the floor geometric shapes, with their significant hidden truths, or spelled out the names of watching princes. As Mark Franko points out, the body that takes its place within the delineation of a whole form has limits placed on its capacity for individual expressivity.[38] Within this physical context, it is not only the dancing body that shows its discipline. Prospero's goddesses have to enter and stand, rather than dance. But their exhibited gait will also presumably be governed by the rules Franko summarizes: 'The correct carriage of the head mirrors that of the eyes and of the body in general.' 'The precepts of physical rectitude, while calling for an immobile stance, preclude rigidity.'[39] They presumably don't wave their arms around in ways which are fast, unexpected or mimetic.

This discipline of the body does ideological work: courtly dance 'could demonstrate measured proportion not only by presenting bodies exemplarily, but also through the ballet's very organization and its choreography. The structured joining of both the different arts and the choreography within and between them produced metaphors of harmony in the aural and sociopolitical senses.'[40] This ideological production from a combination of elements can be exemplified from a masque that was produced close in time to *The Tempest*. Ben Jonson's *Masque of Queens* (1609) has already received a great deal of critical attention[41] so I shall do little more than sketch in the points which exemplify the main

argument here. The masque is celebrated for introducing an antemasque: witches do a magical dance 'full of praeposterous change, and gesticulation'.[42] The 'confused noise' at their entrance is accompanied by visual confusion. They make strange gestures – using those forbidden arms – and carry a clutter of spindles, timbrels and rattles; attention is called to the strange movements by their noise. The queens replace the witches with dances at the end that are 'euen, and apt' (line 754), 'as if Mathematicians had lost proportion, they might there haue found it' (lines 754–6) – inscribing order on the ungoverned physicality. Jones's drawings of the queens depict heads with elaborate crowns and helmets, their breasts and torsos enclosed in stage armour. Thus, apart from the learnt decorums of courtly dance, the upper body was also costumed into stillness, its muscles tensed to bear the loads upon them. With its high centre of gravity, the body is enacting control, balance, highness.

(Woodbridge, 1984); John C. Meagher, *Method and Meaning in Jonson's Masques* (Notre Dame, 1966).

[36] Howard, *Politics*, p. 103.

[37] Arbeau quoted by Mark Franko, 'Renaissance Conduct Literature and the Basse Dance: The Kinesis of *Bonne Grace*', in *Persons in Groups: Social Behaviour as Identity Formation in Medieval and Renaissance Europe* (Binghampton, New York, 1985).

[38] Franko, *Dance as Text*, pp. 30–1.

[39] Franko, 'Renaissance Conduct Literature', 57, 58.

[40] Franko, *Dance as Text*, p. 32.

[41] Much of the recent debate has been about the masque's production of female- or male-centredness: Susan Gossett, '"Man-maid, begone!": Women in Masques', *ELR* 18 (1988), 96–113; Margaret Maurer, 'Reading Ben Jonson's *Queens*', in *Seeking the Woman in Late Medieval and Renaissance Writings: Essays in Feminist Contextual Criticism*, ed. Sheila Fisher and Janet E. Halley (Knoxville, 1989); Stephen Orgel, 'Jonson and the Amazons', in *Soliciting Interpretation*, ed. Elizabeth Harvey and Katharine Eisaman Maus (Chicago, 1990); Barbara Lewalski, 'Anne of Denmark and the Subversion of Masquing', *Criticism* 35 (1993); Peter Holbrook, 'Jacobean Masques and the Jacobean Peace' in *The Politics of the Stuart Court Masque*, ed. David Bevington and Peter Holbrook (Cambridge, 1998); Howard, *Politics*, pp. 118–24.

[42] Ben Jonson, *The Masque of Queens* in *Ben Jonson*, vol. 7, ed. C. H. Herford and P. and E. Simpson (Oxford, 1941), lines 35–6. Line references hereafter to this text.

The attentive spectator in turn absorbs this high virtue. Sir Thomas Elyot describes a form of dancing which displays 'prudence', and remarks that this will be 'well perceyved, as well by the daunsers as by them which standinge by, wyll be diligent beholders and markers'.[43] The geometric and allegorical shapes were meant to be read by spectators. This act of close concentration, this diligence, has the effect, in John Meagher's words, of 'imparting moral improvement to the beholder'.[44] Or, indeed, political 'improvement': the political job of the aesthetics, says Franko, was 'the cultivation of a malleable, hyperreceptive subject-as-spectator'.[45] In the case of the masques for James the close reading of the choreography was situated within, and reinforced by, the visual rhetoric of Jones's stage design. The measured bodies spoke and danced in front of scenery which gradually intensified its focus on a magical vanishing point. In the antemasque to Queens Jones's designs for the House of Fame which replaces the witches' scene have a strong emphasis on the vertical columns. This emphasis is replicated by the upright, column-like bodies of the queens, in their hard casings.[46] As the masque proceeds the vanishing point was in turn lined up with the precise position of the watching monarch.[47] He was not only the single best-placed recipient of this spectacle; he was also, in the terms of its ideological rhetoric, the only begetter of all that noble symmetry. The vanishing point is opposite what has to be taken as the point of origin.

Now, although Prospero the magician is more truly the point of origin than James I ever was, the staged circumstances of The Tempest masque relax the rigorous system of visual focus. Prospero invents the masque as a gift for Miranda and Ferdinand – their responses to it are as interesting as his, and perhaps gesturally more foregrounded since they will be enacting wonder while he presumably watches it and them. Now in itself the prince's look at the masque audience is wholly in keeping with this sort of event – as Franko says, 'his subjects inhabit – actually constitute – the geometry of the ballet's landscape as his ideal field of vision'.[48] But if Prospero is watching Ferdinand and Miranda, so too is the theatre audience,

particularly if, as I suggest, those two are gesturally foregrounded. So in what we might call the *theatricalized* masque of The Tempest the princely perspective elides with that of the paying spectator. We shall return to this elision of class positions later. The second, brutally obvious, point is that this is all a fiction. Masques for James could be upstaged any moment by eruptions within the delicately maintained network of diplomatic allegiances, by mere nuances of disquiet from those who possessed the power to dispossess. The spectacle of the masque, however splendid, always existed in relation to the spectacle of the audience, where there were very few neutral observers. At the same time that staged splendour had a one-night-only transience combined with an elevated indifference to the potential problems of its circumstances. As such it offered its spectator a tense but deep engagement. By contrast Prospero's masque is a much less complicated source of pleasure. Its spectacle, filling the stage physically and aurally, offers plenitude – plenitude organized by choreography and harmony so that the fullness does not bewilder the senses, and is repeatable day after day. In a sense, of course, it is a gesture towards, even a laconic simulacrum of, plenitude.

Most famously something happens to this masque which seems never to have happened at this point to James's. The climax of mythic splendour is forestalled; its originator closes it down. In

---

[43] Sir Thomas Elyot, *The Boke Named The Governour* (1531), intr. F. Watson (London, 1907), p. 97.

[44] John C. Meagher, 'The Dance and Masques of Ben Jonson', *Journal of the Warburg and Courtauld Institutes* 25 (1962), 258–77; pp. 265–6.

[45] Franko, *Dance as Text*, p. 35.

[46] On the relationships of sex, body and building, see Eugene R. Cunnar, '(En)gendering Architectural Poetics in Jonson's *Masque of Queens*' *Literature Interpretation Theory* 4 (1993), 145–60; on the gestural stillness of the upper body, and on constraints upon it, see Franko, 'Renaissance Conduct Literature', pp. 57–8; Howard, *Politics*, pp. 60, 101; Vigarello, 'Upward Training'.

[47] Stephen Orgel, *The Illusion of Power: Political Theater in the English Renaissance* (Berkeley, 1975).

[48] Franko, *Dance as Text*, p. 39.

the innovatory *Masque of Queens* the rough people, the witches, were part of the antemasque, which gives way to the masque proper; here the reverse happens. Far from resolving disorderly elements, this masque is broken apart by them. The artifice, always slightly too relaxed fully to entrain our focus, must yield place to that which seems much more 'real' – the world of the masque's audience, its creator and the plot against him.

At the moment at which the masque is aborted the theatre audience might have a sense of two sorts of action on stage: that of the artifice of the courtly entertainment, and that of the 'real'. We probably knew deeply, anyway, that the masque's apparent fullness was only a quotation of plenitude. By contrast the really authentic matter is the operation on a human being of thought and emotion (of which more later). The 'real' is felt to be superior because this is the narrative which affects people we have come to care about, or at least be interested in; and indeed it is superior because it can abolish masques.

LOW CENTRES OF GRAVITY

Once we concentrate on the plot against Prospero, we discover other ways of feeling about the stage action. Most audiences guess that the plot won't work because it relies on the assistance of clowns. These clowns are seen to be people who easily succumb to their own most base desires. They are clumsy in what they do and without purpose in achieving the objectives set. It is in relation to them and their appearance that an audience might well have – consciously or not – another sense of two sorts of action on stage. This time the division is not between artifice and 'real' but between clowning and the seriousness of Prospero.

What precisely does the clowning here involve? A certain amount of physical comedy is required by two separate routines in relation to a concealed Caliban. First there is Trinculo's discovery of a creature beneath a gaberdine, and his attempts to identify what it is; next there is Stephano's encounter with what has now become a 'monster', a thing with four legs and two voices (Trinculo concealed with Caliban) (2.2.18–102). The physical comedy in each case is predicated upon simple but unremitting emotional drives. Trinculo needs to escape from a darkly threatening storm. Lines are given to the actor early in his entrance to enable him to establish the precise location of the storm over his head (20–1): he can look toward it, his body can adopt an attitude toward it, he can cower away from it and we shall still know it's there. Since there's a storm, of which he is terrified, he needs shelter. The logic is simple, almost hydraulic. But the *only* shelter that is available already has some horribly smelly creature underneath it (25–7). Strong smell is a richly productive ruse for comic performance, much more so perhaps than straightforward curiosity or even fear. The source of the smell provokes curiosity of course, but it also defines a threshold at which the smell becomes repellent: there's a nicely precise line at which the nose sniffing inquisitively becomes the nostrils filled with stinking air, and then the business of struggling through stench to get closer to the source. The extra push towards the repellent smell is provided in this instance by the threat of the storm. The Trinculo actor is thus supplied with a drive to seek shelter, and an obstacle to that drive which is almost intolerable. The business of the interplay between fear and disgust can continue for as long as the actor can sustain it. Lines are, of course, not necessary.

Stephano is also in the grip of a monolithic drive. He drinks alcohol as a solution to the problems which confront him. Once again there is an available physical structure: each problem makes him drink; the drunker he gets, the more problematic and imponderable the problems become; as the problems get apparently bigger, his response gets more urgent and simultaneously more incapacitated. He has the additional advantage of a stage prop – the bottle – which commences on its own journey around the stage space (2.2.72ff). The habit whereby Stephano pours drink into his own mouth leads him to pour drink into other available mouths – the monster's when he finds it (80), and then the second 'mouth' (90). This has little to do with greed, then, but with a logic that requires all orifices to be filled.

The presence of a single dominant drive is a defining element of the mode of characterization here. It is a shape which remains in place even though the drive changes. Trinculo moves from being fearful in the first half of this scene when he discovers the monster through to a mocking contempt for it (2.2.138ff); in the next of his scenes (Act 3 Scene 2) he has become jealous of the monster's relationship with Stephano. The emotion may change in relation to the object but what remains constant is the obsessive force with which it governs the person – the jealousy has the same single-mindedness as the fear.

The mode of acting required of the Trinculo actor (as too with Stephano) is that he be completely taken over, as it were possessed, by a dominant drive. A model for this sort of acting is the commedia dell' arte, an improvised form based on various stock personas. Although there is little evidence, one way or another, to suggest that Trinculo was actually acted as a commedia persona, current opinion does now lean towards the belief that, in general, Shakespeare and his actors were influenced by commedia dell' arte.[49] Commedia types have been identified by a number of scholars in Shakespeare's work,[50] and it has been suggested that, since Italian troupes had been visiting England since 1573, performers had become familiar with the form: 'most of the actors who were to work with Shakespeare – and perhaps Shakespeare himself – were not only acquainted with the stock characters of *commedia dell' arte*, but may actually have been using its comic conventions and the technique of improvisation in the plays they were performing'.[51] The residual presence of improvisatory method is detected by Richard Andrews in the 'elastic' gag, 'capable of being protracted or curtailed at will, according to the audience response'.[52] On the other hand, Shakespeare has Hamlet express hostility to the disruptive activities of clowns, and, if David Wiles is right, the person playing opposite the Trinculo actor in the role of Caliban was Robert Armin, a performer whose hallmark was a quality of intellectualism.[53] With this caution in place, it might still be productive to explore commedia – not to argue the case

for a hidden performance history but to try and formulate some general points about the clowning body.

The commedia personas all had their own specific physical characteristics and routines.[54] In the early days they may not have actually worn face masks – Richards and Richards say that references

---

[49] K. M. Lea, *Italian Popular Comedy: A Study in the commedia dell'arte, 1560–1620 with Special Reference to the English Stage* (Oxford, 1934) argued that the whole plot of *The Tempest* had similarities to the pastoral tradition in commedia. For more recent opinion, see Eugene Steele, 'Shakespeare, Goldoni, and the Clowns', *Comparative Drama* 11:3 (1977), 209–26; Louise George Clubb, 'Shakespeare's Comedy and Late Cinquecento Mixed Genres', in *Shakespearean Comedy*, ed. Maurice Charney (New York, 1980); Ninian Mellamphy, 'Pantaloons and Zanies: Shakespeare's "Apprenticeship" to Italian Professional Comedy Troupes', in *Shakespearean Comedy*, ed. Maurice Charney; Richard Andrews, 'Scripted Theatre and the Commedia dell' Arte', in *Theatre of the English and Italian Renaissance*, ed. J. R. Mulryne and Margaret Shewring (Basingstoke, 1991); Andrew Grewar, 'Shakespeare and the Actors of the *Commedia dell' Arte*', in *Studies in the Commedia dell' Arte*, ed. David J. George and Christopher J. Gossip (Cardiff, 1993) and 'The Old Man's Spectacles and Other Traces of the Commedia dell' Arte in Early Shakespearean Comedy', in *Scenery, Set and Staging in the Italian Renaissance: Studies in the Practice of Theatre*, ed. Christopher Cairns (Lewiston, 1996). The contrary view has been put by Kenneth Richards, 'Inigo Jones and the Commedia dell' Arte', in *The Commedia dell' Arte from the Renaissance to Dario Fo*, ed. Christopher Cairns (Lewiston, 1989) and 'Elizabethan Perceptions of the *Commedia dell' Arte*', in *Cultural Exchange between European Nations during the Renaissance*, ed. Gunnar Sorelius and Michael Svigley (Uppsala, 1994).

[50] See, in addition to references listed in note above, O. J. Campbell, '*Two Gentlemen of Verona* and Italian Comedy', *University of Michigan Publications* 1 (1925), 49–63 and 'The Italianate Background to *The Merry Wives of Windsor*', *University of Michigan Publications* 8 (1932), 81–117; Frances A. Yates, *A Study of* Love's Labour's Lost (Cambridge, 1936); John Robert Moore, 'Pantaloon as Shylock', *Boston Public Library Quarterly* 1 (1949), 33–42; Robert C. Melzi, 'From Lelia to Viola', *Renaissance Drama* 9 (1966), 67–81.

[51] Grewar, 'Shakespeare and the Actors', p. 18.

[52] Andrews, 'Scripted Theatre', p. 26.

[53] David Wiles, *Shakespeare's Clown* (Cambridge, 1987) p. 155.

[54] There is a sense in which the personas hardened into stock types as commedia developed into and beyond the late seventeenth century. For general descriptions see John Rudlin, *Commedia dell' Arte: An Actor's Handbook* (London, 1994).

to masked actors and the mask itself were rare.[55] But, if a persona has physical characteristics, when performers take on their persona they put on, as it were, a particular muscular organization, a bodily attitude. The shapes of these bodily attitudes seem to be visually memorialized in the conventions for graphically depicting commedia routines. This muscular organization is something very different from the learnt, and naturalized, behaviour that we refer to as habitus[56] in that it is *put on* and then *relinquished*; it thus may be said to operate as a mask. What is this operation? In modern maskwork when the performer puts on the mask she or he becomes taken over by it, so that there is a sense of being 'led' by the mask; not looking through its eye-holes but looking *with* it, having one's belly or nose conduct negotiations with the world, seeing as the mask sees. In part this psychic effect is produced from a respect meticulously given to the mask, a willing submission of 'everyday' subjectivity to something indistinctly 'other', projected onto the mask. This may be strengthened by contemplation of a face mask in the mirror, and is almost always sustained in place by the responses of other masks.

'[A *Zanni* or Pulcinella] should be ridiculous in his movements: in the way he puts on a hat, walks, runs, affects gravity or haste in his deportment. He should be ridiculous in the tone of his voice, which ought to be excessively shrill, or out of tune, or raucous. He should be ridiculous' – rather like Stephano perhaps – 'in the dignified roles in which a blockhead incompetently pretends to be a prince, a captain, and so on.'[57] Once a performer is in the mask the characteristic actions which derive from the mask continually re-produce and re-emphasize the shapes and muscular tensions which construct the force of the identity. As Laughlin, McManus and d'Aquili say, 'sustained and intense concentration on a physical activity' leads both to psychic energy and an experience of greater energy flow in the body; later on they observe that 'an excited somatic system produces an excited consciousness, and vice versa'.[58] In the range of physical disciplines which comprise what we have very loosely to call 'masked clowning' a new sense

of the body emerges from zones foregrounded by muscular focus, perhaps a changed centre of gravity, new points of tension and energy. In turn this changed muscular arrangement produces a different relationship to the space around the body and to other individuals. One's sense of one's body in space has bearing on the formation of subjectivity.[59] It is thus in a very developed sense that we speak of the person being taken over or possessed by the mask – a seemingly new subjectivity is not merely licensed but produced while the mask is worn.

This subjectivity of the mask has bearing on both agent and effect of performance. In their work on ritual, Webber, Stephens and Laughlin endeavour to explain how symbols 'operate both to organise and to transform consciousness and cognition'. There are some symbols which 'direct the flow of experience, focus attention, and integrate information' on a scale that exceeds our conscious awareness. When symbols of this sort penetrate the brain they use their information 'to activate neural structures not ordinarily accessible to normal consciousness'. A key concept in their 'biogenetic structuralist' argument is the tri-une brain in which there remain older brain forms from an earlier stage of evolutionary development, together with traces of archaic experiences. A potent symbol can evoke neural models of a 'genetically older date', hence its power. The reason that the authors spend time

[55] Kenneth Richards and Laura Richards, *The Commedia dell' Arte: A Documentary History* (Oxford, 1990), p. 114.

[56] The classic texts are Marcel Mauss, 'Techniques of the Body', *Economy and Society* 2 (1973); Pierre Bourdieu, *Outline of a Theory of Practice*, trs. Richard Nice (Cambridge, 1977) and *Distinction: A Social Critique of the Judgement of Taste*, trs. Richard Nice (London, 1986).

[57] Perucci (1699) in Richards and Richards, *Commedia dell' Arte*, p. 137.

[58] Charles D. Laughlin, Jr, John McManus and Eugene D. d'Aquili, *Brain, Symbol and Experience* (Boston and Shaftesbury, 1990), pp. 299, 319.

[59] See Roger Callois, 'Mimicry and Legendary Psychaesthenia', trs. J. Shepley *October* 31 (1984), 17–32; Henri Lefebvre, *The Production of Space* (1974), trs. D. Nicholson-Smith (Oxford, 1991); and Steve Pile, *The Body and the City: Psychoanalysis, Space and Subjectivity* (London, 1996). This topic is material for another essay, which I am currently writing.

on the discussion of symbols is because the ritual mask is an outward transformation of the sort of potent symbol which crosses cultures and evokes archetypes.[60]

Webber, Stephens and Laughlin are writing about masked ritual, indeed ritual in the Americas. So it's a far cry from the rather European clowning of *The Tempest*, and the student of Shakespeare may feel well justified in putting to one side both ritual ceremony and the tri-une brain. But the biogenetic structuralist work gives emphasis to two key points: first, it re-affirms the depth of the possible relationship between mask and brain, where the brain must not be seen as functioning in the same way in different sorts of performing – where masked clowning may activate a different aspect of the brain. And second, it insists, irrespective of one's views on the tri-une brain, on the power of that which is archetypal, not just in ritual but also in clowning. Alongside, and partly hidden by, the picture of Armin's intellectualism we have to retrieve a sense of the gag being bigger than the clown – where the clown actor is triggered, in a way not necessarily conscious, into what feels like the physical and somatic logic of a routine. In short, there's a mode of comic playing where the rational, and indeed the conscious, are disprivileged.

One of the classic markers of the force of unconscious desire in commedia dell' arte is that it ruptures proprieties: masks usually find themselves in territory which is bawdy, obscene, scatalogical. Indeed one of Thomas Nashe's complaints against Italian clowns or zanni is that they were given to impropriety.[61] The impropriety is usually so studiedly in your face because it grows logically out of given circumstances. Thus when Stephano discovers a monster with, apparently, four legs and two voices he carefully distinguishes between the 'forward' voice and the 'backward voice' which 'is to utter foul speeches and to detract' (2.2.87). Where there are two voices in a body, the backward voice uttering foul speeches can only be the arse. Into this 'mouth' Stephano also pours alcohol. The temporary blurring together of the functions of arse and mouth feels a lot more improper than Stephano's likening of Trinculo, once he has pulled

him free, to the 'siege' or shit of the monster (101). It works a nice variation on the stories of being (re)born from the sea – not here from foam or a fish's mouth but from a monster's arse. But it brings to an end the arse jokes; it produces no new action. In the next scene the obscenity (if obscene it be) is mainly around pissing. In a short, and highly obscure, group of four lines, Trinculo expresses his jealousy of Stephano through puns alluding to urination and defaecation:

STEPHANO Thou shalt be my lieutenant – monster, or my standard.
TRINCULO Your lieutenant if you list; he's no standard.
STEPHANO We'll not run, Monsieur Monster.
TRINCULO Nor go neither; but you'll lie like dogs, and yet say nothing neither.   (3.2.14–19)

If you blink you miss them – it's a mere token gesture towards the traditional obscenity of clowns, but it helps to make more appropriate the later drenching of these three in horse piss. At this juncture a schematic summary of clowning and masque bodies might be useful. In the received conventions of depicting commedia performance – with its possible links to the Shakespearian stage – the clown is angled at the hips, bent forward or back, arse or genitals out, knees bent, twists to the shoulders. The angles tend to be off the vertical, spines curved, shoulders rarely horizontal; the centre of gravity has to be low enough to allow bent knee postures. These might be said to be not only low in physical terms, but morally 'low': 'the prominent choreographer Fabritio Caroso', says Barbara Ravelhofer, 'harbours deep suspicions of knees spread too far apart as if "to urinate".'[62] The chin is thrust forward, the nose exaggerated. In the drawings Inigo

---

[60] Mark Webber, Christopher Stephens and Charles D. Laughlin Jr, 'Masks: A Re-examination, or "Masks? You mean they affect the brain?"' *The Power of Symbols: Masks and Masquerade in the Americas*, ed. N. R. Crumrine and M. Halpin (Vancouver, 1983) pp. 204, 211.

[61] Thomas Nashe, *Pierce Penilesse his Supplication to the Divell* (1592), quoted in E. K. Chambers, *The Elizabethan Stage*, vol. 4, (Oxford, 1923, repr. 1965), p. 239.

[62] Ravelhofer, ' "Virgin Wax" ', 250. See also Paster, *Body Embarrassed* on grotesque bodies.

Jones did for masques, by contrast, the forehead and cheekbones are important – and the bodies are vertical. The limbs of the masque dancers conform to geometric patterns, imaging cosmic order; what they do is not a picture of geometry but geometry itself, abstract. Vitruvius, whom Jones followed, says, in John Peacock's words, that 'units of measurement which the architect uses are derived from parts of the body . . . these various measures go together to make the perfect number'.[63] The dancer is taken over by a network of relations and patterns, a geometric figure; the clown is unable to be taken over by the 'proper' sense of relations because s/he misunderstands, the body does not enact poise or balance.

There is a kinaesthetic empathy between spectators' musculature and performers. In addition, the courtly masque body produces in the spectator a sense of that which is 'high'. It is an art that deals in the capacity of the body to seem 'abstract'. Watching it involves the work of precise looking, a valuation of accuracy and wit and poise. In turn, the watcher becomes poised. We are engaged with an art that is abstracted, disciplined, otherworldly. Far from being abstract, the clown body is indecorous. Its appetite leads it into repeated attempts to achieve satisfaction. This then leads to a sense of superfluous – because repeated – activity. In *The Tempest*, furthermore, the clownish drives don't take us into exciting and risky areas. Stephano and Trinculo are actually pretty dull. Experience of their activity can lead to a feeling that the physical is both superfluous and tiresome – or, in the classic petty bourgeois formulation, unnecessary.

AN ANTI-THEATRICAL COUP

With this clowning around we are hardly in the presence of carnival. If you're reading the play you may note that the scripting of the comedy is pretty straitlaced, but in performance we are also aware always of the presence of Prospero and his agent Ariel. Alongside them the clowning feels trivial, almost pointless – especially in its more obscure moments. While the clowns are later distracted by some clothes – 'glistering apparel' – hung on a line,

which Prospero describes as 'trumpery', he himself is pursuing his mission for justice and true order. While the clowns waste time trying on the robes they've found, Prospero is alert to the 'minute' of their plot (4.1.141). In our reflection on this division between the parties we should pause and note that Caliban too is dismissive of that glistering apparel, which he calls 'trash' (223), and that he worries that the activities with the robes will 'lose our time' (248). He, as much as Prospero, has a sense of mission. If Wiles is right about Armin playing this role, then the casting gives force to the distinction being posited here. Armin the intellectual is not one for trumpery.

That trumpery enables Stephano and Trinculo to play at the roles of king and subject – with Stephano in a robe giving jerkins as rewards to Trinculo. The wardrobe that they find is very like a theatrical wardrobe in that it is associated with the performance of fictional roles.[64] This glistering apparel is the stuff of the stage: as Peter Stallybrass says, 'the theater insisted upon staging the magic of clothes', much to the disapproval of antitheatricalists.[65] Prospero, a man who knows when to end revels, traps his enemies with the apparatus of playing. The bait is very precisely in line with the activities of one who can cause actors to melt into thin air, who can cause an insubstantial pageant to fade . . . or indeed with someone who can give an instruction that some trumpery be fetched, and, when it appears, it turns out to be glistering apparel.

[63] John Peacock, 'Inigo Jones as a Figurative Artist' in *Renaissance Bodies: The Human Figure in English Culture c. 1540–1660*, ed. Lucy Gent and Nigel Llewellyn (London, 1990), p. 160. See also Vigarello, 'Upward Training', on verticality.

[64] Rosemary Wright, 'Prospero's Lime Tree and the Pursuit of "Vanitas"', *Shakespeare Survey 37* (1984), pp. 133–40, argues that this episode recalls 'the late Gothic device of the pedlar and the apes' (page 134). Mary Beth Rose, 'Women in Men's Clothing: Apparel and Social Stability in *The Roaring Girl*', *ELR* 14:3 (1984), 367–91, links propriety of dress and the coherence of society.

[65] Peter Stallybrass, 'Worn Worlds: Clothes and Identity on the Renaissance Stage', in *Subject and Object in Renaissance Culture*, ed. Margreta de Grazia, Maureen Quilligan, Peter Stallybrass (Cambridge, 1996), p. 307.

But how far does that sort of moment really position Prospero as anti-theatre? When that apparel appears it may well exceed what an audience expected – it has a similar sort of visual splendour, unexpectedness, even fullness, as other apparitions in the play, albeit on a smaller scale. And its appearance works to enhance the status of Prospero, for not only can he cause such stuff to be produced but at the same time he also regards it as trumpery. The more an audience is delighted with its appearance the stronger seem Prospero's magic and cynicism. The glistering apparel may be a minor *coup de théâtre* but it is superceded by Prospero's attitude to it, thus achieving a sort of coup of anti-theatre.

Anti-theatrical as the attitude might be, that coup works to enhance the status and indeed charisma of Prospero. As an audience temporarily delights in that glistering texture and surface, Prospero is a step behind that surface, somewhere less accessible, putting on a show, inviting others to delight in the surface which doesn't impress him. His charisma consists not in surface but in depth. Prospero is a fictional creation that seems unimpressed by the apparatus of fiction. To the extent that he has both charisma and authority, in which an audience believes, he must himself – despite his pronouncements (or perhaps because of them) – be a very substantial piece of theatre.

Saying that leads us to a remarkably obvious point. When Prospero ends the masque, the entertainment, pleasurable in itself, is replaced by something much more pleasurable – the emotional seriousness, the apparent psychic depth, that speaks great poetry. It is the speech about the ending of revels that we know and love, not the revels themselves.

THE VARIOUS BODIES

In one sequence, in Act 4, we see masque performance, a man in the grip of a passion that 'works him strongly' (4.1.144) and clowns playing with robes. Each of these elements in the sequence requires a *specific and distinct bodily discipline*. That of the masque and the clowning I have described at length, with the assumption that the interaction between Prospero and his 'family' is in a more familiar, more documented mode. These are not, then, just different social groups: they are different ways of being on stage, different registers, differently used bodies. The moments of transition between one mode and another are marked both by the acting out of aggression – Prospero's passion, his intention to plague the clowns – and by theatrical devices which deliberately uglify – the 'confused noise' which replaces graceful music, the clowns 'all wet'. So there is a feeling of contest, rather than symbiosis, between these modes. And that contest sees one of the three victorious.

The relationship between these modes of playing may, with hindsight, be seen to be working itself out in a domain more extensive than that merely of *The Tempest*. The company performing the play, the King's Men, had, since the opening of their Globe theatre, made a pitch for artistic and social pre-eminence. Richard Wilson has argued that the opening scene of the opening play at the Globe, *Julius Caesar*, enacts a distaste for a low-class audience: 'The first words on the stage of the Globe can be interpreted, then, as a manoeuvre in the campaign to legitimise the Shakespearian stage and dissociate it from the subversiveness of London's artisanal culture'.[66] At that time an amphitheatre such as the Globe may have been supposed to cater for poorer audiences by contrast with the more expensive fare on offer at the hall playhouses, with their literary, satiric plays and their wealthy, culturally sophisticated audiences. But, when Hamlet hears news of the fashionable boy players, *Hamlet* shows that it is up with the fashions. Its literary protagonist also has views on modes of performance, warning against old-fashioned gesticulation and the dangers of letting clowns upstage you. Spoken at the Globe this advice shows circumspection about the traditional fare of amphitheatres, with their jigs and clowns. Put simply, it is as if the theatrical world of both Hamlet and *Hamlet* positions itself between the clowns of the vulgar and the coterie plays of the

---

[66] Richard Wilson, *Will Power: Essays on Shakespearean Authority* (New York, 1993), p. 47.

rich. Ten or so years later, the King's Men owned one of those elite hall theatres (and did *The Tempest* in it), though they still also played the Globe. But by then a different mode and venue had come to typify the performances of the most seriously elite. Under James, the court masque had rapidly acquired a pre-eminence.

None of the foregoing is meant to imply that the King's Men were excluded from court performance: they were not (and they were, after all, the King's Men). The argument is not solely about social status; it is also about artistic forms and artistic identity (which eventually leads us back into the social). The King's Men seem to have been making a bid for pre-eminence in playing a form of serious and 'real' drama; their star, Richard Burbage, was praised for becoming his parts (rather than assimilating them to his star identity, as did Edward Alleyn).[67] As Andrew Gurr puts it, they chose, somewhat riskily, to perform 'a new kind of repertoire', rejecting Henslowe's appeal to old-fashioned citizen taste.[68] At about the time of that choice, the viewpoint spoken by Hamlet was not too far removed from the dramaturgy of his tragedy – drama should be purposeful rather than extravagant, functional rather than distracting. At a much later date, after Shakespeare's death, two established members of the company, in role in Massinger's *Roman Actor* (1626), have a conversation in which they emphasize how their performances

> endeuour
> To build their mindes vp faire, and on the Stage
> Decipher to the life what honours waite
> On good, and glorious actions.

And, another adds – for this is fiction – 'For the profit *Paris*, / And mercinarie gaine they are things beneath vs'. Later in the play Paris recalls playing a tragedy of theirs in which an enacted murder produces a display of troubled conscience in a guilty watcher: Hamlet's functionality still celebrated, by the company, in 1626.[69]

In *The Tempest* we can perhaps glimpse one moment in the process whereby Shakespeare's company define themselves and their mode of playing against other modes – the clowning of vulgar am-

phitheatres, the masquing revels of a tightly circumscribed royal court. The fictional gesture by which revels are ended is made by a star actor working with a company that had high artistic ambitions in a world of entrepreneurial contest between companies. The King's Men wished to dissociate themselves from the vulgar while also exercising a freedom to experiment artistically, without being bound by absolutist authority and its circumscribed world of compliant expensive masques.

A GENTLE START

In my schematic account the three modes – masque, clowning and serious 'real' – all co-exist as possible options, possible body stagings. This is not, however, the experience of *The Tempest* audience. The narrative and dramaturgy of the play work to produce a sense of Prospero's natural superiority. The way he and his 'family' behave on stage seems to be something we should take as authentic, real, as against the artifice or insubstantiality of masque and clowns. With Prospero we come to acknowledge, with poised resignation, that there comes a time when revels need to be ended.

When Prospero interrupts the masque he 'starts suddenly'. He is in a 'passion'. Ferdinand invites Miranda, and the audience, to observe how the passion works Prospero 'strongly'. For a brief interval, unusually, we look *at* Prospero, rather than with him. What we see is as much a performance as the masquing was, but it's a performance which sets up, assumes, produces, a very different relationship between movement and motivation of that movement. The masquing figures adopted formal movements and dance measures because those were the conventions of the masque – they move according to appropriate ceremony. This ceremonial

---

[67] See Andrew Gurr, 'Who Strutted and Bellowed?' *Shakespeare Survey 16* (1963), pp. 95–102.

[68] Andrew Gurr, *Playgoing in Shakespeare's London* (Cambridge, 1987), p.151

[69] Philip Massinger, *The Roman Actor* (1626) in *Plays and Poems*, vol. 3, ed. P. Edwards and C. Gibson (Oxford, 1976), 1.1.21–4, 26–7.

movement seeks to be an image of something outside the human being – measure, 'highness'; it is
movement made abstract. When we see the passion
working strongly on Prospero we see the outer behaviour as the direct result of inner emotion – this
is movement that expresses something from inside
the person. The contrast here between ceremonial,
abstracted movement and what we might call motivated movement gains significance from contemporary attacks on ceremony and custom – modes of
behaviour that are not natural (where this term, like
several others, is to be recognized as ideological).

The work of the French philosopher Montaigne
offers us, in hindsight, a useful gloss on the relationship between passion and ceremony. Montaigne
dislikes the artificiality of ceremony in general and
elaborate dancing in particular:

some Ladies make a better shew of their countenances in
those dances, wherein are divers changes, cuttings, turn-
ings, and agitations of the body, than in some dances of
state and gravity, where they need but simply to tread
a naturall measure, represent an unaffected cariage, and
their ordinary grace; And as I have also seen some excellent Lourdans, or Clownes attired in their worky-day
clothes, and with a common homely countenance, af-
fourd us all the pleasure that may be had from their art.

Against ceremonial behaviour, which is acquired,
learnt, Montaigne places spontaneous feeling. He
recommends that the body express such feeling,
however ungraceful or indecorous the movement
might be: 'If the body be any whit eased by complaining, let him doe it: If stirring or agitation
please him, let him turne, rowle and tosse himselfe as long as he list.' [70] (Similarly one should not
fear to raise one's voice if to do so will allay grief.)
The very clumsiness of a movement resulting from
pain, its conspicuously unplanned agitation, is a
sign of the authenticity and *naturalness* of the emotion which motivates the movement. Within the
religious and political debates at the turn of the
century in England, this authenticity – or as we
might call it this purity of feeling – was a combination of nature and godhead speaking through the
individual. To puritan polemicists ceremony was

associated with both idolatrous state religion and
established courtly wealth.

Set against the masque Prospero's passion displays his naturalness, his distance from empty – or
duplicitous – ceremony. But there's also another
possible contrast at work. When the Prospero actor
gives a display of passion working on the character
he is doing something similar, albeit fleetingly, to
the clown who enters in the grip of a dominant
emotion. The difference, however, is that when
Trinculo and Stephano are emotionally possessed
and driven they are in the grip of physical needs, appetite, which they need to satisfy; their needs don't
relate to a mind. Prospero's passion, by contrast,
arises because he has forgotten a deadline – 'The
minute of their plot / Is almost come' (4.1.141–2).
For the short period that passion works on him we
see the rage for order. As Prospero does his passion, the spirits depart and Ferdinand and Miranda
look on. The stage is being cleared of its artifice,
returned to truth, but we don't yet know what action Prospero will take. We are not looking at action
so much as reaction. The outcome of this passion
will be a course of action that prevents something
happening, a plan to forestall someone else's plan.

But we are not immediately told what that pre-
ventative plan will be. Instead Prospero gives a display of how to control passion. It is turned into,
or replaced by, poetry. The speech about ending
revels seems to be intended to cheer up Ferdinand,
who is looking dismayed. His dismay is presumably
a response to the sight of Prospero's passion. So by
cheering up Ferdinand, the passion is also cleared
away. Of course, it is a strange recipe for cheerful-
ness: a confirmation that the playing is over and a
vision of the littleness of life. But once he has spoken this vision, Prospero can acknowledge that he
is old and vexed. Speaking that speech seems not
just to be emotionally motivated – coming from
an old man's vexation – but it is also part of the
process of moving from passion to repose. The demolition of pageants, indeed the very poetry itself,

---

[70] Michel de Montaigne, *Essayes*, trs. J. Florio, intr. T. Sec-
combe, book 2 (London, 1908), pp. 116, 619.

have a higher function – serving to establish individual repose, individual resignation in the face of life's decay.

At the end of the speech he sends Miranda and Ferdinand away so that he can walk alone, to 'still' his beating mind. That desire to be alone contrasts with the behaviour of the clowns. Trinculo would rather be under Caliban's gaberdine than face the storm: the dramaturgy of their first scene impels each into the company of another. And that scene tends to disturb rather than promote stillness. We have already noted the range and sorts of movement – responses to rain, stench, drunkenness. If their movements highlight appetite and gut instinct, if their centres of gravity are low, if they joke about shit and piss, then they might be seen as corresponding to lower body parts. In relation to them Prospero's movement can be seen as purposeful and functional, rather than driven and wasteful. It is a response to his higher body parts, specifically his mind: after a passion has gripped him he then says he will walk to still his beating mind. Contributing to a whole tradition of acting as the display of bodily inhibition,[71] Prospero will move in order to make himself more still.

What Prospero dislikes about Caliban is that his mind is governed by his body – as his body grows more aged the mind becomes more cankered, he says. The episode of Prospero's passion shows how the mind can control strong emotion and how body movement is beneficial when controlled; to walk to still the mind is to move with plan and purpose. The contrast between Prospero's mode of being on stage and that of the clowns schematically arranges itself as a contrast between high and low, where the action against the clowns expresses not merely a distaste for lower body parts but revenge against them. It also expresses a contempt for waste. Prospero and Ariel watch, invisible, as the clowns' appetite for trumpery wastes their time – and in doing so keeps Prospero's plan right on schedule.

The contrast between the body stagings is, unsurprisingly, a contrast between sets of values. The contrast enables a definition of what in its 'naturalness' and 'realism' would otherwise be pretty slippery to pin down. Prospero's way of being, his place and values are defined as what the others are not. On the one hand there is the courtly masque, on the other clowns; each is felt to be artificial, digressive from the main business. More precisely, in terms of values, there is fragile ceremony on one hand and on the other ill-disciplined appetite and waste. Prospero, fictionally a duke, is located elsewhere by the scheme of body stagings. His mode of being is between courtliness and lower orders. He moves in a way which is 'natural', since it is not meretriciously ornamental; disciplined and orderly, since it is not wastefully overcome by appetite; more passionate than geometric, more rational than possessed; not caught into patterns or lazzi, but vertically still. Neither courtly nor clown, Prospero presides over a sort of household with servants; but it is a household which does not manufacture or produce – he does not labour or trade. His position is that of the gentleman.

Clearly that assertion is nonsense in terms of what Shakespeare scripts. Prospero, as I said above, is an aristocrat – with, we could add, kingly powers. But what the story-line offers us is, I suggest, contradicted, albeit silently, by the – how shall we put it? – body language. In the mode of acting done by Prospero and his family – or, to be more precise, in what that acting is not – it is the *gentle* body which is felt to be authentic, natural, real. The position which is, nominally, princely is concretely embodied as something different. The mode of that embodiment, and its behaviour, imply – without the need for verbalization – the triviality of the courtly on one hand and, on the other, the contemptibility of the clownish. Separated as much from what is higher as from the low, its attachment to discipline, measure, individuality, purpose and time-keeping show how amenable it is to a vision that we have later come to characterize as bourgeois.

This scheme of contrasts produces a sense of the authenticity of Prospero's position. The clowns, on the other hand, are ridiculous because they aspire above their social rank. And there is a parallel, if less ridiculous, piece of social blurring in the

---

[71] On actors learning to acquire inhibition, see Roach, *Player's Passion*, p. 52.

masque. This occurs in the dance, which now at last we need to look at. Nymphs and reapers dance 'country footing'. But they do so within a courtly masque. The stage direction requires not only that the reapers be 'properly' habited, but also that the dance is 'graceful'. Alan Brissenden notes how unusual it is for a Shakespearian stage direction to describe a dance in this way, and conjectures that it 'possibly indicates an insistence that this dance should be particularly attractive and orderly'.[72] Contemporary notions of gracefulness in dance would inhibit the dancers from showing the irregularity and 'freedom' that Skiles Howard associates with real country dancing.[73] We are, in short, watching courtly dancing playing at being 'country' – sliding down in degree just as the clowns aspire upwards.

The inauthenticity with regard to social position may for some in the audience have been adumbrated by more general prejudices not only about clownish wastefulness but about meretricious dancing. To a puritan such as Prynne dancing was both wasteful and scandalous, and the dancing he had in mind was also imported from France.[74] While Prynne's voice was particularly strident, the attitudes about courtly decadence and foreignness were not uncommon among the London mercantile and manufacturing communities.[75] This might give significance to the tendency for city masques to abstain from dance. Where an antipathy against dancing comes into alignment with a valuing of productive work in relation to degree, it might find everything it opposed condensed in the sight of grace-full dancers dressed as reapers.

Prospero enacts for us the destruction of this masquing fantasy. So too he terminates the folly of clowns. But although these things are demolished within the fictional narrative, Shakespeare's text has a deep need of them. For those clown scenes supply one of the parameters which places, defines, that otherwise slippery thing which I've called Prospero's realism. By successfully defining that realism the clown scenes give authority to the values which come with the realism – discipline, measure, etc. (And quickly, having said that, we have to recall that, in the dialectical scheme here, Prospero's

measure is felt to be functional – unlike the ceremonial discipline of masque movement.) Once established, these 'realist' values confirm the waste and triviality of the clown mode. There's something going on which is back-to-front.

Which brings us back to the revels speech. What the speech doesn't tell us is what Prospero has got planned for the next ten minutes. He is certainly not resigned to the Caliban plot and will take action against it. The dramaturgy suggests that the plan is already formed in his mind for, when he sends Miranda and Ferdinand away, even before thanking them for their farewell wishes he has summoned Ariel:

> FERDINAND AND MIRANDA We wish your peace.
> *Exeunt.*
> PROSPERO Come with a thought! – I thank thee. –
> Ariel, come!   (4.1.164–5)

While we may dwell, with Ferdinand, on the beautiful necessity of the revels' ending, and then pity an old man who confronts his own infirmity, we have missed something. The old man has a plan in his head and is yet moving towards the full achievement of his revenge. Far from stilling his mind, he has launched into a new action; far from being resigned, he is going to plague the plotters 'Even to roaring'. And while the 'insubstantial pageant' might have faded, he has sent for a set of glistering apparel to be spread out attractively for a new audience.

Theatrical activity will carry on. But it has been obscured by a rhetorical gesture that invites us to contemplate the ending of revels. It is this gesture

---

[72] Brissenden, *Shakespeare and Dance*, p. 100 (he also notes that the earlier dance of Shapes, with its 'gentle actions', is also orderly).

[73] Howard, *Politics*, p. 2; see Franko, 'Renaissance Conduct Literature', on grace.

[74] See Ravelhofer, '"Virgin Wax"' on both Prynne and Frenchness; Peter Holman, *Four and Twenty Fiddlers: The Violin at the English Court 1540–1690* (Oxford, 1993) and Ward, 'Newly Devis'd Measures' both detail the emergence and influence of French dancing-masters.

[75] Margot Heinemann, *Puritanism and Theatre: Thomas Middleton and Opposition Drama under the Early Stuarts* (Cambridge, 1980).

which has caught the imaginations of so many commentators on the play. What is happening here is that Prospero's contempt is being elided with that of Shakespeare, so that the play appears to be acting out the abandonment not merely of revels but of clowning too. That leaves us with the serious part of the play, which is the 'realist' part – the part that denies its own theatricality, or at least has contempt for trumpery. That part is most closely associated with Prospero, the man who ends revels. At the heart of *The Tempest*, then, is a mode of theatrical playing which identifies itself as anti-theatre. That anti-theatre is attractive and familiar because it gives defining form to the gentle, and later bourgeois, body. While it modestly demurs at the theatrical the gentle body finds in the vigilant maintenance of its tidy uprightness a spectacle that is, as it were, highly satisfactory.

'TAKING JUST CARE OF THE IMPRESSION': EDITORIAL INTERVENTION IN SHAKESPEARE'S FOURTH FOLIO, 1685

SONIA MASSAI

Nicholas Rowe is still widely regarded as the first professional editor of Shakespeare. Because significant seventeenth-century contributions to the editorial tradition were systematically overlooked, disregarded or silently absorbed by Rowe and his successors, he remains the 'father' of Shakespearian editing. The predominant view, according to which Shakespeare's seventeenth-century editors were simple-minded printers' correctors is similarly short-sighted. Though anonymous, they were theatrically minded specialists, whose work is much closer to current editorial practices than is Rowe's interventionist editing in his 1709 edition of Shakespeare's *Complete Works*.

Evidence of editorial intervention can be found in a range of seventeenth-century texts, including Quarto and Folio editions, promptbooks, acting editions and adaptations, manuscript annotations and transcriptions. Restoration adaptations, for example, anticipate 'all the activities that editors of Shakespeare still undertake . . . – the modernization of spelling, the introduction of stage directions . . . , the drawing up of a list of *dramatis personae*, and, that highest of all editorial activities, the collation of quarto and folio variants'.[1] The practical advantages of regarding seventeenth-century adapters as the precursors of eighteenth-century editors are manifold. The editors of *Macbeth* in the Complete Oxford Shakespeare (1986), for example, include two songs, which the Folio fails to preserve in full. The editors believe that these two songs were regularly performed, as suggested by the fact that Davenant, who used a independent theatrical document as

source-text for his 1674 adaptation, preserves them. The Oxford editors therefore import the songs from their probable source, Middleton's *The Witch*, while referring to the Restoration adaptation as control text.[2] A similar use of Restoration adaptations can be found in Jonathan Bate's New Arden edition of *Titus Andronicus* (1995), where Ravenscroft's 1687 *Titus Andronicus, or The Rape of Lavinia* is used as a precedent to support some interesting editorial choices. Most of Bate's borrowings are stage directions introduced by Ravenscroft in the opening scene to clarify the stage action. As a result, Bate's edition highlights the complex and sophisticated blocking implied by the dialogue of the first scene, thus vindicating a text that earlier editors had dismissed as a piece of embarrassing juvenilia. My recent work on Nahum Tate's 1681 adaptation of *King Lear* provides new evidence to support the theory of internal revision in Shakespeare. A contrastive analysis of Quarto and Folio *King Lear* alongside Tate's adaptation shows that Tate regarded his Quarto and Folio sources as two independent texts and used their variants according

---

I would like to thank Thomas L. Berger, who inspired me to write this article, Giles Mandelbrote, who helped me improve my understanding of the book-trade in the early modern period, and Mike Foster for being such a helpful reader and arbiter of style.

[1] J. Bate and S. Massai, 'Adaptation as Edition', in *The Margins of the Text*, ed. by D. C. Greetham (Ann Arbor, 1997), pp. 132–3.
[2] S. Wells and G. Taylor, with J. Jowett and W. Montgomery, *William Shakespeare: A Textual Companion* (Oxford, 1987), p. 543.

to what source text better suited his own strategy of revision.[3]

Seventeenth-century transcripts occasionally preserve a similar range of early editorial interventions. According to Blakemore Evans, the editor–revisers of the six Shakespearian transcripts included in the Douai Manuscript (1694–5) 'work with thought and some knowledge of the plays . . . and show considerable intelligence in dealing with corrupt or difficult passages, or in correcting what seemed to them slight inconsistencies in the text'.[4] As a result, the transcripts provide 'numerous readings which . . . anticipate the emendations proposed by the later eighteenth and nineteenth-century editors of Shakespeare'.[5] While rectifying some of Evans's assumptions about the copy texts of the Douai transcripts, Ann Mari Hedbäck points out that the non-Shakespearian transcripts in the Douai Manuscript also preserve some interesting variants. For example, Hedbäck regards one variant in Davenant's *2 The Siege of Rhodes* as a 'more convincing emendation of a faulty word in the early editions than any of those suggested by later editions'.[6]

Among the so-called 'Players' Quartos', the 1676 and the 1683 Quarto editions of *Hamlet* are similarly representative of the sophisticated level of correction undergone by texts clearly meant to be used as scripts for performance. Ann Thompson has recently argued that at least 'one alteration [in the 1683 Quarto] seems . . . to suggest that someone had finally turned to the folio tradition'.[7] Thompson therefore calls into question the traditional assumption that the 'Players' Quartos' 'run on, heedless except very rarely of the Folios, and then almost invariably with every appearance of causal coincidence'.[8] Focusing on earlier acting editions, Thomas Berger has similarly demonstrated that the 1630 Quarto edition of *Othello* 'represents the first 'conflated' text of [the play], probably the first consistently conflated text of any Shakespearian play'.[9]

Considerable attention has been devoted to Shakespeare's First and Second Folios. In 1991, Howard-Hill observed that the First Folio 'was just the kind of compilation that involved activities that

we can now properly characterize as "editorial" '.[10] After attributing instances of editorial intervention in the First Folio to Ralph Crane,[11] Howard-Hill concluded that

[Crane's] involvement with the First Folio was so extensive and of such a kind that it is [he] rather than the playwright Nicholas Rowe whom we should acknowledge as the first person to confront the problems of translating Shakespeare's plays from stage to the study: Shakespeare's first editor.[12]

At the beginning of the last century, Alfred Pollard made a strong case in favour of the hypothesis of editorial intervention in the Second Folio of 1632. Pollard believed that

the Second Folio did not merely alter the First in order now and again to make the colloquial syntax more regular . . . but in a real sense began the work of lawful and necessary emendation . . . it was in 1632 that a start was made in re-editing the First Folio, and thus no survey of the history of Shakespeare's text can be complete which does not take into account the work of these anonymous compositors and correctors.[13]

[3] S. Massai, 'Tate's Revision of Shakespeare's *King Lears*', *Studies in English Literature* 40 (2000), pp. 435–50.
[4] G. Blakemore Evans, 'The Douai Manuscript – Six Shakespearian Transcripts (1694–95)', *Philological Quarterly*, 41 (1962), pp. 164–5.
[5] G. Blakemore Evans, 'The Douai Manuscript', p. 166.
[6] A. M. Hedbäck, 'The Douai Manuscript Re-examined', *Papers of the Bibliographical Society of America* 73 (1979), 16.
[7] A. Thompson, ' "I'll have grounds / More relative than this": The Puzzle of John Ward's *Hamlet* Promptbooks', *The Yearbook of English Studies* 29 (1999), 141.
[8] H. Spencer, *Shakespeare Improved: The Restoration Versions in Quarto and on the Stage* (Cambridge, MA, 1927), p. 175.
[9] T. L. Berger, 'The Second Quarto of *Othello* and the Question of Textual "Authority"', *Analytical and Enumerative Bibliography* 2 (1988), 141–59, p. 145.
[10] T. H. Howard-Hill, 'Shakespeare's Earliest Editor: Ralph Crane', *Shakespeare Survey 44* (1991), p. 113.
[11] For earlier research on the role played by the 'transcriber-editor' in the Folio text of *2 Henry IV*, see E. Prosser, *Shakespeare's Anonymous Editors* (Stanford, 1981).
[12] Howard-Hill, 'Shakespeare's Earliest Editor', p. 129.
[13] A. W. Pollard, *Shakespeare Folios and Quartos: A Study in the Bibliography of Shakespeare's Plays, 1594–1685* (London, 1909), p. 157.

Pollard's views were endorsed and reinforced by Nicoll in the 1920s[14] and by Black and Shaaber in the 1930s.[15] Finally, in 1951, Giles Dawson demonstrated that a batch of seventy unruled pages in some copies of F 4, now generally referred to as F 5, had been reset and reprinted around 1700.[16] Eric Rasmussen has recently established that 'renewed attention to the reprinted Fifth Folio pages reveals that the person responsible for the text behaved very much like an eighteenth-century editor'.[17]

The Fourth Folio (henceforth F 4) has so far received little attention, despite the fact that Rowe used it as his copy-text in 1709 and that later eighteenth-century editors followed their immediate predecessors, until Dr Johnson decided to go back to F 1 in 1765. Although, as Barbara Mowat has pointed out, Rowe was responsible for the introduction of conventions which affected the structuring and presentation of Shakespeare's plays till the early 1980s,[18] the text of Rowe's influential edition often left its copy-text fundamentally unaltered. If there is evidence to argue that Rowe sometimes combined Quarto and Folio texts to make up a text of his own, it is also clear that whenever he dealt with texts which had appeared only in Folio editions, his intervention was cosmetic. Rowe silently adopted most F 4 corrections, which then, in turn, were inherited by his successors. As the evidence analysed below shows, F 4 corrections were the result of a thorough exercise in modernization and normalization of the text, one which clearly goes beyond the tampering of a solicitous printer's corrector.

Current perceptions of F 4 as a mere reprint of F 3 derive mainly from Black and Shaaber's, *Shakespeare's Seventeenth-Century Editors, 1632–1685.* They argue that, because the text of F 4 falls into three very distinctive divisions, 'some or all of the changes found in F 4 may be the work of three different correctors of the press, each regularly employed in one of the three printing offices involved'. Although they consider the alternative that an editor 'probably unconnected with the printing trade . . . superseded the regular correctors of the three printing houses', they believe that the theory of three different press-correctors is the more likely.[19]

Black and Shaaber's conclusions are questionable. Their lists of textual alterations draw from the collations of the Furness–Variorum edition, and, for the plays which had not been issued in it, the collations of the second edition of the Cambridge Shakespeare (1891–3). Black and Shaaber themselves admit that 'the Cambridge editors collated [F 4] somewhat negligently', and that they 'doubt that [their] own data do it full justice'.[20] A fresh collation of a selection of texts as they appear in F 3 and F 4 shows that the too hastily dismissed alternative theory according to which an editor, 'probably unconnected with the printing trade . . . superseded the regular correctors of the three printing houses', is in fact the more likely.

Black and Shaaber ignored three defining aspects of the internal evidence provided by F 4, which suggest editorial intervention rather than compositorial tampering or press-corrections: consistency of intervention, frequency of intervention, and consistency of procedures. Before considering each aspect more closely, I will discuss three F 4 variants, which suggest the high level of correction and normalisation undergone by F 3. Although the quality of F 4 variants is clearly suggestive of editorial intervention, by itself it is not a determining factor. Only when the quality of the intervention

[14] A. Nicoll, 'The Editors of Shakespeare from First Folio to Malone', in *Studies in the First Folio* (London and Oxford, 1924), 163–6.

[15] M. W. Black and M. A. Shaaber, *Shakespeare's Seventeenth-Century Editors, 1632–1685* (New York, 1937).

[16] G. E. Dawson, 'Some Bibliographical Irregularities in the Shakespeare's Fourth Folio', *Studies in Bibliography* 4 (1951), 93–104.

[17] E. Rasmussen, 'Anonimity and the Erasure of Shakespeare's First Eighteenth-Century Editor', in *Reading Readings: Essays on Shakespeare Editing in the Eighteenth Century*, ed. by J. Gondris (Madison and London, 1998), p. 319.

[18] B. A. Mowat, 'Nicholas Rowe and the Twentieth-Century Shakespeare Text', in *Shakespeare and Cultural Traditions: The Selected Proceedings of the International Shakespeare Association World Congress, Tokyo, 1991*, ed. by T. Kishi, R. Pringle and S. Wells, pp. 314–22.

[19] Black and Shaaber, *Shakespeare's Seventeenth-Century Editors*, p. 29.

[20] Ibid., p. 65.

in F4 is considered alongside their consistency and frequency does the contribution of an editor 'probably unconnected with the printing trade' appear as the most likely explanation to account for their origin.

Some of the best examples of editorial intervention in F4 come from *Coriolanus*. In Act 4, the eponymous Roman leader, who is forced to seek shelter among his former enemies, reflects on the fickleness of allegiance:

> Oh World, thy slippery turnes! Friends now fast sworn,
> Whose double bosomes seemes to weare one heart,
>   ...   shall within this houre,
> On a dissention of a Doit, breake out
> To bitterest Enmity.   (TLN 2638–44)

The F2 compositor mangled the second line into: 'Whose double bosomes seene weare on heart'. F3 leaves F2 unaltered, whereas F4 shrewdly restores F1, modernizing the number of the verb: 'Whose double bosoms seem to wear one Heart'. This line in F4 is more likely to be the result of speculative intervention rather than an actual restoration of F1, given that on other occasions mistakes first introduced in F2 or F3 are not emended according to F1.

The hypothesis of speculative intervention is reinforced by a variant reading later in the same speech. F1 is clearly corrupt when Coriolanus argues:

> So with me,
> My Birth-place haue I, and my loues vpon
> This Enemie Towne: lle enter, if he slay me
> He does faire Iustice: (TLN 2648–51)

F2 makes things worse by dropping the first letter in 'place' and turning 'loues' into 'lover'. F3 reprints the nonsensical version provided by F2. F4 offers the best alternative, restoring 'Birth-place', adding 'left' after 'Lover', and revising the punctuation, which now establishes a link between the preposition 'upon' and the verb 'enter' in the following line – 'My Birth-place have I, and my Lover left; upon / This Enemy's Town I'le enter, if . . .'. Modern editions follow Capell by emending 'have' into

'hate' – 'my birthplace hate I' – and the unusual plural 'loves' into the abbreviated 'and my love is upon / This Enemie Town.' The solution provided by F4 is, again, obviously speculative and not as satisfactory as Capell's. F4's emendation must have been regarded as perfectly acceptable, however, since it was endorsed by all eighteenth-century editors up to Capell, including Nicholas Rowe.

Another example of sophisticated editorial intervention occurs in Act 5. After Coriolanus has given in to Volumnia's request to spare Rome, it is Aufidius's turn to reflect on the fickleness of allegiance. In F1, Aufidius's lines read as follows:

> ...   I tooke him [Coriolanus],
> Made him ioynt-seruant with me: Gaue him way
> In all his owne desires: Nay, let him choose
> Out of my Files, his proiects, to accomplish
> My best and freshest men, seru'd his designements
> In mine owne person: holpe to reape the Fame
> Which he did end all his; and tooke some pride
> To do my selfe this wrong: (TLN 3684–91)

Irregular punctuation probably led to tampering in F2 and F3, where 'holpe', a form occasionally used as the past tense or past participle of the verb to 'help', is replaced by 'hope'. F4 could not restore 'holpe' from 'hope', but nevertheless normalised the tense of the verb by turning 'hope' into 'hop'd' as well as making the sense of this sentence more explicit by replacing the unusual 'end' with 'make' – 'hop'd to reap the Fame / Which he did make all his'. Once again, the solution provided by F4, though speculative and far from satisfactory, was obviously good enough for Rowe and his successors, who silently endorsed it.

The text of *Coriolanus* as it appears in F4 provides many other examples of sophisticated editorial intervention. Suffice it to say that the number of F4 variants recently adopted in scholarly editions of the play range from about twenty in the New Cambridge to around fifty in the second edition of the *Riverside Shakespeare*. These variants are unlikely to be the result of press-correction, as intimated by Black and Shaaber. As J. K. Moore's analysis of extant seventeenth-century proof-sheets reveals, 'all proof-readers were concerned with the appearance of the printed page and invariably notified typographical errors, such as raised spaces, wrong fount, pied type and turned letters. However', Moore specifies, 'many corrections derive from the copy[-text] and could not have been made at the initiative of the reader'.[21] The substantive emendations in the text of *Coriolanus* as it appears in F4 would seem to fall into this category. Nevertheless, all these examples of editorial intervention fail to provide definitive evidence that an editor, 'probably unconnected with the printing trade . . . superseded the regular correctors of the three printing houses'. The three aspects I mentioned earlier, however, corroborate this theory.

The first aspect is the consistency of the editorial intervention. In the text of *Coriolanus* as it appears in F4, Titus Lartius, one of the two generals in the wars against the Volscies, is renamed Titus Lucius. The Arden 2 editor warns us that the name 'Titus Lucius' is a mistake and that Titus Lartius is, historically and bibliographically, the correct alternative.[22] What is significant, though, is that the decision to replace the name 'Titus Lartius' with the name 'Titus Lucius' must have been taken before the F4 compositor began to set his text. The spurious alternative 'Titus Lucius' was probably prompted by TLN 262 in F1 to F3, where Titus Lartius is mistakenly addressed as Titus Lucius. It seems unlikely that a compositor should have decided to emend all the other occasions where Titus's second name is Lartius, as well as speech-headings and stage directions. It seems even more unlikely that a compositor would have chosen to adopt the one spurious occurrence of the name Titus Lucius in F3 and emend all the other occurences of the name Titus Lartius not only after TLN 262, but also retrospectively (see Table 1).

It seems more likely that the compositor was setting his text from an annotated copy of F3 where the name Lartius had consistently been crossed out from dialogue, speech-headings, and stage directions and replaced by Lucius.[23]

Even more significant is the attention devoted to making sure that the proper names, which occur in the stage directions and speech-headings, are consistent with their counterparts in the dialogue. The

Table 1

	F3	F4
TLN 245	Titus Lartius	Titus Lucius
TLN 262	**Lucius**	**Lucius**
TLN 327	Lartius	Lucius
TLN 462	Lartius	Lucius
TLN 478	Lartius	Lucius
TLN 547	Lartius	Lucius
TLN 615	Lartius	Lucius
TLN 644	Lartius	Lucius
TLN 710	Lartius	Lucius
TLN 796	Lartius	Lucius
TLN 832	Lartius	Lucius
TLN 1024	Lartius	Lucius
TLN 1060	Lartius	Lucius
TLN 1245	Lartius	Lucius
TLN 1672	Lartius	Lucius

stage direction which prompts the first entrance of the generals and the Tribunes of the people in Act 1 – '*Enter Sicinius Velutus, Annius Brutus Cominisu* (sic)*, Titus / Lartius, with other Senatours*' – is emended in F4 by replacing '*Annius Brutus*' with 'Junius Brutus'. F4 therefore ensures consistency between this stage direction and an earlier speech in the same scene, where Coriolanus mentions that Sicinius Velutus and Junius Brutus are two of the five tribunes the people of Rome have been granted in order 'to defend', as Coriolanus puts it, 'their vulgar wisdoms'. In F4, this stage direction is in keeping with the dialogue for the first time.

---

[21] J. K. Moore, *Primary Materials Relating to Copy and Print in English Books of the Sixteenth and Seventeenth Centuries* (Oxford, 1992), p. 65.

[22] P. Brockbank (ed.), *Coriolanus, The Arden Shakespeare* (London and New York, 1976), pp. 21–2.

[23] Similarly suggestive is the consistency in the normalization of proper names. Auffidius is consistently spelt Aufidius, and Volcies, Volcians and Volcian are consistently spelt Volscies, Volscians and Volscian. The name Aufidius occurs forty-four times; the names and adjective Volscies, Volscians and Volscian occur thirty-two times. Although this type of consistency often reflects a compositorial habit, the fact that these proper names and adjective are normalized without exception on all of the seventy-six occasions on which they occur could also suggest that the compositor of F4 *Coriolanus* was working from an annotated copy of F3.

Table 2

	Syntax**	Apostrophe***	Modernised Spelling
*Merchant of Venice** (I Div.)	31	9	46
*Coriolanus** (II Div.)	91	64	50
*Hamlet** (III Div.)	69	7	50
*The Northern Lass**[25]	5	3	2
*A Jovial Crew**[26]	—	1	25

* Occurrences in Act I.
** Improvements through addition and omission of commas.
*** Use of the apostrophe to indicate possession and to normalize contractions.

The second defining aspect to suggest editorial intervention as opposed to compositorial tampering in F4 is the distribution and frequency of substantive corrections. If, as Black and Shaaber suggest, F4 variants were 'the work of three different correctors of the press, each regularly employed in one of the three printing offices involved', one would expect a pretty consistent pattern of corrections in all the texts included in the same division. The texts of *Coriolanus* and *Richard II* occur in the same division. Yet the number of corrections introduced in these two texts varies considerably. The frequent and sophisticated emendations introduced in *Coriolanus* are matched by half a dozen obvious corrections in *Richard II*.[24] The sporadic distribution of substantive emendations in the second division of F4 can best be explained in terms of editorial intervention, because its frequency, unlike the tampering of a compositor or press-corrector, is determined by such circumstantial factors as the editor's familiarity with a specific text, or the intrinsic quality of his copy-text.

The third and final defining aspect of the textual evidence provided by F4 is the consistency of procedures across its three divisions – the comedies (first division); the histories and the tragedies including *Romeo and Juliet* (second division); the remaining tragedies and the seven plays first added to F3 in 1664 (third division). F4 improves the syntax as it appears in F3 by consistently adding or removing commas. Contractions are systematically normalized through the addition of the apostrophe. The apostrophe is also used almost

without fail to indicate possession. The spelling is thoroughly modernized.

One might argue that these improvements reflect the contemporary evolution and normalisation of the English language. Table 2 above shows that when a selection of texts drawn from the three divisions in F4 is compared to texts printed in the 1660s and then reprinted in the 1680s, the level of correction and normalization in F4 is exceptional.

The persistence across the three divisions of idiosyncratic procedures, such as the consistent removal of the still widely used ampersand or the hyphenation of compound words at a time when the use of the hyphen was in steady decline, also suggests that the consistency of conventions in F4 does not simply reflect the evolution of the English language between the 1660s and the 1680s.

The fact that both *A Jovial Crew* and *The Northern Lass* were first published in the early 1630s and 1650s and that F1 dates back to the early 1620s

---

[24] What follows is a list of the main emendations introduced in the text of *Richard II* as it appears in F4: 1. TLN 237 'vaded' (F3); 'faded' (F4). 2. TLN 732 'no men' (F3); 'no, men' (F4). 3. TLN 1767 'Jides' (F3); 'Jades' (F4). 4. TLN 1997 'A' (F3); 'As' (F4). 5. TLN 2240 'sights' (F3); 'sight' (F4). 6. TLN 2255 'Heart' (F3); 'Hearts' (F4).

[25] *The Northern Lasse. A Comoedy....Written by Richard Brome....London. Printed for A. Moseley* (1663); *The Northern Lass. A Comedy...By Richard Brome, Gent. London, Printed for D. Newman* (1684).

[26] *A Joviall Crew: Or, The Merry Beggars...By Richard Brome, Gent...London. Printed for Henry Brome at the Gun in Ivy-Lane* (1661); *A Jovial Crew: Or, The Merry Beggars...By Richard Brome, Gent....London. Printed for Joseph Hindmarsh at the Black Bull in Cornhill* (1684).

does not affect the validity of the evidence shown in Table 2. Both those responsible for issuing a third edition of *A Jovial Crew* and *The Northern Lass* in 1684 and the editor / annotator of F4, who was working from a copy of F3, were editing texts which were about twenty years old. Furthermore, the reputation of the publishers of the 1684 editions of *A Jovial Crew* and *The Northern Lass* reinforces the sense of an exceptional level of normalization and correction in F4, as shown in Table 2. *The Northern Lass* was reprinted for Dorman Newman, one of the largest publishers of his time;[27] Joseph Hindmarsh, the publisher of the 1684 edition of *A Jovial Crew*, started his activity later than Newman, but was also well-established by 1684.[28] The cheaper Quarto format of these two editions, rather than the lack of resources or expertise on the part of their publishers, seems to have determined the smaller amount of editorial effort bestowed upon them.

The exceptional level of correction and the consistency of idiosyncrasies across the three divisions in F4 can best be explained not in terms of the evolution and progressive normalisation of the English language but in terms of editorial guidelines. By editorial guidelines I mean specific conventions set by the editor / annotator of F4 for the three printing houses to follow.

External evidence supports the results of my collations, indicating that seventeenth-century publishers bestowed a great amount of care on the printing of *belles-lettres*, including the appointment of 'editorial assistants'. There is a danger of imposing an anachronistic function on these figures, since the term 'editor' as it is understood today was first used at the beginning of the eighteenth century.[29] Besides, the roles of the several parties involved in the book-trade – the printer, the publisher, the editor, the bookseller – often overlapped until the end of the seventeenth century and into the eighteenth. However, the evidence analysed below shows that editorship was already perceived as a specific and crucial function throughout the sixteenth and the seventeenth centuries.

Several seventeenth-century authors, including Samuel Daniel,[30] Ben Jonson,[31] Thomas Heywood,[32] Robert Burton, William Cartwright, William Davenant[33] and John Milton,[34] supervised

[27] H. R. Plomer, *A Dictionary of the Booksellers and Printers who were at work in England, Scotland and Ireland from 1668–1725* (London, 1922), p. 217

[28] Ibid., pp. 156–7.

[29] The first recorded use of the term 'editor' indicating 'one who prepares the literary work of another person . . . for publication' dates back to 1712 (*Oxford English Dictionary*).

[30] Samuel Daniel collaborated closely with his publisher and friend Simon Waterson. Following the piratical publication of twenty-seven of Daniel sonnets at the end of Sir Philip Sidney's 1591 edition of *Astrophil and Stella*, Waterson published two editions of Daniel's *Delia* in 1592 and a third edition in 1594, all of which contain detailed authorial revisions and corrections of typographical errors. For more details on Daniel's collaboration with his publisher and printers, see, for example, C. C. Seronsy, *Samuel Daniel* (New York, 1967).

[31] Jonson claimed a higher status for his dramatic works than normally granted to theatrical scripts in the early seventeenth century by publishing them alongside his poetical works in the 1616 Folio edition, which appealed to a selected and sophisticated reading audience. Jonson was personally involved with the printing of both the 1616 Folio and the two-volume Folio edition, which was eventually published posthumously in 1640. Jonson is reported to have complained about his printer John Beale: 'My printer and I shall afford subject enough for a tragi-comedy, for with his delays and vexation, I am almost become blind.' Quoted in W. D. Kay, *Ben Jonson: A Literary Life* (London, 1995), p. 182.

[32] Although in 'The Address to the Reader' prefixed to *The English Traveller* (1633) Heywood makes some irony at Jonson's expenses by claiming that 'it never was any great ambition in me to be in this kind voluminously read', in *A Prologue to the Play of Queene Elizabeth* (1623) he reports how piracy forced him to publish authoritative editions of his works: 'Some by stenography drew / The plot: put it in print: (scarce one word trew:) / And in that lamenesse it hath limp't so long, / The author now to vindicate that wrong / Hath tooke the paines, upright upon its feete / To teach it walke, so please you sit, and see't.'

[33] For extant proof-sheets suggesting that Cartwright, Burton and Davenant corrected at the press, see J. K. Moore, *Primary Materials* and also Percy Simpson, *Proof-Reading in the Sixteenth, Seventeenth and Eighteenth Centuries* (London, 1935); *The Anatomy of Melancholy*, ed. T. C. Faulkner, et al. (Oxford, 1989); and Ann-Mari Hedbäck, 'The Printing of *The Siege of Rhodes*', *Studia Neophilologica* 45 (1973), 68–79.

[34] With the exception of Richard Bentley, who believed that Milton's blindness prevented him from supervising the printing of *Paradise Lost*, most critics and editors of Milton have regarded the early printed texts as reliable and authoritative.

the printing of their works themselves, initiating a wide variety of press corrections and other editorial activities. Authors of non-fiction also supervised the impression of their works. The divine Thomas Fuller, for example, is reported to have '[seen] through the press his Exeter Sermon, *Feare of London and the Old Light*, and the third edition of *Good Thoughts in Bad Times*, . . . while he was under the shelter of his publisher's roof in London'.[35] In *Life* (1661), Fuller's anonymous biographer also mentions his 'constant attendance on the Press in the edition of his Books', as evidence of an 'Active and Industrious Mind'.[36]

The extraordinary evidence provided by the correspondence between William Holder and John Baynard, the 'editor' of Holder's treatise on *The Natural Grounds and Principles of Harmony* (1694),[37] shows that when the author could not supervise the impression of his works himself, he would be expected to appoint an 'editorial assistant'. John Carr, Holder's publisher, sent him the first sheet of the treatise fresh from John Heptinstall's press. Carr warned Holder that the 'gentleman that [he] intended should have examined [it]' being 'out of Town', he should examine the sheet himself or appoint 'some other person' to do it for him. Holder, who did not reside in London, appointed John Baynard to assist him with the correction of the proofs. The latter produced extended commentary on the minute changes, corrections and revisions, which then had to get Holder's approval before the proofs could be returned to the printer via Carr. Baynard was a professional instrumentalist. He had a large library and mixed with the most prominent intellectual figures of his time. Despite his credentials, he recruited scholar George Tollett as an adviser. The deployment of such a range of expertise to absolve the editorial tasks, which Holder could not carry out himself, suggests how established a function editorship had become by the late seventeenth century.

The evidence provided by prefatory matters to earlier printed texts similarly suggests that, after the author's death, the publishers would appoint someone to perform a range of editorial activities. However, the identity and the specific tasks performed by seventeenth-century editorial assistants are often referred to only in passing or indirectly. As W. W. Greg observed about Heminges and Condell and the publication of F1,

It is perhaps natural that they should say little about their more detailed duties of editorship. However, in the dedication they speak of Shakespeare's plays 'out-liuing him, and he not hauing the fate, common with some, to be exequutor to his owne writings', which implies the need for someone to do the office for him.[38]

Heminges and Condell's reluctance to dwell on the 'detailed duties of editorship' can be effectively explained in terms of the 'awkward transition between collaboration and single, patriarchal and absolutist authorship',[39] which led seventeenth-century publishers to conceal any spurious interference with the text following the author's death.

Not all duties of editorship were regarded with suspicion. The supervision of the impression, which was aimed to remove any accidental tampering the copy text might undergo in the printing house, was widely advertised in the prefatory material to expensive Folio collections as well as in less ambitious publishing ventures. In his address 'To the Readers', in *Five New Playes, . . . By Richard Brome. . . . Printed for A. Crook and H. Brome* (1659), the editor of the volume, Alexander Brome, who was no relation either of Richard, the dramatist,

---

Edward Capell in particular reports that 'the great Author bestow'd no little attention upon the first impression [of *Paradise Lost*]; and sent it into the world in a state of perfection that is truly admirable, considering his condition.' Quoted in M. Walsh, *Shakespeare, Milton, and Eighteenth-Century Literary Editing* (Cambridge, 1997), p. 65.

[35] 'A Bibliography of Thomas Fuller', ed. by S. Gibson, with an introduction by G. Keynes, in *Oxford Bibliographical Society* 4 (1934–5), pp. 75–6.

[36] Ibid., p. 87.

[37] H. E. Poole, 'The Printing of William Holder's "Principles of Harmony" ', *Proceedings of the Royal Musical Association* 101 (1974–5), pp. 31–57.

[38] W. W. Greg, *The Shakespeare First Folio: The Bibliographical and Textual History* (Oxford, 1955), pp. 78.

[39] J. Masten, *Textual Intercourse: Collaboration, Authorship, and Sexualities in Renaissance Drama* (Cambridge, 1997).

or Henry, the stationer, explains that the Stationers 'hav[e] been more watchful over the Printers common negligence, than such work as this hath usually obtained' (A 5v). James Shirley, the editor of Beaumont and Fletcher's First Folio (1647), supports Humphrey Moseley's claim that much care was bestowed on the removal of the 'literall Errors committed by the Printers', by reassuring his readers that 'not one indiscretion... branded this Paper in all the Lines.' In the prefatory material to *A Memorial for the Learned* (1686), Nahum Tate explains that, 'being sent [this treatise] from a conceal'd author, with permission to make it publick, [he] found a double care incumbent upon [him], both *to secure it from errors of the press*, and procure its recommendation to the world, by the patronage of some honourable person' (italics mine). Tate makes a similar remark in the preface to *The Four Epistles of A. G. Busbequius*, published by Taylor and Wyat in 1694: 'the translator of this ingenious and most useful piece not surviving to see it publish'd, upon perusal of the copy, I found the excellent performance and merit of the work did not only deserve *just care of the impression*, but also some eminent person to recommend its appearance in the world.' (A 2r; italics mine) Sometimes the supervision of the press is documented by lists of errata, which draw the reader's attention to mistakes the proof-corrector failed to correct at the press. The emendations included in these lists were regularly used to rectify subsequent editions, as illustrated by the second (1671) and third (1684) editions of John Denham's *Poems and Translations, With the Sophy... London*, which was first published by Henry Herringman in 1668.

Conversely, the annotation of the copy text prior to its submission to the printers was very rarely recorded. The paucity of evidence concerning the annotation of a copy text which was published after the author's death or without authorial consent suggests that editorial intervention had started to be perceived as a necessary but ideologically controversial practice to be silently performed. The practice of editing the copy text is mentioned only when a direct link with the author's holograph makes it unnecessary. Alexander

Brome, for example, boasts that the publishers of *Five New Playes, ... By Richard Brome* (1659) 'had [their copies] from the Author; not suffering any false or busy hand to adde or make the least mutilation' (A 5v). Editorial annotations in acting versions were also introduced silently. The 1683 Quarto edition of *Hamlet*, which, according to H. N. Paul was annotated and emended by Dryden,[40] inherited extensive theatrical cuts and several verbal changes from the 1676 Quarto used by Davenant in the early 1660s. Both Hazelton Spencer and Ann Thompson observe that the editor of the earlier Quarto, possibly Davenant himself, 'felt called upon, not merely to adapt the text to the stage', but to emend the whole text, including those passages which had been marked for omission.[41]

It is worth stressing that Davenant's and Dryden's roles as annotators / editors of seventeenth-century acting versions of *Hamlet* were never explicitly advertised and can only be inferred from internal evidence and from their involvement with the acting companies which produced the 1676 and the 1683 Quarto versions of *Hamlet*. However, a survey of the printing practices in the sixteenth and seventeenth centuries shows that non-authorial editorial intervention in the copy-text prior to its submission to the press was routinely performed by prominent literary figures and intellectuals, hired on a free-lance basis by large printers and/or publishing booksellers.

L. Voet explains that 'in the period 1563–7, Plantin', the first of several generations of successful printers, publishers and booksellers based in Antwerp, 'frequently called in what would now be termed free-lance workers to rewrite texts, translate, or collate, to compile indexes or glossaries, or to carry out similar tasks'.[42] Voet stresses that these

---

[40] H. N. Paul, 'Quartos and Duodecimos of *Hamlet*', *Modern Language Note* 49 (1934), pp. 369–75.

[41] Spencer, *Shakespeare Improved*, p. 177 and Thompson, 'John Ward's *Hamlet* Promptbooks', p. 141.

[42] L. Voet, *The Golden Compasses: A History and Evaluation of the Printing and Publishing Activities of the Officina Plantiniana at Antwerp* (Amsterdam, London and New York, 1972), p. 175.

professional 'correctors' should not be confused with the proof-readers regularly employed by the master printer. Their tasks would go beyond the ordinary correction of the proofs or the preparation of copy for printing carried out by the compositer, as described in seventeenth-century manuals, such as Moxon's *Mechanick Exercises on the Whole Art of Printing (1683–4)*.[43] According to Voet, their tasks 'included rewriting, collating, and correcting manuscripts, making indexes, compiling glossaries, and so on'.[44] These non-resident 'correctors' normally received board and lodging from their employers. Some of them, including Cornelius Kiliaan and Victor Giselinus, became established humanist scholars.[45]

The scale of Plantin's business meant that he did not only serve but could draw on an international scholarly community and sustain the costs of sophisticated machinery and human resources. However, the practice of hiring eminent scholarly figures to perform a range of editorial activities was not exceptional. Elizabeth Eisenstein reports that 'the remarkable output of the Aldine press [in sixteenth-century Venice] owed to aid furnished by Cretans and other Greek exiles'. The latter did not only 'become the nucleus of the printer's academy and members of his household; . . . [they were also] engaged in processing copy for the press'.[46] Eisenstein also points out that even 'obscure young monks like Erasmus and Rabelais could rise in the world without staying in clerical orders, [because] they could find more congenial work in print shops and fully exploit the talents that won them patrons and fame'.[47]

The book-trade came to London mostly via Antwerp and Amsterdam. The English printers and bookseller seem to have reproduced the techniques and practices they learnt from their European competitors, although on a smaller scale. Nicholas Okes and his son John, who printed and published from 1606 to 1639 and from 1627 to 1640, did not only publish a substantial number of Thomas Heywood's own works but also hired him to supervise the printing of some of the copies they owned. In A. C. Clark's bibliography of Thomas Heywood, a separate section is devoted to those works, which

the latter edited, as opposed to those for which he simply provided commendatory verses or prefatory material.[48] Among these, *A Shoemaker a Gentleman* and *The Martyred Soldier*, both published in 1638, were probably edited by Heywood, who contributed prefatory matter to both and introduced extensive revisions in the second. Heywood, like his European predecessors, must have offered his editorial services on a free-lance basis. In the 1631 edition of *The Felicity of Man*, published by Richard Royston, Heywood chose the shorter 1598 edition, as opposed to a longer version published in 1603, as his copy-text. Clark points out that Heywood also 'wrote the illustration of the title-page, the dedication to Somerset, the note of one misprint, the analyses of the chapters, the translations of most of the quotations, the marginalia, and index'.[49]

In *A History of European Printing*, Colin Clair points out that 'by the beginning of the sixteenth century a gradual separation of the various functions [of the book trade] was taking place, and the most financially rewarding one . . . was that

---

43 *Mechanick Exercises on the Whole Art of Printing (1683–4)*, ed. by H. Davis and H. Carter (London, 1958). See p. 233: 'The *Proof* being made, the *Press-man* brings the *Proof* . . . [to] the *Correcter*; the *Proof* . . . being *Corrected*, the *Correcter* gives it again to the *Compositer* to *Correct* the *Form* by'. See also pp. 238–9 'Having placed the *Pages* in their right places, [the compositer] again lays the *Chase* about them, and *Locks* them up again. . . . Then he carries the *Form* to the *Press*, and lays it on the *Stone* for a *Second Proof*, and sometimes for a *Third Proof*; which having *Corrected*, he at last brings the *Form* to the *Press*, and again lays it on the *Stone* . . . After all this *Correcting* a *Revise* is made, and if any *Faults* are found in any *Quarter* of it, or in all the *Quarters*, he calls to the *Press-man* to *Unlock* that *Quarter*, or the whole *Form*, that he may *Correct* those *Faults*.' See also P. Gaskell, *A New Introduction to Bibliography* (Oxford, 1972), p. 40.
44 Voet, *The Golden Compasses*, p. 187.
45 Ibid., pp. 189–91.
46 Elizabeth Eisenstein, *The Printing Press as an Agent of Change* (Cambridge, 1979), pp. 220–23.
47 Ibid., p. 400.
48 A. C. Clark, 'A Bibliography of Thomas Heywood', in *Oxford Bibliographical Society: Proceedings and Papers*, vol. 1, 1922–26 (Oxford, 1927), pp. 97–158.
49 Ibid., p. 143.

of publisher.'[50] This might explain why in the late seventeenth century, eminent literary figures, who acted as editorial assistants, were connected to prominent publishers, rather than printer-booksellers, as it had been the case up to the first half of the century.

Documentary evidence suggests that at the beginning of his career Henry Herringman, the publisher of F4, was already benefiting from the services of some of the most prominent literary figures of his time. In *The Medall of John Bayes* (1682), Thomas Shadwell insinuated that Dryden had 'turn'd a Journey-man t'a Bookseller; / Writ Prefaces to Books for Meat and Drink, / And as he paid, he would both write and think'.[51] The address 'To the Reader' in Robert Howard's collection of *Poems*, which was published by Herringman in 1660, actually suggests that Dryden's duties towards Herringman extended beyond those of a journey-man or a literary hack. In his address 'To the Reader', Howard acknowledges 'having prevailed with a worthy Friend to take so much view of my blotted Copies, as to free me from grosse Errors'. According to James Winn, Dryden's biographer, 'Dryden is the likeliest person to have performed such editorial services' for his publisher.[52] James Osborn anticipated Winn's theory by arguing that Dryden was 'one of the bookseller's [Herringman's] staff'.[53] Although Shadwell's claim that Dryden lodged with Herringman cannot be verified,[54] the arrangement between Dryden and his publisher would reflect an established European tradition of professional, free-lance 'correctors' who received board and lodging from their employers.

Seventeenth-century publishers were unlikely to annotate and supervise the printing of their copy texts themselves. Humphrey Moseley and Henry Herringman, the publishers of the main Folio editions of Shakespeare, Jonson and Beaumont and Fletcher, and most *belles-lettres* in the second half of the seventeenth century, have their imprints on three-hundred-and-fourteen and five-hundred-and-thirty-two publications respectively (*ESTC*). The sheer number of publishing ventures undertaken by these two publishers and booksellers suggests that they most probably delegated the annotation of their copy texts and supervision of the press to someone whose expertise they could trust.

It is, however, worth stressing that Herringman's career took a peculiar turn in 1684, when he sold his bookshop, a popular rendezvous of literary men on the Strand which Pepys mentions several times in his *Diary*, to the retailers Joseph Knight and Francis Saunders. From 1684 Herringman devoted himself to the publication of elegant and expensive Folio collections of literary works,[55] and thus became, as Edward Arber puts it, 'the first London Wholesale Publisher, in the modern sense of those words.'[56] It is also significant that only three years after Herringman's publication of Shakespeare's F4, Jacob Tonson, the publisher, played a crucial role in the editing of the 1688 Folio edition of Milton's *Paradise Lost*, as recorded in his letters published in the *Grub Street Journal* in January 1732. According to Stuart Bennett, the external evidence provided by the 1732 letters is substantiated by a contrastive analysis of Tonson's edition and earlier editions of *Paradise Lost*, which reveals 'how incisive his insights into the problems of editorship were' and 'how intimate his involvement was in this and, doubtless, many of his other important publishing projects.'[57] After turning the retailing side of his business to Knight and Saunders, Herringman,

---

[50] Colin Clair, *A History of European Printing* (London, New York, San Francisco, 1976), p. 125–6.

[51] Quoted in J. A. Winn, *John Dryden and His World* (New Haven and London, 1987), p. 95

[52] Ibid., p. 99.

[53] J. M. Osborn, *John Dryden: Some Biographical Facts and Problems* (New York, 1940), p. 175.

[54] Winn, *John Dryden*, p. 95.

[55] For more details, see H. R. Plomer, *A Dictionary of the Booksellers and Printers who were at work in England, Scotland and Ireland from 1641 to 1667* (London, 1907), pp. 96–7; H. B. Wheatley, 'Dryden's Publishers', in *Transactions of the Bibliographical Society*, 11 (1909–11), pp. 17–38; and C. W. Miller, 'Henry Herringman, Restoration Bookseller-Publisher', in *The Papers of the Bibliographical Society of America* (New York, 1948), pp. 292–306.

[56] *The Term Catalogues* (London, 1905), vol. 2, p. 642.

[57] S. Bennett, 'Jacob Tonson: An Early Editor of *Paradise Lost*', *The Library, Sixth Series* 10 (1988), 247–52.

Table 3

	Syntax**	Apostrophe***	Modernized spelling
*Merchant of Venice** (I Div.)	31	9	46
*Coriolanus** (II Div.)	91	64	50
*Hamlet** (III Div.)	69	7	50
*The Northern Lass**	5	3	2
*A Jovial Crew**	—	1	25
*Cutter of Cole-man Street**	15	11	31

* Occurrences in Act I.
** Improvements through addition and omission of commas.
*** Use of the apostrophe to indicate possession and to normalize contractions.

like Tonson, might have had the leisure to devote time to the preparation of his copies for the press and to supervise the printing process himself. Unfortunately archival evidence concerning Herringman's management of his business is limited to a number of deeds held at the Westminster Archives and records of court cases with which Herringman was involved.[58] No private correspondence survives. It is therefore difficult to speculate about Herringman's involvement in the publication of his Folio collections of literary and dramatic works after 1684. There is however enough internal and external evidence to argue that when Herringman published F4 in 1684, he was still relying on the editorial services provided by his literary friends and associates.[59]

The third part of the eighth edition of Abraham Cowley's *Works*, which Herringman published in 1693, includes *Six Books of Plants*, which had been 'made in English by several Hands', including Tate's. It is interesting that Tate, rather than the other translators, should write the dedication and a short prefatory essay on the Classical influences in Cowley's Latin work. It is even more significant that the *errata* listed at the end of the preliminary matters should include only corrections in Books IV and V, the two translated by Tate. It is also worth noting that the level of modernization of spelling and syntax in the text of *Cutter of Cole-man Street*, which was reset from a 1663 quarto edition prior to its inclusion in Herringman's 1693 collection, is remarkable.[60] The new figures for *Cutter of Cole-man Street* added to the figures presented above in

Table 2 show that the level of modernization is higher than in *The Northern Lasse* or in *A Jovial Crew* and closer to the standards reached in F4 (see Table 3).

The number of substantive emendations is also remarkable. Compared to Act I in *The Northern Lass* and in *A Jovial Crew*, where there are no substantive variants, Act I in the 1693 edition of *Cutter of Cole-man Street* provides eleven original emendations, including the normalization of stage-directions. As in the text of *Coriolanus* in F4, the editor of *Cutter of Cole-man Street* pays particular attention to improving the consistency between stage directions and speech-headings. At B1r line 3, the speech-heading 'Truman Jun.', which was missing in the 1663 edition, is supplied; at B2v line 11, the attribute 'jun.' is added to the original speech-heading 'Truman' in order to avoid a potential ambiguity. Tate's extensive involvement with the publication of Cowley's *Works* would seem to

---

[58] See, for example, Chancery Proceedings. PRO, Mitford, Bundle 298, MS 169.

[59] We know that Moseley, Herringman's predecessor, had six assistants, and no more than three at any one time, working for him, as well as the support and advice of the literary 'friends' he names in the preface to Robert Heath's *Clarastella*, which he published in 1650. For more details, see J. C. Reed, 'Humphrey Moseley, Publisher', *The Oxford Bibliographical Society* 2 (1927–30), 57–142.

[60] *Cutter of Cole-man Street. A Comedy . . . Written by Abraham Cowley. London. Printed for Henry Herringman* (1663); *Cutter of Cole-man Street. A Comedy . . . Written by Abraham Cowley. London. Printed for Henry Herringman* (1693) (In Collection).

suggest that Herringman kept employing his literary friends and editorial assistants even after he turned wholesale publisher in the mid-1680s, when he published F4.

Both the internal and the external evidence analysed in this article in relation to the publication of F4 suggest that Herringman relied on the editorial services provided by some of the most prominent literary figures of his time. Herringman's failure to advertise their contribution is likely to be the result of the cultural silence surrounding editorial practices which went beyond the supervision of the press, as well as Herringman's decision to reprint the prefatory material from the earlier Folios. The available evidence is too limited to support a definitive conclusion as regards the identity of the editor(s) of F4, although Nahum Tate seems to be the most likely candidate. It is suggestive, for example, that by the time Herringman published F4 in 1685, Dryden was working for different publishers, including Tonson, who would become Dryden's exclusive publisher for the rest of his literary career. It is also significant that Dryden had started delegating unwanted work to Tate from around 1682. Given Tate's involvement with the publication of Cowley's *Works* in 1693, an earlier collaboration with Herringman in the mid-1680s should not be ruled out.

Internal evidence confirms that Tate might have replaced Dryden as Herringman's editorial assistant and that he might have played a role in the editing of F4. Tate's 1682 adaptation, *The Ingratitude of a Common-Wealth*,[61] anticipates some of the substantive emendations subsequently introduced in the text of *Coriolanus* as it appears in F4. For example, the belly in Menenius's parable, which replies 'taintingly' in F1 and 'tantingly' in F2 and F3, is finally allowed to reply 'tauntingly' to the 'discontented members, the mutinous parts' of the body politic in F4 (TLN 112), following Tate's emendation in *The Ingratitude* at B2r lines 21-2. The same belly is reported to answer in the past tense only in Tate's adaptation at B2r line 17 and in F4 at TLN 107. The First Senator's defiant warning to the Romans led by Coriolanus as it appears in F4 – 'our Gates, / Which yet seem shut, we have but pinn'd

with Rushes' (TLN 507) – is anticipated by Tate's correspondent line at C2r line 3, which emends the alternative 'pin'd' preserved in the earlier Folios.

These parallels between Tate's 1682 adaptation and the text of *Coriolanus* as it appears in F4 are significant but do not prove Tate's involvement in the editing of F4 because they are not beyond the scope of a solicitous compositor or press corrector. Other variants, however, are gratuitous changes as opposed to necessary emendations, and are therefore more difficult to account for as the result of press-correction. Tate added two references to 'the Commons' in his adaptation of *King Lear* at E1v line 16 and H4v line 30, where his Shakespearian originals contain none. As Richard Strier points out, '[Tate] says "the Commons" here, not the crowd, the multitude, or the rabble, [because] he conceives of this group politically and respectfully'.[62] When he adapted *Coriolanus* in 1682, Tate chose the more topical title, *The Ingratitude of a Common-Wealth*, which, still according to Strier, suggests a 'different view of politics, . . . [once] both the parliamentary and the popular movement had been defeated'.[63] Independently of whether Tate's attitude to the Exclusion Crisis changed between 1680–1 and 1682, the term 'Commons', as opposed to 'crowd', 'multitude' or 'rabble', retains its highly topical and political connotations. Besides the title, Tate also changed the Shakespearian original twice from 'the People' at TLN 1380 to 'the Commons' at D2r line 25 and from 'the Common' at TLN 1709 to 'the Commons' at E1r line 23. The staggered entrances at the beginning of Act 2 in Shakespeare, including the 'two Tribunes of the People' at TLN 896, are replaced by one group entrance at C4r lines 8–9 and C4r line 13, where the Tribunes of the People are not mentioned individually but as

---

61 All citations from Nahum Tate's *The Ingratitude of a Common-Wealth* are followed by line-reference to the original edition, printed for Joseph Hindmarsh in 1682.

62 R. Strier, 'Impossible Radicalism and Impossible Value: Nahum Tate's *King Lear*', in *Resistant Structures: Particularity, Radicalism, and Renaissance Texts* (Berkeley, Los Angeles and London, 1995), p. 223.

63 Ibid., p. 206.

part of the 'Commons of Rome'. It is interesting that F4 should similarly emend 'Commoners' at TLN 3735 in order to introduce an extra reference to the 'Commons' in a play where the people of Rome have such a crucial role and yet are referred to as 'the commons' only three times.

According to Gary Taylor, the anonymity of seventeenth-century editors has prevented a systematic survey of their contributions. 'Literary historians,' Taylor explains, 'usually regard Nicholas Rowe as Shakespeare's first editor, because he is

the first we can confidently name'.[64] The internal and external evidence analysed in this article shows that, however speculative the identity of Rowe's predecessors remains, the silence surrounding their work is ideological rather than documentary and can be effectively broken through a systematic survey of their influential and extensive contributions to the editorial tradition.

---

[64] *A Textual Companion*, p. 53.

'A WORLD ELSEWHERE':
SHAKESPEARE IN SOUTH AFRICA

JONATHAN HOLMES

I

Between 1945 and 1957 every English-speaking theatrical union in the world agreed to a boycott of the South African stage in response to the outrage of apartheid. This move was officially ratified in 1969 by the United Nations, which requested its member states to suspend 'cultural, educational, sports and other exchanges with the racist regime'.[1] A consequence of this was that many South African actors were forced abroad to find work, though most left willingly to distance themselves from the political situation in their homeland. Two such actors are Janet Suzman and Antony Sher. Suzman left at 22 to attend LAMDA in 1959 and Sher followed a decade later, aged nineteen, to study at The Webber Douglas Academy of Dramatic Art.

Both actors came from wealthy, middle-class Jewish backgrounds in Johannesburg (Suzman) and Cape Town (Sher). Both have since become pillars of the British theatrical establishment, assimilated completely in terms of accent, training and their participation in an explicitly English acting tradition. Both chose in early middle age to return to South Africa to stage productions of the only two Shakespearian plays to feature characters of colour (Moors in both cases) in leading roles.[2] Both subsequently wrote at length of their experiences. Suzman talked of directing *Othello* in several articles, particularly 'South Africa in *Othello*'.[3] Sher co-wrote *Woza Shakespeare!* with his partner and director Gregory Doran – an account of producing *Titus Andronicus*.[4]

Both productions were staged at the Market Theatre, Johannesburg, an institution of 'dissident prestige'.[5] Both featured a similar backstage cast of names, principally those of Barney Simon and John Kani, and even shared one cast member – Dorothy Gould (Emilia and Tamora). They also invoked a similar politico-theatrical rhetoric in both their conceptual aims and performance practice.

It is this rhetoric that is the subject of the ensuing discussion. Despite the many circumstantial similarities between the two events, the productions themselves could hardly have differed more. Suzman's *Othello* was Elizabethan dress, traditionally staged with, apart from Kani as Othello, a cast using English received pronunciation. The Sher/Doran *Titus Andronicus* on the other hand was

---

[1] Quoted in Antony Sher and Gregory Doran, *Woza Shakespeare!* (London, 1996), p. 218.

[2] Janet Suzman's production of *Othello* with John Kani and Richard Haddon Haines opened at the Market Theatre, Johannesburg, in June 1987. Anthony Sher and Gregory Doran's production of *Titus Andronicus* with Sher as Titus opened at the same theatre in March 1995.

[3] In Jonathan Bate, Jill L. Levenson and Dieter Mehl (eds.) *Shakespeare and the Twentieth Century*, Selected Proceedings of the International Shakespeare Association World Congress, Los Angeles, 1996 (New York, 1996), pp. 23–40.

[4] Antony Sher and Gregory Doran, *Woza Shakespeare! Titus Andronicus in South Africa* (London, 1996) hereafter abbreviated to *WS*.

[5] Loren Kruger, '"That Fluctuating Moment of National Consciousness" – Protest, Publicity and Postcolonial Theatre in South Africa', in J. Ellen Grainer (ed.) *Imperialism and Theatre – Essays on World Theatre, Drama and Performance* (London, 1995) pp. 148–63, 156.

eclectic in dress and design with a multi-racial cast of diverse prior experience ranging from music to stand-up comedy, and it was performed in predominantly South African accents. Perhaps most significantly of all, *Othello* was staged seven years before apartheid began to be dismantled, at a time when the regime seemed almost invulnerable, whilst *Titus* was performed exactly one year after the election of Nelson Mandela as president.

Both ventures came from similar origins and belief structures but were highly individual in their response to these structures and distinct in the general environment of their reception. This essay will focus on the manner in which the texts detailing these processes negotiate aspects of genre, politics and colour within the larger engagement with two major authorities – Shakespeare and apartheid.[6] It is the implied antithesis between these forces that lends both sets of accounts their power and the writers their moral authority. What becomes evident is a moral crusade in the name of Shakespeare against what Derrida has called the 'archival record of the unnameable'.[7]

In this way, both apartheid – given a face (or faces) in the texts through names such as B. J. Vorster, P. W. Botha and above all Eugene Terre'Blanche – and Shakespeare become the author-functions of a tragedy. This is summed up by Janet Suzman: 'Tragedy, in Africa, is not a conventional form in the theatre, although God knows it is on the streets.'[8] Taxonomy is invoked both as agent of repression and agent of emancipation through virtue of its appropriation and authority. The tragic action within Shakespeare is performed, as Raymond Williams suggests, as a revolutionary action, directly opposed to acts of tragedy in reality: 'The tragic action, in its deepest sense, is not the confirmation of disorder, but its experience, its comprehension, and its resolution. In our own time, this action is general, and its common name is revolution.'[9]

Commenting upon systems of repression in his native Brazil not dissimilar to those in operation in South Africa, Augusto Boal writes more pessimistically that it is necessary for dominant regimes to ensure that the populace remain, if not uniformly satisfied, 'at least uniformly passive with respect to criteria of inequality. How to achieve this? Through many forms of repression: politics, bureaucracy, habits, customs – and tragedy.'[10] A South African version of this theory is supplied by Doreen Mazibuko, who writes that 'it is very important to note that culture in South Africa has been state-controlled all along ... Black culture was never given a chance to develop.'[11] Similarly, Boal's view is that the cathartic aim of tragedy produces also a catharsis of the revolutionary spirit, an abandonment of agency in favour of fate that lends itself strongly to autocratic ideologies. Sher and Suzman attempt to appropriate the universalist humanism of the Shakespearian logos in the name of a revolutionary action, the aim of which is to disturb a strikingly similar humanistic universalism at work within a political system.

The result is a fascinating and complex blurring of conventional boundaries, or genres, between politics, art, performance and action. Apartheid, in its processes of segregation and limitation, becomes a genre of politics just as the plays performed are genres of drama. The characterization of both as tragedies enables the actor/writers to create a performance intertext that mixes the now equal and equated discourses in the name of a theatrical politics and an emphatically political theatre.

---

[6] I agree with Tzvetan Todorov in his distrust of the word 'race' to describe a phenomenon that, in biological terms, has no connection to this noun. I have therefore followed Todorov, where it has not been possible to avoid using the word, placing it in inverted commas, and in general choosing alternatives such as 'colour'. See his article ' "Race", Writing, Culture', trans. Loulou Mack, *Critical Inquiry* 12 (Autumn 1986), pp. 170–82, for elucidation.

[7] Jacques Derrida, 'Racism's Last Word', trans. P. Kamuf, *Critical Inquiry* 12 (1985), pp. 290–300, 291.

[8] Janet Suzman, *Acting With Shakespeare: Three Comedies* (New York, 1996) 58.

[9] Raymond Williams, *Modern Tragedy* (London, 1966) 83.

[10] Augusto Boal, 'Aristotle's Coercive System of Tragedy', in *Theater of the Oppressed,* trans. Charles A. and Maria-Odilia Leal McBride (New York, 1979) 37.

[11] Doreen Mazibuko, 'Theatre – The Political Weapon in South Africa', in Geoffrey V. Davis and Anne Fuchs (eds.) *Theatre and Change in South Africa* (Amsterdam, 1996) pp. 219–224, 219.

II

The position of Shakespeare in South Africa is unsurprisingly problematic. On the one hand, there is the colonial impetus of appropriating Shakespeare as agent of respectability and repression; on the other, an anecdote told by Suzman of being unable to find a copy of *Othello* in the whole of Johannesburg. As Martin Orkin says, Shakespeare 'has been primarily appropriated by most amongst the English-speaking educated members of the ruling classes as a means of evidencing their affiliations with the imperial and colonial centres'.[12]

As a result of the use of Shakespeare in both education and theatre to propagate repressive ideologies, the Market Theatre had no real history of staging Shakespeare before Suzman's *Othello*, preferring indigenous dramatists such as Athol Fugard or new, devised work. Their classic author of choice, insofar as they had one, was Chekhov, whose more overt politics, ensemble casts and dependency on unspoken – therefore uncensorable – subtext made him suitable material.

Janet Suzman's decision to stage *Othello* was prompted by many factors, principally the desire to direct (something she had never done before), to return to her South African theatrical roots, to stage Shakespeare in a country with little experience of the dramatist, and finally to give John Kani the opportunity to play a role she felt he was literally born to play, thus infiltrating real otherness into Anglicized Shakespeare. On her choice of leading actor Suzman explained:

There have been great American actors play the part, but English is their mother tongue. There have been great European actors play the part, but their skins are the wrong colour. Here we have, for the first time to my knowledge, the REAL THING. This is the man who can say 'Rude am I in my speech' without false modesty. Not 'rude am I' in my intelligence, or vocabulary, or my imagination – but speech. In other words English is a second language to him.[13]

For Suzman, Kani was authentic, despite being neither a Moor nor a soldier (or, for that matter, an Italian). Playing the role three decades earlier at Stratford, Paul Robeson also resorted to a discourse of authenticity, which in his case involved also invoking Shakespeare:

I feel the play is so modern, for the problem is the problem of my own people. It is a tragedy of racial conflict, a tragedy of honour rather than of jealousy... The fact that he is an alien among white people makes his mind work more quickly. He feels dishonour more deeply. His colour heightens the tragedy.[14]

Furthermore, when confronted with established performance traditions he was expected to continue, but with which he disagreed, Robeson made his colour an emphatic scene of authorial presence. He felt that 'in some cases their Othello didn't think or act as I believed a great Negro warrior would do and in these cases I played it my way'.[15]

The invocation is twofold. First, Shakespeare's genius allows for a remarkably truthful presentation of racial conflict, and second, where interpretation of this is problematic the colour of the actor becomes a final, unquestionable arbitrator. What becomes evident are claims for a simultaneous authorial universality and a performative particularity when invoking the Bard, a strange combination of poetic essentialism and naturalistic realism that allows the dramatist to become African and the actor to become Shakespearian, summed up by Suzman's revealing coinage 'othelloid'.[16] John Kani explodes these tendencies more pithily, remarking 'there goes the native causing more trouble, and this time he has Shakespeare to do it for him'.[17] For Kani, performing Othello never ceases to be a political act, one that involves the appropriation of the canonical genius of colonial culture as a weapon

---

[12] Martin Orkin, *Drama and the South African State* (Manchester, 1991), p. 235.

[13] Suzman, '*Othello* – A Belated Reply', in *Shakespeare in South Africa,* vol. 2, 1988, pp. 90–6, 95.

[14] Robeson, in Judith Cook, *Shakespeare's Players* (London, 1983), p. 124.

[15] Ibid., p. 125.

[16] Suzman, quoted in Barbara Hodgdon, 'Race-ing Othello: Re-engendering White-out', in Lynda Boose and Richard Burt, *Shakespeare and the Moving Image*, (London, 1997), pp. 23–45, 26.

[17] Kani, quoted in Hodgdon, 'Race-ing Othello', p. 27.

in its subversion. He himself never succumbs to a mythology of authenticity, seeing the production for what it was – a courageous moment in a modern political struggle.

For Suzman, Kani's authenticity resided in his colour and his language, the two things that mark Othello out from his fellow Venetians. They are also the two factors identified by apartheid as essentially other and therefore requiring segregation. Not only black Africans, but also those of mixed ethnicity, Indians, East Asians and Jews were ghettoized by successive South African governments.[18] By casting Kani, Suzman in a sense reinforces the essential validity of the arguments used by the discourse she is attacking. In short, she runs a danger of, in Albie Sachs' phrase, remaining 'trapped in the multiple ghettos of the apartheid imagination'.[19]

Casting Kani also cemented Suzman's commitment to a venue, the Market Theatre, which in 1987 was co-directed by Kani and Barney Simon. Suzman herself is a co-founder and a trustee of the theatre, which was for many years the only independent, political performance venue in South Africa. A former fruit and livestock market as the name suggests, the choice of performance space offered a political, radical and specifically protest interpretation of the play before any conceptual decisions had been made. This fitted in with Suzman's recasting of the play as protest theatre:

No great poetry was around to take the measure of the wanton destruction that apartheid spawned. This play could attempt it for us. Thus Shakespeare's vision found its time and place. 'Thus the whirligig of time brings in its revenges' – thank God.[20]

Suzman simultaneously claims for the play and her production a timeless universality and a local habitation and a name – apartheid. This rhetorical operation is encapsulated perfectly by Greg Doran in his response to the Market Theatre in *Woza Shakespeare!*

The Market is a truly Shakespearean space. Standing on the stage you feel that, if the auditorium were full you could shake hands with everyone without having to stretch . . . I want the space to allow any location. Not 'Nowhere-in-general' but 'Everywhere-in-particular'.[21]

The situation of the Market is in reality considerably more complex. Unquestionably opposed to apartheid, the venue was also dependent on corporate sponsorship, supplied often by pro-apartheid companies. It became an unwitting symbol to the world of the regime's apparent leniency and cultural freedom, whilst unwillingly becoming a vehicle for the suppression of other such enterprises. As Anne Fuchs comments: 'It was a superstructure which secreted all the ideological contradictions of the regime, but was itself in its cultural aspirations opposed to that regime'.[22] Despite the best efforts of Barney Simon and, earlier, Mannie Manim, the theatre generally played to majority white audiences. This is a fact acknowledged from the start by Simon, who opened the Market in 1976 with a production of Chekhov's *The Seagull*, which might not only be supposed to be more attractive to white audiences but which also included a quotation from Chekhov in the programme: 'I wanted to tell people honestly: Look at yourselves. Just see how absurdly you live.'

The success of the Market in reaching black communities usually resides in their touring projects – with the notable and famous exception of Percy Mtwa and Mbongeni Ngema's *Woza Albert!* perhaps the most important play hitherto staged at the theatre, as Percy Mtwa recalls:

People would see *Woza Albert!* in the townships and they would follow us right there to the Market . . . we started to break the whole [white dominated] thing. We would

---

[18] This process of wholesale 'racism' was tempered in the 1960s by the South African government's realization that it undermined their claims of natural isolation for racial groups. Vorster compromised by to some extent allowing Jewish, Chinese and Indian communities to assimilate and acquire rights in order to reinforce the general anti-black policies.

[19] Albie Sachs, 'Preparing Ourselves for Freedom: Culture and the ANC Guidelines' in Ingrid de Kok and Karen Press (eds.) *Spring is Rebellious: Arguments about Cultural Freedom by Albie Sachs and Respondents* (Johannesburg, 1990) pp. 19–20, 20.

[20] Suzman, *Acting With Shakespeare: Three Comedies* (New York, 1996), p. 59.

[21] *WS*, 46.

[22] Fuchs, *Playing the Market* (Amsterdam, 1990), p. 135.

find even sometimes during the week that we had a 50–50 black and white mix.[23]

This play is obviously cited within the title to Sher and Doran's book, which combines the specifically South African – 'woza' meaning 'arise' – with the universal name of the great humanist writer. *Woza Albert!* described the fantasy of Christ's return to South Africa, and concluded with his call to the great leaders of the liberation struggle, including Albert Luthuli, to rise from the dead. Shakespeare here becomes part of this genealogy of resistance, an activist against apartheid, his name collocated with Luthuli, Biko and Mandela. Canonicity sanctions ideology and topicality validates performance, creating a rhetoric of righteous immediacy.

In a word, this serves to create relevance, the point of which for *Othello* is pinpointed further by Suzman:

The story of a black man and a white girl, deeply in love, whose marriage is destroyed by Iago just because he feels like it, had profound resonances in a South Africa where Mandela had not yet walked free.[24]

The method by which these resonances would be communicated to an audience is also described by Suzman, who urges that we should treat Shakespeare less 'academically', and 'more as an event releasing, by metaphor, the political and social reverberations of the place in which it is performed'.[25] The playtext becomes a metaphor for apartheid, a prefiguration. Speaking of apartheid, Derrida calls it 'a memory in advance',[26] referring to the power of the name to encapsulate a moment in history in much the same way as the Holocaust has come to do. In Suzman's terms, *Othello* itself becomes a memory in advance of apartheid, a way of recalling, in language that precedes the event by 350 years, an abhorrent socio-political event.

Memory becomes a significant factor in Suzman's project, as she consciously attempts to marry two dissonant cultural traditions:

It was going to be up to me to release that race memory [in John Kani] via the incomparable verse of the Chief Dead White European Male; a nice paradox ... What a fascinating reversal it would be to have an African thinking 'black', while desperately trying to think 'white'.[27]

Once again 'racial' difference is enshrined as absolute, even having its own collective memory system. The agent of its expression, however, is the great interpreter Shakespeare. Not only is the dubious notion of 'race' memory implicitly assumed, Shakespeare's transcendent ability to contain within the text a full capacity to express such otherness is also taken somewhat for granted. Suzman becomes a Desdemona to Kani's Othello, arguing for him in the court of opinion while idealistically believing that a seamless marriage of time and tradition is entirely possible.

Suzman's strong sense of place, both in terms of venue and geographical location, also finds echoes within the play, in which the Venetians are dislocated to Cyprus, a place of otherness that allows the tragic events of the second half of the text to unfold. Othello's position in Cyprus is as governor of a Venetian colony – far from being the other, his position is as representative of order and sameness. Kani's position within the Market is somewhat similar, as administrator of an institution reliant on benevolent capitalism for its existence. As Kruger comments, this can lead to an over-simplification of the theatre's role:

The generality of protest and the immediate assent it demands from its audience not only misrepresents the actual conflicts and divided loyalties of people struggling with apartheid capitalism but also undermines attempts to build solidarity on the recognition of difference and dissent.[28]

In other words, the universalizing rhetoric of Suzman's appropriation of Shakespeare actually diminishes its power to embody the nuances of a political situation and leaves the metaphor hollow.

---

[23] Percy Mtwa, quoted in Fuchs, *Playing the Market*, p. 83.
[24] Suzman, *Acting With Shakespeare*, p. 57.
[25] Suzman, '*Othello* – A Belated Reply,' p. 96.
[26] Derrida, 'Racism's Last Word', p. 290.
[27] Suzman, 'South Africa in *Othello*,' p. 26.
[28] Kruger, 'That Fluctuating Moment', p. 151.

The restrictive vocabulary of protest theatre limits the connotative power of the production, suppressing signification more effectively than could censorship. By 1995 Kani himself had realised this and had modified his own rhetoric appropriately: 'Protest theatre? Is that what we were doing all those years? Man, we didn't even know how to spell "protest". We were just telling the stories of our lives.'[29]

Despite the intriguing similarities here with Othello's own storytelling, Suzman's *Othello*, crucially, did not tell the story of their lives. At its most relevant, it was a direct and powerful response to the Immorality Act that prohibited any kind of sexual relationship between individuals of different colour, and which had been repealed only the year before, effectively allowing this production to go ahead. Tellingly, it was the aspects of the production that showed the relationship between Othello and Desdemona to be loving, affectionate and above all physical that caused the most controversy and the most media attention. Even favourable reviews could not quite accept this:

The temptation to play to a specifically South African audience led the director into the error of allowing Othello and Desdemona to exhibit their sexual bond in public . . . for the notion of a 'lascivious Moor' exists only in Iago's racial fantasies, and any suggestion that Othello is parading his sexual conquest robs Iago's insinuations of their calumny and the tragedy of the part of its dignity.[30]

Suzman's own perceptive reply to this comment correctly identifies the agenda hidden within it:

Well, well. The notion of a 'lascivious Moor' is Roderigo's little hang-up, by the way. But be that as it may, I just cannot see why a langourous and tactile relationship should 'rob the tragedy of its dignity'. Prudery gone mad! I suspect it's a specifically South African critic talking here.[31]

Even John Kani found the 'interracial' physical affection problematic, expressing his difficulties in typically forthright style: 'I can understand the agony, but I can't do the love – I was taught to hate those white bastards when I was a kid.'[32] It was the physicality of the romance that had the biggest

impact on the majority-black audience. The production became not a metaphor for apartheid as a system but a commentary on one, albeit powerful, aspect of it.

III

Joel Fineman makes a direct correlation between the operations of the metaphorical and those of the mimetic, commenting that both function through a process of likeness: 'Verisimilar likeness or resemblance in the first case [mimesis], the likeness of figural comparison and similitude in the second [metaphor].'[33] In her rhetoric of justification for the production, Suzman employs both procedures. On the one hand, she claims for Kani's Othello a mimetic truth, he is the 'real thing', he is so biologically like the character he plays that his performance becomes a mirror image of the Shakespearean word, his physical self an embodiment of the text. At the same time, the world of that text is 'a metaphor' for the world of late capitalist apartheid in 1980s South Africa, which becomes metaphorically akin to a Jacobean representation of a colony of a late renaissance mercantile European power. Such comparisons are reducible to the image of an 'interracial' kiss only through the avoidance of a panoply of other factors, just as Kani's supposed identity with a sixteenth-century Moorish general is as tenuous as that of a white American actor with Richard III.

Suzman's simplification of the cultural operations of a four-hundred-year-old play text in a highly politically charged environment is evident also in her description of other characters in the play:

It seemed to me that the play's characters divide neatly into a microcosm of not only South Africa, but perhaps

29 *WS*, 221.
30 Elizabeth Lickendorf, 'The Verse Music of Suzman's *Othello*', in *Shakespeare in South Africa*, vol. 1, 1987, pp. 69–71, 70.
31 Suzman, '*Othello*, A Belated Reply', in *Shakespeare in South Africa*, vol. 2, 1988, pp. 89–96, 95.
32 Suzman, 'South Africa in *Othello*', p. 34.
33 Joel Fineman, *Shakespeare's Perjur'd Eye* (Berkeley, 1986), p. 3.

of any society in the West: The out-and-out bigots (Iago, Roderigo); the armchair liberals (Brabantio, Gratiano); the pragmatists who judge things on their merits (Emilia, Lodovico); and those who simply don't see colour at all (Desdemona, Cassio).[34]

The playworld is now a microcosm of the world at large, the characters becoming metaphors for sectors of society and the text as a whole forming a mimetic relationship with the South African world. This inverts the processes of identification established earlier, where character construction was mimetic and textual interpretation metaphorical. Suzman is moving between thinking of the text as performance and the performance as cultural artefact in her speech, while still maintaining the rhetoric of Shakespearean transcendence:

Since theatre is metaphorical, and need not be limited by an imposed realism, we decided that nothing like that [modern dress] should take people's minds off the dreadful story, nor should we adopt any contemporary anachronisms that might hinder their self-recognition.[35]

By removing any hint of modernity within the design of the production, Suzman is claiming paradoxically that an enhanced sense of the production's relevance will emerge. The play's timeless universality will be clearly visible without the obfuscation of design interpretation. This ideological ellipsis is in fact functioning on two levels. Firstly there is the assumption that historically specific Elizabethan dress is somehow free from cultural connotations whereas modern dress is not. But more insidiously there is Suzman's repeated submergence of interpretation. A continuous discourse of authenticity becomes increasingly evident in Suzman's prose – she appears to be claiming a kind of return to origin for the production, a performance that is as close to Shakespeare's intention as is possible. This is a fidelity not to the conditions of original production, but to the spirit of the play, a fantasy of the play as it should be performed.

Suzman's blurring of the operations of mimesis and metaphor enables her to claim at once the production's historical relevance and the play's timeless universality, focusing on the repercussions of a black actor in the title role but also unavoidably

implicated in more problematic attitudes towards the body of John Kani. As Dympna Callaghan has written, talking of a nineteenth-century black Othello:

When the distance between Shakespeare's Othello and Ira Aldridge is diminished by being performed by an African-American, the performance becomes an exhibition as opposed to 'art'; it ceases to be acting, becoming not the representation of the-thing-itself but, instead, the-thing-in-itself.[36]

The signified of the actor's body overrides the signifier of the performed text, unbalancing the mimetic act. Yet this operation is still sanctioned by reference to Shakespearean authority, resulting in the fact of the actor's body being presented as an authorial invention. Contemporary politics becomes subordinate to the larger ideological construct of the Shakespearian name – a construction evident in a review of the production by Bernard Levin: 'If South Africa's leaders can awake, a tiny part of the credit will go to Shakespeare and Miss Suzman.'[37] Apartheid, the struggle against it, 'racial' difference and humanist sameness are all authored by the transcendent power of Shakespeare.

Suzman's own account of the production's triumphant reception also privileges author over authorities, as she tells how the audience 'leaned forward in their seats like baby birds, their mouths open',[38] ready to receive, it is implied, the essential nourishment they are prevented from obtaining for themselves. This superiority also, for Suzman, tells against attempts to censor or prohibit the production – it would, remarked Suzman in a revealing choice of simile, be 'like banning *Black Beauty*'.[39]

The privileging of the synchronic over the diachronic, whole over part, marks out Suzman's

---

[34] Suzman, 'South Africa in *Othello*', 29.

[35] Suzman, 'South Africa in *Othello*', p. 33.

[36] Dympna Callaghan, *Shakespeare Without Women: Representing Gender and Race on the Renaissance Stage* (London, 200), p. 91.

[37] Bernard Levin, 'Kissing Apartheid Adieu', *The Times*, 26.10.87.

[38] Janet Suzman interviewed by Angela Brooks, *The Times*, 30.10.87.

[39] Ibid.

project as univeralist, essentialist and prescriptive – exactly the features that characterize the very different (in content) ideological operations of apartheid. Suzman's strong identification of a modern, South African act with a historical, English series of actions in a play works to unify her project, direct interpretation and control meaning. Apartheid and Shakespearian production share a particular concern with boundaries, limitations and genre that is devoted towards establishing a universalism, a final transcendence, but which inevitably only establishes an imperialism and a reliance on that which exists outside various taxonomic orders.

Despite the paradoxes of her ideological position, there is no doubting the sincerity of Suzman's politics and her desire for change. In many ways, the strength of the production originated from the similarities with apartheid outlined above – in its likeness to the regime it sets out to criticise, the production had a clearer and more direct resonance for its audience. Suzman takes this view further in her comments on costume, where, as we have seen, she justifies her choice of Elizabethan dress by remarking that she should avoid adopting 'any contemporary anachronisms that might hinder their [the audience's] self recognition'.[40] The assumed transcendence that period dress holds is coupled as well with an implication that South Africa is also somehow Elizabethan, a view that can similarly be detected in Doran's description of the Market, quoted earlier, as 'Shakespearian'.

IV

In *Woza Shakespeare!* Doran makes connections between Shakespeare and South Africa not just through the venue, but also through the violence contained within them:

Whereas it can be absurd and revolting elsewhere, doing the play [*Titus Andronicus*] here in South Africa, a society which has suffered decades of atrocious violence, a strange reversal occurs. The acts of violence, instead of being gratuitous or extreme, seem only too familiar.[41]

Not only does this become a case of the familiarization of violence, it also becomes, once again,

an 'Elizabethanism' of South Africa, as Doran finds that 'the rhythms of Elizabethan and African society are strangely compatible: the violence and beauty and humour in both'.[42]

The identification between eras is cast in a slightly different light here, perhaps because Doran is a product of the nation that also produced Shakespeare and thus feels some proprietorial rights, or perhaps because he is not a returning exile but a briefly expatriate Lancastrian in an alien environment. The identity posited here is not familiar, but other. Doran is noting a similitude of otherness, a distance elided by Suzman. He consciously reflects on this:

Am I not just a tourist too? How can I direct a play here? Well, South Africa does seem to have been part of my life with Tony . . . But surely, to be relevant, theatre must have an umbilical connection to the lives of the people watching it. How can I provide that? I suppose the answer is that I won't. Shakespeare will. I'm just a facilitator.[43]

An interesting rhetorical contradiction is evident here. Doran reasonably doubts the integrity of his connection with the socio-political otherness of South Africa. Yet he assumes an identity with the world of Shakespeare, a world he has just identified as being equally as alien as that of the country he's working in, but to which he assumes the position of facilitating oracle. Once again, the paradox is explained by positing the universalism and transcendence of Shakespeare, and particularly of tragedy, which effects a continual sublimation of disparity.

The movement here is to elide recognition of the other in a perpetuation of the same. In establishing a rhetoric of metaphorical resonance and mimetic similitude, Suzman and Doran work to expunge all otherness and difference from their writing in favour of a universal humanist sameness which in reality is the province of a few western Europeans.

---

[40] Suzman, 'South Africa in *Othello*', p. 33.
[41] *WS*, 150.
[42] *WS*, 19.
[43] *WS*, 34.

Within South African Shakespeare production this is most evident through the continual comparison and identification of place. Elizabethan England and apartheid South Africa become one, which in turn affects notions of time and history, which are compressed to say the least.

The politics of place, onstage and off, are central to *Woza Shakespeare!*, in particular in the discussions of the play's reception in Johannesburg. A debate is sparked off by newspaper critic Digbi Ricci in an article in which he writes:

The accents. Why, there's the rub. Nobody is demanding the crystaline voices of a Vanessa Redgrave or a John Gielgud from a local cast, but it does seem wilfully perverse of a director to rob most lines of beauty, grandeur or even meaning by an insistence on relentlessly rolling Rs and pancake-flat vowels.[44]

Sher rightly criticizes the assumption that there is 'a secret blueprint of how the play ought to be done', yet invokes something very close to a blueprint of Shakespearian authority to sanction the relevance of *Titus*. His perspective is summarized by a piece in *The Sunday Times* by Michael Kustow: 'Shakespeare wrote templates for times to come, and this play has found its time and place.'[45] Unfortunately the audience did not always agree, and the production was starved of spectators, in stark contrast to Suzman's *Othello*, which was sold-out. Appropriately for the southern hemisphere, all expectations operate in reverse, with lowest attendance occurring at weekends: 'This odd, upside-down syndrome (in the UK, all shows pick up at the weekend) is apparently caused by security fears; Jo'burg, the murder capital, turns into a ghost town on Saturday and Sunday nights.'[46] The combination of an eclectic, accented, localized *Titus* with its place in post-apartheid South African mayhem deprived it of an audience. So often the subject of a cultural boycott themselves, South Africans now boycotted the immigrant Shakespeare.

The political stance of both productions, and of the rhetoric their initiators employ, is very much a stance of place and time. The title of Suzman's main article – 'South Africa in *Othello*' – is indicative of the ultimately metonymic relationship the real South Africa has with the productions themselves. This othered nation, politically ostracized and economically sidelined, becomes also the other of Shakespeare, an other that is ultimately contained within this final artistic signified, tamed and reduced to two characters and a rhetoric of violence. The tragedy of South Africa becomes that of the individual against authority, the will against the law. Saturninus/Iago becomes Terre'Blanche, Othello, even Aaron, becomes – if not Biko or Mandela, then a symbol of black South Africa. Worryingly, this is a symbol that is male, patriarchal and a participant in the system, one that is ultimately violent and itself destroyed. By reducing South Africa to these characters, Suzman, Sher and Doran diminish both political and artistic discourses.

In contrast, there can be few plays in any culture so obsessed with dissonant metonymic relations, whether they be that of the individual with the state, the individual with the family, the child with the parent or even an organ with the body, as *Titus Andronicus*. *Titus* literally dissects the autonomy of the individual, who is revealed as in fact highly 'dividual' indeed. Such is the emphasis within the text on conflict and contradiction that it has become famously difficult for twentieth-century actors to play. Sher was no exception, and imposed continuity of symbolism was echoed in a commitment to sameness within characterisation. As Doran explains:

We reached a crucial decision. We'll be cutting the death of Mutius. How do you find any journey for Titus to go on, if he's barking mad to start with? From a close study of the text, it seems that the death of Mutius might have been an afterthought, a late rewrite. It interrupts a conversation, and Marcus is given the clumsiest segue imaginable in an attempt to get back to the plot: 'My lord, to step out of these dreary dumps ...' Mutius is for the chop.[47]

---

44 Digbi Ricci, 'Titus topples into the Relevant Pit', First printed in *Mail and Guardian* II (14) 31.03.95, Reprinted in *Shakespeare in Southern Africa*, vol. 8, 1995, pp. 81–3, 82.

45 *WS*, 208.

46 *WS*, 220.

47 *WS*, 111.

The result of this is that, as Sher says: 'Now that we've cut his hysteria in scene 1, killing his own son, I think I can map out an interesting journey for him – from rock-solid pillar of the community to outcast to wounded animal to psychotic avenger.'[48] The principal of the production thus becomes an elimination of difference in favour of identification and a kind of post-Stanislavskian psychological continuity. This operates not just in the sense of a submergence of the otherness of South Africa, but also as a denial of the otherness of Shakespeare. Doran recounts how, early on in rehearsal, he scribbled 'Titus Andronicus was written yesterday' on the wall, 'not just to stop a lot of classical posturing, but to get the actors to approach the text as if the ink was still wet, as if the author was writing about their lives here and now. Holding the mirror up to show them their own reflection.'[49]

The actors – from a massive cross-section of backgrounds including almost all the myriad forms of distinction of identity in South Africa – can 'find themselves' in the text. But, importantly, only the authentic text. The 'later rewrites' clearly don't have this reflective ability and are excised. Ironically, it is more likely that these rewrites are by Shakespeare than the text being rewritten, which was possibly the work of George Peele.[50] Authenticity becomes a matter of psychologized consistency, with Shakespearian authority appropriated by late twentieth century European acting methodologies.

The massive contrasts in language, culture, nationality, sexuality, gender, class, age, experience and even occupation evident among the cast are also elided in favour of a post-1960s English, broadly RSC, approach to Shakespeare. The cast is imported to London for sessions with Cicely Berry and John Barton in which this approach is reinforced and hammered home, to the extent of the cast repeating, rote, acting homilies necessary for the performance of Shakespeare. Having been successfully homogenised, the group is then encouraged to use their 'native' accents. Sher describes his approach to character as follows:

Approaching a role from the outside and inside simultaneously. In other words, a combination of assuming the

superficial behaviour of other people, their mannerisms, their accents, with things that really matter, things from your own heart.[51]

Yet it is the 'things that really matter', the deep-rooted approaches of many of the cast, that are altered while the superficialities of accent remain. The Sher/Doran Titus is in many ways just as universalist as the Suzman Othello, because, as Tzvetan Todorov remarks, 'what has been presented as universality has in fact been a fair description of white males in a few Western European countries'.[52]

V

The fact remains however that the production did use South African actors of diverse backgrounds and did actively provide the opportunity for these actors to perform in a different and unusual way. From a traditionally English performance background, difference was suppressed, but from a South African perspective the actors were engaging with a discourse of extreme otherness. What was perhaps less radical than was supposed from the point of view of Shakespeare production in England was extremely new from the point of view of South African performance traditions. Suzman remarks that: 'tragedy is an unknown form in Africa. They [black African spectators] are not as well-schooled as whites in the manners of the theatre. Thank God.'[53] The received view of tragedy in Western Europe may incline towards the universalist, but in South Africa it remains an isolated and largely peripheral genre, not part of

---

48 WS, 117.

49 WS, 110.

50 Dover Wilson's 1948 edition was the first to suggest this possibility, of which Gary Taylor in William Shakespeare: A Textual Companion (ed. Wells and Taylor, with Jowett and Montgomery, Oxford, 1987) approves (see p. 115). Jonathan Bate disagrees, however, and in his 1995 Arden III edition (London: Routledge) of the play removes Peele from the equation entirely (see Bate, pp. 78–83).

51 WS, 118.

52 Todorov, '"Race", Writing, Culture', 175.

53 Suzman, private letter, quoted in Hodgdon, 'Race-ing Othello', 42, n.13.

the state apparatus of theatrical repression because not performed. South Africa is not in *Othello* or *Titus Andronicus*; these plays were briefly in and briefly addressed South Africa. As the reviewer Mark Gevisser commented:

As racial or political allegory it does not work. Far more successful is the production's attempt to render itself accessible by localising the action in South Africa: this production of *Titus Andronicus* fails as The Story of South Africa, but it works as a story set in South Africa, with South African themes.[54]

The power they projected was to do with a metonymy of action enabled by timing and positionality. As Loren Kruger remarks:

Cultural forms, in this case theatrical conventions, have no intrinsic aesthetic value but draw their significance from the occasion and place of their performance and the acknowledgement on the part of the audience and performers of the significance of the occasion.[55]

Shakespeare in South Africa on this occasion acquired its impact not through the power of the Shakespearian word but through the aptness of the performance occasion. For all the displacement of authority onto Shakespeare, it was the excellence of two groups of actors, whose bodies became highly politicized, buttressed by a general cultural–economic reputation that gave the plays their significance.

Political bodies are central to both plays, with the semiotic status of physicality – whether that denotes age, sex or 'race' – assuming a pathological importance. The physicality of the actors present on stage is therefore, as Suzman realized, an extremely powerful sign. Doran notes this during his audition process:

The play deals with issues of race and therefore we do need to be precise about the colour of actors we choose. Aaron has to be isolated in his blackness. Saturninus and Tamora have to be white, otherwise there would be no scandal when Tamora produces a black child. Nevertheless, since we know Tamora has a penchant for black men, her three other sons don't need to be white as well.[56]

In terms of the play, casting has no need to be so 'precise' – beyond Aaron's colour, and the Caucasian imperial family, actors in the play have no need to be colour-specific. For South Africa, however, these factors are central and Doran does have to be careful, which raises interesting issues in regards to supposedly colour-blind casting. As Herbert Blau comments:

Where the issue is race the pressing question remains as to whether we should be colour blind or, as an articulation of value, colour conscious. In either case we are left with various unresolved questions about the specificity of history: just how material we want it to be in the theatre's signifying practice ... for it is surely of material consequence to insist that the colour we're seeing is not what we're seeing.[57]

Doran's own theatrical practice is here at odds with his ideological programme. As it turned out, white actors were in the minority in the production, with only the Andronici, Saturninus and Tamora played white. Even Bassianus was coloured, implying the brothers' mother herself prefigured the Queen of the Goths in her sexual preferences. The relationships between individuals and the socio-cultural conditioning of each character combined to tell of the relationship between individual and state. The most important process by which this complex system of relations is presented is stage positioning:

The blocking and the gestus of the actors tell the fable in such a way that one could discover what is happening even if one couldn't hear anything. Transformations in the dialectic are marked on stage through transformations in blocking.[58]

On a split-level stage, this factor is enhanced further. On the Market stage, with virtually no wing

---

[54] Mark Gevisser, 'What's Wrong with Relevance? *Titus Andronicus* at the Market Theatre', *Mail and Guardian* II (15) 7.4.95, reprinted in *Shakespeare in Southern Africa*, vol. 8, 1995, pp. 83–4, 83.

[55] Kruger, 'That Fluctuating Moment', p. 156.

[56] *WS*, 32.

[57] Herbert Blau, *To All Appearances: Ideology and Performance* (London, 1992), p. 145.

[58] John Rouse, 'Brecht and the Contradictory Actor', in Philip. B. Zarilli (ed.) *Acting (Re)Considered* (London, 1995), pp. 229–42, 233.

space, blocking was dictated in a certain way for *Titus*, with its scenes of processions and crowds. No ability to wait in line in the wings meant that such scenes had to originate onstage, and when they did begin offstage, it was with a certain trepidation. The use of a jeep for Titus' triumphant first entrance proved fraught, with the result that on the first preview night Sher careered off in the wrong direction, remarking wryly that 'I've waited twenty-seven years to step onto a South African stage, and what happens? I crash.'[59] The wing space thus affected blocking which affected characterization – the emphasis on constructing scenes onstage meant the actors had to do most of the nightly stage-management and interact with each other more. This created a highly Brechtian series of relationships between the cast:

Brecht rarely spoke about individual characters in isolation. Rather he exhorted his actors to create their characters dialectically with each other, to react rather than act: 'The smallest social unit is not the individual, but two people. We create each other in life, too.'[60]

VI

For Sher, the production was as much an analysis of his own identity as that of *Titus*. *Woza Shakespeare!* is as much about the construction of his relationship with Doran, with South Africa, and his identity as a gay, Jewish expatriate as it is about Shakespeare. As a member of 'four minority groups' (the fourth being that of actor), any discussion of otherness is extremely relevant to his own life. The book becomes about 'creating each other in life, too', the medium of creation being Shakespeare. When Doran remarks that Shakespeare is the 'facilitator', it is a role more appropriate to his personal than professional life. Interestingly, it is a role in which Doran also casts himself during a question and answer session he chairs with Sher and Ian McKellen responding to questions about their respective Richard IIIs. Doran remarks, smuttily, 'I give good facilitation', briefly linking Shakespeare to an appropriately bawdy and slightly camp tradition of innuendo.

Sher modelled part of his Titus on his father, and the stay in South Africa was partly to facilitate a decision as to whether or not he should return there to live. John Rouse comments that, according to Brecht, 'the actor's ultimate goal in performance is to achieve a dialectical unity between the gestural presentation of the character in his social relationships and a realistic emotional foundation won through identification'.[61] For Sher, this becomes the object of both his personal and professional journeys, the dual roles of South African citizen and Shakespearian actor requiring the same preparation. Once again, the relationship between art and life is one of metonymy. Sher's persona as narrator of and character in a book in which he is also co-author is as constructed as his persona as actor, and perhaps even more sophisticated. The reader sees him play his several parts – prodigal son, lover, artist, novelist, South African, Englishman, actor, player of Titus Andronicus – and the rhetoric of identification employed in each one builds as a system of metonymy devoted to his superordinate role of, on this occasion, narrator. He openly and systematically progresses through the factors that construct himself in exactly this Brechtian/Shakespearian fashion.

This is exemplified several times in the early sections of the book, perhaps most completely by Doran in his account of first meeting Sher, then playing Shylock in Bill Alexander's 1987 RSC production, in which Doran played Solanio. According to Doran, 'in tackling the part, [Sher] explored his own experience of prejudice, as a Jew, as a gay man, as a South African, and lent Shylock the voice of his own anger'.[62] Not only did the Sher identity form that of Shylock, but also the play itself was appropriated for political ends when the South African Ambassador attended on Shakespeare's birthday. Sher aimed most of the play directly at the Ambassador:

---

[59] *WS*, 191.
[60] Rouse, 'Brecht and the Contradictory Actor', p. 240.
[61] Ibid.
[62] *WS*, 27.

Line by line hit home. The 'Hath not a Jew eyes?' speech reverberated round the auditorium; and in the court scene, as Shylock pleads with the Duke, Tony grabbed one of the court attendants (played by a black actor), dragged him to the front and, eyes sparking, directed this speech at the hapless attaché:

> You have among you many a purchased slave,
> Which like your asses and your dogs and mules
> You use in abject and in slavish part . . .

The play itself spoke our objections louder than any boycott action could possibly have done.[63]

Interestingly, this powerful moment was not, as Doran claims, a spontaneous statement conceived by a Sher gripped with blazing indignation, but an established and long-standing part of the blocking of that production. Doran appropriates a moment that gained added resonance on the occasion described above and attributes it to a gesture of authorial creation by Sher in the spirit of Shakespeare.[64]

The Merchant of Venice here not only operates to establish Sher's identity but is appropriated on behalf of his political agenda, his physical and professional position onstage underscoring his ideological stance. It is this movement that really makes overt the operations discernible within the rhetoric of both Suzman and Sher, which are essentially operations of appropriation. The text becomes a property, a vehicle for political positioning much like the Market itself. *Woza Shakespeare!* is a paradigm of political, individual, theatrical and authorial positioning, appropriating several systems of authority in order to produce an authorial identity for its writers.

VII

The freedom posited by these writers and that spuriously offered by the pre-1996 government of South Africa operates precisely on such grounds of property and propriety. The great and painful irony of the disenfranchised black majority being contained within imposed 'Homelands' is an example of how such rhetoric can become a deceitful propagandist move. Positioning and place in these texts comes to focus almost obsessively upon

ownership – unsurprisingly considering the connections their authors have with this country.

This ownership of positionality, occupation of place, is discernible in the Market itself, through its unavoidable participation in the national economy. As Kruger remarks:

Most Soweto theatre ventures . . . have had to rely on the Market Theatre and its liberal capitalist backers for financial support and, until very recently, had to rely on the prestige of the central and conspicuous location of the metropolitan theatre as a way of escaping the police.[65]

The Market became a market for the ideology trade, operating a system of essentially economic transactions with the authorities to enable them to continue staging protest plays. The commodification of positionality that takes place under a capitalist system imposes a doctrine of sameness and negotiation rather than a recognition of otherness. Theatre, as always, becomes an exemplar of dominant ideological forces – in this case, Market forces – as does the rhetoric that emerges from within it. Its constant self-reflexivity ensures a commentary on the process of its own production as well as the more overt ideologies presented on stage.

Both writers are well aware of this, and Doran makes it clear at the beginning of his book by reflecting on a lecture by Richard Eyre in which he remarked that post-Thatcher Arts in Britain were terrorized by 'the three horsemen of the contemporary apocalypse: money, management and marketing'.[66] It is without any irony that, halfway through the book, Sher complains at the incompetent management, lack of money and 'no marketing at the market'.[67] The system is unavoidable and all-pervasive, the reality of contemporary theatre being so imbued that Sher and Doran find themselves

---

[63] *WS*, 27.
[64] See James Bulman, *The Merchant of Venice* (Shakespeare in Performance Series, Manchester, 1991), particularly p. 124, for an account of this moment in the production's history.
[65] Kruger, 'That Fluctuating Moment', p. 155.
[66] *WS*, 16.
[67] *WS*, 154.

wishing that South African economics would catch up with English Thatcherite capitalism.

The literal appropriation of place and action by the operations of contemporary capitalism is the single largest split between the Elizabethan world and that of modern theatre, the former having become a commodity in the latter, commenting from within. The presence of the Shakespearian text is thus doubly composed of absence: denying a final signified and irrecoverable in its alterity. In this it mimics the act of performance, in which the actor's self is physically present yet always under erasure due to the presence of the character, but the character itself is simply a signifier without a real referent. Presence, like the present, 'in order to be presence and self-presence has always already begun to represent itself'. In other words, 'what is tragic is not the impossibility but the necessity of repetition'.[68] Repetition, reproduction, re-presentation is the nature of theatre and also of politics.

In this way we can see the repetition of performances as containing potentially striking political resonance, as was the case with the South African ambassador's attendance at that particular performance of *The Merchant of Venice*. The operations evident in Sher's confrontation, channelled through the text of *The Merchant of Venice*, are perhaps not quite as straightforward as they appear. Indeed, the rhetoric can be seen as being all the stronger, and having more to do with Shakespeare, precisely because Sher's action was not, as Doran claims, spontaneous, but in fact the reproduction

of an act that had occurred dozens of times before. The blocking used by Sher to accompany Shylock's words in the trial scene, when a merchant scornfully indicts the hypocrisy of a mercantile economy, is apt and powerful. It is indicative of an effective interpretation of the play, and it is also justified by the text. In the context of the unexpected (when the move was blocked) appearance of a representative of apartheid, it becomes an action that gains its strength through a reading of the text and temporarily endows the moment with greater significance than the whole. Closure is denied and the frame subsumed by its content.

The importance of the moment lies in the restoration of agency to the individual: to Sher, to the ambassador, to the slave hauled into close proximity to him. Sher attempted here not to possess the text or its spiralling connotations, but to invoke its authority for an individual and continuously repeated moment. It was a moment that became tragic in a manner that was unrestricted to generic boundaries and achieved the proximity and liminal performativity desired by Sher, Doran and Suzman in their South African Shakespeare productions, but which was finally compromised by their unwitting ideological connections to the discourses they were attacking.

---

[68] Derrida, 'The Theatre of Cruelty and the Closure of Representation', in Alan Bass (trans.), *Writing and Difference* (London, 1979), pp. 231–50, 249.

SHAKESPEARE PERFORMANCES
IN ENGLAND, 2001

MICHAEL DOBSON

The year 2001 has been eventful for the Shakespearian theatre in England, and despite some strong productions which are likely to influence views of their respective plays for some time to come – notably the RSC's *Hamlet* in the Royal Shakespeare Theatre and the RNT's *The Winter's Tale* in the Olivier – it has been on the whole a rather depressing one. The terrorist attacks of September 11th – which had a side-effect of galvanizing the casts and audiences of the RSC's *Hamlet* and *King John*, bringing an unwelcome but energizing topicality to those public discussions of bereavement and vengeance – all but halted the flow of the American tourists who can normally be relied upon to subsidize Shakespearian productions in London and Stratford, and with many companies who revived Shakespeare plays for the millennial year of 2000 now unable to afford such large-cast extravagance for some time to come, there is less Shakespeare on offer in the English professional theatre in the autumn of 2001 than I for one can remember. In the whole of greater London, for example, there's a low-budget RSC *Merchant of Venice* about to leave the Pit on a provincial tour, a fringe *Taming of the Shrew* in a basement near King's Cross Station, and a small-cast *Richard III* at the Drayton Court theatre in West Ealing, but otherwise nothing.

Much more disturbing than this current post-millennial hangover and thin spell, however, are the long-term implications of two announcements made this year by the RSC's management, in late May and late October respectively. The first, made just before new European regulations on consulting workers before laying them off would have made it illegal, declared that the RSC would no longer put together a company of actors on 14-month contracts to appear across a range of shows in Stratford which would then transfer to London via Plymouth and Newcastle: instead of being a repertory company reinventing itself annually, the RSC would fire many of its Stratford and Barbican-based employees and become a subsidized conventional impresario, mounting free-standing productions for short runs, often at West End venues hired just for the occasion. One reason given for this is that it should make it easier for the company to attract big-name actors back to Shakespeare in between lucrative film contracts: many fear that this may promptly transform the RSC from being the company in which one sees actors on the way up to being the company in which one sees actors on the way down. (A less publicized factor behind this change of policy is that the proposed set-up will obviate the need for different directors to share actors and thus agree together about casting a whole season, something the RSC's current semi-resident directorate have been finding increasingly difficult to do). The second press release, in October, announced plans to demolish the Royal Shakespeare Theatre and build a new auditorium on the same site as part of a 'theatre village' incorporating a shopping mall; during the completion of this monument, operations are to be transferred to another new theatre, to be built at implausible speed on what is now the Other Place car park. At the time of going to press it is not at all clear what the next RSC season will look like, nor whether these building plans are practically or economically feasible (or even legally so, given that the RST is a listed building). At the moment the whole project – the brain-child of an Artistic Director, Adrian Noble, who hasn't directed a production in an RSC repertory season since 1998, and has thus seemed to the present ensemble more like a remote and authoritarian corporate manager than a member of an artistic team – still looks worryingly like a massive gamble aimed at attracting people who don't actually like live Shakespeare very much at the expense of the RSC's long-term core audience and staff who do, but we shall see. What is already certain is that the damage caused to the RSC's morale by a summer of uncertainty and of rapidly enforced redundancies – with an acting company, a backstage staff and indeed a mailing list in a state of profound anger and disbelief – may never be fully repaired. In the short term, the transfer of the 2001 Stratford season to London is set to be disrupted by strikes, staged by support staff understandably unhappy about the company's plans to forsake its purpose-built Barbican premises entirely. (The whole project, incidentally, is known as 'Fleet' – but as in speedy, or as in the debtors' prison?) More will have become clear by the time this edition of *Survey* appears: in the meantime it should be part of the record of the 2001 season that the atmosphere in Stratford over the summer – endless discussions as to whose job was safe and whose wasn't, announcements and rumours that a percentage of employees would be retained (albeit on a casualized basis) carefully timed to avert possible industrial action – was a depressingly familiar one to anyone who, like me, entered the British university system at the same time that the blessed Margaret, patron saint of down-sizing, entered Downing Street. The mood and tenor of the whole season is perhaps best exemplified by the way in which the description of the Royal Shakespeare Company supplied as a preface to the programmes of every production was silently altered during June and July, as if on the instructions of the Ministry of Truth. The sentence 'Despite continual change, the RSC is still at heart an ensemble company, and the continuation of this great tradition informs the work of all its members' disappeared, to be replaced by 'Despite continual change, direc-

tors, actors, dramatists and theatre practioners all continue to collaborate in the creation of the RSC's distinctive and unmistakable approach to theatre.' With this quiet erasure from on high of its great ensemble tradition, in 2001 the RSC appeared to be on the verge of becoming an un-company.

Despite a temptation to chart this momentous year in chronological fashion, I will remain faithful to this slot's own great tradition of classifying productions by genre, though not necessarily in the Folio's preferred order – this time histories, tragedies, comedies, romances. If nothing else, this will enable me to finish on a much more optimistic note than that on which I have begun, with a genuinely interesting *Cymbeline* at the Globe, two impressive *Tempests* (in the Pit and at the Almeida respectively), and a sometimes magnificent *The Winter's Tale* which augurs well for its director Nicholas Hytner's tenure at the National when he takes over the Artistic Directorship from Trevor Nunn in 2002.

HISTORIES

I begin, though, with what in retrospect may have been the last flowering of the RSC as we thought we knew it: the productions of *1*, *2* and *3 Henry VI* and *Richard III* staged by Michael Boyd in the Swan as the culmination of 2000's 'This England' project, and the production of *King John* staged by Greg Doran in the same theatre in the spring of 2001 as a sort of postscript or afterthought to it. Boyd started 'This England' afresh, using a separate ensemble of actors for the whole of the second tetralogy instead of carrying over the survivors from Edward Hall's *Henry V*, and employing his usual designer, Tom Piper, whose version of the medieval owed nothing to the white-box modernity employed in Stephen Pimlott's *Richard II*, the mud-and-religion effects of Michael Attenborough's *1* and *2 Henry IV* or the modern dress embraced by Hall's post-D-Day vision of Harfleur and Agincourt.

Boyd supplied the three *Henry VI* plays with new subtitles – respectively 'The War Against France', 'England's Fall' and 'The Chaos' – but if this reflected any lack of confidence in their texts, the sense of a need to impose some added thematic coherence on their potentially miscellaneous and episodic contents, he needn't have worried. As always, these three plays, even the much-disparaged part 1, emerged in performance as compellingly vivid and engaging drama, and as possessed throughout their immense scope by a powerful argumentative logic, albeit of a different kind to the more heavily psychologized patterns developed in the second tetralogy and already just visible in *Richard III*. Boyd used the Swan's stage and indeed its height to full effect throughout – few modern theatres are as well-adapted to the realization of ex-Rose Theatre stage-directions such as 'The French leap over the walls in their shirts', and the great embossed city gates at the centre-rear of the stage for most of part 1 looked just as imposing when transferred to the Young Vic in London. (In this venue the Jack Cade sequence, with its invocation of a mutinous South Bank, seemed particularly at home.) A sense of vertigo, of a society clinging desperately and ultimately in vain to a precarious vertical hierarchy, was realized in part by some striking uses of flying and indeed scattering – at the opening of the cycle, for example, the props for Henry V's funeral, including his cereclothed corpse, were just visible suspended as if among the rafters, descending as if from some frighteningly misplaced underworld at the opening of the action, and at intervals throughout all three Henry VI plays white and red feathers fell in showers from on high under a single spotlight, especially during uncanny moments of quiet in battle sequences, like ambiguously compassionate or mocking commentaries from a distant and otherwise aloof God. Red and white are fairly inescapable colours in the Henry VI plays in any production, and the visual impact of this whole sequence was largely created by the brilliant lighting of very richly coloured and richly textured robes against a black and uncluttered background: a white robe under a gorgeously rich gold surcoat and tall gold crown on Henry VI (giving place to a white tunic for his final defeat in part 3); a cream tunic, later with a breastplate, for Joan La Pucelle; an exquisite high-collared burgundy robe embroidered with gold roses for Queen Margaret;

cardinal red for Winchester, sombre black for his adversary Duke Humphrey; red for York in his days of loyalty to Henry, giving place to black and finally a white shirt for his slow and bloody death; green for the Kentish rebel Cade; black, black and more black for crook-back Richard. Whether the characters wearing these colours – coded, but always detailed and beautiful in their own right – were attacking cities on ropes, offering peace terms from the rear circle or butchering one another centre stage, this was always a sumptuous but at the same time lucid and unfussy production to look at, full of intelligent visual ideas. (Piper, the costume supervisor Howard Raynor and the lighting designer Heather Carson all deserve great credit.) One such idea, for example, was the convention Boyd and Piper adopted for dramatizing proxy wooings, whereby the character being described *in absentia* would pose at the rear of the stage in a full-sized, wheeled picture-frame, as if the speaker were exhibiting a portrait: this effect reached a comical climax in part 3 where Warwick, wooing Lady Bona on behalf of King Edward in 3.3, received the news of Edward's marriage to Lady Gray, at which the 'portrait' Edward was joined in his frame by Gray, both smiling and waving as if in mockery.

The chief and defining effects of this whole sequence, though, were produced not so much by the design as by the casting. This was very much an ensemble piece throughout: if anything, it was those roles which most obviously lend themselves to being treated as sustained individual star turns – Margaret of Anjou and Richard of Gloucester – which seemed underpowered and slightly out of place. Both the actors involved were perhaps hindered by the fact that they played different characters in part 1, for which they consequently had to reserve parts of their range which might otherwise have enriched their larger roles. Fiona Bell made a tough, spiky, Scots-accented young Joan in part 1 (her status as the only woman among the French reinforced by the casting of her three fiends as young women, inclined to sing uncanny harmonies in what looked and sounded like a deliberate allusion to the Medieval Baebes), but the task of growing old as an anglicized Margaret across

11   *3 Henry VI*, directed by Michael Boyd for the Royal Shakespeare Company. David Oyelowo as King Henry, Fiona Bell as Queen Margaret.

the next three whole plays defeated both her and the make-up department. She seemed to get into a grey-permed, implausibly lined rut at about forty, and could find little to give even to the great curses in *Richard III* that didn't seem like a repetition of earlier effects. Aidan McArdle played the Dauphin in part 1 in what sounded like a slightly camper imitation of Anthony Sher, and unfortunately that was the keynote of his Richard too, an oddly lightweight tyrant who could be petulant but never very frightening. Clive Wood held attention much more readily as a cropped-blonde, sour, stolid York, despite finding little more variety in the part, but then York matters more for what he does than for what he feels (until his death scene, for which Wood had saved up a lot of power to very moving effect): the interest of his scenes is a function less of

characterization than of the plays' structure, and it was this to which Boyd gave full weight throughout. There was a strong feeling, for example, of how York acted as an active counterpart to his passive antagonist King Henry, here played with grace, nuance and intelligence by David Oyelowo: with no change of make-up and very little of costume, Oyelowo's transformation from uncertain but still eager and hopeful boy-king to the mature tortured conscience of his entire realm – bitterly conscious of his failure to find any alternative to war except submission to it – put his queen's efforts into the shade.

The main point of the sequence in Boyd's hands, though, was not to provide a framework for a series of virtuoso character-sketches or individual poetic and dramatic set-pieces but to exhibit the playing-out of conflicts and processes larger than any single figure caught up in them, and this was deliberately underlined throughout by doubling. If none of these characters was a fully interiorized individual in his or her own right, all were figures in one another's dreams, or in the same collective nightmare, the repressed continually returning in another guise to fight another day. As in his *Romeo and Juliet* the previous season, Boyd allowed some of the dead to make periodic unscripted returns as ghosts (sometimes literally, sometimes through the effects of casting), with the difference that here – since the technique is borrowed from the end of *Richard III* anyway – these effects seemed perfectly in keeping with the plays' own vision. Hence York was made especially vicious during the collective taunting and murder of Joan in part 1 (brutally stabbing her between her legs with a dagger), as if founding in advance his enmity with Margaret, the same actress, who would avenge it in kind in part 3; the other French enemy the Dauphin similarly returned as the enemy within, Richard; the ghost of Humphrey Duke of Gloucester reappeared as Beaufort's hangman; the betrayed, heroic Talbot (a superbly cast oak-like Keith Bartlett) returned as Suffolk's nemesis Walter Whitmore, and both Talbot and his son returned as apparitions conjured by Eleanor of Gloucester, and still later as the father who has killed his son and the son who has killed his father in part 3. The dead of part 1 marched across the battlefields of parts 2 and 3, and the dead Clarence, Margaret, Edward, York and King Henry were all present in Richard III's (interpolated) coronation procession. Boyd, in effect, backdated the eve of Bosworth Field, for which an ever-increasing army of ghosts was already in intermittent rehearsal as far back as the end of part 1. This held the Henry VI plays together wonderfully, but if anything it made the ghosts' customary appearance in Richard's tent something of an anticlimax, or at least much less of a surprise. In fact as so often happens when these plays are performed in sequence, *Richard III* as a whole seemed a rather slow and constrained postscript to the Wars of the Roses, in a way it never does when performed on its own. It ended, however, in

grand style, with Bosworth the culminating specimen of the superbly choreographed ghost-haunted battles for which the audience were by now almost nostalgic, pining throughout the indoor London-centred intrigues of *Richard III* for the expansive military excitement of the *Henry VI* plays. Boyd displayed a predictable lack of confidence in the Tudors at its conclusion: his final tableau showed Richmond (a last return for Talbot's valiant son, Sam Troughton, a strong family likeness linking this second tetralogy back to his father David's Bolingbroke in the first) rather overshadowed by what ought to have been the real royal family, the murdered little York princes, visible on the balcony above him. So ended 'This England', and for a brief period in March real afficionados, moving from Pit to Barbican main house to Young Vic, could see all eight plays in sequence over the space of four days. Despite its many pleasures and achievements, 'This England' left something of a confused impression, across all eight miscellaneously designed and directed plays, of a company no longer willing or able to agree which England it was either depicting or playing to. It's of some interest that the second tetralogy had to be heavily subsidized by an American institution, the University of Michigan, Ann Arbor, which it visited in between its Stratford and London runs: This England seems yet again to need transatlantic cash to survive.

The subsequent RSC season got off to a promising start in the spring of 2001 with Greg Doran's pendant production of *King John* in the same space, the Swan. Very much in the mode of the same director's *Henry VIII* here in 1997, it played the text as a sort of handsome but sceptical historical pageant, a mass of beautifully waved and suspended heraldic flags which were always in danger of collapsing crumpled and deflated to the ground. Visually akin to Boyd's *Henry VI* in its vivid uses of colour, of medieval dress and of the Swan's height (it's a great shame, incidentally, that the botched transfer of this season to the Barbican will mean that London audiences will only see *King John* in redesigned format in the cramped, low-ceilinged Pit, when it would have suited the Barbican main stage perfectly), this production revealed *King John* as a fundamentally

12 *King John*, directed by Gregory Doran for the Royal Shakespeare Company. Guy Henry as King John.

we are kept guessing as to whether *King John's* half-satiric version of history is closer to comedy, like *Henry V*, or to tragedy, like *Richard II*. What Henry seemed to have done, whether by chance or design, was to internalize this uncertainty, offering a fascinating portrait of a monarch who, because unsure as to his own legitimacy as such, didn't know how seriously to take either himself or the trappings of his own kingship. He lacked the confidence to inhabit the crown as a sacred symbol, much as he might have half-liked to, and hence derived no Richard II-style gravitas from any of his impending defeats or even from his own death: it was the fact that even his deathbed lacked dignity that made it so pitiful. Instead John was forever half-mocking both the crown and himself by donning it as though it were merely an expression of the personal vanity which alone seemed to keep him going – though even as such it irritatingly didn't quite fit, and was likely to be taken off and hung jauntily on one point of the bleak, commode-like central throne.

If John didn't know how seriously to take himself, he didn't know how seriously to take other people either, and we never really knew whether his comically late first entrance for his interview with Chatillon, and his request for a prompt as to the ambassador's name, were pieces of calculated diplomatic rudeness or just symptoms of the petulant near-solipsism into which this king was perpetually liable to lapse. There was another splendid example of this aspect of the king's curious mind-set in 4.2, when the English lords had just stormed off in anger after John had told them of the death of Arthur: here Henry played a line apparently written as soliloquy, designed to reveal an internal change of heart, as something uncertainly poised between soliloquy and aborted rhetoric. John, gawkily waving the orb and sceptre towards the lords' departing backs like a camp preying mantis, called out 'I repent' in accents which were somehow already in an adolescent sulk with both the nobles and himself because they had neither seen the gesture nor heard the line, and the mock-despairing sigh that followed tried to put the blame on the absent lords for the fact that this little performance had convinced nobody. This John, though haunted by a disabling

different kind of chronicle play, treating its battles with far more irony and taking a much more individualistic interest in the inner workings of its characters. Although the cast worked perfectly together, the production was accordingly dominated by a central performance, from Guy Henry as John, which was at once idiosyncratic and searching, at once funny and sad.

Henry's John suffered, for example, from a wonderful sense of physical discomfort with his crown, which looked like a preening parody of the rather grimmer business which David Troughton developed with his as Bolingbroke in *Richard II* and *Henry IV*. The aspect of the script to which Henry responded most unexpectedly and most illuminatingly was something which in the past has interested literary critics much more than performers, namely the play's generic ambiguity, the sense that self-consciousness throughout, didn't have the self-assurance even to have a proper soliloquy, and his attempts at regal public speech, as before Angers, equally failed to sound anything more than kitsch. Pathetically aware of how ineffectual he sounded and how unpopular he was, he could only take still further refuge in the childish, wounded egotism which was itself half the cause of the problem. What Henry teased and flounced out of Shakespeare's text was less a supplement to the King John of Holinshed than a perfect impersonation of the King John of A.A. Milne: 'King John was not a good man – / He had his little ways . . .'

With its central performance thus more interested in some very quirky psychology than in public history, Doran's whole production eschewed obvious topicality throughout. Its French characters weren't Eurosceptic stereotypes, even when they invaded England, and if anything one of them, the Dauphin, another nicely observed study in narcissism in the first half of the show (strongly played by a complete newcomer, John Hopkins), carried an unusual amount of moral weight in the second when he finally lost his temper and renounced the realpolitik he had earlier learned from his erstwhile mentor Pandulph (played as a superb, sibilant would-be seducer by David Collings). This is in part, though, because the character who usually carries that burden, the Bastard, seemed so oddly insubstantial and distant from the third act onwards, displaced so thoroughly from the centre of the stage that he delivered many of his lines from the shadows of the auditorium. Jo Stone-Fewings was perfectly effective in the first movement of the play, guiding the audience along with him as far as the 'Commodity' speech at the end of 2.1, but after this he strangely faded out, leaving only a faint impression of his uninspired costume, a completely generic RSC bastard black leather jacket. This near-disappearance was so marked that when John was so relieved to see the Bastard again on his deathbed it looked like another of his eccentricities, the last and most eerily touching of his little ways.

Not that those little ways died with John, either: the moments after John's death in this production were as fascinating as his life. The nobles and the Bastard all anxiously waited to see which way the cat would jump before suddenly rushing to pledge allegiance to John's son, and when they finally did so King Henry's whimsical, put-upon sigh, upon which the blackout fell, seemed to promise a regal performance just like his father's. Nor was John's family the only one to have its little ways in this show. Constance, for example, in Kelly Hunter's frighteningly convincing performance, became not only a tragic personification of maternal Grief but yet another study in neurotic self-absorption. In this reading she never did refute King Philip's remark that she was as fond of grief as of her child, since from her first scene onwards she was evidently so obsessed with the injustice of her position that she was more preoccupied with the fantasy of a vindicated, crowned Arthur than with the real boy. He himself was terrified of her anger, and much better at calming her sufferings than she was at comforting him, notably when he cried on 'I am not worth this coil that's made for me.' It's interesting, I think, that Arthur's death in this production was merely an accident rather than the half-suicide it appears to be in the script: heart-stoppingly, he tightrope-walked along the balcony of the Swan's above-stage gallery before slipping inadvertently inwards, to be replaced by a dummy of himself which plummeted to the stage. (This, I admit, may have been the result of sheer practicality – if Arthur had jumped off that balcony outwards instead of falling inwards, obviously, the RSC would have needed a lot more than two alternating child actors to get them through the season, and both Joshua McGuire and Benjamin Darlington were far too good to throw away). It must have been intentional, though, that Arthur's escape from Hubert's intended blinding seemed to be the result of a very peasant Hubert's superstition about the hot iron visibly going out, rather than the expression of a moral change of heart: if the battery-operated light-up poker failed once, apparently, this Hubert could no more bring himself to try again than a hangman used to be allowed to make a second attempt on a condemned criminal if the rope broke the first time. It was this interest in a sometimes reductive, if nonetheless satisfyingly complex account of human motivation that made

Doran's *King John* rather caustic as well as funny: this production showed once again – as, even more signally, did Hytner's *Winter's Tale* thereafter – that if you play Shakespeare's characters for psychological realism throughout, one of the things that is likely to vanish is the possibility of redemption. Use every man according to his Stanislavskyan deserts, and who shall 'scape whipping?

TRAGEDIES

If 2001's *King John* looked like a continuation from 2000's 'This England', the production which opened the RSC season in the main house – Stephen Pimlott's *Hamlet* – marked a continuation, too, and in more ways than one. It followed on from the previous year's incipient boom in *Hamlet*s, which shows no sign of giving off: summer 2000 saw Simon Russell Beale open at the National (in a much-toured and much-extended production which closed only in July 2001), while Mark Rylance played the Prince at the Globe; the autumn saw Richard McCabe's Birmingham Rep Hamlet (described in *Survey* 53) revived for a national tour, and late December in Paris saw the opening performances of Peter Brook's *The Tragedy of Hamlet* (which finished a world tour at the Young Vic in the late summer of 2001, and of which more later). *Hamlet* was even revived over the winter of 2000–1 by the Creation Theatre Company in Oxford, in a production (by Zoe Seaton) sponsored by BMW, acted in a massive, bitterly cold shed at their car factory in Cowley. It's true that the RSC's last *Hamlet*, with Alex Jennings, was sponsored by Citroen, but this latest instance of commercial support for the theatre occasioned much more disquiet about what happens when the classics get into bed with the corporate. Good as some of Seaton's cast were – especially Marie McCarthy as Gertrude – the play here became much less a vehicle for them than a vehicle for some vehicles. Claudius and Gertrude arrived for 1.2 fondling one another in the back seat of a chauffeur-driven black BMW limousine; Rosencrantz and Guildenstern arrived from Wittenberg on a tandem but were subsequently rewarded for their good offices with a prototype of

the new BMW Mini, much shown-off during their dialogue with the Prince in 2.2; and the final duel was fought in part not with rapier and dagger but with spanner and hub-cap. The rest was silence, apart from the chance to inspect that Mini on the way out and even book a test-drive. Such a sight as this may become the Motor Show, but here shows much amiss.

Pimlott's *Hamlet*, though just as keen to offer a modern-dress, corporate Claudius who would clearly have been perfectly at home in a BMW, was rather more chaste in its use of props. It followed on from 'This England' no less than from the *Hamlet*s which immediately preceded it, adopting the same contemporary white-box look of Pimlott's *Richard II*, and using the same actor in the title role, Samuel West. (In between the two roles, West, among other things, directed a *Hamlet* of his own in the Other Place in September 2000 as part of the RSC Fringe, rehearsed in just two weeks while its Prince, Adrian Schiller, was also playing Mercutio, Touchstone and Fluellen). There are, however, great differences between the tiny Other Place and the full-sized RST, and these have been still further increased by a cosmetic make-over, as a result of which the theatre currently has the largest acting area it has ever known. The new stage was advertised as a 'shared space', supposedly developed with the interests of all three of this season's main-house productions equally in mind, but in practice that isn't really how it has turned out. The alterations to the auditorium and stage just happen to have been planned by the same person, Alison Chitty, who was also designer for Pimlott's *Hamlet*, and what has really happened is that all three productions have shared a space modified with that show in mind. (This is much what happened last season at the Other Place, where all the productions seemed to be taking place on a set purpose-made for Pimlott's *Richard II*). What Chitty has done is to push the front of the stage about four rows forward into the stalls, raising the stalls floor at the same time, with the newly enlarged area of the stage in front of the proscenium arch extending the full width of the auditorium. Every square foot, back to the rear wall of the theatre all the way upstage, has been painted an uncompromising sterile pale grey, as have the walls of the auditorium right up into the balcony area, where Chitty appears to have run out of paint, leaving the previous deep purple exposed above a ragged front of roller-strokes. This is said to be a spontaneous feature produced quite inadvertently because the decorating budget ran out before the whole theatre was covered, but it looks artfully deliberate, since the whole effect of the alterations is to present the stage as a vast, daunting, freshly prepared blank canvas. This exposure of one edge to its white ground, with the rough shadings still visible along one extremity, just makes the provisionality of it all helpfully explicit.

Viewed from the central upstage entrance used from time to time in *Hamlet*, what Chitty has produced is about as imposing a stage as any agoraphobic actor could dread to see, a comfortless snowbound prairie that from here makes even the faraway-looking proscenium arch seem like a cosily small doorway into a yet more aching void. Beyond the proscenium, and above that further emptiness, framed in the arch, all visible space is completely full of audience. The wings, themselves strangely empty this season with so little scenery to change over between only three shows (since the company decided to economize on main-house productions in order to pay for the make-over), are miles away to either side, and if you're setting out downstage towards the front of the acting area, as West does to deliver 'To be, or not to be', you've a good sixty lonely feet to cover before you get there. (In fact there's nothing to stop him going even further than that if he wants to, since a ramp extends the stage yet further into the stage-right aisle of the stalls: if you include that, the acting area must be at least as deep as half the building's total length). The most visible support and companionship which West has on the first stage of this solitary trek is, unprecedentedly, robotic, since upstage of the proscenium arch are a new and extremely costly set of what are in the fullest sense of the word performing lights, capable of moving up and down and to and fro along rails, and of changing their own colour-filters, all by remote control. These are American-made, designed for use in stadium rock concerts but looking like accessories from Hollywood, and from the auditorium they serve to underline the new playing space's marked resemblance, when not in use, to a cavernously empty sound-stage, actively waiting for something large and cinematic to happen. Orson Welles once described a film studio as 'the best toy-set a boy could ever have', and that's something of the feeling that these alterations have brought to a Royal Shakespeare Theatre which has too often been described in the past as stuffy and inert. It's true that these adjustments have made very little difference to either the view or the acoustics from the most overpriced seats in the house, the ones at the rear of the stalls right under the overhang of the circle, where the increase to the width of the stage has only exacerbated the strong impression one always did get from back there of watching the show in letterbox format while wearing ear-muffs. But from the front stalls the height and rake of the stage are about perfect, and few would have believed the difference which the forward extension of the acting area has made to the perspective from the circle. Suddenly the circle feels as though it is in the same room as the actors, even when they aren't blowing fanfares from the side-seating or abseiling over the front rail (as they do in *Julius Caesar*, described below). One ex-RSC director, hearing about Chitty's modifications, remarked wearily that 'people have been tinkering with that theatre for as long as I've known it, but nothing they can do to the stage and the décor can change the nature of the beast beneath – in its heart of hearts it will always be an Odeon'. But it's an Odeon which is currently doing a very good job of looking like a place where dreams are made rather than one where they are merely projected – and in any case an Odeon which has played host to Komisarjevsky's *Comedy of Errors* and Gielgud's Angelo and Olivier's Coriolanus and Hall and Barton's *Wars of the Roses* and Dench's Viola and Brook's *Dream* and Sher's Richard III probably isn't all bad anyway. It was nice to think, when *Hamlet* opened in the spring, that Chitty's remodelling might have been helping the company's management to fall in love with the Royal Shakespeare Theatre all over again, but alas, apparently not. But if this auditorium is marked for death, it is at least on its way out with a terrific stage and a very fine production of *Hamlet*.

I haven't always liked Pimlott's work in the past, but over these last two seasons he has really seemed to be getting somewhere – specifically, he has found one route of his own away from the Perfectly Composed Production. By 'Perfectly Composed Production' I mean to denote what is still the dominant style of subsidized Shakespeare at both the RSC and the National, a style perhaps best exemplified by the work of Trevor Nunn, or by Nicholas Hytner's *The Winter's Tale* in the Olivier, of which more in due course. In a Perfectly Composed Production, or PCP for short, the director and designer between them hit upon some specific time and place in which to set the play, and decide on a couple of important motifs to underline, and from this they work up a set and a range of costumes: and then much later on they bring in some actors who devise a set of performances to fit in with it all. It doesn't matter whether the chosen setting is Elizabethan or modern, Jacobean or Regency: the crucial thing for a PCP is that absolutely everything should match, with the same level of unreal perfection as the reproduction furniture in one of those National Trust stately homes that has been deemed only to have been truly itself in 1727 and has thus had all traces of pre-1727 and post-1727 life carefully removed. The lettering in a PCP's programme; the stitching of its buttons; the extensive incidental music; the voices; the bodies; the business; it all matches. Though there may be some slight variations in manner according to which setting has been chosen, the acting in a PCP is almost invariably Stanislavskyan method acting throughout, the style of realism-with-aspirations-towards-naturalism with whose rigid codes we are all intimately familiar from the cinema and television. The volume and gestures may be adjusted upward or downward on a scale running approximately between *Barchester Towers* and *EastEnders*, but the emphasis will always be on playing Shakespeare's lines as though they all just belonged to those characters in those costumes on that set. Some of the script may, in the context of that set, sound unexpectedly like local social comment, but, whether this emerges or not, most of it will be played relentlessly for local psychological depth, every last metaphor conscientiously appropriated as a revelation about what that particular character had for breakfast that day and why it reminded him or her of a childhood trauma intensely relevant to one of the production's chosen motifs. The most important thing for the actors in a PCP to remember – and for most of them, trained as juvenile delinquents in *The Bill* as nearly all of them nowadays are, it is axiomatic and instinctive anyway – is that Shakespeare's language, however extravagant and inconsistent and magical, should be meticulously nailed down flat against the perfectly composed production's chosen realist setting. The words may be beautifully spoken; they may even sound recognizably like verse; but they will all be exclusively about the characters' inner lives, their social situations, and their immediate objectives. In a PCP there should never be a moment when the actors aren't simulating everyday behaviour, when the audience aren't being shown exactly what they should be feeling about it, and when the critics aren't being told exactly what it should mean. This isn't necessarily a bad approach – playing Shakespeare as if it were really big-budget Chekhov can produce revelatory results, as, most literally, Nunn's *All's Well That Ends Well* demonstrated back in 1981. But seeing Shakespeare's plays being given the PCP treatment one after another, carefully tied down to a great consistent realist machine of stage business and lighting and sound cues and programme notes, can after a while feel a bit like watching generations of dolphins being harnessed to tow barges. The exercise certainly reveals the wonderful strength of the dolphins' swimming, and it's good that what's in the barges should be delivered efficiently, but there are perhaps some less predictable, more poetic things which the poor brutes might occasionally be allowed to do instead. A big flashy barge of an RSC production can, after all, be driven entirely by mechanical means, without anything really alive being involved at all – as their ghastly musical of *The Secret Garden* showed over Christmas 2000–1, and as *Les Misérables* has been demonstrating for years.

Pimlott is hardly an exponent of the rough theatre like some other previous RSC exponents of the non-PCP production before him, such as Buzz Goodbody or the young Deborah Warner – he has come back to Shakespeare over the last few years via a completely different route, via *Carousel* and *Sunday in the Park with George* and *Joseph and the Amazing Technicolour Dreamcoat* and, speaking of animals and machines, *Dr Doolittle*. But in his own fastidious way he has emerged nonetheless as a sort of Brechtian: an undogmatic, arch, designer Brechtian, admittedly, and one extremely skilled at working up a beautifully co-ordinated realist action sequence when the pacing of a show needs one, but a director more than happy to make space for a cast and an audience to think for themselves instead of laying on perfectly pre-programmed didactic illusions. The costumes and props for Pimlott's *Hamlet* are, broadly speaking, contemporary: the setting is an off-white void traversed by surveillance cameras; and that's it. All sorts of inventive uses are made of the wonderful split-new box of tricks that is the stage (such as the moment in the nunnery scene when the surveillance cameras, activated by the offstage Claudius, begin for the first time to follow Hamlet's movements), all of them exactly as exuberant and clever-clever and self-congratulatory as Samuel West's Hamlet himself (and at the same time just as serious): but both the design and the central performance always give the impression of welcoming meanings in rather than projecting them pre-conceivedly outwards. Like the setting in which Pimlott directed West's Richard II last season, the *mise-en-scène* for this production exists in the time of its audience without being in any way a hermetically sealed mechanical simulacrum of that time. This stage is mercifully indifferent to what style the cast may wish to play in: from moment to moment, as their performances choose to guide us, we can, if we wish, read it at the show's opening as a real-life platform from which real anxious armed sentries are shining dazzling searchlights in fear of an unknown enemy's soldiers, or we can read it, *and* we can read it, as the newly enlarged stage platform that it is, the platform where we watched, from which some actors are shining what are visibly stage lights at us – as Shakespeare's *Hamlet* once more sets out to read us far more searchingly than we will ever read it. The actors can emote away as intricately and introvertedly as they like, but against this chilly and unreinforcing background there is no risk of our merely understanding the play as a soap-opera that happens to be written in blank verse: conversely, they can rant and recite away as grandly as they like, but under these pitiless and surgical lights we are unlikely to think of the show as merely a barnstorming melodrama or a set of ancestral poetical gestures. In itself icily chic, this *Hamlet's* design is exquisitely non-committal about what or how we may wish to think about it. Self-consciously clever and modern it may be, but it isn't reading us a lecture about the play over the heads of the actors.

That this is nonetheless the most wittingly, dangerously political *Hamlet* the RSC has staged for years is in some ways a direct concomitant of what I've already described, since the emancipation of the script from the confines of set-dictated televisual realism is also its emancipation from a sense that it can only be about the personal – or perhaps from the sense that the personal *is* only personal. The wide range of possible resonances that this cast have so far been able to explore over this production's run (during which it has evolved considerably, something the short stand-alone productions of the RSC's envisaged future will not have the chance to do) include, at the most obvious level, a good deal of immediate topicality. It was the good fortune of this show to go into rehearsal at exactly the time that the Florida electoral fiasco was just being settled in favour of the presidential candidate who got the most accidental votes from his opponents – a time when all those arguments which scholars used to have about whether Shakespeare's Denmark had an elective or a hereditary monarchy were suddenly available for recycling in the newspapers as arguments over whether George Bush's America had an elective or a hereditary presidency. Claudius's regime, the personal identities of its willing servants reduced to the identity badges they wear at the lapels of their dark-grey business suits, is to all intents and purposes a one-party state just as are the pseudo-democratic, de facto royal presidency of modern-day America and the pseudo-democratic, de facto presidential monarchy of Blair's Britain: the fact that its appurtenances and security procedures and structures of feeling look as much like those of any transnational corporation as they do like those of any Western government in itself makes a political point.

Played in this unlocalized political lobby – a little more than white, if less than a house – all sorts of long-dormant aspects of *Hamlet* wake up and leap into sharp focus. With Denmark not just a prison but a prison full of interns, the text's Renaissance anxieties about the rise of the professional courtier suddenly cease to be quaint period allusions to Machiavelli, just as Wittenberg suddenly ceases to be somewhere obscurely to do with religion and becomes a real-life university, full of students who may or may not be trying to postpone the day when they are obliged to grow up into compliant suits in the administration. Rosencrantz and Guildenstern profit most obviously from this, played by Wayne Cater and Sean Hannaway as a comical but believable-looking partnership between a Hardy-like swot and a hungrier, more athletic Laurel. Some newspaper critics bemoaned the joint they share to celebrate their reunion with Hamlet in 2.2 as a cheap modern-dress gimmick, but it seems to me to be witty in the best and fullest sense of the word. Not only does 'What a piece of work is a man!' play superbly well as the sort of thing someone might come out with very late at night among some old college intimates over a roach, but Guildenstern's discreet, watchful abstinence perfectly illustrates the real careerist purpose of this little vignette from *The Big Chill*: as they sit together on the ground on an outspread overcoat, passing the joint to one another at intervals, he accepts and detains it each time it comes to him but never actually takes a drag, keeping his mind clear and on the job and keeping open the option of telling the press later on that he didn't inhale. The other, less celebrated little double act at Claudius's court, too, gets just as telling a treatment: here at last is a *Hamlet* in which Voltemand and Cornelius, too often cut along with the rest of

the Fortinbras plot, receive their due. The scene of their return from their diplomatic mission, to the applause of their loyal colleagues, with Voltemand waving Norway's letter like Chamberlain's piece of paper and putting the best possible spin on it, is a masterpiece, every bit as expertly and excitingly staged as the panic that tears through Elsinore's west wing during Laertes' for once genuinely threatening rebellion in Act 4: what is particularly acute is the way in which throughout Voltemand's statement Cornelius (Chuk Iwuji), handcuffed to his diplomatic briefcase, doesn't quite dare to voice his palpable sense that Fortinbras's army is an imminent danger despite the press-release claiming that he is only entering Denmark in order to attack the Poles. When he does arrive, too, Fortinbras is as strong a figure here as his name suggests, in part because his impersonator, Finn Caldwell, doubles a First Player who takes the role of Lucianus instead of that of Player King, and is thus already marked as a double or proxy for Hamlet. At the close of Act 5 the surviving members of Claudius's government eagerly applaud his takeover, just as they lined up across the width of the stage to applaud Claudius's own coup in 1.2: the point of this reprise – that apparatchiks accustomed to serving suave civilian hypocrisy will just as willingly or cravenly serve naked militarism – may be made crudely, but it certainly sticks, and it deliberately prompts some nice reflections on what our own role is as mutes or audience to this act.

The one member of this palace staff who stands out by her willingness to insist that her superior *does* face a crisis, unexpectedly, is Gertrude's nameless attendant lady in Act 4. This four-hour production of the play gets two intervals (one at the end of Act 2, one at the end of 4.4: it's remarkable how much this comparatively unfamiliar punctuation freshens the whole play), and the last third of the play fades in at Ophelia's mad scene, which here interrupts a dreary party at which a broken Gertrude, as if trying unsuccessfully to prolong the interval indefinitely so as not to have to confront her troubles, is drowning her sorrows and looking for comfort in a cheek-to-cheek dance with Hamlet's substitute the First Player. (This conjuring of an entire, crowded social event as a context is one of many ways in which Pimlott seeks to fill the vast stage despite the text's preference for scenes between only two or three characters at a time: elsewhere, in 2.2, he uses what has previously seemed something of a directorial mannerism, having Polonius place chairs for Claudius and Gertrude facing each other from opposite edges of the stage, from which their occupants play the dialogue as if they were intimately close together regardless.) The gentlewoman forces her way across the dance-floor to Gertrude to speak Horatio's lines demanding access for the mad Ophelia, which she delivers with a real attempt at moral authority: this role of messenger-in-waiting may be Pimlott's invention, but the actress (another newcomer, Hattie Morahan) makes an exemplary job of it, forceful and tactful at once. The question such little scenes pose about what choice these apparently compliant governmental functionaries really have – of how much agency agents Guildenstern and Cornelius and Morahan can actually have in this world, where there doesn't seem to be any secure ground from which to offer moral resistance to the tyranny of ordinary political expediency – beautifully restates and underlines the questions posed more fully and more eloquently by the ex-student Hamlet in their midst.

Ex-student he may be, but it clearly isn't that long since he finished his BA. Compared to Simon Russell Beale's recent Hamlet at the National, who looked more as though he wanted to get back to Wittenberg to continue a well-established career as a well-meaning theology don, West's Prince still hasn't found a role for himself since graduating when the play opens, sulking in a black hooded jacket that wouldn't disgrace a sullen athlete or a would-be black teenager. It is one of his great strengths in this part that while he actually has years of theatrical experience behind him, and as conscientiously developed a vocal technique as any actor of his generation, Sam West can still plausibly simulate the body-language of a dangerously fit malcontented 25-year-old, scruffily unshaven but perfectly capable of holding his own with a rapier against Errol Flynn in his prime. There are all sorts of brilliantly illuminating incidental touches to this

13 *Hamlet*, directed by Steven Pimlott for the Royal Shakespeare Company. Kerry Condon as Ophelia.

performance – his at once affectionate and mocking removal of a stray eyelash from Gertrude's cheek while she implores him not to leave the court in 1.2, for example, or his cowering and hiding his face on the ground as the appallingly needy ghost of his father confronts him with the horrible rash produced by Claudius's poison, and almost smothers him with his embrace in 1.4, during an interview in which father and son alternate in their inadequate attempts to console one another. (More cunning thematic casting here, incidentally: Christopher Good doubles the territory-gambling old Hamlet with the play's other landowner Osric, and is thus made the recipient of Hamlet's scornful, futility-conscious dying insistence that the crown should pass from his extinct dynasty and into the hands of Fortinbras.) This Hamlet dares Polonius to kill him with a flick-knife on 'Except my life', and he has a lovely piece of black-comedy business with the same knife when Rosencrantz confiscates it after the murder of Polonius: Hamlet first has to show him how to put the blade away, and then while he is so occupied he pulls his pistol on him, going on to assert his superiority by surrendering the gun instead of using it. What shines most about West's performance, though, is the clarity with which it plots its trajectory, the lucidity with which West shows Hamlet's conscious self-distancing from the hackneyed revenge plot in which he finds himself. (He even evolves a little gesture to indicate when he is talking about 'violent action' as if in quotation marks, right fist drawn back behind right ear as if to strike a comic-book knockout punch – a gesture which turns bathetically and self-castigatingly into the vulgar visual slang for 'masturbator' at one point during 'O what a rogue and peasant slave am I'.) This is a performance which begins comfortably within the customary expressive range of the PCP but blossoms into all sorts of territory well beyond it. His first soliloquy, for example, 'O that this too too solid flesh would melt', doesn't open out to us at all: instead of turning with relief to confide in the audience after the constraints of the previous public dialogue with his mother and stepfather, West reserves that effect for later, and plays this speech strictly as self-involved Stanislavskyan psychology, the inadvertent revelation of a genuinely suicidal state of mind. It is only the coming of Horatio that prevents him actually killing himself (with the pistol he has been cherishing in his inner pocket), and that rouses him into a sense that he is in a play that offers other possibilities, and the much shorter soliloquy at the very end of the scene, 'My father's spirit in arms!' is played with a much greater consciousness of being on a stage before an audience. By the time we get to the end of 'O what a rogue and peasant slave am I', during which he melodramatically leaps from the stage to harangue the front rows before dismissing such ranting as emotional self-indulgence, West's ability to move at will between the extremes of naturalism and of open rhetoric has already been superbly demonstrated – from the utter conviction with which he makes an

involuntary throwaway exclamation out of 'Angels and ministers of grace defend us', rapidly spoken completely under his breath, as though he himself isn't conscious of saying it, to the self-conscious, complicity-demanding 'About, my brain'. Most arresting of all, quite literally, is the treatment given to 'To be, or not to be', which West, unlike any other Hamlet for years, plays not as a symptom but for its content. He appears at the centre rear entrance and takes that sixty-foot walk straight down the stage, with a sense of urgency that has nothing to do with simulating personal emotion: he acknowledges that he is aware of the presence of Ophelia, but carries straight on, arriving right in front of us with something to say which he is clearly convinced is much more important than anything contained within the framework of the play's fiction. So important is this message, in fact, that he temporarily stops the play, bringing up the house lights, and with a straight-down-the-line purely lucid diction that would satisfy the most exacting classical elocution teacher, he forces the fact of our mortality in our faces. Hamlet's authority, West's authority, here completely trumps that of the *mise-en-scène* around him. If this production ever had a constricting frame, it is dramatically broken here, to a devastating effect which no PCP could ever hope to rival.

Such metatheatrical effects only proliferate and deepen from here onwards – the similar, brief use of the house lights when the actors (with whom Hamlet personally mingles, visibly keen to be one of them) turn to face us over their shoulders on 'the mirror up to nature'; the turning of one of Claudius's representational weapons on himself during the play scene as Hamlet arms Horatio with a video camera, which relays a close-up of him onto the screen behind which Polonius will subsequently hide ('O, the recorder' becomes a request to see the playback); the spotlight by which a knowingly complicit First Player enhances the stagey, self-dramatizing quality of ''Tis now the very witching time of night'; or the echo of a wonderfully corny mock-retro-rock-musical dumb show in the closet scene, as Hamlet adopts a posture hitherto assumed by Lucianus all over the

Player Queen. It's true that this is perhaps a regrettable and needless fossil of the long-outmoded sub-Freudian account of *Hamlet* – the Ghost predictably arrives dead on visual cue, just as the prince is getting aggressively on top of Gertrude – as if Pimlott had here and only here lapsed into directorial autopilot. It's true, too, that as usual Hamlet largely surrenders the extra-theatrical self with which he has been mutinously experimenting when he returns from his abortive voyage to England for Act 5 – though the narrative explanation for his return, those wonderfully convenient pirates, is here made with a deliberate perfunctoriness apparently designed to show it up as a thin theatrical pretext. The prince has a last defiant burst of mischief in the gravediggers' scene, when after finishing the sandwich he has accepted from the First Gravedigger (Alan David, here with Tupperware lunch box) he invites the younger Second to join him in the apocryphal game of 'skullruggery', and suddenly kicks Yorick's skull across the stage, clearly fully aware that this piece of extra-textual youthful high spirits will annoy half of the audience. But then West's Hamlet is an absolute virtuoso at irritating people, always hoping to needle the compromised characters around him into being as real as he suspects he may be himself, forever hoping to break through the court's mere knowingness into some sort of genuine knowledge. This is a restless, smart-alec performance of a restless, smart-alec Hamlet, fatally able to see the black comedy in his own tragedy: he relishes the absurd vanity of his own satisfaction at finally using his pistol on Claudius, even after he has already fatally wounded him with an envenomed rapier and made him drink poison, and the first three words of 'O God, Horatio, what a wounded name . . . ' are delivered as an appalled laugh, in a sort of comic disbelief that any day could turn out so spectacularly badly as this one has. Forever looking for an authentic way of being in a Denmark which is visibly a moral vacuum, he dies with all sorts of quizzical energies tragically but miraculously unexhausted.

If West's central performance often reaches triumphantly beyond the limits of the average PCP, this is nonetheless a production which among its many cocky intellectual tricks and gestures has all the virtues of a good specimen of that genre. One of those virtues is that sacred cow of the drama schools, emotional truth, which the supporting performances in this production have in spades. Marty Cruickshank is a genuine, plausibly shallow Gertrude with no spiritual resources at all to draw upon as things go from bad to worse. Larry Lamb's Claudius wants to persuade himself as much as the recipients of his PR that he isn't essentially a bad man despite what he has done, almost playing 'O, my offence is rank!' like a rehearsal for one of those press conferences in which a politician says 'yes, *mea culpa*, and now you can see how wonderfully sincere I really am'. Hamlet's sustained defiance, though, eventually provokes him into abandoning this illusion about himself, bear-hugging and kissing the Prince aggressively after his insolent performance under interrogation about Polonius's body (much-enhanced by the insertion of lots of repetitions of 'father' into Hamlet's answers, from the first quarto), and Claudius finally shows his true primary colours during the sword duel, when he himself deliberately switches the rapiers to make sure that Laertes doesn't survive to tell tales. This makes such improved narrative sense that I can't think why I've never seen a Claudius do it before.

In Elsinore's other dysfunctional family, meanwhile, Alan David's tense, possessive Polonius, a far cry from the genial buffoon we have come to expect, makes equally good sense throughout, not only of the sometimes unconvincing relationship with Ophelia, but as a placeman haunted by a sense of the integrity he knows he has surrendered: 'This above all – to thine own self be true' here isn't a piece of comic sententiousness but the desperate, emphatic cry of a lost soul just about sustained by the forlorn hope that his children may somehow find a way of remaining immune to the general corruption in which he has long been implicated. His loss of memory in his dialogue with Reynaldo – 'By the mass, I was about to say something' – is not a cute piece of stereotypical old-bufferishness but a genuine and frightening symptom of implicit Alzheimer's disease: there's a real sense that Polonius may at any minute literally forget whatever self

14 *Hamlet*, directed by Steven Pimlott for the Royal Shakespeare Company. Sam West as Hamlet, Marty Cruickshank as Gertrude,
Christopher Good as the Ghost.

it was he once aspired to be true to. Ben Meyjes'
touchingly naive Laertes, still a fresher compared to
Hamlet's shop-soiled bachelor of arts, even looks
as though he might actually be Ophelia's brother
rather than just someone who regards the Prince
as a rival for her attention, and the pitifully clean
and dutiful new blue anorak in which he sets off
for Paris beautifully matches his thin, diffident sister's line in cardigans. The most heartbreakingly
eloquent prop of the show, though, must surely be
the shoebox in which Ophelia has been keeping
Hamlet's letters in the nunnery scene, all decorated
with Gallery Five stickers and little pictures cut out
of magazines. You don't get very long in which
to establish who Ophelia is and what her relations
with Hamlet have been like, and this beautifully observed adolescent treasure – just grown out of, but
still not thrown away – helps Kerry Condon and
Sam West between them produce one of the more

convincing and upsetting accounts of the nunnery
scene in recent memory. She is inexperienced and
trusting enough to hero-worship Hamlet but still
to think her father knows best about the sinister
directions their relationship might take (Condon
is the youngest actress the RSC have ever cast as
Ophelia, one of the few players around to look
young enough to seem plausibly virginal in modern dress): he is at once intellectually arrogant and
personally insecure enough to bask in the adoration of someone still working on her A-levels, and
at the same time he hopes to find in her innocence,
just as Polonius does, a possible last refuge from the
compromises and crimes of the public sphere. The
stakes are thus easily high enough for Hamlet to
snap horribly when she obediently jilts him, not
only in the petulant spirit of 'well, I chuck you first
then, you slag', though that is certainly there, but in
the realization that so far from being exempt from

the corruptions of Claudius's court she too has here become a tool of the regime. In her madness she seems almost serene, voluntarily taking refuge in insanity, led into Gertrude's party in just a short coat (later soaked in water, as if in a premonition of her death), looking for all the world like a child who has come downstairs into the grown-ups' alien evening and needs taking back to bed: the indecency of her songs, and her assault on Claudius's buttons while she sings, are genuinely shocking. There is nothing cosy about the doubling of Polonius and the Gravedigger in this production: it turns out that he has been digging Ophelia's grave all along. This is a show which received mixed reviews (always a better sign than universal mild praise) – some found it gimmicky, some monotonously monochromatic, some complained that its Prince lacked tragic dignity – but which I personally found one of the most stimulating and affecting productions to have graced the RST for a long time, and certainly one of the most intellectually cogent of the many recent re-readings of *Hamlet*.

To my own surprise I can muster far less enthusiasm about a show which by comparison has enjoyed well-nigh universal praise, not just in London but in Paris, Vienna and New York. *The Tragedy of Hamlet*, 'adaption and direction by Peter Brook', played for a much-anticipated short run at the Young Vic in late August and early September, and appeared to have everything going for it – most obviously, a legendary director, working with some actors who have been his disciples for decades (Natasha Parry, Bruce Myers) and some whose impressive credentials promised to bring in new scope from elsewhere (Adrian Lester and Scott Handy, reprising their Rosalind and Orlando from Cheek by Jowl's early 1990s *As You Like It* as Hamlet and Horatio). But while Pimlott's *Hamlet* took up what seemed the shortest four hours I have spent in a theatre in years, Brook's occupied about the longest two and a half, though to be fair this was a deliberately slow-moving, time-stopping, pensive *Hamlet*, less political thriller than metaphysical riddle. A cast of eight performed a drastically cut and often re-arranged interval-free version of Shakespeare's play, or perhaps didn't so much perform *Hamlet* as

15   *The Tragedy of Hamlet*, directed by Peter Brook at the Bouffes du Nord, Paris. The closet scene: Adrian Lester as Hamlet, Natasha Parry as Gertrude.

carry out a sort of trance-like religious meditation upon it. As with Brook's earlier Francophone *Hamlet* piece *Qui est là?*, all began as ever with 'Who's there?', but here it was spoken by Hamlet as the way into his dialogue with the Ghost; then came 'O that this too too sullied flesh would melt', then a little of the court scene that usually precedes it; later 'To be or not to be' came only after Hamlet's despatch towards England. 'This adaptation seeks to prune away the inessential, for beneath the surface lies a myth', explained one of Brook's programme notes. 'This is the mystery that we will attempt to explore.'

It's odd how dated the very word 'myth' sounds nowadays, a throwback via Northrop Frye to second-hand copies of *The Golden Bough* and student essays on *The Waste Land*, and if any single aspect of this production seemed like a belated twentieth-century survival into a less optimistic era it was its aspiration towards universality. By contrast with the National's firm setting of *Hamlet* into a context of late sixteenth-century Christianity the previous year, or Pimlott's vision of a godless contemporary Western public sphere during this, Brook's production sought in *Hamlet* for a set of pan-religious spiritual truths supposedly accessible to all cultures at once, attempting to set the play timelessly and everywhere. The First Player was Japanese, the Gravedigger Irish, Ophelia Indian; the music was predominantly East Asian, the principal set an orange Persian carpet. The gestures were slow, and clear, and graceful, and deliberately carried overtones of ritual, with hints of Noh drama: taken together with the carpet, the Irish gravedigger and the emphasis on myth, the actors' stylized movements suggested a *Hamlet* reimagined by Yeats for performance in Lady Gregory's drawing room. A flexible rod was solemnly lifted sword-like for ''Tis now the very witching time of night'; the slow waving of a flag illustrated Hamlet's narration of his encounter with the pirate ship; Hamlet made Gertrude carry out a meticulous checking of his own pulse in the closet scene, recapitulated at the opening of 'To be or not to be'; a skull was propped on a stick during the gravedigger scene, played with like a silent ventriloquist's dummy for 'Alas, poor Yorick', and allowed to fall, to be draped with a cloth, to illustrate 'Imperious Caesar, dead and turned to clay'. At the end of the play, before Horatio and the rest of the cast (the dead rising from the floor) suddenly cut back to Act 1 to conclude by raptly contemplating the morn in russet mantle clad walking o'er the dew of some high eastern hill beyond the audience, the main action was concluded by a duel with rods, a duel which consisted mainly of a particularly slow, reverent specimen of that familiar move which *The Art of Coarse Acting* terms The Eternal Parry.

By this point in the evening, as the very fact that this phrase crossed my mind may suggest, I have to admit that I was beginning to find all this elaborately paraded simplicity, all this intensely un-coarse acting, rather wearing, and was wondering once again whether the quest for universal spiritual truth wasn't best left to rich hippies. It isn't that Lester's Hamlet wasn't powerful: if anything, he was too powerful, so consciously the tallest, most beautiful and most dangerous-looking specimen in a court without courtiers, never mind guards, that he never appeared to be in any physical danger whatsoever. He was much more a threat to those around him than at risk from them, a nobly statuesque bully: it was his own body he contemplated on 'What a piece of work is man', stripping to the waist (in marked constrast to West's ironic gesture towards a tubby, familiar Rosencrantz). Understandably, this Hamlet scared Polonius half to death in their 'fishmonger' exchange in 2.2, and he physically rather than emotionally overpowered Ophelia in the nunnery scene, practically suffocating her by effortlessly holding her mouth shut on 'I say we will have no more marriages' (just as he forced a recorder into Guildenstern's mouth after the play scene). Nor did Lester show any psychological turmoil: he was a little dour, perhaps, but uncannily calm throughout. He seemed to be performing a combination of spiritual stillness and physical self-mastery, more like a long-matured Kung Fu expert than a young man with problems: accordingly he died on his feet, his poise and dignity uncompromised, not so much collapsing as gliding very, very slowly to his knees with a smoothness that spoke more eloquently of fetishistically-maintained muscle tone than of death. This was a Hamlet who was always already outside everything – as was most of this production, not so much taking place everywhere as taking place nowhere. There may be something to be said for cutting to the heart of a play, but it may be a good idea to leave it some limbs, to allow it to preserve the odd vulgarism like narrative or suspense: the people presented here were so far beyond mortal suffering that nothing appeared to matter whatsoever. 'This must be so', intoned Claudius, welcoming Hamlet's sword. If both the villain and the protagonist had apparently attained Nirvana years ago, what was supposed to be at stake in what survived of the story? I was unable to answer this question to my own satisfaction, beautiful though this production was to contemplate

(*Hamlet* as Zen koan?). It must be significant, however, that the one part of the text which Brook scarcely cut at all was the closet scene (so that a production that left Laertes with little more than three speeches nonetheless included, very unusually, the unpegged basket and the famous ape), and that Jeffery Kissoon doubled Claudius and Old Hamlet. Perhaps, in keeping with his enterprise's thoroughly early twentieth-century tone, the myth that Brook had found under the surface of *Hamlet* was just dear old Oedipus yet again after all. If this was an exercise in getting beyond Shakespeare's surfaces, I am afraid it left me keener than ever on Shakespeare's more superficial aspects.

Elsewhere on the south side of the Thames, the 2001 Globe season was offering what sounded from its publicity materials like a much more localized perspective on Shakespearian tragedy. 'The Celtic Season' consisted of *King Lear*, *Macbeth* and *Cymbeline*, and surely no one looking at that choice of plays can have expected them to have been played as anything less than tales for these devolutionary and pro- and anti-European times. Spurious as the notion of a 'Celtic Season' may have been, given that Shakespeare never himself used the word 'Celt' and probably didn't have the concept either ('The Kerns and Galloglasses Season'?), it at least seemed to promise something topical and likely to bring into discussion the very questions of national identity which the entire Globe project has raised. One play about Britain being divided into three, one about an English-backed reconquest of Scotland, and one about Britain renegotiating its membership of the Roman empire, and all this at a theatre haunted by locals and tourists alike in search of authentic Britishness? But this turned out to be a Globe season in purposeful denial about this venue's status as part of ye olde heritage industry, and all three productions scrupulously eschewed the am-dram aesthetic of tights and enforced merriness which has been the Globe's dominant Shakespearian mode to date, in ways which mandated completely un-topical takes on this set of plays.

The season's opening production, Barry Kyle's *King Lear*, though the closest of the three to the Globe's established house style, signalled its desire for independence from that style from the outset by having a design of its own. Instead of playing *Lear* in front of the gaily-painted *frons scaena* and around the faux-marble pillars as usual, Kyle's designer Hayden Griffin had them all boarded up, and he had placed a tall wooden post in the yard, surmounted by a horizontal cartwheel (to suggest Fortune? or just the wreckage left after a particularly violent cart accident?). Kyle had also insisted on certain changes to the auditorium which were retained throughout all three productions: the fronts of the galleries were decorated with swags of dried flowers and herbs in bunches, and the bluish industrial arc-lights hitherto used to light evening performances were replaced by warmer spotlights on the stage and the yard, while the audience in the galleries were kept lit and visible by little fairy-lights strung along under the roofs. The overall result was that while the stage looked a lot bleaker than usual, in keeping with this play, the rest of the theatre looked less so, liable during the evenings to remind spectators of pleasant beer-gardens outside rural pubs. But then this was in many respects a ruralist *Lear*, responsive to the play's pastoral elements even in the opening scene: the eclectic costumes on the male courtiers – mainly Jacobean-cum-Tsarist tunic shapes, riding-breeches, thick serge in dark colours – spoke of mud and long cross-country journeys, and Lear's regal cloak was ornamented with flowers, feathers and sea-shells. The Globe hasn't been hospitable to this sort of visual effect before, and to some extent Kyle appeared to be working against its grain, treating it as though he were trying to direct a Perfectly Composed Production in the RST in the 1970s or 1980s. But the plain blank boards did make a difference, able to tell us we were in a rough, wood-hewn sort of Britain matched by this show's props – Lear divided his map, for example, on a crude, almost cylindrical wooden table that didn't look out of place when it reappeared in the hovel later on.

As ever at the Globe, though, what defined this production was not the stage but the yard, and predictably the character in the play best-placed to fulfill the expectations which seem to be built-in to open-air theatre in full daylight – of broad asides, vigorous comedy, interaction with potential

16   *King Lear*, directed by Barry Kyle for Shakespeare's Globe. Paul Brennen's Edgar, as Poor Tom, takes refuge up the pole in the yard.

hecklers – was Edmund. Kyle played up to this, placing Edmund actually in the yard (half-way up the wooden post) throughout the first scene of the play, until on the line 'Legitimate Edgar, I must have your land' in 1.2 he laid claim to the stage itself, from which Edgar duly found himself banished in due course, driven not just round the bend as Poor Tom but up the pole as well. Michael Gould was so successful at endearing himself to the crowd as a swaggering, confiding villain that in effect the whole play was overbalanced by him: Paul Brennen's initially bookish Edgar, merely baffling as a Poor Tom who seemed to have forgotten entirely that his antics were supposed at one level at least to be a disguise, never succeeded in engaging the crowd's attention and interest to anything like the same extent, and sadly neither did Julian Glover's middleweight, colonel-like Lear. The trajectory one watched was of the whole play being invaded and colonized by pantomime, as Regan and Goneril gradually became the Ugly Sisters, as if learning to flirt energizingly with the audience from their beloved Edmund: the second half of the play was largely dominated by Felicity Deane's exuberant Regan, reborn after the interval in a magnificent tight black dress that by some structural miracle managed to be nearly all cleavage. This aspect of the show certainly worked, but it left large parts of the play drained of energy by comparison, and they seemed drained of clarity too – there were all sorts of intricate things going on, but none quite seemed to add up or to take the audience with them. Poor Tom kept putting a noose around his neck and taking it off again; Lear and the Fool – Peter McEnery in melancholy George Formby mode – hung onto a red rope during the storm, with which the Fool hanged himself after the joint-stool scene (this was a Quarto-based production, mainly keeping to Stanley Wells' new Oxford text but here adding this drastic new stage direction to explain the Fool's subsequent disappearance); Cordelia wore glasses for some of the time, and was briefly visible above the tiring-house during the storm; both Lear and Poor Tom wore large white loin-cloths suggestive of Crucifixions. These things clearly meant a lot to somebody, but it wasn't the audience, who were left pretty cold by Lear's griefs: every time I saw this show, the line 'Her voice was ever soft, / Gentle, and low, an excellent thing in woman' got a laugh – in part compassionately wry ('o the poor devil, he *still* hasn't got it') but in part just completely unsympathetic ('what an unbelievable old sexist!'). This was a serious production, and richer than most that this stage has so far seen, but the main story it told was not of the defeat of King Lear but of the victory of an audience more eager for a certain kind of rough theatrical fun than for high tragedy.

The Globe's other tragedy this season also decided against doublet and hose, and even more dramatically. Tim Carroll's *Macbeth* was played in evening dress, to the strains of big-band swing music, with the cast often sitting on rearranged straight lines of chairs (and hence looking exactly like the Jack Parnell Band without their instruments). They enacted killings not by one actor feigning to stab another with a dagger but by one removing a pebble from the other's jacket pocket and putting it into a galvanized tin bucket. Predictably, this outraged those who go to the Globe in the hope of seeing what they regard as 'traditional' Shakespeare (occasioning a heated debate in the pages of the house magazine *Around the Globe*), and it wasn't at all obvious what it was supposed to offer to anyone else either: the play's ethics and politics and much even of its narrative disappeared entirely, leaving a slick but vacuous spectacle that looked as though it had been devised by bored art students during the small hours of an overlong May ball. Eve Best gamely stuck with it and gave the sort of large-scale performance as Lady Macbeth that she'd probably have given in any other production, but all in vain: she kept getting interrupted by Jasper Britton as Macbeth, whose performance may have been reaching for tragic self-knowledge but achieved only comic self-importance. This was a production to add to the catalogue of great *Macbeth* disasters, and then leave well alone.

During the autumn and early spring, Tim Supple's RNT *Romeo and Juliet* at the Olivier received reviews which the cast of Carroll's *Macbeth* might have envied but which by normal standards were only lukewarm, and deservedly so. Robert Innes

Hopkins' set worked beautifully – curved segments of wall, capable of being rearranged into simple, suggestive patterns as needed – but in other respects the design of this production was based on some very tired ideas indeed. Verona was a white-boy's Baccardi-advert fantasy of the Caribbean, with a mardi-gras-like ball chez Capulet and calypso-based pop music punctuating the action elsewhere too (excessive incidental music has long been a vice of Supple's, here most regrettable at Mercutio's death). All was more-or-less modern dress, with the inevitable open-air café for the brawl scenes, and the weapons were a mixture of guns and machetes. The Capulets wore white linen suits and were predominantly white, and the Montagues didn't and were predominantly black, a racial divide about which the play's characters of course remained mysteriously silent. This crude system of non-blind casting looked worse than dated – can it still be even legal to deny an actor a role as a Capulet on the grounds that he isn't white? – and did little to help the play. Beverly Klein was an excellent Nurse, Lloyd Hutchinson an interestingly and properly untrustworthy whisky-priest of a Friar Laurence (and what was in that cigarette he was smoking? had he been in touch with Rosencrantz?). Chiwetel Ejiofor made a graceful, sensuous Romeo who grew in stature as the evening progressed, though his verse-speaking began to sound monotonous in the tomb. But this play depends much more heavily on Juliet, and Charlotte Randle just wasn't quite up to the job; she affected quick, very small steps to suggest youth, looking merely nervy rather than imaginatively excited, and played the great set-pieces – notably 'Gallop apace' – as if girlishly embarrassed by them, in this instance lying back on a sofa and giggling at herself for making such a fuss. Poor alone, her voice cracking repeatedly in what sounded like an overdone imitation of Harriet Walter, she was even less convincing with Romeo, who was in a different play running on a different heartbeat: as one of my students remarked, it was as if she was on amphetamines while he had been sharing some of the Friar's marijuana. The school parties duly came, but I doubt if it did very much for them.

The last major production of a Shakespeare tragedy to open in 2001 was Edward Hall's powerfully and elegantly staged *Julius Caesar* back in Stratford in July, another exercise in modern dress, though a rather more successful one. Taking up some motifs from *King John* in the Swan and the *Hamlet* that had preceded it in the RST, this production too seemed in part to be about the possibility of redemption, albeit of a limited kind. The play's conclusion, however, remained as bleak as always, and its depiction of Roman civil society was here considerably bleaker. Deciding to play the text without the interval which always threatens to make the events after Caesar's funeral seem like an anticlimax (just as his father Peter did in 1996), Hall cut the text heavily, and his very purposeful omissions, together with the pointed and repeated insertion of a new song, made this show almost an adaptation of Shakespeare's tragedy rather than simply a revival of it.

The tribunes Flavius and Marullus, together with the punning cobbler and his proletarian peers, were the first casualties. What we got instead, as our sole prelude to Caesar's triumphal first massive entry into the spacious white-marble forum constituted by the unadorned new stage, was the Soothsayer anxiously inspecting some entrails; above him was a large, partly-graffiti'd stone plaque represented on a gauze, bearing the slogan 'Peace, Freedom and Liberty' (later illuminated as a neon sign at the rear of the stage instead); and soon the soothsayer was supplanted by the performance, by a boy and girl in the uniform of what was evidently the Caesar Youth, of a new anthem about how the republic which we all serve makes us strong. (This neo-classical rewrite of *Cabaret*'s 'Tomorrow belongs to me' was considerately performed first in Latin and then in English – as was the lullaby supplied for Lucius in Act 4 – presumably for the benefit of any ancient Romans in the audience.)

Evidently, Hall had been reading up about Orson Welles' famous pre-war production at the Mercury in New York, which dressed all of Caesar's supporters in the uniforms of Mussolini's fascists, but as the spectacular procession that accompanied Ian Hogg's avuncular, Stalinesque Caesar onto the stage came fully into view, under a shower of paper petals, it became clear that Hall was a good deal less optimistic than Welles was about the possibility of political change. In this Rome, everybody was wearing a fascist uniform, but with token togas draped around the arms of the senators (rather in the manner of the Peacham drawing). Like the unruly and flippant plebeians of the cut 1.1, all non-Party members seemed to have been expelled from the city long ago, and with all the script's references to Pompey deleted apart from one passing allusion to his statue (as if Caesar's former rival had undergone an Orwellesque deletion from official history) there apparently never had been an opposition. Rome in this reading was just as much a one-party state as Pimlott's Denmark: even the words which Brutus and Cassius mean to proclaim after the assassination, 'Peace, freedom, and liberty', were, according to the neon sign visible throughout the first three acts (and partly extinguished only during the thunderstorm the night before the murder) already the official slogan of Caesar's regime anyway.

This account of Rome, needless to say, turns much of the play as we thought we knew it inside out. The killing of Caesar, rather than an expression of one strand of popular feeling, became strictly a palace revolution, to be announced as if from the Tiananmen gate as a fait accompli. Sure enough, the speeches at Caesar's funeral and their immediate aftermath, which have generally been treated as the play's climax, were here strangely muted. They were beautifully staged, mind: from a raised platform across the front centre of the stage, Brutus and Antony took turns to address the whole auditorium, which had been seeded with cast members who awoke the whole building by banging rhythmically on the balcony and circle rails, and some of whom descended into the stalls and thence stage on ropes for the display of Caesar's mantle and the reading of his will. But all of these extras, too, were uniformed, giving the impression that Antony's audience was not a potentially mutinous crowd but an attentive team of professional *agents provocateurs*. Tom Mannion, accordingly, played his great oration less as a cynical, calculated exercise

in full-on rabble-rousing than as a perfectly sincere, rather subdued briefing of the party faithful, which took a turn he just possibly hadn't completely foreseen himself. I was at first inclined to view Mannion's restrained delivery of this speech as an accidental side-effect of the decision that he should play Mark Antony in RP rather than in his native Scots – as a symptom of the constraint which anyone who would normally talk about 'Rrohm' and 'Rrohmans' is bound to experience if they are perpetually having to remember to say 'Reome' and 'Reomans'. But it must have been deliberate: it was certainly matched by the solemnity with which his onstage audience reverently performed Caesar's cremation down the stairs towards the rear, and the equally sullen, unfrenzied way in which they then killed Cinna the poet and dutifully suspended him by his ankles from a chain. In this production, this wasn't an expression of mob violence, but of ideological dogmatism: Cinna was the only person on stage wearing civilian clothes rather than the *res publica's* uniform, and as a poet he was evidently under suspicion anyway of being a bourgeois intellectual insufficiently committed to the cultural revolution.

The removal of the portly body at the centre of this production's massively organized and inflexible state, then, looked less likely than ever to make very much difference to the political status quo, and Hogg's Caesar, an eminently replaceable figurehead for the party machine, only looked really tyrannous with Calphurnia when abruptly persuaded to dismiss her dream. The assassination's unintended transformation of him into a figure of indestructible dignity was accordingly very marked in this production. 'Et tu, Brute' was played not as the despairing cry of a man realizing he has been stabbed by his friend, but as an appeal for an actual personal relation with his chief assassin: Brutus had so far been hanging uncertainly back while his colleagues attacked, but Caesar steadily confronted him on this line, insisting that Brutus should face up to his share of the work. The two maintained eye contact as Brutus obediently stepped slowly forward and finished Caesar in what was almost an embrace: it seemed almost as much a response to this proper man-to-man farewell as to this last stab-wound that the emperor collapsed on 'Then fall, Caesar.'

Here, as elsewhere, this production seemed to be about not political change, which looked substantially impossible, but about whether any authentic personal relationships can survive in a world in which the public sphere is completely given over to mere expediency and personal ambition: in this it had a good deal in common with Doran's *King John*, and still more with Pimlott's *Hamlet*. As in the *Hamlet*, this question was most thoroughly focused by a single central performance, and it was another deeply non-PCP piece of work, greatly assisted by the receptive empty whiteness of Alison Chitty's stage. As Brutus, Greg Hicks offered the most thoroughly stylized piece of Shakespearian acting all year, and it is very difficult to imagine any more mimetic set than this on which it wouldn't look surreally out of place. After a conspicuously lithe and serpentine youth, years of playing classical tragedy seem practically to have ossified Hicks, setting his body into a small repertoire of hollow-bodied, statuesque, balletic postures, and freezing his face into a single, rigidly serious expression, as if it had permanently taken on the contours of the tragic masks he wore in the *Oedipus* plays and the *Oresteia* and *Tantalus*. His voice, meanwhile, seems equally to have forgotten all gears except the intensely tragic, playing each line with a metallic tremor which at times produces a sound something like that of an unexpectedly sensitive and suffering Dalek: *it must be by his death, exterminate.*

But casting Hicks as Brutus worked superbly: whatever suspense and drama *Julius Caesar* may have lost from its depiction of public life relocated itself around the question as to whether anything that could happen in Rome could make this rigidly-principled stoical robot start behaving like a human being. And how tensely Hicks kept us waiting for it. The orchard scene didn't come close: Brutus's decision to join the conspiracy seemed as mechanical as the ingenious ripple-machine which ruffled the stage pool's surface until he made up his mind, and Portia barely even reached his side of the water, never mind his innermost self; and though Caesar's insistence

17　*Julius Caesar*, directed by Edward Hall for the Royal Shakespeare Company. Greg Hicks as Brutus.

on being personally murdered shook him briefly, Brutus settled back into his customary granite-like mode for the funeral. The really electrifying scene in this production, probably for about the first time since the days of Thomas Betterton, was in fact the quarrel scene, 4.2. Here Brutus not only wore his top button undone, a breakthrough, but, though of course he didn't smile – I'm not at all sure Hicks would still be physically capable of that – he had a small wry joke with Cassius (4.2.175–9). More importantly, Brutus got involved in a real row, and it came as an incredible relief that he did. When Brutus admitted to Tim Piggott-Smith's excellent foil of a Cassius that he had been ill-tempered, we suspected there might still be a person in there after all: when he was so provoked by the intrusion of the poet that he smashed a wineglass, we were convinced of it, and it's extraordinary how touching the spectacle of this redemptive anger was. The effect was not unlike that of the Dauphin's rage at Pandulph in *King John*, the welcome irruption into the play's discourse of an emotion which at last reached to something deep inside the character that wouldn't be entirely subordinated to the ego or the superego or to political interest.

Redeemed into humanity this Brutus might be, but he was of course still doomed, he and Cassius alike killed off with particular swiftness in this production's efficacious rendering of Philippi and its aftermath. The public world currently belonged to Mark Antony, who from his brief moment of sincerity after Caesar's death had quickly vanished under a military helmet into the usual machiavellian business of maintaining power, but the future of Rome lay with the efficient Octavius. The triumvirs were less sympathetic than usual in this reading, if only because so cut: they despatched the proscription scene at a terrific pace, as though sentencing members of their families to death meant nothing to them. Furthermore, Octavius' insolent insistence on commanding the right flank of their army revealed very clearly that he was as at least as egotistically ambitious as Caesar ever was, destined to personify and sway the *res publica* far more ruthlessly than did the unappeased ghost who remained visible at the close of this exceptionally lucid and original reading of *Julius Caesar*. Octavius was forcefully played by John Hopkins, who was also impressive as the Dauphin in *King John*; perhaps the greatest tragedy of the current RSC situation is that there may no longer be a repertory system for the likes of Hopkins and this season's other remarkable novices – Hattie Morahan, Finn Caldwell and all – to rise through over the coming years.

COMEDIES

2000–1 was a good year for the late romances – with a major production of *Cymbeline*, two notable *Tempest*s and an important *The Winter's Tale*, of which more later – but among the other comedies few theatre managements were in a mood for experimentation, sticking to well-tried favourites.

In Manchester, Helena Kaut-Howson directed a characteristically lively and inventive *The Taming of the Shrew* at the Royal Exchange, and in the Open Air Theatre, Regent's Park, Rachel Kavanaugh staged a play which has always been a favourite of that venue, *Love's Labour's Lost*, with Adrian Schiller as Biron and a *mise-en-scène* which appeared to pun on his surname, setting the play in stocks and cravats as if in Weimar around 1800. But the only other comedies to receive any major outings at all were two so popular that they are in severe danger of over-exposure, namely *A Midsummer Night's Dream* (which came out in a whole rash of Bottoms during the spring and early summer, at the National's education department, in a commercial production at the Albery in the West End, in Regent's Park and at the Barbican Hall), and *Twelfth Night*.

It's perhaps a sign of the dangerous level of familiarity that *Twelfth Night* currently enjoys that both of this year's productions should have had so much in common, not only with each other but with Trevor Nunn's film version of 1996. Bill Alexander directed the play for Birmingham Repertory Theatre (of which he has now been Artistic Director for almost a decade) in a modest, capable production which toured during the autumn of 2000 back-to-back with his *Hamlet*, using most of the same cast; the set was economical, the stage mainly plain white, but the setting suggested an Edwardian country house. Lindsay Posner directed the play for the RSC in their summer season in 2001, in the Royal Shakespeare Theatre; the set was not very economical, but the stage, as modified for Pimlott's *Hamlet*, was very largely plain white, against which the setting did what it could to suggest an Edwardian country house.

This has become such an ordinary way of dealing with *Twelfth Night* that neither production achieved anything that felt like a revelation, though Posner's had some ideas, and Alexander's had some admirable execution – with exquisite lighting, by Tim Mitchell and Sarah Rushton, fine costumes by Ruari Murchison (with definite touches of Cecil Beaton's designs for *My Fair Lady*), and some strong ensemble playing. Jayne McKenna, as

Olivia, managed to be at least as interesting as the divine hat and veil in which she first encountered Cesario suggested, and she achieved real poignancy at the play's ending, which was as conscious of who hadn't won Cesario as it was of who had wound up with Rakie Ayola's shrill but endearing Viola. Toby Belch and Andrew Aguecheek came, as they often do, from somewhere between P. G. Wodehouse and *Toad of Toad Hall*, but elsewhere in the subplot there were two less conventional pieces of casting. David Hargreaves was an old, white-bearded Feste, which gave added point to his singing 'Youth's a stuff will not endure' (to the Morley tune, for once), even if his singing voice isn't what it was. Gerard Murphy was a physically powerful, sinister Malvolio played in his own native Belfast accent, but his performance foundered, as post-Elizabethan Malvolios often do, on the problem of his cross-gartering: in the trouser era, showing one's socks at all looks a good deal more transgressive in itself than just changing the colour of one's hose used to, and the risk of overdoing this scene is accordingly much larger. Both Murchison and Murphy lost their own and the play's sense of decorum entirely here, with Malvolio coming out (and I choose the phrase advisedly) in a full-scale pseudo-Elizabethan fetish outfit which he must have been keeping in a closet all along – a medallion, yellow mock-hose with suspenders, even a corset. The effect of his postures in this ensemble was more of a self-involved, bafflingly mock-Tudor Elvis impersonator at a gay disco than of an otherwise puritanical steward betraying his social and sexual aspirations to his mistress: it was too grotesque to be either funny or plausible in its context, and struck the one fatally wrong note in an otherwise palatable if unsurprising Perfectly Composed Production.

Posner's RSC production similarly had a Wodehousian Belch and Aguecheek (though Barry Stanton's Sir Toby, who at his first entrance went beyond belching into actual vomiting, was probably worse-behaved than anyone in Wodehouse would actually have tolerated), and it too had a sadly overacted cross-garter scene. Guy Henry's Malvolio was initially plausible enough as a prudish lower-middle-class Northern baptist struggling to

camouflage his accent so as to fit his position as Olivia's chief servant, but from the letter scene onwards he seemed to forget the social constraints of the production's chosen historical moment, *c.* 1910, with baffling rapidity. A steward's chain would have helped: it might have reminded us why Maria resents him so much (this Maria, Alison Fiske, who played Eleanor in *King John* in similar style, looked as though she could have bitten his head off at will), and it might at least have saved Henry from the predictable vulgarity of treating the line 'playing with ... some rich jewel' as a masturbation joke. By then, though, this was already turning into such a disproportionately vulgar performance that even a straitjacket would have been hard put to keep Henry from going over the top, never mind a chain. One might just about have bought the idea that this Malvolio could have imagined that the Olivia whom he believed to be in love with him was a closet libertine who would have enjoyed some fairly rough and explicit advances, but where this Malvolio was supposed to have picked up the ideas about libertine behaviour which he acted grossly out all over the cross-gartered scene it is hard to imagine.

This very full display of Malvolio's explicit fantasy life, though unfunny, was, however, in keeping with the production's main line of ideas, since Posner was attempting to slant his particular Edwardian PCP of *Twelfth Night* in the direction of self-conscious sexual experimentation on the artistic fringes of Bloomsbury. (Hence Zoe Waites' firm-chinned Viola was put into a high-collared tunic with her hair slicked back as Cesario, looking like a generic butch lesbian in a Kurt Weill cabaret, though her convincingly lovelorn, depressive performance wanted nothing to do with the design's hints of playful bisexuality.) Posner's ideas for the play would probably have best fitted a big revolve like the one in the Olivier, where one massively detailed set representing Orsino's domestic interior could have alternated swiftly with another representing Olivia's. As it was, however, faced with the great white blank of Chitty's stage, all Posner and his designer Ashley Martin-Davis had been able to do was to build fragments of those two respective sets, which huddled in either corner in front of the proscenium, signifying as loudly and desperately as they possibly could to make up for the void in between. Stage right, chez Orsino, an implausible collection of very famous early twentieth-century paintings and a chaise longue shouted 'Sensual Late Imperial Exoticism': stage left, chez Olivia, a grandfather clock and some black-and-white family portraits supplemented by two newly installed Aubrey Beardsley prints (hugely enlarged from their orginal format as illustrations in the *Yellow Book*) shouted 'My Parents Were Respectable Victorians But I Want To Be Advanced'. In between was a great hole, gamely plugged by a backdrop of a huge black-and-white photo of the sea at its rear (not unlike those that sometimes used to adorn the walls of old fish and chip shops), but more often blocked out entirely by large shutters. Thanks to these, hardly any action took place upstage of the proscenium arch at all, and this was as a result the most monotonously lateral piece of directing I think I've ever seen. As far as its blocking went, it was like watching Mr and Mrs Noah on an old-fashioned barometer: Jo Stone-Fewings' tongue-in-cheek old Eastern hand of an Orsino and his household came out from stage right and their scene spread across to about stage centre, and then they went off through their door stage right again, and then Matilda Ziegler's elegant, thin-voiced Olivia and her household came out from their door stage left and got about as far as stage centre before going off stage left again. And so it went on.

The year's various takes on that other favourite *A Midsummer Night's Dream*, by contrast, were worlds apart, and offered a nice cross-section of the styles of Shakespeare currently on offer at different levels of the theatrical marketplace. At the low-budget end, as in Sean Holmes' production for the National's education department – briefly visible in the Cottesloe in Spring before touring the nation's schools – all is ugly grunge minimalism. A cast of eight worked in the round more or less in rehearsal clothes (with any additions for fairies and donkeys made from twisted wire coat-hangers, matching the shop-rail on castors on which Tom

Anderson's yobbish Puck scooted on and off), and they seemed to be doing their utmost to camouflage the play's beauty and verbal richness in case it seemed too unlike the drearily impoverished imagined lives of their target audience. Karen Tomlin, as Hippolyta, Titania and Snug, could cope with Shakespeare's syntax only by breaking it unmetrically and nonsensically into very short units (hence her exclamation on first hearing Bottom's voice ran 'What angel? Wakes me from my flowery bed?'), but all of this cast, as some pre-show educational exercises revealed, were keen to apologize for Shakespeare's poetry in any case: 'these people *have* to use poetry because their experiences are so weird . . . Shakespeare's time was verbal, they didn't have TV, they had to make pictures of feelings with words'. This was all very worthily meant, no doubt, but liable to be wholly counter-productive: make Shakespeare as unglamorous and non-escapist and would-be real as *Grange Hill* and teenagers may as well watch *Grange Hill* instead, a programme, incidentally, which is sometimes a good deal funnier than was this production. It wasn't at all obvious that these actors thought the mechanicals were wrong to want to show their audience a real wall and real moonlight: this team showed rather less faith in the possibilities of theatrical make-believe than Quince did.

More expensive, if even less stimulating to the imagination, was Matthew Francis's *Dream* at the Albery, a vehicle for the comedienne Dawn French, who played Bottom – supplied with a dangling, tassel-like penis along with the rest of her hairy ass outfit in the wood for the diversion of the Fairy Queen, though it's hard to see why a production willing to accommodate a female Bottom should have had any trouble with a bisexual Titania. This appendage was of a piece with this production's middlebrow literal-mindedness throughout, which went far beyond that of its mechanicals: by Act 5 Francis was in no position to ask us to laugh at their taste in real walls and real moonshine, having by then given us a real wood, a real pond (and with it the usual tedious wait to see which of the characters was going to be obliged to fall in – Lysander, eventually), and all the efficiently simulated realist moonshine his lighting designer Mark Henderson could lay on. Expecting an audience drawn in by French's television-based celebrity, Francis too seemed anxious about Shakespeare's poetry: hence generic ethereal 1970s-style synthesizer music was played over any long set-piece speeches, such as 'I know a bank' and Puck's epilogue. This music matched the heavy-metal satyr look favoured by Michael Siberry as Oberon well enough, but had nothing to do with the novel setting which Francis had elsewhere imposed on the play, nor the interpolated jive dance-routines which came with it. Theseus' palace was, according to its noticeboard, 'Athens House', an English stately home requisitioned for some obscure military purpose during the Second World War (and apparently blown apart by a bomb to reveal the wood at the end of the first act, though it was miraculously intact again for the last). It wasn't clear what Theseus was exactly doing for the war effort, nor in what theatre of the conflict he had defeated Jemma Redgrave's perfectly English-sounding Hippolyta, but Lysander and Demetrius looked nice enough in their respective army and RAF uniforms – even if one was left wondering why they weren't worried about getting shot as deserters for running off into the wood. By the end of the first scene, though, one was envisaging this possible outcome with some pleasure, as Francis and his cast made the classic mistake of anxiously straining to find laugh-aloud sight-gags long before Shakespeare has finished the serious exposition without which none of the rest of the comedy will work.

The same distracting quest for irrelevant incidental mugging bedevilled the mechanicals' scenes throughout, which the wartime setting did little to assist. Mrs Bottom, as she was intermittently known, was part of an amateur theatre group which boasted only one man, Paul Rider's camp Northern Snug, who in order to preserve the script's own cross-dressing jokes went on to play Thisbe to her Pyramus. By the time they got to their performance, one was well past objecting that no such troupe would have dreamed of casting their only male actor in their only female role, since everything else about this supposed portrait of am dram on the Home Front was wrong too: as Quince, Selina Cadell had a class accent which didn't match either her uniform or her behaviour (and she made an unbearable long, slow, self-indulgent, unfunny hash of her Prologue), and the company's props were for the 1940s absurdly lavish of materials: Bottom's immense comedy breastplate was clearly made of anachronistic plastic anyway, but if it had really been metal it would have long ago been melted down in a munitions factory. To be fair, French herself worked very hard to carry what she could of the ungainly and incoherent show that had been built around her, and when left to herself was very funny: she has a great deal of presence, speaks Shakespeare very well and can warm up an auditorium just by walking onto the stage. But there was little this one glowing performance could do to make sense of a *mise-en-scène* which had less than nothing to say to Shakespeare's script, tripping up and confusing its narrative and adding only inexplicably irrelevant connotations to its poetry. Why, for example, did the fairies (the smaller ones played by adults dressed in fragments of 1940s school uniforms, a trick pinched from Dennis Potter's *Blue Remembered Hills*) worry at such length about the bad weather the mortals were having and the conflict between Oberon and Titania, but say absolutely nothing about the fall of France or the problem of how to stave off the Blitz? One gave up imagining that Francis might have an answer to any such question fairly early in the evening. Audiences wanting a cogent middlebrow mass-market *Dream* with a few ideas of its own (and an even more real wood) were much better advised to skip this one and head for the Open Air Theatre in Regent's Park to see its revival of Alan Strachan's production from 2000 (described in *Survey 55*).

Wilfully ugly, poverty-look minimalism at the bottom; literal-minded set-dominated realism in the middle; and at the top of the range, back to a different tone of minimalism altogether, the expense and the special effects not scorned but all translated into sheer professionalism. On 20 March 2001, the City of London Sinfonia celebrated its 30th anniversary by performing Mendelssohn's incidental music to *A Midsummer Night's Dream*, in the Barbican Hall, and they not only called in Dame Janet Baker to make a few introductory remarks but borrowed a team of nine actors to give a one-off gala performance of Shakespeare's play to go with the music. These nine actors, directed by Jonathan Best, were drawn from what was then still a Barbican-based organization, the RSC: some were veterans called in from outside the current season (such as Alex Jennings, reprising his fastidious Theseus/Oberon from Adrian Noble's version of 1996, and Samantha Bond, playing Hippolyta/Titania for the first time), but most had by then been acting together in the 2000 season for over a year. They can only have had a very brief rehearsal period for this show (David Tennant, for example, learned his Lysander and Flute in between playing Romeo, Antipholus and Jack Absolute), and they had what looked like an unpromising space to work in – the shallow, wide gap left at the front of a stage otherwise full of musicians. But as the note about the RSC in the evening's programme could then still say, 'the company today continues to function very much as an ensemble of actors and actresses', and this performance turned out to be one of those miracles that only really hardworking, accomplished actors who have grown used to playing together over a long period can possibly achieve. In deference to the Mendelssohn, the actors, visible throughout, wore early Victorian dress clothes, arriving to group themselves on and around two chaise-longues at either side of a dark Turkey carpet, and helping themselves to what looked like claret from decanters when they weren't performing. There were no costume changes (unless you count the slippers Ian Hughes as Puck affixed vertically alongside Desmond Barritt's own ears with a headband to indicate his transformation as Bottom, and an apron-like instant dress for Thisbe); no lighting effects; and the barest minimum of props. But Mendelssohn's music itself supplies all the imaginary gauze wings anyone could desire, and it here provided the frame and occasion for an astoundingly elegant, almost nonchalant performance of *A Midsummer Night's Dream*, dashed wittily and intricately off as if it were just a virtuoso after-dinner charade being played by nine

close colleagues for their own amusement. I suppose that after the last forty years the RSC ought indeed to be able to field a team of nine actors at short notice capable of polishing off a funny, profound, eloquent and moving little *Dream* without a second thought, but when they do it is still an astonishing and dazzling and joyful thing: the only other performance I saw all year to approach the level of instinctive skill and teamwork and timing and style on display on 20 March was given by the Chinese State Circus. No other theatre company I've ever seen could have done it, and it was glorious.

ROMANCES

The minimalism of this particular one-off production (if one can use such a term of an evening that employed the top-class soprano Susan Gritton, the equally eminent mezzo Pamela Stephen, Dame Janet Baker as prologue, and one of the world's better small orchestras) looked accidental – no set could have been accommodated on the City of London Sinfonia's stage anyway, no exits and re-entrances were feasible, and no gesture towards the kind of visually elaborate *Dream* envisaged by this score, beyond Nina Garner's single set of Victorian costumes, could possibly have been made. The effect would have been utterly different had these restrictions been deliberately adopted back in the Barbican main house, just as Brook's decision to stage only a cut-down *Hamlet* with a tiny cast on another carpet was different in kind at the Young Vic. At the Barbican Hall, the audience were given the full exhilarating thrill of seeing a company at the top of their form effortlessly transcending the apparent limitations under which they were working, but they weren't necessarily asked to feel intellectually and spiritually better about themselves, as Brook's audience perhaps were, for having deliberately been denied the more customary and worldly pleasures of a busier and more colourful stage. I'm not at all sure myself that the prosaic mimetic realism of Matthew Francis's *Dream* and the flaunted highbrow asceticism of Brook's *Hamlet* aren't equally inappropriate to the immense range and vitality of

18 *Cymbeline*, directed by Mike Alfreds for Shakespeare's Globe. The reconciliation scene, in cream silk pyjamas: (from left to right) Fergus O'Donnell as Guiderius, Jane Arnfield as Imogen, Richard Hope as Cymbeline and Abigail Thaw as Arviragus.

Shakespeare's stagecraft, unconfined as it is by either good taste or bad, though I emerged from 2001's other exercise in wilful minimalism, Mike Alfreds' *Cymbeline* at the Globe, with considerable respect for an utterly counter-intuitive set of directorial choices boldly sustained.

Alfreds' production, though rooted in his own distinguished work with Shared Experience, seemed to have picked up a number of its tics from Brook (and perhaps from Ariane Mnouchkine): here again, for example, were the onstage accompanists commenting on the action on assorted Asian instruments (here mainly percussion), and here again was the single carpet used to define the acting area – orientalist almost to the point of self-parody,

as if Kai Lung had just unrolled his mat. Here too was the surprisingly small number of performers: six, to perform a play with at least twenty-seven speaking parts. This *Cymbeline*, though, was at once more fussy than Brook's *Hamlet* and less so. It was more so with letters and props, of which there are more than enough in *Cymbeline* for this to matter: Alfreds adopted an intrusive practice whereby props were never carried on by the performer who would use them but were supplied only at the moment they were needed, handed swiftly to the character by a currently non-performing actor – the whole transaction further underlined by a percussive noise from the accompanist. (The props were themselves stylized, pseudo-Asian percussion instruments, most memorably a sort of miniaturized washboard of a notepad on which Iachimo scratched with a stylus in Imogen's bedroom.) It was much less so, though, when it came to costumes: the six actors and two musicians, who remained in full view of the audience throughout, wore cream silk pyjama suits the entire time.

The results were very impressive, but very impressive in the same way that seeing a passage from *Swan Lake* danced charmingly to the accompaniment of a single penny whistle by a ballerina who has chosen to wear leg-irons throughout might be very impressive. It was a fascinating exercise in seeing what might be left of the play if you took away all its more vulgar elements, such as characterization (since for the most part the actors were compelled to concentrate solely on the simplest requirements of storytelling, making big coded signals with voice and body language to indicate which of their roles they were playing at any given moment), or spectacle (for once one knew from the very beginning of a *Cymbeline* exactly what Jupiter's descent on the eagle was going to look like: it was going to look like six actors in cream silk pyjamas), or any of those cheap theatrical effects that Shakespeare will insist on using and thinking-through that involve disguise – though the comic non-disguising of Imogen as a man and of Cloten as Posthumus, when each merely changed into another identical pair of cream silk pyjamas, here became a new cheap effect in its own right. What was left, in startlingly clear relief, was structure: I admit, for instance, that it shouldn't have taken the playing of Imogen's bedchamber scene and of the scene of Fidele's supposed funeral and its aftermath and the scene of Posthumus's dream by the same small group of actors in cream silk pyjamas to point forcefully out to me how thoroughly this play revolves around scenes in which significant things happen to the main characters while they are unconscious, but it did. The other benefit of this production's chosen method was a remarkable focusing of its audience's attention, rarely achieved before in this space: less confident that they'd know what they were supposed to be

enjoying if they didn't follow this unfamiliar play and this unfamiliar set of procedures very carefully, the whole house was in an unusual state of concentration, and if there was a certain amount of self-congratulation involved in having managed to follow the plot despite all the trebling and quadrupling of roles and the complete absence of costume changes, there was genuine satisfaction at following the narrative closely to its resolution too.

I still left the theatre, though, more conscious of what had been lost – and what I had been asked to congratulate myself on tastefully going without – than of what had been gained. For all its angular and intricate and naturalism-defying structure, there is a far wider and more intimate range of writing in the main roles of *Cymbeline* than this method could accommodate: one always knew, for example, exactly what emotions Jane Arnfield's Imogen was signalling by her emphatic ballet-school-teacher gestures of hands and face (and would have done so from half a mile further away), but it was never very detailed or very engaging. Mark Rylance produced some impressive work as Posthumus and Cloten, but he was in some respects hindered by the doubling rather than helped: he reserved all his darker side for an interesting, musclebound Cloten who pathetically half-knew how awful he was (and who spoke out of only one side of his apparently numbed mouth, as if just back from the dentist), and didn't allow Posthumus ever to be seriously dangerous or unpleasant at all, throwing away 'Is there no way for men to be...?' as if embarrassed by it. His penitence after Imogen's death (which helpfully comes after Cloten's too) was, however, extremely moving, and the little scene between him and the sour jailer in 5.5 was delightful. This may have less to do with the acting, though, than with the fact that this exchange is sufficiently still, and sufficiently removed from the needs of the narrative, for one to have actually started listening here to what the play itself was talking about: the line 'I would that we were all of one mind, and one mind good', for example, rang out like a bell. Elsewhere, though, this was a spectacle almost entirely about its own perversely-selected method of telling the story of *Cymbeline*: one was entertained throughout by the ingenuity with which the six players in their cream silk pyjamas switched roles – which of course reached a mad and delightful climax in the last scene – but at the expense of very much emotional or intellectual engagement with the play's content. (When Britons, Romans and Italians, men, boys and women, ghosts, gods and mortals, are all the same six would-be Orientals in cream silk pyjamas, it's hard to feel that one is being drawn into any very searching or urgent discussion about identity and difference.) There were some splendid effects in this show, but I wasn't sure that they couldn't have been achieved just as well or even better by only one performer in cream silk pyjamas, standing perfectly still and reading out the entire script from the book.

The question of good theatrical taste and how much to represent materially was also raised this year by two productions of *The Tempest*, seen in London during the autumn of 2000, one at the Pit and one at the Almeida. In the Pit, James Macdonald's RSC production (which subsequently toured small venues throughout the country) made what for this company was a fairly daring use of video, projecting footage of real sea and clouds onto a blank white screen behind the acting area (at first as if through a telescope, as if showing Prospero's view from the island as he looks for Alonzo and Antonio's ship), and later displaying some rather beautiful images of wheat and of peacock feathers to indicate Ceres and Juno during Prospero's masque. In case anyone suspected the production of inclining towards cinematic realism, however, all the highly-stylized music in this production (composed, to great effect, by Orlando Gough) was chanted by visible singers who encircled the acting area from time to time, and there was nothing very naturalistic about its central performance. As Prospero, Philip Voss was seraphic throughout: he spoke his lines beautifully, but gave every impression that the beautiful speaking of his lines was all that he had on his mind, never seeming very troubled or vengeful or anxious, and in his epilogue he sounded more rather than less actorish without his magic than he had done with it. What shone in this production, unexpectedly, were not so much the customarily

showy Ariel (though Gilz Terera's eerily sensual and remote creature was fascinating enough, especially in the silvery night-club-chanteuse dress he wore as a nymph of the sea) or Caliban (Zubin Varla, and a lot of make-up), but the scenes between Alonzo, Antonio, Sebastian and Gonzalo – Alonso's remorseful near-breakdown over the supposed loss of Ferdinand was rendered with real complexity and force by Paul McLeary. This was a prettily designed production in a clean-lined, modern manner, but despite much to enjoy around its perimeter it lacked a central conflict to animate and drive it.

This pattern was reversed by Jonathan Kent's production at the Almeida, where nearly all the psychological complexity, depth and conflict were Prospero's, and where an equally impressive set's flirtation with potential vulgarity took the form not of photographically represented water but of the real thing. The performance began with an abrupt blackout simultaneous with a deafening clap of thunder and the first hissings of some real hose-pipe simulated rain, and as the lights gradually rose they revealed an acting area largely submerged under gallons of water. For this last show before the company moved out during refurbishments, Paul Brown had stripped the Almeida's stage area down to something that resembled a building site, or rather a derelict theatre awaiting demolition, and had then flooded it, leaving little piles of masonry just sketching the outlines of what seemed to be a rock pool on Prospero's island. The effect of this was generally to keep the newcomers to the island at a distance, compelled to spend a lot of time behind the central pool (often acting up and down a narrow diagonal ramp set against the raw brick back wall of the building) while Prospero and Miranda, more accustomed to this terrain, commanded the house from the rocks further forward. But the character with the closest relationship with this pool was the part-time sea-nymph Ariel, played by a very fit if not especially well-spoken Aidan Gillen, who made his first entrance in 1.2 by air – flown in from above, dangling upside-down from a rope – but his first exit by water, diving perpendicularly down from the rope and vanishing completely under the pool's surface. This splendid effect, repeated at intervals, read quite differently according to where one was in the auditorium: from the circle one could see Gillen swim away towards the wings through an underwater doorway, but the audience in the stalls had no way of knowing for sure that he hadn't drowned until his next entrance, when he bobbed up like a seal in the middle of the pool (as, later, did the delusive magic banquet tantalizingly offered to Alonzo and his party).

It's an immense tribute to Ian McDiarmid that his performance as Prospero wasn't completely upstaged by all this, but it never was. To McDiarmid and Kent, the play was not a lyrical meditation but an exercise in psychological suspense, its central drama not so much Prospero's recollected renunciation of his god-like magic as his struggle to rehabilitate himself, mentally and spiritually, for normal life among other human beings. In dishevelled modern dress in 1.2, he was more like Ben Gunn than Merlin, his twisted, angry reiteration of his wrongs the voicing of an obsession that over the preceding twelve years of exile had all but eaten him alive. Anna Livia Ryan's strong Miranda, accordingly, spent this scene not just feeding obedient cues and sounding naively astonished about the plot, but trying anxiously to manage her father's near-madness, still playing the role Prospero remembered her playing at three when they were cast adrift, when only her presence in the boat enabled him to avoid complete despair (1.2.151–8), and evidently not yet knowing whether or not to believe anything that he was telling her. She appeared to offer the last hold on sanity and the last possibility of human interaction to a man otherwise trapped in the past, spiritually ossified by anger and vindictiveness. (Malcolm Storry's Caliban, intriguingly, was almost Prospero's age, and the magus had already recognized him as part of himself well before the last scene, introvertedly referring to 'the beast Caliban' at his interruption to the masque as if in self-reproach). This strategy of playing Prospero as someone at first not obviously capable of subduing his enemies at all, or even of speaking cogently with them, one who over the course of the play pulled himself together at terrible personal cost, worked

extraordinarily well: the play here offered the very moving spectacle of a man gradually and only just managing to heal himself, giving up his staff as reluctantly a convalescent might give up a crutch. The stages of his parting from Ariel were particularly well marked. At the end of the spirit's narration of his musical misleading of Caliban, Stefano and Trinculo (4.1.184), Ariel hung from his rope with a gesture of inviting applause for what he knew would be one of his last opportunities to show off, and after a little pause it suddenly occurred to Prospero to acknowledge him, meeting his eyes as never before, and beginning to clap. 'This was well done, my bird' was a belated hello as well as the beginning of a goodbye. Prospero's parting from the audience was as hard-won and emotional, too: the house-lights came on for Prospero/McDiarmid's epilogue, the dilapidated old theatre apologetically bidden farewell to along with the role, and at the end of it the entire audience rose to their feet to applaud, something I have very rarely seen a London crowd do. This production may largely have been a vehicle for McDiarmid, but his wonderfully intelligent and articulate performance amply deserved it.

Kent's production left one with the option of regarding all Prospero's magic as a metaphor for his psychological state, or as the staged realization of a fantasy-life he was tentatively learning to live without, but it didn't make any effort to preclude the possibility that he really was a magician and that these his actors really were spirits. The last and most widely praised of the year's revivals of the late plays, however, left no such option open for how to read Shakespeare's dealings with the supernatural, but meticulously played *The Winter's Tale* as a depiction of strictly secular events, each minutely explained as far as could possibly be managed in the terms of a rational modern world. Nicholas Hytner's expensive, glossy show, which played in repertory in the Olivier between May and August, was the Perfectly Composed Production *par excellence*, designed and thought-out to within an inch of its life, and sustained by some excellent acting, some intelligent if not always consistent directorial reading, and a text whose ending turns out to play almost as movingly as an unmagical, unredemptive tragedy as it does as a miraculous blessing.

The good PCP always starts with a thematic keynote message from its director, and this one was no exception: instead of opening with Archidamus and Camillo's little diplomatic conversation before the arrival of the principals, this production offered the spectacle of what turned out to be Mamillius dressed as Time, complete with wings and scythe, reciting sonnet 12 ('When I do count the clock that tells the time...'). The lights came up at the sonnet's close to find Leontes, Hermione, Polixenes and attendants all politely and enthusiastically applauding this little performance, evidently a party-piece to impress his parents' associates, and Archidamus and Camillo only got into their opening dialogue aside while Mamillius further enchanted most of the party nearer the back of the stage with another display of his accomplishments, playing a classical study on the grand piano. The designer Ashley Martin-Davis had been given a much freer hand to create a domestic interior for Leontes than he had been given to set up house for Orsino and Olivia in Stratford, and by the look of it a much larger budget too. Most of the Olivier stage was taken up with representing a large and expensive modern apartment, complete with leather sofa and armchairs: shelves bore silver trophies, and the walls were decorated with framed photos of Leontes and Polixenes playing rugby and cricket together as schoolboys, pictures which were ominously just a little larger than those of Leontes and Hermione getting married. This apparently was an 'apartment' rather than a 'flat', too, since although no one in this cast had an American accent the painted buildings visible through a window looked like Manhattan, the clothes on Leontes and Polixenes were more preppie than aristocratic English (Ralph Lauren as opposed to Jermyn Street, with Alex Jennings' Leontes at first sporting a roll-neck jersey which might as well have had New England Casual written all over it), and the wheeled truck on which Mamillius had piled some of the many expensive toys that littered the carpet was a Radio Flyer – identical in shape to the little truck Ellen Terry towed as Mamillius at the Princess's in

1856, as Hytner probably knew, but made in Illinois and currently sold only in the United States. These puzzling transatlantic details at first encouraged a suspicion that this setting was intended to be half-satiric, as if we were to understand that this Leontes and Hermione were forever desperately trying to look like one of those unbelievably perfect couples seen in expensive home-furnishings catalogues in Massachusetts, and that their unbearably precocious little boy was obliged to look continuously happy and over-achieving in front of his parents' friends like this so as to vindicate their choice of prep-school for him. But there was no mistaking the earnestness with which Jennings' Leontes slipped suddenly into his jealousy, nor the reality of the tenderness he was still intermittently able to show Mamillius (even if his throwing of a rugby ball to him on 'Go play, boy, play' was slightly less convincing than the trophies might have led one to expect). Indeed once Alex Jennings' characteristically lucid performance got into its stride the setting soon ceased to distract, if it ever had. Wherever we were, it was dangerously at the mercy of this man's paranoia, and the carefully assembled status symbols dwindled in importance compared to the tyranny of his mania. Such is the size of the Olivier's stage that for the arrest of Hermione and her separation from her son Ashley-Davis was able to supply a games room, bringing on a full-scale ping-pong table (under cover of two gauzed, potentially translucent screens, which slid across to meet at right angles centre stage to allow for the changing of the set behind continuous action), so that the king's shocking intrusion could interrupt not only Mamillius's tale of sprites and goblins but a game between the two ladies-in-waiting; later (at the start of 2.3) the area behind the gauze screens became the boy's sick room, with the driven, tormented, insomniac Leontes pacing outside.

The character made-over most thoroughly to fit the social setting of the first three acts was Paulina, who was here of the same generation as Clare Skinner's instantly sympathetic, poised Hermione, and just as attractive. A high-maintenance dyed-blonde lady-in-waiting-who-lunches, Deborah Findlay arrived to comfort Hermione in the jail bearing a clutch of designer shopping bags, evidently full of treats carefully chosen from the friends' favourite department stores, and her performance was perfectly socially placed throughout and no less moving or forceful for it. Her re-entry in the trial scene bearing the news of Hermione's death was the more shocking for its sudden abandonment of all decorum, and it formed part of one of the most impressive and moving sequences of this production's first half. The trial was beautifully staged throughout: Hermione was required to sit in a solitary chair behind an enormous desk, from which, scorning the official microphone set on a low stand before her, she rose to deliver her defence, at first a little shakily, then with terrible, numb composure, then shakily again. When the court subsequently broke up into disorder on the news of Mamillius's death – the attendants released with relief from their dutiful obedience to Leontes by the oracle's verdict and rushing with relief to the assistance of the collapsing Hermione – Leontes began to stagger, and after her removal he eventually subsided remorsefully into the condemned chair which his queen had vacated, covering his face with his hands. A long, horrified silence supervened before, head bowed, he began to pray for forgiveness, then another before he very, very slowly and painfully made confession of his attempted murder of Polixenes over the tannoy system, breathing unsteadily into the microphone through his clenched fingers. Paulina returned to deliver the tirade that prefaces the news of Hermione's death from the position the king had adopted as prosecuting counsel, and Leontes was unable to remove his hands from his face and look up – to reveal features that appeared to have aged by years – until 'Prithee bring me / To the dead bodies of my queen and son' some fifty or sixty lines later.

So far, everything more or less matched: we were in a present-day parallel universe in which absolute monarchies looked like the executive suites of multinational corporations, a sort of domesticated equivalent of Pimlott's Elsinore, but in which the Delphic oracle could deliver a judgement from which there was clearly no appeal to any Supreme Court. A first slightly off-key note was hit by this

PCP, however, at the entrance of the Old Shepherd in the following scene. John Normington looked fine – wearing a quilted jacket and tweed cap, he could have stepped straight out of a Range Rover – but when he opened his mouth, it became clear that he might as well have been wearing the usual stock-costume smock, since his accent was standard Mummerset. The costume was contemporary, but the conception of English rural life was antediluvian. This came to matter much more in the second half of the show, and before the shepherd's reappearance after the interval Hytner made what seemed to me another error of judgement, bringing Mamillius back in his Time costume to speak the Act 4 chorus. This seemed a mistake on two counts, firstly because it seemed to imply that the character wasn't really dead, and secondly because although both of the children the production used could just about cope with a sonnet they became inaudible and hard to follow over sixteen rather complicated rhyming couplets.

All thoughts of Time were soon banished, however, by Autolycus, a character to whom Hytner was prepared to sacrifice most of the fourth act. Finding a modern-day analogy to the strolling ballad-singers of the seventeenth century in the figure of the folk-rocker, Hytner supplied Phil Daniels' snapper-up of unconsidered trifles with an old Telecaster and a microphone stand, and re-worked the entire sheep-shearing festival around him as The Sheep-Shearing Festival, a caricature of Glastonbury, complete with a village of tents, a crowd of gormless-looking bead-stringing extras and a painted backdrop of an implausibly sunlit English hillside. This worked beautifully for Autolycus – who peddled souvenir products from a wheeled barrow, performed his songs in a cod-Dylanesque style (strangely, to the slick accompaniment of an offstage band and through an unseen amplifier, instead of through a small portable amp in the manner of a real busker), paraphrased and supplemented some of his lines, and generally revelled in all the incidental satirical jokes this setting made possible. But it was fatal to the rest of the act's characters, who were either upstaged or placed into various false positions or both. The

Old Shepherd seemed to own the land on which the pop festival was taking place, but he didn't talk like a present-day landowner (or like very many shepherds nowadays), and he didn't look at all like the sort of middle-aged man who turns up at such festivals for any other reason: he wasn't even given the pretext of coming to fetch his cut of the money from the organizers in used fivers. Camillo had the sense to disguise himself, albeit badly, as an old hippy, but Polixenes, bafflingly, dressed up for the occasion as another misplaced old-style farmer. Daniel Roberts' slight Florizel didn't seem to know quite what he was doing there: he was dressed in impeccable fawn Oxford bags, and it looked as though his sole concession to the counter-culture had been to undo the top button of his expensive white shirt and remove his Eton prefect's tie. Worst of all, Melanie Clark Pullen's Perdita, despite the educated syntax and vocabulary the script gives her, had grown up speaking the same apocryphal West Country dialect as her adoptive father, with the result that she sounded, frankly, rather stupid, just like Brenda Tucker in *The Archers*. In her dialogue with Polixenes, her resistance to the cross-breeding of flowers sounded like a sullen attack on genetically modified crops naively parroted from elsewhere, and unusually she really did seem to be leading Florizel astray much as his father claims. At the beginning of their conversation at the start of 4.4 she passed him what was evidently the prince's first joint, so that his opening remark, as he stared wide-eyed at her through the smoke, became an outrageous pun: 'These your unusual weeds to each part of you / Does give a life . . . ' (2001 was a year in which Shakespeare's characters seemed topically to have entered the legalization debate in force). It was all very funny and good-tempered – though the extension of the Autolycus–Mopsa–Dorcas trio 'Get you hence, for I must go' into a dated pastiche of rap music, with added lyrics quoting from lots of other Shakespeare plays, got fairly tedious – but so lightweight that the emotional momentum of the first three acts, instead of being transmuted and continued by other means, was simply lost, and the anticipated resolution of the off-centred Florizel and Perdita plot threatened to

diminish the force of the ensuing act rather than compound it.

Back in Sicilia, the plain walls behind Leontes and Paulina at the start of Act 5 bore immense poster-sized portraits of Mamillius and Hermione (a mistake, this, since they ought to have pre-empted Perdita's curiosity to see the statue in order to find out what her mother had looked like, and seemed again to be slightly satirical at Leontes' expense in a way which Jennings' performance of unaffected sincerity did nothing to invite, hinting that his grief was all a public show). A large table-like black marble slab bore an elaborate inscription detailing his wife and son's fates and his responsibility for them (as promised at 3.2.231–42: the epitaph ended, cutely enough, by quoting 'Fear no more the heat o' the sun'). During his conversation with a much-mellowed Paulina – during which the two often touched each other affectionately, looking slightly like a married couple – he sat down at this slab, as if his family's grave had become his office job. Jennings had greyed his hair slightly, and a slightly stiff upper-class manner and a much more old-fashioned suit than he had worn for his previous appearance at the trial seemed deliberately to suggest another royal guiltily overshadowed by a dead wife, Prince Charles. This allusion became as good as explicit at the opening of the statue scene, when the king, entering past a completely empty plinth at the back of the stage which was clearly the last of many conceptual works in Paulina's private gallery, constrainedly thanked his hostess for having hitherto shown the royal party 'many – *singularities*' (5.3.12), as though this were a polite euphemism for the modern art which Charles famously loathes. Perhaps this was another gentle dig in a long-running amicable difference of opinion on the subject between two old friends, about to be parted: certainly Hytner's wonderfully intense and unusually desolating take on the statue scene was marked at first by what looked like a valedictory reluctance on Paulina's part to let go of Leontes and give him back to his (first?) wife. But she knew she had to go through with it, if only for the sake of the rustic-sounding young stranger awkwardly in their midst, and at 5.3.87 her promise to make the statue move indeed, descend, 'and take *you* by the hand' was specifically addressed to Perdita. Paulina already knew that Hermione's reappearance was not for her husband. As we should have anticipated all along, and perfectly in keeping with this production's secular logic, there was no magic here, no miraculous restoration, and whatever was restored of Hermione was restored only to her daughter. Unveiled, Hermione knelt, mermaid-on-the-rock style, in a white dress, her eyes cast down, an image of fixed and inconsolable grief. Deeply damaged, and only now just willing to face other people at all, she was reluctant to stir at Paulina's bidding, and when she finally embraced Leontes she did so quite briefly, and as if not quite sure of what she was doing. His immediate response was of indignation at having been duped into thinking her dead (hence 'O, she's warm' sounded baffled and almost angry); this appeared to give place to sheer terror at the prospect of having to face Hermione after all; in any case only a very small proportion of what passed across his face above her shoulder looked like joy. When Hermione was shown the kneeling Perdita, she just tentatively managed her one speech before kneeling too and embracing her, both weeping in silence, both in effect turned inaccessibly back into the grieving statue. An awkward pause supervened, and Leontes' suggestion that the forlorn Paulina should marry Camillo came as a completely unconvincing attempt, confronted by this spectacle and completely excluded from it, to talk his way back into the centre of the scene: it failed dismally. Paulina and Camillo looked profoundly embarrassed, holding hands only under compulsion to humour him for the time being, before, with one devastated last look over his shoulder, an embarrassed Leontes led them away, leaving the audience with the tableau of scarred mother and lost daughter crying as if forever for all that could never be recovered. Meanwhile the incidental music recapitulated the dead Mamillius's piano study from the first scene. The last scene of *The Winter's Tale* usually leaves an audience in tears, as this did, but rarely in the contemplation of such an empty, desolate future for all the play's major characters.

The future of the National under Hytner may be rosier: whatever minor reservations some of his ideas for this play may have occasioned, he has lost nothing of his ability to tease rich, intense performances from his actors, and the work shown here by Jennings, Skinner and Findlay in particular was as good as anything the Olivier has seen. But elsewhere at the end of 2001, the future of the English subsidized classical theatre looks far less assured. Watch this space.

PROFESSIONAL SHAKESPEARE PRODUCTIONS IN THE BRITISH ISLES JANUARY–DECEMBER 2000

NIKY RATHBONE

Most of the productions listed are by professional or semi-professional companies. Productions originating in 1999 or earlier have only been included if there is new information. Details are mainly taken from newspaper reviews held in the Birmingham Shakespeare Library. Many of the companies listed were involved in small-scale tours; where neither review nor listings mark these as professional they are starred. I have also included the principal annual Shakespeare festivals, both professional and amateur.

ALL'S WELL THAT ENDS WELL

Stray Dogs, tour: July 2000
Director: Simon Godwin

ANTONY AND CLEOPATRA

Adaptation

All for Love by John Dryden
Artifice, Twickenham, at Battersea Arts Centre: September 2000
This new company intends to produce non-naturalistic plays, including plays written in verse.

AS YOU LIKE IT

The Crucible Theatre, Sheffield and the Lyric Theatre, Hammersmith: February 2000
Director: Michael Grandage
Designer: Christopher Oram
Music: Julian Philips

Rosalind: Victoria Hamilton
Victoria Hamilton won the Barclays Regional Theatre award for Best Actress.

The Gate Theatre, Dublin: February 2000
Director: Jonathan Miller
Designer: Bruno Schwengl

Heartbreak Productions, Leamington Spa, tour with *The Tempest*: June 2000
Director: Maddy Kerr

Pentameters Theatre Club, Hampstead*: June 2000
Directed by Matthew Brenher
Played in repertory with *Henry V*. The company hopes to tour America.

Manchester Royal Exchange: July 2000
Director: Marianne Elliot
Designer: Liz Ascroft
Seen as a journey from tyranny to religious reconciliation and emphasizing the androgynous attraction of Rosalind.

The RSC at the Royal Shakespeare Theatre, Stratford: March 2000
Director: Greg Doran
Designer: Kaffe Fassett
Rosalind: Alexandra Gilbreath

Ballet

As You Like It
Cwmni Ballet, Gwent, tour: May 2000

Artistic director: Darius James
Choreographed for eight dancers.

THE COMEDY OF ERRORS

The RSC at the Royal Shakespeare Theatre, Stratford: April 2000
Director: Lynne Parker
Designer: Blaithin Sheerin
Music: Bell Helicopter

OpenHand at the Cambridge Shakespeare Festival: July 2000
Producer: David Crilly

Pendley Manor, Tring: July 2000
Director: John Branston
Annual Shakespeare production with professional casts.

CORIOLANUS

The Almeida Theatre at the Gainsborough Studios, Islington, London and New York: June 2000
Director: Jonathan Kent
Designer: Paul Brown
Music: Jonathan Dove
Lighting: Mark Henderson
Coriolanus: Ralph Fiennes
Aufidius: Linus Roache
Set in the shell of the old film studios, against a jagged, riven wall of brick, symbolizing the disunity of the state. Played in repertory with *Richard II*.

HAMLET

Fifth Column at the Oval House Theatre, Kennington: March 2000
In this production, influenced by Meyerhold, two actors played Hamlet to suggest his dual nature.

Shakespeare's Globe, London: May 2000
Director: Giles Block
Designer: Jenny Tiramani
Music: Claire van Kampen
Hamlet: Mark Rylance

Claudius: Tim Woodward
Gertrude: Joanna McCallum
Rylance's performance refined on his previous creation of the role with the RSC.

Galleon Theatre Company at Greenwich Playhouse, London: June 2000
Director: Bruce Jamieson
Designer: Lily Elms
Hamlet: Rupert Fawcett
The political elements of the plot were cut in a production focused on family relationships.

Stamford Shakespeare Company, Tolethorpe Hall, Rutland: June 2000
Annual amateur Shakespeare production.

The Original Shakespeare Company at The Bothy, North London: June 2000
Directed by Patrick Tucker
Intended to reproduce the conditions of Elizabethan unrehearsed performance.

The Royal National Theatre, London and tour: July 2000
Director: John Caird
Designer: Tim Hatley
Music: John Cameron
Lighting: Paul Pyant
Hamlet: Simon Russell Beale
Polonius/Grave-digger: Denis Quilley
Claudius: Peter McEnery

Wellmade Theatre Company, tour of open-air venues in East Sussex: July 2000

The Deutsches Schauspielhaus, Hamburg at the Edinburgh Festival: August 2000
Director: Peter Zadek
Designer: Wilfred Minks
Hamlet: Angela Winkler
A co-production with the Wiener Festwachen, Schaubuhne am Lehniner Platz, Theatre National de Strasbourg, Zuricher Festspiel, Theaterformen, first produced at EXPO, Hanover, 2000.

PinPoint productions, tour of open-air venues: August 2000
Director: Mike Dodsworth
Played in modern casual dress.

The RSC Fringe Festival, TOP, September 2000
Director: Sam West
Hamlet: Adrian Schiller
A fast-moving production played on the bare white set used for *Richard II.*

Adaptations

Shamlet
In Touch Theatre Company* at the Edinburgh Fringe Festival: August 2000
Rosencrantz and Guildenstern play *Hamlet* as the cast of an amateur production fail to turn up.

Films

Hamlet
Director: Michael Almeryeda
Distributors: Channel Four Films. Film Four, Miramax
Hamlet: Ethan Hawke
Set in modern Manhattan. Denmark is depicted as a USA corporation.
USA release April 2000, UK release December 2000.

The Freethorpe Hamlet
National Museum of Photography, Film and TV, Bradford: October 2000*
A film short made by children from Freethorpe County Primary School, Yarmouth, directed by Roger Hawkins, and based on the 'To be or not to be' soliloquy.

HENRY IV PART 1

The RSC at the Swan Theatre, Stratford: April 2000
Director: Michael Attenborough
Designer: Es Devlin

Music: Paddy Cunneen
Henry IV: David Troughton
Prince Hal: William Houston
Falstaff: Desmond Barrit
Produced as part of the RSC's Millennium season: *This England: The Histories.*

HENRY IV PART 2

The RSC at the Swan Theatre, Stratford: June 2000
Director: Michael Attenborough
Designer: Es Devlin
Music: Paddy Cunneen
Henry IV: David Troughton
Prince Hal: William Houston
Falstaff: Desmond Barrit
Produced as part of the RSC's Millennium season: *This England: The Histories.*

HENRY V

Pentameters Theatre Club*, Hampstead: June 2000
Henry: Matthew Brenher
In repertory with *As You Like It.* The company hopes to tour America.

The Union Theatre*, London Fringe: July 2000
Directors: Marshall Griffin and Matthew Ashwood
Henry: Marshall Griffin

Tour de Force Theatre Company at Arundel Castle, Arundel Festival: August 2000
Director: Joe Harmston
Music: Andy Whelan
Henry: James Simmons
A pro-am production.

The RSC at the Royal Shakespeare Theatre, Stratford: August 2000
Director: Edward Hall
Designer: Michael Pavelka
Music: Simon Slater
Henry: William Houston

Produced as part of the RSC's Millennium season: *This England: The Histories.*

JULIUS CAESAR

Tenth Planet* upstairs at the Gatehouse, London Fringe: August 2000
Director: Craig Giovanelli
Set in 1930s New York.

The Young Vic, London: September 2000
Director: David Lan
Designer: Stephen Brimson Lewis
Music: John Harle
A modern-dress production focused on personal relationships.

The Crypt Arts Centre, Dublin Castle, Ireland: September 2000
Director: Joe Devlin
Designer: Sandra Walsh

Troy Productions at Baron's Court Theatre, London: October 2000
Director: Jonathan Price
Designer: Rebecca Chadwick
The production experimented with gender reversal; Caesar, Cassius and Antony were played by women.

KING LEAR

Shakespeare at the Tobacco Factory, Bedminster, Bristol: February 2000
Director: Andrew Hilton
Music: John Telfer
Lear: Roland Oliver
A traditional production in a new, intimate theatre.

OpenHand Theatre Company at the Cambridge Shakespeare Festival: August 2000

Bristol Old Vic: October 2000
Director: Jan Sergent
Lear: Bill Wallis
Kent: Jimmy Yuill
A modern-dress production.

Opera

King Lear
The Alexander Theatre, Helsinki, Finland: September 2000
Producer: Kari Heiskanen
Conductor: Okko Kana
Designer: Markka Hakari
Composer/Lear: Matti Sallinen
A new Finnish opera, using Rossin's translation into Finnish. Included for interest.

LOVE'S LABOUR'S LOST

Southend Shakespeare Company, tour of Essex: July 2000
Amateur Shakespeare company.

Film

Love's Labour's Lost
Intermedia Films and the Shakespeare Film Company, Pathe Films, Miramax
Director/Berowne: Kenneth Branagh
A 1930s musical version set to music by Cole Porter and Irving Berlin.
The Shakespeare Film Company has been set up to produce compelling and exciting films of Shakespeare.
Release date: March 2000

MACBETH

The RSC
The 1999 production starring Antony Sher and Harriet Walter toured to New York and Boston, and returned to the Young Vic, London. It was also shown on TV in January 2001. See *Shakespeare Survey 54.*

Maquama Theatre Company, Southwark Playhouse, London and national tour: February 2000
Director: Alan Whetham
Designer: Rebecca Core
A modern-dress production.

Theatre Unlimited, London and tour: February 2000
Director: Christopher Geelan
Designer: Kate Burnett
Macbeth: Rupert Wickham
Touring with *Measure for Measure* as part of the community project, *Take the Stage.*

Theatre Nomad, the Astor Theatre, Deal, local tour and world tour: February 2000
First performed at the Hong Kong Festival. The actors come from various countries and re-interpret classic texts in a non-traditional way.

Two-Way Mirror*, London Fringe: March 2000
Director: Ricardo Pinto.

Battersea Arts Club: March 2000
Director: Tom Morris
Designer: Ti Green
Macbeth: Corin Redgrave
Lady Macbeth: Amanda Harris

Sandyback Theatre, MAC, Birmingham and tour: April 2000
Director: Maria Ring
First performance, Cherbourg, France.
A modern-dress production set among drug dealers, combining film with live performance.

The Citizens Theatre, Glasgow and tour of Scotland: May 2000
Director: Mary McCluskey
Designer: David Carter
The set comprised white and scarlet drapes.

Shakespeare at the George, Huntingdon: June 2000
Annual amateur Shakespeare production.

Rainbow Theatre Company, tour of open-air venues around Worthing: July 2000
Tour, with *Much Ado About Nothing.*

Dolce Vita Theatre Company, tour of open-air venues: August 2000
Played in traditional Scottish costume.

The Long Overdue Theatre Company, Theatr El, Dyfed, Wales and tour of Ireland: September 2000
A multicultural production for school audiences which included Zulu war dances, Balinese masks and visual pyrotechnics.

Fluellen, Swansea; Cardiff and tour of South Wales: September 2000
Director: Peter Richards
UK and European tours are planned for 2001.

Bitesize Theatre Company, tour of UK schools and colleges: October 2000
Played using Scottish accents.

Adaptations

Macbeth, False Memory by Dorothy Levy
The Actors Touring Company, Waterman's Arts Centre, London, Lyric Hammersmith and tour: March 2000
Director: Nick Phillipou
Designer: Zelina Hughes
A play about murder, guilt and revenge based on Shakespeare's play and its sources, set in the world of business.

Macbeth
Movingstage on the Barge Theatre, London Fringe: March 2000
Director: Gren Middleton
A puppet production with Toby Stephens recorded as the voice of Macbeth.

Macbeth
In Fieri*, the Studios, Beckenham, Kent and tour: April 2000
An adaptation for three actors using puppets, masks and performance art.

Makinde by Femi Elafowojo Jr.
The Oval House Theatre, Kennington, London: April 2000
A play set in the Nigerian civil war, inspired by *Macbeth* and West African theatre traditions.

Macbeth 2000
Albany in Education with Little Fish Films, The Deptford Albany, London Fringe: April 2000
A semi-promenade production focused on modern warfare.

Macbeth
The Shakespeare Company of Japan at the Edinburgh Fringe Festival: August 2000
Adapted by Shimodate, in Japanese.

MacHomer
Rick Miller one-man show, Edinburgh Fringe Festival: August 2000
The Simpsons play *Macbeth*. A very successful show from the USA.

Macbeth-Moment
ITI Theatre at the Edinburgh Fringe Festival: August 2000
Described as a collage of scenes and reflections on *Macbeth* performed by an international cast led by directors from Russia, Romania, USA and UK.

MacBeth
Shakespeare 4 Kidz, tour: September 2000
Adapted by Julian Chenery
A musical and puppet adaptation for children aged four to seven.

Macbeth
One-man performance adapted and presented by Simon Floyd, Thetford: September 2000.

Macbeth
Red Pear Theatre at the Kings Head, Islington, London: November 2000
An American actors' collective of seven actors. The actors remained on stage, observing the action.

Radio

Macbeth
BBC Radio 3: September 2000
Directed by Richard Eyre

Macbeth: Ken Stott
Lady Macbeth: Phyllis Logan

MEASURE FOR MEASURE

Theatre Unlimited, tour with *Macbeth*: February 2000
Director: Christopher Geelan
Designer: Kate Burnett
Angelo: Rupert Wickham

The Library Theatre, Manchester: February 2000
Director: Chris Honer
Designer: Michael Pavelka
A modern-dress production which used pornographic video footage to suggest the depravity of Vienna.

Adaptation

A Millennium Measure for Measure
Siege Perilous Project at the Edinburgh Fringe Festival and the Hill Street Theatre, London Fringe: August 2000
A contemporary adaptation; sexual harassment in the boardroom.

THE MERCHANT OF VENICE

The Palace Theatre, Southend: March 2000
Director: Roy Marsden
Designer: Simon Scallion
Shylock: Robert Demeger
Sumptuous period costumes and a simple white set.

Adaptation

BareBones Theatre, tour: March 2000
A group of Jewish converts at the court of Queen Elizabeth I enact the play using music, songs and stories.

THE MERRY WIVES OF WINDSOR

OpenHand in Cambridge college gardens for the Cambridge Shakespeare Festival: July 2000
Producer: David Crilly

Opera

Falstaff by Giuseppe Verdi
Opera North, tour: 2000
Director: Caroline Giles
Conductor: Steven Sloane
Falstaff: Cinal Coud
A revival of the 1997 production.

Falstaff by Giuseppe Verdi
The Royal Opera House, Covent Garden, London:
January 2000
Director: Graham Vick
Designer: Paul Brown
Conductor: Bernard Haitink
Falstaff: Paolo Gavanelli
Production opened December 1999.

A MIDSUMMER NIGHT'S DREAM

The Arches Theatre Company, Citizens Theatre,
Glasgow and tour of Scotland: March 2000
Director: Andy Arnold
A very physical production set in the fifties with
music provided by the actors on stage.

Shakespeare at the Tobacco Factory, Bedminster,
Bristol: March 2000
Director: Andrew Hilton
A new 200-seat theatre in a converted warehouse,
dedicated to producing Shakespeare.

Theatre Set Up, tour: June 2000
Director: Wendy McPhee

The Southsea Shakespeare Actors the New Theatre
Royal, Plymouth: June 2000
Amateur Shakespeare company.

The New Shakespeare Company at the Open Air
Theatre, Regent's Park, London: June 2000
Director: Alan Strachan
Designer: Kit Surrey
Music: Catherine Jayes

The British Touring Shakespeare Company*, tour
of west country open-air venues, with *Much Ado
About Nothing*: June 2000

C'est Tous, Marsden Theatre, Worden Park,
Leyden, Lancs, tour: June 2000

Wales Actors Company, Gwent, tour of open-air
venues in Wales: July 2000
Director: Paul Garnault

The Northcott Theatre, Exeter, in Rougemont
Gardens: July 2000
Director: Ben Crocker

Cannizaro Park Open Air Theatre, Wimbledon:
August 2000
Director: Jenny Lee
Annual Shakespeare festival production.

Lincoln Shakespeare Company, Lincoln Castle:
August 2000
Director: Rob Smith
A pro-am production.

OpenHand in Trinity College gardens for the
Cambridge Shakespeare Festival: August 2000.
Producer: David Crilly

Nottingham Playhouse: September 2000
Director: Richard Barton
Designer: Edward Lipscomb
Played in repertory with J. M. Barrie's *Dear Brutus*,
a fantasia on *A Midsummer Night's Dream*.

The Original Shakespeare Company at Elmbridge
Arts Festival: September 2000
Director: Graham Pountney
An all-female cast.

Almond Rock Theatre Company* at the Man in
the Moon, King's Road, London: November 2000
Director: Peter Gallagher.
Modern dress.

Adaptations

Brenddwyd Noswyl Ifan
Welsh translation by Gwyn Thomas
Ysgol Glanaethwy private drama school, Bangor at
Theatre Gwynedd, Bangor: April 2000

Commissioned and published by the Welsh Joint Education Committee.

A Midsummer Night's Dream
Oddsocks tour: June 2000
Director/Adaptor: Andy Barrow
A vigorous, comical production played on and around a touring wagon stage and presented as though played by a company of Elizabethan strolling actors.

A Midsummer Night's Dream
Shakespeare 4 Kidz, New Theatre Royal, Plymouth Shakespeare Festival and tour: July 2000
Presented with workshops for children.

The Donkey Show
Project 400 Theatre Group, New York City Pyramid Club at the Edinburgh Fringe Festival: August 2000
Director: Randy Weiner
A gender bending cult show set in Club Oberon. A UK tour is planned for 2001.

Dear Brutus by J. M. Barrie
Nottingham Playhouse: September 2000
Director: Richard Baron
Designer: Edward Lipscomb
A revival of Barrie's play. A mysterious old man manipulates the minds of his guests on Midsummer Night. Played in repertory with *A Midsummer Night's Dream*.

The Dream, adapted for children by Cornelius and James
Guildhall Theatre, Derby: October 2000
Director: Susan Leech
Will: Neil Canham
Set outside the Globe. With the help of puppets, actor Will Kemp explains the play which is taking place inside.

A Midsummer Night's Dream
Shakespeare Unplugged; Royal National Theatre schools tour: November 2000.
An adaptation for eight actors.

MUCH ADO ABOUT NOTHING

Northern Broadsides, Halifax, West Yorkshire Playhouse and tour: February 2000
Director: Barrie Rutter.

Mad Dogs and Englishmen, tour: June 2000.

The British Touring Shakespeare Company*, tour of open-air venues in the West Country, with *A Midsummer Night's Dream*: June 2000.

The R. J. Williamson Company, tour of open-air Shakespeare festivals: July 2000
Director/Benedick: R. J. Williamson

The New Shakespeare Company, the Open Air Theatre, Regent's Park: July 2000
Director: Rachel Kavanaugh
Designer: Kit Surrey
Music: Terry Davies
Beatrice: Nicole Redmond
Benedick: Tom Mannion
A World War II setting in the grounds of an English country house.

Rainbow Theatre Company, tour of open-air venues around Worthing with *Macbeth*: July 2000

OpenHand in Girton college gardens for the Cambridge Shakespeare Festival: August 2000

OTHELLO

Sixty Six Theatre Company* at the Etcetera Theatre, London Fringe: June 2000
Director: Robert Deering
A minimalist white backdrop and bureaucratic setting.

The Groundlings Theatre Company, New Theatre Royal, Portsmouth and tour of Shakespeare festivals with *Twelfth Night*: July 2000
Director: Bruce Wall

Opera

Othello by Gioachino Rossini
The Royal Opera House, Covent Garden, London: January 2000

Director/designer: Pier Luigi Pizzi
Artistic director: Patric Schmid
Conductor: Gianluigi Gelmetti
Othello: Bruce Ford
Desdemona: Elizabeth Futral
First performance of this production: Teatro Rossini, Pesaro, Italy, 1998.

PERICLES

Ludlow Castle, the Ludlow Festival: June 2000
Director: James Roose-Evans
Designer: Bruno Santini
Pericles: Stephen Beckett

A and BC Theatre Company, North Lawn, Lincoln's Inn, London and Canterbury: August 2000
Directors: Gregory Thompson and May Jepson
Pericles: Paul Lecoux
An open-air production played around an audience seated on upturned oil drums.

Adaptations

Islands by Anita Sullivan
The RSC Fringe Festival, TOP: September 2000
Described as an epic, surreal journey through Shakespeare's *Pericles* and the personal and political dilemmas of modern life.

RICHARD II

The Almeida Theatre at the Gainsborough Studios, Islington, London: March 2000
Director: Jonathan Kent
Designer: Paul Brown
Music: Jonathan Dove
Lighting: Mark Henderson
Richard: Ralph Fiennes
Bolingbroke: Linus Roache

The RSC at the Other Place, Stratford: March 2000
Director: Steven Pimlott
Designer: Sue Willmington
Music: Jason Carr
Richard: Sam West
Bolingbroke: David Troughton

Adaptation

Richard II
Lancaster Castle: October 2000*
Director: Stephen Tomlin
A promenade production cut to ninety minutes and focusing on the history of Lancaster.

RICHARD III

NU Chamberlain's Men*, Hull, tour: January 2000
Director: Mike Carter

The Artemis Project at St. Luke's Church, London Fringe: March 2000
Director: Bryan Tofeh
Richard: Sonia Ritter
This new company has been formed to allow women the opportunity to play classic roles.

Galleon Theatre Company, Greenwich Playhouse, London: October 2000
Director: Stephen Wisker
Richard: Tom Rushforth
Set in a bare space dominated by a broken mirror; reflecting Richard's fractured personality.

Adaptation

Richard III
The 1am Theatre Company* at the Edinburgh Fringe Festival, August 2000
Described as a shortened version for a new ensemble.

ROMEO AND JULIET

Showscape Productions* and the United Spirits Theatre*, Westminster Theatre, London: January 2000
Director: Martin Scott Gilmore
Designer: Annabel Hill
The designs were influenced by Japanese theatre.

Norwich Theatre Royal: February 2000

Leicester Haymarket: February 2000
Director: Nona Shepphard

Designer: Marsha Roddy
Set in seventeenth-century India with the Montagues played as white Christians and the Capulets as Moslems.

Illyria, tour of National Trust open-air venues: May 2000
Director: Oliver Gray
The production toured to Canada and the USA in 1999 and 2000.

Chapterhouse Theatre Company, tour of open-air venues: June 2000
The company perform traditional productions of Shakespeare.

The RSC at the Royal Shakespeare Theatre, Stratford: June 2000
Director: Michael Boyd
Designer: Tom Piper
Music: Stephen Warbeck
Romeo: David Tennant
Juliet: Alexandra Gilbreath

OpenHand in Cambridge college gardens for the Cambridge Shakespeare Festival: July 2000
Producer: David Crilly.

The Royal National Theatre: September 2000
Directors: Tim Supple and Trevor Nunn
Designer: Robert Innes Hopkins
Romeo: Chiwetel Ejiofor
Juliet: Charlotte Readle
Set in post-colonial Africa with the Capulets played as white and the Montagues as black.

The Original Shakespeare Company at the Elmbridge Festival: September 2000
Director: Graham Pountney.
The company also performed *A Midsummer Night's Dream*.

The Royal Lyceum Theatre, Edinburgh: October 2000
Director: Kenny Ireland

Designer: Hayden Griffin
Romeo: Kanana Kirimi
Juliet: Garry Collins
Set in a modern Middle East war zone with the Montagues and Capulets played as Christians and Moslems.

Adaptations

Romeo and Juliet
Theatre by the Lake*, Keswick: April 2000
Director: Ian Forrest
Designer: Martin Johns
Played in the round by seven actors.

Romeo and Juliet
Chicken Shed Theatre*, Southgate, London: July 2000
Chicken Shed are a community theatre working with young people and linked to the music group.

Romeu & Julieta
Grupo Galapao, Minas Gerias, Brazil at Shakespeare's Globe, Bankside, London: July 2000
A commedia dell' arte street theatre production performed in Portuguese using a 1930s translation by Onestado de Pennaforte.

Ballet

Romeo and Juliet
The Scottish Ballet at the Festival Theatre, Edinburgh and tour: June 2000
Choreography: Robert North
Music: Sergei Prokofiev
Romeo: Adam Cooper
Juliet: Mia Johansson

Romeo and Juliet
The Preljocaj Ballet at Sadlers Wells, London: October 2000
Choreography: Angelia Preljocaj
Music: Sergei Prokofiev
A one-act ballet about socio-political repression set in a modern totalitarian state.

Film adaptation

Romeo Must Die
Warner Brothers
Script: Mitchell Kapner
Director: Andrzej Bartkowiak
Music: Stanley Clarke and Timberland
Romeo: Jet Li: Han Singh
Juliet: Aaliyah: Trish O'Day
A martial arts film, loosely related to *Romeo and Juliet*, about corruption in the Hong Kong construction business.
Release date: October 2000

THE TAMING OF THE SHREW

The RSC, world tour
Director: Lindsay Posner
See *Shakespeare Survey 54*

THE TEMPEST

The Abbey Theatre, Dublin: January 2000
Director: Conal Morrison
Costumes: Joan O"Cleary
Music: Conor Linehan
Prospero: Lorcan Cranitch
Set in the Victorian period.

Gloriana Productions, Richmond tour: February 2000

A and BC Theatre Company, Bath Shakespeare Festival, the Edinburgh Fringe Festival and tour to Prague and Gdansk: March 2000.
See *Shakespeare Survey 54*.

Logos Theatre Company, Wimbledon Studio Theatre: April 2000
Director: Melissa Holston

Shakespeare's Globe, Southwark, London: May 2000
Director: Lenka Udovicki
Prospero: Vanessa Redgrave
Caliban: Jasper Britton
A modern-dress production.

Heartbreak Productions, Leamington Spa, tour with *As You Like It*: June 2000
Director: Barry Stanton.

Stamford Shakespeare company, Tolethorpe Hall, Rutland: July 2000
Annual amateur Shakespeare festival in a purpose-built theatre.

Pendley Manor, Tring: July 2000
Director: Mark Oldknow
Annual Shakespeare production using professional casts.

The Festival Players, tour of open-air venues: August 2000

The Nuffield Theatre, Southampton: October 2000
Director: Patrick Sandford
Prospero: Julian Glover

The RSC at The Pit Theatre, Barbican, London, TOP, Stratford and tour: October 2000
Director: James Macdonald
Designer: Jeremy Herbert
Prospero: Philip Voss
Set on a curving white plywood floor and using video projections to suggest location.

The Almeida Theatre, Islington, London: December 2000
Director: Jonathan Kent
Designer: Paul Brown
Music: Jonathan Dove
Lighting: Mark Henderson
Prospero: Ian McDiairmid
Ariel: Aiden Gillen
Caliban: Malcolm Storry
Set in the flooded shell of the old theatre, using air and water to remarkable effect.

Adaptations

The Tempest
Polka Theatre for Children, Wimbledon at The Broadway, Wimbledon: May 2000

Director: Kate Beales
Designer: Ruth Finn
Music: Jack Pinter
A production which used puppets and actors, played as part of the Shakespeare Centre Millennium Link project.

Caliban and Miranda
Common Ground* at the Ludlow Festival: July 2000
A prequel to *The Tempest* using giant puppets, dance and film.

This Rough Magic
An adaptation by Polly Wiseman and Anton Binder Fireraisers Theatre Company, performing on an oil rig off the West Pier, Brighton beach: 19 August 2000
Director: J. J. Waller
A cast of hundreds took part in this lottery-funded free event which included video, computer imagery and soundtrack. Five actors played Shakespeare's characters. J. J. Waller is a member of the French performance art circus Archaos.

The Tempest
Signal to Noise Theatre Company*, Edinburgh Fringe Festival: August 2000
Director: Chris Goode
The cast of six offer to perform their adaptation in private houses.

TITUS ANDRONICUS

Flexible Deadlock Company*, Glasgow at the Botanic Gardens, Glasgow: July 2000
Director: Leah Altman
A promenade production making dramatic use of torches in the fading light of the evening.

TWELFTH NIGHT

The Brunton Theatre, Musselburgh: February 2000
Director: David Mark Thompson
Designer: Edward Lipscomb

A modern-dress production with Olivia portrayed as the head of a couture fashion house.

Compass Theatre Company, Sheffield, tour: April 2000
Director: Neil Sissons
Designer: Neil Irish
Music: Christopher Madin
Performed by eight actors, doubling, and using a mirror set.

Now and Then Productions* at the CBSO Centre, Birmingham: July 2000
Director: Ben Oldfield
Music: Frank Moon
Performed to a jazz score.

The R. J. Williamson company, tour of open-air venues: July 2000.

The Groundlings Theatre Company at the New Theatre Royal, Portsmouth Shakespeare Festival and tour of open air venues in the south, with *Othello:* July 2000
Director: Alison King.

Stafford Castle: July 2000
Director: Julia Stafford Northcott
Viola: Chloe Newsome
Malvolio: John Challis

Miracle Theatre Company, tour of open-air venues in Dorset: August 2000
Performed by eight actors, doubling.

Birmingham Repertory Theatre: September 2000
Director: Bill Alexander
Designer: Ruari Murchison
Viola: Rakie Ayola
Played in repertory with a revival of the 1998 *Hamlet.*

Adaptations

Twelfth Night
Over the Edge* at the Edinburgh Fringe Festival: August 2000

A five-man company from Zimbabwe, performing an adaptation set in South Africa.

Six Eggs Productions, Cambridge, the ADC Theatre, Cambridge: December 2000
A new company of five professional actors.

TWO GENTLEMEN OF VERONA

Rude Mechanicals Theatre Company, Eastbourne, Theatre of the Green tour of open-air venues in South East England: July 2000
Director: Pete Talbot
Designer: Izzie Hall
A tour of small rural communities.

THE WINTER'S TALE

The European Theatre Group*, the ADC Theatre, Cambridge and European tour: January 2000
Music: Iain Morrison
Leontes: Ben Silverstone
A company of Cambridge students. Ben Silverstone was well known as a child actor.

Salisbury Playhouse: February 2000
Director: Joanna Read
Designer: Nancy Surman
A set which made clever use of lighting to suggest Leontes is imprisoned by his thoughts.

Stamford Shakespeare Company, Tolethorpe Hall, Rutland: June 2000
Annual amateur Shakespeare festival in purpose-built theatre.

Southwark Playhouse, London: June 2000
Director: Erica Whyman
Designer: Sandra Gilmour
Hermione: Victoria Finney
Paulina: Lucy Briers
The action was set before and after Word War I.

Opera

Wintermärchen
Theatre de la Monnaie, Brussels: December 2000

Libretto: Luc Bondy and Marie-Louise Bischofberger
Director: Luc Bondy
Designer: Erich Wonder
Performed in German, with Act 3 in English. Included for interest.

ATTRIBUTED PLAYS

TWO NOBLE KINSMEN

Shakespeare's Globe, Bankside, London: July 2000
Director: Tim Carroll
Designer: Roger Butlin
Music: Corin Buckeridge
Palamon: Jasper Britton
Arcite: Will Keen

The Grace Theatre, London: November 2000
Director: Bronwen Carr
Designer: Jennifer Wilson
Set in the aftermath of World War I, using period songs, and with Palamon and Arcite played as German prisoners of war.

POEMS AND SONNETS

Venus and Adonis
Turlygood Theatre Company* at the Edinburgh Fringe Festival: August 2000
An adaptation in which Shakespeare's Venus goes to Edinburgh.

MISCELLANEOUS

An Act of Will, the Secret Life of William Shakespeare by Michael McEvoy
One-man touring production: February 2000
Set in Stratford in 1613 and concerning Shakespeare's religious beliefs.

Cressida by Nicholas Wright
The Almeida Theatre at the Albery Theatre, London: March 2000
Director: Nicholas Hytner
Designer: Bob Crowley

With Michael Gambon and Charles Kay
Set in the 1630s; a fascinating exploration of the craft of acting at that time.

By Royal Command by Reg Mitchell
King Edward's School, Stratford: April 2000*
A comedy concerning Sir John Falstaff and the writing of *The Merry Wives of Windsor*.

The Millennium Link Project.: The Shakespeare Centre, Stratford, April 2000*
A project linking young people around the world in performances of Shakespeare.

A Celebration Concert
The Swan Theatre, Stratford: May 2000
Five-minute musical pieces, performed as a coda to the Shakespeare Birthday Celebrations, with readings by Harriet Walter and Malcolm Storry. Music composed by Django Bates, Jason Carr, Shaun Davey, Anne Dudley, Dominic Muldowney, Stephen Warbeck, Ilona Sekacz, Mark Anthony Turnage, Guy Wolfenden and Huw Warren.

Dreams
The Leeds Shakespeare Festival: June 2000
Opera North, the English Northern Philharmonia Orchestra and Intake, the Leeds school for the performing arts performing dream sequences from *A Midsummer Night's Dream*, *Richard III* and *The Tempest*.

Romans
Crew of Patches*, tour: June 2000
A comic review based on *Antony and Cleopatra*, *Titus Andronicus* and *Julius Caesar*.

Madman William by Naomi Wallace
ACTual Reality Theatre Company* at Stratford Civic Hall and the Edinburgh Fringe Festival: July 2000
Described as intellectual farce. A confrontation between Shakespeare and his characters. The production is expected to tour the USA in 2001.

Shakespeare Translated: The Bard's 60 minutes of fame
Mithras Productions* at the Edinburgh Fringe Festival: August 2000
TV executives resurrect Shakespeare to boost falling ratings.

My Son Will by Colin George and Anthony Naylor
One-man show, Stratford and proposed tour of American universities: November 2000.

1. CRITICAL STUDIES

reviewed by EDWARD PECHTER

Stephen Greenblatt's *Hamlet in Purgatory* is more about Purgatory than about *Hamlet*; the play, though 'the subtext of this entire book' (p. 157), is given sustained treatment only in the fifth and final chapter. In the first three (the fourth is on ghosts elsewhere in Shakespeare), Greenblatt focuses on the earliest imaginings and theological foundations of Purgatory and its elimination in Reformation England. He acknowledges the venal system of indulgences that served the material interests of a clerical elite but concentrates on the psychic fears and desires which Purgatory answered to and provoked – anxieties about one's own afterlife but also, as a ritualized process to maintain connection with others who have died, a remediation for trauma. Purgatory 'gave mourners something constructive to do with their feelings of grief . . . abandonment and anger' (pp. 102, 103). Greenblatt's *Hamlet* responds to the deprivation that followed the eradication of Purgatory, resituating in the theatre an experience of commemoration and belief – 'the communal ritual assistance given to the dead by the living' (p. 246) – no longer accessible in its original theological and ecclesiastical sites.

This will not seem strikingly new; that 'the power of Shakespeare's theater' is 'linked to its appropriation of weakened or damaged institutional structures' (pp. 253–4) is a claim Greenblatt has already pursued. *Hamlet in Purgatory*, moreover, goes with the flow of current work focused on the

powerful residuum of Catholic sentiment in Renaissance England. To be sure, Greenblatt helped to create this interest; he took religion seriously when it was still largely ignored. But in any case he is not here trying to break new ground or make any boldly original claim about *Hamlet*. Innovative idiosyncrasy – a Lutheran *Hamlet*, say, or a Catholic author – would work against his basic argument that this play appeals across a wide range of fragmented feeling and belief in its original (and subsequent) audiences. Although a Catholic Shakespeare clearly intrigues him, the 'point is surely not to settle issues that Shakespeare has clearly gone out of his way to unsettle or render ambiguous' (p. 244). Even this claim for a functional ambiguity independent of any personal authorial belief has been, as Greenblatt insouciantly grants, anticipated by 'quite a few critics' (p. 308). The blurb puffs *Hamlet in Purgatory* as a 'capacious new reading' of the play, but novelty is just what Greenblatt has to avoid in order to achieve capaciousness.

The autobiographical framing of *Hamlet in Purgatory* works in a similar way. The dust jacket shows Greenblatt beside a road sign, *PURGATORIO (Fraz. di Custonaci)*, and the Prologue revisits memories of his father, the subject of sustained reminiscence in *Learning to Curse*, now extended back to the story of his grandfather's 'dreadful' death, 'clinging to his son and begging for help' (p. 6). Faced with the unabashed confessionality of someone 'incapable of simply bracketing my own origins' (p. 5), Greenblatt trackers will have no trouble tracing a line from 'I want to die' at the end of *Renaissance Self-Fashioning* (p. 255) to 'I began with the desire to speak with the dead' at the beginning of *Shakespearean Negotiations* (p. 1) to the 'lightly ironic piety' that a secular Jew who 'scarcely know[s] how to pray' for a dead father or anyone else offers as 'the personal starting point' for this book (p. 9). Yet in what sense is this personal? The death of fathers and grandfathers (that father lost, lost his) is as common as any the most vulgar thing to sense (Claudius 'usurps not only the kingship but also the language of Protestant mourning' (p. 247)). Greenblatt is not testifying to any special knowledge or experience; we have all been to the border of Purgatory (if not now, yet it will come). His peculiar beliefs can hardly count more than Shakespeare's; Foucault's question applies equally to critical personality: 'what difference does it make who is speaking?' (p. 160).

What Greenblatt does 'want to bear witness to', however, is 'the intensity of *Hamlet*' or, more generally, 'the compelling imaginative interest' of 'literary power', the 'disturbing and vivid' ways in which fiction works on the imagination to take hold of belief in the form of a reciprocally intense and affective – and in this sense personal – response (p. 4). From this base, Greenblatt accounts for Purgatory as 'A Poet's Fable' (Tyndale's phrase). Under the complex institutional apparatus, Purgatory established itself in 'the way that fables seize hold of the mind, create vast unreal spaces, and people those spaces with imaginary beings and detailed events' (p. 33). Narrative is particularly 'serviceable': not just 'an abstract principle of successive events in time but the adventures of a named hero' and 'the principal home of eyewitnessing', it claims 'to record a direct, personal encounter' (p. 86). Hence the knightly protagonist of *Saint Patrick's Purgatory* (Owein Miles his name, Northumberland his local habitation), 'acting as a reader's surrogate, insists' despite councils of caution 'upon a direct encounter, and the reader accordingly follows him into the black hole' of Purgatory (p. 82). In *The Gast of Gy*, a much translated and circulated

fourteenth-century narrative about a haunting, the climax alludes to an unspecified sin committed in the very site of the haunting but known only to the ghost and his widow. In this 'insistence on the personal, the particular, and the experiential against the more abstract and theoretical' (p. 130), the 'enormous institutional structure' of Purgatory is located not at 'the high altar in the church or the papal court of Avignon or the royal throne' but in 'the bedroom in a bourgeois house in a provincial town' (p. 131).

Both the bedroom and the rashness ('My fate cries out...') have counterparts in *Hamlet*, but Greenblatt does not bother to point them out. He seems more concerned with the details in and about the unfamiliar medieval texts – that the haunting 'took place in 1323 (or 1324) in the town of Alès, near Avignon', for instance (p. 105) – than with any interpretive conclusion he might draw about *Hamlet* or anything else. This book has a high proportion of narrative to argument, but narrative dilation is a kind of argument; and when it comes to death, as *Scheherazade* suggests, it may be the best one available.

In this year's other *Hamlet* book, John Lee argues that the 'sense of interiority or inner life' is central to this play and to Shakespearian interest in general. In the second of the book's three parts, Lee offers a detailed history of the first two centuries of *Hamlet* commentary as it developed around 'the concept of character' (p. 1). Against those for whom 'the *Hamlet* problem' does not arise 'until the end of the eighteenth century' (p. 96), Lee argues for continuity, so that Coleridge and Hazlitt are located at a climactic point in the middle rather than at the beginning of an epistemic shift to a new paradigm. More particularly, Lee argues for Hazlitt's pre-eminence. Where Coleridge locates Hamlet's character in a 'germ' or fixed essence, Hazlitt makes the 'constructivist' claim (p. 139) that Hamlet's 'inner variety mirrors the variety of his personal roles, each shaping the other'. Hamlet's interiority is thus developmental or 'processional', a speculative capacity entailing growth rather than an ontologically fixed phenomenon – not 'a question of self-mastery', as for Coleridge, 'but of self-exploration' (p. 143). In the third part, Lee takes on board a variety of arguments about interiority and identity from literary criticism (Anne Ferry, Katharine Maus, et al.), philosophy (Charles Taylor) and psychology (George Kelly's 'personal construct theory' (p. 171)). The main emphasis here is historical – acknowledging the distance between ourselves and any concept of inner character available when the play was first performed, but insisting that lexical deficiency does not preclude the concept's existence.

In seeking to reclaim character as a legitimate topic of interest and to set up Hazlitt rather than Coleridge as the foundation of modern literary study, Lee shares in recent revisionary thought. He chooses, though, to locate his work rather in an adversarial context. The first hundred pages of *Shakespeare's 'Hamlet' and the Controversies of Self* mount a take-no-prisoners assault on New Historicism and Cultural Materialism. The ostensible purpose is to undermine the 'central' claim of such criticism 'to diffuse the "I"', whether 'of dramatic person, text, critic, reader, or author' (p. 30). But decentered subjectivity has been largely relegated to the margins of current work; and elsewhere, too, Lee seems to be flogging dead horses. He claims that 'Althusser's definition of ideology' is 'central to New Historicist' criticism (p. 31) but cannot cite current work. Censuring the 'continued influence' of the 'thoroughly superseded' Lawrence Stone, he has trouble citing any work at all, current or otherwise, admitting that 'this use' is only 'implicit' and so 'hard to footnote', and citing only Jean Howard, who in fact 'quibbles' with Stone – and would probably be amused to find her criticism lumped into 'New Historicist writing' (pp. 38, 39).

Lee claims to be interested in progress, so that 'the literary-critical debate staged here may be moved forward' (p. 149), but his strongest motivation seems to be victory at any cost. In an earlier piece attacking Greenblatt for getting his facts wrong, Lee was so driven by the desire, in Paul Stevens's description, 'more than anything else' to 'nail Greenblatt, to put him in his place', that in the process he got his own facts wrong and was required to apologize in print. Amazingly – obsessively – Lee

reprints and carries on here with this same embarrassing business and with similarly embarrassing results. The problem with nailing people is that it invites them to nail you, and given the fact that interpretation always involves selectivity, they can always find a basis to get you back. Those who live by the *gotcha!* perish by the *gotcha!*, and sometimes historical process itself rather than any critical adversary administers the *coup de grâce*. Lee claims from the outset that 'the absence of *Hamlet*' from New Historicist critics is 'evidence of their tendency to banish the critical and historical past' (p. 1), and he hammers home the point later on. 'This absence' is 'all the more remarkable' given the centrality of 'notions of subjectivity' to New Historicist work. '*Hamlet*, then, plays the ghost in New Historicism's drama, but it is a ghost to which New Historicism has not spoken' (p. 51). That *Hamlet in Purgatory* follows so hard upon these triumphant assertions is bad luck for Lee, but something like it was bound to happen sooner or later. Lee's interests would have been better served trying to find bases of common cause with the critics he seeks so ferociously to discredit. *Survey* readers may want to skip the first section of *Shakespeare's 'Hamlet' and the Controversies of Self* in order to concentrate on the considerable value and interest of the latter two.

Everyone, though, should take delight all the way through *Shakespeare's Noise*. Kenneth Gross looks at *Hamlet*, *Measure*, *Othello*, *Coriolanus* and *Lear* in terms of 'their violent or disorderly forms of speaking: slander, defamation, insult, vituperation, malediction, and curse' (p. 1). 'Slander' gets pride of position here and a chapter to itself, ranging across judicial, theological and ethical commentary as well as poetry and drama to suggest 'the period's larger preoccupation with damaging words' (p. 37) – a virtually obsessive 'culture of slander' (p. 6). Slander, though, 'barely catches the darker motivations for Hamlet' (p. 16); the 'more telling' register of Hamlet's 'way of speaking' is as 'a strange herald for what the Renaissance saw as the shadow world of rumor' (p. 12). In a similar way, curse in *Lear* 'often seems to wander about homeless, without clear aim' (p. 163), so that by 'extending the range of the word' (p. 173), we discover the same 'labile freedom' found in 'the workings of rumor and slander' (p. 163). For Gross, then, Shakespearian noise is the marker of an existential situation, the acoustic embodiment of epistemological uncertainty. 'Rumor and gossip play a part as well', he adds after his opening catalogue of 'disorderly forms of speaking'; but more than bit players, these are the star turns in a drama driven by profound anxiety about a volatile, ungovernable and essentially unknowable external world.

Gross points to a painful double bind in the 'flood of slander litigations entering the courts during the sixteenth century' (p. 55): affirming one's 'common fame' (p. 37) only reinforces dependence on external voices. Attempts to extricate the self from the public world exacerbate vulnerability. Gross analyzes this traumatic situation as 'a measure of Shakespeare's difficulty': where ' "scandal given" and "scandal taken" ' are 'intricately bound up together, even as we are relentlessly, unendingly tasked with sorting them out', the plays 'enact the dance of our soiled knowledge of the world, and of ourselves' (p. 67). Given the fragility of reputation, a retreat into inner selfhood seems the obviously therapeutic response, but introspection and Stoic self-sufficiency did not answer to Renaissance hopes. Acting as though a man were author of himself, Shakespearian protagonists lost their occupations, became titleless – nothing. Hamlet's problem was not just the inevitable soilings of self-knowledge (you cannot 'see yourself'), but an unshakable certainty about the self's own uncleanness. Slander in this radically Protestant world was so painful because of its intuited truth. Feeding 'the soul's prior, archaic attachment to images of its own weakness' and answering 'the rumors of the soul's self-loathing', one 'runs to stand on the exact spot where the arrow shot at random can hit the heart' (p. 50).

In his Introduction to *Shakespeare and Modernity*, one of three engaging Accents on Shakespeare collections this year, Hugh Grady locates the contributions in a set of Enlightenment-generated problems – subjectivity; race, identity and otherness; the aesthetic; and historical periodization: Stephen Cohen analyzes Elizabeth's deployment

of gender 'and the emergence of modern subjectivity' (p. 20), and John Drakakis analyzes textual slippages in speech prefixes, 'Shylock' vs 'Jew', traversing 'the gulf between stereotype and individuated "character" which in part signals the birth of the modern' (p. 110). Lisa Freinkel distinguishes the theological–conversionist anti-semitism of the Renaissance from social–eliminationist versions later on; Eric Mallen keys on the 'Jewish invader' in sci-fi movies (p. 142). Charles Whitney claims that post-Enlightenment concepts of the aesthetic are not relevant to the pragmatic Renaissance, but John Joughin argues we can still get use out of them. Douglas Bruster analyzes 'Renaissance' versus 'Early Modern' in terms of 'the end of history' (p. 168), and Linda Charnes describes the evacuation of the political in postmodern *Hamlet*s.

There are striking similarities between Grady's collection and John Joughin's *Philosophical Shakespeares*. As Grady includes an essay by Joughin, Joughin includes one by Grady as well as another Charnes piece, 'We Were Never Early Modern', revisiting *Hamlet* as the site now of historical evacuation. Her Latour echo is meant to ring the same kinds of changes as in Grady's Introduction on modernity – early, late, and post – and many of Joughin's other contributors are motivated by interests similar to those of Grady as well. Michael Bristol takes on issues of subjectivity, character and interpretation, as does Grady himself arguing 'the need for a differentiated theory of (early) modern subjects' ('On the Need', p. 34). Even Joughin's title reflects continuity with Grady: the 'conflict of the faculties' implied between *Philosophical* and *Shakespeares* is yet another Enlightenment-spawned topic, treated as such by Stanley Cavell in a Foreword regretting that philosophy and literature regard each other 'with indifference or suspicion' (p. xii), and by Joughin in his own Introduction, lamenting that the 'ordering of English' is so 'deeply entrenched' (p. 3).

Cultural analysis has by now mellowed into an established middle age, and despite marketing claims – 'expanding the horizons', 'challenging the preconceptions', 'forefront of critical activity', etc. (Hawkes, 'General Editor's Preface,' p. x and

p. xi) – *Shakespeare and Modernity* and *Philosophical Shakespeares* tend to travel established routes in familiar territory. To suggest routinization, however, would be misleading. Freinkel's sharp analysis of both continuities and discontinuities between Renaissance and modern racial thought should help to advance beyond the polemics in which this vexed subject is currently stalled. Some contributors have negotiated the success of their own preferred practice for an innovative self-reflection and self-criticism. Joughin cautiously withdraws from the tendency in 'recent criticism' to neglect 'the distinctively qualitative aspects of literary meaning', arguing that the 'time is now ripe for a re-examination of the aesthetic' ('Shakespeare, Modernity and the Aesthetic', pp. 65, 66, 62). Grady makes similarly recuperative gestures in the direction of 'the subject', claiming that the critique 'of "liberal humanism" finally collapses' because 'it tries to unify too many contradictory, differentiated social practices' ('On the Need', p. 38). And Michael Bristol sets out more boldly to oppose the 'rudimentary insight' of 'professional scholars' that 'persons are not texts or vice versa', arguing that 'it is reasonable to think about literary characters the way we think about real people' because this is 'what ordinary readers do when they participate in the institution of make-believe' ('How Many Children', p. 19). Bristol is so light-handed and direct that readers may miss his sophisticated complexity. This too is a new thing. Unlike the brain-numbing abstraction cultural critics felt compelled to use in the recent past, the proportion of accessible prose here suggests a justified self-confidence.

This same relaxation, though, can allow for some problematic slippage. Bristol assumes that the 'we' who are 'professional scholars' should be absorbed into the 'we' who are 'ordinary readers', and in his *Survey* piece this year on 'Vernacular Criticism', arguing again on behalf of 'ordinary, or as we might say, vernacular ethical standards' (p. 97), Bristol reiterates his conviction that 'the interpretive practice of expert readers can be brought into a closer approximation to a vernacular criticism' (p. 95). But the differences may be too great to bridge (to describe Gail Paster's work as 'pretty close to Bradley's' (p. 95) pushes intellectual generosity rather far); and even if we could span the gap, it is not clear that we should. 'General intuitions' and 'default assumptions' (p. 90) can lead to banality – what Macbeth 'performs upon the unguarded Duncan is done in careless indifference to the integrity and the life of another person' (p. 101). If formalists and historicists have become too disengaged from Shakespearian characters, their claims for 'defamiliarization' and historical distance acknowledge a Shakespearian strangeness and exceptionality it is our job to protect.

Charnes's attractive pieces produce similar slippages. About 'the Shakespearian fragments' that, 'like "button mushrooms"', are 'popping up' through the 'forest of rotting wood' we call 'contemporary mass culture', she allows as how 'we might speculate' that their ghostly 'presence reassuringly enables us to "infer" that underneath all the historical "debris", behind the fragmenting claims and postures of "postmodernity", there is still "a there there"' ('We Were Never Early Modern', p. 66). But the 'us' reassured by this Bardic Big Cahoona is not identical to the 'we' who speculate anxiously about the need for such reassurance in a world from which historical consciousness has effectively disappeared. Like many contributors to these volumes, Charnes is weighed down with Hegel, who 'crystallized for posterity the notion of Shakespeare as an inaugurator of modernity' and 'enshrined the idea of a progression toward modernity' (Grady, Introduction, p. 3). Hence her felt need for teleological diachrony, meaning in sequence. Anyone who begins one paragraph with 'Some thirty years ago, Norman Rabkin argued' and the next with 'The problem is not, as Francis Barker argued over a decade ago' ('We Were Never Early Modern', pp. 58, 59) will get cold comfort from the amorphous globality in which all those vernacular-speaking Valley Girls delightedly drift. On the other hand, even 'professional scholars', no matter how critically we have assimilated everything from Homer to Žižek, are floating in the same Sargasso Sea. *Le chair est triste, hélas, et j'ai lu tous les livres.* Charnes acknowledges both her qualms and her *jouissances*, sometimes both at once, so that we (or at least I) cannot tell where she is coming from. When 'show me the money' is annotated as a phrase 'immortalized' in 'the 1997 film *Jerry McGuire*' ('Hamlet', p. 209), *immortalized* cannot be taken at face value, but to which of the *we*'s from which this note emanates does the irony belong? Or maybe, to recall Foucault from the beginning, it makes no difference who is speaking.

The third Accents collection, Jean Howard and Scott Shershow's *Marxist Shakespeares*, includes a piece by Kiernan Ryan arguing that 'Marxism has more to learn from Shakespeare today than ever before' (p. 230), chiefly the 'utopian spirit' at home in 'the realm of art' but now systematically 're-pressed' in most Marxist commentary (pp. 228–9). In 'Shakespeare Beyond Shakespeare', however, Shershow dismisses claims for 'esthetic universality' as a 'historical construction' (p. 245) which 'seals itself off from "economic" considerations' only to allow them 'free reign everywhere else'; as in Bourdieu, ' "art for art's sake" is just another way of saying "business is business" ' (pp. 248–9). Also working out of Bourdieu, Richard Wilson similarly disallows claims about aesthetic autonomy: Shakespeare's plays 'in fact remind us that "over that art" which they say "adds" to commerce, is an art that commerce makes' (p. 176).

These divergent perspectives on the aesthetic replay differences between Joughin and Whitney, but the larger context of debate has disappeared. Ryan is the odd man out in *Marxist Shakespeares*, which nowhere else exhibits the revisionist tendencies evident in *Shakespeare and Modernity* or *Philosophical Shakespeares*. The unequivocal tone is set by the Introduction which, in contrast to Grady and Joughin's accommodation, sees an 'unholy alliance between the Enlightenment will to knowledge and the continuing global "drive" of capitalist exploitation' (p. 6) and worries that 'the pure gaze of Enlightenment knowledge' has motivated 'a slippage back to idealist formations' in current criticism, of which 'the aesthetic itself' is 'especially' regrettable (p. 8). Hence Howard and Shershow display almost no interest in accounting for Shakespearian theatrical excitement, focusing rather on a variety of concerns in materialist theory – the

'insufficiently political nature of *American* cultural studies' (pp. 1–2; their emphasis), problems of scientism, economism, the determinacy of class, etc.

The contributors reflect similar priorities. Peter Stallybrass keys on parodic and farcical elements in *The Eighteenth Brumaire*, speculating that Marx's avowed appreciation of such qualities in *Hamlet* may have contributed. For Richard Halpern, *Hamlet* furnishes a metaphorology (ghosts, skulls, haunting) that served both Marx and Derrida and that Halpern himself now uses to reveal Derrida's 'political project' as 'undialectical, and, as a result, self-congratulatory' (p. 51). Dympna Callaghan argues that 'an absolute distinction between aesthetic and productive labor . . . certainly postdates the Renaissance' – an assertion *Othello* is twice called upon to 'demonstrate' (pp. 78, 79). Natasha Korda, reflecting on the ' "marriage" between Marxism and feminism' (p. 82), thinks we ought to focus more on exceptions to the Renaissance law of coverture in order to avoid reproducing patriarchal privilege. Barbara Bowen locates 'a radical political imaginary' in *Salve Deus Rex Judaeorum* (p. 105) where Aemilia Lanyer includes 'a single line' embedded as 'a quotation from Shakespeare's *Rape of Lucrece*' (p. 107) to revise the story's orthodox version (political order founded on rape). Walter Cohen focuses on 'successive but overlapping orientations' of Renaissance trade, arguing that 'even in socio-economic discussions of Renaissance literature and theater', the subordination of 'state policy' to 'economic interests and especially mercantile ones' is inadequately understood (p. 131). Crystal Bartolovich enters a debate about globalization – the nation-state is 'depleted or imperilled' vs. 'the states of the North still maintain a neo-imperial stronghold' ('Shakespeare's Globe', p. 203) – using *Henry V* to argue that language and culture always extend beyond the borders of a ' "possessive nationalism" ' (p. 196). Denise Albanese, analysing recent movies in terms of 'the US imaginary', plays off Branagh's 'regressive formations around the aesthetic' (p. 209) against Luhrmann's 'brilliantly polished, exciting and troubling' (p. 215) alternative to 'the conventional trappings of "quality cinema" and an elite theatrical tradition' (p. 210).

Marxist Shakespeare is thus nothing if not consistent, but whether consistently good or bad is hard to say. Its sustaining values are reversible. If the aesthetic is just an ideological construct, so is sociology; 'Marx' is entitled to the same scare quotes as 'Shakespeare'. As Walter Cohen recognizes, 'hyperbolic claims' for his own kind of analysis will not displace aesthetics or discredit other modes, because the 'accessibility of the plays' and 'cumulative heritage of Shakespearean criticism' will 'render suspect hermetic and previously unimaginable interpretations' (p. 193). Such detachment is rare in a book set up with its own 'self-congratulatory' claims for the power of a 'fully dialectical' methodology to reveal 'actual social relations' (Howard and Shershow, 'Introduction,' p. 11). But critics cannot be expected to deconstruct their own practice (unless their practice is deconstruction). The more important question is how they do what they do, and the answer here is – with consistent brilliance. The essays are all richly informative and strongly argued, not a clunker in the bunch. Readers predisposed to a sociological approach will be especially happy, but even others should be able to suspend disbelief, registering the purposivity under all the noise about political purpose, and taking pleasure in the universal beauty of the book.

Working from a similar agenda, Peter Stallybrass has edited a symposium on 'Material Culture' – twenty-two contributions grouped under the rubrics 'Material Texts', 'Clothes, Properties, Textiles', and 'Languages of Materiality'. As Stallybrass sees it, our professional history imagines culture to transcend materiality, so 'Material Culture' looks like an oxymoron. New bibliographers examined 'paper and ink and binding' only (he claims) to 'find the traces of Shakespeare himself behind the materials' that 'hide and deform him' (p. 123). This editorial position may explain why only four contributors focus on Shakespeare, but *Survey* readers will find this material interesting nonetheless, not least 'The Triumph of King James and His Descendants', a parody of the modes seriously on display in the symposium attributed to

one 'Ana Mary Armygram' – unidentified in the Contributors but possibly one of Randall McLeod's aliases (if it matters).

In one of the Shakespearian pieces, Patricia Parker reflects on the editorial and critical suppression of the location for Q1 *Hamlet*'s 'Mousetrap' not in Vienna but '*guyana*'. 'Guyana' prompts characteristically brilliant associationism from which, however, Parker finally retreats: 'All of this may be immaterial', when 'all that matters' is getting the variant back into view so 'that this occulted murder in guyana will out' (p. 173). In a similar mode, Jonathan Goldberg writes about *King Lear*'s letters (in many different senses), re-calling (his pun) his own earlier writing in order 'to encourage work that might further specify the connections between textual conditions, textual properties, and textuality in its broadest sense' (p. 248). The two other Shakespearian pieces discuss Caliban. Gary Tomlinson analyses the 'famous set-piece' on the island's musical noises in the context of Renaissance magic (p. 239), and Ian Smith locates Caliban with relation to inherited ideas about the linguistic and rational skills of barbarians and Africans, arguing that the play 'throws into sharp relief the colonial implications of Prospero's island regime' soon to be more fully realized in actual experience (p. 255).

The Tempest is the subject of five other essays this year. The play was a main attraction in Margaret Fuller's father's library, and Phyllis McBride describes the canniness with which Fuller appropriated its material, establishing 'credibility with her male readers' (p. 132) in order 'to subvert patriarchal *literary* texts to her advantage' (p. 133, McBride's emphasis). Paul Cefalu argues that recent New World *Tempest*s have 'overlooked' the 'embattled economic relationships' among 'the European colonists themselves' as recorded in 'some central early modern "colonialist" texts' (p. 85). In 'Creature Caliban', Julia Lupton analyses the etymologically indefinite status of 'creature', arguing that Caliban functions as a category-breaking figure of thought, taking 'shape beneath the arc of wonder that moves throughout the play...between animate beings in general and their realization in the form of humanity' (p. 2). Julia Griffin comes to a similar conclusion, though about Ariel. She describes 'one small episode' in *Tempest*'s 'afterlife' (p. 137), in which 'filmy, epicene fantasies' (p. 150) about Prospero/Ariel provided 'an image of extraordinary suggestiveness and appeal' to some 'once-scandalous' modernist writers (p. 137), chiefly Ronald Firbank and Frederick Rolfe, 'Baron Corvo', but also Auden, Thomas Mann and J. M. Barrie et al., with Oscar Wilde a consistent shadowy presence. This piece is about a love that might dare to but simply cannot speak the name of its object, because Creature Ariel is not quite male or female – or even human. Ruth Morse boldly goes to the (for now) final frontier of *Tempest*-inspired recreations; her science fiction 'story – a posterity of pulp – is less well known than the one post-colonialists have told' but speaks across eras and modes from *Robinson Crusoe* to *Blade Runner* (p. 164). Morse would 'go beyond Shakespeare's play' to assess its influence in 'other contexts' but insists on regularizing protocols 'as a control on ostensible "recognition"' (p. 165). She is reluctant to hold *The Tempest* responsible for its own afterlife: 'imitation is not only the sincerest form of flattery, it is the most contagious'; after 'one recreative imitation, inertia may well take over' (p. 174).

'*The Tempest*' and its Travels* may convince readers to think otherwise. Peter Hulme and William Sherman's exciting collection is dedicated to the proposition that the play travels well, and its tripartite distinction – 'Local Knowledge', 'European and Mediterranean Crossroads', 'Transatlantic Routes' – traces 'a journey which proceeds steadily outwards' to the New World 'where it has certainly received some of its most powerful readings' (Preface, p. xi). '*The Tempest*' and its Travels* negotiates more than half its business there: offering pieces on colonial and postcolonial themes; considering Caribbean and Latin American writers who have drawn inspiration from the play; and, in a section 'On the World's Stage', including excerpts from the first English production of Aimé Césaire's *Une tempête* in 1998, a Cuban spinoff called *Otra Tempestad* brought to London also in 1998, and a 1999 Copenhagen production of *Tempest(s)*, staged 'as part of a five year cultural and arts development plan' by the Terra Nova Theatre Institute (Allsopp, '*Tempest(s)*', p. 162).

But in current criticism (like the Cefalu piece just discussed), the trajectory has been more inward than 'outwards'. The editors acknowledge 'recent' efforts to bring 'domestic discourses to bear on *The Tempest*' both 'alongside' the '"colonial reading"' and 'often as a backlash against it' (Introduction, 'Local Knowledge', p. 4). At the same time, they do not want a diminished concept of 'the historical' to restrict interpretive activity, and as a way to keep all positions open, Hulme and Sherman emphasize the play's 'extraordinary ability (even by Shakespearean standards) to translate and be translated' as testimony not just to the 'appropriative' momentum of critical history, but to the play's own capacity to regenerate interpretive interest. 'The power and mobility of its language and themes' along with its 'endlessly malleable' theatricality 'have made it a renewable resource like few other texts'. By virtue, then, of literary/theatrical power – an '"openness"' so 'full of "blanks" that it "tempts us to fill in"' – audiences across space and time have been enabled to bring meanings outside the play's initial purview back into its original orbit so that 'the play itself' may be said to exist 'in many places at once' (Preface, pp. xi–xiii).

Contributors regularly confirm editorial claims about the play's 'uncanny' ability 'to anticipate later texts and events' (Hulme and Sherman, Introduction, 'European and Mediterranean Crossroads', p. 74). For Barbara Mowat, 'traces' of earlier texts 'weave themselves' into 'an intricate intertextual melange', extending 'the play's geographical and temporal boundaries far beyond its apparent limits' (p. 27). She rejects the view that 'colonial readings' are 'historically anachronistic and geographically restrictive'; the play's 'voyage infracontexts' require 'a broadening of these implications' (p. 34). Jeremy Brotton agrees: the Mediterranean *Tempest* is meant 'not to dismiss the New World dimension' but 'to suggest' a 'more complex and overdetermined awareness of geography' (p. 132). For

Elizabeth Fowler, the play's 'openness' is derived from conventional topoi – the ship of state, the drifting boat – 'designed to draw the audience into an activity, a habit of cognition and affection – not a *what* to think and feel, but a *how*' (p. 40). Roland Greene develops a similar idea around 'island logic': not just a geographical but a 'conceptual formation that proposes an imagined resolution to a social contradiction' (p. 140), a place where 'encounters unregulated by a stable world horizon introduce the prospect of something new' (p. 141). Greene's 'spectators are encouraged to apply an island logic to the play itself', obliged 'to elaborate it, criticize it, and – what is illusory – complete it' (p. 145).

In two tightly sealed completions, Donna Hamilton's play uses Virgil to support James's international policy (finding a 'proper' Protestant husband for Princess Elizabeth) while criticizing his domestic absolutism (p. 110), and Andrew Hess's 'play itself' endeavours to 'avoid' any 'detailed engagement with the Ottoman Empire' (p. 121) in order to occlude England's anxious triangulation between Muslim and Catholic interests. But even these pointedly focused interpretations get caught up in the centrifugal forces of this book's critical energies. Hamilton can reach her conclusion only through an *Aeneid* used by both Catholics and Protestants for contradictory purposes, and Hess's 'Coda: Prospero and the Refashioning of Mediterranean Identities', contrasts Islam to the 'play of imagination' by which Shakespeare and other 'modern European' texts (p. 130) seem to encourage an extended interpretive afterlife. Joseph Roach focuses on one example in the theatrical innovations by which Restoration audiences acquired visual mastery: the 'flying machines and pyrotechnics' in Shadwell's *Enchanted Island* 'expanded the franchise of a privileged spectatorial position – the right to see everything, even mysteries, clearly' (p. 61). Roach develops this idea through to Bardolatry, in which 'the veneration of the author as the eventual touristic centrepiece of the "heritage industry"' constructs ' "Shakespeare" ' as 'the scenic vanishing-point of the world's authentic secrets' (p. 70). Here an expansive afterlife has also become an evidently contracted one.

In the book's opening piece, Crystal Bartolovich describes the 'moral crisis in the social order' created by an emergent market economy, arguing that 'through' Prospero's 'magical auspices, the play' produces 'a powerful fantasy of control' ('Baseless Fabric', p. 25). This piece goes against the flow of much that follows, which regularly assumes not an identity but 'a "difference" between Prospero's play and Shakespeare's' (Gillies, 'Figure of the New World,' p. 199). For Robin Kirkpatrick, 'much that Prospero refers to' in 'Ye elves of hills . . .' and elsewhere 'seems in excess of – or irrelevant to – the action that the audience has witnessed' (p. 94). Other contributors are similarly disinclined to endow Prospero's 'magical auspices' with unequivocal authority. Gillies sees Prospero as contaminatingly 'linked to Sycorax by a subterrene set of correspondences' (p. 199), and Marina Warner claims that Sycorax's 'mysterious, indeterminate story and character suffuses *The Tempest*' (p. 97), producing an 'emotional link between Prospero and Sycorax' (p. 98) that tends to collapse differentiation. 'Shakespeare condemned these Circean powers and annexed them for his own art', Warner suggests, in a 'grotesque' mode that combines 'the newly discovered with the newfangled to produce hybrids and monsters' (p. 114). But while these later contributions contradict Bartolovich's powerfully interesting argument, they never erase it. '*The Tempest' and its Travels* may thus seem to mirror its subject, offering in its first action a mode of belief precipitously reframed by what follows and then inviting its audience to occupy different critical regions at the same time.

Critical Essays on Shakespeare's 'Richard III' includes twenty-four pieces, mostly modern but extending back to Hazlitt and Schlegel. In providing convenient access to so much of the play's complex critical history, Hugh Richmond has also exercised extraordinary editorial discretion in the packaging. In Richmond's view, the play writes us into an affective engagement with the protagonist which it then gradually requires us to diminish and finally relinquish. This interpretation is plausible but presented as the only one legitimately available. The play's theatrical history thus turns into an unbroken line of error in which 'theater professionals' have 'protracted their own delight in Richard' through to the end, refusing the pattern of 'Richard's decline' that 'the morally and aesthetically scrupulous' Shakespeare had so carefully written into the text (Introduction, p. 4). This process, starting with the 'facile melodrama' and 'aesthetic failure' of 'Cibber's rewriting' ('*Richard III* Recognized', p. 115), carries on to 'our own era's postmodern contempt for authorial and textual integrity', in which Antony Sher 'and his cohorts' – Ian McKellen ('greater extravagance'), Al Pacino ('could hardly be more wrong') and Charles Marowitz ('witty cynicism') – all 'reject' the 'complex structure of the original script' (Introduction, pp. 4–5, 7). A similar 'self-indulgence' characterizes the 'many critics' who are 'merely betraying their own predispositions' instead of 'offering objective insights into the text' (p. 10), so that to a 'surprising degree, this rather facile interpretation' holds 'the critical foreground' as well as the stage for four centuries.

In the one notable exception, a 'reaffirmation of English identity . . . provoked by World War II' led Tillyard to treat the histories as a 'national epic meriting serious political investigation' ('*Richard III* Reinvented', p. 74). Tillyard-'derived' work allowed for a '20-year' respite during which 'the goal' of 'serious scholarship' was 'the accurate description of objective phenomena' ('*Richard III* Contextualized', p. 15). Richmond installs this work as the first body of material in the collection, before going back to eighteenth-century and Romantic rewriting ('*Richard III* Reinvented'). The third and longest section, '*Richard III* Recognized', begins with Tillyard himself, and the eleven pieces grouped there are said 'to validate the original play' (p. 115), but only to regress into the postmodern subjectivism of excerpts illustrating the 'subordination of texts to feminist preconceptions' and 'of Reformation subjectivity to Marxist determinism' ('*Richard III* Deconstructed', p. 255).

The distinction on which all these claims are based – original play vs. subsequent interpretation – is unsustainable. If 'from the start' Richard's 'obsessional fascination' has provoked 'compulsive behavior' in 'actors and audiences' (Introduction, p. 2) and if 'the earliest published versions' indicate that 'the text was subject to substantial modifications from the start' ('*Richard III* Reinvented', p. 73), there is no way to separate the initial play itself from its reception history. As Richmond's own World War II scenario suggests, the Tillyard-'derived' view simply extends the tradition that began with the play's 'first performances' in which 'each generation must rework to validate its own prejudices and preoccupations' ('*Richard III* Recognized', p. 116). Any preference for Tillyard's followers over Sher's 'cohorts' must be based on beliefs buried underneath the claims for disinterested scholarship, and Richmond seems to hint at what they are in describing the 'postmodern multiculturalism' of the Sher–Alexander production: initiated by Ron Daniels, 'originally from Brazil'; with program notes 'by a scholar from Canada'; 'an Australian' Lady Anne, interested in 'aboriginal witchcraft'; and with Sher himself, 'a South African, of Russian extraction', influenced by his psychotherapist, 'also a South African, "originally from good Communist Jewish stock" ' ('Postmodern Renderings', p. 257, quoting Sher). What a falling off from the 'English identity' celebrated by Tillyard! In 'betraying' these 'prejudices and preconceptions', however, Richmond does no more than expand on his disarming acknowledgement that 'I too feel an obsessive interest in *Richard III*' (Introduction, p. 10). In its enactment of historical resentments, this play seems to get us all.

Shakespearians continue to be fascinated with the Catholic connection, and Velma Richmond aligns *Shakespeare, Catholicism, and Romance* with the renewed respect for Catholic residues in Shakespeare's England. A chapter on 'The Shakespeares of Stratford' sums up the strong evidence, but Richmond does not 'believe it is possible' to ' "prove" that Shakespeare was a Catholic' (p. 208), claiming only that his Romances and Romance elements emanated from 'a man plainly Catholic in habit of mind' (p. 16, quoting Hillaire Belloc). Mental habits, though, are hard to define, and topics that Richmond associates with Catholicism – the pilgrimage quest and an invigoratingly unpredictable sense of divine intercession – found their ways into Spenser and Herbert, for whom Rome held no appeal. Richmond amasses references to Catholic practices and beliefs in the plays, but their mere existence is inert unless made part of a dramatic effect or interpretive scheme. Ruth Vanita's piece on 'Mariological Memory in *The Winter's Tale* and *Henry VIII*' helps to clarify this matter. Vanita provides confirming evidence for Richmond in pointing to the generous presence of 'Marian mythology' in these plays, but for Vanita (as for Greenblatt), the plays 'reinscribe' elements of 'the old religion' not merely to identify with the values of the past but to 'replace the cultural power of communal church ritual and practice' (pp. 311–12). The 'practical effect' of Shakespearian performance thus may 'have been to encourage the expansion and evaluation of options'. Vanita acknowledges that her protofeminist Shakespeare, with plays 'directed to the general audience, especially to women', does not preclude their being 'directed to a royal patron' as well (p. 331). Catholic residues in the plays must have served different needs for a variously constituted general audience, but even the Catholic spectators Richmond has in mind, watching and listening for coded messages, would have had their understanding in some measure shaped by the theatrical coding.

'Without Class' in the title of Donald Hedrick and Bryan Reynolds' lively collection does not claim that Shakespeare transcends social difference, and 'Misappropriation' in the subtitle is not meant to separate legitimate from illegitimate response. On the contrary, *Shakespeare Without Class: Misappropriations of Cultural Capital* seeks to blur the boundaries by which Shakespearian interpretations are sorted into fixed categories. Hedrick and Reynolds argue that there is no way to stabilize response as hegemonic or transgressive, offering the 'transversal' instead, as a category designed to respect the 'dynamic' possibilities available in 'Shakespace' – that volatile and indefinite area within which Shakespearian interpretation happens. In the first group of essays, 'Acting Out

from Under Authority', Robert Weimann redeems the 'bad' *Hamlet* quarto by means of his always dialectically bifold authority; and William Over offers a fascinating look at the New York African Theatre – black-managed, with black actors playing to a mostly black audience, performing Shakespeare as well as original black plays in New York during the 1820s. Under the rubric 'Adapting Ideologies', Curtis Perry compares what Shakespeare did to and with Seneca with what Jarry and Ionesco did to and with Shakespeare – taking 'us beyond stoic hostility' to 'celebrate instead the more immediate desires and satisfactions of the body' (p. 104); and Reynolds claims that *Coriolanus*'s 'radical potential' exists 'prior to any alterations made by Brecht' (p. 126). 'Loving Otherwise' includes Laurie Osborne on the uses of Shakespeare by romance writers and Richard Burt on the 'extensive gay and lesbian performance history of *Romeo and Juliet*' in recent stage and screen versions (p. 154). Gender bending is also an issue in 'Disfilming Power', but James Andreas looks at *Prospero's Books* and Matt Bergbusch at *My Own Private Idaho* more in terms of technological mastery and cinematic technique. In the final section, 'Teaching Transversally', Leslie Katz describes her experience conducting 'two "witch workshops," one at Amherst College, the other at the University of Rochester' (p. 229), and Hedrick engages with 'a nervousness about teaching Shakespeare in relation to the market value of our stock' ('Shakespeare's Enduring Immorality', p. 241).

Julia Lupton's Afterword, 'Shakespace on Marloan', looks back to Hedrick and Reynolds's opening reflection on how Stephen Greenblatt almost got the moguls to do the movie his way, as *Shakespeare in Love – With Marlowe*. Lupton acknowledges that the film declines a bent bard, 'the lurid or scandalous (a risk that, admit it, usually pays off these days)' (p. 277), but in her view it amply compensates by accepting 'rather the risk of allusiveness, the gamble not of *the literal*, but of *the literate*', thereby opening up the 'transversal Shakespace' the editors describe, where the 'shifting history of Shakespearean appropriation is itself shot through and set into motion by the originary encounter, whether physical or purely cognitive, between these playwrights' (p. 278). From this angle, 'Shakespace' and 'transversality' constitute not so much a textual as an interpretive category – the place where we engage an overdetermined text with our own overdetermined capacities for response. However Shakespeare knew Marlowe, we know Marlowe, and the knowledge kicks in when we read Shakespeare, though it works the other way around as well: we know Marlowe through Shakespeare; they are both each other's pretexts.

Is 'Shakespace', then, a new word for 'intertextuality'? The question hangs over three books attempting to assess Italian, Senecan, and Ovidian presences in Shakespeare. In *Shakespeare and Intertextuality*, Michele Marrapodi collects sixteen essays, most based on papers delivered to a 1999 Palermo conference. This book – wide-ranging, informative, and generously complemented with a substantial bibliography – answers the 'Shakespace' question with a resounding 'maybe'. It depends on what you mean by 'intertextuality', and since the 'methodological premises and disciplinary confines' for this term are 'far from being univocally established', its meaning can be fixed only negatively – a phenomenon not limited to the 'positivistic source studies' of the recent critical past (Marrapodi, Introduction, pp. 20, 11). This distinction between more and less specific categories structures the book's opening piece. Robert Miola differentiates between an intertextuality in which 'specific books or texts' are 'mediated directly through the author' (p. 24) and another kind in which 'traditions' of such complexity proceed along so many 'indirect routes' that, for all we know, '*the originary text may never have been read by the author at all*' (p. 33, his emphasis). The same ideas are sustained through to the end of the book where Keir Elam reiterates the claim that intertextuality 'is a dynamic concept' that 'is constantly changing' ('Welcome', p. 295). Looking back at the Palermo conference on the same subject 'four or five years ago', though, Elam sees a clear trajectory amidst all the changes – a 'shift' away from Miola's 'book on the shelf category', involving 'source studies and therefore one-to-one relationships', toward 'an

endless sort of productivity of textual exchange without limits and without predefined boundaries' (p. 296).

The pieces sandwiched between the 'Introduction' and the 'Round Table' explore the 'multiplicity of views and critical strategies' (Marrapodi, p. 20) associated with intertextuality in its currently more flexible form. Elam examines English (as contrasted to continental) bodies on the Shakespearian stage, concluding that, though 'somewhat battered from these meetings, the body of early modern England affirms itself not least through its ironical acts of theatrical self-representation' ('The continent', p. 68). Mario Domenichelli, interested in 'the crisis of the aristocracy' (p. 87), keys on *Troilus*'s treatment of the ' "handsome" death *topos*' (p. 89) as reflected/refracted from Franco-Italian traditions. Marrapodi, Jason Lawrence and Charlotte Pressler trace the blurry-wavy lines by which Italian dramatic and narrative conventions make their way into *Measure*, *Othello* and *Twelfth Night*. For Anthony Barthelemy and Pamela Brown, Italy itself serves as intertext for *Merchant* and *Othello*; as the place of the sexual and racial other, Venice encourages English audiences to displace anxiety. Anxiety figures prominently for P. A. Skantze too, who associates Isabella's enforced improvisations in *Measure* 2.2 with *comedia* acting styles. Skantze's is one of four pieces on 'Stage and Spectacle' at the end of the book, including J. R. Mulryne on the migration of pageants from Italian theatrical practice through Inigo Jones and masques into *Antony*'s *mise-en-scène*.

Expanding thus beyond an authors-and-sources approach, the contributors nonetheless retain the emphasis on historical sequence from which the old model was generated. Marrapodi's opening claim that current work has 'examined the theatrical ancestry of the plays outside positivistic sources' stays– with 'ancestry' and with 'legacies' a few words later on – inside the framework of values inherited through time (Introduction, p. 11). Elam's 'textual exchange' at the end is not really 'without limits' or 'predefined categories'. Though no longer mapped directly onto individual agents, the process retains the securely humanized historical agency with which earlier causes produce later effects. The effects, moreover, restore the individual agency supposedly renounced: when Elam distinguishes the new intertextuality from the old as 'not so much' interested in 'Shakespeare's use of text' as in 'Shakespeare's use of the cultural archetypes or stereotypes' (p. 297), he retains his fundamental interest in the author's art – 'Shakespeare's use'. This continuity is even more evident once the Round Table gets going. The first contributor sets the tone, acknowledging that he is 'suspicious' of 'the "brave new world" of intertextuality', with its 'endless arrays of texts', where if 'everything is equally meaningful' then 'everything is equally meaningless'. The second contributor, surveying what he takes to be the narcissistic nihilism of postmodern textual theory ('we are so smart . . . we are extremely brilliant in false etymologies, false everything'), declares 'I'm really fed up' (pp. 300–02). These are critics for whom the question 'who is speaking?' retains an absolute primacy.

Working within a diachronic and author-centered model of textual transmission, most contributors to this volume would not be comfortable with the deliberate 'privileging' of 'the spatial over the temporal' in Hedrick and Reynolds's 'transversal' model of textual reception ('Shakespace', p. 11). There are two notable exceptions. Fernando Cioni, reviewing the complexities involved in determining priority between *the* and *a Shrew*, finally embraces the intertext according to Barthes – a 'palimpsest of quotations, versions and translations', a 'boundless intertextuality, with its codes of "already seen/already written"' (p. 161), simultaneously (or at least synchronically) available to interpreters for whom all reading is rereading. Jeffrey Netto focuses on the chess game in *The Tempest* and pictorial art. His eight exemplary paintings date mostly from the Renaissance and include Karel van Mander's ravishing Shakespeare-Jonson portrait; but he brings in later pictures as well, and even with the earlier ones his aim is 'not simply to suggest that there are "allusions to painting in Shakespeare," or vice versa', but that 'Shakespeare's play participates in the play of reiterations, of cultural revisions and rehearsals, that is

necessarily at work behind every act of signification, aesthetic or otherwise' (p. 288).

In *Fated Sky*, M. L. Stapleton takes on Seneca's presence in Shakespeare, claiming that the '*femina furens*' in *Seneca's Ten Plays* is visible behind a variety of Shakespearian women. Joan, Margaret of Anjou and Tamora represent 'a "transposition" or "reanimation" of the Senecan and Studleyan Medea' (p. 41). A 'capacity for self-will or even self-transcendence' in Kate and Portia suggests the 'autarchy' which 'describes *femina furens*' (p. 63). Helena's 'passionate speeches and her crushing plot to bed' Bertram 'reveal her as another manifestation' with particular affiliations to Studley's Phaedra (p. 77). Cleopatra 'represents Shakespeare's most detailed and triumphant reanimation of *femina furens*'; Jasper Heywood's Juno and Megaera and Studley's Deianira and Medea 'inform his conception' (p. 96). A final chapter argues that if the recapitulative qualities of the romances extend to the Senecan material, the Queen and Imogen in *Cymbeline* represent 'an exorcism' of various aspects of *femina furens* earlier in Joan and Cleopatra (p. 113).

The 'dramatic classical topos that I call *femina furens*' (p. 14) does not appear to have the substantive recognizability of, say, love-death or *miles gloriosus*, and stretching it to fit so many different phenomena (Joan, Helena, Imogen) may lose its shape – a least common denominator of 'strong women' without great critical leverage. Shrews and learned women come into Shakespeare from literary material quite apart from Seneca – maybe even from Renaissance life itself. Most generally, the whole question of Senecan presence is particularly vexed. Beyond methodological and theoretical uncertainties, critics have been unable to agree whether there *is* a Senecan presence of any consequence on the Renaissance stage. But Stapleton, who represents the debate fully and fairly, and who has critical judgment to supplement his learning, intends his claims to keep the conversation moving along in interesting directions – which they should do.

There is no vexing question about Ovid's presence in Shakespeare. The editor of *Shakespeare's Ovid* and four of his contributors confidently declare that Ovid is Shakespeare's 'favourite' poet (Taylor, Introduction, p. 3; Peyré, 'Niobe', p. 126; Lyne, 'Ovid', p. 150; Velz, 'Shakespeare's Ovid' p. 185; Martindale, 'Shakespeare's Ovid', p. 212), echoing a consensus that goes back to R. K. Root if not to Francis Meres. As a result, most of the contributors – nine of the thirteen, grouped under the rubric 'The *Metamorphoses* in the Plays and Poems' – are free to avoid theoretical implications in favour of practical criticism, describing what Shakespeare does with or to Ovid in this or that work. In the first of these, William Carroll argues that Proteus's attempted rape and Valentine's offer of Sylvia to his repentant friend mirror each other in 'a dark, essentially Ovidian view of masculine desire, figured by the possession of the female body' (p. 62). Carroll's Ovid is a straightforward presence in Shakespeare, serving to produce a protofeminist rather than misogynist text reassuringly consistent with current values. Elsewhere in this collection, though, discomfort – about Ovid, Shakespeare, and their relation – tends to prevail. The *Metamorphoses* was an awkward poem before Shakespeare, requiring moralization in the Middle Ages and in the humanist-cum-Calvinist claims Golding was at such pains to make in the prefatory material to his translation. R. W. Maslen looks at early sixteenth-century Ovidian poems to show how writers became gradually aware of the 'dangerous matter' (p. 16) of this 'duplicitous text' (p. 17), learning to 'exploit the philosophical gravitas accorded to Ovid's witty fables' as 'a means of meddling with impunity in the affairs of the rich and powerful' (p. 28). An empowering Ovid also figures centrally for John Roe: both *Hero and Leander* and *Venus and Adonis* 'gain a considerable degree of imaginative freedom' through their Ovidian material. Roe, however, emphasizes the differences between the 'brilliantly acerbic' Marlowe and a 'more tender' Shakespeare who, in shifting tone at the end to Venus's maternal grief, more fully 'acknowledges the contemporary human obligations that the gift' of Ovidian liberation 'incurs' (p. 45).

Similar contrasts are replayed in other pieces. A. D. Nuttall takes the equivocal judgement of 'brilliantly acerbic' to an unequivocal conclusion.

His *Winter's Tale*, having 'woven together' Ovidian stories of Proserpina, Orpheus and Pygmalion, changes their tone from the 'strangely hard playfulness' and 'cool elaboration' in the original to 'a serious beauty'; beyond tonal difference, the 'Christian terms' with which Shakespeare's play is infused have 'inverted Ovid's myth and made death the loser', revealing 'in comparison' an Ovid who 'with all his glittering "proto-Freudian" expertise does not actually know what love is' (pp. 141–2). Pauline Kiernan is equally unequivocal on the other side. Like Roe, she focuses on tonal shifts in *Venus*, but in her view when the 'undignified' Venus 'is allowed her moment of tragic decorum' at the end, the effect is not to anchor the poem in a final tenderness so much as produce a delighted realization of the possibilities of metamorphosis itself: a 'useful lesson to have learned for manipulating the responses of a play audience' (p. 94). Kiernan's view finds support in two *Survey* pieces on the poem this year. For Margaret Tudeau-Clayton, *Venus and Adonis* embodies a Shakespearian 'poetics of recreative licence, a stepping out from narrative and syntactic linearity in a discursive equivalent to the intemperance of holiday' (p. 12). Peter Smith claims that the poem casts 'the reader in the role of an Antony', a sexually adventurous crossdresser, 'rather than an Adonis', as suggested in C. S. Lewis's 'prudish' and 'obtuse' response (p. 31). For these critics too, Kiernan's 'techniques of impropriety used to meaningful effect' (p. 87) count for more than the 'human obligations' proper to the tender hearted.

Taylor's own contribution splits the difference – or, better, magnifies the contradictions. Although the metamorphosis from human to bestial 'is clearly Ovidian' in *Titus*, the idea is 'moralized, implicitly by Lavinia' ('Animals', p. 69), whose 'moral outrage, framed in terms of "grace", humanity, and tenderness', departs from Ovid in favour of 'decent civilized values' signaled in Christian terms (p. 75). But then the play 'ironically undermines its own moralizing', putting this normative tenderness into the vicious mouth of Lucius at the end, returning us to the 'nightmarish vision' of a world metamorphosing into bestial savagery (p. 78). Taylor does not say whether we ought to like the play for being so Ovidian, but then it is hard to know, given 'that ambivalent tone that is so elusive, but so important aesthetically' (Velz, 'Shakespeare's Ovid', p. 194), whether an 'essentially Ovidian view' exists. In his piece on the *Sonnets*, Gordon Braden claims that an Ovidian sense of a regenerative metamorphosis (notably from Book 15) tends to diminish into an equally Ovidian sense of *degenerative* metamorphosis (notably from Medea in Book 7, whose inability to follow what she knows to be the better is generalized into the 'more inclusive terms' of Sonnet 129 (p. 110)). Since an essentially Shakespearian view is equally elusive, there can be no hope for establishing a stable and straightforward Ovid–Shakespeare relationship. Peyré gets at this point, when, after describing *Hamlet*'s radical transformation of Ovid's Hercules to 'a few fossilized ruins' (a Christian moralization, in effect, though Peyré does not say so), he surprisingly concludes that, 'In fact, the Ovidian imagery of metamorphosis is very much alive' as 'the radiating power of myth reactivates its own imaginative structures within the play' (p. 133). The transformation of Ovid is thus itself Ovidian, because transformation is the still point on the *Metamorphoses*' still turning wheel.

Theory thus manages to get into these interpretive essays after all, and in Charles Martindale's brilliantly sophisticated Postscript, 'methodological' questions compel sustained reflection on the values with which intertextual relations are conceptualized and assessed. Martindale has no use for the 'historical positivism' behind claims to read Shakespeare's Ovid the way Shakespeare might have (p. 201). Convinced that the 'desire of critics to arrive at an original meaning that is apparently "in the text"' is 'deluded' (p. 202), Martindale demurs from 'most contributors to this book', who 'foreground sameness (partly from a "humanist" belief in the continuity of human nature and concerns)', proposing 'an alternative analysis that *rigorously* foregrounds difference'. Before proceeding with any comparison of Shakespeare and Ovid we need to ask, ' "*Whose* Shakespeare is like/unlike *which* Ovid?" ' (p. 210, his emphases). But these questions are less likely to preface interpretation than to preclude it, or to produce a discourse so resolutely committed to undecidability as to put at risk the kind of detailed speculation – about Ovid, Shakespeare and their relation – abundantly available in this wonderful book.

That theory should not block practice is central to Andy Mousley's *Renaissance Drama and Contemporary Literary Theory*, one of five books this year written with teaching in mind. Mousley begins with 'the differences that modern literary theory has made to literary studies' (p. 1). He identifies pre-theoretical criticism with humanist self-realization: through affectively engaged reading, we 'find ourselves lovingly mirrored in the text' and experience 'the pleasure of identification' (p. 3). Recent theory, suspecting that 'identification seduces us into passive and uncritical acceptance' (p. 6), and that there is no stable self to identify prior to the socially determined system of language, replaces affective engagement with a detached 'critical consciousness' (p. 7). The patness of this 'stark opposition' (p. 8) motivates Mousley's chief aim, 'to explore the continuities' between 'old and new critical approaches' (p. 1). Although some current modes (structuralism, some 'varieties of Marxism and poststructuralism') can be 'unremittingly anti-humanist' in the rigour with which they treat 'language and society as impersonal systems', others (including 'feminist, historicist, psychoanalytic and again Marxist and poststructuralist' modes), by '*writing the psyche back into society, language and history*' at the same time as '*writing society, language and history back into the psyche*', manage to 'decentre the self while retaining a humanist dimension'. Reading thus still 'catalyses an intense and meaningful relationship between text and reader but broadens it' (p. 10; his emphases).

Mousley develops these ideas by laying out the defining differences and continuities in each mode, then moving over to Renaissance plays (by Marlowe, Dekker, Beaumont, Jonson, Webster, Middleton and Ford as well as Shakespeare). He is careful not to conceive the plays as passive recipients of theoretical insights: if the contrary desires of current theory – engagement and detachment, enchantment and estrangement – may be traced back to Renaissance drama, then the plays are as much the true begetter as the product of a dialectical contemporary criticism. In trying 'to build bridges between the old and new' (p. 9), Mousley speculates that 'the balance' Lear 'seeks' might reside in a 'third option...somewhere between extreme androcentric and theocentric, or humanist and anti-humanist perspectives' (p. 64). *Lear*, however, seems more inclined to take us to the edge of confine than to any middle ground. *Bartholmew Fair* is a better candidate, but to speak of 'the delicately poised mean' (p. 120) of its 'neoclassical balance' (p. 121) may abstract a concept of achieved stability from a theatrical experience characterized rather by intense contradiction. Some differences just cannot be mediated, and the project of mediation itself can be called into question. In the 'Marxism' chapter at the end, for instance, trying 'to reconcile' the 'humanisms and anti-humanisms' in 'different strains of Marxist thought', Mousley laconically remarks that it 'should come as no surprise by now to find that the place of their reconciliation is that traditionally humanist discourse, literature' (p. 192). Reconciliation is here identified with one of the categories to be reconciled and is therefore, arguably, recuperative.

Mousley's commitment to mediation will thus bother some readers, but he always leaves ample room for disagreement – not just to theorists committed to different beliefs, but to students who may not know what to believe. Mousley writes with an undergraduate audience in mind: bulleted summary points; patient explanation; information professional Shakespearians will take for granted; above all, a demystifying accessibility that refuses to simplify complex material or to dazzle with the sophistication of his own critical intelligence. This book, though, should be substantially useful not just to students, but even to those readers for whom the foot-and-a-half long words of high theory come trippingly off the tongue.

The eighteen pieces Maurice Hunt collects in *Approaches to Teaching Shakespeare's 'Romeo and Juliet'* are provocative and smart, but whether the book fulfills its declared pedagogical purpose – offering 'a sourcebook of material, information, and ideas on teaching the subject of the volume to undergraduates' in order to encourage 'discussion of the aims and methods of teaching literature' (Gibaldi, p. ix) – is not clear. This book seems to be about *Romeo and Juliet* rather than about teaching *Romeo and Juliet*. Hunt's introductory assessment of 'Materials' is informative and analytically shrewd but hard to distinguish in kind from essays introducing collections without specifically pedagogical designs. The contributions, though frequently interspersed with a teaching narrative ('I offer students the alternative...' (Moisan, '"Now Art Thou What Thou Art"', p. 49)), typically proceed along the same interpretive lines as do journal articles, beginning with a foundational claim of disconfirmation. The first contributor's opening sets the tone: Arthur Kinney 'arms' his students with close reading skills so they 'are not readily accepting of glib critics who, over the years, have lifted phrases like "star-crossed lovers" out of context' (p. 31). The same predication appears with remarkable consistency at the beginning of subsequent contributions: 'ask students to resist'; 'asking students to move...away from'; 'encourage students to rethink'; 'undermine the preconception...most students have' (Kamps, '"I Love You Madly"', p. 38; Low, p. 75; Kehler, 'Teaching *Romeo and Juliet*', p. 78; Hirsh, p. 163, etc.). You find the same predication in *ELR*'s *Romeo* piece this year, in which Chris Fitter urges us to key on 'the play's immediate political context', its 'sustained populist sensitization to social inequity', as a dimension 'obscured by a long tradition of appropriation' emphasizing 'romantic "transcendence"' (pp. 155, 177).

Disconfirmation may be inherent in all critical work (if not all speech), but works differently in journals and in classrooms. Fitter's readers are mostly anonymous equals; teachers and students are not equals and their relation more directly affective. That teaching has an erotic charge is attested to by linguistic origins (education and seduction) and by a long line of authorities going back to Plato. This book reflects different styles of seduction, from a relatively tough love requiring argumentative coercion to a relative mutuality in which teachers and students can be convinced at least for a passing moment that they are 'fellow explorers' (Porter, 'The Wild Goose Chase', p. 145). Mapping these styles onto the play we ask, who seduces whom in *Romeo and Juliet*, who's on top? We could ask the same question about Beatrice and DeFlores or Lolita and Humbert Humbert, but in *Romeo and Juliet* the concept of seduction itself, with a top and a bottom, seems inappropriate, as if the lovers find a place that in fact transcends power. Since the classroom domain is shaped by due dates and grades, we can't get there from here, but neither did the protagonists of the tragedy – except perhaps for a passing moment.

Before we service student needs we have to determine what they are, and the contributors do not speak with a single voice on this matter. The dominant claim – the default position, urged on with missionary zeal – is that, prone to romantic sentimentality, the students require our disillusioning discipline. Some contributors, though, think it is student 'cynicism' we need to dislodge: 'twenty-year-old students seem way too young to disbelieve utterly in the possibility of love'; they 'need' an 'expanded sense of context' allowing them 'to feel the pathos of young love' as well as 'to observe love's follies' (Marshall, ' "Who Wrote the Book of Love" ', p. 99). For Karl Zender, this is what we *all* need, 'if we are to engage fully with the play's emotional power', students and teachers alike. Before 'we see the young lovers as flawed, ... we need to see them as valuable', to 'empathize strongly (and unashamedly) with their hopes and tribulations', 'to love Shakespeare's lovers' (p. 137).

In *Shakespeare, Feminism and Gender*, Kate Chedgzoy collects eleven essays, ten from the 1990s, as 'a snapshot of a decade when feminist criticism of Shakespeare's plays both flourished and diversified' (Introduction, p. 6). The contributors include some of the most compelling critics on the current scene (Hodgdon, Howard, Loomba,

McLuskie, Sinfield, Thompson, Traub, et al.), and readers are bound to find pieces that have had a decisive personal and professional impact. Chedgzoy's incisive introduction emphasizes the political dimension: beginning with the 1994 Jane Brown affair ('Head bans *Romeo and Juliet*') in which, as 'so often', Shakespeare is 'the site where élite, popular and national interests converged' (p. 2), she 'underlines' the 'responsibility of feminist Shakespeare scholars to continue to make critical interventions' in 'the world outside', of which 'the academy is a part' (pp. 5, 6). American feminists, who tend to negotiate their practical business within a more narrowly (or sharply) defined professional and academic framework, may not be comfortable with the conclusions drawn here. Chedgzoy is interested not just in 'the education system' as a 'primary site' where 'practices of inclusion and exclusion are elaborated' and 'cultural privilege is sustained' (p. 4), but more pointedly in pedagogical practice, the specifically 'radical potential' of Luhrmann's *Romeo*, for instance, as something which 'teachers in schools and colleges are constantly realising' (p. 5). But the question remains how and by whom pop culture is deployed and understood. To say that the Luhrmann movie 'has proved a fruitful way of enabling' students 'to bring their complex understandings of representational politics to bear on the less immediately accessible Renaissance text' (p. 3) reinforces the claim of student empowerment – 'encourage students to extend their own ideas' (Peck and Coyle, 'General Editors' Preface', p. ix) – with which the New Casebooks Series identifies itself. But if *William Shakespeare's Romeo + Juliet* belongs to the students, the 'complex understandings of representational politics' sounds more like a teacher than a student-generated value. In concluding that *10 Things I Hate About You* is 'a funny and thoughtful exploration' that 'teachers and students of Shakespeare will no doubt quickly incorporate' into 'debates about the sexual politics of Shakespeare' (p. 17), Chedgzoy represents the 'sexual politics of Shakespeare' as an interpretive agenda determined collectively among equals; but it is a complex critical construct developed over many years by a sophisticated and highly trained professional cadre – an élite – who pursue their interests (including, of course, a sincere regard for what they take to be student interests) in a way that inevitably involves 'inclusion and exclusion' and 'cultural privilege' (grades and degrees are conferred differentially). We are back to those irritating questions about identities and needs, the students' and our own, from which no consensus is likely to emerge.

These are just the questions to which Sharon O'Dair gives an unflinchingly intelligent look in *Class, Critics, and Shakespeare*. O'Dair is sceptical about the egalitarian critical claims made these days – not so much their intentions as their effects, emanating from an intellectual and professional elite, the stewards of an educational system that is itself aimed at 'establishing and maintaining class distinction or inequality' (p. 2). The first three of her four main chapters couple a discussion of educational institutions with *The Tempest*, economic institutions with *Timon*, and political institutions with *Coriolanus*. The fourth analyses the politics of land use in Oregon as contested by environmentalists and loggers, in the context of the Ashland Shakespeare Festival and theories of pastoral. The Shakespearian connections, though always informed and smart, are sometimes perfunctory, but since O'Dair wishes to 'enter an ongoing debate about the politics of academic literary study and of the academy more generally', she targets 'readers whose specialties are not necessarily Shakespeare or early modern English literature or indeed who are not academics at all' (pp. 17–18).

Though never mean-spirited, O'Dair's analysis leaves no ox ungored. The cultural left will not be happy with her critique of critique. Under its contempt for the market economy, O'Dair detects an identification with residual aristocratic interests, 'an idealization of the old order of feudalism, of economic irrationality, and of stratification by status' (p. 59): no shopkeepers we, let alone bin persons. Implying that most currently self-designated political criticism is deluded or hypocritical cant, she nonetheless positions herself firmly on the left,

concluding not that we should tone down the political for the professional but the other way around. Since the 'academy – and perhaps especially its humanists and artists – protects and perpetuates the cultural structure that guarantees the irksomeness of labor and of laborers', and since we 'cannot subvert it without subverting ourselves', this 'is exactly what we should do: reduce the power of formal education to determine what people will lead good lives' (p. 4). This counter-intuitive conclusion is bound to meet with resistance – 'why on earth should anyone expect University professors willingly to' diminish their own position? (p. 130) – but she sticks to it 'because it is right' and because it is consistent with 'our own bottom line, which is to protect our intellectual work and freedom' (p. 131). Since the same social order that maintains and is now (she claims) increasing class and income differences has also significantly reduced funding to the humanities and the humanist professoriate in favour of vocational education, something needs to be adjusted in O'Dair's analysis. Maybe we are less complicit than she claims – or maybe the system more benign. All *Survey* readers will want to engage with this invigorating book and decide for themselves.

Reading Shakespeare's Dramatic Language: A Guide, this year's last teaching book, is designed to 'help its readers to attend more closely to what Shakespeare does with words, to understand something of the linguistic context of those words, and to find their own words for engaging in informed discussion of the issues' (Thompson, 'Heightened Language', p. 15). Sylvia Adamson and the other editors divide their material into three parts. 'The Language of Shakespeare's Plays' includes twelve contributions ranging from local details (figurative language, puns, scansion) to larger structural components and rhetorical strategies (description, narrative, persuasion). The last three essays here extend to performance: how opening sequences establish interest; vocal stress in delivery; and the phenomenology of performance experienced through the ' "meaning" of the body on stage' (Elam, 'Language', p. 173). The next four essays, grouped as 'Reading Shakespeare's English', focus on the pronunciation, grammar, and various sociolects and idiolects specific to Elizabethan English. Finally, 'Resources for Readers' offers an alphabetical list defining and illustrating the 'main rhetorical devices used by Shakespeare' (Wales, 'An A–Z', p. 272).

According to Ann Thompson at the beginning, the popularity of Luhrmann's *Romeo* 'testifies to the continuing ability of ordinary people (including many young people) to follow the language in a performance context' and suggests 'a considerable degree of continuity between Shakespeare's dramatic language and everyday modern language' (p. 6). Subsequent contributions strike a similar note – 'little difference' and 'we too shift our speech' (Magnusson, 'Style', pp. 19, 24); 'reminiscent' of 'actual life' (Wright, 'Shakespeare's Metre Scanned', p. 59) – but these reassuring claims are not sustained for long. Thompson admits that the Luhrmann example may demonstrate not so much Shakespearian accessibility as linguistic 'redundan[cy]' if, in the face of overwhelmingly spectacular effects, audiences are left wondering 'why' the actors are 'taking so long to tell us' things 'when we can see and hear it all before they tell us?' (p. 14). Lynette Hunter's claim for shared rhetorical interests, 'just as we do today', (p. 115) gives way to an acknowledgement that 'the sixteenth century knew better than today' the 'complexity of persuasion' available through the rhetorical *paideia* (p. 128). A persistent scepticism – how can these 'ordinary ... young people', rapped and hiphopped beyond linguistic nuance, distinguish 'the authentic grand style' from 'bombast' (Adamson, 'Grand Style', p. 48), or 'insidious parody' from 'due decorum' (Nash, 'Puns and Parody', p. 84) – develops into explicit emphasis on the remoteness of Shakespeare's language – those 'unfamiliar features' by 'which it differs from our own' (Adamson et al., Introduction, p. 191), and those misleadingly familiar ones which leave us, like Shaw's British and Americans, ' "divided by a common language" ' (quoted Adamson, 'Understanding', p. 211). By the end, Roger Lass concludes that a 'modern listener' at a Renaissance performance 'would probably find

the (probably rather small) part of the language that was comprehensible at all both surprising and rather confusing' (p. 257).

Always accommodating in tone, the contributors nonetheless urge students to reach beyond their own ideas to engage with historical difference. But historicism is not the prime motivation here. As Lass wryly remarks, you could produce Shakespeare 'in a reconstructed original pronunciation', but no one would come; 'literary and historical appreciation', he adds, 'are not the same thing' (p. 264), and the editors make it clear that the latter is driving the work in this book, arguing that historical knowledge serves the 'more important' goal of 'heighten[ing] students' enjoyment and appreciation of the plays' (Adamson et al., Introduction, p. 191). Magnusson thus emphasizes Shakespeare's 'showmanship in language' and 'the age's love affair with copia' (pp. 17, 22); for Kastan, 'Shakespeare orchestrates' his 'multiple voices' to 'produce stories that are almost uniquely memorable and meaningful' (p. 111); for Wales, 'Shakespeare's artistry' is to bring various 'idiolects, sociolects, dialects' from 'ordinary speech' into 'the overriding genre of poetry', whose 'rhythms secure their memorability' and 'resonate through time' ('Varieties', p. 208).

Aimed at heightening aesthetic pleasure, this book is a resounding success – one wonderfully smart and detailed discussion after another of Shakespearian passages themselves running over with expressive richness and vitality. But the contributors are not sure that aesthetic pleasure is enough. For Magnusson, 'a dramatic language cannot be merely an exhibitionist one', and Shakespeare 'strikes a fine and imaginative balance between the love and embellishment of words for their own sake and the functional matching of words to situations' ('Style', pp. 24, 28). But this transfer from figurative to narrative orchestration still leaves us in the position of appreciating an exhibition – Penshurst now instead of Hilliard. Magnusson later tries more of a vertical move, suggesting that the situational and dialogic variety in Shakespeare 'has certainly contributed to' Shakespeare's staying power, 'whether' by 'promoting' the 'toleration of differences' or 'offering everyone a point of agreement' ('Dialogue', p. 135). Nash too, writing on the puns in which he takes an informed and infectious delight, worries himself into larger-sounding claims. Haunted by Dr Johnson (see pp. 78, 79, and 87, where the 'fatal Cleopatra' remark is quoted), Nash feels he must rise above 'the merely picturesque' in order to answer the questions, 'What does the Shakespearean pun *do*? . . . what's the point?' (p. 71, his emphasis), concluding that it contributes to an 'ultimately compassionate laughter' (p. 87). In Kastan's conclusion, Shakespearian orchestration is 'part of what makes us fully and complexly human' (p. 111).

Compassion, toleration, *consensus gentium*, humanity – these are the values with which Kant systematized aesthetic experience, and you have to wonder about their relevance to a 'profession' which, in Greenblatt's view, 'has become so oddly diffident and even phobic about literary power, so suspicious and tense, that it risks losing sight' of the 'whole reason anyone bothers with the enterprise in the first place' (*Hamlet*, p. 4). If we have really seen through the 'idealist formations' of 'Enlightenment knowledge' (Howard and Shershow, Introduction, p. 8), these values cannot provide a solid foundation for current work. But Greenblatt's discontents with professional norms have in the past generated whole schools of criticism, and classroom practice may not be able to afford the luxury of theoretical correctness. Keep teaching, stay tuned.

Shakespeare on Love and Friendship is excerpted from Allan Bloom's posthumous *Love and Friendship* (1993). As a free-standing Shakespearian study, this book is a marketing fiction. But the point can be given a positive spin: *Shakespeare on Love and Friendship* assumes a perspective larger than ordinary Shakespeare criticism; Bloom does interdisciplinary work. This is just the claim put forward on the dust jacket of Paul Kahn's *Law and Love: The Trials of 'King Lear'*: 'More than a contribution to literary criticism . . . the best interdisciplinary work'. Books like these make it hard to sustain claims about a 'deeply entrenched' hostility to interdisciplinarity (Joughin, Introduction, p. 3). In conjunction with Tim Spiekerman's similarly interdisciplinary study of *Shakespeare's Political*

Realism, they allow for some reflection about the expectations reasonable for such work.

Survey readers probably hear Bloom's title in the context of queer theory, and Bloom works this territory in his last two chapters: Polixenes and Leontes' friendship versus the anxiety-filled desires of marriage; Hal–Falstaff as a relation largely independent of desire, utility, social or political advantage. But this interest is absorbed into a broad historical framework spanning a radical divide: friendship is associated with antiquity, an expansive masculine realm focused on the polity, into which love enters with the advent of Christianity, bringing a feminized ideal located in private and domestic spaces. In earlier chapters these mighty opposites shape discussions of *Romeo*, *Antony*, *Measure* and *Troilus*. Hence the 'Shakespeare on' formula in the title, though presumably editorial invention, is apt nonetheless: Bloom's Shakespeare is a thinker, 'the first philosopher of history' (p. 29), whose 'divine gifts' allow him to 'discipline his thoughts' so that their 'different aspects' in various plays form 'a total vision' (p. 79) – a sort of de Rougemont-cum-Burckhardt, aware of his participation in a major transformation and sharing his conflicted and complexly nuanced historical consciousness with an apparently equally reflective audience.

Tim Spiekerman analyses *King John* and the second tetralogy plays from the assumption that 'Shakespeare is an author from whom we can learn something significant about politics' (p. 4). Like Machiavelli, Spiekerman's Shakespeare is unillusioned about the practical value of transcendent ideals, but unlike Machiavelli, he represents these ideals as deeply ingrained in human need: we 'love the old' because we 'think, or would like to think, that it is good' and 'God-given' (p. 155). This atavistic need for a transcendent legitimation means that a strategically self-interested Machiavellian rule is unsustainable. The best you get is Henry V at Agincourt, but 'built on fraud and ambition and self-deception', even 'this political peak' is bound to be 'short-lived' (p. 150). If 'the key' to Shakespeare's 'political teaching lies in his presentation of a seemingly irresolvable conflict between ambition and justice' (p. 154), then 'Shakespeare's view of politics is tragic' (p. 164), with the implicit *contemptu mundi* moral often emphasized in conservative readings of tragedy: looking even on *Henry V* 'isn't to say one must be impressed. There are other things . . . besides politics' (p. 150).

Spiekerman acknowledges Bloom's formative influence as 'everywhere evident' in *Shakespeare's Political Realism* (p. ix) and, like his mentor, centres discussion on a self-consciously analytical author whose beliefs are accessible to and valuable for a current readership. As 'a practical matter', we can go 'about unearthing Shakespeare's views', by observing 'the signs of the maker in what he's made. If a given character appears admirable or amusing', we can 'infer that Shakespeare himself admires or is amused by him' (p. 14). In assuming we can determine who is speaking and thus the value of what is said, Bloom and Spiekerman work at a considerable remove from the current norms of Shakespearian commentary. Paul Kahn's *Lear* book occupies an equally distant site. It builds on the idea that the 'destruction of love by law and of law by love' is the play's 'central theme' (p. xi), a 'very large theme' indeed (p. xvii), 'situate[d] squarely within the Judeo-Christian tradition' (p. xii), and thus extending far beyond *Lear* or Shakespeare to include pretty much everything: 'a central claim of this work is that love is not a particular emotional experience but a form of experience from within which we can view the entire social and political world' (p. xvi). Like Bloom, Kahn paints in broad strokes. He proceeds sequentially through the play, teasing out the 'large conceptual blocks' (p. xvii) of law/love conflicts as they culminate in the knowledge that 'Man must die to power if he is to love purely' (p. 1). Coming 'with the epiphany of grace' to Lear on the heath, this supreme insight allows Lear to understand 'at that moment of complete vision that he is beyond good and evil, and that forgiveness is the only free act of which a king – or anyone else – is capable' (p. 134).

In his disdain for the political realm, Kahn is generally like Spiekerman and more specifically like Bradley, for whom Cordelia retired from the field in triumph and felicity. In both cases, Kahn is disconnected from the beliefs dominating current Shakespearian commentary, in which love and law, the 'personal and the political', are not mutually exclusive but indissolubly intertwined orders of being. Kahn is aware of his difference from 'contemporary literary criticism', which seeks to relate texts to 'specific historical controversies' (p. xvii), but given his declared interest in 'generalities', historical specificity is inconsequential (p. xviii). He acknowledges current editorial concern with textual variation between early *Lear* texts, but having 'approached all of the controversies over text by asking how various readings would fit the general interpretation of the play I offer', he finds that 'In general . . . most of the controversies do not bear on the interpretation' (p. xx). Insouciantly reasserting generality in the face of arguments against it, Kahn evidently feels he can wear his difference without rue. He writes with disciplinary and institutional impunity, not as a Shakespearian but as a Professor of Law and the Humanities at Yale Law School, where they are free to do things differently. But the freedom comes at a certain cost – in relevance, consequence, utility. Despite the blurb's 'original . . . and extremely useful', usefulness is what the book lacks, and precisely *because* of Kahn's originality – its remoteness, that is, from the assumptions, values and procedures of those situated inside the Shakespearian tent.

Bloom, who taught in Chicago's School of Social Thought, and Spiekerman, who was educated in the same School and currently teaches in a political science department, share the same freedom with Kahn. Neither feels it necessary to engage more than perfunctorily with current Shakespearian work, but then we are equally free to ignore them as we proceed along the established routes of our own work. Despite current advocacy, then, interdisciplinarity may not be what people really want – not an alternative to disciplinary specialization, that is, but rather an alternative kind of specialization (Bourdieu instead of Coleridge, say) and hence a redefined form of professional correctness. This is not to deny the pleasures and understandings available in engaging with these three books, especially Bloom's, which is richly suggestive about a range of thinkers from Plato to

Saul Bellow. Its usefulness to professional Shake-spearians is limited, but Shakespearian work is not the be-all and end-all even for those of us who do it for a living.

Manhood, good manhood, is not forgot upon the face of the earth, to judge from Bruce Smith's *Shakespeare and Masculinity* and Robin Headlam Wells's *Shakespeare on Masculinity*. ' "Masculinity" ', according to Smith, is 'as much a social construction as "femininity" ' (p. 2), 'not a natural given' but 'an achievement' (p. 131). From this perspective he argues not for the non-existence of the category, distancing himself from recent critics who have 'stressed the nothing' (p. 132) – anxiety, depression, impotence – but for a various and multiple existence, requiring 'a rounded view', coming at 'the subject' not 'just from *one* critical vantage-point' (p. 5, his emphasis). In a chapter on 'Persons', masculinity emerges as 'a function of body chemistry' (p. 15). 'Ideals' examines the many diverse character types – 'chivalrous knight', 'Herculean hero', 'humanist man of moderation', 'merchant prince', 'saucy jack' (p. 56) – available for masculine realization. 'Passages' charts the trans-formative narratives in Shakespeare that 'manifest a variety of ways of understanding masculinity as something that happens in time' (p. 97). 'Others' discusses women, foreigners, persons of lower so-cial rank and sodomites as deviations against which masculine norms may be formed. A final chap-ter, 'Coalescences', looks at theatrical production across time and space to suggest Shakespeare's use-fulness in enabling us 'to imagine visions of mas-culinity more equitable and more fulfilling than those we already know' (p. 161).

Smith's commitment to diversity can produce surprising results. After a detailed exposition of Galenic balance and moderation, he veers into a coda endorsing Leeds Barroll's ' "Renaissance tran-scendentalism" ' in which ' "the desideratum for the human personality" must be, not the integra-tion of soul and body, but their separation' (p. 27). The use of 'human' here, even borrowed, is po-tentially contentious, and Smith's own discussion frequently tends toward a generally human – as distinct from strictly masculine – experience. If

Renaissance hierarchy 'meant that men were always defining themselves *vis-à-vis* men above them and below them', the William Gouge passage enlisted in support of this claim – just as the 'master that hath servants under him may be under the authority of a magistrate', so the 'wife, though mother of chil-dren, is under her husband' (p. 118) – suggests that women too experienced selfhood as an ambiva-lent positionality. Smith does not stress the simi-larity and is not about to call his book *Shakespeare and Humanity*, but he is not averse to risk. Despite the strong current advocacies for either one- or two-sex theories, Smith admits evidence for both (pp. 15–16, p. 106). Either/or is not his mode; he rejects 'essentialism versus constructionism' as an 'all-or-nothing proposition' (p. 132), and 'coales-cence' is meant to acknowledge the real – if always incomplete and unstable – achievements of mascu-line identity on the Shakespearian stage. Smith's glasses (or perhaps, in this context, his bags) are half full. His upbeat conclusions may not always be convincing: that the self-mastery of theatri-cal performance constitutes a masculine achieve-ment (pp. 32–36) seems more like a current than a Renaissance take. But Smith's large minded in-telligence communicates an abundance of useful knowledge in an accessible and consistently attrac-tive manner.

Among many beliefs he shares with Smith, Wells has no use for current claims that masculinity is an inevitably anxiety-fraught condition, (p. 5, pp. 212–14), but instead of surveying the exten-sive range of masculine possibility, Wells keys on a particular debate: on one side, a martial ideal, associated with Sidney and the Protestant party, ag-gressively interventionist in foreign policy during Elizabeth's reign, regrouping after the Essex fiasco around Prince Henry; on the other, a relatively pacifist ideal, represented by Burghley, Elizabeth and James himself, who sought an accommoda-tion among European religious and national dif-ferences. In effect, Wells examines the conflict between a residual value, associated with a declin-ing aristocracy, and an emergent or dominant ide-ology, associated with humanist educational goals, in which a civilizing Orphic harmony trumps the order produced by conquest. In Smith's terms, the 'Herculean hero' is displaced by the 'humanist man of moderation'.

Wells's *Henry V/ Troilus* chapter keys on 'the dangers of single-minded idealism' reflected in Henry's 'missionary zeal' (p. 43). In the Essex references, 'Shakespeare had to tread with extreme caution'. 'Returning to satirize the false ideals of masculine chivalry' in *Troilus* after Essex's disgrace, he 'could afford to drop his guard' (p. 51). *Hamlet* stages a conflict between the 'incompatible cultures' of 'classical epic and Norse saga' and 'the modern world of Christian humanist values' (p. 73). Othello and Coriolanus come out badly as part of an increasingly overt scepticism about heroic ideals. *Macbeth* is more ambiguous. Its neo-Virgilian equivocation between 'mutually opposed conceptions' – 'heroic epic' and 'the Gospels' – refuses to declare the 'superiority' of 'one set of values over another', because they are mutually dependent. 'Duncan's piety would be helpless without Macbeth's ferocity, and Macbeth's *virtus* mere barbarism without Duncan's *civilitas*' (p. 140). In Wells's final chapter, *The Tempest* complements Shakespeare's 'series of pessimistic analyses of the Herculean warrior-hero' with positive alternatives: 'the sensitive Ferdinand as a contrast to the harsh masculinity of the warrior-hero' (p. 201); and Prospero as 'an Orphic political leader' (p. 185) who resolves 'to suppress Herculean fury' for 'a rarer kind of virtue' (p. 195).

This interpretive structure – chapters on individual plays in chronological order – coincides with the title (another 'Shakespeare on . . .') to represent Wells's assumption of an author writing out of developing conviction. But Wells recognizes that theatrical texts are not windows onto authorial belief. He concedes that stage protagonists have an affective appeal independent of the values imputed to the playwright (pp. 80–5) and consistently accommodates 'the distinguished line of twentieth-century critics' for whom (although not wholly indifferent to the question, 'who is speaking?') 'the quality that is most characteristic of Shakespeare's plays is their ambivalence' (p. 24; see also pp. 122 and 210). Perhaps as a result of the same situatedness

as a Shakespearian, Wells sustains a running argument against the 'presentism' he finds in current criticism (pp. 18, 55–6, 57, 122, 123, 124, 133, 137, 170 and 207–18). Since the central historical thesis coincides precisely with Wells's own present beliefs ('I think the "ethic of heroism" has no place in the modern world . . . I suspect that Shakespeare probably felt the same' (p. 207)), his bona fides as a hard historicist may not be totally convincing; but his interpretations are interestingly persuasive quite apart from theoretical claims about their authentic cognitive status.

Good womanhood does not fare well on the Jacobean stage where, as Karen Bamford observes, female characters are regularly 'cursed, beaten, tortured, raped, pursued to death, pursued beyond death' (p. 161). *Sexual Violence on the Jacobean Stage* argues that the obsessive interest in rape shared by playwrights and audiences coincided with 'contemporary anxiety' about disorder (p. 12). As the consensual beliefs disintegrated on which social stability seemed to depend, the female body became symbolically central – the location for an intuited chaos come again, at once the origin of the problem (the whore, witch or shrew requiring punitive containment) and its solution ('the chaste victim of sexual aggression providing a scapegoat for an anxious patriarchal society' (p. 22)). Bamford identifies three scenarios in which Jacobean stage rapes performed the 'cultural work' of 'managing patriarchal anxieties' (p. 24). In descending order of importance: 'the heroine's suffering redeems her community from its bondage to the tyrant-rapist' – *Rape of Lucrece, Appius and Virginia, Revenger's Tragedy, Cymbeline, Second Maiden's Tragedy, Valentinian*, et al.; the heroine's 'triumphant chastity redeems the men around them' – *Pericles, Virgin Martyr, Martyred Soldier* et al.; 'the rapist, rather than the community, is redeemed', rescued from his own lust and forgiven 'by the providential craft of a benevolent older man' – *Measure for Measure, Queen of Corinth, Spanish Gypsy* (p. 23).

Bamford acknowledges that 'a diverse group of dramatists, with varied skills and interests' were not working to produce 'a conscious and unified ideological project' (p. 22). Willing, though, to ignore the 'peculiar' qualities of plays 'read individually' in favour of the 'mutually illuminating and congruent...patterns' that emerge when 'read collectively' (pp. 22, 23), she is sometimes quick to translate theatrical impressions into the master discourse of ideological effect. Hence of possible *Titus* echoes in *The Revenger's Tragedy*: in 'spite of the wide differences in tone', they 'emerge from the same paradigm of gender and rebellion' (p. 85). Or again, while 'consent or lack of consent to sexual intercourse' is 'theatrically and dramatically significant', it is 'wholly irrelevant to the question of "honor"', that 'emerges most clearly' from her synoptic view (p. 155). But if in drama 'the impression is the fact', it would work the other way around: 'honor' and other ideological values are shaped by the higher authority of theatrical effect. As Kathleen McLuskie argues, 'the direct link between cultural forms and social forms is broken by the particular characteristics of the theatre as a mode of cultural production' (quoted p. 11). This is not to deny that Renaissance plays 'performed cultural work', but to insist on the relative autonomy of theatre as an ideological apparatus and on the finesse required of those who log on and fill out the time sheets. Bamford understands the problem (she is the one quoting McLuskie, after all), and despite my niggles, her wide-ranging discussion sets a standard for many others who will want to follow her into this troubling and important subject.

Putting History to the Question collects fifteen essays Michael Neill has published during the last twenty-plus years. Neill organizes the material thematically rather than chronologically: 'The Stage and Social Order' includes essays on service, legitimacy and social mobility in *Arden*, Massinger, Middleton et al.; 'Race, Nation, Empire' has pieces on *Othello*, *Henry V*, *The Tempest* and Fletcher's *Island Princess*. The Introduction concedes the difficulties of 'historicist criticism': the remoteness and sometimes intentional ambiguity of Renaissance theatrical texts gives the metaphor of 'interrogating' the past, 'a certain uneasy appropriateness' (p. 1). But despite the book's sceptical title (taken from an uncharacteristically argumentative piece about Greenblatt), Neill claims that the enterprise

'need not be as difficult as it sounds' (p. 5). Remoteness is not inaccessibility; Foucaultian epistemic rupture was meant not as an 'irreducible truth' but as a corrective to the 'complacencies' by which 'Whig history' articulated smooth continuity (p. 5). Continuities remain in the 'structures of feeling' which, though no longer 'quite our own', contribute 'as surely as the genetic histories imprinted in every cell of our bodies...to what we are' (p. 9). Neill accommodates equivocal textuality with the kinds of arguments Raymond Williams employed to define 'structures of feeling'. Though Renaissance plays may not provide reliable information about material conditions, 'they are unfailingly sensitive registers of social attitudes and assumptions, fears and desires', 'what people *thought* was happening'; and 'since what people believe to be true is typically what determines the way they act', the plays are a 'remarkably illuminating' source of historical knowledge (pp. 3–4, Neill's emphasis).

These claims can themselves be put to the question. The 'structures of feeling' argument runs into the problem we have just encountered – no direct link between theatrical and social forms. Neill takes Massinger as his best case scenario, since 'no one who reads' him 'with any attentiveness can doubt that anxiety' about social instability 'was one of the abiding preoccupations of this society' (p. 3). But recent work by Wayne, Butler, and Leinwand has done just that, rethinking the relation between drama and society so that 'anxiety' is replaced by a more positive if not altogether celebratory response to the dynamic possibilities of the new socio-economic order. Behind this particular disagreement lurk those intractable theoretical problems Neill wants to dismiss. Maybe Foucault really meant it – the past is readable only as appropriation – and maybe the genetic imprint argument is just the last infirmity of humanist mind. Neill claims that 'the past can be as *eloquent in its troubling familiarity as it is taciturn in alterity* – and that the business of historical criticism is to trade as tactfully as possible between these contraries' (p. 5, my emphasis). But the thing about contraries is that they are not amenable to negotiation, no matter how tactful. There is a certain reliance here on rhetoric in the pejorative sense – the chiasmic style under-lined just above central to so much New Historicist writing: ('the textuality of history, the historicity of texts') – whose power to persuade withers under theoretical scrutiny.

But again, this is what theory does – preclude practice, or restrict it to its own discourse. Presentism vs. historicism constitutes an irresolv-able debate, and Neill does not want to go down this endless road. Even the few pages of methodological lucubration in his Introduction seem to be wrested from him, and he moves over with evident relief to a beautifully nuanced read-ing of pronouns in *Lear*, whose interest far exceeds any purportedly illustrative function. Like Green-blatt, who has nothing against 'methodological self-consciousness' but does not consider it 'inherently necessary or virtuous' (*Learning to Curse*, p. 167), Neill just wants to do historically inflected practical criticism. And he does it wonderfully well. 'Tact' may be one way to explain his success, or 'intel-ligence', Eliot's main criterion for good criticism, to which is added an abundantly detailed historical knowledge, derived evidently from lots of painstak-ing archival research. However we explain it, Neill's work has been consistently useful over the years, to judge from the regular allusions to these essays in the notes and parentheses of those who follow in his wake. By making this material more accessible, *Putting History to the Question* is bound to increase Neill's presence in ongoing work – a good thing.

Clayton MacKenzie is interested in the icono-graphic representations of mortality resonating throughout Renaissance culture. *Emblems of Mor-tality*, one of three books this year focusing on Shakespeare's tragedies or general tragic concerns, provides sustained readings of *Romeo* (an 'arresting conjunction of Love and Death' (p. 71)), the mid-dle histories ('the idea of "life in death"' functions ironically to qualify suggestions that magnanimity or grandeur of state can compensate for the loss of Eden (p. 15)), and *Hamlet* (*memento mori*, the Death's Head, the *danse macabre*). MacKenzie dis-cusses many details in other plays by Shakespeare as well as by Kyd, Marlowe, Dekker, Middleton, et al., and in non-dramatic literature (Spenser, Donne,

et al.). He ranges widely across emblem books, painting (lots of Holbein) and church monuments, including twenty-six plates. The book is generously responsive to current work and communicates con-siderable knowledge and critical intelligence with clarity and grace.

In *Shakespeare's Tragic Form: Spirit in the Wheel*, Richard Lanier Reid takes on the idea of struc-tural pattern. He concentrates on *Lear* and *Macbeth*, though his interest in formal integrity takes him beyond tragedy across the entire Shakespeare canon and extends (as his subtitle suggests) to psycho-logical and ontological effects as well. This last connection entails (among other matters) a com-parison of Shakespearian with Spenserian Platon-ism and spirituality. Reid pursues his interests with a broad knowledge of classical traditions and of modern critical interpretations from Baldwin on. He acknowledges that to 'seek a simple, singular form in Shakespeare's plays is to court frustration' (p. 13), and the felt need to complicate and qual-ify his claims makes this book impossible to sum-marize and sometimes hard to read. But like the poetic rhythms that make Shakespearian language so memorable, the structural patterns in the plays are of major consequence and deserve the kind of attention furnished here.

Charismatic Authority in Early Modern English Tragedy builds from 'the central paradox of charisma and group function': 'a group ideal tends to de-stroy the individuality of the human being at the group's core' even as 'the autonomy of an indi-vidual charismatic leader destroys the group ideal' (p. 1). Raphael Falco amplifies this idea with his-torical knowledge (the Pauline basis for charisma in Corinthians) and theoretical sophistication (the extent to which charismatic authority inherently transgresses established norms). The treatment of 'early modern subjectivity' in current literary crit-icism, including 'only a dusting of anthropologi-cal or sociological theory', reduces the topic to a 'polarizing either/or' between an essentially auto-nomous interiority and a socially determined dis-continuity. Working out of Max Weber and his followers, Falco insists rather on a 'dialectical and irresolvable' situation: 'normative' social structures and 'individual identity' are mutually constitutive as well as inherently antagonistic (pp. 10–11). This interdependence is not meant to deny the centrality of the protagonist to tragic experience. In contrast to the ' "oversocialized" ' modes of comedy and romance, tragedy works 'to recapitulate the relation of the individual to society by examining the power of choice and interpretation in fostering action' (p. 23). But since 'little critical attention has been paid to group dissolution' and 'the isolation of tragic figures dominates our analyses' (p. 1), Falco urges a corrective emphasis on group needs.

The book's main chapters focus on *Tamburlaine, Richard II, Hamlet* and *Othello, Samson Agonistes,* and *Cleopatra* (in Daniel, Shakespeare, Sedley, May and Dryden). His *Tamburlaine* integrates the two parts into a story about the routinization of charisma; the protagonist's authority 'little by little' becomes 'less revolutionary and more conventionally imperialistic' (p. 29; revolutions fail by succeeding: 'New Presbyter is but old Priest writ large'). *Richard II* shows how Richard's 'lineage' and Bolingbroke's 'personal' charismas 'conflict' and, at the same time, 'interpenetrate and overlap, producing ambiguous figures of shifting status' (p. 65). Charisma is an odd term for the laconic and pragmatic Bolingbroke, who buys loyalty with promises to respect prerogatives, and whose followers seem motivated by strategic self-interest rather than magical authority. With *Hamlet* and *Othello*, Falco takes on hard cases and knows it. Since 'group experience contributes less than individual revelation' in these plays (p. 101), his emphasis on Hamlet 'as a group leader' or 'the center of a group experience' (p. 103) is 'counterintuitive', not least because 'it is difficult . . . to identify specific members of a charismatic group responsive to Hamlet' (p. 104). The *Othello* discussion centers on a similarly provocative claim: the protagonist's 'individuation through marriage . . . isolates him from his group', disturbs 'the aim-inhibited libidinal ties that bound his army group together' (p. 120) and leads ultimately 'to the disintegration of his charismatic band' (p. 124). These strongly revisionary emphases may lose Falco some of his readership group, but risk-taking authorial leadership is appropriate to the subject,

and the book never relinquishes its suggestive power.

Lyell Asher takes on charisma too, though his word for it is 'lateness'. Lateness has many applications to tragic action and experience in general, but Asher is interested in its special relevance to King Lear's age. Lear discovers not only that he has no future (true of all tragic protagonists), but no past either – nothing specially heroic or transgressive in the vast expanse of personal history he carries with him into the action of the play. The 'peculiar trajectory of Lear's fall', thus (p. 218), is horizontal rather than vertical, like Gloucester's deluded leap. Asher Kottifies the play, transposing main and subplots, and the consequence (handy dandy) is to de-charismatize the protagonist. Instead of sensing a magical power they would fain call master, Asher's spectators discover kinship with Lear's belated status – 'themselves too late for a world of tragic grandeur, a world that has always already retreated into the bronze light of the past' – as folks to whom nothing special has happened. Asher thinks this a comforting recognition. 'Let us be the spectators of tragedy rather than the subject of one; let stamina, in other words, trump stature' (p. 227). In this triumph of normative group needs over individual transcendence, we cash in tragic nostalgia (there were giants in those days) for post-tragic relief (happy is the land that needs no heroes). Like Bradley's 'reconciliation', lateness serves the anaesthetizing function as parodied in an old *Simpsons*: camera pans cartoon faces wincing in horror at car crashes in a safe driving film, coming to rest on Homer's idiot grin: 'I'm laughing because it didn't happen to me.' The paradox of tragic pleasure is an important topic and Asher's piece as provocative and analytically powerful as anything I have read this year, but Dr Johnson's 'unendurable shock' will endure.

On September 5, 1607, *Hamlet* was performed aboard an English vessel harboured in what is now Freeport, Sierra Leone, before an audience that included four native guests – the first time Shakespeare was performed outside Europe. In an informative and shrewdly speculative essay, Gary Taylor reflects on the circumstances – local and immediate, global and historical – that defined this event, leading up to and away from it down to our own situated interests today. Like Greenblatt earlier on, Taylor focuses less on *Hamlet* than on its location. Taylor's emphasis on Africa is designed to correct the 'cultural imperialism' by which 'even in the 1990s, Shakespeare scholars who mention this incident treat Africa not as a subject of interest in itself' and even ignore or mistake significant facts about the episode. 'Shakespearians all know what "Africa" means, right?' Taylor asks (p. 224), after two notable *gotcha!*s, in the up-close-and-personally-challenging tone sustained engagingly throughout the piece. The tone works well here, because its immediate impact conceals unwanted complexities. While error is always regrettable, that Shakespearians are interested chiefly in Shakespeare is, after all, too much of a professional obligation to be a disgrace. Elsewhere the immediate impact of the personal creates problems, rather than disguising them. Speculating on what the four Africans aboard ship might have heard in the 'racially prejudiced' uses of 'black' in *Hamlet*, Taylor confesses that teaching at a university 'where one-sixth of our undergraduates are African-American students, I cannot help but be embarrassed by such images' (p. 238). Does this mean he would not be embarrassed teaching at Antioch, say, or Newcastle-upon-Tyne? Like Shaw, admitting that 'no man with any decency of feeling can sit [*Shrew*] out in the company of a woman without being extremely ashamed', Taylor seems to imply that the presence of the other, mixed company, is what creates the problem. These unintended implications tell us more about language and difference than about Taylor or GBS; but once you get started with the personal, where do you stop? Maybe the trick is not to get started. After all, *what difference does it make who is speaking?*

A big difference, according to Richard Wheeler, whose 'Deaths in the Family' undertakes both to practise and to justify biographical criticism. The practice connects Shakespeare's 'response to the death of his young son' to the histories, where repeatedly 'a young boy's death produces a volatile mix of parental grief, distraction, helplessness,

recrimination, rage', and to the comedies, which complete 'the movement from youth into early adulthood' denied Hamnet (p. 145). In the justification, Wheeler argues that 'Notions of the author ... enter into all interpretation', so we wind up doing biographical criticism anyway (p. 130). This allows for too much slippage between forms of authorial presence. While interpretation is always grounded in human intention, the face we put on this intention need not be Shakespeare the grieving father. It could be Shakespeare the secret (or lapsed) Catholic, or a multitude of non-biographical faces as well – reinforcer of the patriarchy, advocate of plebian interests, etc. This feeds into Wheeler's second defense-that there is no compelling reason why 'the fairly extensive information we have about Shakespeare's life' should not be allowed, like other historical data, to contribute to interpretive conclusions (p. 130). True enough: biographical criticism is as legitimate as the other kinds – or the other kinds as illegitimate as it. There is no firm theoretical basis for choosing between biographical and non-biographical modes, or between different kinds of biographical or non-biographical modes. What we need, though, is not theoretical legitimacy but a critical mass of people inside the tent disposed to what we want to do. Given the number of Shakespearians excited by the new portrait, Hoghton Tower, and the Peter Elegy, invited even now as I write to attend a conference on new directions in biographical criticism, scheduled for the very room where Thomas Jenkins may have introduced our favourite author to his favourite author, Wheeler has nothing to worry about.

WORKS REVIEWED

Adamson, Sylvia, 'The Grand Style', in Adamson et al., *Reading Shakespeare's Dramatic Language*, pp. 31–50.

'Understanding Shakespeare's Grammar: Studies in Small Words', in Adamson, et al., *Reading Shakespeare's Dramatic Language*, pp. 210–36.

Lynette Hunter, Lynne Magnusson, Ann Thompson, and Katie Wales, Introduction: 'Reading Shakespeare's English', in Adamson et al., *Reading Shakespeare's Dramatic Language*, p. 191.

Lynette Hunter, Lynne Magnusson, Ann Thompson, and Katie Wales, eds., *Reading Shakespeare's Dramatic Language: A Guide* (London, 2001).

Albanese, Denise, 'The Shakespeare Film and the Americanization of Culture', in Howard and Shershow, *Marxist Shakespeares*, pp. 206–26.

Allsopp, Ric, '*Tempest(s)* at Terra Nova Theatre Institute', in Hulme and Sherman, '*The Tempest' and its Travels*, pp. 162–67.

Asher, Lyell, 'Lateness in *King Lear*', *Yale Journal of Criticism* 13 (2000), 209–28.

Bamford, Karen, *Sexual Violence on the Jacobean Stage* (London, 2000).

Bartolovich, Crystal, ' "Baseless Fabric": London as a "World City" ', in Hulme and Sherman, '*The Tempest' and its Travels*, pp. 13–26.

'Shakespeare's Globe?', in Howard and Shershow, *Marxist Shakespeares*, pp. 178–205.

Bloom, Allan, *Shakespeare on Love and Friendship* (Chicago, 2000).

Bowen, Barbara E., 'The Rape of Jesus: Aemilia Lanyer's *Lucrece*', in Howard and Shershow, *Marxist Shakespeares*, pp. 104–27.

Braden, Gordon, 'Ovid, Petrarch, and Shakespeare's Sonnets', in Taylor, *Shakespeare's Ovid*, pp. 96–112.

Bristol, Michael D., 'How Many Children Did She Have?', in Joughin, *Philosophical Shakespeares*, pp. 18–33.

'Vernacular Criticism and the Scenes Shakespeare Never Wrote', *Shakespeare Survey 53* (Cambridge, 2000), pp. 89–102.

Brotton, Jeremy, 'Carthage and Tunis, *The Tempest* and Tapestries', in Hulme and Sherman, '*The Tempest' and its Travels*, pp. 132–37.

Bruster, Douglas, 'Shakespeare and the End of History: Period as Brand Name', in Grady, *Shakespeare and Modernity*, pp. 168–88.

Burt, Richard, 'No Holes Bard: Homonormativity and the Gay and Lesbian Romance with *Romeo and Juliet*', in Hedrick and Reynolds, *Shakespeare Without Class*, pp. 153–86.

Callaghan, Dympna, 'Looking Well to Linens: Women and Cultural Production in *Othello* and Shakespeare's England', in Howard and Shershow, *Marxist Shakespeares*, pp. 53–81.

Carroll, William C., ' "And love you 'gainst the nature of love": Ovid, Rape, and *The Two Gentlemen of Verona*', in Taylor, *Shakespeare's Ovid*, pp. 49–65.

Cavell, Stanley, 'Foreword', in Joughin, *Philosophical Shakespeares*, pp. xii–xvi.

Cefalu, Paul A., 'Rethinking the Discourse of Colonialism in Economic Terms: Shakespeare's *The Tempest*, Captain John Smith's Virginia Narratives, and the English Response to Vagrancy', *Shakespeare Studies* 28 (2000), pp. 85–119.

Charnes, Linda, 'The Hamlet Formerly Known as Prince', in Grady, *Shakespeare and Modernity*, pp. 189–210.

'We Were Never Early Modern', in Joughin, *Philosophical Shakespeares*, pp. 51–67.

Chedgzoy, Kate, Introduction, in Chedgzoy, *Shakespeare, Feminism and Gender*, pp. 1–23.

ed., *Shakespeare, Feminism and Gender: Contemporary Critical Essays*. New Casebooks (Basingstoke and New York, 2001).

Cioni, Fernando, 'Shakespeare's Italian Intertexts: *The Taming of the/a Shrew*', in Marrapodi, *Shakespeare and Intertextuality*, pp. 149–61.

Cohen, Stephen, '(Post)modern Elizabeth: Gender, Politics and the Emergence of Modern Subjectivity', in Grady, *Shakespeare and Modernity*, pp. 20–39.

Cohen, Walter, 'The Undiscovered Country: Shakespeare and Mercantile Geography', in Howard and Shershow, *Marxist Shakespeares*, pp. 128–58.

Domenichelli, Mario, 'Renaissance Chivalry and "Handsome Death" in Shakespeare's *Troilus and Cressida*', in Marrapodi, *Shakespeare and Intertextuality*, pp. 85–99.

Drakakis, John, ' "*Jew*. Shylock is my Name": Speech Prefixes in *The Merchant of Venice* as Symptoms of the Early Modern', in Grady, *Shakespeare and Modernity*, pp. 105–21.

Elam, Keir, ' "The continent of what part a gentleman would see": English Bodies in European Habits', in Marrapodi, *Shakespeare and Intertextuality*, pp. 39–68.

'Language and the Body', in Adamson et al., *Reading Shakespeare's Dramatic Language*, pp. 173–87.

'Welcome to the Round Table', in Marrapodi, *Shakespeare and Intertextuality*, pp. 295–310.

Falco, Raphael, *Charismatic Authority in Early Modern English Tragedy* (Baltimore and London, 2000).

Fitter, Chris, ' "The Quarrel is Between Our Masters and Us Their Men": *Romeo and Juliet*, Dearth, and the London Riots', *English Literary Renaissance* 30 (2000), 154–83.

Foucault, Michel, 'What is an Author?', in Josué V. Harari, ed., *Textual Strategies: Perspectives in Post-Structuralist Criticism* (Ithaca, 1979), pp. 141–60.

Fowler, Elizabeth, 'The Ship Adrift', in Hulme and Sherman, '*The Tempest' and Its Travels*, pp. 37–40.

Gillies, John, 'The Figure of the New World in *The Tempest*', in Hulme and Sherman, '*The Tempest' and Its Travels*, pp. 180–200.

Goldberg, Jonathan, 'Shakespeare Writing Matter Again: Objects and Their Detachments', *Shakespeare Studies*, 28 (2000), 248–51.

Grady, Hugh, 'Introduction: Shakespeare and Modernity', in Grady, *Shakespeare and Modernity*, 1–19.

'On the Need for a Differentiated Theory of (Early) Modern Subjects', in Joughin, *Philosophical Shakespeares*, pp. 34–50.

ed., *Shakespeare and Modernity: Early Modern to Millennium*. Accents on Shakespeare (London and New York, 2000).

Greenblatt, Stephen, *Hamlet in Purgatory* (Princeton, 2001).

Learning to Curse: Essays in Early Modern Culture (New York and London, 1990).

Renaissance Self-Fashioning: From More to Shakespeare (Chicago, 1980).

Shakespearean Negotiations: The Circulation of Social Energy in Renaissance England (Berkeley and Los Angeles, 1988).

Greene, Roland, 'Island Logic', in Hulme and Sherman, '*The Tempest' and its Travels*, pp. 138–45.

Griffin, Julia, 'The Magician in Love', *Shakespeare Survey 53* (Cambridge, 2000), pp. 137–50.

Gross, Kenneth, *Shakespeare's Noise* (Chicago, 2001).

Halpern, Richard, 'An Impure History of Ghosts: Derrida, Marx, Shakespeare', in Howard and Shershow, *Marxist Shakespeares*, pp. 31–52.

Hamilton, Donna B., 'Re-Engineering Virgil: *The Tempest* and the Printed English *Aeneid*', in Hulme and Sherman, '*The Tempest' and its Travels*, pp. 114–20.

Hawkes, Terence, 'General Editor's Preface', in Grady, *Shakespeare and Modernity*, pp. ix–x, Howard and Shershow, pp. xi–xii, and in Joughin, *Philosophical Shakespeares*, pp. x–xi.

Hedrick, Donald, 'Shakespeare's Enduring Immorality: the Ethical vs. the Performative Turn, or Toward a Transversal Pedagogy', in Hedrick and Reynolds, *Shakespeare Without Class*, pp. 241–74.

Hedrick, Donald and Bryan Reynolds, 'Shakespace and Transversal Power', in Hedrick and Reynolds, *Shakespeare Without Class*, pp. 3–47.

eds., *Shakespeare Without Class: Misappropriations of Cultural Capital* (New York and Houndsmill, Basingstoke, 2000).

Hess, Andrew C., 'The Mediterranean and Shakespeare's Geopolitical Imagination', in Hulme and Sherman, '*The Tempest' and its Travels*, pp. 121–30.

Howard, Jean E. and Scott Cutler Shershow, 'Introduction: Marxism Now, Shakespeare Now', in Howard and Shershow, *Marxist Shakespeares*, pp. 1–15.

eds., *Marxist Shakespeares*. Accents on Shakespeare (London and New York, 2000).

Hulme, Peter and William T. Sherman, Introduction: 'European and Mediterranean Crossroads', in Hulme and Sherman, '*The Tempest' and its Travels*, pp. 73–77.

Introduction: 'Local Knowledge', in Hulme and Sherman, '*The Tempest' and its Travels*, pp. 3–11.

'Preface', in Hulme and Sherman, '*The Tempest' and its Travels*, pp. xi–xiv.

eds., "*The Tempest' and its Travels*. Critical Views (London, 2000).

Hunt, Maurice, *Approaches to Teaching Shakespeare's 'Romeo and Juliet'* (New York, 2000).

Hunter, Lynette, 'Persuasion', in Adamson et al., *Reading Shakespeare's Dramatic Language*, pp. 113–29.

Joughin, John J., 'Philosophical Shakespeares: an Introduction', in Joughin, *Philosophical Shakespeares*, pp. 1–17.

'Shakespeare, Modernity and the Aesthetic: Art, Truth and Judgement in *The Winter's Tale*', in Grady, *Shakespeare and Modernity*, pp. 61–84.

ed., *Philosophical Shakespeares*. Accents on Shakespeare (London and New York, 2000).

Kahn, Paul W., *Law and Love: The Trials of 'King Lear'* (New Haven and London, 2000).

Kamps, Ivo, ' "I Love You Madly, I Love You to Death": Erotomania and *Liebestod* in *Romeo and Juliet*', in Hunt, *Approaches to Teaching Shakespeare's 'Romeo and Juliet'*, pp. 37–46.

Katz, Leslie, 'Rehearsing the Weird Sisters: The Word as Fetish in *Macbeth*', in Hedrick and Reynolds, *Shakespeare Without Class*, pp. 229–39.

Kehler, Dorothea, 'Teaching *Romeo and Juliet* Historically', in Hunt, *Approaches to Teaching Shakespeare's 'Romeo and Juliet'*, pp. 78–84.

Kidnie, Margaret Jane, 'Text, Performance, and the Editors: Staging Shakespeare's Drama', *Shakespeare Quarterly*, 51 (2000), 456–73.

Kiernan, Pauline, '*Venus and Adonis* and Ovidian Indecorous Wit', in Taylor, *Shakespeare's Ovid*, pp. 81–95.

Kinney, Arthur F., 'Authority in *Romeo and Juliet*', in Hunt, *Approaches to Teaching Shakespeare's 'Romeo and Juliet'*, pp. 29–36.

Kirkpatrick, Robin, 'The Italy of *The Tempest*', in Hulme and Sherman, '*The Tempest' and its Travels*, pp. 78–96.

Korda, Natasha, '"Judicious oeillades": Supervising Marital Property in *The Merry Wives of Windsor*', in Howard and Shershow, *Marxist Shakespeares*, pp. 82–103.

Lass, Roger, 'Shakespeare's Sounds', in Adamson et al., *Reading Shakespeare's Dramatic Language*, pp. 256–68.

Lee, John, *Shakespeare's 'Hamlet' and the Controversies of Self* (Oxford and New York, 2000).

Lupton, Julia Reinhard, 'Afterword: Shakespace on Marloan', in Hedrick and Reynolds, *Shakespeare Without Class*, pp. 277–85.

'Creature Caliban', *Shakespeare Quarterly*, 51 (2000), 1–23.

Lyne, Raphael, 'Ovid, Golding and the "Rough Magic" of *The Tempest*', in Taylor, *Shakespeare's Ovid*, pp. 150–64.

MacKenzie, Clayton G., *Emblems of Mortality: Iconographic Experiments in Shakespeare's Theatre* (Lanham, Maryland and Oxford, 2000).

Magnusson, Lynne, 'Dialogue', in Adamson et al., *Reading Shakespeare's Dramatic Language*, pp. 130–43.

'Style, Rhetoric and Decorum', in Adamson et al., *Reading Shakespeare's Dramatic Language*, pp. 17–30.

Mallin, Eric S., 'Jewish Invader and the Soul of State: *The Merchant of Venice* and Science Fiction Movies', in Grady, *Shakespeare and Modernity*, pp. 142–67.

Marrapodi, Michele, 'Introduction: Intertextualising Shakespeare's Text', in Marrapodi, *Shakespeare and Intertextuality*, pp. 11–20.

ed., *Shakespeare and Intertextuality: The Transition of Cultures Between Italy and England in the Early Modern Period* (Rome, 2000).

Marshall, Cynthia, '"Who Wrote the Book of Love?": Teaching *Romeo and Juliet* with Early Rock Music', in Hunt, *Approaches to Teaching Shakespeare's 'Romeo and Juliet'*, pp. 98–107.

Martindale, Charles. 'Shakespeare's Ovid, Ovid's Shakespeare: A Methodological Postscript', in Taylor, *Shakespeare's Ovid*, pp. 198–215.

Maslen, R. W., 'Myths Exploited: the Metamorphoses of Ovid in Early Elizabethan England', in Taylor, *Shakespeare's Ovid*, pp. 15–30.

McBride, Phyllis, 'In Her Father's Library: Margaret Fuller and the Making of the American Miranda', *Shakespeare Survey 53* (Cambridge, 2000), pp. 127–36.

Miola, Robert S., 'Seven Types of Intertextuality', in Marrapodi, *Shakespeare and Intertextuality*, pp. 23–38.

Moisan, Thomas, '"Now Art Thou What Thou Art": or, Being Sociable in Verona: Teaching Gender and Desire in *Romeo and Juliet*', in Hunt, *Approaches to Teaching Shakespeare's 'Romeo and Juliet'*, pp. 47–58.

Morse, Ruth, 'Monsters, Magicians, Movies: *The Tempest* and the Final Frontier', *Shakespeare Survey 53* (Cambridge, 2000), pp. 164–75.

Mousley, Andy, *Renaissance Drama and Contemporary Literary Theory* (London and New York, 2000).

Mowat, Barbara, '"Knowing I loved my books": Reading *The Tempest* Intertextually', in Hulme and Sherman, '*The Tempest' and Its Travels*, pp. 27–36.

Nash, Walter, 'Puns and Parody', in Adamson et al., *Reading Shakespeare's Dramatic Language*, pp. 71–88.

Neill, Michael, Introduction, in Neill, *Putting History to the Question*, pp. 1–9.

Putting History to the Question: Power, Politics and Society in English Renaissance Drama (New York, 2000).

Netto, Jeffrey A., 'Sensuous Games: The Iconography of Chess in *The Tempest*', in Marrapodi, *Shakespeare and Intertextuality*, pp. 257–70.

Nuttall, A. D., '*The Winter's Tale*: Ovid Transformed', in Taylor, *Shakespeare's Ovid*, pp. 135–49.

O'Dair, Sharon, *Class, Critics, and Shakespeare: Bottom Lines on the Culture Wars* (Ann Arbor, 2000).

Parker, Patricia, 'Murder in Guyana', *Shakespeare Studies* 28 (2000), 169–74.

Peck, John, and Martin Coyle, 'General Editors' Preface', in Chedgzoy, *Shakespeare, Feminism and Gender*, p.ix.

Perry, Curtis, 'Vaulting Ambitions and Killing Machines: Shakespeare, Jarry, Ionesco, and the Senecan Absurd', in Hedrick and Reynolds, *Shakespeare Without Class*, pp. 85–106.

Peyré, Yves, 'Niobe and the Nemean Lion: reading *Hamlet* in the Light of Ovid's *Metamorphoses*', in Taylor, *Shakespeare's Ovid*, pp. 126–34.

Porter, Joseph A., 'The Wild Goose Chase: Teaching Metaphor in *Romeo and Juliet*', in Hunt, *Approaches to Teaching Shakespeare's 'Romeo and Juliet'*, pp. 144–52.

Reid, Robert Lanier, *Shakespeare's Tragic Form: Spirit in the Wheel* (Newark, Delaware and London, 2000).

Reynolds, Bryan, '"What is the city but the people?": Transversal Performance and Radical Politics in Shakespeare's *Coriolanus* and Brecht's *Coriolan*', in Hedrick and Reynolds, *Shakespeare Without Class*, pp. 107–32.

Richmond, Hugh Macrae, Introduction: '*Richard III* Restored', in Richmond, *Critical Essays on Shakespeare's 'Richard III'*, pp. 1–14.

'Postmodern Renderings of *Richard III*', in Richmond, *Critical Essays*, pp. 257–66.

'*Richard III* Contextualized', in Richmond, *Critical Essays*, pp. 15–16.

'*Richard III* Deconstructed', in Richmond, *Critical Essays*, pp. 255–6.

'*Richard III* Recognized', in Richmond, *Critical Essays*, pp. 115–16.

'*Richard III* Reinvented', in Richmond, *Critical Essays*, pp. 73–4.

ed., *Critical Essays on Shakespeare's 'Richard III'*. Critical Essays on British Literature (New York, 1999).

Richmond, Velma Bourgeois, *Shakespeare, Catholicism, and Romance* (New York and London, 2000).

Roach, Joseph, 'The Enchanted Island: Vicarious Tourism in Restoration Adaptations of *The Tempest*', in Hulme and Sherman, '*The Tempest*' and its *Travels*, pp. 60–70.

Roe, John, 'Ovid "renascent" in *Venus and Adonis* and *Hero and Leander*', in Taylor, *Shakespeare's Ovid*, pp. 31–46.

Ryan, Kiernan, '*Measure for Measure*: Marxism Before Marx', in Howard and Shershow, *Marxist Shakespeares*, pp. 227–44.

Shershow, Scott Cutler, 'Shakespeare Beyond Shakespeare', in Howard and Shershow, *Marxist Shakespeares*, pp. 245–64.

Smith, Bruce R., *Shakespeare and Masculinity*. Oxford Shakespeare Topics (Oxford, 2000).

Smith, Ian. 'When We Were Capital, or Lessons in Language: Finding Caliban's Roots', *Shakespeare Studies* 28 (2000), 252–6.

Smith, Peter J., 'A "Consummation Devoutly to be Wished": The Erotics of Narration in *Venus and Adonis*', *Shakespeare Survey 53* (Cambridge, 2000), pp. 25–38.

Spiekerman, Tim, *Shakespeare's Political Realism: The English History Plays* (Albany, N Y., 2001).

Stallybrass, Peter. 'Material Culture: Introduction', *Shakespeare Studies* 28 (2000), 123–9.

Stapleton, M. L., *Fated Sky: The 'Femina Furens' in Shakespeare* (Newark, Delaware and London, 2000).

Stevens, Paul, 'Pretending to be Real: Stephen Greenblatt and the Legacy of Popular Existentialism', *New Literary History* 33 (2002).

Taylor, A. B., 'Animals in "manly Shape as Too the Outward Showe": Moralizing and Metamorphosis in *Titus Andronicus*', in Taylor, *Shakespeare's Ovid*, pp. 66–80.

Introduction, in Taylor, *Shakespeare's Ovid*, pp. 1–12.

ed., *Shakespeare's Ovid: The 'Metamorphoses' in the Plays and Poems* (Cambridge, 2000).

Taylor, Gary, '*Hamlet* in Africa 1607', in Ivo Kamps and Jyotsna G. Singh, eds., *Travel Knowledge: European 'Discoveries' in the Early Modern Period* (New York, 2001), pp. 223–48.

Thompson, Ann, 'Heightened Language', in Adamson et al., *Reading Shakespeare's Dramatic Language*, pp. 5–16.

Tomlinson, Gary, 'The Matter of Sounds', *Shakespeare Studies* 28 (2000), 236–9.

Tudeau-Clayton, Margaret, 'Stepping out of Narrative Line: A Bit of World, and Horse, Play in *Venus and Adonis*', *Shakespeare Survey 53* (Cambridge, 2000), pp. 12–38.

Vanita, Ruth, 'Mariological Memory in *The Winter's Tale* and *Henry VIII*', *Studies in English Literature 1500–1900* 40 (2000), 311–37.

Velz, John W., 'Shakespeare's Ovid in the Twentieth Century: A Critical Survey', in Taylor, *Shakespeare's Ovid*, pp. 181–94.

Wales, Katie, 'An A–Z of Rhetorical Terms', in Adamson et al., *Reading Shakespeare's Dramatic Language*, pp. 271–301.

'Varieties and Variation', in Adamson et al., *Reading Shakespeare's Dramatic Language*, pp. 192–209.

Warner, Marina, ' "The foul witch" and Her "freckled whelp": Circean Mutations in the New World', in Hulme and Sherman, '*The Tempest*' and its *Travels*, pp. 97–113.

Wells, Robin Headlam, *Shakespeare on Masculinity* (Cambridge, 2000).

Wheeler, Richard P., 'Deaths in the Family: The Loss of a Son and the Rise of Shakespearean Comedy', *Shakespeare Quarterly* 51 (2000), 127–53.

Wilson, Richard, 'The Management of Mirth: Shakespeare via Bourdieu', in Howard and Shershow, *Marxist Shakespeares*, pp. 159–77.

Wright, George T., 'Shakespeare's Metre Scanned', in Adamson et al., *Reading Shakespeare's Dramatic Language*, pp. 51–70.

Zender, Karl F., 'Loving Shakespeare's Lovers: Character Growth in *Romeo and Juliet*', in Hunt, *Approaches to Teaching Shakespeare's 'Romeo and Juliet'*, pp. 137–43.

2. SHAKESPEARE'S LIFE, TIMES AND STAGE

reviewed by LESLIE THOMSON

I

For a group of books as miscellaneous as this review section attracts, no principle of organization really works, but the title's terms 'life', 'times' and 'stage' are a place to start. A problem of disproportion nevertheless remains, since for obvious reasons there is little new to say about Shakespeare's biography. This has not, however, deterred Katherine Duncan-Jones from writing *Ungentle Shakespeare: Scenes from his Life*. Under the imprint of Arden Shakespeare, but very much displaying the commercial auspices of Thomson Learning, the material object seems to be saying 'this is an important book' – large and heavy, with a very red cover, glossy pages, and numerous (often tangential) illustrations. As the title's emphasis on 'ungentle' indicates, Duncan-Jones's aim is to 'bring Shakespeare down from the lofty isolation to which he has been customarily elevated, and to show him as a man among men, a writer among writers', whose brilliance elicited envy rather than admiration (p. x). Further, she says her purpose is 'to explore some of the areas of Shakespeare's life' neglected by Schoenbaum and others, and that she has chosen 'generally, for preference, the road less travelled' (p. ix). In a territory as over-explored as Shakespearian biography, if a road has remained largely untravelled there is usually a good reason why so many others have avoided it. Duncan-Jones's chief concerns are 'social class, sex and money', topics she describes as previously 'taboo' in Shakespeare biography (p. xi). Typically her strategy is to weave a web of interrelated arguments in which an idea introduced as a possibility in one paragraph or chapter becomes a fact in the next, then the basis for a new speculation and so on; the result is a circular tour de force of guesswork and invention.

The second chapter, for example, is devoted to Duncan-Jones's belief that Shakespeare was a member of the Queen's Men between 1589 and 1592,

a belief 'suggested . . . by the abundant evidence of his close and intimate knowledge of their plays'. She argues that '*If* Heminge and Shakespeare were for a time among Leicester's Men, their service *may have been* fairly brief. An exciting possibility is that they *could have been* part of that large group of Leicester's performers . . . who *went* to the Netherlands in his train, and *performed* at Utrecht on St George's Day 1586' (p. 31, my italics). The intrepid reader who negotiates the subsequent maze of conjecture will soon be given a new signpost: 'The rest of this chapter will be based on the *supposition* that from about 1588 Shakespeare *was indeed* a Queen's Man' (p. 36, my italics). When Duncan-Jones later criticizes R. B. McKerrow for offering 'a rather strained hypothesis' (p. 69), she seems unaware how often she does exactly that. Speculation is rampant throughout, with heavy use of the usual qualifiers – seems, perhaps, possibly, I believe, I think – although one frequently gets the impression that Duncan-Jones has no doubts, and conjecture is often stated as fact. At the start, she thanks various people, but asserts 'I have in many instances stuck stubbornly to my guns, against their sage advice' (p. xiv). No one who reads even part of her book will doubt the truth of this defiant statement. By interpreting Shakespeare's works in terms of 'scenes from his life' and inserting his life into his plays and poems, this book reduces the products of genius to something more like episodes in a soap opera.

Although, as Robert S. Miola notes, 'we cannot confidently identify a single volume as belonging to [Shakespeare]' (p. 164), his *Shakespeare's Reading* offers far more satisfying (and plausible) explanations for various aspects of Shakespeare's works. An addition to the Oxford Shakespeare Topics series, this is not simply another source study but an explication of influences from classical and other literature, informed by Miola's thorough knowledge of Greek, Latin and Italian. The result is a series of pithy yet comprehensive analyses of Shakespeare's works and his use of sources. The book is organized around not the plays but the texts and traditions – the 'inherited strategies and expectations about character and action' (p. 15) – upon which Shakespeare drew. Two tables at the end of the first chapter set out the principal sources and traditions along with the Shakespeare works to be covered: the sources are Ovid's *Metamorphoses* and *Fasti*, Holinshed's *Chronicles*, Plautus's *Menaechmi*, Fiorentino's *Il Pecorone*, Plutarch's *Lives*, the anonymous *King Leir*, Greene's *Pandosto* and Chaucer's *Canterbury Tales*; the traditions are Italian love poetry, the vice figure, the classical conflict between fathers and lovers, Senecan revenge, and pastoral (p. 16). This method of organization admittedly produces a stimulating, multi-faceted survey, but it also necessitates some jumping back and forth, which results in a tendency to repetition.

Miola's discussion of Shakespeare's sonnets illustrates his point that they 'derive demonstrably from his reading, whatever other biographical inspirations may have once existed' (p. 27), with Italian love poetry being a central influence. But he also documents Shakespeare's reworking of source material for his own purposes. Several times we are shown how he expanded the role of women in a source, as with Portia in *The Merchant of Venice*. In his consideration of the father/lover conflict, Miola naturally looks mostly at comedies, but also at *Othello*, noting that Brabantio's 'anguish, animated with the ache of betrayal, reformulates the classic comic conflict. Shakespeare turns the comic stereotype inside out and presents us with a serious, tragic *senex*' (p. 95). He shows how, in *Julius Caesar*, Plutarch contributes 'a defining perspective to Shakespeare's balanced and ambivalent play' (p. 100), while the discussion of *Hamlet* reveals how 'From the beginning . . . Shakespeare exploits and subverts Senecan revenge traditions' (p. 121). At the end, Miola provides a clear summary, confirming the impression that although echoes or influence are the starting point of his discussions, this book is often as much or more a series of perceptive analyses of what Shakespeare wrote than simply of what he read.

A timely complement to Miola's study is *Shakespeare's Books: A Dictionary of Shakespeare Sources*, by Stuart Gillespie. At over 500 pages, it updates previous reference works on the topic and, unlike them, is organized by source as a dictionary. Citing Miola, Gillespie includes in his idea of a source 'intertextuality more loosely conceived' (p. 2). The arrangement of entries is explained in the introduction, the format being generally that of other Athlone Shakespeare dictionaries. The first section of an entry gives factual details about the source author and/or work(s); in the second, Shakespeare's probable knowledge of and access to the source is assessed; the third deals with the relationship between the source and Shakespeare's plays and poems. The final section is a bibliography. A shorter form of entry is used for subjects considered to be only minor or doubtful sources. For instance, William Caxton receives four pages for having translated the *Recuyell of the Historyes of Troye*: we are given the publishing history, cross references to Homer and to Lydgate among others, a sizeable segment in original spelling, a mention of the other two main sources of the Troy legend, and a list of eleven references. By contrast, the entry for Cervantes which follows is a mere four lines, noting that the tale of Cardenio and Luscinda in *Don Quixote* is the source for the lost *History of Cardenio*, and providing one reference. Among the sources given extensive entries are the Bible, Cicero, Daniel, Erasmus, Greene, Harsnett, Homilies, Montaigne, Morality Tradition, Mystery Plays, Seneca, and *Tottel's Miscellany*. As the world known as 'Shakespeare' enlarges exponentially, reference works are not just helpful but absolutely necessary; many of us will doubtless be grateful for this one.

II

Martin Wiggins's *Shakespeare and the Drama of his Time*, another in the Oxford Shakespeare Topics series, is an informed and engaging story of the evolution of early modern drama, not at all merely a summary of what has already been said. As the title indicates, Wiggins links 'Shakespeare'

with 'the drama of his time'; as a welcome consequence, probably as much attention is given to
other plays as to his. In discussing *Tamburlaine*, *The
Spanish Tragedy*, and *Dr. Faustus*, Wiggins observes
that with these plays 'Tragedy had begun to ask
its audiences to respond with humane subjectivity;
the essence of the experience was now a relationship with another human being' (p. 42). He charts
the genre's evolution under the influence of humanism and its emphasis on right choice, describing the process very effectively through the analysis of specific plays and tragic protagonists. Among
Wiggins's cogent observations is that 'During the
1590s, Shakespeare became the London theatre's
pre-eminent dramatist not only through talent but
also by default' (p. 53). Arguing that in 1597, between the writing of the two parts of *Henry IV*,
'drama became self-consciously modern' (p. 56),
he cites *Every Man in His Humour* as an example
of how 'Dramatic speech turned from the high
style to the low' and how 'Plotting and characterization underwent a corresponding change of
focus' to private matters and petty humanity, initiating the turn in taste towards comedy (pp. 56–7).
In the penultimate chapter, 'How to Write a Play',
Wiggins explains the accepted conventions of playwriting and why they were not always followed.
He accurately observes that 'a play's themes were
as much a part of its structural make-up as was
its story: the "rhetorical" patterning of the action contributes not only to the play's narrative
exposition but also to the audiences's apprehen-
sion of its conceptual argument' (p. 84). The discussion of tragi-comedy considers such matters as
how inductions and other framing devices mark
a change to greater self-consciousness in drama.
Wiggins concludes by describing a 'King's Men
style' (p. 127), which reflected later playwrights'
awareness that they were 'post-Shakespearian', the
result being 'a drama with a broad streak of nostalgia
and a noticeable dependence on recycled materials' (p. 130). He observes that 'Shakespeare did not
open out new and influential modes of drama in
the way that Marlowe and Chapman and Marston
had done, enabling later writers to exercise their
own creativity in different ways; he only provided

them with a treasure-house of new source material'
(p. 132).

Shakespeare's relationships with his contemporaries are also the concern of James P. Bednarz
in *Shakespeare and the Poets' War*, which begins
by asserting that 'The legend of Shakespeare and
Jonson's wit-combats is unarguably the most famous case of poetic rivalry in the annals of English
literature' (p. 1). This confident tone is indicative of
what is to come: Bednarz has no doubt that there
was a 'poets' war' and that Shakespeare was one of
the chief combatants. Readers who already share
his view will likely find this detailed study very satisfying; those who know little about what seemed
an arcane topic will be enlightened by the generally
clear discussion and analysis – while those who do
not believe that there was a *poetomachia* will probably react in frustration to Bednarz's assertions and
conclusions (a problem of which he is aware, p. 5).
His 'goal is to present the first comprehensive account of the Poets' War as a crisis of legitimation,
a literary civil war during which Jonson's vanguard
project [which Bednarz defines as 'to establish for
himself and for his age a new paradigm of poetic
authority'] clashed with the skepticism of Marston,
Shakespeare and Dekker, who literally laughed him
off the stage' (p. 3). In support of this interpretation he provides a chart of the chronology of
the plays in the battle and an appendix in which
the posited sequence is explained. Briefly, he sees
'three phases, each of which was initiated by one
of Jonson's comical satires followed by responses to
it' from the other three playwrights (p. 10).

Like both Duncan-Jones and Wiggins, but from
yet another angle, Bednarz seeks to counter previously accepted ideas of Shakespeare, arguing 'for
a shift in the contemporary meaning of "Shakespeare," ... away from the myth of the anonymous
and remote creator, ... to the engaged, partisan in-
ventor of witty, deconstructive paradoxes that still
attest in our eyes to his superiority over Jonson'
(p. 16). The book begins and ends with *Troilus and
Cressida* as Shakespeare's answer to Jonson's challenge to his kind of comedy – the 'purge' referred to in *2 Return from Parnassus* being Ajax
('a jakes' or privy). Perhaps inevitably, given the

nature of the subject, Bednarz traces a sometimes tortuous course of allusions from play to play, theatre to theatre, and playwright to playwright, which I suspect few will follow from beginning to end. Nevertheless, while many of the points have been made previously by others, his project is a more thorough-going analysis with new connections. The book ends on an anticlimactic note with the view that rather than having a winner, the Poets' War left a legacy: 'the legend of Shakespeare and Jonson as mighty opposites upon whose antagonism our conception of literature depends' (p. 264).

Interestingly, Bednarz touches on many of the same topics as does Robert Weimann in *Author's Pen and Actor's Voice: Playing and Writing in Shakespeare's Theatre* (edited by Helen Higbee and William West). Much of Weimann's material has appeared in earlier versions as articles; gathered into a book it becomes both a rather repetitious and dauntingly dense argument that sometimes verges on the incomprehensible and which no summary could pretend to convey. Its considerable complexities are not helped by the style, which has a strong tendency to abstractions, repetitions and paraphrases of the same points, extensive mid-sentence citations and references, and such textual tics of po-mo critical practice as the pretence that single and double quotation marks mean different things and the use of parentheses to create multiple, often contradictory words at once – such as (dis)continuity and (dis)similar. The numerous references to other critics both in the text and in the notes, as well as a long list of works cited, testify to the wide range of authorities who contribute to Weimann's argument. Referring to his title, Weimann says that 'The deliberate criss-crossing between title and subtitle underlines the idea that, in Shakespeare's theatre, "author's pen" is in "actor's voice" just as players' voices and bodies, with all their contrariety, resonate in the writings of the pen' (p. xi). The study ostensibly seeks to answer what is in fact a rhetorical question: 'Was the Elizabethan purpose of playing, perhaps, predicated upon far more fluid, direct, and less "representative" premises than mainstream

twentieth-century criticism ever allowed for?' (p. 4). More particularly, it is an 'attempt to reassess Elizabethan performance practice' by focusing on the various kinds and uses of 'authority' in the Elizabethan theatre (p. 7).

Weimann gives extended attention to the Q1, Q2 and Folio *Hamlet*s. Q1's 'To be or not to be' is studied 'semantically', 'dramaturgically', and with reference to 'audience response' (pp. 20–1), to demonstrate its 'blurring of boundaries between dramatic action and theatrical display, representation and presentation' (p. 22). Shakespeare is the main focus throughout, especially *Henry V*, *Macbeth*, *Richard III*, *Timon of Athens*, and *Troilus and Cressida*. Not surprisingly, Weimann returns to the concepts for which he is already well known: 'I shall work with and develop further my earlier distinction between the *locus* as a fairly specific imaginary locale or self-contained space in the world of the play and the *platea* as an opening in *mise-en-scène* through which the place and time of the stage-as-stage and the cultural occasion itself are made either to assist or resist the socially and verbally elevated, spatially and temporally remote representation' (p. 181). The question I am left with is why any writer would couch his or her ideas in prose so obfuscating that only the really determined would persist in trying to comprehend the ideas being expressed.

In *Theatre and Empire: Great Britain on the London Stages under James VI and I*, Tristan Marshall begins by acknowledging 'a danger that historians can be too zealous in trying to fit plays into convenient boxes in response to literary criticism's attempts either to fit square pegs into round historical holes or ignore potential aspects of topicality altogether', quipping that 'sometimes a play is just a play' (pp. 4–5). On the evidence of the book, however, this is a warning he forgot as he himself became seduced into seeing allusions. Marshall 'looks at the interrelationship between nationalism and theatre in the Jacobean period', especially at 'the creation of a British identity brought about by the accession of King James VI of Scotland to the English throne' (p. 1). Key ideas are that James succeeded in 'popularising the idea of "Britain" as a cultural entity' and that 'the most significant political legacy of James's national project was the creation of an emphatically British identity among the settlers from both England and Scotland who planted Ulster' (p. 2). The book gives welcome attention to Jacobean theatre and to some otherwise neglected and obscure plays and masques, with Shakespeare considered as 'his work fits into a wider framework of dramatic material discoursing on not just the Union but on issues of war, religion and overseas exploration' (p. 6). Central to Marshall's study are two terms, *empire* and *imperium*, which he differentiates as 'overseas colonising' on the one hand and 'the internal sovereign national state' on the other (p. 11). He dates the idea of imperium from the union of England and Scotland under James, and that of empire from the founding of the Virginia Company in 1606. In addition, 'identification with Rome was a prelude to overseas expansion – the idea of overseas conquest being derived ultimately from Roman imperial rule over large territories' (p. 18).

Marshall discusses *King Lear*, *Nobody and Somebody* and *Macbeth* because 'plays set in Scotland and in ancient Britain were fertile ground for commentary on James Stuart's rule' (p. 56). Shakespeare's changes to his sources are explained in terms of the argument being made; here, that what makes *King Lear* 'an implicitly British play is the fact that, where Holinshed provides two of the corners of the island, Cornwall and Albany, Shakespeare adds the third' – and he then 'effectively squares the triangle' by adding Kent and the action at Dover. Furthermore, of the Q1 ending in which Albany succeeds Lear, Marshall observes that 'Out of the chaos ensuing from the demise of the royal line a Scot will restore order' (p. 57). He concludes that *Macbeth* is 'a very British play', in part because 'Macbeth betrays his country, yet in so doing prefigures the union of the kingdoms' (p. 64). Such statements are indicative of the book's very narrow and superficial treatment of the plays, which acknowledges other critics' views of a work's political implications only to contradict them. *Cymbeline* not surprisingly receives extensive treatment, with its 'concentration on marriage' argued as being 'strongly reminiscent of the reunion of the kingdoms of England and Scotland' (p. 70).

The Tempest is seen as 'a compromise' that 'gave its public audience a glimpse of the mysteries and excitement of acquiring strange new lands – [Prince] Henry's interest – while remaining firmly fixed within a familiar Jacobean world' (p. 95). In this interpretation, the island of the play is an allusion to 'Britain as a distinct island kingdom replete with a past steeped in ancient history' (p. 96). Marshall's discussion of the play demonstrates no grasp of it as a coherent work of art, but it is fully representative of both his approach and tone of superior insights; his certainty that he is right and all other critics are either wrong or at best over-interpretive. They, however, might call his approach reductionist.

Renaissance Clothing and the Materials of Memory by Ann Rosalind Jones and Peter Stallybrass is very much a collaborative project: the authors repeatedly acknowledge discussions with and contributions from others. Furthermore, much of the material has been presented orally or in print elsewhere and includes additions and modifications resulting from this circulation of ideas. Wide-ranging research is organized into a series of stimulating variations on a theme rather than a sustained through-line of one argument, with the essential idea of clothing as a 'material reminder' being developed from numerous perspectives. As if in acknowledgement of the many topics covered and the rather loose connections between them, each chapter begins with an overview of its argument and an indication of its relation to the rest. Typically the vast array of evidence drawn together by Jones and Stallybrass is treated selectively, and interpreted in ways that serve the purposes of their arguments; while this is virtually inevitable in such a project, and probably in any attempt today to make sense of the past, periodic acknowledgement that at least some of their conclusions might be tentative would be helpful. 'Clothing' here means anything worn, including jewellery, armour, etc. The authors quote Hal's 'I will deeply put the Fashion on, / And weare it in my heart' (*Henry IV, part 2*, 5.2) as an articulation of their key point that 'clothes permeate the wearer, fashioning him or her within' (p. 2). They also explore the etymology and meanings of 'fetish' and 'fashion', terms that recur. A central concept is 'livery', originally a term for various kinds of non-monetary payment, but which gradually came to mean 'not just clothing but *marked* clothing' worn by retainers in the servant–master relationship (p. 17, original italics). The authors also emphasize the differences between modern ideas of clothing and those of the Renaissance, when, we are told, clothes 'were closer both to a second skin, a skin that names you, and to money' than clothes we wear today, so that 'The tension between clothes as mnemonics and clothes as cash is one of the most fertile sources of cultural analysis in the Renaissance' (p. 32). The topics covered are various – clothes as 'coin' or wealth, clothes in portraits, yellow starch and xenophobia, women's spinning and needlework, ghosts' clothing – but always the main interest is the reciprocal relationship between the meaning invested in clothing and the meaning clothing imposes on its wearers.

For example, Jones and Stallybrass look at the complicated history and significance of yellow starch: 'Saffron dye was associated both with the foreign (whether Spanish, French, Irish, or Scottish) and with a woman (Mrs Turner), and this association was equally true in the case of starch' (p. 67). Starch was also demonized because, being made from the bran of wheat, it was seen as a threat when harvests were poor, and because the duke of Northumberland (who had the starch monopoly) was a Howard, a Catholic, and implicated in the Overbury murder. The authors comment that 'In yellow starch, republican theorists found a fashion accessory that combined all that they detested in the court: its permeability by the "foreign" and above all by Catholic influences; its vanity, pride, and sexual corruption; its supposed fashioning (like starch) by the hands of women' (p. 76). The typical complexity of this discussion is hinted at by one of its concluding sentences: 'The now-dead metaphors of habit (clothing and custom), of costume/custom, of bodies/bodice were given vital and conflictual force in the narrations of the Overbury affair' (p. 85).

In turning to the theatre, Jones and Stallybrass observe that 'professional London companies were . . . organized around costumes, costumes

that were . . . part of a more general circulation of clothing' (p. 177). Indeed, they argue, costumes were more valuable than the plays they were used in, hence they were a considerable investment for a theatre company, so much so that 'a labor force grew up around the theatre because of the value of its clothes' (p. 178). More generally, 'To run a theatre was not only to build playhouses but also to own, lend, and sell costumes or to lend the money with which to acquire them' (p. 179). Philip Henslowe is offered as the most obvious, and successful, example since not only did he need costumes for his actors, he was also a pawnbroker and fripperer (dealer in second-hand clothes). Henslowe's records are, as often, the primary evidence, but in this case his expenditures on costumes are the focus. Drawing on the research of Susan Cerasano, Jones and Stallybrass give figures showing how clothing was a form of money on which loans could be obtained, and at usurious rates. They suggest that 'the economic relations of the theatre to the clothing trade help to illuminate both the repertory of the companies and the process by which roles and identities were defined on the stage' (p. 195). This point is effectively illustrated in discussions of such matters as kinds of costume and doubling in plays including *Volpone*, *Twelfth Night*, *Cymbeline*, *The Widow*, *Troilus and Cressida*, and *Othello*.

A series of speculations about the body of the boy actor beneath women's clothing is far less successful, especially in the suggestion that boy actors undressed onstage and wore prosthetic breasts. No evidence is adduced, although there is a discussion of eighteenth-century illustrations of bed scenes, such as that in *Othello* in which Desdemona's breast is partly exposed. As the authors note, however, such illustrations do not necessarily reflect stage practice and by then the women in the beds were no longer being played by boys. Here (though seldom elsewhere in the book) there is a disappointing insistence on interpretations that are possible only if one accepts all the implausible premises on which they are built.

Material London, ca. 1600, edited by Lena Cowen Orlin, contains an impressive group of essays offering numerous enlightening analyses of historical records. The collection originated in an equally impressive 1995 conference organized by Orlin at the Folger Shakespeare Library. Concerned not with Shakespeare or Queen Elizabeth as such, the book offers a revisionist approach by finding 'other ways of making meaning in our historical narratives' (p. 6). First comes 'London's Dominion: The Metropolis, the Market Economy, and the State' by David Harris Sacks, who links the otherwise separate figures of Will Kemp and the Earl of Essex in two 'tales of metropolitan dominion' (p. 26). He begins with Essex's 'abortive coup d'etat' in 1601, focusing on the earl's 'misapprehensions about London' (p. 29), which led him to believe he could be successful, and on 'the city's role in thwarting him' (p. 30), and shows how 'The Essex affair demonstrates the potential power of London in the state and the capacity it had to sustain its organization and shape its political agenda' (p. 35). Sacks's second tale actually came first chronologically: 'Kemp's famous nine days' wonder, his Morris dance from London to Norwich, during Lent 1600' (p. 26). He develops the idea of the Morris dance as a celebration of ancient virtues in contrast to present corruption, in particular the idea of how Kemp 'evokes Norwich as a harmonious domain of civic virtue' (p. 39), in contrast to London's abandonment of established values. The city's growth, a concern of several of the essays, is the subject of 'Material London in Time and Space' by Derek Keene, who argues that 'the decisive stage in the development of the city as the focus of national power and expenditure was in the late thirteenth century rather than in the sixteenth' (p. 58). He considers particularly the importance of Antwerp and the Low Countries in the gradual development of London's commercial and cultural relationship with Europe, especially in relation to the cloth trade – also a recurring concern in this collection. With Alan Sinfield's 'Poetaster, the Author, and the Perils of Cultural Production' the focus narrows to recent critical theories. It begins by charting the evolution from 'materialism' to 'material' as a preliminary to 'disputing a reactionary view of Ben Jonson and crediting him with

a critical stance toward authority, ideology, and the functions of the author at the metropolitan center of power' so as to reassert the 'Marxian political' or 'materialist edge' (p. 75).

Part 2 opens with Joan Thirsk's question, 'England's Provinces: Did They Serve or Drive Material London?' Although one might think that the smaller towns were subservient to the larger city, Thirsk provides ample evidence of how the 'Scattered provincial centers offered diversity, which is the very lifeblood of consumerism' (p. 102). Here the focus is on goods imported not from abroad but from the provinces – the output of their indigenous cultures, industries, and agricultural production that made 'material London' possible. Thirsk demonstrates her expertise as 'a historian of the agrarian economy and rural society' (p. 97) in her explanation of the details of local production and her 'close to the ground' research. The same can be said of Jane Schneider, whose 'Fantastical Colors in Foggy London: The New Fashion Potential of the Late Sixteenth Century' establishes 1600 as the dividing point between a time of 'sad' or dark colours and one of 'peacock splendor' (p. 110). Among the related subjects she discusses are methods of dyeing, the importance of purples and especially reds, the close association between London's leading citizens and the woollen textile industry, Puritans and colour, and the abandonment of sumptuary laws. Clothing is also the concern of Ann Rosalind Jones and Peter Stallybrass in '"Rugges of London and the Diuell's Band": Irish Mantles and Yellow Starch as Hybrid London Fashion', a topic also discussed in their book reviewed above. Jean E. Howard's 'Women, Foreigners, and the Regulation of Urban Space in Westward Ho' argues that city comedies can be 'read as a renegotiation, through a focus on the urban site, of England's self-definition and its position in a global arena' which succeed the history play as 'a genre of national self-definition' (p. 152). In these comedies, therefore, 'discourses of foreignness became part of the stage's resources for posing and for providing imaginary solutions to the problems of its urban site of production' (p. 153). The essay's purpose is to map the 'urban geography' of *Westward Ho* to show 'the way a discourse of national difference helps to articulate and resolve the problems of urban life which the play foregrounds' (p. 154).

The third section also starts with a question – 'Material Londoners?' – this one from Ian W. Archer. His survey of answers provides examples of the 'explosion of consumer goods in the metropolis around 1600' (p. 176), generated by the growth in demand from the middle and upper classes. But he also shows that the 'celebration of wealth did not go unchallenged' by the voices of Christian morality (p. 178). Archer covers a lot of territory very effectively, offering examples from contemporary documents and suggesting how to understand them, while also painting a clear picture of the commercialization of London and its consequences. Between them, this essay and Gail Kern Paster's 'Purgation as the Allure of Mastery: Early Modern Medicine and the Technology of the Self' give a good sense of the kinds and range of approaches to the topic of material London in this collection. In contrast to Archer's broad sweep over the commercial city, Paster's essay links the use of purgation as revenge in *The Family of Love* to wider social implications of the practice of purgation generally. Her interest is in 'purgation as early modern culture's signifying practice upon the social body as a whole' and as 'a freely willed act of rational consumption akin to the purchase of other goods and services' (p. 195). In 'London's Vagrant Economy: Making Space for "Low" Subjectivity', Patricia Fumerton offers a complex argument which is not helped by the overuse of historicist jargon. She observes that the rapid growth in London would have most severely affected servants and apprentices, the group 'most prone to vagrancy' (p. 210); but, she argues, this group also included pedlars and chapmen, part of 'a new category of poor – neither deserving impotent nor undeserving sturdy rogue, but deserving, sturdy indigent who sought but could not find work' (p. 213).

First in part 4 is Alice T. Friedman's 'Inside/Out: Women, Domesticity, and the Pleasures of the City', which considers the country house as both place and concept. Friedman's particular interest

is the 'Profound changes in the ideology of gender among men and women of the upper classes' (p. 234) when, although the rules of the past required women to stay on country estates, they were increasingly mobile. Andrew Gurr returns us to London in 'The Authority of the Globe and the Fortune'. A focal idea here is that both theatres were 'second-best choices' (p. 251) because 'their design must have been ... a distinctly retrograde step' (p. 252) in that they were modelled on marketplace scaffolds, making them poor substitutes for indoor venues such as the town halls where travelling players performed for a mayor's approval. Gurr summarizes 'the Privy Council's attempt to regulate the professional playing companies between 1594 and 1600' (p. 253), quoting the June 1600 order which made the Fortune and Globe London's only authorized theatres. He argues that the 'the security of a "home" base for professional companies from 1594 ... has a role to play in the story of the major surviving records, the play-texts, and the question of how much their composition was determined by the venues they were written for' (p. 261). In 'Building, Buying, and Collecting in London, 1600–1625', Linda Levy Peck addresses the very different material interests of the nobility, gentry and upwardly mobile merchants. She observes that 'In 1600 the English elite lagged fifty years behind their Continental counterparts both in wealth and display. But, by 1625 that elite had embraced the material culture of Italy, France, and the Netherlands' (p. 271). Peck argues that 'construction of Jacobean culture was shaped by gender', on the one hand echoing Alice Friedman's point that women were the shoppers, but also showing that men such as Robert Carr and George Villiers led a 'new type of collecting that was *not* effeminate' (p. 272, original italics).

The last group of essays begins with John Schofield on 'The Topography and Buildings of London, ca. 1600'. This extensive 'tour of London' looks at virtually every aspect of physical London before offering three main conclusions: 'expansion of London was aided by the dissolution of the monasteries'; London buildings 'were occasionally exceptional because the place was so large and displayed features peculiar to a capital city'; and 'no style seems to have been prevalent' (p. 318). His final point, that 'In 1600, London was a medieval city on the edge of spectacular expansion in the century to come' (p. 319), is supported in different ways by many of the other pieces in this collection. In 'John Day and the Bookshop That Never Was', Peter W. M. Blayney traces a long-hidden path of evidence. He shows that a power struggle between City and Church authorities for control of St Paul's Churchyard lay behind an attempt by the archbishop of Canterbury to have Day build a shop there. Having discovered the highly descriptive lease for the site, Blayney conjecturally reconstructs the shop and places it in the churchyard to show that it 'would have been not so much a bookshop as a street corner' (p. 340). In a similar demonstration of how the analysis of early documents can produce new information, Lena Cowen Orlin investigates 'Boundary Disputes in Early Modern London', her purpose being 'to make material the abstract numbers of demographic calculations and to illustrate some of the consequences of urban density for the everyday lives of sixteenth- and seventeenth-century Londoners' (p. 345). Her principal evidence is the surveys of Ralph Treswell, paired with the reports of the London Viewers – 'a group of four men, generally men from the building trades, commissioned by the city to adjudicate property disputes' (p. 349). Among Orlin's discoveries is that 'old and sometimes eccentric property agreements were rigorously enforced long after the original parties to them were gone' (p. 353). As a conclusion to this collection, Orlin's essay exemplifies its merits. Everyone interested in early modern London will find much to learn about different kinds of extant records and methods of analysis from the studies here.

III

Many who consider investigating early performance conditions doubtless dissuade themselves, believing that there is nothing new to find or say. Clearly Tiffany Stern thought otherwise, the result being *Rehearsal from Shakespeare to Sheridan*, which looks at the whole business of rehearsal from 1576 to 1780. The focus here will be on the first third of the book, up to the closing of the theatres, but the idea of continuity is one on which Stern puts considerable weight. Her study of the evidence has led her to conclude that 'From the sixteenth to eighteenth centuries, different plays were put on every few days, sometimes every day, during the theatrical season, meaning that often an actor had to learn or relearn a part during the day for the evening's performance. For this reason, the stages of rehearsal were skewed quite differently [from today]: the emphasis of preparation was on "private" or "individual" rehearsal (also called "study"), during which the actor worked on his or her own "part" for performance' (p. 10). While the essentials of this conclusion are not altogether new, Stern's intensive collection and analysis of the evidence make her interpretations seem more convincing than heretofore; whether or not they are correct is almost impossible to say, given the paucity of hard facts. Two points follow from her main ones: the performance of a part became 'fixed' for all subsequent productions and because a new actor was 'taught to mimic precisely the manner in which the part had first been acted' little rehearsal was necessary. The 'part', therefore, was the basic unit, and this, Stern argues, affected how plays were written: 'Divided back down into parts, plays reveal an internal logic of prose and verse, long and short sentences, changing modes of address, that are somewhere between literary points and lost stage directions' (p. 11). Stern's sources for the early period are 'account books, prompt-books, court records, academic records, overseas records, legal documents, plays-within-plays, letters, play prefaces, prologues and epilogues' (p. 18); this, however, adds up to much less than the list suggests.

According to Stern, the basic meaning of 'rehearse' was to repeat, imitate, or mimic, and 'a "rehearsal" could consist of important bits rather than a whole' (p. 25). Acknowledging that the question of how much time was given to preparation of a new play for performance is 'a vexed issue' (p. 54), Stern accurately observes that our modern predisposition is to look for and expect evidence that supports a substantial period of preparation. In fact, she says, the evidence indicates that 'plays could be allotted a varying amount of time for preparation depending on when they were put on within the theatrical season, and that different kinds of play were allotted different portions of preparation time: more for a tragedy; less for a farce' (p. 55). She concludes that anywhere from three days to five weeks were given to 'preparation' of a new play but that 'For revivals of stock plays, or repetitions of plays within the season, there is no suggestion that "refresher" rehearsals took place' (p. 57). Unfortunately, however, the evidence is meagre – a few Henslowe records, lines in several plays, one actor's 'part' – and the conclusions therefore necessarily speculative. At the heart of Stern's argument is the idea that the parts 'contained the information players needed for solo practice' that would result in integration with other parts on stage (p. 65). This is also where the real problems begin, since her examples do not invite ready agreement. For instance, Stern suggests that when in *Twelfth Night* Olivia switches from prose to verse, she thereby signals that she has fallen in love with Viola: 'The transformation from prose to verse marks a change in the pace and tempo of the scene, but it is also an actor's stage direction, visually obvious from the arrangement of speeches on the part.' From this it follows that '"Actual" stage directions . . . are simply other ways of conveying the same information in Renaissance texts' (p. 65). This raises more questions than it answers, such as whether *all* shifts between prose and verse in plays of the period are also stage directions.

Turning to 'group rehearsal', Stern states that 'Both university and provincial players had as a rule only one general rehearsal, and I am inclined to think that the same is roughly true also of the public theatre' (p. 76). Her evidence here, however – the staged rehearsal of plays-within-plays – hardly proves that real plays received no more group preparation than did fictional ones. Similarly, Stern says the prompter directed blocking and timing, making rehearsal unnecessary, and (based on four vague references in plays) posits the existence of 'call-boys and stage attendants' (p. 97)

who helped during performance. Having created these figures, she then proceeds to argue that 'The "plat" or "plot" that hung in the tiring house – a plan containing a scene-by-scene account of entrances and exits – was almost certainly prepared for call-boys rather than for actors, as is sometimes claimed'. She continues that since the wording of plots 'recalls prompt-book stage directions . . . the prompter will hardly have duplicated information he already had for himself' (p. 98) – *ergo*, call-boys. But nobody has claimed that the bookholder wrote the plot 'for himself', and the wording of plots is in fact quite different from that of annotated playtexts. Other points are more convincing; for example, Stern offers persuasive evidence that revisions were 'part based', showing how cuts retained cues so parts would not have to be rewritten. Such cuts, she suggests, were frequently made during the first performance of a play, which was 'the audition-like "rehearsal" of the text' (p. 112). The later chapters focus on rehearsal in the theatres of Betterton, Cibber and Garrick. Overall, this book is about more than rehearsal; often it is as much about performance and performances, albeit usually as a context for information and speculation about rehearsal and preparation more generally. Certainly Stern has gathered and coherently organized a lot of material, and her analysis of it has produced many provocative suggestions and conclusions which theatre and performance specialists in particular will want to consider.

Those with an interest in early theatre apart from Shakespeare have good reason to appreciate the existence of *Medieval and Renaissance Drama in England*, one of the few journals that is largely a Shakespeare-free zone. Volume 13 demonstrates once again its value as a forum for research on and interpretation of the whole period of early modern drama. But sadly this uneven collection is marred by very careless editing; such sloppiness does not inspire confidence in the accuracy of the information provided, which is especially unfortunate since new information is largely what this journal is about. The topics covered in this volume include 'A Fifteenth-Century Saint Play in Winchester: Some Problems of Interpretation' by

Jane Cowling, who examines Winchester records referring to an otherwise unknown play of St Agnes performed there in 1409. Cowling describes and analyses evidence, including court records and pictures on an ornate cup in the British Museum, to suggest what a play of St Agnes might have consisted of. Alison Shell's 'Autodidacticism in English Jesuit Drama: The Writings and Career of Joseph Simons' highlights otherwise neglected Jesuit dramas, written to foster 'moral and spiritual self-education in their writers and performers as well as in their viewers' (p. 34). Her plausible premise is that 'Jesuit drama is written on the assumption that the boy actors would assent to the models on offer, actively internalizing them in readiness for occasions when real-life exemplary behavior was needed' (p. 35). Shell works to counter criticism of Jesuit drama as lacking 'psychological complexity', insisting that 'To complain about the flatness of the characters in Jesuit drama is to miss the point: if to imagine an exemplary character is to create a stereotype, then the Jesuits were aiming to create stereotypes in real life' (p. 48). June Schlueter has a more worldly topic in 'Celebrating Queen Elizabeth's German Godchild: The Documentary Record', the child in question being Elizabeth, the second of the four children of Landgrave Moritz of Hesse and his wife Agnes. There are two pieces by S. P. Cerasano: 'The Patronage Network of Philip Henslowe and Edward Alleyn' followed by 'Edward Alleyn: His Brothel's Keeper?' After these is Herbert Berry's 'Where Was the Playhouse in Which the Boy Choristers of St Paul's Cathedral Performed Plays?', but unfortunately the whirligig of publication timing has resulted in his question having already been answered by Roger Bowers in *Theatre Notebook* 54 (reviewed briefly last year). While both authors correctly locate the playhouse in the Almonry building, Berry apparently places it too close to the cathedral nave, and on the second floor of a part of the building that Bowers (p. 77) shows to have been only a single story high. Overall, Bowers's article is more precise, better illustrated, and more convincing. In '*Enter out*: Perplexing Signals in some Elizabethan Stage Directions', Michela Calore surveys a number of the enigmatic

directions typical of early modern playtexts, making the well-taken but unsurprising point that it is 'impractical and illusory . . . to hope that general truths about theatrical practices of the age can be recovered once and for all' (p. 125).

Individual plays are the focus of the next essays, beginning with Fenella MacFarlane's 'To "Try What London Prentices Can Do": Merchant Chivalry as Representational Strategy in Thomas Heywood's *The Four Prentices of London*'. In my one reading I caught a dozen typographical errors, leaving me wondering how many more important errors of fact and reference are waiting to mislead the unwary. MacFarlane's essay is followed by '"So much English by the Mother": Gender, Foreigners, and the Mother Tongue in William Haughton's *Englishmen for My Money*', by Emma Smith. Then comes probably the most ambitious and significant piece in this volume, Ronda A. Arab's 'Work, Bodies, and Gender in *The Shoemaker's Holiday*'. She develops her idea that in Dekker's play 'the household workshop and the artisan men who inhabit it are represented as the energy and strength of England and the source of the major assets of the emerging nation: work, productivity, and patriotism'. Noting that 'The bodies of the lauded artisans are foregrounded again and again, and are usually engaged in some kind of vigorous activity' (p. 182), Arab shows how the play 'answers the turmoil of the work world with a whitewashed fantasy that masks both the very real divisions within artisan society and the extensive social fears of dangerous, rebellious and politicized artisans' (p. 193). The idea of the 'grotesque body' is developed in relation to gender: 'Women in the artisan household [of the play] are marked as grotesque bodies because they are a threat to the idea of a male-dominated society based on the power and authority of the distinctly masculine artisan body' (p. 201). In passing, I would note that although Arab repeatedly uses the term 'guild', neither Dekker nor contemporary London records ever do so: 'company' was, and is, the correct term for a sixteenth-century London craft association. Such quibbles aside, though, this essay is an effective combination of old-fashioned close textual analysis within a new-historicist approach that situates the play in the world of early modern London's emergent capitalism. The final piece is Meg Powers Livingston's study of 'Herbert's Censorship of Female Power in Fletcher's *The Woman's Prize*'. Here another obscure play is given welcome attention, this one being of interest both because it exists in printed and manuscript versions and because it is a response to *The Taming of the Shrew*. Livingston argues, first, that Herbert censored the play to remove suggestions of female power that might have fed 'growing disquiet concerning Queen Henrietta Maria's religious practices and her influence on the royal court' and, second, that Fletcher managed to circumvent Herbert's alterations, thereby illustrating 'Fletcher's resources as a playwright' as much as 'Herbert's difficulties as a censor' (p. 214). This too is a detailed examination of textual evidence, one which in this case successfully demonstrates what can be achieved by combining bibliographical and literary analyses.

The practice of boys playing women is the concern of several authors this year, chief among them Mary Bly, in her very thought-provoking *Queer Virgins and Virgin Queans on the Early Modern Stage*. The rather strange and oblique title does little to convey the book's multiple interests – linguistic theory, theatrical scholarship, and queer theory. These are integrated into an innovative and notably jargon-free study that aims to give voice to a submerged segment of writers, actors, and spectators concentrated in one London theatre. Bly 'focuses on silenced laughter: on puns whose acrobatics no longer please, and indeed are hardly intelligible' because 'Puns naturally erupt in taboo cultural arenas' (p. 1); in particular, her interest is the 'creation and reception' of what she terms 'queer' puns: 'puns that carry homoerotic resonances and speak to homoerotic desires' (p. 2). These are studied in the few plays written for performance at the short-lived Whitefriars theatre, plays which are 'obscene, coarse, and gross' (p. 2), with the male body their special focus. In 1607–8, the amateur playwrights who ran the company wrote and produced seven comedies and one tragedy; Bly singles out 'bawdy virgins' in five comedies, characters anomalous because they are 'female romantic heroines' whose

dialogue is 'ripe with phallic puns' (p. 4). Her concomitant broader argument, relevant to all eight plays, is that 'the Whitefriars syndicate sought to exploit an identifiable group of men, and that when those men gathered together in the theatre, the nature of punning suggests that a sense of community formed around their shared laughter' (p. 5).

Bly posits three interrelated related 'communities' – playgoers, writers, boy actors – with the bawdy pun the means of communication among them. She analyses the language of five marriageable virgins in Whitefriars plays – e.g. Florimell in John Day's *Humour out of Breath* – who speak in double entendres. Although, as Bly acknowledges, the verbal jokes of another time are notoriously difficult to explicate, her treatments of the puns and their cultural, social and theatrical contexts are quite masterful, not only explaining the jokes but also suggesting how and why they worked. One reason for the success of these explications is that they do not try to limit a pun to one set of referents but, on the contrary, show how the possible meanings are always multiple and often dependent on who is speaking in what context. At the same time, central to Bly's argument is the premise that the puns in these plays were especially addressed to and appreciated by a significant 'homoerotic community' in the audience at least in part because there is safety in language that says two things at once: 'The cross-dressed boy, as he linguistically disrobes, creates a community of two with the auditor who catches his puns' (p. 23). Among Bly's key premises are that Whitefriars plays 'were read *for* their puns, which constitute their primary characteristic as a group' (p. 30, original italics) and that 'By staging bawdy virgins, Whitefriars authors challenge verbal taboos rather than royal authority' (p. 36). She further argues that 'The Whitefriars syndicate perceived an audience for plays specializing in phallic puns, and the resemblance between Whitefriars plays is a sign of wilful, economically driven thought' (p. 45). As a way of illustrating and confirming her concept of a Whitefriars audience receptive to queer puns, Bly uses two non-Whitefriars plays, *Greene's Tu Quoque*, and *A Christian Turn'd Turke*, to demonstrate that 'When queer puns are not a logical selling point, they are ruthlessly effaced' (p. 131). Given the care and clarity with which Bly sets out her thesis, these ideas will doubtless influence any future considerations of not only the Whitefriars milieu itself, but more generally of puns and their seductive, subversive uses as a means of undermining taboos and giving voice to desires.

Boys playing women is one of several related concerns in Carol Chillington Rutter's *Enter the Body: Women and Representation on Shakespeare's Stage*, which, despite what the title implies, also deals with modern productions. The copy I received has pages 47 to 74 duplicated and 75 to 107 missing; fortunately, I suppose, the latter segment is from chapter 3, which (I discovered with no help from any acknowledgement in either book) is also in *Shakespeare in Performance*, reviewed later. More seriously offputting, *Enter the Body* bears all the marks of pretentiousness I have come to associate with Routledge publications: jargon, neologisms, and self-indulgent wordplay that adds little to a reader's understanding of the argument. Rutter's engagement with and enthusiasm for her topic are abundantly apparent, and she is a strong presence, with a plentiful use of the first person and a prose style that is often ironic, sarcastic, and combative, making this very much a personal response to texts and performances. Certainly, this is an over-managed book: a two-part title for a book is still, it seems, *de rigeur*, but here each chapter also has a title, subtitle, and several quotations at the start, followed by divisions titled in bold and sometimes subdivisions titled in italic. Thus while this study might be termed 'wide-ranging', it is also choppy – constantly moving from topic to topic, past to present, stage to film. The general aim is to combine historical research focused on the 'body consciousness' (p. xiii) of Shakespeare's culture with considerations of modern stage and film productions, though the latter dominate. Rutter makes no bones about her purpose and its context: 'a corrective to feminist criticism's preoccupation with discursive bodies, and materialist and performance criticism's exaggerated attention on men. The former derives from a fascination with

power, the latter from a logocentric fascination with Shakespeare's words as the bearers of authorial meanings; as everyone knows, men have more to say in Shakespeare than women do' (p. xiv). Among the characters and topics discussed are Cordelia and the staging of 'dead' female bodies, Ophelia in the grave, Cleopatra's colour, Helen of Troy's beauty, and the role of Emilia in *Othello*.

If titles matter (and undoubtedly they do), Joy Leslie Gibson's *Squeaking Cleopatras: The Elizabethan Boy Player* is surely among the least successful, especially since the implications of 'squeaking' are directly contrary to the positive view of boy players set out in the book. Also problematic is the frontispiece illustration and credit: 'The Fortune Theatre: a reconstruction from the builder's contract. From the Royal National Theatre's programme for *Rosencrantz and Guildenstern are Dead*, 1995'. It resembles no credible illustration of any Elizabethan theatre. The first chapters summarize much of what is already known about boy players in preparation for Gibson's 'valid discoveries' (p. xi) derived from her analysis of speeches written for boys' roles. The foremost of these discoveries is that 'Shakespeare never gave his boy players any speeches that were not within the breath span of a trained boy's voice – about twenty-eight syllables seems to be the longest phrase he expected to be spoken on one breath' (p. 73). Gibson takes a number of speeches by female characters and breaks them up into segments as 'proof' of her theory; but the examples make the problems immediately obvious: probably no two readers would divide the texts in the same way, and some of her suggestions seem bizarre in the extreme. If spoken as Gibson hypothesises, the speeches become words in strings only long enough for a boy to speak, not words spoken to convey character and emotion. Despite the many examples, her evidence is not at all persuasive.

In *Women and Dramatic Production 1550–1700*, by Alison Findlay and Stephanie Hodgson-Wright with Gweno Williams, a broad definition of 'dramatic production' is applied, since so far as is known many of the works discussed were never performed publicly and may not have been written for performance. Indeed, an important point is that 'Taking account of alternative types of drama staged in the royal court or in the country house or in non-official venues like the street, obliges us to re-think our definitions of theatre' (p. 6). Each of the seven essays – by one or two of the three authors – puts a positive, feminist spin on almost every aspect of works which are said to 'show women taking the stage in order to foreground interests particular to their sex' (p. 1). Among the topics covered are Tudor women's translation of Latin plays, Mary Sidney's *The Tragedie of Antonie*, masques written for Anna of Denmark and Henrietta Maria, *The Tragedy of Mariam* by Elizabeth Cary, and *Love's Victory* by Mary Wroth. Included in the many significant points are Hodgson-Wright's assertion that 'What we find throughout women's dramatic activity in the early seventeenth century is an initial seizing of masculine prerogative, followed by a gradual shift towards the validation of feminine virtues and values on equal terms with masculine virtues' (p. 67). Findlay notes that 'from women's point of view' the closing of the public theatres 'creat[ed] a newly-levelled playing field' and further that 'The ways in which women participated as authors, directors, actors and protesters in various performances and rituals suggests that they understood the power of drama as a means of self-presentation or persuasion' (pp. 68–9). She looks at 'The proliferation of theatre . . . in the streets or market place, in places of worship or in the courtroom', places where women could 'express ideas which were often radical' (p. 81). Williams discusses the work of Margaret Cavendish as 'protofeminist' (p. 100), arguing that 'Indications of household performance possibilities within individual plays support a reading of her plays as actual or potential performance texts for aristocratic women' (p. 96). Hodgson-Wright studies the use of discovery scenes by Aphra Behn and how Behn exploits the fact that 'By the Restoration, the term "whore" was demonstrably impoverished as a means of classifying and castigating women' (p. 160). With extensive references to other critics and a detailed bibliography, this book is a very good resource, especially for those feminist readers with previous knowledge of at least some of the

figures and works discussed, who will probably find the book more satisfying and persuasive than the uninitiated.

The most recent contribution to Cambridge's Shakespeare in Production series is *The Tempest*, edited by Christine Dymkowski. Not surprisingly, it is a hefty volume offering detailed information about staging, sets, cuts, additions, interpolations, revisions, different directors' approaches, and contrasting responses from critics. There is an easy-reference chart of the productions cited, listing director, company, venue, designer, composer and date of first performance, as well as a chart of the principal players in each production and an extensive bibliography. Although the emphasis is on twentieth-century productions, for which there is obviously an enormous and detailed record, Dymkowski researched something like 130 different productions, from the first in 1610 to several in early 1999, about 100 of which were in London or elsewhere in the United Kingdom. As a Canadian I couldn't but note that, aside from a brief mention, Stratford Ontario is ignored. Perhaps the reason is the notorious difficulty of doing archival research there, but Dymkowski doesn't say. Her sizeable introduction is divided into sections dealing with the original play; long-lived Restoration adaptations; changes in the roles of Prospero, Ariel and Caliban over time; and representations of the storm scene and the island. These topics are considered further in the commentary to the text itself, where, for example, twelve pages are devoted to the shipwreck and storm, giving information about productions over the past three centuries by, among others, Kemble, Tree, Garrick, Healey, Miller, Strehler, and Hytner. Some of the topics receiving detailed and often fascinating discussion are the colour of Prospero's cloak and when or if he sits and stands in the second scene; the representation of magic, of course; the discovery of Miranda and Ferdinand at chess; the freeing of Ariel. The evidence presented by Dymkowski certainly illustrates her initial point that Shakespeare's 'last play seems unusually elastic, its almost miraculous flexibility allowing it to embody radically different interpretations, characterizations and emphases' (p. 1).

Shakespeare in Performance, edited by Grace Ioppolo, is a collection honouring Reg Foakes and reflecting his interests in theatre history, textual analysis, and performance both past and present. It contains eight essays on performances in Shakespeare's time and eight on performances in our time, with an afterword by Stanley Wells. To begin, Jonathan Bate asks whether Shakespeare had a 'philosophy of life' (p. 20) and answers by looking at *King Lear* in the light of especially Montaigne's essays and Erasmus's *Praise of Folly*. Of the play he concludes: 'in despite of the pagan setting, those essentials of the Erasmian and Montaignian – that is to say the counter-Renaissance – Christian vision, are still there: folly and love'; of the Shakespeare who wrote the play he asserts: 'He was not a historian. He was not a philosopher. He was a FOOLOSOPHER' (p. 31). M. M. Mahood follows with a thought-provoking study of character entrances and exits in which she suggests that 'in the Elizabethan theatre there operated upon playwrights, actors and audiences alike an unvoiced and almost unconscious distinction between "outward" and "inward" entrances and exits, especially in interior and urban scenes' (p. 34). More broadly, she argues that 'a steady awareness of the conventions of Elizabethan domestic architecture and of the social significance of space which they embody is essential to our understanding of the manner in which interior scenes are orientated in Shakespeare's plays' (pp. 34–5). If Mahood's thesis is even only partly right, it adds an important new dimension to what we can imagine an early modern audience's experience of a play to have been. Also included in the first section are an essay by Peter Davison on the Chamberlain's Men's tour of the provinces in 1597 and the possibility that they performed at great houses along the way; a study by Peter M. Wright of the stage directions for music and sound effects in *1* and *2 Henry VI*; an exploration by Philip Edwards of 'the inscrutability of language' and 'the impossibility of distinguishing sincerity from insincerity, truth from falsehood' in Shakespeare's plays (p. 128); and E. A. J. Honigmann on the first 'performances' of the sonnets (the quotation marks are his, and indicate how the meaning of 'performance' is being stretched in a

piece actually about identifying the Young Man and the Dark Lady). Ian Donaldson uses the contrasting examples of *Julius Caesar* and *Sejanus* to pose questions about the 'hermeneutic limits' of 'reading between the lines' in search of contemporary allusions which have evaded censorship. He demonstrates that while for Jonson's play such an approach is 'apt and highly suggestive', Shakespeare's is 'curiously resistant to approaches ... which seek to understand the play's obscurities by reference to contemporary political events' (p. 89). He focuses particularly on the 'interpretative riddles, mysteries, and misunderstandings' (p. 96) in both plays, but also broadens the discussion to ask, 'What kind of "conversation" was going on between Shakespeare and Jonson on the topic of Roman history, and how, if at all, are their Roman plays linked?' (p. 101). Alexander Leggatt looks at 'detachable scenes' in three tragedies: *Titus Andronicus* 3.2 (the fly-killing scene), *Richard II* 4.1 (the deposition scene), and the large segment of *Hamlet* 4.4 (scrutinizing Fortinbras), which exists in Q2 but not in the Folio. Several times appositely quoting Foakes, Leggatt's analyses show how these scenes 'are placed in the thick of the action, in it as well as out of it, stopping the forward movement for a period of thought. What that thought in each case uncovers is absurdity: the absurdity of grief, of revenge, of action; the emptiness of the signs of power and identity; the blocking of language, the frustration of thought.' His insightful conclusion is that in tragedy such absurdity forestalls an audience's easy emotional release because 'It should not be too easy for us to weep at suffering or applaud revenge' (p. 120).

The section on modern performances begins appropriately with John Russell Brown on writing about Shakespeare's plays in performance. Noting that the experience of attending the theatre involves 'All our senses, instincts, and memories', he asks, '"How can we best describe or report on a theatre experience, and what do we gain by this exercise?"' (p. 151). His answer is a credo of sorts: 'Writing about performances of Shakespeare's plays should not be limited to a collection of momentary details about what individual actors have said and done so that they can be used to support, without defending, the writer's own critical views. Nor should it be guided solely by an uncritical acceptance of the writer's own predilections' (pp. 160–1). In the essays that follow, Richard Proudfoot remembers a production of *Measure for Measure* at the Old Vic in 1957–8, paying particular attention to the effects of cuts; Grace Ioppolo discusses the 1997 Royal National Theatre production of *King Lear*, focusing on what happens when directors and actors 'reject the "reading" texts provided by literary editors, such as Foakes, and instead act as the play's editors by producing their own theatrical texts' (p. 180). A central issue is the preference (perhaps by now indestructible) for a conflation of Q1 and the Folio, in this case by Richard Eyre, whom Ioppolo interviewed about his production. *Lear* is also the focus for Michael Hattaway, who uses Stephen Greenblatt's 'attempt[s] to historicize the references to devils in the play' (p. 198) as the context for a consideration of how to perform Edgar, especially his seeming possession as Poor Tom; this section also includes the piece by Carol Chillington Rutter on *Troilus and Cressida* which, with some revisions, also serves as the third chapter in her book reviewed above; and Alan Brissenden contributes a historical survey of 'Australian Shakespeare' which particularly emphasizes parallels between that country's political maturation and cultural self-confidence.

Two of the essays deal with filmed Shakespeare, a form of performance which by the end of the twentieth century had come to be seen as worthy of serious attention and to which much of the rest of this review will be devoted. The first piece is by Marliss C. Desens on cuts to the women's roles in the Olivier and Loncraine-McKellen films of *Richard III*; in a series of comparisons between the two, Desens shows how 'In the Olivier film, the female characters are portrayed as sympathetic victims, helpless against the force of Richard's evil. Their brief moment of community centers on their victimization rather than their empowerment. In the Loncraine film, the cuts result in a depiction of neurotic women for whom we have little sympathy, and who never draw together as a community' (p. 261). Desens also calls attention to how the cuts affect this play in particular: 'In no other history play did Shakespeare give female characters such prominence. It is time that directors start asking why' (p. 269). In the final essay Peter Holland looks at the treatment of Ophelia in Kenneth Branagh's *Hamlet* to illustrate the unreliability of screenplays as accurate witnesses. He also considers the implications of Branagh's decision to film the 'full text' of the play – actually 'plays', since although his script was based on F1 it included additions from Q2 – and the related desire to make it all comprehensible to film audiences everywhere. The consequence is that 'Rather than editing the text by altering language, Branagh's film edits by adding explanatory visuals, as if to represent the play more fully' (p. 290). The collection concludes with an afterword by Stanley Wells surveying both Reg Foakes's productive career and his influence on other scholars – many more, of course, than have paid their own tributes in this volume.

The publication of *The Cambridge Companion to Shakespeare on Film* signals that the topic has indeed officially arrived, and certainly Russell Jackson has put together a collection that goes some way in confirming this status. Following an informative introduction from Jackson are seventeen essays under the headings of adaptation, genres, directors, and critical issues. Jackson begins with 'From playscript to screenplay', a look at both conservative and radical adaptations. He illustrates, for example, the consequences of a desired running time of under two hours by describing various approaches to making cuts. Jackson also emphasizes the important fact that whereas a theatregoer can choose where on the stage to look, a filmgoer must look where the camera does, with 'the effect of limiting the audience's options and with them, arguably, the scope of its reactions' (p. 24). Particularly effective in illustrating the differences between the two media is Jackson's discussion of how the theatrical conventions of observation scene and soliloquy are treated. He also considers the consequences of film's emphasis on the visual in contrast to theatre's on the verbal, describing instances when narration in a play becomes action in the film. Citing Zeffirelli's and Luhrmann's versions of *Romeo and Juliet* as examples, Jackson concludes by observing that 'One crude but persistent truth about making films out of these Elizabethan plays seems to reassert itself . . . : the ending needs to show, rather than promise, something to the audience' (p. 31). Other essays in this section survey different aspects of the adaptation process: Michèle Willems on 'Video and its paradoxes'; Barbara Freedman on 'Critical junctures in Shakespeare screen history: the case of *Richard III*' and Harry Keyishian on 'Shakespeare and movie genre: the case of *Hamlet*'.

The second section includes 'Filming Shakespeare's History: Three Films of *Richard III*' by H. R. Coursen, '*Hamlet*, *Macbeth*, and *King Lear* on film' by J. Lawrence Guntner, 'The Tragedies of Love on Film' by Patricia Tatspaugh, and 'The Comedies on Film' by Michael Hattaway. In the last, Hattaway offers a mostly negative evaluation as he considers why the comedies have proven the most difficult Shakespeare genre to film. Among the problems, Hattaway suggests, is that of 'place' because in contrast to the histories and tragedies, 'Characters in the comedies . . . tend to the typical rather than the individuated and require settings that are neither wholly exterior nor wholly interiorized. The stories are enacted in distinctive fictional worlds which were designed for representation within the frames of a specifically theatrical architecture' (p. 86). Films of *As You Like It*, *A Midsummer Night's Dream*, *Twelfth Night* and *The Taming of the Shrew* are used as evidence of this point. A related problem, according to Hattaway, is 'space', particularly apparent in the comedies' use of overhearing scenes and inset plays, because 'On stage, actors playing characters who serve as spectators or overhearers have a special relationship with the audience, helping the other actors to manipulate audience response' but such positioning 'is difficult to re-create in the cinema since an actor cannot be both in and out of shot at the same time' (p. 88). As he notes, 'Theatre is an actor's medium, film a director's medium, and it is a director, with a totalising control of *mise-en-scène*, and, with his editor, master of not only pace but of sequence, who inevitably displaces the author and becomes the *auteur* of the film' (p. 95).

Among the directors of Shakespeare films considered is Grigori Kozintsev, whose *Hamlet* and *King Lear* are analysed by Mark Sokolyansky. He looks at these two remarkable films in the light of the differing political climates in which each was undertaken, with some reference to topical resonances. Subjects covered include the casting of actors whose first language was not Russian; the music by Dmitri Shostakovich; the creation of a 'universe' for *Hamlet*, which 'determine[s] Hamlet's tragedy as that of an unsleeping conscience' (p. 203); and how in his *King Lear*, 'the director and his team made a protest against the cynical, Edmundian view of life and stated that there are real moral values in this world – and that every epoch begets defenders of those values' (p. 209). Particularly valuable are the translations by Sokolyansky of interviews with Kozintsev and writing by him. The other directors discussed are Lawrence Olivier by Anthony Davies, Orson Welles by Pamela Mason, Franco Zeffirelli by Deborah Cartmell, and Kenneth Branagh by Samuel Crowl.

The critical issues raised in the final section include Shakespeare's women on film by Carol Chillington Rutter, national and racial stereotypes by Neil Taylor, cinematic offshoots by Tony Howard, and 'Shakespeare the illusionist: filming the supernatural' by Neil Forsyth. In the latter, Forsyth contrasts the different illusionistic possibilities of theatre and film, a difference first explored by Georges Méliès, 'a stage magician turned *cinéaste*' (p. 274), whose early work on film illusion is the essay's point of departure. Forsyth also remarks on a general 'discomfort with pictorial illusion', which 'has something to do with the fact that film art grew up with Modernism, in which high and low art-forms were fiercely separated, so that "special effects" are for children or certain subgenres, horror and sci-fi, not the serious mainstream' (pp. 276–7). He describes and assesses film treatments of Old Hamlet's ghost, of the weird sisters, and of Banquo's ghost and the apparitions in *Macbeth*, giving extended attention to the films by Polanski, Welles and Kurosawa.

Deliberately narrower in focus than the *Companion* is *Shakespeare, Film, Fin de Siècle*, edited by Mark

Thornton Burnett and Ramona Wray. As the title indicates, the concern here is recent Shakespearian films, the governing idea being the rather large claim that they 'are key instruments with which western culture confronts the anxieties attendant upon the transition from one century to another' (p. 4). Not surprisingly, Kenneth Branagh is prominent: his double image as Hamlet looking in a mirror is on the cover, he appears as actor and/or director in three of the twelve essays, and he is the subject of an interview with the editors (he is also on the cover of the *Cambridge Companion*, with others from the cast of *Love's Labour's Lost*). Here, virtually no one is critical of the film he or she discusses, although certainly not everyone would agree with all, or even most, of the positive views on offer, and some of the analyses read as special pleading.

In 'Shakespeare Meets *The Godfather*: The Postmodern Populism of Al Pacino's *Looking for Richard*', Neil Sinyard considers the film as 'a new cinematic form of the filmed essay' (p. 59) on the meaning of Shakespeare at the end of the twentieth century. He is especially interested in Pacino's approach to the relation between technology and text and his desire to make the filmed version accessible to an American audience. In Sinyard's view, Pacino's previous success in playing characters with criminal connections means that 'In screen acting terms, one could not have a better guide across the character contours of Richard III than Al Pacino, nor one who can so effectively exploit his screen persona to make a remote Shakespearian hero seem so modern and living and "real"' (p. 68). Sinyard suggests that this innovative amalgam of man-in-the street interviews, academic talking heads, rehearsals, etc., is perhaps 'the most radical and far-reaching strategy of them all' (p. 69). Amelia Marriette's 'Urban Dystopias: Reapproaching Christine Edzard's *As You Like It*', discusses a film that was neither a commercial nor critical success – she notes that the film, released in 1992, has never been shown in the US, and that Disney, which holds the rights, has 'deleted' it (p. 86, n. 1). Marriette draws on a personal interview with Edzard to concentrate

on her film's 'distinctive relocations, its utopian aspirations and its doubling arrangements' and to argue that it must be 'assessed in its own avantgarde terms as a postmodern experiment attendant upon, and sensitive to, a *fin-de-siècle* moment' (p. 73). Mariette remarks how the references to modern urban culture are emphasized by contemporary dress, but at the same time, Shakespeare's language is retained. The thrust of the discussion is positive and only at the end does Marriette venture explanations for the film's failure to survive in the modern marketplace: 'the director's resistance to lifting the film's mood and enticing the viewer makes it somewhat incompatible with a comedic core' (pp. 85–6), and the film's 'insistence on portraying *fin-de siècle* societies as dystopian might also seem overly morose' (p. 86).

In ' "The Way the World is Now": Love in the Troma Zone', Margaret Jane Kidnie bravely wades into Lloyd Kaufman's 1996 parody, *Tromeo and Juliet*, arguing that 'the classic status of *Romeo and Juliet* allows Kaufman to exploit the gap between conventional ideological constructions of both romantic love and Shakespeare, and the reconstruction of those discursive categories' in the film (p. 103). Noting that Kaufman's intention was to disturb audiences, Kidnie describes how the film uses analogies, such as between the meat industry and marriage. The result, she observes, is that 'A power base founded on canonical literature, capitalist markets and the brutal assertion of patriarchal authority is thus explicitly set in opposition to a supposedly degenerate youth culture' (p. 111). Finally, in 'Virgin and Ape, Venetian and Infidel: Labellings of Otherness in Oliver Parker's *Othello*', Judith Buchanan argues that 'Parker's *Othello* (1995) aligns itself with the placement of Othello as a man willing to advertise his resistance to his environment more than with productions that present a man trying to minimize his distinction from it' (p. 182). She looks at several related issues, including 'how the manipulation of the subjectivized gaze contributes to notions of belonging and alterity' (p. 180).

Another culture rather than a different medium is the context for *Performing Shakespeare in Japan*, edited by Minami Ryuta, Ian Carruthers and John Gillies. If the 'language' and conventions of cinema necessarily alter the original play, this collection gives the impression that such is perhaps even more radically the case when the language is Japanese and the conventions those of Kabuki, Noh and other Japanese performance styles. The first group of essays describes and explains early modern and traditional productions, the second group shifts the focus to post-World War II productions, and the last section consists of interviews with five Japanese directors of Shakespeare plays. Since, as this brief summary indicates, different approaches are the main concern, we also learn much about Japanese theatre conventions and the challenges that performing Shakespeare has presented to traditional ways. It becomes clear that adaptation is here a two-way process with some very unconventional results.

I conclude by noting that the disproportion referred to at the start is equally apparent here at the end, except that the number of works gathered under 'stage' is by far the largest, with 'times' coming a rather distant second. While the reasons bear thinking about and are no doubt various, it seems a safe bet that the many manifestations of Shakespeare in performance, especially in the twentieth century, will be a central focus of criticism for some time to come – but not, one hopes, at the expense of investigations into the plays' origins.

WORKS REVIEWED

Bednarz, James P., *Shakespeare and the Poets' War* (New York, 2001).

Bly, Mary, *Queer Virgins and Virgin Queans on the Early Modern Stage* (Oxford, 2000).

Burnett, Mark Thornton and Ramona Wray, eds., *Shakespeare, Film, Fin de Siècle* (London and New York, 2000).

Duncan-Jones, Katherine, *Ungentle Shakespeare: Scenes from his Life* (London, 2001).

Dymkowski, Christine, ed., *The Tempest* (Cambridge, 2000).

Findlay, Alison and Stephanie Hodgson-Wright with Gweno Williams, *Women and Dramatic Production 1550–1700* (Harlow, Essex, 2000).

Gibson, Joy Leslie, *Squeaking Cleopatras: The Elizabethan Boy Player* (Stroud, Glos., 2000).

Gillespie, Stuart, *Shakespeare's Books: A Dictionary of Shakespeare Sources* (London and New Brunswick, NJ, 2001).

Ioppolo, Grace, ed., *Shakespeare in Performance* (Newark and London, 2000).

Jackson, Russell, ed., *The Cambridge Companion to Shakespeare on Film* (Cambridge, 2000).

Jones, Ann Rosalind and Peter Stallybrass, *Renaissance Clothing and the Materials of Memory* (Cambridge, 2000).

Marshall, Tristan, *Theatre and Empire: Great Britain on the London Stages under James VI and I* (Manchester and New York, 2000).

Medieval and Renaissance Drama in England 13 (2001).

Miola, Robert S., *Shakespeare's Reading* (Oxford, 2000).

Orlin, Lena Cowen, ed., *Material London, ca. 1600* (Philadelphia, 2000).

Rutter, Carol Chillington, *Enter the Body: Women and Representation on Shakespeare's Stage* (London and New York, 2001).

Ryuta, Minami, Ian Carruthers, and John Gillies, eds., *Performing Shakespeare in Japan* (Cambridge, 2001).

Stern, Tiffany, *Rehearsal from Shakespeare to Sheridan* (Oxford, 2000).

Weimann, Robert, *Author's Pen and Actor's Voice: Playing and Writing in Shakespeare's Theatre* (Cambridge, 2000).

Wiggins, Martin, *Shakespeare and the Drama of his Time* (Oxford, 2000).

3. EDITIONS AND TEXTUAL STUDIES (1)

reviewed by ERIC RASMUSSEN

Genuinely monumental studies of Shakespeare's texts tend to appear, with curious regularity, once every nineteen years: the recent milestones being 1963 (Hinman's *Printing and Proof-reading of the First Folio of Shakespeare*), 1982 (Blayney's *The Texts of 'King Lear' and Their Origins*), and now 2001 with the publication of Anthony James West's *The Shakespeare First Folio: The History of the Book*, the first of four projected volumes presenting the results of West's decade-long census of the extant copies of the First Folio. Through a combination of careful archival research and tireless legwork, West has located 228 copies – a remarkable seventy more than were listed in Sidney Lee's 1902 *Census of Extant Copies*. The first volume in West's study reports on the sales and prices of copies of the First Folio since it left the press in 1623 through 2000; the forthcoming Volume II will provide concise descriptions of each extant copy including its location, condition, provenance, and binding; West is currently engaged in the further Herculean labour of collating all of the 228 copies world-wide and recording full bibliographical descriptions of each, to be presented in Volume III; Volume IV will then round out the project with a cultural history of the First Folio, a biography of the book.

This is an essential reference work for Shakespearians, librarians, book-collectors, and antiquarian book dealers. The first volume – consisting of detailed tabular listings of auction records for sales of F1 as well as more scaled-down listings of sales of F2, F3, and F4 – will probably have more specialist users than casual readers, but the narrative sections have some fascinating stories to tell about the history of Folio prices (from £1 in the seventeenth century to $1,000,000 at the close of the twentieth) and the mass migration of copies to the United States (which occurred despite Sidney Lee's admonition that 'if English millionaires don't bestir themselves, there is a likelihood that all the forty privately owned copies of the volume still in this country will make tracks across the Atlantic').

West introduces a new numbering system based on each book's current geographical location, with numbers 1–44 assigned to copies in the United Kingdom; number 45 to the copy in Ireland; numbers 46–190 to copies in the United States; number 191 to the copy in Canada; numbers 192–217 to copies in the rest of the world; and numbers 218–228 to 'unfound' copies (the rationale for including these missing copies in the census will be supplied in Volume II). Lee had sorted copies into categories based on his (often highly subjective) appraisal of their relative quality. Although a good case can be made for West's decision to sort by location instead, it's not clear that the preference given to English-speaking nations is entirely appropriate. Why do Ireland and Canada, with one copy each, deserve separate headings, while Japan, which boasts fifteen copies (twelve at Meisei University), is lumped in with the rest of the world? One also wonders whether the copy that is currently on the market (West 217) will have to be renumbered, according to the address of the new owner, once it is purchased.

A previously unpublished list of the prices that Henry Clay Folger paid for his First Folios enables West to provide fresh insight into the process by which Folger accumulated his 82 copies over three and a half decades. But I suspect that a few of the conventions that West adopts in dealing with the Folger purchases may puzzle some readers. For example, although West reports that A. S. W. Rosenbach's 'bid of £8,600 for the Daniel copy' set 'a new record' in 1922 (p. 46), this figure does not appear in the tabular summary of prices of the First Folio, 1900 to the present, on pages 125–6. The reason for this omission is that in those instances in which a First Folio was bought at auction by a dealer who then sold it to Folger within a few months, West has not recorded the auction price in his table, so as to avoid 'double counting'. Thus, because Rosenbach sold the Daniel copy (Folger 5, Lee 5, West 63) to Folger shortly after he had acquired it, the price recorded in West's table is the $52,070 (£10,414) that Folger paid. It could be argued that an accurate historical record of prices of the First Folio ought to include both sales, since each represents the market value of the Daniel copy at a particular moment in time.

Shortly after West's volume appeared, the Berland copy of the First Folio fetched $6,166,000 (£4,301,883) at Christie's New York in October 2001. This remarkable price shatters the previous record by more than sixfold and establishes a new context for West's data. Interestingly, the penultimate record price is somewhat uncertain. In 1989, a set of all four Folios (F1, F2, F3, and F4) from the collection of Garden Ltd, Books sold at Sotheby's New York for $1.9 million. If the First Folio's value was approximately 56 per cent of the total (the percentage employed by Lee in such cases), then the price of the Garden F1 came to more than $1 million (£691,040). This is significantly above the previous record of $580,000 (£411,348). As West points out, however, Lee selected the 56 per cent figure quite arbitrarily; one could just as easily say that the Garden F1 was worth 70 per cent of the total paid for the four Folios, or 40 per cent, for that matter. So although West's table listing 'New record prices of the First Folio' gives an appearance of precision, a careful reader will be aware of the indeterminacy surrounding the figures he provides.

The issue of 'buyer's premiums' presents another problem. Beginning in the 1970s, the major auction houses added a buyer's premium – generally 10 per cent of the successful bid – to the price of each lot sold, payable by the purchaser. Although West sees some merit in the view that 'price plus premium is a better measure of what the buyer, at least the sophisticated buyer, is willing to pay and therefore of value', he concludes that 'consistency of price data, and comparisons with previous periods, are better served by excluding the premium'. I wonder whether this decision does not actually make comparison more difficult. A user of these tables might assume that the Folio sold at Sotheby's

in 1967 for £4,500 fetched more than the copy sold at Sotheby's in 1978 for £4,200; whereas, in fact, because a buyer's premium was added to the latter, its real price was £4,620. Consider also the $1.9 million hammer price of the Garden Folios. The ten per cent buyer's premium was $190,000. If the 8.25% New York State sales tax is included, the actual cost of the Garden set was over $2.2 million.[1] In a study entitled *An Account of the First Folio Based on its Sales and Prices*, surely it would be worth drawing attention to the fact that the prices First Folios fetched in subsequent years – £95,000 at Christie's London in 1990, $90,000 at Christie's New York in 1991, $225,000 at Sotheby's New York in 1996 – do not even equal the amount of the tax and buyer's premium paid on the Garden Folios.

West's discussion of the earliest owners of the First Folio – an earl, two bishops, a baron, a knight, a herald, a lawyer, a mayor, and a Norfolk gentleman – makes no mention of a particularly intriguing possible early owner: one of Shakespeare's fellow players. A copy in the Folger Shakespeare Library (Folger 12, West 70) contains the signature of Samuel Gilburne, a member of the King's Men whose name appears in the F1 list of the names of the principal actors. Although the attribution to Gilburne is somewhat uncertain, this association copy was one of Henry Folger's most prized possessions, and the fact that it goes unmentioned in West's introductory essay is difficult to explain.

West's synthesis of the archival records of auction catalogues dating back three centuries is an invaluable resource; the tables herein contain an enormous amount of data. However, my spot-check of one of West's primary sources, *American Book Prices Current* for the years 1897–1901, revealed a few gaps. The copy sold at a Bangs & Co sale in New York on 18 January 1897, which is described in some detail in *ABPC*,[2] is nowhere

---

[1] Had the Garden Folios sold in London (where VAT is charged only on the buyer's premium, not on the hammer price for books), the tax would only have amounted to $33,250 whereas the New York sales tax was $172,425.

[2] 'Mr William Shakespeare's Comedies, Histories, and Tragedies, published according to the True Originall Copies. The

mentioned by West. Moreover, West's entries for the 20 March 1900 sale of Lee 33 and for the April 1901 sale of Lee 140 list the auctioneers as unknown, but *ABPC* specifies that the auctioneers were American Art Galleries and John Anderson Jr, respectively. A minor erratum to supplement a monumental achievement.[3]

Michael Hattaway's New Cambridge edition of *As You Like It* presents a crisply intelligent introduction, reminding overly analytical readers that 'comedy should be fun' while warning against sentimental readings of a play that is both 'more dangerous and more cautious' than it might appear. Among the many gems to be found in Hattaway's commentary is the splendid gloss on Le Beau's description of Celia as 'taller' (1.2.224). The Folio reading is often thought to be an error, since Rosalind elsewhere describes herself as 'tall' whereas Celia is 'low', or to represent a revision made to match the heights of a new group of boy actors. But Hattaway effectively renders these editorial theories both untenable and unnecessary by observing that 'tall' can also mean 'more spirited or handsome'. Elsewhere, Hattaway notes that the 'holy bell knolled to church' at 2.7.121 may be a glance at the pre-Reformation custom of ringing the 'holy bell' to help the souls of the recently dead out of purgatory, a practice decried by John Foxe and other Protestant commentators; this may be an indication, Hattaway provocatively suggests, that there are Puritans in the forest. The forest itself is here designated 'Arden' rather than 'Ardenne', but Hattaway cautions readers to 'remember that this is an imaginary location, as "French" as it is "English", as fantastic as it is familiar'.

Those of us who admire (indeed revere) Hattaway's previous editorial work will be surprised and disappointed, however, by the text of this edition. I note twenty-two minor errors in the collations[4] and several more serious omissions.[5] Most perplexingly, some emendations that are the commonest of common property are claimed to be unique to this edition. The alteration of the Folio reading 'man:' to 'man!' (3.3.46), for instance, which has been made by editors ranging from Theobald, Warburton, Capell, Johnson-Steevens, and Malone in

the eighteenth century to the Arden, the Riverside, and the Pelican in the twentieth, is unaccountably marked as original to '*This Edn*' (the abbreviation used for 'innovations'). The emendations 'thee;' to 'thee,' (3.6.91) and 'love,' to 'love;' (3.6.92), here claimed as unique, were both made in Clark and Wright's Cambridge edition and in Dover Wilson's New Cambridge Shakespeare. Many of the added stage directions that are identified as innovations were anticipated in previous editions: the added *Aside* (1.2.201), *To Celia* (1.2.204), *To Touchstone* (2.4.62), *Aside* (3.4.82), and *To Rosalind* (5.2.87) all appear verbatim in the Oxford Complete Works;

First Folio. London, 1623. Folio, levant morocco, gilt edges by H. Stamper. Lines before the title reprinted; title-page (except the portrait, which was probably from a later edition and inlaid) in facsimile; preliminary leaves to the catalogue, partly from other copies and partly in facsimile; and last four leaves of Cymbeline in facsimile. Bang's, Jan. 18, 1897. (3422) $500.00'. *American Book-Prices Current*, ed. Luther S. Livingston (New York, 1897), p. 392

[3] In the quotation from the Stationers' Register on page 5, for 'many' read 'manie'; the 13 November 1922 sale of Lee copy 26 for £5,900 is inadvertently omitted from the tabular 'Summary of First Folio prices, 1900 to the present' on page 126; the sources I have checked record the 1960 hammer price of the Perkins-Law copy as 350,000 DM rather than the 310,000 DM listed on page 120.

[4] 1.2.6 citation of F reading for 'Herein' read 'Heerein'; 1.2.66 citation of F reading for 'enough' read 'enough;'; 1.2.117–18 for 'forwardnesse' read 'forwardnesse.'; 1.3.79 for '*duke, etc.*' read '*Duke, &c.*'; 2.4.0 SD 1–2 for '*alias*' read 'alias'; 2.5.34–7 for '*see*' read '*see.*'; 2.5.34–7 lemma should read '35–7' and in the lemma for 'Come' read 'Here'; 2.7.167–70 for '*Du.*' read '*Du*'; 2.7.175–8 for '*ingratitude:*' read '*ingratitude*'; 3.3.94 for 'graff' read 'graffe'; 3.3.100 for 'bee,' read '*bee,*'; 3.3.213–16 for '*Iaq.*' read '*Iaq*'; 3.4.72 for 'thee' read 'thee.'; 3.6.66–9 for 'sheell' read 'shee'll'; 4.1.22 for 'travail' read 'trauaile'; 4.1.69–70 for 'suite' read 'suite:'; 4.1.124 for 'hyen' read 'Hyen'; 4.3.4 SD square bracket needs to be moved to after the lemma; 4.3.157 for 'arme' read 'arme.'; 4.3.158–9 for '*Rose.*' read '*Ros.*'; 5.3.16, 24, 32, 40 for 'rang' read '*rang*'; 5.3.17–18, 25–6, 33–4, 41–2 for 'sing, hey' read '*sing, hey*'; 5.3.23–7, 31–5, 39–43 for 'In spring time, etc.' read '*In spring time, &c*'; 5.4.98 for 'hether' read '*hether*'

[5] The added stage directions at 1.1.50, 3.3.197, 3.4.54, 3.6.66, 4.3.12, 5.4.106–8, 5.4.114–118, are not collated; the relineations of 2.5.41–2, 2.7.180–1, 2.7.182–3 are not collated; at 2.7.38 the emendation of F1 'braiue' to F2's 'brain' is not collated.

the added stage directions *To Silvus* (3.6.73) and *with a letter* (4.3.4) appear verbatim in Bevington.

Tracking down the source of emended readings in an edited text can be a massive task and one that many editors dread. Nevertheless, as Bowers observed, 'it is customary for an editor to credit the earliest document with the emendation (or correction) he has adopted'; doing so is 'partly a courtesy but chiefly an act of historical scholarship' in that it establishes 'the precise details of the refinement of a textual tradition'.[6] The false claims to originality in the Cambridge *As You Like It* not only misrepresent the textual tradition, but obscure Hattaway's genuine contributions to it, such as the compelling emendation of the F1 crux at 2.7.55 from 'Seem senseless of the bob, if not' to 'If he seem senseless of the bob, if not'.

Many of the '*This Edn*' claims that do not stand up to scrutiny should probably be regarded as typographical errors. Since Hattaway surely did not intend to assert that his edition is the first in history to render the Folio's '*Actus primus. Scoena Prima*' as '1.1', '*Actus Secundus. Scoena Prima*' as '2.1', and the like, one must assume that these and other editorially added act and scene numbers (1.3, 2.2, 2.3, 2.4, 2.5, 2.6, 2.7, 3.1, 3.2, 3.3, 3.4, 3.5, 3.6, 4.1, 4.2, 4.3, 5.1, 5.2, 5.3, and 5.4) were accidentally marked '*This edn*' rather than '*Eds.*', the abbreviation used for 'insignificant and obvious editorial practices'. Only '1.2' is correctly attributed to '*Eds.*' (Since Hattaway marks a scene break after the tenth line of 3.2, where most editors do not, the newly numbered scene 3.3 might have a legitimate claim to being an innovation were it not that Pope, Warburton, and other early editors also marked 3.3 as beginning at the same spot.)

Printers' devils also seem to have been at work on Andrew Gurr's edition of Q1 *Henry V* in the Cambridge Early Quartos Series. Gurr presents a provocative narrative of the quarto's textual origins in a manuscript recorded by dictation specifically for the press; the players of Exeter and Gower are identified as the agents given this task by the acting company. The dictation yielded a record of 'a shorter, brisker, simpler play' than the full version found in the Folio, and one that, Gurr argues,

'repays minutely detailed and scrupulous study'. Such detailed study of the quarto text might be hampered, however, by the errors in this edition,[7] most significantly at 9.56, where Gower is made to refer to 'such and such a scene'. Gurr's collation notes the variant reading 'Sconce' in Q3 and F; since the word in question in Q1 (sig. D1r30) has six letters, the third of which is rather faintly printed and somewhat obscure, the word may be either 'sconce' or 'scence' but it is certainly not 'scene'. (My examination of the British Library copy – one of the two copies that Gurr used in preparing his text – corroborates Greg's reading 'sconce'.)[8] This slip is exacerbated by an extended discussion in the introductory essay of the possible origins of the supposed alteration of Q1's 'scene' to Q3's 'sconce'. Gurr wonders whether the Q3 compositor had 'privileged access to the manuscript he was later to use to set F', or whether the alteration was 'an inspired guess'. This is a moot point, of course, if Q1, Q3, and F all read 'sconce'.

There are gaffes in this edition that one simply does not expect to find in Gurr's work. On the same page in which he cites Thomas Berger's 'careful analysis of the printing' of Q1 *Henry V*, Gurr asserts that none of the extant copies of the quarto reveal 'any corrections made while the work was in press', thus overlooking the press variant that Berger identified, a dropped speech prefix on C2v of the Bodleian copy.[9] Similarly, when Gurr discusses Q3

---

[6] 'The Historical Collation in an Old-Spelling Shakespeare edition: Another view', *Studies in Bibliography* 35 (1982), 237.

[7] In the 2.25 collation, for '*Nims.*' read '*Nims,*'; 10.22.1 SD for '*Exit*' read '*Exit Pistol*'; 11.69 SH the emendation of Q1's '3 *Lord.*' to '3 SOLDIER' is not collated; 14.15–20 line numbering is off by one; 16.28 for 'e'er' read 'ere'; 19.76.1 SD for '*and all the Lords*' read '*and the Lords*'; p. 78, note 25, the Q1 readings are not '*Pharamount*' and '*Pharamont*' but '*Faramount*' and '*Faramont*'; prose lines are indented as verse at 2.42, 14.4, 14.9, and 14.14.

[8] In introducing the Clarendon Shakespeare Quarto Facsimile of *Henry V*, Greg noted that 'few readings are really obscure in the original; it may, however, be worth while to confirm the following…D1 recto, 1. 30 sconce' (Oxford, 1957), p. viii.

[9] 'The Printing of *Henry V*, Q1', *The Library*, 6th series, 1 (1979), 116 n. 16.

Henry V, one of the so-called Pavier quartos printed in 1619 but dated '1608', he incorrectly claims that Pavier's quartos were 'all printed . . . with similarly false dates'. In fact, Pavier's quarto reprints of *The Merry Wives of Windsor, Pericles*, and *A Yorkshire Tragedy* are all correctly dated '1619'.

In October of 1999, Richard Proudfoot gave a series of remarkable lectures: one at Stationers' Hall to mark the centenary of the publication of the Arden Shakespeare, one to commemorate the 400th anniversary of the opening of the first Globe Theatre on Bankside, and one at King's College London on the occasion of his retirement from the English Department. These lectures, now published in *Shakespeare: Text, Stage, and Canon*, offer an engaging introduction to the issues of editing Shakespeare's texts, staging his plays, and assessing questions of attribution and authorship. This trim volume, at less than a hundred pages, is packed with more information than some reference works many times its size. Even advanced scholars will be indebted to Proudfoot, not merely for reminding us (as reviewers' parlance would have it) of certain facts, but also for telling us facts we did not know. For my own part, I was unaware before reading these lectures that at least five hundred copies of Shakespearian quartos printed before 1623 are known to survive today, and that the Globe Theatre is not named on the title-page of any play quarto published before 1608, the date of the King's Men's repossession of the Blackfriars, after which it apparently began to be necessary to remind purchasers which of the King's Men's two houses had been the site of performances of the play they were about to buy.

These superbly crafted lectures are a joy to read. Proudfoot moves deftly from ringing *occupatio* ('I do not intend to tell of the vision, persistence and courage of Sam Wanamaker . . . I shall not tell of those exciting months in the spring and summer of 1989 . . . Nor shall I, finally, recall the wonder') to quiet moments of humour (gently kicking himself for publishing an edition of *The Two Noble Kinsmen* which gave the names of its authors as 'John Fletcher and William Shakespeare,' in that order: 'I have a suspicion that it might have earned

more royalties over the years if I had been less scrupulous and put the big name first').

Having served as general editor for both the Malone Society and the Arden Shakespeare, Proudfoot is perhaps uniquely qualified to comment authoritatively on the fortunes of Shakespearian editing in the twentieth century. This he does with wit and insight, as when he characterizes the original Arden series as 'an understated English response to the academic overkill and heavyweight bulk of the American New Variorum edition'. In tracing the history of the old-spelling edition commissioned by Clarendon Press in the 1930s, Proudfoot notes the unfortunate irony that R. B. McKerrow, having published his *Prolegomena for the Oxford Shakespeare* in 1939, died the following year, and that his successor, Alice Walker, never completed the edition either – having concluded, 'as she worked on the early volumes and on her study of *Textual Problems in the First Folio* (1953), that the presentation of Shakespeare to modern users in the orthography of the early editions was intolerable'. Although Proudfoot celebrates the Oxford Shakespeare ultimately produced in 1986 by Stanley Wells, Gary Taylor, John Jowett and William Montgomery, and its *Textual Companion* (1987) – 'at last an epilogue rather than a further set of prolegomena' – he questions the procedures of the Oxford old-spelling edition. Specifically, since the orthographic forms in the early editions owe as much to the habits of individual compositors and their adjustment of spelling in order to produce a tight line of type as they do to the orthography found in the printers' copy, Proudfoot argues that 'to divorce the spelling of a printed text from the constraints of lining and page layout that were among its formative conditions is, in any event, to present readers with much insignificant detail whose *raison d'etre* is concealed by modern typography and layout'.

For Proudfoot, the Oxford Shakespeare 'embodies the ideal . . . of a "definitive" edition of Shakespeare', but he notes that 'by a paradox of timing, it was completed and published at a time when that ideal began to be redefined as a mirage'. Some editorial theorists who have recently championed the view that editing is an impossible, or even theoretically improper, activity have found themselves, as Proudfoot puts it, 'in a deeply cleft stick' when they are commissioned to prepare an edition for a series. Proudfoot observes, with obvious satisfaction, that 'practicality appears usually to have won – to the benefit of the users of their editions'.

Having ranged skilfully over the editorial past, Proudfoot offers valuable advice to editors of the future. He challenges publishers and readers 'to contemplate other criteria than the sometimes slippery one of authorship for constructing collections of plays' – proposing, for instance, volumes of plays associated with particular acting companies, or with particular playhouses. He also envisions editions of early modern plays which present a carefully prepared facsimile and a fully modernized edited text on facing pages, thereby cutting through 'the clutter of textual apparatus familiar in current editions by allowing readers to see for themselves what the editors had done with the early text on which their own was based'. A neat hybrid, one might observe, of the conventions of the two editing projects, the Malone Society reprints and the Arden Shakespeare, with which Proudfoot has so long been associated.

Proudfoot identifies the Norton facsimile of the First Folio as 'the first indispensable book for the library of any serious student of Shakespeare'. The second essential volume might well be *Shakespeare: Text, Stage, and Canon*, a lucid synthesis of the central issues in the profession of Shakespearian editing written by one of its most distinguished practitioners.

A reasonable facsimile of Proudfoot's vision of an ideal edition can be found in *The Shakespeare Folios*, a new series under the general editorship of Nick de Somogyi. The volumes in this series – *Hamlet*, *Twelfth Night*, and *Henry V* have now appeared; *Measure for Measure*, *Othello*, and *Richard III* are in preparation – offer a diplomatic transcript of the First Folio on each recto page and a modernized text on the facing verso. Voicing concern that 'the Folio's antiquated typography and cramped layout make it remote and inaccessible to modern eyes', the editors have attempted to 'scrupulously reproduce in modern type the exact spelling, punctuation, and layout' of the First Folio, thereby 'dissolving the patina of age that any mere facsimile would necessarily present'. But just as the act of cleaning an Old Master painting necessarily risks losing some of the original, so too, some elements of the Folio text almost invariably get lost in transcription. I randomly checked two pages of the *Hamlet* transcript against F1 and found four errors;[10] if the typos on these pages are representative, then there are potentially more than two hundred errors in the transcript of the Folio text of this play. There's nothing inherently wrong, of course, with providing a diplomatic transcript in lieu of a facsimile, but the series' bold claims about being the first to do so ('combining for the first time the authenticity of the First Folio with the accessibility of modern type... in a way that has *never been done before*') are simply wrong. In fact, an edition published in 1906 made a similar claim: 'What is reproduced, and reproduced with exact fidelity, is the text of the First Folio, the only variation being the substitution of modern type'.[11]

The Malone Society reprint series – which has of late moved away from diplomatic transcripts in favour of facsimile reproductions – has reached an important milestone. The project to make all of the Shakespearian play quartos available in single-text facsimile editions, which began with the Clarendon Shakespeare Quarto Facsimiles in the 1950s and has been carried on by the Malone Society, has now been completed with the publication of volume 163, a facsimile of the Huntington copy of Q1 *Romeo and Juliet* (1597) supplemented by pages from the Trinity College, Cambridge copy. Jill L. Levenson and Barry Gaines provide a superlative introduction to the complex printing history of this text. To their good discussion of the rows of

---

10 For 'Hamlet' read '*Hamlet*' (TLN 1963), for 'yeere' read 'yeare' (TLN 1986), for '*unto*' read '*vnto*' (TLN 1992), for '*dcclines*' read '*declines*' (TLN 1993). It should be noted that *The Shakespeare Folios* do not provide line numbers, making citation difficult and, I should think, use in the theatre rather problematic.

11 *The Complete Works of William Shakespeare Reprinted from the First Folio*, ed. Charlotte Porter and H. A. Clarke (London, 1906), p. iii.

printer's ornaments across the pages which begin on G2v of Edward Allde's section of the quarto, I would like to add that these ornaments generally appear where a new scene begins, making Q1 *Romeo and Juliet* the only Shakespearian quarto that is (at least partially) divided into scenes.

According to the most recent count, Shakespeare's works have been translated into 95 languages.[12] But it is too often the case that foreign translations are based on critically outdated English editions. Jean-Michel Déprats's recent French translation of *Cymbeline* is based on J. M. Nosworthy's 1955 Arden edition. Similarly, a new translation of *King Lear* into Brazilian Portuguese by Aila de Oliveira Gomes is presented on facing pages with Kenneth Muir's 1952 Arden text. Although Muir's edition offers a perfectly serviceable version of the play, in recent decades textual critics have revealed some serious problems with the practice – all but standard when Muir produced his edition – of conflating the Q and F texts. Readers in Rio de Janeiro may be legitimately confused about the Gentleman (*Fidalgo*) in 4.7 who hears Cordelia address Kent by name ('O meu bondoso Kent'), as in F, but later – in lines that only appear in Q – seems to believe that Kent is in Germany ('Conde de Kent na Alemanha'). It is no doubt easier to secure the rights to reproduce these outmoded texts, but one wonders if there couldn't be more of an effort made to provide readers of Shakespeare in translation with the best that textual and editorial scholarship has to offer.

WORKS REVIEWED

Proudfoot, Richard, *Shakespeare: Text, Stage, and Canon*, The Arden Shakespeare (London, 2001).

Shakespeare, William, *As You Like It*, ed. by Michael Hattaway, New Cambridge Shakespeare (Cambridge, 2000).

  Cymbeline, trans. Jean-Michel Déprats ed. by Margaret Jones-Davies (Paris, 2000).

  Hamlet, ed. by Nick de Somogyi, The Shakespeare Folios (London, 2001).

  The First Quarto of King Henry V, ed. by Andrew Gurr, New Cambridge Shakespeare: The Early Quartos (Cambridge, 2000).

  Henry V, ed. by Nick de Somogyi, The Shakespeare Folios (London, 2001).

  Rei Lear, Edição Bilíngüe [English and Brazilian Portuguese], trans. by Aila de Oliveira Gomes (Rio de Janeiro, 2000).

  Romeo and Juliet 1597, ed. by Jill L. Levenson and Barry Gaines; checked by Thomas L. Berger and G. R. Proudfoot, Malone Society Reprints, vol. 163 (Oxford, 2000).

  Twelfth Night, ed. by Nick de Somogyi, The Shakespeare Folios (London, 2001).

West, Anthony James, *The Shakespeare First Folio: The History of the Book. Volume I: An Account of the First Folio Based on its Sales and Prices, 1623–2000* (Oxford, 2001).

---

[12] See David Scott Kastan, *Shakespeare After Theory* (New York, London, 1999), p. 76.

3. EDITIONS AND TEXTUAL STUDIES (2)

reviewed by JOHN JOWETT

Two major new editions of *3 Henry VI* in the Arden 3 and Oxford series happen to have reached an advanced stage of production at exactly the same time. Eric Rasmussen has been engaged on the Arden 3 alongside his work reviewing textual studies and editions for *Shakespeare Survey*. In standing in to review these editions, I cannot fail to recall Rasmussen's generous account of my own

editing of *Richard III*, but my long-standing association with the Oxford Shakespeare offsets any potential partiality. To quote Shakespeare's words on the deferral of both favour and judgement, 'both alike we like'. It is not the case, however, that, in the Citizen of Angers's previous words, 'Both are alike'. These are two distinctive and different editions. In a world of bookshelves rather than crowns and kingdoms there is no need to declare victory for one and defeat for the other. These distinguished editions both deserve a place.

Rasmussen and his collaborator John D. Cox have prepared a book longer than Ardens such as *Othello* or *King Lear* with a far denser history of reception than *3 Henry VI*. They present an organized and astonishingly comprehensive account of the play's reception in criticism and on stage. In it, they point to continuity between earlier and recent responses, and emphasize the value of bringing this historical depth to a current engagement with the play. After some forty pages discussing the play as a performance work, their introduction evolves into a survey of its critical reception, in eight sections with headings such as 'Historical criticism', 'Psychoanalytic criticism', and so on. The heart of the Introduction reads virtually as a review of trends in Shakespeare criticism as a whole, taking *3 Henry VI* as the test case. The relative rarity of major critical studies on this play works very much to the editors' advantage, for they are able to able to construct a wide-ranging and thorough account of reactions to the play that aims for and achieves historical depth as well as critical currency.

The account is enlivened and enriched with the editors' own critical intelligence and perception. Reviewing the RSC 1999–2000 production, they refer to its 'magic realism and spiritual pilgrimage' (p. 33), which are are tellingly compared with the politics of Tony Blair in a comment whose complexion is remarkably changed and deepened since Blair's even more recent emergence as a rhetorician of war. They later ask 'what kind of moral thinking the play exhibits' (p. 56), drawing attention usefully to examples of 'magical thinking' such as belief in 'spells, incantations, curses, and blessings' as examples of an 'on-again, off-again quality of magical thinking' (p. 59), a phrase that connects interestingly with their allusion to Blair.

In the Oxford edition, Martin positions himself much closer to the play, unfolding a sustained critical viewpoint informed at all points with a concern for the play's effect on the stage and giving detailed attention to different strands, episodes and roles. Instead of providing a formal stage history, Martin

gives interest and immediacy to his critical exploration by weaving theatre history into it. The core of Martin's introduction consists of sections relating to a greater or lesser extent to the major dramatic roles. The scope of these sections is far-ranging, and they make repeated reference to literary, dramatic, social, and political contexts. For instance, Henry VI is addressed by way of taking the play's title as the section title; the discussion covers the scope and genre of the play as a whole, with subsections on 'An Elizabethan civil war play', 'Civic and royal pageantry', and so forth. '*Edward IV*' attends not only to the role of Edward as an alternative focus point, but also to the play about Edward IV performed at Coventry in 1591; it goes on to explore the Warwickshire topicalities of *3 Henry VI*. In 'Margaret's story' Martin suggests that the theatre has discovered an 'unwritten tragedy' of Queen Margaret in the First Tetralogy. The overall achievement of these sections is to provide a strong critical account of *3 Henry VI*'s rich multifocality.

Both editions reassess the Octavo and Folio texts. Following a wider trend in questioning or at least narrowing the scope for the operation of memorial reconstruction in O, they nevertheless stop significantly short, at different points, of rejecting the theory outright. The Arden editors destabilize the customary explanation of O in terms of memorial reconstruction by showing that in some details it is closer to the source material in the chronicles than is F – though in a footnote (p. 164) they make the significant concession that in principle a memorially reconstructed text could subsequently be corrected by referring to Hall. Another common assumption is challenged when they point out that the large number of actors required for *True Tragedy* deprives it of a leading characteristic that would be expected of a text used by a troupe of players on provincial tour. The editors do nevertheless accept that 'memory may have played a role in the transmission' of O (p. 165). Following Peter Blayney, they suggest that it might be based on a transcript by actors incorporating theatre cuts. Whether this provides an adequate explanation for the aural errors they identify is not entirely clear, and the demonstration of O's sporadic proximity to Hall needs some further assimilation into this hypothesis. In the face of these residual difficulties, the editors' saving grace is that they do not strongly commit themselves to any particular hypothesis, but rather show the vulnerability of some of the hypotheses that have been current, aiming to leave our understanding less sure than it has been.

Much the same applies to Cox and Rasmussen's treatment of F. Their account of the appearance in F of what are apparently the actors' names 'Humfrey', 'Gabriel', and 'Sinklo' is properly sceptical: no secure inference as to the nature of the copy manuscript can be drawn. The editors point out that variation in the speech headings in F for Lady Gray between 'Lady Gray' and 'Wid[ow]' is not necessarily evidence of foul papers, as such variation might possibly survive in a playbook. They suggest further that the switch from the stage direction '*Lady Gray*' to speech-prefix '*Wid.*' in 3.2 might be due to the change of compositors at the intervening page-break. The case would be stronger if a speech-prefix for Lady Gray appeared before the page-break, but there is no opportunity for it to do so. This is a speculative line of argument that goes against what one would most readily expect of compositorial type-setting, but the editors nevertheless succeed in raising significant questions as to whether the Folio copy can be identified with any confidence as 'foul papers'.

Cox and Rasmussen advertise that 'we do not want to prejudice interpretation by pronouncing one text more authoritative than the other or even by attaching labels such as *original* and *revision*'. That might well be a cogent point on which to close a textual discussion, but it does not provide a platform for editing. One text, F, becomes the basis for the play we read, and for the vast majority of the edition's discussion and commentary. Cox and Rasmussen follow the Arden policy of including facsimiles of 'short' or 'bad' texts. This certainly pulls O into view as an artefact, and is to be strongly commended on this account, but in terms of presenting *True Tragedy* as a text for reading, criticism, and performance it is only a concession. If the textual discussion is non-prejudicial, the editing definitively cannot follow suit, for editing is about making choices. Significantly, the edition offers no account of the editorial procedures to provide a bridge between textual analysis and execution.

Though the consequences for establishing the text are in practice limited, Martin's approach eschews the scepticism of Cox and Rasmussen. He seeks out in the more optimistic spirit of W. W. Greg to know as much as can reasonably be known, or at least inferred, and proceeds to the task of editing on that basis. It is argued firmly that '*True Tragedy* is a memorially reported version of the play' put together by actors from Pembroke's Men, and Martin adds that 'Nothing underhanded is implied' in the actors' making of the report (p. 109).

In support of O's memorial character, Martin endorses the more persuasive of the arguments raised by earlier critics such as Peter Alexander, and notes that O's error 'Lord *Bonfield*' introduces a fictional name found also in the historical romance *George a Greene*. This intertextual slippage may well be suggestive of a memorial error, though Martin's belief that O's mistake in calling Edward Brooke '*Edmund*' is implausible as an authorial error seems to me to be less well founded, and the mistake could alternatively result from a simple misreading of the abbreviation 'Edw' as 'Edm'.

Making a significant revision of the accepted view, he adds that the Folio text is based on Shakespeare's later and substantial revision of the play. Memorial reconstruction in O and revision in F have usually been seen as alternative ways of explaining the relationship between the two texts, with the former view prevailing. For Martin they coexist. Most editors see F as the earlier version, whereas Martin regards the text behind O as coming first. In arguing this case, he notes that memorial reconstruction fails to provide a full explanation for O. Yet he points to the inadequacy of other ways of accounting for this text as a derivative from the longer Folio version. He observes, as do the Arden editors, that *True Tragedy* does not particularly save on the number of actors needed to perform it, and adds that if it had been prepared simply to offer a shorter script the alterations would have been much simpler. Nor can censorship offer an adequate explanation. From these essentially negative considerations Martin proceeds to develop his alternative theory that as a script that existed before memorial reconstruction O was Shakespeare's first version of the play. He makes the same case as Cox and Rasmussen in citing instances where O is closer to the source material than is F. There is some overlap between their independent findings (which in Martin's case will be stated more fully in a forthcoming article), though the overall argument they make between them is more extensive and therefore stronger than its two separate constituents.

Following up this important breakthrough in identifying F as the product of a revision of the play, Martin goes so far as to date it, provisionally, and on the basis of circumstantial arguments, to about 1595. If the date is right, it might be asked whether any consequences arise from the revision being close to the publication of O. Moreover, if, as seems plausible, the theory of revision is right, Martin might have built it into his curiously unmodified account of F as an authorial 'pre-performance' text. By his own hypothesis, F must be in important respects post-performance too.

Both editions present a text generally close to F. Both read, for example, 'his passions moves' at 1.4.150, a lack of concord between subject and verb that most editors have emended since the Second Folio introduced the change in 1634. In the Arden edition, an exception to the general conservatism is at 1.1.46, where F's 'hee' is emended to O's more literary 'bird'. In line with the reticence in explaining editorial procedure already noted, this emendation is not discussed in the commentary. The dialogue in Martin's edition is occasionally underpunctuated, especially around vocatives. For example, when Warwick turns his address from Lewis to Margaret it would help to resolve a syntactic ambiguity by having a comma after 'queen': 'My noble queen let former grudges pass'. This and similar examples perhaps reflect a deliberate light touch, but if so the policy has been taken too far.

It is in the editorial treatment of stage directions and speech-prefixes that the two editions most obviously differ textually. The Arden edition introduces titles of royalty where they are missing in the copy-text; this is not extended to aristocrats such as

Oxford and Warwick, though F's '*Bona*' becomes '[*Lady*] *Bona*'. Square brackets are used in this fashion in stage directions. The speech prefixes, however, are susceptible to expansion without brackets or record in the collation. These silent emendations are of some significance to the reader, as entitlement, particularly to the crown, is itself very much in question. For instance, in the opening of 1.3 Lewis addresses Margaret as 'Fair Queen of England, worthy Margaret', to which Margaret, or in the Arden edition 'QUEEN MARGARET', replies 'No, mighty King of France: now Margaret/Must strike her sail and learn awhile to serve/Where kings command'.

In matters of theatrical substance Cox and Rasmussen follow the stage-direction wording of the early texts. '*Exeunt. March. Warwick and his company follows*' at the end of 5.1 is a case in point. Who is left on stage after the exeunt, does '*March*' refer to actions, music, or both, and in what sense does Warwick follow the figures on the main stage when he is '*upon the walls*'? Cox and Rasmussen defer the matter to the commentary. In contrast, Martin follows the Pelican and other editions in printing the highly elaborated '*Exeunt King Edward and his company. March. Warwick and his company exeunt above, re-enter below, and follow King Edward*'. Neither edition points out that '*March*' is crucial to the envisaged staging because it allows for offstage drumming while Warwick and company descend within to the main stage.

In contrast with his liberality in making the stage direction theatrically meaningful *in situ*, Martin is exceptionally cautious about absorbing information from O's stage directions into his text. He declines to adopt the famous stipulation that Clifford enters with an arrow in his neck in 2.6, pointing to this as an example of F's more subtle staging (p. 36); nor does he accept O's 'Three sunnes appeare in the aire' at 2.1.20. The editorial stage direction '*He shows a red rose*' (5.1.81.1) both reflects and minimizes a stage direction in O, which reads 'Sound a Parlie, and *Richard* and *Clarence* whispers togither, and then Clarence takes his red Rose out of his hat, and throwes it at *Warwike*'. Martin understandably rejects the option of pasting in O's direction wholesale, or the Arden option of selecting the details relating to the rose without modification. Whilst often providing a full account of the Folio staging in his editorial modifications, he thus shows a strong sense of the staging proper to F as a textual version. It is indeterminable whether F actually preserves a more restrained staging or is merely more reticent in its verbal stipulations. I'm not sure that Martin is right in accepting the former view, but in the present period initiated by the two-text *King Lear* his approach is certainly defensible theoretically.

In the cases of the exeunt in 5.1, the red rose direction before it, and elsewhere, it would have been helpful to direct the reader to the uncertainty surrounding the stage action by printing the direction in brackets. Martin has interpreted liberally the Oxford policy of reserving brackets for contentious stage directions. In a similar spirit, in the stage direction at 3.3.110.1 he translates F's '*aloofe*' to '*apart*', an explanation that might well have been left to the commentary. However, the collation line is a reliable record of Martin's alterations, and his interventions add to the theatrical cogency of the script rather than attending to details of presentation.

Cox and Rasmussen do not print extended extracts from the sources, but the commentary devotes much of its space to relating the play to the historical events. An appendix presents a table listing the historical battles and the location of their treatment in the play; another provides four pages of genealogical tables. Martin appends a 'Commentary on Historical Sources', which stands midway between commentary notes and the traditional appendix of extracts from source material. Effective in itself, it also frees up the commentary for generously detailed and attentive annotation of other matters. The commentary is a particularly strong point of his edition. Like his introduction, it is alert to matters of theatre, and selectively draws on an extensive knowledge of the play's history of staging. Where the opportunity arises,

Martin is also good on the literary qualities of the language.

Both editions are reliable, highly accurate, and usually conservative in their treatment of the copytext. A local exception to the general accuracy is that the Arden edition has a series of superscript 'r's for 'recto' that should read 'v' for 'verso' in its tabulation of compositors' stints on pp. 156–7.

I will probably more often consult Cox and Rasmussen as a source of information, but I may well more often read the play in Martin's edition. Any such distribution of preference is, of course, personal, and both editions can be strongly recommended on account of their particular strengths. As I have suggested, the differences might be summarized in terms such as 'sceptical' versus 'engaged', or perhaps 'accumulative' versus 'performative'. Obviously, these are crude polarities, and in reality both editions display a range of characteristics across the spectrum that such terms bound. Nevertheless, the editions usefully illustrate two contrasting tendencies, one of which makes the edition an instrument of record in a tradition going back to the Variorum, the other treating the edition as an instrument of more individuated and critical mediation. These can be different routes to the same end, which in the case of these editions of *3 Henry VI* is to provide a strong platform for the play as part of a larger sequence but also, more importantly, as a text that commands attention in its own right. Both editions are unapologetic and powerful acts of advocacy for the play – or at least for the Folio version of the play that provides their copy.

WORKS REVIEWED

Shakespeare, William, *Henry VI, Part Three*, ed. by Randall Martin, The Oxford Shakespeare (Oxford, 2001).

King Henry VI Part 3, ed. by John D. Cox and Eric Rasmussen, The Arden Shakespeare (London, 2001).

BOOKS RECEIVED

The list includes all books received between September 2000 and September 2001 which are not reviewed in this volume of *Shakespeare Survey*. The appearance of a book in this list does not preclude its review in a subsequent volume.

Belsey, Catherine, *Shakespeare and the Loss of Eden* (Basingstoke, 1999).

Daybell, James, ed., *Early Modern Women's Letter Writing, 1450–1700* (Basingstoke, 2001).

Gertz, SunHee Kim, *Chaucer to Shakespeare 1337–1580* (Basingstoke, 2001).

Ghosh, Gauri Prasad, *The Insubstantial Pageant: A Study of the Development of Shakespeare's Life-vision* (Calcutta, 2001).

Gibson, Rex, *Stepping into Shakespeare: Practical Ways of Teaching Shakespeare to Younger Learners* (Cambridge, 2000).

Knight, G. Wilson, *The Wheel of Fire* (Oxford, 1930; 4th edn 1949; repr. London, 1989 and 2001).

Harp, Richard and Stanley Stewert, eds., *The Cambridge Companion to Ben Jonson* (Cambridge, 2000).

O'Meara, John, *Othello's Sacrifice: Essays on Shakespeare and Romantic Tradition* (Toronto, 1996).

Partridge, Eric, *Shakespeare's Bawdy* (London, 1947; 2nd edn 1955; repr. 2001).

Simkin, Stevie, *Marlowe: The Plays* (Basingstoke, 2001).

Simkin, Stevie, ed., *Revenge Tragedy: Contemporary Critical Essays*, New Casebooks (Basingstoke, 2001).

Shakespeare, William, *Richard III*, ed. by Pat Baldwin and Tom Baldwin, Cambridge School Shakespeare (Cambridge, 2000).

INDEX

No book titles are included in this index, but the names of the authors are given. Book titles in the review articles are listed alphabetically at the end of each article.

INDEX

INDEX

INDEX

INDEX

INDEX

INDEX

INDEX